THE
PRESIDENCY

ABOUT THE AUTHORS

Jeffrey E. Cohen received his Ph. D. in Political Science from the University of Michigan in 1979 and specializes in American politics and public policy with an emphasis on the Presidency. He has published articles in the *American Political Science Review, the American Journal of Political Science,* and the *Journal of Politics* and is co-editor of *American Political Parties: Resurgence and Decline* (2001). In addition Jeff Cohen has written numerous books, including *Politics and Economic Policy in the United States,* 2nd edition (2000), and *Presidential Responsiveness and Public Policy Making: The Public and the Policies that Presidents Make* (1997), which won the 1998 Richard E. Neustadt Award from the Presidency Research Group of the American Political Science Association.

David C. Nice received his Ph. D. in Political Science from the University of Michigan in 1979 and specializes in American politics and public policy making. Before joining the faculty at Washington State University, he taught at Indiana University and the University of Georgia. His research has appeared in the *American Journal of Political Science,* the *Journal of Politics, Public Administration Review,* and a number of other scholarly journals. He is the author of *Public Budgeting, Politics and Policies in States and Communities,* 7th edition (with John Harrigan), *Amtrak,* and *The Politics of Intergovernmental Relations,* 2nd edition (with Patricia Fredericksen).

To Ruth and Phyllis

BRIEF CONTENTS

CONTENTS

PREFACE

We chose to write this textbook on the presidency for several reasons. First, the major textbooks are now quite old, into several editions, and we did not feel that they had kept up with many of the major changes in the presidency and thinking about the presidency as they retained their same perspectives. Thus, on a content level, none of the existing textbooks dealt much with the president and interest groups, though this relationship has become an increasingly important concern of modern presidents. Similarly, there has been new thinking about the office, especially from the perspectives of institutionalists and rational choice theorists. Current textbooks do not make much use of these ideas, and while we are not necessarily proponents of those perspectives, they have informed our thinking about the presidency, and we think that students should be introduced to these ideas. Lastly, none of the textbooks on the market do a very good job of introducing students to how social scientists go about studying the presidency. While we do not belabor the point in our text, we wanted to give students some insight into this by talking about collecting evidence and assessing how good that evidence is. In conjunction with this perspective, we also wanted to introduce students to some of the controversies among political scientists about the presidency. We hope that doing this will help raise students' curiosity about the office and show them that learning about the office is not a matter of digesting the wisdom and facts from authorities but of being actively involved in trying to understand the presidency.

Our book can be roughly categorized into four major sections. In the first several chapters, we discuss the constitutional nature and historical evolution of the office. The next section looks at presidential relations with what we can think of as presidential constituencies: voters, public opinion, the mass media, parties, and interest groups. Unique to our text are the extended discussions of interest groups and the mass media. The next section emphasizes the presidency in government, with a discussion of the organization of the White House and the relationships between the president and Congress, the judiciary, and the bureaucracy. Finally, we explore presidential policy making, with one chapter discussing presidential decision making more generally and separate chapters on economic and foreign policy making. The decision-making chapter includes an extended discussion on agenda setting.

We view our book as a comprehensive overview of what we know and what political scientists think about the presidency. We use a definite theme, which we apply to as many of the topics as is relevant. That theme begins with the notion that the Constitution sets the framework within which the presidency operates. Over time, however, the political context of the presidency has changed. In particular, expectations for presidential leadership have grown. The problem for the president is how to provide leadership in a constitutional system that often limits his leadership resources.

In our approach to studying the presidency, we try to offer a balanced constitutional understanding of the office, with its historical evolution, as well as a social science perspective. For each topic, we spend some time laying out the constitutional foundations and historical development of the office; those factors are important, but controversial, influences on the presidency of today. We also incorporate relatively modern social science techniques to help students understand the dynamics of the contemporary presidency and to show them how political scientists think about the presidency. Our aim is not to be highly technical but rather to give students a sense of how to scientifically study the presidency.

We also on occasion introduce students to some of the theoretical controversies about the presidency, especially the debate between Neustadt's presidential persuasion model and Terry Moe's unilateral action model. We do not act as advocates when introducing such controversies but offer students an idea of why the proponents of the different perspectives think the way that they do.

The presidency is often a controversial office, in part because presidents deal with issues that touch people's lives, especially in the modern era, and because we often disagree with one another regarding those issues. We do not expect everyone to feel the same way about particular presidents or particular presidential decisions, but we hope to help students understand the dynamics of the office and its interactions with other parts of the American political system.

To complement the topics of this text, we have edited an accompanying reader entitled *The Presidency: Classic and Contemporary Readings*. We hope that students will draw connections between the current scholarship within the text and the primary source readings in the reader. To help students make this connection, we have placed icons in the margins of the text indicating the appropriate correlating reading. At the end of each chapter, we also have included discussion questions, a list of key terms, and a list of other secondary sources that students can turn to for further enlightenment.

In addition to this, McGraw-Hill has developed a custom-crafted website on which students may find Internet links and simulations on the presidency. We hope that all of these tools together will give students a full and rich picture of the presidency.

A great many people have contributed to this book in many ways. We owe a great debt to the many scholars who have studied the presidency over the years, and to the reviewers who examined drafts of the books. The crew at McGraw-Hill, especially Monica Eckman and Angela Kao, worked heroically to bring the book to completion. The authors wish to thank their respective universities, Fordham University and Washington State University, for providing a wide range of institutional support that helped us to complete this book. Our students have also helped to sharpen our thinking about the presidency in countless ways. We also offer a special thanks to Professor George Grassmuck, who did a great deal to introduce both of us to the American presidency.

We are grateful to the reviewers who examined drafts of this book. The following were integral to the development of this first edition:

Martin Gruberg, University of Wisconsin, Oshkosh
Joseph Unekis, Kansas State University
Andrew Merrifield, Sonoma State University
Thomas Wolf, Indiana University Southeast
Theodore Hindson, Southwest Texas State University
J. Kevin Corder, Western Michigan University
Paul Quirk, University of Illinois, Urbana-Champaign
James McDowell, Indiana State University
Cary Covington, University of Iowa
Ryan Barrileaux, Miami University of Ohio
John McAdams, Marquette University
Jeffrey Kraus, Wagner College
Robert Bresler, Penn State-Harrisburg
Paul R. Petterson, Central Connecticut State University
Dan Tichenor, Rutgers University
Gary Lee Malecha, University of Portland
Robert Shapiro, Columbia University
Richard Pious, Barnard College
Mark Byrnes, Middle Tennessee State University
Lori Cox Han, Austin College
Kathleen Kemp, Florida State University
Thomas Langston, Tulane University
Robert Spitzer, State University of New York-Cortland

1

THE PRESIDENCY AND
THE CONSTITUTION

During the several years before the United States' entry into World War II in December 1941, President Franklin Roosevelt was apprehensive about American security. The war began in September 1939, when Nazi Germany invaded Poland. Within a year (June 1940), France had fallen, Germany had overrun most of Europe, and Great Britain was the lone European democracy combating Nazi Germany. FDR's greatest fear was that if Great Britain also fell, the United States would become the world's only major democracy. Then the United States might be dragged into a war with Germany without allies. The prospect of a world dominated by Germany loomed as a possibility.

Thus, FDR wanted to do anything that he could to help Great Britain in its struggle with Germany. One option, that of entering the war on Great Britain's side, was ruled out American public opinion, despite great sympathy with Great Britain, strongly opposed entry into the war. Moreover, strong isolationist sentiment in Congress precluded passage of a declaration of war against Germany.

As a substitute policy, FDR hoped that he could bolster Great Britain with the arms and matériel of warfare, thus not having to risk American lives. Here, too, FDR was hamstrung because of restrictions in the Neutrality Act and other related laws that were enacted in the mid-1930s. The Neutrality Act of 1935 prohibited the United States from selling arms or loaning money to any belligerent nation, aggressor or not, once war broke out. In 1937, "cash and carry" provisions were placed on nonmilitary items, like oil and raw materials. "Cash and carry" required that purchases had to be paid for in cash and transported by the purchasing nation from American ports. U.S. merchant vessels could not transport any good to a warring nation.

FDR sought a way around the restrictions of the neutrality laws to support Great Britain once the war broke out, but the strength of isolationist sentiment in the nation, and especially in Congress, raised the specter of impeachment if he violated or tried to skirt or evade the law. As the urgency of the situation in Europe heightened, FDR did manage to get the neutrality laws reformed in late 1939, with the arms embargo lifted, but the "cash and carry" provisions remained. With Great Britain's war debt mounting and the laws prohibiting the United States from extending credit to belligerents, Britain lacked the finances it needed to buy enough U.S.–produced arms to defend itself as it desired. It was not until late 1940 that Congress passed the Lend-Lease Act, in which the United States would loan "surplus" armaments to Britain, to be returned or paid for in kind at war's end.

Even here, Congress imposed limitations by prohibiting U.S. vessels from convoying the lend-lease goods to Britain. Thus, even with lend-lease, FDR was unable to help Britain as much as he wanted to and thought was necessary if Britain was to be able to defeat Germany.[1]

This example illustrates the major themes of this book, themes that hold today even as they did at the dawn of U.S. entry into World War II. First, FDR probably did more to build up the presidency as a leadership institution than any other modern president, yet he was constrained by a Congress that opposed, and was often hostile to, the policies that he thought necessary for the nation's security. Moreover, here was a president restricted in the area of foreign and defense policy, realms thought by most to be the areas of public policy in which the president commands the greatest discretion, leadership, and power. Here, the constitutional structure of our political system, which requires congressional cooperation, constrained FDR's policy options.

The Constitution does not tell the entire story of the presidency, although it lays an important foundation for understanding it. As we will see, public and political expectations for presidential leadership (that is, how much other participants in the political system want the president to play a leadership role in policy making and governing) are also important. By the time of FDR, a strong expectation had developed that the president would provide leadership across a large array of issues and concerns.[2]

In this book, we offer an understanding of the presidency that emphasizes the impact of the constitutional structure and public expectations on presidential behavior and accomplishment. While we agree with those who think the person in office can also make a difference, equally, if not more, important is the constitutional structure of our governmental system in the United States and how that structure mixes with the public's expectations of government performance. In particular, our Madisonian system of **separation of powers, checks and balances,** and federalism determines to a significant extent what a president can or cannot accomplish in office and how he will go about trying to attain his goals.

In our constitutional system, the president does not govern alone. He cannot simply command the creation of new legislation or policy, no matter how well intentioned, designed, or beneficial that course of action may be. Instead, to see his policies enacted and implemented, the president often requires the cooperation of Congress, the courts, and the federal bureaucracy. Such cooperation is not easily forthcoming for a host of reasons, many of which have to do with our constitutional structure. Throughout this book, we will detail these as they come up.

Thus, much of presidential behavior in office is an attempt to accommodate, compensate for, or overcome the confines that our constitutional system imposes on the president. In this book, we will learn how presidents come to grips with

---

[1] On FDR's foreign policy plight before the Second World War, see David M. Kennedy, *Freedom from Fear.* (New York: Oxford University Press, 1999), esp. pp. 394–406, 428–34, 469–76.

[2] Also, the manner of the person in office, his beliefs, ambitions, and talents make a difference in what a president does.

the constitutional system, a system that requires great effort if presidents are to have an impact on the nation's policies.

The limitations, but also the potential, that the Constitution provides for presidents were not an accident or oversight of those who drafted that document in Philadelphia in 1787. Rather, they were by design and on purpose. While the framers of the Constitution clearly could not foresee every development that would occur or every application of their ideas, they still had a plan for what government would look like. They did not intend that governing would be easy for those who sat in positions of authority, whether those seats be in Congress, the judiciary, or the executive.

For the most part, as long as not too much was expected from presidents, the constitutional system did not pose too great of an issue for the chief executive. Many presidents of the nineteenth and early twentieth centuries interpreted their job narrowly and offered little in the way of policy leadership to the nation. And in times of emergency, such as war and civil war, presidents could call on the doctrine of **"executive prerogative"** to justify their heightened leadership activity. Essentially, executive prerogative asserted that in time of great emergency, the president was not bound by either the Constitution or existing law when dealing with the emergency. However, such prerogative powers were also viewed as temporary and specific to the emergency in question. And in the few incidents when presidents seemed to overstep what was considered an acceptable or legitimate use of executive prerogative, action by the other constitutional branches, Congress, or the Supreme Court, effectively brought the president back into line. Thus, as long as presidents did not deem it their responsibility to provide active leadership on most matters of policy, presidents could and did operate relatively comfortably within the strictures of the constitutional system of separation of powers and checks and balances.

However, beginning sometime near the end of the nineteenth century or the beginning of the twentieth, presidents began to think that it was their responsibility to become a leader. Presidential leadership means actively offering policy directions to deal with the nation's problems and issues, galvanizing public and political support behind those policy intentions, and endeavoring to see that these policy proposals are adopted and implemented. By the 1930s, with the election of Franklin Roosevelt to the presidency, this new, active, **modern presidency** had been realized. In short order, the entirety of the political system, from leaders in Congress to the voter, now expected the president to take the lead in governing. All presidents subsequent to FDR would feel the pressure of such expectations for leadership, and many relished the idea of providing such leadership.[3]

The constitutional system, however, had not changed much from the days before the institution of this modern presidency. While the public might expect the president to solve the nation's problems, the constitutional structure limited the president. He could not legislate, for instance; only Congress could. And Congress

---

[3]Great debate exists over the timing of the appearance of the modern presidency, as well as the meaning and nature of the modern presidency. In Chapter 2, we will deal with these issues in more detail.

would not always agree with the policy solutions that the president suggested, nor would it always act as speedily as the president would prefer.

In a sense, a gap grew between the expectations placed on the president and the governmental authority to act. This gap is in many senses a key frustration to presidents, especially those who strive to live up to these newfound expectations for presidential leadership and governing responsibilities.[4]

As we will show in this book, some presidents devised creative approaches to overcoming the limitations that derive from the Constitution. Some, for instance, have acted unilaterally to make policy. Unilateral actions are those that the president takes alone, such as issuing **executive orders** and proclamations. Thus, unilateral actions bypass the normal routines of the legislative process. The eminent historian Forest McDonald calls these "presidential legislation."[5] Also, presidents have tried to acquire as much political support as possible in an attempt to use that support to motivate other policy makers to comply with their wishes. Few, however, have tried to narrow the gap by trying to lower public expectations, and we should not expect ambitious politicians to pursue such a strategy of lessened expectations.

Trying to supply policy leadership and governing the nation in a system that is designed to limit executive authority is the theme of our book. The constitutional system, public and political expectations for presidential leadership, and the preferences and talents of presidents themselves become the major ingredients in trying to explain what presidents do, what they can accomplish, and the nature of the presidency and our political system. The rest of this chapter looks at the constitutional foundation of the presidency. Chapter 2 addresses the evolution of the presidency from these constitutional foundations.

THE CONSTITUTION'S IMPRINT ON THE PRESIDENCY

One cannot understand the presidency without looking to its constitutional nature. The Constitution greatly affects the character of the presidency, providing the governmental structure within which the president will act. Through the Constitution, certain powers are granted to the president. But certain limitations are also placed on the office, the most critical one being the system of separation of powers and checks and balances.[6]

---

[4]On this expectations gap, see Richard W. Waterman, ed. *The Presidency Reconsidered*. (Itasca, Ill.: F. E. Peacock, 1993).

[5]Congress and the Supreme Court can overturn executive orders and the like, but they rarely do so. Forest McDonald, *The American Presidency: An Intellectual History* (Lawrence: University Press of Kansas, 1994), pp. 293–98. Also see Terry M. Moe and William G. Howell, "Unilateral Action and Presidential Behavior: A Theory," *Presidential Studies Quarterly* 29 (December 1999): 850–72.

[6]On the constitutional foundations of the presidency, see Joseph M. Bessette and Jeffrey Tulis, eds., *The Presidency in the Constitutional Order* (Baton Rouge: Louisiana State University Press, 1981); Thomas E. Cronin, ed., *Inventing the American Presidency* (Lawrence: University Press of Kansas, 1989); and the Spring 1987 volume (17, no. 2) of *Presidential Studies Quarterly,* which is devoted to this issue.

Separation of powers and checks and balances constrain presidential action and discretion. The theory of separation of powers and checks and balances requires cooperation among the branches of government for government to take action. Each of the three branches of government has some ability to block or impede the actions of the other branches, which often means that cooperation across the branches is required for government to take action. Such consent is not always forthcoming, as each branch has its own institutional boundaries to protect and different constituents and interests to serve. Thus, conflict among the branches is as common, if not more so, than cooperation.[7] As a consequence, over the course of U.S. history, there have been many instances when presidents wished they were free or tried to free themselves of this structural constraint.

Our constitutional system also means that government overall shall be limited, that it shall not unduly abridge the liberties of its citizens, such as freedom of speech, association, and religion, and the other rights granted to them in the Bill of Rights. The combination of limited government and separation of powers strikes at the core of what has historically been considered executive powers. Much of the character of the presidency and our government is molded by this system of constitutionally limited government and separation of powers and checks and balances.

A third consideration of the constitutional foundation of the presidency and the government relates to the framers' attitudes toward democracy. Bluntly put, they were suspicious of democracy. Their suspicions grew from several sources.

First, they likened democracy to a mob, fearing that demagogues could rouse the mass public through fear and other base emotions, not through rationality or reason, the mode of political problem solving that the framers preferred. Sensing the potential power and destructiveness of a mobilized mass public, the framers designed the presidency, and the Constitution overall, in such a way as to channel the voice of the mass public into representative political institutions. One of their greatest fears was that a mobilized mass would destroy liberty and, out of jealousy and envy, would appropriate the private property of those who had accumulated some wealth. To insulate government and policy making from such threats, elected and appointed political leaders would govern for fixed terms of office. But they would be held accountable to the public, through election and other recruitment devices, for what they did in office. A republic, not direct democracy, characterizes the governmental system that the framers designed.

The presidency, especially in the modern age, has run up against the republican nature of this constitutional framework. First, the presidency, along with some other political institutions, has been evolving in a democratic direction. We see this in the early changes in the electoral college and the rise of presidential primaries to nominate candidates for the office. We also see this democratizing trend in presidential use of the modern mass media to communicate to the public directly and

---

[7]A good account of the implications of the system of separation of powers and checks and balances is found in Nelson W. Polsby, *Congress and the Presidency,* 3d ed. (Englewood Cliffs, N.J.: Prentice-Hall, 1976), pp. 176–98.

in the increasing reliance of presidents on public opinion polls in deciding policy directions.[8] In this sense, a tension exists between the aspirations of the occupants of the modern, twenty-first-century presidency and its constitutional moorings and foundations. This tension, which will be explored in more detail throughout this text, illustrates why a constitutional perspective provides us with an important starting point in understanding the presidency. However, a fuller, more complete understanding of the nature of the presidency and presidential behavior must also take into account the climate of public and political expectations regarding the office of the presidency and the beliefs, goals, and talent of individual presidents.

Another important feature of the constitutional framework is that Article II of the Constitution does not provide a very clear description of the president's power and duties. Over half of that article is devoted to the presidential selection process, including qualifications for the office, and the remaining sections cover less than a page of a standard college textbook. One consequence of the lack of constitutional clarity about the office is that from time to time, presidents have been criticized for exceeding their authority, failing to meet their obligations, or otherwise not following the Constitution. At the same time, this lack of constitutional clarity has enabled the presidency to develop, evolve, and adapt to new circumstances over time.

In the sections to follow, we will detail the constitutional nature of the office. We will discuss the factors that affected the design of the presidency, such as the revolt against British monarchy, the failure of the Articles of Confederation, and strengths and weaknesses of the office of governor of the states. Then we will discuss the constitutional powers of the presidency and the debates during the constitutional era over the presidency.

THE ORIGINS OF THE PRESIDENCY

Although they were drafting the first of its kind, without a prototype to follow, the designers of the Constitution and the presidency looked to history, their experience in government and politics, and the ideas of important political thinkers and philosophers to guide them in creating the presidency and the Constitution. We begin by discussing why a new constitution was needed in 1787.

The Need for a Constitution and a Presidency

The need for a presidency and a new government arose from the chaos and discord of the first few years of the existence of the new nation under the **Articles of Confederation.**[9] The confederation proved ineffective in dealing with the new

---

[8]On the rise of polling in the presidency, see Lawrence R. Jacobs and Robert Y. Shapiro, "The Rise of Presidential Polling: The Nixon White House in Historical Perspective," *Public Opinion Quarterly* 59 (Summer 1995): 163–95.

[9]For an overview of the period of the articles, see the classic Merrill Jensen, *The New Nation: A History of the United States During the Confederation, 1781–1789* (New York: Knopf, 1950), and Jack N. Rakove, *The Beginnings of National Politics: An Interpretive History of the Continental Congress* (Baltimore: Johns Hopkins University Press, 1979).

nation's problems; a stronger government was required. Yet the memory of the British monarchy and the "tyranny" that Americans felt they had suffered under the British made many people fearful of a strong national government. The delegates to the Constitutional Convention were determined to build a government that was strong enough to govern but not so strong as to become tyrannical and override liberties. The presidency was one important part of that design, answering many of the faults that were identified with the Articles of Confederation.

The Articles of Confederation were adopted in 1781[10] just two years before the American colonies won their independence from Great Britain. Merely four years after independence was won in 1783, circumstances were so dire that the Constitutional Convention was convened. How could matters go so wrong in such short order?

First, let us consider the nature of government under the Articles of Confederation. The articles provided for a weak central government and can perhaps be better viewed as a defense alliance among the thirteen states aspiring for freedom from British colonial rule than as a government capable of forging a nation. Outside of the United States, the term *state* generally refers to a country and its national government, whereas in it, *state* has come to mean a subnational unit of government, a level of government that is not an independent player in the international political system. During the early postcolonial period, many people regarded the states as sovereign and independent political units, much like the way the term is used outside of the United States.

The weakness of the central government under the articles is readily apparent from listing their provisions. Only one branch of government existed under the articles—Congress. Within the national legislature, each state was granted one vote, and each state was allowed to determine how to select its legislators. The president served merely as presiding officer of Congress, and while Congress eventually created departments to handle matters such as finance, diplomacy, and military decisions during the Revolutionary War, the departments were heavily scrutinized by Congress.[11]

Passing legislation under the articles was difficult. A supermajority of nine of the thirteen states was required to enact important legislation; finding a minority of five to block legislation was generally easy, and little legislation emerged from Congress. Moreover, amending the articles was nearly impossible, as unanimity was required. This provision had important implications later when the delegates to the Constitutional Convention met, leading them to jettison the articles in favor of the more pliable Constitution.

[10]The articles were written in 1776 and ratified by the Continental Congress on November 17, 1777, but it took until 1781 for all of the states to ratify them. All but Maryland had ratified the articles by 1789; Maryland did so in 1781. On the Articles of Confederation, see Merrill Jensen, "The Articles of Confederation: A Re-Interpretation," *Pacific History Review* 6 (1936):120–42; Jack Greene, "The Background of the Articles of Confederation," *Publius* 12 (1982): 15–44; Jack Rakove, "The Legacy of the Articles of Confederation," *Publius* 12 (1982): 45–66; Peter S. Onuf, "The First Federal Constitution: The Articles of Confederation," in *The Framing and Ratification of the Constitution,* ed. Leonard S. Levy and Dennis J. Mahoney (New York: Macmillan, 1987); and Jensen, "Articles of Confederation."

[11]Richard B. Morris, "The Origins of the Presidency," *Presidential Studies Quarterly* 17 (Fall 1987): 673–88.

Still, government and Congress under the articles were granted wide responsibilities, although often without the requisite powers to carry them out. For instance, Congress under the articles was granted the power to declare war, make treaties, enter alliances with other nations, raise a military, regulate and borrow money, oversee affairs with Indian populations, set up a post office, and adjudicate disputes between the states.

But Congress's ability to meet these responsibilities was severely restrained because of the required supermajority. Equally important, Congress's ability to raise revenue to operate government was negligible. It could impose tariffs on imported goods, but it could not gather the necessary legislative majority to do so. Another route to raising revenue—taxes—was not open to Congress, as it could not levy taxes directly. Instead, Congress had to rely on voluntary contributions from the states. They were usually unwilling to contribute, and only when immediately threatened by British troops during the Revolutionary War did the states come up with funds for the national government. The national government, as a consequence, was in debt and seemingly unable to find a way out of its debt, a point we will elaborate on in the "Crises Under the Articles" section.

Under the Articles of Confederation, the states were the critical and important level of government, not the national regime; the states reigned supreme over the national government through their ability to block the national government from taking legislative action and the national government's inability to force the states into action. The states, thus, maintained their autonomy and independence under the articles.

Crises Under the Articles

Given the weakness of the central government under the articles, it is not surprising that the central government did not have the resources to cope with important emerging and worsening problems. A host of problems, from a distressed economy to internal civil unrest to external threats, stands out. Together, they amounted to a daunting task for the feeble government under the articles, or for any government for that matter. Moreover, they potentially threatened the existence of the nation.

Economic Issues   The economy was in a shambles. Much of the economic problem stemmed from the costs of the Revolutionary War, the inability of the government to collect revenue to pay its debts, and economic competition across the states. First, the Revolutionary War had tremendous impact on the economy of the new nation. The national government was deeply in debt, owing creditors who had loaned it money for the war effort. Foreign creditors, especially France and the Netherlands, held over $10 million in U.S. notes, and the United States owed about $1.8 million in unpaid interest payments. The U.S. treasury held less than one-third of the interest owed in 1786. Foreign creditors were refusing further credit to the United States and were threatening to cease trade with the young nation if the debts were not paid.[12]

---

[12]These figures come from Sidney M. Milkis and Michael Nelson, *The American Presidency: Origins and Development, 1776–1990* (Washington, D.C.: Congressional Quarterly Press 1990), p. 7.

Also, the nation lacked a uniform currency because the articles allowed states to print their own money. Many did, without backing in gold or silver, as they responded to political pressures from farmers, who were often unable to pay their debts. In several states, farmers, who made up the bulk of the work force and the core of the U.S. economy at this time, took control of the state's legislature. They implemented "easy money" policies by printing large volumes of money, which flooded their economies with paper currency. Massive inflation resulted as the value of this new currency eroded nearly as soon as it entered the economy.

Adding to the inflationary and national debt woes was an American buying spree of imported goods, mostly from Britain. Americans used their private silver and gold to pay for these imports, consisting mostly of household items like clocks, glassware, and furniture. A silver and gold shortage within the United States resulted, further exacerbating the currency crisis. The scarcity of specie, that is, gold and silver, in the economy made it even more difficult for debtors, like farmers, to secure loans so that they could pay off their debts and continue their operations. This added to the pressure from farmers and other debtors to inflate the economy with "cheap" money. Creditors, like banks, naturally detested such a policy, which would destroy the value of the assets that they held in the form of loans to farmers and others.

The lack of a uniform currency and questions about the value of currency of some states impeded trade among the states. In several instances, trade wars erupted, as states entered individual trade agreements with foreign nations, in part because of Congress's inability to negotiate and ratify treaties. New York required shippers from New Jersey and Connecticut to pay to enter its ports. New Jersey retaliated by taxing a New York lighthouse built on New Jersey soil. These trade barriers stifled commerce, adding to the nation's economic woes. Other conflicts broke out as states claimed the same lands in the west. In one such incident, settlers from Connecticut clashed with Pennsylvania troops.

Internal Civil Unrest   Civil violence and unrest erupted as well. In several instances, farmers took up arms against their creditors. The most famous case was Shays's Rebellion in western Massachusetts. Unlike farmers in Rhode Island, Massachusetts farmers were unable to win political control of the statehouse. Instead of policies to ease the plight of farm debt, as discussed in the section on economic issues, the Massachusetts legislature passed laws favorable to creditors, like banks, who foreclosed on farmers unable to meet their debt. As farm debt was common, tensions rose, and in some areas, armed conflict between farmers and creditors resulted.

Shays's Rebellion began in 1786. Daniel Shays, a former army officer, led about fifteen hundred armed farmers against courthouses and other establishments in western Massachusetts. The aim was to stop creditors' seizure of farmers' property. Shays's movement, however, was quelled by a state militia that was privately financed by creditor interests. In the state elections the next year, farmers successfully captured the statehouse and implemented policies more favorable to them. This eased immediate tensions, but fear of mass insurrection throughout the nation rose as a consequence of the highly publicized uprising.

Unrest also existed in the military ranks, centering on the issue of back pay. Unable to collect revenues, Congress was unable to pay its troops. In 1782, in Newburgh, New York, one group threatened mutiny over the back pay issue. They even attempted to make George Washington king. Washington refused to participate in the mutiny, however, and the movement quickly aborted.[13] The next year, troops in Philadelphia vandalized arsenals there, forcing Congress, which held its sessions at the time in Philadelphia, to flee. Without a reliable military, the central government was unable to respond to the civil uprisings, such as Shays's Rebellion.

External Threats   Threats along the nation's border also plagued the country. The British had not relinquished their hold on several Great Lakes forts, as the treaty ending the Revolutionary War required. In addition, the British stirred up Indian populations on the western frontier against American settlements and closed its Canadian and West Indian colonies to U.S. trade. Toward the south and southwest, Spain closed the Mississippi River to U.S. traffic, laid claim to lands east of the river that the United States also claimed, and incited Florida Indians to attack settlements in Georgia. On top of these threats, pirates in the Mediterranean Sea were attacking U.S. merchant ships.

People were rapidly losing faith in the central government under the Articles of Confederation. One indication of this loss of faith was that the nation's leaders began to correspond and talk to each other about changing the government to strengthen it. As early as 1783, Alexander Hamilton began calling for Congress to call a convention to reform the articles. Amending the articles did not seem to be the best road to take because of the unanimity provision that was required for such action. Initially, only a handful of states supported the idea, including important Virginia, but Shays's Rebellion sparked a feeling of emergency and crisis, and in 1787, Congress called for a convention to be held in Philadelphia. At Philadelphia, the delegates quickly decided to scrap the articles in their entirety and replace them with a new constitutional government.

INFLUENCES ON THE DECISIONS AT THE CONSTITUTIONAL CONVENTION

The problems that the Constitutional Convention delegates had to face in devising a new government were legion. They had to create a new government strong enough to govern but not so strong as to threaten liberties. Also, they had to create a government that would find popular approval and support. Important to these constitution writers was preserving the principles of constitutionalism, republicanism, and limited government—principles that were so hard fought for and won by the Revolutionary War—while also avoiding tyranny or mobocracy.

---

[13]On the Newburgh mutiny, see Richard H. Kohn, "Inside History of the Newburgh Conspiracy," *William and Mary Quarterly* 28 (1970): 187–220. Also, Richard M. Pious, *The Presidency* (New York: Allyn and Bacon, 1996), p. 21.

The Impact of the Colonial Experience

Colonial governors were the primary instruments of British administration of the American colonies. They became an important foundation for the presidency, more as an example of what the founders did not want in a presidency than as a positive example.[14] Colonial government was composed of three governmental offices: the governor, a council, and a legislature. The governor was appointed by the King, and the council was formally appointed by the King, based on the governor's recommendation. The legislative body, in contrast, was popularly elected. These three governmental bodies paralleled the British system, with the governor being the functional equivalent of the King, the council acting as the upper chamber (the House of Lords), and the legislature being similar to the lower legislative chamber (the House of Commons).

Governors of the colonies tended to hold formidable powers. In most cases, the governor possessed an absolute veto over legislation, could create courts and appoint judges, and could dissolve the legislature. Together with the council, the governor exerted tremendous power over the colonies, which many colonials often felt verged on abuse of power. As a result, upon rebellion, the newly organized state governments shifted power away from the executive and toward the state legislature.

The State Governor as a Model

During the Revolutionary War and Articles of Confederation periods, the governors of most states were quite weak, with most power resting in the hands of the legislature. Commonly, the governor was appointed to office by the legislature for a very short term, in most cases merely one year, and rarely was the incumbent eligible for reappointment. A council also tended to share powers with the governor; those powers were likely to be meager. Few state governors held veto or appointment powers, either. In sum, the governors of the states were weak and ineffectual, while the state legislatures were dominant.[15]

One governor, however, stood out as a strong leader and served in many respects as the model for the future presidency: the governor of New York.[16] The office of New York governor was among the last to be created (in 1777), and therefore, the New York constitution writers could look to the experiences of the other states when designing their governor's office.

Unlike other governors, the New York governor held a reasonably long term of office (three years), was popularly elected, and was eligible for unlimited

[14]On the colonial experience, see Louis Koenig, *The Chief Executive,* 5th ed. (New York: Harcourt, Brace, Jovanovich, 1986), p. 22, and Milkis and Nelson, *American Presidency,* pp. 2–3.

[15]Interestingly, in many states, the governor was titled "president." On the powers of the state governors, see Milkis and Nelson, *American Presidency,* pp. 3–5.

[16]Charles C. Thach, *The Creation of the Presidency, 1775–1789* (Baltimore: Johns Hopkins University Press, 1922).

reelection.[17] Thus, New York governors did not owe their position to the state legislature, and their power came from popular approval. Moreover, the New York governor did not share his powers with a council; it was truly a unitary office. This concentrated gubernatorial powers and authority in the hands of one person, the incumbent. The office also had important powers: a qualified veto power (subject to legislative override) and a qualified appointment power (again subject to legislative confirmation).

The substantive powers of the governor were also ample. He was commander in chief of the army and navy, on extraordinary occasions was allowed to call the legislature into session, and could issue pardons and reprieves. He was also expected to report to the legislature on the state of the state, was allowed to make recommendations for matters to be considered by the legislature, and was required to see that the laws were faithfully executed. New York's experience was a strong influence on the design of the presidency. In many instances, wording was lifted from the New York constitution and used in the national Constitution's article on the presidency.

The Importance of Ideas

Not only did colonial and early state experience inform the decisions of those who attended the convention in Philadelphia, but the ideas of thinkers and philosophers were also critical. The basic issue that the founders faced was how to create a strong national government yet preserve liberties, which was the primary justification for seeking independence from Great Britain.[18]

Before attending the Constitutional Convention, several of those designated to participate, such as James Madison, prepared themselves for the task that they were about to undertake by reading widely from history and political thought in search of some lessons and guidance. The ancient democracies, especially Athens and Rome, as well as the British experience, provided historical lessons, while the ideas of three political philosophers stood out in terms of influencing the thinking of the Constitution's framers. These three thinkers were William Blackstone, John Locke, and Charles-Louis Montesquieu.[19] From their writings, the framers identified important problems as well as possible solutions to those problems.

---

[17]On the New York governor, see Koenig, *Chief Executive,* pp. 22–23, and Milkis and Nelson, *American Democracy,* pp. 4–5.

[18]Different perspectives on the importance of ideas and the revolutionary and constitutional periods can be found in Bernard Bailyn, *Ideological Origins of the American Revolution* (Cambridge: Harvard University Press, 1967); Gordon Wood, *The Creation of the American Republic, 1776–1787* (New York: Norton, 1972); Forrest McDonald, *Novus Ordo Seclorum: The Intellectual Origins of the Constitution* (Lawrence: University Press of Kansas, 1987); and Forrest McDonald, *The American Presidency: An Intellectual History* (Lawrence: University Press of Kansas, 1994).

[19]An interesting study of the variety of thinkers who influenced the framers' ideas about government is found in Donald S. Lutz, "The Relative Influence of European Writers on Late Eighteenth-Century American Political Thought," *American Political Science Review* 78 (March 1984): 189–97.

Charles-Louis Montesquieu (1689–1755) was a French nobleman who was highly critical of absolute monarchy, chiefly because it suppressed liberty and paved the way for tyranny. In his most famous work, *Espirit des Lois* (*Spirit of the Laws,* 1748), Montesquieu argued that the best way to preserve liberty was to disperse power, and dispersed power was best realized through separation of powers. Moreover, Montesquieu felt that balanced government was necessary because politics was fundamentally about conflict between classes with different interests, such as nobles versus commoners, and nobles and commoners against the Crown. Balanced government, in Montesquieu's estimation, was best realized through a system of checks and balances.

Similarly important was the British jurist William Blackstone (1723–1780), whose most influential work was the *Commentaries on the Laws of England,* four volumes, published from 1765 to 1769. Blackstone described the "genius" of the British system as deriving from the limitations put on the monarchy through the rule of law and the systems of checks that the parliamentary system provided. The "Commentaries" became the foundation for all legal education in both Great Britain and the United States until the late nineteenth century. A strong believer in liberty, Blackstone is credited with the famous dictum that "It is better that ten guilty persons escape than that one innocent suffer."

Perhaps the most influential thinker of the period, at least with respect to framing the Constitution, was British philosopher John Locke (1632–1704), whose most relevant work in this regard was *Two Treatises on Government* (1690). Locke attacked the doctrine of divine right of kings, arguing that sovereignty resided with the people, not the monarchy. He also argued that the state must respect natural law, that is, no civil law could be made that alienated people from what was natural. To Locke, liberty and private property were natural, liberty could not exist without protection of private property, and thus, among the highest callings for government was protection of private property. Locke also possessed a well-developed and refined sense of separation of powers. He distinguished legislative or lawmaking power from executive or law-enforcing power and both from the "federated" powers that related to issues of war, peace, and foreign relations, where legislative and executive powers would be fused.

These thinkers, and others, influenced the framers of the Constitution profoundly. Concepts such as separation of powers, checks and balances, liberty, private property, republican versus directly democratic forms of government, and the rule of law can all be located in their thinking, and all are important values found in the Constitution. Rather than being founded on one key idea, the Constitution mixes and balances many ideas. Some ideas that the Constitution tried to incorporate are seemingly contradictory, such as a strong but limited government.

Two other ideas that are seemingly in great tension, separation of powers and checks and balances, provide the major underlying framework for the structure of the federal government under the Constitution. The combination of these two ideas also has important implications for the presidency.

Strictly speaking, separation of powers theory argues that one can distinguish the three major powers or activities of government—legislative, executive, and judicial—and that these three powers can be located in their respective institutions. The rationale behind separation of power is the preservation of liberty. Dividing governmental functions and powers in this way and locating each function in separate bodies helps prevent the concentration of power, which is thought to be the greatest threat to liberty by adherents of the strict separation of powers doctrine. Further, the theory of separation of powers bars encroachment of one branch on another and officials serving in one branch from serving in another.[20]

However, separation of powers theory is incompatible with another theory, that of mixed government, which is also concerned about threats to liberty. Checks and balances is one way to structure a mixed or balanced government. The idea behind checks and balances is that society is composed of several interests, each of which should find representation in the halls of government so that no one interest or class may dominate or rule. Furthermore, to inhibit the ability of any one interest from ruling or dominating, each interest is given a method of checking the powers and actions of another. Under checks and balances regimes, each branch and institution of government is designed to represent some interests better than another branch. And each branch would be given some power that would check the power of another branch, representing a different interest. For example, the president possesses a qualified veto, and the Senate has the power to confirm presidential nominees for judicial and executive branch posts. Thus, checks and balances preserves liberty through the power of one branch to check the actions of another.

Unlike separation of powers, checks and balances blends powers across governing institutions. In the examples offered above, is the presidential veto power legislative or executive? Clearly, it has strong legislative elements. Similarly, is the senatorial confirmation power legislative, executive, or judicial? Clearly, it has strong executive and judicial aspects.

However, it is not correct to characterize our constitutional system as merely mixed government. The bulk of the major functions of government fall to their respective branches. Furthermore, and most critically, there is strict separation in the officials who serve in government. Membership in Congress precludes holding a post in the executive or judicial branches, and incumbents in the executive and judicial are restricted to serving in those branches. What we have is most aptly put by political scientist Richard Neustadt: a system of "separated institutions sharing powers."[21] Thus, it is not that separation of powers exists, but rather that people who serve in government are separated into the different branches of government, each branch with different emphases and bases of power but also possessing some powers that overlap with the powers of the other branches of government. As a result, jealousy across the branches of government is fostered because of the possibility of one

---

[20]A good discussion of the strict or pure theory of separation of powers can be found in David N. Mayer, "Thomas Jefferson and the Separation of Powers," in *The Presidency Then and Now,* ed. Phillip G. Henderson (Lanham, Md.: Rowman and Littlefield, 2000), pp. 14–15.

[21]Richard E. Neustadt, *Presidential Power and the Modern Presidents: The Politics of Leadership from Roosevelt to Reagan* (New York: Free Press, 1990), p. 29. Also see Charles O. Jones, *The Presidency in a Separated System* (Washington, D.C.: Brookings Institution, 1994).

branch encroaching upon the others. In response, each branch will become diligent in protecting itself from possible encroachments by the other branches. A perpetual state of tension and competition will exist across the branches of government.

The framers of the Constitution built such a governmental system, with its separations and checks, not only to ensure liberty and limit government but also because they held a cynical view of human nature. Generally, they did not believe that one could rely on good people doing good work. Their view of human nature was darker. Baser emotions and motivations, such as jealousy, greed, ambition, and power hunger, would also affect behavior, and one could never be certain when a good or not-so-good person would serve in government. The founders built a system that would allow the expression of those baser motivations without undermining the ultimate goal of strong government that does not threaten liberty. In effect, the Constitution put into practice Madison's dictum from *Federalist* No. 51 that "Ambition must be made to counteract ambition."

INFLUENTIALS AT THE CONSTITUTIONAL CONVENTION

Several of the people who attended the Constitutional Convention were especially influential with regard to the presidency. James Wilson and Gouverneur Morris argued most vigorously for a strong executive, while James Madison, perhaps the most influential participant at the convention, came around to the idea of a relatively strong presidency only after initial misgivings. In the background, George Washington and John Adams the first and second presidents, also influenced the shape of the presidency. In fact, had there not been a consensus that George Washington would be the first president, it is entirely likely that the office would have emerged as a much weaker version than it ultimately did. Lastly, lest we overstate the idea that the constitutional presidency is without qualification a strong office, Alexander Hamilton, who argued for the strongest version of the presidency, an elected monarchy, had little influence, and with little debate his notions were summarily rejected by the convention.

James Madison

Historians regard James Madison (1751–1836) as the single most influential person at the Constitutional Convention in Philadelphia. A Virginian, Madison came to the convention with wide political experience despite his youth. He authored the bulk of the **Virginia plan,** discussed in the section on "Decision Making at the Constitutional Convention," and he was instrumental in forging many of the compromises that were necessary to attain majority support for specific provisions and the Constitution overall.

However, Madison did not come to the convention with any well-thought-out ideas about the nature or structure of the executive.[22] His major concern centered

---

[22]Jack N. Rakove and Susan Zlomke, "James Madison and the Independent Executive," *Presidential Studies Quarterly* 17 (Spring 1987): 293–300.

on checking the abuses of the legislative branch, exemplified by the actions of many of the state legislatures that caved in to the demands of radical farmers to inflate their economies by printing worthless paper money.[23] These examples tempered Madison's belief in democracy, and he feared that popularly elected legislatures would undermine liberties and private property. John Locke's ideas strongly influencing him, Madison thought that to protect liberties in general required protecting private property.

James Wilson

Like Madison, James Wilson (1742–1798) was quite young and politically experienced when he came to the Philadelphia convention. Unlike Madison, Wilson had definite ideas about the presidency, being a forceful advocate of a strong and popularly based presidency.[24]

Wilson proposed a strong, unitary presidency with unlimited reeligibility and a popular base. According to Wilson, only a strong presidency could check the potential abuses that might come from a popularly elected legislature. Also, unlike many of the time, he saw the presidency as being a republican, that is, representative institution and not another name for monarchy.

Wilson thought this representativeness could come about if the president were held accountable. Accountability, in turn, was possible only with a unitary executive who owed his position to the public and who could be returned to office so that he would care about the public. Consequently, Wilson advocated direct election of the president—one of the few positions he held that did not carry the day. The electoral college compromise mollified Wilson, however, by eliminating legislative appointment of the executive, which he thought would undermine the president's independence from the legislature. The electoral college also allowed the president to point to his popular and wide base of public support, being elected at least indirectly by the public from across the nation. Thus, the president would serve in the people's interest, the national interest, unlike Congress, which Wilson thought was more likely to be captive to local and narrow interests.

Wilson not only viewed the presidency in accountability terms but agreed with Hamilton that energy and dispatch were needed in the executive. The basis of Wilson's reasoning was that national emergencies required quick responses, something possible only in a unitary office. Congress, by its collective nature, would be more deliberative, a virtue when time was not of the essence but, according to Wilson, a potential disaster if time was short for taking effective action.

---

[23]Fear of legislative tyranny was a major cause of concern among those, such as Madison, Wilson, and Morris, who advocated a strong executive as a check. See Judith A. Best, "Legislative Tyranny and the Liberation of the Executive: A View from the Founding," *Presidential Studies Quarterly* 17 (Fall 1987): 697–709.

[24]Robert E. DiClerico, "James Wilson's Presidency," *Presidential Studies Quarterly* 17 (Spring 1987): 301–17, and Daniel J. McCarthy, "James Wilson and the Creation of the Presidency," *Presidential Studies Quarterly* 17 (Fall 1987): 696–98.

Gouverneur Morris

Gouverneur Morris (1752–1816), like Wilson and Madison, was quite young (thirty-five) when he appeared as a delegate to the Constitutional Convention. At the convention, no one spoke more often than Morris—173 times, according to Madison's notes of the convention's debates.[25] In general, Morris and Wilson teamed together to fight for a strong unitary executive of unlimited reeligibility and directly elected by the people.

Like Wilson, Morris feared that the legislature would become the bastion of special interests. In particular, Morris contended that in a republic that fostered commercial activity, propertied interests would become the most powerful class and would dominate the legislature. To reset the balance away from narrow interests and toward a national interest, a strong presidency with ties to the nation at large, including the public overall, was required. Thus, to Morris, the president could become the tribune of the people and guardian of the national interest, but only if the office were made independent and tied to the populace. Hence, Morris's support for a unitary, popularly elected president.

Moreover, Morris supported a strong, active executive by substituting the word *duty* for *may* in the clause instructing the president to report to Congress on the state of the union. He did not want anyone to stand in the president's way of becoming active in the policy making process. Similarly, he objected to any attempt to limit presidential control of top-level administration by making, for example, the nation's treasurer subject to joint appointment by the president and Congress.[26]

Adams, Washington, and Hamilton

Whereas Madison, Wilson, and Morris were outspoken activists at the Constitutional Convention, plainly leaving their fingerprints on the document, others were influential in more subtle ways. For instance, John Adams helped frame the Constitution and the doctrine of checks and balances, which provides much of the foundation on which the details of the Constitution are built, despite his less prominent presence at the Convention. Adams made a strong case for checks and balances in his book, *Defense of the Constitution of the United States of America Against the Attack of Mr. Turgott*. He viewed society as being divided into three conflicting classes—the monarchy, the aristocracy, and the masses—each capable, if given the power, of tyrannizing the others. Through the system of checks and balances, a strong government that would not undermine liberties could be created.

Alexander Hamilton was an ardent advocate of assembling a convention to rewrite the Articles of Confederation. But his influence at the convention, despite

---

[25]Cited in Donald L. Robinson, 'Gouverneur Morris and the Design of the American Presidency," *Presidential Studies Quarterly* 17 (Spring 1987): 319–28 (p. 322).

[26]Robinson, "Gouverneur Morris," p. 326.

his political prominence, was mild, owing to his decision to bolt from the convention early in its deliberations. While not supportive of a hereditary monarchy, Hamilton argued that once elected, the president should serve for life to ensure an independent executive, one that would not be brought into the petty political squabbles of the day but would be on the lookout for the broader national interest.

No one else at the convention, however, thought that such a presidency could be sold to the public after having fought a long and costly war against the British monarchy. To the majority of delegates, gaining any type of presidency was seen as an uphill fight. Hamilton's proposal was too far out of step with the prevailing mood for acceptance, and if included in the Constitution, would doom its chances for ratification. In a huff, Hamilton left the convention, although he became an ardent supporter of the Constitution during the ratification debates that followed, authoring the *Federalist Papers* that in particular dealt with the presidency (discussed in Chapter 2).

Washington, unlike Madison, Wilson, and Morris, was a towering, if silent, influence on the Constitution Convention. Part of Hamilton's justification for his presidential proposal was the notion that Washington would serve as the first president and that a long term of service by the first occupant would help ensure a necessary period of political stability.

No one was more respected than Washington, who served as the convention's presiding officer. Everyone present assumed that Washington would become the nation's first president, a prospect that emboldened supporters of a strong executive to press their point. In part, then, the presidency was being designed with Washington in mind. As South Carolina delegate Pierce Butler observed, "I do [not] believe they [the executive powers] would have been so great had not so many members cast their eyes toward General Washington as President; and shaped their Ideas of the Powers to be given the President, by their opinions of his Virtue."[27] Washington, too, seemed to support a strong executive.[28] Rarely speaking at the convention, he also rarely voted on measures before the delegates. But in the few instances of his voting, he supported a strong executive. Thus, he voted for a unitary office and against a proposal that restricted reeligibility.

DECISION MAKING AT THE CONSTITUTIONAL CONVENTION

The Constitution is a document that attempts to implement a set of ideas through the structure of government. We should not, however, leap to the conclusion that the delegates to the Constitutional Convention were starry-eyed idealists. Many were experienced politicians who understood that compromise is often required

[27]Quoted in Koenig, *Chief Executive,* p. 29.

[28]Glenn A. Phelps, "George Washington and the Founding of the Presidency," *Presidential Studies Quarterly* 17 (Spring 1987): 345–63, and Glenn A. Phelps, "George Washington: Precedent Setter," in *Inventing the American Presidency,* ed. Thomas E. Cronin (Lawrence: University Press of Kansas, 1989), pp. 259–81.

to forge majority support for proposals. Compromise was required at the Constitutional Convention because significant divisions existed among the states and the delegates over important issues.

The Philadelphia convention convened on May 25, 1787.[29] Two decisions in the early business meetings were crucial. First, the debates were to be kept secret in an effort to allow free debate without the constraints of public or outside pressure and to keep delegates from playing to the crowds. Second, any decision could be reconsidered. No decision was final until the entire constitutional document was accepted. This was to allow forces that lost on a decision to bring it up for reconsideration, to convince others to change their minds, and, most important, to keep anyone from walking out of the convention over a dispute.

On May 29, substantive business and debate began with the introduction of the Virginia plan, which included provisions relevant to the presidency. Across the next several weeks, three other plans were introduced for debate, the New Jersey plan and plans by Alexander Hamilton and Charles Pinckney of South Carolina.

The Virginia plan, authored mainly by James Madison, was the first proposal submitted to the convention for debate. Under the plan, three branches of government were to be created, and the new national government was to reign supreme over the states by having the power to veto state laws that conflicted with the Constitution. The core of government was to be a bicameral legislature. It was to choose the executive, thereby giving the legislature strong control over the proposed executive. The executive, with the judiciary, was granted the power to veto legislation in what was termed a "council of revision," subject to legislative override. Otherwise, the Virginia plan was quite vague about the executive. For instance, it did not specify either the length of term or the composition of the executive (plural or unitary).

The representative bias of the Virginia plan was toward the big states. Both houses of the legislature were to be apportioned by population, with the lower house choosing members of the upper chamber. The small states opposed the Virginia proposal, which they countered with their own, called the **New Jersey plan.** Under that plan, each state was given equal representation in the legislature. And while the Virginia plan was presented as a new constitution, the New Jersey plan was submitted as amendments to the Articles of Confederation. Beyond these, there was little difference between these two initial plans.

Alexander Hamilton proposed the most radical departure with his plan that was submitted to the convention on June 18, just several days after the submission of the New Jersey plan. Hamilton proposed the strongest of all governmental forms, modeled on the British parliamentary system, which included a monarchy. He did not propose a hereditary monarchy but rather one in which electors would select the monarch for lifetime tenure. Moreover, Hamilton's elected monarch was given wide powers, including an absolute veto on legislation, direction of war, exclusive appointment power of department heads, and

---

[29]A very good discussion of the Constitutional Convention is found in Milkis and Nelson, *American Presidency,* pp. 8–23, which I rely on heavily in this section.

pardoning power for all cases except treason. Only treaty-making power was to be shared, with the Senate. Hamilton's plan was quickly disregarded by the convention, the monarchial provision being the most repugnant to the delegates, and Hamilton left the convention.

Charles Pinckney of South Carolina offered the last plan, which aimed more at revising the articles than creating a new constitution. Still, it heavily relied on the New York governorship as a model for the new presidency, except that under Pinckney's plan, the presidency was to be elected by the legislature.[30]

On June 19, the New Jersey plan was defeated and the Virginia plan accepted and sent from the "committee of the whole" to the convention, where each clause was to be scrutinized, debated, and, if needed, modified. This process, which began on June 20, extended until late July. A major sticking point was the apportionment of large and small states in the legislature. The most important changes associated with the presidency included dropping the provision for legislative election of the presidency, but no solution to presidential selection appeared during this month-long debate.

The document that emerged was sent on July 24 to the Committee of Detail. That committee fleshed out the Constitution as reported to it by the convention; the resulting Constitution was about three times as long.[31] The five-member committee also incorporated ideas and wordings from the New Jersey plan, the Articles of Confederation, the Pinckney plan, and the state constitutions of New York and Massachusetts.

Yet the committee placed its own stamp on the document by enumerating some grants of power not previously detailed and replacing several provisions. With regard to the presidency, the committee added to the powers of the presidency: to recommend legislation to Congress, make executive appointments, receive ambassadors, issue pardons, command the armed forces, and see that "the laws were faithfully executed."

The committee reported back to the convention on August 6, and another round of debate commenced, lasting till the end of the month. It was during this stage that many of the most momentous decisions were made, including the issues of counting a slave as three-fifths of a vote in the apportionment of Congress,[32] the prohibition against laws that would restrict the importation of slaves before 1808, and the compromise on the representation of states in the House and Senate.

Another subcommittee, the Committee on Postponed Matters, took up its task during the week of August 31 to September 8, fleshing out many unresolved issues regarding the presidency. The term of office was reduced from seven to

---

[30]On the Pinckney plan, see Koenig, *Chief Executive,* p. 25.

[31]Milkis and Nelson, *American Presidency,* p. 17.

[32]In deciding on how to count the population of states, the founders determined that a slave was to be counted as three-fifths of a person.

four years, with unlimited reeligibility and election by the electoral college. Some responsibilities were assigned to the vice president, who was to be the candidate who received the second largest number of electoral votes, the president being the one who gained the most votes *and* majority support. Also, if no candidate received a majority, the House of Representatives was to make the final choice from among the top five candidates. Qualifications for holding the office were also specified.

The convention quickly took action on this committee report, making only minor adjustments. It added to the presidency the powers to make treaties and appoint ambassadors, Supreme Court justices, and other high-level officials, with the advice and consent of the Senate. The impeachment process was also delineated. On September 9, the Committee on Style convened to work on wording, and the convention continued to work on remaining matters, such as amendment procedures. Finally, on September 17, the Constitution was approved by forty-one of the original fifty-five delegates. Only three of those who remained to the end refused to sign. In Chapter 2, we assess the constitutional presidency.

KEY TERMS

Articles of Confederation   6
checks and balances   2
executive order   4
executive prerogative   3

modern presidency   3
New Jersey plan   19
separation of powers   2
Virginia plan   15

DISCUSSION QUESTIONS

1. How do checks and balances and separation of powers affect the presidency?
2. How is the modern presidency different from the presidency of earlier years?
3. What historical and philosophical factors influenced the original design of the presidency?
4. Which delegates to the Constitutional Convention had the most influence on the original design of the presidency?

SUGGESTED READINGS

Joseph Bessette and Jeffrey Tulis, eds., *The Presidency in the Constitutional Order*. Baton Rouge: Louisiana State University Press, 1981.

Thomas Cronin, *Inventing the American Presidency*. Lawrence: University Press of Kansas, 1989.

Daniel Farber and Suzanna Sherry, *A History of the American Constitution*. St. Paul, Minn.: West Publishing, 1990.

2

ASSESSING THE CONSTITUTIONAL PRESIDENCY

In Chapter 1, we discussed the forces that led to the creation of the presidency and the Constitution. In this chapter, we follow up on that discussion by assessing the constitutional nature of the presidency. We begin by outlining the powers of the presidency as established in the Constitution. Then we review the debates between the Federalists and Antifederalists over the presidency during the campaign to ratify the Constitution. We conclude this chapter by comparing the presidency to other chief executives, the state governors, and presidents of other nations in our attempt to gain further perspective on the nature of the constitutional presidency.

THE CONSTITUTIONAL STRUCTURE AND POWERS OF THE PRESIDENCY

Americans like to think of the presidency as the strongest office in the land and the world. Most presidents would disagree, feeling that the office is greatly confined, mostly because of the separation of powers and checks and balances. In this section, we delineate the major constitutional characteristics and powers of the presidency at the time of its inception in 1787. This will help us get a sense of how the framers of the Constitution conceptualized the presidency and the governmental role that they envisioned the presidency would play.

Single or Plural Executive?

Should the executive be a unitary or plural office? If unitary, should the executive have to consult with a council or other body before taking action? These questions were among the first and most important concerning the presidency raised at the Constitutional Convention.

James Wilson of Pennsylvania proposed a unitary executive. His argument was that only an unitary executive could act with "energy" and "dispatch." Further, Wilson maintained that it was easier to hold a single executive accountable than a plural executive. For instance, should we hold one of the members of the plural executive accountable for an action taken by the body when that executive opposed the action? How should the executive proceed in the face of splits in opinion among its members? What would happen to the conduct of foreign affairs or military operations if a nation belligerent to the United States were aware of division within the executive?

Despite the argument that accountability was clearer with a unitary executive, not all delegates initially supported that idea. Some, such as Edmund Randolph of Virginia, viewed a unitary executive as a threat to liberty. He contended that in time, the office would evolve into a monarchy, a danger that outweighed any advantage that a unitary executive would provide. Randolph proposed instead that the executive be composed of a three-person committee. Others felt that the issue should not be defined in the Constitution but rather that Congress should be allowed to determine the unitary-plural nature of the executive. Proponents of this idea would have allowed Congress to restructure the executive as events and necessity dictated. These "congressionalists" held that Congress should be the seat of power in government and that the executive should be the servant of the legislature.

The chaos of weak government under the Articles of Confederation and Wilson's arguments, especially those pertaining to accountability, proved persuasive, however, and the convention, which originally had only the vaguest notion of what the executive should look like, adopted the unitary executive approach.

A related issue was whether the executive should be required to consult with a council before taking action. Like a plural executive, a consultative council dispersed the authority and power of the executive, and potentially interfered with the executive's ability to take quick and decisive action. Indirectly, consultation with a council also raised the accountability issue. If the executive could not take action until after consulting with such a council, who was responsible for whatever action was finally taken?

One council proposal suggested, for instance, that the president be required to consult with the judiciary, but opponents of this position argued that such a joint executive-judicial arrangement might overwhelm the legislature, disrupt the balance among the three branches that was being sought, while also undermining any sense of separation of powers. In the end, the convention was unable to find a council formula that a consensus could support, and the idea was dropped.

A related issue involved the idea of a cabinet. The framers were familiar with cabinet government, which was already in use in the British parliamentary system. Also, the U.S. government had used executive departments, such as State, War, and Treasury, during the Revolutionary War and Articles of Confederation periods. Moreover, the appointment provisions in the Constitution—presidential nomination with senatorial confirmation—provide a more concrete expression to the notion that the framers intended executive departments to exist in the new regime. Thus, while the Constitution makes no formal provision for a cabinet, it appears that the framers intended, if not a cabinet, at least government departments.

However, the framers decided to hold off on designing the cabinet and the rest of the executive branch until after the ratification of the Constitution. They reserved this decision for the newly installed government. But this lack of action on a cabinet implies that the framers did not intend the cabinet to become a council, as discussed above, nor a site for collective, executive responsibility. Such responsibility was to be the president's alone.

Method of Election

The unitary nature of the presidency provided one element of a strong executive. How the executive would be selected would also affect the strength of the office. This issue being among the most controversial regarding the presidency, two options were debated: election by the legislature and election by the people.

A number of delegates believed that selection by the legislature would inherently weaken the executive, whether it be unitary or plural. They doubted that Congress would select a strong executive if it was granted the power to choose the president. More likely, Congress would select someone easily controlled. For an executive to be strong and to act with the energy and dispatch that James Wilson and his supporters sought in a unitary presidency, the executive must somehow be independent of Congress. In essence, a strong presidency requires an independent power base. The most likely source of such power resides in the mass public. Thus, several delegates, again including Wilson, argued for popular election by the voting public. Several forces at the convention argued against popular election, however.

First, some, but not all, of the delegates feared so much popular participation. The public, it was argued, expressed itself in the election of representatives to the lower chamber of Congress. Giving them such a clear voice in the executive could tilt the new government too far in the direction of a popular versus a representative government. Part of the rationale for balanced government through checks and balances was to allow popular voice and participation but not to allow that popular voice to dominate. Therefore, while the House of Representatives was seen as the body most closely tied to popular politics, the other branches of government, the presidency included, should be somewhat insulated from the popular pressures.

Still, advocates of a strong presidency saw it as the "guardian of the people," (Gouverneur Morris of Pennsylvania's term), with the House acting as the representative of localities and the Senate the representative of upper-class and statewide interests. The presidency was envisioned as representing the larger, public interest, not small, geographic, sectoral, or class interests. How could they construct a presidency that would represent the national interest without being overly responsive to popular passions? The answer would come with the electoral college.

But before discussing the electoral college, we need to make note of other forces that opposed direct election of the president. These mainly came from the small states, which feared that the large states would dominate the vote for president. This and the power of the large states in the House of Representatives, delegates from small states feared, would tilt the balance of power too far to the advantage of the large states over the small. Others, such as George Mason of Virginia, argued that given the size of the nation and the primitive communications system, the public would be unable to make a reasoned choice about the president because few would know who was qualified for the job.

A compromise solution emerged with the **electoral college.** Some viewed the electoral college as a way to check popular opinion, arising from the distrust that the founders had with democracy.[1] Others saw it as a pragmatic solution to a nagging problem.[2] It is hard from the vantage point of our mass media-drenched society to view the electoral college as a democratic institution, but that is how most of the founders saw it.[3]

The mechanics of the electoral college are far from simple and are described at length in Article II, Section 1 of the Constitution. First, each state's electoral college vote was based on the number of *senators and representatives* that the state sent to Congress. Thus, the apportionment of Congress, which aimed at meeting the representation needs of both large and small states, is replicated in the electoral college.

However, the Constitution is silent on the method of selection of the presidential electors other than that no senator, representative, or "Person holding an Office of Trust or Profit under the United States" could be an elector. The Constitution allows each state to devise its own system of appointing electors. Initially, the state legislatures selected the electors, but popular voting for electors quickly gained support. By 1800, five of the fifteen states chose electors by popular vote, and by 1828, all but Delaware and South Carolina did so.

Another feature of the electoral college was that the electors in each state shall vote for at least two persons one of whom must not be a resident of the state, and that a list of all persons who received a vote for president shall be transmitted to the Senate. The designers of the electoral college thought that in general, no one would receive a majority of electoral votes, which would turn the election over to the House of Representatives. In effect, the electoral college system was envisioned as a winnowing process by which a small number of viable candidates for the office would be sent to Congress for final selection.

Still, the framers in general viewed the electoral college as fundamentally a popular process that would provide the president with a popular base and a power base that was independent of Congress. It also helped overcome some other problems of selecting the national executive in a country as geographically vast as the United States which at the time possessed at best a crude communications infrastructure.

The electoral college effectively dealt with the problem of rudimentary communications across a far-flung territory limiting the public's ability to gather enough information to make a reasoned choice. Institutions like national political parties did not yet exist, and it was assumed that people would vote based on the reputations of people. Knowledge of reputations was easier to assess in

---

[1]For instance, Charles A. Beard, *An Economic Interpretation of the Constitution of the United States* (New York: Macmillan, 1913).

[2]John P. Roche, "The Founding Fathers: A Reform Caucus in Action," *American Political Science Review* 55 (December 1961): 799–816.

[3]This line of argument is articulated in Shlomo Slonim, "Designing the Electoral College," in *Inventing the American Presidency,* ed. Thomas E. Cronin (Lawrence: University Press of Kansas, 1989), pp. 33–60.

small units, where the average citizen was likely to know or be aware of the important notables.

The framers assumed that the electors would be more familiar with the notables around the nation than average citizens, being more involved in politics and other activities that would broaden their acquaintances. Thus, the electors were viewed as important intermediaries in carrying out the people's wishes with regard to presidential selection. In effect, the electors could be considered to be the agents of the public.

Thus, like the unitary executive, which provided for a strong presidency, the choice of the electoral college also helped to provide for a strong executive by ensuring that election would be independent of the legislature. Through the electoral college were established the popular roots and bases of the power of the presidency, which would be greatly enhanced in the future development of the office. But the electoral college also fit in with the founders' republican conception of government by keeping the people one step removed from the selection of the president. This, it was hoped, would help steer the presidency away from demagoguery and populism, while still making the president the voice of the national interest and the people at large.

Length of Term, Reeligibility, and Other Qualifications for Office

Popular governments, whether democracies or republics, are based on the notion that the people are sovereign. Thus, political leaders serve at the pleasure of the people for a limited time and do not possess a property right of the office that they hold. Still, the power that an office confers upon its occupant is partly a function of how long that person is allowed to serve—the longer the service, the greater the power. A consequential decision for the designers of the Constitution was how long incumbents would be allowed to hold their offices.

Consistent with the ideas of the separation of powers, dispersal of political power and authority, and limitations of popular rule, the Constitution's designers gave each branch of government a different term of office, as they had given each a different constituency. The House of Representatives, which many viewed as potentially being the most powerful branch of government due to its small constituencies and direct popular election, was limited by frequent election. The Senate, with its larger constituencies and nonpopular election, was provided with a long tenure of six years. Judges, who were insulated from popular pressures through the complex nomination and confirmation process, were given lifetime tenure. The presidency was granted a moderately long term of four years.

Four years exceeded the two-year terms that most of the weak state governors possessed and the three-year term of the stronger New York governor. By this reasoning, we can think of the presidency as a moderately strong office, much in accord with the reasoning discussed concerning the electoral college in the section on "Method of Election."

The Constitution's designers also decided to grant the president unlimited eligibility for reelection. As long as the president proved to be a good president, he should be allowed to stay in office, without the Constitution artificially restricting his service. Viewing politicians as ambitious men, the designers of the Constitution reckoned that reeligibility would serve as an incentive for incumbents to offer wise government, to stay within the boundaries of the Constitution, and to be responsive to outside demands for responsible, effective government. This they would have to do to retain the power and prestige that the office conferred upon them.

A term-limited office, it was supposed, would uncouple the president, as well as legislators, from this type of incentive, perhaps motivating the president to make decisions that either would serve his own self-interest or would violate the constitutional balance among the branches. In extreme circumstances, presidents bent on retaining power but limited in eligibility might threaten to dispense with the constitutional regime altogether. Reeligibility could fuel the ambitions of politicians, while also keeping them in check.

But what should be done if a president proved ineffective or corrupt before his term of office expired? The designers of the Constitution dealt with this eventuality with an impeachment process. However, they were wary of allowing the impeachment process to be used for narrow political reasons, such as to remove from office a political competitor or one who espoused policies that a majority of members of Congress disagreed with.

The Impeachment Process   Like many constitutional processes, the impeachment process is both cumbersome and at times ambiguous and lacking in direction. Invoking the process must begin with an understanding of impeachable offenses. The framers' view of impeachment rested with offenses that would undermine the constitutional order. Impeachment was not to be used as a political device. Thus, the famous but ambiguous phrase describing impeachable offenses: "treason, bribery, or other high crimes and misdemeanors" (Article 2, Section 4, Paragraph 1).

The process begins in the House of Representatives, which must vote on articles of impeachment. Upon a majority vote, the impeachment charges are sent to the Senate, which acts as jury. The House of Representatives plays the role of prosecutor as it tries to convince the Senate that the president is guilty of the charges that it has levied against him. The chief justice of the Supreme Court sits much like a judge in any other judicial proceeding. The fact, however, that it requires a two-thirds majority of the Senate to convict the president and not a simple majority attests to the framers' intention that the process not be used for partisan or political purposes but only for higher reasons, such as to defend against the undermining of the constitutional order. If convicted, the president is removed from office and is ineligible for future office holding. Lastly, other than removal from office, impeachment carried with it no other penalties, although the impeached officeholder could "be liable and subject to indictment, trial, judgement and punishment, according to law" (Article 1, Section 3, Paragraph 7). This last provision ensured that public servants would not be held above the law but would be subject to it, as all citizens are. We will discuss impeachment in more detail, including its historical use against presidents Andrew Johnson, Richard Nixon, and Bill Clinton, in Chapter 10 on presidential-legislative relations.

Executive Powers and Enumerated Powers

The Constitution provides the president with a long list of powers and responsibilities. It is ambiguous, however, about whether or not this list exhausts the powers of the presidency. This confusion stems from the phrase, "The Executive Power shall be vested in a president of the United States of America" (Article 2, Section 1, Paragraph 1). Nowhere is the term *executive power* defined.

Indications exist, however, that the delegates at the Constitutional Convention did not intend the presidency to be limited to the enumerated powers (to be described more fully in the following paragraphs). James Madison argued at the Constitutional Convention that the powers of the president should be defined, but his view was rejected for the more general and ambiguous "executive power" phrase. Disagreement has existed over whether this phrase refers merely to the powers of the presidency that are enumerated, mostly in Section 2 of Article 2 of the Constitution, or whether this ambiguously worded phrase allows the expansion of presidential powers beyond the enumerated powers. Despite the dispute, the presidency has evolved beyond the enumerated powers.

Article 2 contains most of the enumerated powers of the presidency. They are listed in table 2-1. Scattered throughout the rest of the Constitution are a few other passages that describe presidential powers, the most important relating to the process of passing legislation, where the president is given the qualified veto (Article 1, Section 7, Paragraph 2).

The **enumerated powers** can be roughly divided into the following categories: relations with Congress and the legislative process; diplomatic and military affairs; and administration of government. With regard to Congress, the president plays a role in the legislative process, not as a legislator but by his power to approve or veto legislation, which Congress can override by a two-thirds vote of both houses (Article 1, Section 7, Paragraph 3). The president is also given a less formal role in the legislative process with his constitutional duty to report on the state of the union and, perhaps more important, to make recommendations for legislative action (Article 2, Section 3, Paragraph 1). This constitutional duty is somewhat vague as to timing and format. Nowhere is the president instructed on how many times or in what manner he must inform the Congress. However, presidents have taken this task seriously. George Washington initiated the annual State of the Union address to fulfill this responsibility, a practice that subsequent presidents have followed, institutionalizing the State of the Union address as a fixture in U.S. politics.[4]

---

[4]The State of the Union address has evolved over time. Whereas Washington presented the address in person to a joint session of Congress, Thomas Jefferson dispensed with the personal appearance, instead sending a written address to Congress. Woodrow Wilson returned to the practice of personal delivery, which has been the tradition ever since.

TABLE 2-1   THE ENUMERATED POWERS OF THE PRESIDENCY
AS SPECIFIED IN THE CONSTITUTION

From Article 1, Section 7, Paragraph 3:

—Every order, resolution, or vote to which the concurrence of the Senate and House of Representatives may be necessary (except on a question of adjournment) shall be presented to the president of the United States, and before the same shall take effect, shall be approved by him

—or, being disapproved by him, shall be re-passed by two-thirds of the Senate and House of Representatives

From Article 2, Section 2, Paragraph 1:

—Commander in chief of the army and navy and of the militia of the several states

—may require the opinions, in writing, of the principal officer in each of the executive departments

—power to grant reprieves and pardons, except in case of impeachment

From Article 2, Section 2, Paragraph 2:

—shall have the power, by and with the advice and consent of the Senate, to make treaties

—shall nominate, and by and with the advice and consent of the Senate, appoint ambassadors, other public ministers, and consuls, judges of the Supreme Court

From Article 2, Section 2, Paragraph 3:

—shall have power to fill up all vacancies that may happen during the recess of the Senate, by granting commissions, which shall expire at the end of the next session

From Article 2, Section 3, Paragraph 1:

—shall, from time to time, give to the Congress information of the state of the union, and recommend for their consideration, such measures as he shall judge necessary and expedient

—may, on extraordinary occasions, convene both houses, or either of them, and in case of disagreement between them, with respect to the time of adjournment, he may adjourn them to such a time as he shall think proper

—shall receive ambassadors and other public ministers

—shall take care that the laws are faithfully executed

—shall commission all of the officers of the United States

Throughout history, executives have dealt with stubborn, antagonistic, and independently minded legislatures by dissolving them and proceeding to direct a nation's affairs unilaterally. The president was given no such power, although when the two houses of Congress could not agree on a time for adjournment, the president was given the power to decide that date (Article 2, Section 3, Paragraph 1). More important, however, was the presidential power to call Congress into session for "extraordinary occasions" (Article 2, Section 3, Paragraph 1). Here, we see the energy and dispatch that the founders intended for the presidency: When times called for it, such as during major emergencies like wars, presidents would lead. It is also from this provision that we see where the presidency's importance to the founders would be located—in foreign affairs, where secrecy, speed, decisiveness, and boldness of action, rather than the deliberateness and debate of a representative legislature, would be required for the nation's security.

Thus, the president's strongest enumerated powers would be in matters of foreign and military affairs. The president would be **commander in chief**

(Article 2, Section 2, Paragraph 1), which would not only secure civilian control over the military, necessary in a democratic republic, but ensure unity of command, which is necessary for effective use of military forces. Furthermore, presidents were to commission the officers of the military (Article 2, Section 3, Paragraph 1), again underscoring their commander-in-chief powers, as well as civilian control of the military.

The president does not have complete control over military matters. The Constitution provides that Congress has the power to declare war, to raise and support military forces, to make rules for their governance, and to make policies regarding the "militia," which we now call the National Guard. Given the expense of military programs in the modern age, congressional powers over money and military finance are also significant. Many constitutional scholars have made a distinction between "making" war and "declaring" war, arguing that the president possesses wide latitude to do the first, but Congress is constitutionally empowered to do the latter. In Chapter 15 on foreign policy, we will discuss this issue in more detail.

Beyond military command, presidents were to take the lead in diplomatic affairs by first receiving ambassadors and other representatives from foreign nations (Article 2, Section 3). But nowhere does the Constitution say that the president shall unilaterally make foreign policy. Although presidents have the power to forge treaties with other nations, the Senate possesses the power to ratify treaties (Article 2, Section 2, Paragraph 2). Ratification requires an extraordinary two-thirds majority, which was intended to force the president to negotiate treaties that the vast majority of the nation could support. Reinforcing the lead that the president was to take in foreign policy was his naming of ambassadors, but again, this power was confined by the necessity of senatorial confirmation (Article 2, Section 2, Paragraph 2).

The other major arena of presidential powers concerned the operation and administration of government. Congress had experience with executive departments during the Revolutionary War and under the Articles of Confederation, and the delegates to the convention assumed that similar agencies and offices would exist under the new Constitution. The experience and chaos of having Congress and its committees run government operations also affected the thinking of the convention delegates—government would be run more effectively, efficiently, and accountably if it were coordinated under the auspices of the president. Thus, we find here some of the president's most sweeping, if not entirely clear, powers.

For instance, the president could require the opinions and advice, in writing, from the lead officials of the government's departments and agencies (Article 2, Section 2, Paragraph 1), officials whom the president appointed to office, although again, with senatorial confirmation in most cases (Article 2, Section 2, Paragraph 2). However, the president could not keep top officials from reporting to Congress because of Congress's power of investigation. Nor did the Constitution say anything about the president's power to fire or remove people from office, an omission that would lead to many legal disputes.

But perhaps the most expansive administrative power derives from the phrase that the president "shall take care that the laws are faithfully executed" (Article 2,

Section 3, Paragraph 1). The exact meaning of this clause is unclear, but presidents have used it to support actions that they want to take, as well as on occasion to bar Congress and others from acting or prohibiting presidential activities. For instance, from this power, presidents have been able to issue executive orders directing bureaucrats to take or not take action.

Presidential Prerogatives?

The enumeration of presidential powers raises the issue of whether the president can act beyond what those powers grant. As indicated, the founders intended that the president not be strictly bound by the enumerated powers. Yet the question remains of how far beyond the enumerated powers a president can venture. Related to this question is whether the president, as an executive, possesses prerogatives of office.[5]

Executive prerogatives are an important foundation for monarchies, even constitutional ones, such as Great Britain. Fundamentally, the prerogative power allows the monarch to disregard the actions of the legislature—in the most extreme instance, dissolving it. But the prerogative power is also the foundation for the modern veto power.

The delegates to the Constitutional Convention were wary of using the term *prerogative* to describe the executive power because of its association with the British monarchy and the supposed abuses of monarchial power that led to the revolution. Thus, advocates of a strong presidency at the Constitutional Convention substituted such words as *energy* and *dispatch* when describing the presidency. Their understanding of executive prerogatives derived from the English philosopher John Locke, who argued that executives may have to take actions without the backing of legislation because the nation may be threatened. In his famous *Second Treatise,* Locke writes:

> many things there are which the law can by no means provide for, and those must necessarily be left to the discretion of him that has the executive power in his hands, to be ordered by him as the public good and advantage shall require; nay, it is fit that the laws themselves should in some cases give way to the executive power, or rather to this fundamental law of Nature and government, viz., that as much as may be all the members of the society are to be preserved.[6]

Locke even goes so far as to argue that the executive can act according to his "discretion, for the public good, without the prescription of the law, and sometimes even against it."[7] The delegates to the Constitutional Convention were clearly thinking of

---

[5]Thomas S. Langston and Michael E. Lind, "John Locke and the Limits of Presidential Prerogative," *Polity* 24 (Fall 1991): 49–68; Pasquale Pasquino, "Locke on King's Prerogative," *Political Theory* 26 (April 1998): 198–208; David R. Weaver, "Leadership, Locke, and the Federalist," *American Journal of Political Science* 41 (April 1997): 420–446; Leonard R. Sorenson, "The Federalist Papers on the Constitutionality of Executive Prerogative," *Presidential Studies Quarterly* 19 (Spring 1989): 267–83.

[6]Quoted in Edward S. Corwin, *The President: Office and Powers,* 4th rev. ed. (New York: New York University Press 1957), p. 7.

[7]Quoted in Richard M. Pious, *The Presidency* (Boston: Allyn and Bacon, 1996), p. 84.

something along these lines, and the authors of the *Federalist Papers* reflected that concern. Federalist Numbers 33 and 34 note that the extent of threat to the nation's security can be difficult to predict, and when people are in danger, the need for protection will overwhelm legal considerations.

Whether presidents possess broad prerogative powers or only limited ones that are to be used just in emergencies and for the sake of preserving the nation, presidents have often acted as if their executive prerogatives are quite broad and constitutionally sanctioned. They have used several types of arguments to support their broad interpretation of the powers that they possess.

Among the most forceful of such arguments has been the claim of emergency powers, which presidents have tended to invoke to preserve the nation, as Lincoln did throughout the Civil War. Similarly, presidents have disobeyed Congress with what are called **dispensing powers,** if they viewed the actions of Congress to be harmful to the nation and if they view laws to be in conflict with each other. Presidents have also claimed inherent powers, based on their reading of the Constitution that makes them head of the executive branch. Another, but not contradictory, reading of the Constitution has led to implied powers, whereby presidents have argued that just as Congress is granted the power to make all laws "necessary and proper," so too has the president a similar power to guide his actions. Thus, presidents boast a panoply of constitutionally styled arguments to allow them to take actions beyond those powers enumerated in the Constitution and beyond legislation. Those arguments are often disputed, however.

Presidents have also relied on a less formal device to expand the scope of their powers—precedent. Precedent is when presidents justify their actions by actions of previous presidents. Not every action of a president can serve as a precedent for future incumbents. Precedent setting is more likely when Congress consents to such actions, when it has passed laws that are consistent with the precedent action, or when it passes laws that support the president's policy.[8]

Constitutional Curbs on the Presidency

Presidents possess a set of enumerated powers, have built the office through the use of executive prerogatives, and have cited precedent to justify their actions. While such a list suggests broad executive power for the president, the Constitution also imposed limits on the presidential exercise of executive power. Thus, we noted that the presidential power of appointment is qualified: for most important offices, senatorial confirmation is required. The veto power, too, is qualified. The president can veto only entire bills. He does not possess the line-item veto, which would allow him to excise disagreeable parts of legislation.[9] Most important, Congress can override the president's veto, although

[8]Ibid., p. 84–85.

[9]President Clinton briefly exercised authority similar to a line-item veto, but that authority was declared unconstitutional by the Supreme Court. See Michael Nelson, ed., *The Evolving Presidency* (Washington, D.C.: Congressional Quarterly, 1999), pp. 247–52.

it takes a two-thirds vote of each house to do so. And despite the president's wide foreign policy making powers, the Congress is given the power to declare war and the Senate must ratify treaties. Lastly, Congress can remove the president through the impeachment process.

Ratification Debates: Federalists versus Antifederalists

On September 15, 1787, after four months of work, the delegates to the Philadelphia convention adopted the Constitution. A vigorous campaign that lasted for months ensued in which supporters and opponents tried to mobilize the public to stand either behind or against the proposed Constitution. If ten of the thirteen states accepted the Constitution, it would replace the Articles of Confederation. As a practical matter, however, ratification by all of the states was needed if the new system was to be accepted and survive.

The Federalists

The two opposing camps have come to be known as the **Federalists** and **Antifederalists.** They later provided the foundation for the political parties of the early era, known as the Federalists and Democratic-Republicans. Alexander Hamilton, James Madison, and John Jay spearheaded the campaign for ratification, each authoring essays that explained how the new government would function. Of the eighty-five or so essays, Hamilton wrote the most, about fifty, with Madison another two dozen, Jay five, and the remainder jointly authored by Hamilton and Madison. These essays first appeared in New York newspapers as part of the campaign led by Hamilton (and others) to secure New York's ratification of the Constitution. They were thought so persuasive and such good explanations of government under the Constitution that they were published in other newspapers, and in 1788, they were collected together into a volume that we now call the *Federalist Papers.*

Federalist Numbers 69 to 77, authored by Hamilton, provide the major exposition concerning the presidency. In particular, numbers 69 and 70 stand out in importance. In Federalist No. 69, Hamilton goes to great pains to explain that despite the fact that the presidency is a unitary office and possesses a qualified veto, in no way is the office comparable to the British monarchy. He points out that unlike the monarchy, the presidency is not a hereditary office; that presidents can be removed from office via impeachment; that they possess only a qualified veto, which Congress may override; that Congress, not the presidency, is granted the power to declare war; that the Senate ratifies treaties; and that major presidential appointments must secure senatorial confirmation.

Federalist No. 70 explains why energy in the executive is so important, after having described the limitations of the office in Federalist No. 69. Hamilton argues in Federalist No. 70 that a strong, energetic executive is required to see to it that the nation is protected from foreign attack, that the laws are administered, and that private property and liberty are guarded, all essential to a well-functioning society in

his estimation. He goes on to describe what he means by "energy in the executive." He means a unitary executive who is assured of some duration in office and
has the requisite powers necessary for the job.

Hamilton is not content, however, to merely describe the rationale for the
strengths of the office; he must also persuade his audience that the presidency
will fit into the republican tradition. Thus, he argues that the president needs to
be dependent on the people but also responsible to the people for his actions.
Again, we see the formula of strength in an executive that is answerable, accountable, and responsible to the people that Wilson and Morris advocated at the
Constitutional Convention.

The Antifederalists

The Antifederalists agreed with the Federalists that the articles needed reform.
They did not agree that a new constitution was necessary. And like the Federalists, they believed that government should protect liberty and that it should have
a popular base. Unlike the Federalists, they believed more strongly in democracy,
which they held was rooted in local governments, especially the states. They also
feared that the proposed government under the Constitution would be too strong,
undermining individual liberties and state governments.[10]

The Antifederalists, in particular, thought that the presidency under the Constitution was flawed. First, they preferred a plural executive, rather than a unitary
one, as well as a council to check the president. Similarly, they thought that the
president's term of office was too long, and they objected to the presidency's provision for unlimited reeligibility. Moreover, in their support of the states as the
most desirable unit of government, one Antifederalist supported the idea of ro-
tating the presidency among the states.

The Antifederalists also saw the Constitution as blending the executive, legislative, and judicial powers among the branches, which they cautioned might lead to
an elite of government officeholders controlling the government and undermining
liberties, freedom, and democracy. To preserve these values, they preferred a
stricter separation of powers than that proposed in the Constitution. Lastly, the
Antifederalists charged that the presidency was given too much power, noting the
vagueness in the definition and description of presidential power, as we have discussed. In all, the Antifederalists saw the presidency, like the Constitution itself, as
being too strong and a threat to liberty and local (state) government.[11]

Much of the potency of the Antifederalist attack evaporated when the Federalists agreed to add a Bill of Rights, which important Antifederalists, such as Thomas

---

[10]Raymond B. Wrabley, Jr, "Anti-federalism and the Presidency," *Presidential Studies Quarterly* 21
(Summer 1991): 459–70. Also, Herbert J. Storing, with the editorial assistance of Murray Dry, *What the
Anti-Federalists Were For* (Chicago: University of Chicago Press, 1981).

[11]Ibid. The "Antifederalist papers" have only recently been collected. Herbert J. Storing, ed., with
the assistance of Murray Dry, *The Complete Anti-Federalist,* 7 vol. (Chicago: University of Chicago
Press, 1981).

Jefferson, recommended. Fearing that they could not gain ratification in all of the states, the Federalists compromised by proposing that once the Constitution was ratified, a Bill of Rights, styled as amendments to the Constitution, would be the first order of business for the new Congress. With this compromise, much of the misgiving about the potential threat of the Constitution subsided, and ratification proceeded swiftly.

THE CONSTITUTIONAL PRESIDENCY IN COMPARATIVE PERSPECTIVE

How powerful was the presidency that the delegates to the Philadelphia convention created? We have given one answer by discussing the inherent nature of the presidency from a constitutional perspective. The presidency, by that view, appears to be moderately powerful, although, as we have stressed, the Constitution is not always very clear in several important respects. Another way of answering this question to compare the presidency with other chief executives. First, we compare the president to the governors of the states. As we will see, the presidency left a lasting legacy on that office. Then we will turn our attention to presidencies around the world. We will see that the Constitution has rather modestly endowed the American presidency with powers compared to many presidencies elsewhere.

Comparing Presidents and Governors

For years, scholars and observers of the American governorship have contended that the greater the institutional resources given the governor, the greater the governor's leadership ability. Such a perspective has won great currency among state-level reformers, who have convinced state policy makers to enhance the governor's powers in many of the states over the past fifty years.[12] One of the useful aspects of this research has been the attempt to measure the degree of institutional, or constitutional, power that the governor possesses. There are significant similarities between presidents and governors, the most important being their shared position in separation of powers systems. We can use these measures of gubernatorial powers to compare the president with the governor and get another fix on just how powerful the presidency is.

The most current and widely used measure of gubernatorial powers has been developed by Thad Beyle (table 2-2). Beyle measures gubernatorial powers along five dimensions that are appropriate for comparison with the American president. These dimensions refer to 1) whether or not offices that one can construe as the cabinet are separately elected, 2) the tenure potential of the governor, 3) appointment power, 4) budget making authority, and 5) veto power. Each dimension, according to Beyle's scheme, is scaled from 1 to 5, with 1 suggesting weak powers and 5 the highest degree of institutional power. Using Beyle's

---

[12]Thad L. Beyle, "Enhancing Executive Leadership in the States," *State and Local Government Review* 27 (Winter 1995): 18–35.

TABLE 2-2   THE INSTITUTIONAL POWERS OF THE PRESIDENT AND THE FIFTY STATE GOVERNORS, 1994

Rank	State	Score	Rank	State	Score
1	New York	21.5	26	Wyoming	17.5
2	Maryland	20.5	27	Colorado	17
3	Pennsylvania	20.5	28	Delaware	17
4	Alaska	20	29	Idaho	17
5	Connecticut	20	30	Kentucky	17
6	Iowa	20	31	Mississippi	17
7	New Jersey	20	32	Montana	17
8	Ohio	20	33	New Mexico	17
9	West Virginia	20	34	Rhode Island	17
10	Hawaii	19.5	35	Arizona	16.5
11	Minnesota	19.5	36	Florida	16.5
12	Nebraska	19	37	California	16
13	Tennessee	19	38	Arkansas	15.5
14	Illinois	18.5	39	Washington	15.5
15	Michigan	18.5	40	Indiana	15
16	North Dakota	18.5	41	Louisiana	15
17	South Dakota	18.5	42	New Hampshire	15
	U.S. president	**18**		Alabama	14.5
18	Kansas	18	43	Georgia	14.5
19	Massachusetts	18	44	Nevada	14
20	Utah	18	45	Oklahoma	14
21	Wisconsin	18	46	South Carolina	13
22	Maine	17.5	47	Texas	13
23	Missouri	17.5	48	Vermont	12.5
24	Oregon	17.5	49	North Carolina	11
25	Virginia	17.5			

Source: Adapted from Thad L. Beyle, "Enhancing Executive Leadership in the States," *State and Local Government Review* 27 (Winter 1995): 29.

scheme, the presidency scores 18 overall, based on the following component scores: separate election of other officials = 5, tenure potential = 4, appointment power = 4, budget power = 3, and veto power = 2. On average, the state governors averaged 17.2, which means that the president is slightly more institutionally powerful than the average state governor. Further, the president ranks nineteenth; eighteen governors possess more institutional power than the president. Again, this places the president somewhere in the middle of the pack of American state chief executives.

In looking at the components of Beyle's scheme, sometimes the president is granted greater institutional power than the average governor, and at other times he is granted much less. Thus, where the president scores highest—separate election of other officials—governors, on average, do not fair as well, with a score of 2.9. In many cases, other important officials in state government, such as the attorney general, lieutenant governor, and secretaries of state and treasury, are elected separately from the governor in statewide races. Only the vice president is also elected at the national level, but this is now on a ticket with the president.

The president's tenure potential is comparable to that of the average governor (Beyle score 4.1), as most governors can now serve only two terms. However, the president tends to possess greater appointment powers than the average state governor (Beyle score 2.8). The common case is that someone other than the governor names the appointee, to which the governor can consent or not, much like the Senate's confirmation power. Presidents and governors on the average share similar budget making authority (Beyle score 3). Each initially constructs a budget proposal that the legislature can change as it sees fit. Lastly, the weakest presidential power relates to the veto, an aspect of considerable gubernatorial power (Beyle score 4.4). Where the president can veto only entire bills, the typical governor possesses a line-item veto. Overall, while presidents have greater control than governors over building their administrations, governors have greater power than the president over the output of the legislature. Despite these differences, the president overall looks like a typical governor, among neither the most nor the least powerful.

Comparing the U.S. President with Other Presidents

The major limitation of comparing presidents with governors is that presidents serve nations, while governors serve subnational governments. Thus, governors have no foreign policy making role, which we have argued was a crucial aspect of the constitutional power of the presidency.[13] We must bear this important difference in mind when making comparisons between presidents and governors, but this point also suggests that it might be instructive to compare the U.S. president with other nationally elected presidents.

One study by Matthew Shugart and John Carey does just this (see table 2-3).[14] Shugart and Carey compare forty-two presidencies, including the United States, that existed by the late 1980s. In making their comparisons, they distinguish between two major dimensions of presidential power: powers that relate to the legislature and those that they term *nonlegislative*. The latter mainly relate to cabinet formation and related functions, which we detail in the following paragraphs. There is great overlap between the Beyle and Shugart-Carey schemes, which suggests some agreement by scholars about the constitutional and institutional powers of executives.

---

[13]Note, however, that governors in the modern era sometimes do become involved in international trade and investment issues, such as trying to promote sales of state products abroad or trying to attract foreign investment in their states.

[14]Matthew Soberg Shugart and John M. Carey, *Presidents and Assemblies: Constitutional Design and Electoral Dynamics* (New York: Cambridge University Press, 1992).

TABLE 2-3   LEGISLATIVE AND NONLEGISLATIVE POWERS OF PRESIDENTS

Country	Legislative power score	Nonlegislative power score
Argentina	2	7
Austria	0	5
Bolivia	2	12
Brazil—1988	9	12
Chile		
1969	12	12
1989	5	15
Colombia—1991	5	8
Costa Rica	1	12
Dominican Republic	2	12
Ecuador	6	8
El Salvador	3	12
Finland	0	8
France	1	4
Guatemala	4	12
Honduras	2	12
Iceland	3	8
Ireland	0	0
Korea		
1962	6	12
1987	6	9
Mexico	5	12
Namibia	2	10
Nicaragua	3	12
Nigeria	2	11
Panama	5	12
Paraguay	6	16
Peru	0	9
Philippines	5	11
Portugal—1982	1.5	6
Sri Lanka	4	12
United States	**2**	**11**
Uruguay	6	11
Venezuela	0	12

Source: Adapted from Matthew Soberg Shugart and John M. Carey, *Presidents and Assemblies: Constitutional Design and Electoral Dynamics* (New York: Cambridge University Press, 1992), p. 155

The Shugart-Carey scheme has six components on the legislative powers dimension: veto and item veto powers, decree powers, budgetary powers, executive power to introduce legislation, and executive power to propose referenda.[15] Each is measured on a 0-to-4 scale; thus, a maximum of 24 points is possible. According to this, the U.S. president receives 2 points because of the qualified veto power. Few nations score high on legislative powers granted to presidents. The whole idea of separation of powers is to curtail executive power in this dimension fundamentally by providing the legislature with the bulk of legislative powers and having the executive act mostly as a check on the legislature. Even the strongest president scored by Shugart and Carey, the Chilean presidency of circa 1969, received only 12 of a possible 24 points, mostly because of that president's strong item veto.

The second dimension, according to the Shugart-Carey scheme, relates to nonlegislative powers, primarily those concerning the formation and continuation of government, especially the executive branch.[16] There are four components here: presidential power to create a cabinet, presidential power to dismiss cabinet officials, the power of the assembly (legislature) to censure the president, and the ability of the president to dissolve the assembly or legislature. Again, each component is scaled from 0 to 4 points. The U.S. president fairs quite well here, gathering 11 of 16 points. Only his inability to dissolve Congress keeps him from being in the top rank of national executives. However, very few rank above him by much, with the common president scoring from 8 to 12 points.

The most common type of presidential arrangement, as calculated by Shugart and Carey, is when presidents are strong in both legislative and nonlegislative powers (twelve of thirty-two cases, or 37.5 percent).[17] Some countries that fall into this category include Chile (1969 and 1989), Brazil (1988), Uruguay, Paraguay, Philippines, Mexico, Panama, Guatemala, and Sri Lanka. Second most common are presidents with strong nonlegislative but weak legislative powers (nine of thirty-two cases, or 28 percent), such as the United States and such nations as Nigeria, El Salvador, Argentina, Dominican Republic, Costa Rica, and Venezuela.

One important point of this exercise is to note that variations in presidencies exist. While all presidencies are situated in separation of powers systems, which differ from parliamentary systems by locating executive and legislative powers in different branches of government, the amount of institutional power given to each branch may vary. Thus, some separation of power systems might lean in a strong legislative but weak executive direction, while others may provide for a strong executive and a weak legislature. Similarly, both presidencies and legislatures may be together weak or strong. The U.S. system is styled somewhere in the middle, with a moderately powerful executive, weak in legislative powers but relatively

[15]Ibid., pp. 150, 155.

[16]Ibid.

[17]Ibid., p. 157.

strong in nonlegislative powers, and a moderately powerful legislature. In this sense, a true balance exists between the legislature and the executive in the United States, something that the framers of the Constitution sought and seemingly were successful in creating. Other countries that have followed the U.S. lead by adopting a presidential system over a parliamentary one have not been as successful in establishing such a balance between the branches, nor have they always been successful enough in establishing a government that is neither too strong nor too weak to govern without undermining liberty and democracy.

STRONG PRESIDENCIES AND DEMOCRACY: AN ASSESSMENT

Critics of the presidency as designed by the framers of the Constitution, such as the Antifederalists, argued that a powerful presidency will threaten liberties and democracy. Our discussion comparing the presidency with U.S. governors and other national presidents does not point to the U.S. president as being overly powerful, at least in a constitutional sense. Still, the Antifederalists may have had a point about strong presidencies and threats to liberty and democracy. The Shugart-Carey classification can allow us to test this implication of the Antifederalist critique of strong presidencies.

Longevity may be an important way of assessing a governmental system's success.[18] Long-lived political systems suggest an ability to adapt to changing conditions, to meet new and varied demands. It also suggests that the political system may possess a reservoir of public support that it can draw on, that it is viewed as legitimate. By such a standard, the U.S. political system and its presidency have indeed been successful, being among the longest-lived of democracies.

This stands in stark contrast to many of the world's political regimes, democratic or not. Recall that the Shugart-Carey presidential scoring scheme classified two types of presidential systems as being most common: the weak legislative but strong nonlegislative presidency, such as that of the United States, and the presidency that is both strong in both the legislative and nonlegislative dimensions. One might venture the point that a stronger governmental system, that is, one in which the presidency is both legislatively and nonlegislatively strong, would be, on average, the more successful. That is not what Shugart and Carey find. Presidential systems like that in the United States had a failure rate of about 25 percent, that is, one-fourth of them stopped being democratic for at least one election or were permanently replaced by nondemocratic regimes. In contrast, one-half of the doubly strong presidential systems failed, not a good record by any measure.[19]

Why should a comparatively weak presidency, especially one that possesses anemic legislative powers, be more stable and long-lived than a legislatively

---

[18]This is not the only noteworthy standard that one can or should employ in comparing political systems. Other standards might look at how often or how successful the nation has been in war, the degree of economic wealth and equity, the ability to weather civil disturbances and political crises, or the fairness and justice accorded the citizenry, to name only some of the more obvious ones.

[19]Shugart and Carey, *Presidents and Assemblies,* p. 157.

strong presidential system? The answer lies in the nature of separation of powers systems. For a separation cf powers system to function and weather political storms and upheavals, both the executive and legislative branches must be able to withstand encroachments from the other branch. Each must be able to maintain its independence from the other, to serve its own constituency and protect its constitutional role.

The stronger the legislative powers that the presidency possesses, the more likely that the president will attack the legislature with the constitutional powers at hand, such as by dissolving it. Given that two branches tend to have different constituencies, defined by either different timing of election, terms of office, or districts, the executive and legislature are bound at some time to come into conflict. Strong presidents, when faced with legislative opposition, seem to have a tendency to end the democracy, either temporarily or more permanently, often by asserting their executive rights or declaring national emergencies.

In contrast, it is less likely that legislatures with strong legislative powers are as able to undermine the executive in the way that the executive with strong legislative powers can undermine the legislature. It is more difficult for the legislature, a collective body, to act in unison about such matters or to be able to take such decisive action against the democratic system. There will always be someone in the legislature who will speak out against such a move to upset the democracy. Government may not operate effectively in a strong legislative-weak presidential system, but the democracy is less threatened than when the executive possesses strong legislative powers.

Thus, the Antifederalists seemed to have a point, but not one in particular about the presidency as designed by the Philadelphia framers. Strong presidencies, especially ones with strong legislative powers, are threats to democracy and perhaps liberties as well, in as much as democracy is necessary to protect liberty. The Antifederalists were wrong about the nature of the presidency in the United States, however. It, in comparative perspective, is not so constitutionally strong as to be a threat to democracy and liberty. And the Antifederalists seemed to forget that a strong legislature can offset a strong presidency. We see the relative strength of the legislative branch in the United States when we note the relatively weak legislative powers that the presidency possesses. However, the Antifederalists were correct about a too strong executive being a threat to democracy.

By comparing the U.S. presidency with other national presidencies, we have been able to learn something about the constitutional nature of the office—its strong nonlegislative but weak legislative basis—as well as about presidential systems more generally. The point about the U.S. presidency's weak legislative powers will become important in understanding the evolution of the presidency into its modern form, as well as the troubles that presidents have in gaining congressional acceptance of their policies. Presidents have sought political resources from other places, such as the public, to compensate for their weak constitutional legislative base.

But before presidents began to search for such resources systematically, they needed a justification or motivation to do so. When the public began to expect the president to provide leadership, which it did in the 1930s, the president had that motivation to seek the resources needed to satisfy the public's expectation. This is the topic of Chapter 3.

KEY TERMS

Antifederalists   33
commander in chief   29
dispensing powers   32

electoral college   24
enumerated powers   28
Federalists   33

DISCUSSION QUESTIONS

1. What are the major constitutional provisions regarding the presidency? How has each provision affected the presidency?
2. What criticisms did the Antifederalists make regarding the Constitution generally and the presidency in particular?
3. How do the American presidency's powers compare with those of the governors? With the powers of presidents in other countries?
4. Are very strong presidents a threat to democracy or the stability of a political system?

SUGGESTED READINGS

Alexander Hamilton, James Madison, and John Jay, *The Federalist Papers*. New York: Bantam Books, 1982.
Jackson Main, *The Anti-federalists*. New York: Norton, 1974.
J. W. Peltason, *Understanding the Constitution,* 13th ed. Fort Worth, Texas: Harcourt Brace College Publishers, 1994.

3

THE EVOLUTION
OF THE PRESIDENCY

Chapters 1 and 2 outlined the constitutional nature of the presidency. The main point in those chapters was that the Constitution is ambiguous about the presidency in at least two senses. First, the Constitution is ambiguous about the meaning of the executive and executive power. In other words, the boundaries of the presidency are not clearly specified, and thus, it may be hard to tell when a president has overstepped his proper role. Second, the Constitution is ambiguous about some of the formal duties of the president.

These ambiguities open up the presidency to differing interpretations, understandings, and expectations. For instance, different presidents may interpret the duties and responsibilities of the office in different ways. Public expectations of the office and its incumbent may differ over time. As these interpretations and expectations change, the office itself may be changed. In this chapter, we will discuss the evolution of the presidency from the office that the founders created to the office that now exists. Although the underlying constitutional foundation of the office has not been altered very much over the history of its existence, the presidency has fundamentally changed.

Two major sources or motivations exist for change in the office: presidents themselves and the expectations of those outside of the office. Presidents may come to office desiring to do things differently from their predecessors or to solve problems that earlier occupants were unable to solve. To effect these solutions, presidents may seek to change the office. How successful presidents are in solving these problems may determine how firmly the changes that they inspired in the office are embedded or how quickly they are discarded. Outside forces, such as the public, interest groups, political parties, Congress, the bureaucracy, and the judiciary, may impel change in the presidency. Outside forces may seek presidential attention for their issues and concerns, making the president responsible for them. Presidents may respond directly to these outside pressures, altering the office and their behavior to meet the demands of these outside forces. Alternatively, these outside forces may be able to compel change in the office by, for instance, legislative mandates, even though the president resisted these alterations. The manner of change in the presidency is complex and comes about in different ways and from differing motivations. The one constant of the presidency, however, is the fact that it is ever changing and evolving.

We begin this chapter with a discussion of the mechanisms through which the presidency changes. Then we will discuss perhaps the most profound change of the presidency, the evolution into the modern, active office that now exists. We will discuss the forces that promoted the change into the modern office, and we will end the chapter with a discussion of the implications of the evolution into the modern office for how presidents behave and conduct themselves.

MECHANISMS FOR CHANGING THE PRESIDENCY

The Constitution's lack of clarity in a number of issues about the presidency, including its powers, has allowed the presidency to change over time. At a most basic level, the office changes through primarily two routes or mechanisms. The first involves informal actions on the part of presidents. When a president does something new or different and it is followed as a practice by succeeding presidents, we can say that a precedent has been established. Not all different or new actions by presidents will be carried on by their successors, though. Precedent becomes institutionalized when rules governing the new behavior are written, when offices and personnel are assigned to those tasks, or when presidents formally set aside some of their time to attend to those matters. We can consider this an informal route for changing the office, at least initially.

The second major route to changing the presidency involves formally altering the office through constitutional amendment, statute, or formal presidential action, such as through the issuance of an executive order. Although some changes that are implemented through this route may be inspired and sought by presidents, at times changes in the presidency brought about this way are stimulated by outside forces, such as Congress and the mass public, who desire to make the office responsive to some need or demand that they feel is important for presidents to attend to. Presidents may like some of these changes but resist others sought by these outside forces.

Thus, in thinking about the sources of change in the presidency, we can make a distinction between presidential and nonpresidential sources of change, as well as formal and informal means of changing the office. Presidents may want to alter the office for a number of reasons, which may include their personal preferences and operating styles, as well as political and policy needs and goals. But presidents may also decide to alter the office in response to nonpresidential forces. These forces may be many and varied, and may include the changing social, economic, political, and technological environment and contexts. It is important to note, as we have mentioned, that these nonpresidential forces may act on the presidency directly through constitutional or statutory means, as well as indirectly, by influencing presidents themselves. Thus, both presidents and outside forces may induce change through formal and informal mechanisms. First, we will discuss the use of formal mechanisms to change the presidency, focusing our attention on the amendment process. Then we will turn our attention to changes that come about informally, primarily through the actions and behaviors of presidents, which serve as precedents for successors to follow.

Changing the Presidency Formally: The Amendment Process

Since ratification, the Constitution has been amended twenty-seven times, including the ten amendments that comprise the Bill of Rights. At least six of these amendments pertain in part or in whole to the presidency. Yet the basic constitutional nature of the office has not changed very much. The evolution of the office of the presidency has come about primarily through means other than constitutional change.

Several amendments deal with qualifications for office, terms of office, and succession patterns. These amendments are listed in table 3-1. The Fourteenth Amendment, ratified in 1868, disqualified those who allied with the South during the Civil War from being electors or from serving as president or vice president. In 1933, the Twentieth Amendment was ratified, which changed the date that the president's term of office begins from March to January 20. That amendment also provided for the succession to the presidency in the event of the death of president-elect before he could take office. The Twenty-third Amendment, which was ratified in 1961, granted the District of Columbia representation in the electoral college in proportion to what it would have were it a state. With the Twenty-fourth Amendment, which was ratified in 1964, poll taxes and other taxes were prohibited as means of keeping people from voting for president. The Twenty-fifth Amendment of 1967 elaborated on succession to the presidency and defined presidential disability. These five amendments have had little practical effect on changing the office of the presidency.

Two others, however, have had a greater, albeit still modest effect on the presidency. The first of these is the Twelfth Amendment, which was ratified in 1804. The aim of this amendment was to deal with ties in the electoral college and selection of the president. Originally, under the Constitution, each elector of the electoral college would vote for two persons (Article 2, Section 1, Paragraph 3). The person with the greatest number of votes would become president if he had a majority, while the second-best vote getter would become vice president. If two persons claimed a majority of votes but were tied, then the House of Representatives would choose who was to become president. In the event no person held a majority, the House would select from among the top five vote getters, with each state granted one vote. Political maneuvers and backroom deals among those jockeying to become president, which some felt might harm the legitimacy of the office, motivated the reforms associated with the Twelfth Amendment.

By 1800, recognizable political parties had developed in the United States—the Democratic-Republicans and the Federalists. Thomas Jefferson and Aaron Burr, both Democratic-Republicans, were nominated by that party's caucus, with the understanding that Jefferson was head of the party. Party discipline among the Democratic-Republicans led to Jefferson and Burr each receiving seventy-three electoral votes, while Federalist and incumbent President John Adams received sixty-five. The Jefferson-Burr tie threw the election into the House of Representatives. However, the House deadlocked, in part because Burr, seeing his chance to attain the presidency, refused to take the number two spot. Thirty-five ballots were held, without resolution, until Federalist Alexander Hamilton threw his

TABLE 3-1   AMENDMENTS TO THE CONSTITUTION THAT PERTAIN TO THE PRESIDENCY

Amendment XII (1804)

The electors shall meet in their respective states and vote by ballot for President and Vice-President, one of whom, at least, shall not be an inhabitant of the same state with themselves; they shall name in their ballots the person voted for as President, and in distinct ballots the person voted for as Vice-President, and they shall make distinct lists of all persons voted for as President, and of all persons voted for as Vice-President, and of the number of votes for each, which lists they shall sign and certify, and transmit sealed to the seat of the government of the United States, directed to the President of the Senate;—The President of the Senate shall, in the presence of the Senate and House of Representatives, open all the certificates and the votes shall then be counted;—the person having the greatest number of votes for President, shall be the President, if such number be a majority of the whole number of electors appointed; and if no person have such majority, then from the persons having the highest numbers not exceeding three on the list of those voted for as President, the House of Representatives shall choose immediately, by ballot, the President. But in choosing the President, the votes shall be taken by states, the representation from each state having one vote; a quorum for this purpose shall consist of a member or members from two-thirds of the states, and a majority of all the states shall be necessary to a choice. And if the House of Representatives shall not choose a President whenever the right of choice shall devolve upon them, before the fourth day of March next following, then the Vice-President shall act as President, as in the case of the death or other constitutional disability of the President. The person having the greatest number of votes as Vice-President, shall be the Vice-President, if such number be a majority of the whole number of electors appointed, and if no person have a majority, then from the two highest numbers on the list, the Senate shall choose the Vice-President; a quorum for the purpose shall consist of two-thirds of the whole number of Senators, and a majority of the whole number shall be necessary to a choice. But no person constitutionally ineligible to the office of President shall be eligible to that of Vice-President of the United States.

Amendment XIV (1868)

Section 3. No person shall be a Senator or Representative in Congress, or elector of President and Vice-President, or hold any office, civil or military, under the United States, or under any state, who, having previously taken an oath, as a member of Congress, or as an officer of the United States, or as a member of any state legislature, or as an executive or judicial officer of any state, to support the Constitution of the United States, shall have engaged in insurrection or rebellion against the same, or given aid or comfort to the enemies thereof. But Congress may by a vote of two-thirds of each House, remove such disability.

Section 4. The validity of the public debt of the United States, authorized by law, including debts incurred for payment of pensions and bounties for services in suppressing insurrection or rebellion, shall not be questioned. But neither the United States nor any state shall assume or pay any debt or obligation incurred in aid of insurrection or rebellion against the United States, or any claim for the loss or emancipation of any slave; but all such debts, obligations and claims shall be held illegal and void.

Amendment XX (1933)

Section 1. The terms of the President and Vice President shall end at noon on the 20th day of January, and the terms of Senators and Representatives at noon on the 3d day of January, of the years in which such terms would have ended if this article had not been ratified; and the terms of their successors shall then begin.

Section 2. The Congress shall assemble at least once in every year, and such meeting shall begin at noon on the 3d day of January, unless they shall by law appoint a different day.

Section 3. If, at the time fixed for the beginning of the term of the President, the President elect shall have died, the Vice-President elect shall become President. If a President shall not have been chosen before the time fixed for the beginning of his term, or if the President elect shall have

TABLE 3-1   CONTINUED

failed to qualify, then the Vice-President elect shall act as President until a President shall have qualified; and the Congress may by law provide for the case wherein neither a President elect nor a Vice-President elect shall have qualified, declaring who shall then act as President, or the manner in which one who is to act shall be selected, and such person shall act accordingly until a President or Vice-President shall have qualified.

Section 4. The Congress may by law provide for the case of the death of any of the persons from whom the House of Representatives may choose a President whenever the right of choice shall have devolved upon them, and for the case of the death of any of the persons from whom the Senate may choose a Vice-President whenever the right of choice shall have devolved upon them.

Amendment XXII (1951)

Section 1. No person shall be elected to the office of the President more than twice, and no person who has held the office of President, or acted as President, for more than two years of a term to which some other person was elected President shall be elected to the office of the President more than once. But this article shall not apply to any person holding the office of President when this article was proposed by the Congress, and shall not prevent any person who may be holding the office of President, or acting as President, during the term within which this article becomes operative from holding the office of President or acting as President during the remainder of such term.

Amendment XXIII (1961)

Section 1. The District constituting the seat of government of the United States shall appoint in such manner as the Congress may direct:

A number of electors of President and Vice-President equal to the whole number of Senators and Representatives in Congress to which the District would be entitled if it were a state, but in no event more than the least populous state; they shall be in addition to those appointed by the states, but they shall be considered, for the purposes of the election of President and Vice-President, to be electors appointed by a state; and they shall meet in the District and perform such duties as provided by the twelfth article of amendment.

Amendment XXIV (1964)

Section 1. The right of citizens of the United States to vote in any primary or other election for President or Vice-President, for electors for President or Vice-President, or for Senator or Representative in Congress, shall not be denied or abridged by the United States or any state by reason of failure to pay any poll tax or other tax.

Amendment XXV (1967)

Section 1. In case of the removal of the President from office or of his death or resignation, the Vice-President shall become President.

Section 2. Whenever there is a vacancy in the office of the Vice-President, the President shall nominate a Vice-President who shall take office upon confirmation by a majority vote of both Houses of Congress.

Section 3. Whenever the President transmits to the President pro tempore of the Senate and the Speaker of the House of Representatives his written declaration that he is unable to discharge the powers and duties of his office, and until he transmits to them a written declaration to the contrary, such powers and duties shall be discharged by the Vice-President as Acting President.

Section 4. Whenever the Vice-President and a majority of either the principal officers of the executive departments or of such other body as Congress may by law provide, transmit to the President pro tempore of the Senate and the Speaker of the House of Representatives their written declaration that the President is unable to discharge the powers and duties of his office, the Vice-President shall immediately assume the powers and duties of the office as Acting President.

TABLE 3-1　CONTINUED

Thereafter, when the President transmits to the President pro tempore of the Senate and the Speaker of the House of Representatives his written declaration that no inability exists, he shall resume the powers and duties of his office unless the Vice-President and a majority of either the principal officers of the executive department or of such other body as Congress may by law provide, transmit within four days to the President pro tempore of the Senate and the Speaker of the House of Representatives their written declaration that the President is unable to discharge the powers and duties of his office. Thereupon Congress shall decide the issue, assembling within forty-eight hours for that purpose if not in session. If the Congress, within twenty-one days after receipt of the latter written declaration, or, if Congress is not in session, within twenty-one days after Congress is required to assemble, determines by two-thirds vote of both Houses that the President is unable to discharge the powers and duties of his office, the Vice-President shall continue to discharge the same as Acting President; otherwise, the President shall resume the powers and duties of his office.

weight and influence behind Jefferson. Hamilton argued to the Federalists that Jefferson was no enemy to the strong executive that the Federalists supported and that Jefferson, unlike Burr, was incorruptible.[1]

Many of the time believed that if another backroom deal was necessary to elect a president, the legitimacy of the electoral college, the election process, and the presidency would be undermined. Such an outcome might even destabilize the constitutional regime, which at the time was but a dozen years old. To rectify the situation, the Twelfth Amendment was ratified. The amendment required electors to designate one vote for president and one for vice president, with the president being the person who received the majority of *presidential* electoral votes. If no one received a majority, the House of Representatives would choose the president from among the top three vote getters, again with each state receiving one vote. A majority again was required to select the president. A majority was also required for the election of the vice president, but if no one received a majority, the Senate would elect the vice president from among the two top vice presidential vote getters.

In effect, the Twelfth Amendment separated the election of president and vice president to avoid the politics and maneuvering of the election of 1800. The most important consequence of the amendment was that it removed a major roadblock to the development of political parties in presidential politics. Still, this amendment did radically alter the basic constitutional nature of the office.

The second amendment with major implications for the presidency was the Twenty-second Amendment, which was ratified in 1951. This amendment limited presidents to two terms. It is not likely, however, that this amendment fundamentally altered accepted political practices that had developed over the years. Rather, it seemed more to institutionalize the tradition of a president serving for only two terms, a tradition that dated back to George Washington, who was credited with beginning it. Despite having unlimited eligibility, George Washington

[1]Sidney M. Milkis and Michael Nelson, *The American Presidency: Origins and Development, 1776–1990* (Washington, D.C.: Congressional Quarterly Press, 1990), pp. 96–97.

stepped down from the presidency at the conclusion of his second term. Every president elected to a second term did the same until Franklin Roosevelt, who was elected president four times. Partly out of partisan calculations, when Republicans took the Congress in the late 1940s, they offered this amendment for consideration. However, this term limitation also found broad public support, even though Roosevelt was very popular during his long term of office. For instance, a National Opinion Research Center Poll conducted in late November and early December 1944 found that 58 percent favored a two-term limit for presidents, with only 37 percent opposing the proposal. Similarly, a Gallup Poll taken in March 1947 found 59 percent supporting a two-term limit for president, with only 41 percent opposing.[2] The fact that all incumbents save Roosevelt respected Washington's example meant that this amendment did little more than reinstitute Washington's voluntary two-term tradition. Moreover, the long historical tradition of limiting oneself to two terms meant that the country had come to believe that it was proper and best if presidents served for only two terms.

Our main point, to repeat, is that the constitutional nature and foundations of the presidency have not been altered very much over the more than two centuries of its existence. Still, the presidency has changed remarkably from what the founders expected of it. The major mechanisms of change of the presidency are not constitutional in nature. Instead, the ambiguity of the Constitution has allowed the office to be reinterpreted across U S. history without having to resort to constitutional amendments to change the office. In this sense, the office has been quite malleable and responsive to changing interpretations and expectations of the presidency.

Changing the Presidency Through Precedent Setting and Presidential Action

Actions such as constitutional amendments and laws may alter the presidency fundamentally. Such formal processes of change tend to have long-lasting effects, as presidents who come to office long after the amendment or law was enacted will have to behave in accord with that amendment or law.

But the presidency may be altered through less formal means, primarily through precedent setting. Precedent setting comes about when one president acts in a novel way, perhaps doing something that previous incumbents have not done or doing something in a different way. If succeeding presidents continue the practice that the preceding president initiated and justify continuing the practice by citing the earlier president's action, then we can say that precedent has been established. Not all novel actions by presidents will be continued by successors. But when they are, depending on the nature of the novel action, the presidency may be fundamentally altered.

The ambiguity of the Constitution, as we have been discussing, allows presidents to reinterpret the office, which may lead them to innovate or do things differently than in the past. Motivation to innovate may come from the president

---

[2]These poll results and others on the two-term limit were found at the Roper Center at University of Connecticut, accessed through Lexis-Nexis Academic Universe.

directly, as a function of his goals, ambitions, policies, and so on. Or the motivation may come from outside forces, such as Congress or the public. Presidential responsiveness to these outer forces may lead to innovative or novel behavior and subsequently to changing the office.

George Washington, as the first president, probably had more impact on the office through the precedent setting route than any other president. Almost by definition, every action that he took was novel or new because it was the first. Washington's prestige and forethought about what he did in office also meant that many of the actions that he took indeed became precedents that later presidents would follow. Washington seemed to sense the importance of his being the first to hold the office and was deliberate in what he did in office. Moreover, it appears that he had a relatively well-thought out notion of what he wanted the presidency to look like, siding with the Federalists and their conception of the presidency as an office of energy and national unity.[3]

We have mentioned that the Constitution is undergirded by two related but ultimately contradictory ideas—separation of powers and checks and balances. The notion of checks and balances is often called "mixed government" in that the several branches of government are "mixed together" by sharing powers and by possessing checks on the powers held by the other branches. The Constitution did not fully resolve this tension between a strict separationist perspective and a checks and balances model of government. Washington pursued both paths, following a separationist path in trying to create an independent executive but also seeking a mixed government model when he thought the national interest called for it.

Among Washington's most important acts with regard to the separation of powers doctrine were those that established the supremacy of the national government and the presidency over issues of public order. For instance, Washington called up the state militia in two actions, the War Against the Six Indian Nations and the Whiskey Rebellion, without an outcry from the involved states or their governors. These actions helped establish federal and presidential supremacy in this regard. Further, he enlisted the state of Pennsylvania to inform him on the activities of French pirates then docked in the state. His authority to do this was never questioned. In matters of national security and public order, then, Washington's actions set the precedent of presidential leadership and primacy.[4]

Washington also extended the presidency with the first issuance of a proclamation, in this case, that the nation should observe a day of thanksgiving. While proclamations do not carry the power of law, Washington's action set the prece-

[3]On Washington's presidency, see Glenn A. Phelps, "George Washington and the Founding of the Presidency," *Presidential Studies Quarterly* 17 (Spring 1987): 345–63; Glenn A. Phelps, "George Washington: Precedent Setter," in *Inventing the American Presidency,* ed. Thomas E. Cronin (Lawrence: University Press of Kansas, 1989), pp. 259–81; Ralph Ketcham, *Presidents Above Party: The First American Presidency, 1789–1829* (Chapel Hill: University of North Carolina Press, 1984); Forest McDonald, *The Presidency of George Washington* (Lawrence: University Press of Kansas, 1974), pp. 209–44; and Milkis and Nelson, *American Presidency,* pp. 68–86.

[4]Phelps, "George Washington," pp. 350–52.

dent not only for such presidential issuances but also for his role as speaking for the nation.[5] In other actions, Washington established protocol with regard to the presidency. Governors were to call upon the president, not vice versa. Presidents were in this regard symbolically superior to the governors, and by implication, the nation was superior to any state. All told, these and other actions by Washington established the national presence of the presidency, a presidency in which the occupant could take actions he deemed necessary, even if they were merely symbolic expressions and possessed no explicit constitutional sanction.

In the area of administration, Washington was perhaps most protective of preserving the independence and authority of the president. Constitutionally, the Senate shares appointment power through the power of confirmation. The Constitution is unclear, however, about the extent of the Senate's role in the appointment process beyond the act of confirmation. Can the Senate, for instance, suggest to the president whom the nominee should be? Washington fought to ensure that the Senate's appointment power would go no further than confirmation. When one of his nominees failed to be confirmed, Washington refused to let the Senate further instruct him. He nominated another candidate without any Senate involvement, thereby securing the independence of presidents to name nominees and build their administration.[6]

Washington also began the controversial practice of **executive privilege,** the withholding of information from Congress, the courts, or the public. His actions were based on concerns for the public interest and constitutional provisions regarding governmental responsibilities. He did not, so far as is known, use executive privilege to conceal misconduct, either by him or by others in his administration.[7]

Washington also understood the limitation of presidential power under the Constitution, while recognizing the importance of building an independent power base for the presidency to ensure it would be an effective office. To this end, he cultivated power and support for the presidency from two sources not directly derived from the Constitution—the presidency as a national symbol and the people.

In part, Washington turned to these sources because the other branches blocked or resisted his attempts to incorporate them into a presidency-led government. For instance, in 1793, as France and Britain, both at war, challenged America's neutrality, Washington sought advice from the Supreme Court about whether a series of hypothetical actions on his part as president would be considered constitutional or not. Previously, he had privately sought and received advice from Chief Justice John Jay, who had even served as a foreign envoy for the administration while also serving on the Court. But in making a formal request to the Court, Washington was rebuffed, with the Court arguing that the separation of powers prohibited such advising and that the president had the heads of departments to which he could turn

---

[5]Ibid., p. 351.

[6]Ibid., p. 360.

[7]Mark Rozell, *Executive Privilege* (Baltimore: Johns Hopkins University Press, 1994), pp. 32–36.

for advice. Further, the Court argued that part of the purpose of creating and staffing the executive departments was to provide such advice to the president.[8]

In 1789, the Senate also refused Washington's request to use that body as an adviser, echoing the behavior of the Supreme Court. Washington had sought Senate advice on several questions relating to negotiating a border dispute between the state of Georgia and the Creek Indians. One senator refused to allow the Senate to respond to Washington's question until Washington presented his plans to the Senate. Washington balked at doing this, arguing that opening his hand to the Senate would undermine his bargaining position.[9] While Washington would continue to seek the counsel of individual senators, he would not realize his hopes that the upper house would play the role of adviser to the president.

With both branches of government closed off to Washington, he sought political support outside of the capital and beyond the formal institutions of government. He turned to the people in hopes of building the presidency into a national office. To effect this image, Washington began his presidency by touring the nation. He purposely lent his personal prestige to the office, and by traveling around the nation, he was symbolically bringing the nation into the president's orbit of concerns and also helping to forge an identity for the nation through the office of the presidency.[10]

Although Washington did not create the public presidency of the modern age of mass media communications, he helped establish the linkage between the people and the office. Further, he planted the idea that the power of the presidency resided as much in the people as in grants of authority from the Constitution. A popular presidency was not foreseen in the Constitution; Washington's imprimatur was critical in establishing this important characteristic of the presidency.

Other presidents followed Washington's example by defining the ambiguity of the Constitution to meet their needs and those of the office by moving the presidency into areas uncharted by the Constitution, thus establishing more precedents for their successors. We find, therefore, Thomas Jefferson asserting his prerogative powers in buying the Louisiana Territories. Later, Andrew Jackson helped establish the patronage role of the presidency with regard to mass-based electoral political parties. Jackson also expanded the use of the veto. Where previous presidents justified vetoing legislation when they considered it to be unconstitutional, Jackson added a policy justification to the presidential veto arsenal. Thus, if a president deemed the policy to be bad policy, according to Jackson and most subsequent presidents, the president could rightfully veto the legislation.[11]

In these and many other instances, the presidency has developed from the foundation laid out in the Constitution. Thus, while the Constitution is significant in un-

[8]Phelps, "George Washington," p. 355.

[9]Ibid., p. 356.

[10]Ibid., p. 350.

[11]On the development of the presidential veto power, see Robert J. Spitzer, *The Presidential Veto: Touchstone of the Presidency* (Albany: State University of New York Press, 1988), esp. pp. 25–70.

derstanding the character of the presidency and the behavior of those in office, it alone cannot explain the presidency and the behavior of presidents. We will discuss other presidential precedents as they come up.

The Emergence of the Modern Presidency   The theory of the modern presidency is a theory about the evolution of the presidency from its early constitutional roots to its modern-day practices. That theory argues that there are two major periods or types of presidencies. The first type, the early or premodern presidency, begins with George Washington and ends when Franklin Roosevelt assumed the office in 1933. Franklin Roosevelt's presidency is thought by many to be the first modern presidency. Four changes in the presidency came with the development into the modern presidency: 1) enhanced presidential staff resources, 2) a greater presidential role in policy making, 3) a stronger relationship with the mass public, and 4) a greater presence in the realm of international politics.

First, the presidency was given enhanced resources to oversee and control the burgeoning bureaucracy and government. One sign of the enhanced responsibilities given to the president was the passage of the **Budget and Accounting Act of 1921.** That act made the president responsible for submitting a budget to Congress each year. The budget would include a review of each government agency's request for funding for the upcoming year. By filtering agency requests through the president's budget document, presidents could gain a measure of control over what agencies were planning to do. To assist the president in building the budget, the Bureau of the Budget was created. The Budget and Accounting Act of 1921 is instructive because it came on line more than a decade before the appearance of the modern presidency and illustrates the idea that aspects of the modern presidency began to appear before its full blooming in the late 1930s.

The **Executive Office of the President (EOP)** in 1939 is another sign of the development of this aspect of the modern presidency. The main idea behind the creation of the EOP was to give presidents help in overseeing the bureaucracy, which had grown during the 1930s as new agencies were created to deal with the Great Depression and its ill effects. Through the EOP, the president was given more staff assistance and a structure in which he could organize the increasingly large and differentiated staff. Over the years, presidents have altered the structure of the EOP to meet their needs. We will discuss the EOP in more detail in Chapter 9. For now, it is important to point out that the EOP increased the president's ability to act on several fronts, including controlling the bureaucracy, making policy, and relating to the public.

Second, Congress and the nation expected a greater role for the president in the policy making process. Presidents have always played a part in the legislative process. The veto power gives presidents a formal constitutional role, though at the end of the process, and throughout history, presidents have used the State of the Union address to request that Congress legislate on certain matters. What changed with the modern presidency was the level of presidential involvement throughout the legislative process. Thus, presidents would send draft legislation to Congress, would lobby members of Congress in support of or opposition to certain legislation, and would mobilize other political forces to influence Congress. By the time of the Truman administration in the late 1940s, presidents began to develop what came to be known as the president's program. The program consisted of all items that the president deemed important enough to single out as priorities for Congress to work on. By the early 1950s, the president's program had become so important to Congress in terms of setting its agenda and giving it some direction as to what to work on, that when Eisenhower did not submit a program to Congress, he was roundly criticized by Congress, the press, and the public. The result of these changes was that the president had become a major actor in the legislative process, a role that he played more peripherally before the era of the modern presidency.

Third, the relationship between the president and the mass public strengthened. The electronic media helped focus public attention on the president, often overwhelming others who would try to gain public attention and favor. The president, in effect, became the center of people's political world. With the advent of the modern mass media, the president stood alone and above all other political figures; consequently, the president was the only figure who, by virtue of the position that he held, could rally the public to his side or direct attention to what he wanted the public to be thinking about. The public became one of the modern president's most important political resources and sources of support. As we will see, the president's increased visibility brings a number of risks as well as potential benefits, to the White House.

Fourth, the president became perhaps the dominant actor on the world stage. This role emerged at the end of the Second World War, as the United States became the most important military, diplomatic, and economic power around the globe. While other nations, like the Soviet Union, developed nuclear weaponry that could challenge that which the United States possessed, only the United States stood so tall on all three international fronts of the military, diplomacy, and economy. And as the war came to an end, it was replaced by another type of the war, the Cold War, a competition between the United States and the Soviet Union and their allies that persisted until the demise of the U.S.S.R. in 1991.

The importance of this shift in the world role of the United States is that the president became not only the most powerful actor on the international stage but also the most prestigious. And Cold War tensions also translated into domestic political advantage for the president. Policies that he encouraged could be justified by the necessities of the Cold War, and challenges to his leadership could be stifled by calls for patriotism and protecting the security of the nation. Lastly, the dangers of the Cold War rivalry allowed the president to classify more and more information as secrets, giving him an information advantage over others who did not have access to such material, such as the public and even many members of Congress. Thus, on many fronts and in many ways, the rise of the United States as a powerful nation and the Cold War rivalry transformed the presidency, helping to secure the modern presidency.

All of this added up to a signal change in expectations for the president and made the president the central actor in the political system. An office that the founders envisioned would be turned to in times of crisis would now be turned to every day, as a matter of course in routine politics. Without constitutionally amending the office in significant ways, the transformation of the presidency into the modern presidency, some have suggested, has upset the constitutional balance among the branches, with the presidency becoming "first among equals."

WHY THE MODERN PRESIDENCY?

The reasons for the evolution into the modern presidency are many, varied, and disputed. One set of reasons looks at the growing size of government in Washington and the shift of governmental responsibilities from the states and localities to the national government. When political power grows and centralizes, as it began doing in the middle of the twentieth century, it often flows to the executive, which in the United States means the presidency.

A related reason for the evolution to the modern presidency is that public conceptions of government changed. Historically, Americans have preferred small government, especially at the national level. But economic changes, such as the industrialization of the nation and the growth of large corporations, provided a rationale for a more active role for the government in regulating the economy and the private sector. The depth and length of the Great Depression of the 1930s underscored this need for some government regulation of the economy. Again, public expectations for leadership in this regard flow to the presidency, rather than Congress.

In part, both of these reasons suggest that a process of nationalization is occurring in the United States. While, theoretically, Congress could have taken the lead here, the design of the presidency may make it a more suitable place for national concerns than Congress. Members of Congress, for one, represent local districts, and thus, their careers are often better served by attending to local matters than national ones. There are few incentives in Congress for members to focus the bulk of their time and energy on national concerns, although it is true that subsets of members of Congress—those in leadership positions and those with ambitions for the presidency—will spend more time on national concerns that the typical member.

In contrast, the fact that presidents are nationally elected gives them an incentive to view issues from a national perspective. Moreover, the fact that the office is unitary means that people will likely turn their attention to the president when demanding that government deal with national crises. Thus, political and economic forces were nationalizing by the middle of the twentieth century, and this process of nationalization impacted the presidency, leading to the development of the modern office.

But one should not forget the impact of an inspired president like Franklin Roosevelt on stimulating the development of the presidency into its modern form. As we have discussed, aspects of modernization of the presidency were apparent before FDR took office. However, his predecessor, Herbert Hoover, resisted many of those forces, in particular demands that the federal government be used to get the country out of the Depression and to ensure that something like the Depression would not happen again.[12] FDR, in contrast, was more willing to expand the office to meet these demands. His success in office (he was elected for an unprecedented four terms) set a model for all succeeding presidents to emulate and be judged by. Thus, FDR's actions became precedents that other presidents would follow, adapt, and elaborate on in building a modern presidency.[13]

THE IMPLICATIONS OF THE MODERN PRESIDENCY FOR PRESIDENTIAL BEHAVIOR

The development of the modern presidency fundamentally altered the role and place of the office in the political system and policy making. Premodern presidents are conventionally thought of as "clerks." William Howard Taft gives a good definition of clerkship presidents.[14] These are presidents who define their job narrowly and confine themselves to actions that the Constitution or a statute explicitly calls on presidents to perform. When the Constitution is silent, the theory of the clerkship presidency argues that presidents should take no action. Only during times of emergencies and wars do premodern presidents act in a less restrained fashion, offering leadership.

The two themes that undergird the development of the modern presidency are increased expectations for presidential leadership and increased presidential capacity to lead. Increased expectations mean that the president is held responsible for public policy to an extent not evident for premodern presidents. The increase in staff and budgeting powers indicates the growing resources and capacity of president to take action and lead in the modern era. Richard Neustadt aptly sums up the difference between presidents in the premodern and modern eras: "A striking feature . . . has been the transformation into routine practice . . . actions we once treated as exceptional. A President may retain liberty, in Woodrow Wilson's phrase, 'to be as big a man as he can.' But nowadays he cannot be as small as he might like."[15]

Neustadt argues further, however, that despite the increase in presidential resources in the modern era, expectations for presidential leadership far outstrip whatever resources have accumulated. In part, this is a function of the lack of constitutional development of the office. No new constitutional authority or power has flowed to the presidency during the modern era.

---

[12]Not everyone agrees that Hoover was so premodern. See Michael Lewis-Beck and Peverill Squire, "The Transformation of the American State: The New Era-New Deal Test," *Journal of Politics* 53 (1991): 106–21.

[13]On the impact of FDR, see William E. Leuchtenburg, *In the Shadow of FDR: From Harry Truman to Ronald Reagan,* 2d ed. (Ithaca, N.Y.: Cornell University Press, 1989).

[14]William Howard Taft, *Our Chief Magistrate and His Powers* (New York: Columbia University Press, 1916).

[15]Richard E. Neustadt, *Presidential Power: The Politics of Leadership* (New York: John Wiley, 1960), p. 5. The next several paragraphs are based on Neustadt's book.

Still, to meet these heightened expectations for leadership, presidents must supplement their meager constitutional and institutional resource base. Neustadt argues that presidents in the modern era, in order to accomplish anything that they set out to do, must become acutely aware of the context in which they operate and the power or influence at their disposal. Presidential power or influence, according to Neustadt, is highly situational, although presidential power is rooted in the president's reputation and prestige.

Reputation is how others in the political world view the president. Is he astute, a strong leader? In essence, what do others expect the president to do in a given situation? Do they expect him to win or lose, to carry out his threats or to compromise? Prestige deals more with public standing. Is the president popular with the public, will the public follow the president's lead? Neustadt argues that a professional reputation and prestige with the public will enhance a president's ability to persuade others to follow his lead, to bargain with others so that they will see it is to their advantage to do as the president wants.

In other words, the fundamental basis of presidential power and influence in the modern era is the president's ability to persuade. Presidents, according to Neustadt, must be highly sensitive to the context in which they attempt to persuade and the likelihood that they can bargain successfully. But presidents must be aware that their power of persuasion is fragile; it can easily be squandered or lost. Losing in one bargaining game may undermine a president's ability to bargain in another. Moreover, presidents have to bargain with everyone, from members of Congress, to bureaucrats, to even their own staffers. They must bargain with everyone because no one else shares the presidential perspective or vantage point and everyone else, including top staffers, has their own agendas and goals, some of which may be at variance with the president's.

In contrast to Neustadt's often pessimistic view of the modern president, Terry Moe argues that modern presidents have considerable resources and strategies at their disposal to meet expectations for leadership.[16] First of all, the president has important structural advantages that derive from the ambiguity of the Constitution and the comparative structures of Congress and the executive. As we have mentioned so often, the ambiguity of the Constitution allows each generation to reinterpret what it expects of presidents, including how they will go about their job.

Moe also see advantages that accrue to the president from the mere fact of being head of the executive branch. Unlike Neustadt, Moe contends that the resources,

[16]Moe's theory has been developed in several chapters and articles. See Terry M. Moe, "The Politicized Presidency," in *The New Direction in American Politics,* ed. John E. Chubb and Paul E.Peterson (Washington, D.C.: Brookings Institution, 1985), pp. 235–72; Terry M. Moe, "The Politics of Bureaucratic Structure," in *Can the Government Govern?* ed. John E. Chubb and Paul E. Peterson (Washington, D.C.: Brookings Institution, 1989), pp. 267–329; Terry M. Moe, "Presidents, Institutions, and Theory," in *Researching the Presidency: Vital Questions, New Approaches,* ed. George C. Edwards, III, John H. Kessel, and Bert A. Rockman (Pittsburgh: University of Pittsburgh Press, 1993), pp. 337–85; Terry M. Moe and Scott A. Wilson, "Presidents and the Politics of Structure," *Law and Contemporary Problems* 57 (Spring 1994): 1–44; Terry M. Moe and William G. Howell, "The Presidential Power of Unilateral Action," *Journal of Law, Economics, and Organization* 15 (1999) 132–79; Terry M. Moe and William G. Howell, "Unilateral Action and Presidential Power: A Theory," *Presidential Studies Quarterly* 29 (December 1999): 850–72.

expertise, experience, and information of the vast executive branch establishment benefit the president. Congress cannot match these resources, even in its own agencies such as the Congressional Research Service or the Congressional Budget Office. Presidents as executives manage the operations of government, giving them a degree of access and control over the bureaucracy denied to others, such as the Congress. Also, as the executive, presidents are often able to act first. This allows presidents to structure the agenda.

But the structure of the executive in comparison to Congress also provides the presidents with important advantages. As a unitary office, presidents can take quick action. Congress, on the other hand, has to coordinate hundreds of members across two chambers before it can take action, such as passing a bill. Furthermore, decision points, such as committees or a filibuster by a one senator, can stop or frustrate Congressional action, even when a majority in Congress supports taking an action.

This structural property of Congress may even make it difficult to stop or overturn actions that presidents have taken. Moe calls these unilateral actions, which often come in the form of executive orders. Rarely does Congress overturn an executive order or other unilateral action, in part because of the collective action problems noted above. This provides presidents with a key advantage. They can take unilateral actions with the knowledge that they will very rarely be overturned by Congress.

Also, in contrast to Neustadt, Moe argues that presidents have strategies that they can use so that they do not have to resort as much to persuasion and bargaining in each situation. One strategy involves politicizing the appointees to office. The idea of politicizing is to ensure that appointees to bureaucratic and EOP slots are loyal to the president. When appointees are loyal, the likelihood that they will have agendas at variance with the president's will decline. Presidents can use these appointees to carry out their decisions and directions without having to engage in the persuasion and bargaining that Neustadt suggests they have to do, even with appointees and staffers.

A second strategy that presidents can use is to centralize decision making. Centralization involves pulling all kinds of decisions, especially those concerning policy making and implementation, into the White House. Doing this increases presidential control over decision and policy making because presidents or loyal staffers are the ones who make the decision under consideration.

Thus, the picture of the modern president that Moe presents differs from Neustadt's. Neustadt's modern president basically stands alone, unable to rely on anyone else systematically, because others have their own agendas. Thus, the Neustadtian president must resort to his own political skills, talents, and bargaining advantages if he is to effect the outcomes that he wants. Moe, in contrast, sees a modern president who possesses important institutional and strategic resources that he can employ to further his ends. Moe's president need not resort to persuasion as much. Instead, he can rely on loyal staff and the institutional advantages of the presidency over the Congress when making policy.

Who is correct, Neustadt or Moe? There is probably a grain of truth in both accounts of the modern president. As Moe observes, the structural nature of the presidency and Congress does afford the president several advantages. Consistent with Moe's account, presidents have engaged in much unilateral action in making policy. Similarly, accounts of modern presidents indicate that they often follow the strategies of politicizing appointments and centralizing responsibility and decision making. But it is also noteworthy that Congress has set requirements for many posts, within both the bureaucracy and the EOP. In some instances, Congress has even created posts that presidents opposed. This suggests that presidential control over appointments is not as complete as Moe's theory contends. Lastly, even if presidents can command loyalty within the executive branch and resort to unilateral forms of policy making, much policy making requires legislative action, the involvement of interest groups, and the participation of civil service bureaucrats, among others. Under such conditions, presidents may have to resort to persuasion and bargaining, much as Neustadt describes. Thus, it is not so much a question of whether Neustadt or Moe is right or wrong but under what circumstances presidents can act with the dispatch and direction of Moe's modern president or have to resort to the persuasion and bargaining of Neustadt's modern president.

ALTERNATIVE THEORIES OF PRESIDENTIAL CHANGE: POSTMODERN PRESIDENCY, RHETORICAL PRESIDENCY, AND CYCLES IN THE PRESIDENCY

Although the theory of the modern presidency is quite widely held, not all political scientists and other scholars of the presidency subscribe to it. Some contend that the modern presidency is not the end of development of the office and that in the late twentieth century, the presidency entered a third phase, which they call the postmodern presidency. Another perspective suggests that the fundamental change of the presidency occurred around the turn of the twentieth century, when the presidential behavior before the public changed. At that time, presidents began to try to rally the public behind their policy initiatives and efforts—a development that is called the rhetorical presidency. A third idea that we will discuss suggests that the office may not change so much in a linear fashion, from premodern to modern, as go through recurring cycles that have a strong pull on what presidents do and what they can accomplish. This cyclical account of the presidency invokes the idea of presidential time.

The Postmodern Presidency and the End of the Modern Presidency?

The discussion of the modern presidency almost makes its emergence seem natural and unavoidable, and suggests the clock cannot be turned back. A less expansive presidency may not be possible ever again, or at least in the foreseeable future. But some have argued that changes in the world will scale back the modern presidency. Such a view does not see a return to the presidency of Washington through Hoover but rather a movement toward a presidency that is not as imposing or dominant as the modern presidency of Franklin Roosevelt through Clinton. In fact, some see the seeds of this new presidency beginning when Ronald Reagan was president, in the 1980s. Proponents of this perspective call this new president the **postmodern presidency.**[17]

Two trends seem most important if a postmodern presidency is a likelihood. First, the end of the Cold War may have critical implications for the presidency. Some saw the power of the modern presidency as being strongly rooted in the politics of the Cold War. It is often the case that during war, nations, even those with limited central governments, allow political power to be collected and centralized in the executive, in order to prosecute the war. Even Lincoln, during the Civil War, amassed impressive power in his office and engaged in practices unthinkable in other times, arguing that preservation of the Republic and the Constitution outweighed other considerations.

With regard to the modern presidency, the Cold War allowed presidents to make claims similar to Lincoln's, suggesting that national security concerns overrode other concerns. Thus, presidents could engage in secret activities, although secrecy in general is inimical to democracy. Presidents, too, could ask for and receive extraordinary emergency powers that could be invoked at will, again because of national security concerns. The specter of nuclear holocaust that might result if relations with the Soviets were not managed ably and incidents like the Cuban Missile Crisis in 1963 made presidential claims for relatively unrestrained power credible to many.

However, the collapse of the Soviet Union in 1991 and the transformation of the Soviet Union and most of the nations in eastern Europe that were once allied with the Soviets into democracies seemingly removed or at least lessened the great threat to world peace. Peaceful coexistence, if not cooperation, with Russia was now possible. The trouble spots in the world were more local than global, which further reduced the prospect of global war and nuclear holocaust. With the end of the Cold War, the United States emerged as the world's unrivaled power, but world power meant less than it did during the nearly forty-five years of Cold War tensions. Domestic politics replaced international issues as the dominant concerns of American voters, and few if any international problems seemed big enough to push domestic concerns off of the public's agenda for long as the Cold War was sometimes able to do. The consequence of this new environment was that presidents could not so convincingly call for power and support as they could during the Cold War era. The wave of terrorist attacks on September 11, 2001, however, led to new assertions of presidential power to protect the nation.

[17]On the end of the modern presidency and the postmodern presidency, see Richard Rose, *The Postmodern President: George Bush Meets the World,* 2d ed. (Chatham, N.J.: Chatham House, 1991); Ryan J. Barilleaux, *The Postmodern Presidency: The Office after Ronald Reagan* (New York: Praeger, 1988); and Michael J. Smith, "Going International: Presidential Activity in the Post-modern Presidency," *Journal of American Studies* 31 (August 1997): 219–33. However, not everyone subscribes to the postmodern presidency thesis. See, for instance, Joseph A. Pika and Norman C. Thomas, "The Presidency Since Mid-century," *Congress and the Presidency* 19 (Spring 1992): 29–46.

George H. W. Bush once remarked that one does not really need a president for domestic affairs The president's importance and power derive from directing international affairs. Bush seemed to sense the power that accrues to the presidency from international politics and tensions. He also seemed to sense the limitations of the presidency in domestic politics, where Congress easily challenges the president, refuses to adopt his policy proposals, or amends them profusely. The end of the Cold War has thus diminished the power and leadership of the presidency.

The end of the era of big government may have also profoundly reshaped the presidency. When speaking of the end of the era of big government, we should not infer that it means that the public wants to scale back the size of government very much but rather that there is little support for new government programs that are big, expensive, and may entail creating a large bureaucracy for their implementation.

During the era of the modern presidency, presidents pursued big domestic political issues, much as they pushed on the foreign policy front. Such big policies generally affected large masses of the population, sometimes restructured the political and economic relationships and positions of many people, and often entailed building large bureaucracies to implement the policies. Thus, under the New Deal policies of Roosevelt in the 1930s, labor unions rose to power, and rich people were taxed and their wealth redistributed through government programs to aid those distressed by the Depression. The important Social Security program was created in the 1930s and was to become the most expensive government program administered by the largest domestic bureaucracy. In the 1960s, major programs to help elderly and poor people pay for medical care were created, and a significant number of regulations were placed on corporations, focusing on their products and production practices. Civil rights legislation passed in that decade had perhaps the most profound impact on how people of different races would relate to each other. Even in the 1980s, the economic package promoted by Ronald Reagan cut back on taxes and restructured the distribution of wealth in the United States as a consequence. Other examples of presidents proposing big domestic policies abound.

Presidents did not always get what they wanted when they proposed major domestic initiatives. As early as Harry Truman's presidency in the late 1940s and early 1950s, we see presidential calls for national health insurance. But the swan song for big presidential domestic policies probably came with Bill Clinton's failed attempt at comprehensive health care reform in 1994. Notably, opponents stressed that Clinton's plan would lead to the creation of new and large federal bureaucracy to administer the program. But the public did not seem in the mood for any new federal bureaucracies of measurable size. Not only was Clinton given his most critical policy defeat with this policy, but the Republicans claimed that they gained control of Congress for the first time since the early 1950s as a result. But most important, Bill Clinton proclaimed in his second inaugural address in 1997 that the "era of big government" was over, at least in the abstract.

If international politics no longer provide a dependable justification for the modern presidency and if big, new domestic programs are no longer possible, what is the need for a modern-style presidency? Presidents might still be important at times, but the changing international and domestic environment may have altered the presidency and its role in the political system.

The Rhetorical Presidency

The **rhetorical presidency** theory argues that there are basically two major types of presidencies, but the two types of the rhetorical presidency differ from those of the modern presidency. The rhetorical presidency theory argues that the first, or constitutional presidency, lasted from the founding of the nation until the late nineteenth century. From then to the present, we are in the period of the rhetorical presidency. Thus, the rhetorical presidency begins some thirty years or so before the modern presidency.

Second, the rhetorical presidency focuses on the relationship between the president and the public and the use of presidential rhetoric or speaking in defining that relationship. In contrast, the modern presidency theory looks at a whole complex of changes in the presidency, as we have discussed, in which the relationship between the president and the mass pubic is but one.

Fundamentally, the rhetorical presidency theory argues that the quantity and quality of presidential rhetoric changed in the late nineteenth and early twentieth centuries. Presidents began to speak more in public, and they began to speak in public about political issues of the day with the objective of rallying public support behind their policy efforts. This is a change in the public rhetoric of presidents, who were previously less likely to take up policies or issues and even less likely to try to mobilize the public behind such causes. Thus, as the nineteenth century drew to a close and the twentieth century began, the relationship between the president and the mass public began to alter. Presidents began more and more to seek public support for policies that they cared about, and in time, "popular or mass rhetoric . . . [became] a principal tool of presidential governance."[18]

Before the twentieth century, presidents involved themselves in policy making, but they communicated their policy positions mostly by sending written messages to Congress. The public was not a prime audience of such communications. Also, presidents would rely on the press, which tended to be highly partisan, to express their policy preferences on issues of the day, but generally, surrogates were used to write those articles, and presidents never personally identified themselves.[19]

Presidents of the nineteenth century also toured the nation, a practice begun by George Washington. Rarely did a president use such tours to make direct policy appeals to the public, and even when a policy agenda motivated a president

[18]Jeffrey K. Tulis, *The Rhetorical Presidency* (Princeton, N. J.: Princeton University Press, 1987).

[19]Mel Laracey, "The Presidential Newspaper: The Forgotten Way of Going Public," in *Speaking to the People: The Rhetorical Presidency in Historical Perspective,* ed. Richard J. Ellis. (Amherst: University of Massachusetts Press, 1998), pp. 66–86.

to tour, he was often indirect and oblique about pressing his issue before the public. For instance, in 1877, Rutherford B. Hayes toured New England, the Midwest, and the South to promote his policy of withdrawing federal troops from the South and allowing local civilian control of government in that region. "But he assiduously avoided explicit references to politics and specific policies" and often told audiences that he was not there to make a "political speech."[20] Together, presidential use of the partisan press, rarity of public rhetoric on policy issues, and presidential tours of the nation give a strong sense of the cultural norm of the nineteenth century that proscribed direct presidential appeals to the public about pressing issues.

Theodore Roosevelt ushered in the rhetorical presidency (1901–1908). By the administration of Woodrow Wilson (1912–1920), a new norm that emphasized presidential leadership of the public in pursuit of policy had taken root in the political system. Changes in the press and the political parties, plus a new set of ideas that provided an ideological justification for popular presidential leadership, led to the transformation of the relationship between the president and the mass public.

First, the press gradually became less partisan and more professional and objective in its reporting of the news. The partisan press was instrumental in educating the public about political issues and thus in helping to mobilize voters behind candidates. As a consequence, much campaigning for office in the nineteenth century revolved around spectacle—rallies, parades, fairs, carnivals, and the like—to rouse the party faithful and get them emotionally involved in the election campaign. The partisan press provided the reasons for voting for a candidate, and the campaign heightened emotional ties between parties and their candidates with the voting public.

The rise of the professional press and the decline of the partisan press forced the parties to find some other forum to educate voters about why they should support the party's candidates for office. Campaigns became one such forum, as did other public events, which campaign managers hoped would generate press coverage. By the turn of the century, the public began to expect popular leadership from the president, not only during presidential election campaign periods but throughout his term of office.[21] An indication of the hold of this new, more public presidency is Theodore Roosevelt's colorful phrase of the presidency as a "bully pulpit."

Although Roosevelt may have been the first rhetorical president, Woodrow Wilson provided the intellectual foundation and justification for such a presidency. Wilson was closely associated with the Progressive movement of the late nineteenth and early twentieth centuries. Progressives were not all of one mind, but in general, they thought that parties were corrupt and that the bosses who ran

---

[20]Gerald Gamm and Renee M. Smith, "Presidents, Parties, and the Public: Evolving Patterns of Interaction, 1877–1929," in *Speaking to the People: The Rhetorical Presidency in Historical Perspective,* ed. Richard J. Ellis. (Amherst: University of Massachusetts Press, 1998), pp. 87–111.

[21]Ibid., pp. 90–92.

them had too much power. They preferred more direct forms of democracy, such as primaries to nominate candidates.[22]

Wilson identified the separation of powers as a fundamental defect in the structure of government.[23] To Wilson, the separation of powers enabled Congress to dominate in policy making. But "congressional government"—a label he would use as the title of one of his famous books on the operation of the U.S. government—meant that special interests, through their hold on congressional committees, would make most policy decisions. As a consequence, national issues or the public interest was not adequately addressed, national leadership from the nation's capital was not forthcoming, nor was there much policy coordination. Perhaps even more important, the public, writ large, had little or no role to play in the governing process.

Wilson, like many Progressives, had great faith in the public, especially if informed and led. Leadership, to Wilson, was a process whereby the leader would "interpret" the people's desires.[24] Thus, unlike the founders, who viewed public opinion as something that leaders instilled in the mass public, Wilson reversed the process, arguing that public opinion began in the hearts and minds of ordinary people, but it was the job of political leadership to give such opinion political and policy meaning and shape. In this process of interpreting, the president became the people's representative, and the process of interpretation involved a "discussion" between the people and its leaders, that is, a deliberation between the two. To Wilson, because of the president's national platform and office, only the president could effectively lead the public.

The founders limited popular democracy in part out of a fear of demagoguery. Wilson answered this charge, too. He felt that political norms could be established such that leaders would be less inclined to seek personal power but would aim to serve the public. Second, and perhaps more important as a safeguard, Wilson felt that the public could judge character. And finally, Wilson argued that the difficulty of changing and moving public opinion would also provide a bulwark against demagoguery. Wilson's ideas provided an important justification for a presidency based on popular leadership of the public for policy objectives, and his ideas are still important to our understanding of the operation of the modern presidency and the functioning of our political system.

Some of the same factors that led to the modern presidency also are identified as stimulating the development of the rhetorical presidency. The nationalization of the economy and the government's role in regulating it are important in boosting the president in the political system. Perhaps as important is the role of the Progressive movement and the ideas that Progressives brought with them to governing, as we detailed in reviewing the ideas of Woodrow Wilson.

---

[22]On the Progressives and their political views, see Richard J. Hofstadter, *The Age of Reform* (New York: Alfred Knopf, 1977). On the impact of Progressives on the presidency, see Lester G. Seligman and Cary R. Covington, *The Coalitional Presidency* (Chicago: Dorsey, 1989), pp. 27–45.

[23]On Wilson and the rhetorical presidency, see Tulis, *Rhetorical Presidency,* pp. 118–32. Much of the following discussion comes from that source.

[24]Ibid., p. 125.

Cycles and the Idea of Presidential Time

Both the modern presidency and rhetorical presidency theories suggest development and change in the office such that presidencies of the different periods are fundamentally different. Some changes in the office may be permanent or at least long lasting. But not all changes will be so permanent. Some will be fleeting, existing for perhaps only one president's term of office. Other types of change will be of short duration but will recur. In other words, there may be recurring cycles that affect the presidency and the behavior of the incumbent in office. A large number of these cycles have been identified: for instance, the first term-second term cycle, the congressional midterm election cycle, and the cycle of decreasing resources but increasing effectiveness.[25] Each of these cycles affects each new presidency, and we will discuss them in more detail as their implications come up in later chapters. Here, our concern is with more epoch cycles—those cycles of history that may affect several presidents and their time in office. The most influential of these is expressed by Stephen Skowronek's theory of **political time.**[26]

Political time is not necessarily a linear concept, but historically, there has been a general progression from one phase to the next that repeats, creating a cycle. The convergence of two contexts determines the president's placement in political time. The first is whether the established (or ruling) political order, which is composed of the dominant political party, allied interest groups, and the issues of concern to them, is in a resilient (or strong) posture or whether it is in a vulnerable (or weak) posture. The second context is the relationship between the president and that established ruling order—whether the president is an affiliate (ally) or an opponent. This creates four possible political time placements for a president, as outlined in table 3-2.

TABLE 3-2   PRESIDENTS AND POLITICAL TIME

Political Time Phase	Status of Ruling Political Order	Relationship of the President to the Ruling Political Order	Examples of Presidents
Reconstruction	Vulnerable	Opponent	Jefferson, Jackson, Lincoln, F. Roosevelt
Articulation	Resilient	Affiliate	Monroe, Polk, L. Johnson
Disjunction	Vulnerable	Affiliate	J.Q. Adams, Pierce, Hoover, Carter
Preemption	Resilient	Opponent	Tyler, A. Johnson, Wilson, Nixon

Source: Adapted from Stephen Skowronek, *The Politics Presidents Make: Leadership from John Adams to George Bush* (Cambridge: Harvard University Press, 1993).

[25]Paul C. Light, *The President's Agenda: Domestic Policy Choice from Kennedy to Carter (with Notes on Ronald Reagan)* (Baltimore: Johns Hopkins University Press, 1982). A wide-ranging discussion of the impact of several types of cycles on the presidency can be found in Bert A. Rockman, *The Leadership Question: The Presidency and the American System* (New York: Praeger, 1984), pp. 83–130.

[26]Stephen Skowronek, *The Politics Presidents Make: Leadership from John Adams to George Bush* (Cambridge: Harvard University Press, 1993). We will consider a related theory—realignment theory—in Chapter 8, when we discuss political parties.

The basic logic behind the cycle from one phase to the next is that the dominant ruling political order is broken up, in part by a president coming along who helps to break it apart and to establish a new ruling political order, until it too is destroyed at some time in the future. Although each president may have strong incentives to make an imprint on the political system, the president's placement in political time, according to Skowronek, heavily affects the president's potential for impact and the actions that he can and may be forced to take while in office.

The first phase of the political time cycle is called the politics of reconstruction. In this phase, a new president is able to attack the established ruling political order, which is vulnerable to attack and has been weakening for some years already. The reconstructive president begins to erect a new ruling political order, which he does in two senses: first, by building a new ruling party to replace the one of the past ruling order, and second, by establishing a new political agenda, which he does by promoting new issues and redefining old ones. Thus, the politics of reconstruction involve a ruling political order that is vulnerable with a president who is an opponent of that weakening political order. Examples of reconstructive presidents include Thomas Jefferson, Andrew Jackson, Abraham Lincoln, and Franklin Roosevelt. It is interesting that these presidents are often counted among the greatest. Skowronek's theory, then, also gives a sense of what makes a great president—it may have less to with the talents of a particular president than with the placement of the president's service in political time.

Reconstructive presidents tend to be followed by articulation presidents. These presidents build on the successes of the reconstructive president, solidifying the gains of the emerging ruling political order that was inaugurated by the reconstructive president. In terms of political time, these presidents are affiliated with the established political order but also serve when that order is resilient and strong. Examples of such presidents include James Monroe, James Polk, and Harry Truman. Generally, the historical reputations of these presidents are also often highly ranked, but not nearly as high as those of the reconstructive presidents. Again, political time makes a great impact on what a president can accomplish and, hence, his historical reputation.

The process of building and maintaining a ruling political order is fragile, however, and over time, fissures among elements of the ruling order begin to widen and can no longer be reconciled or compromised. The emergence of new issues and groups may further weaken the ruling political order. Presidents of disjunction preside during these perilous times as they try to keep the ruling political order together. Rather than accomplishing great things or consolidating a powerful ruling order, disjunctive presidents are usually on the defensive, being attacked from inside and outside of the ruling order as that order weakens. Such presidents are primarily concerned with making themselves and their ruling order credible, a task that is undermined by the weakening of their ruling order. Finally, the ruling order breaks down, and a reconstructive president emerges. Examples of such plagued presidents include John Quincy Adams, Franklin Pierce, Herbert Hoover, and Jimmy Carter. The historical reputation of all is weak, owing perhaps to their political time setting more than to their own lack of talents or abilities.

Punctuated at points when the ruling political order is resilient will be circumstances in which presidents opposed to that dominant political order come to office, often because of some combination of short-term political forces, perhaps including their own personal attractiveness to voters. Skowronek calls them preemptive presidents. Their accomplishments are often modest, owing to the strength of the ruling political order, as they seek to become reconstructive presidents and replace the ruling political order with a new one. But the existing political order is just too strong to shake fully, though the efforts of preemptive presidents may help to weaken the established ruling political order. Examples of such presidents are John Tyler, Andrew Johnson, Woodrow Wilson, and Richard Nixon. The historical reputations of preemptive presidents are mixed, but in almost all cases, they are not thought to have lived up to their potential. The theory of political time, however, suggests another reason for their mixed reviews—the times were stacked against them.

The theory of political time suggests that much of how we think about presidents should be viewed not solely from the perspective of the individual in office but also from the context of the times in which a president serves. Skowronek's theory also takes note of another important development in government that affects presidents and what they can accomplish. This is the growth of government, both in size and in its ties to important elements of society. As government has grown stronger and has established stronger alliances with people and forces outside of government, it is harder to upset, change, replace, or get rid of those parts of government, as new presidents and new political forces might like to do. Thus, we may see the disappearance of the reconstructive president, because opposition presidents will not have the authority, power, and political support to change the political system as radically as previous presidents did. This may help account for why we did not mention Ronald Reagan among the reconstructive presidents. His ability to impact the political system was limited when compared to the last reconstructive president, Franklin Roosevelt. Future presidents may be no more successful than the preemptive variety, suggesting that our presidential experience in the future will be quite mixed, with few, if any, presidents living up to their "potential."

CONCLUSION

In this chapter, we have discussed how the presidency has evolved and changed over time. Ambiguity in the Constitution regarding the presidency has opened the office to much redefinition and change. Both formal and informal mechanisms may account for how the presidency changes, while the stimulus for change can come from presidents as well as outside forces.

We have also discussed a variety of notions about the nature of presidential change: whether the early presidency has become a modern office, whether that modern office has transformed into a postmodern office, whether the whole notion of a modern presidency is at all useful, whether the idea of a rhetorical presidency is a better way of understanding the office. Further, we have discussed whether cycles across time have had a stronger impact on the office than the evolutionary trends. The main point to our discussion is that the office is highly dynamic and in many regards has drifted from the founders' vision.

KEY TERMS

Budget and Accounting
   Act of 1921   53
Executive Office of
   the President   53
executive privilege   51

political time   65
postmodern presidency   60
rhetorical presidency   62

DISCUSSION QUESTIONS

1. What processes are used to change the presidency?
2. How did George Washington shape the presidency?
3. What are the main features of the modern presidency? Why did it emerge?
4. How important is the power of persuasion for presidents?
5. What structural advantages does the president have over Congress?
6. How did the end of the Cold War affect the presidency?
7. How does political time affect a president's ability to accomplish things?

SUGGESTED READINGS

Sidney Milkis and Michael Nelson, *The American Presidency: Origins and Development,* 3d ed. Washington, D.C.: Congressional Quarterly Press, 1999.

Michael Nelson, ed., *The Evolving Presidency.* Washington, D.C.: Congressional Quarterly Press, 1999.

Richard Neustadt, *Presidential Power and the Modern Presidents.* New York: Free Press, 1990.

Richard Rose, *The Postmodern President,* 2d ed. Chatham, N.J.: Chatham House, 1991.

4

THE PRESIDENTIAL
SELECTION PROCESS

The process used to select America's president is one of the most complex leadership selection systems in the world. Some of the complexity stems from the structure of the American political system generally. Because of that structure, presidential selection is governed by national laws, national party rules and regulations (which are somewhat different for each of the parties), fifty sets of state laws, and at least one hundred sets of state party rules (assuming two parties in each state). In addition, local governments and local party organizations are involved in a variety of ways, a fact that was driven home to many Americans by the wrangling in Florida after the 2000 presidential election. Voting systems in Florida, as well as a number of other states, vary somewhat from one locality to another. Keeping track of the many rules and regulations is a formidable task.

Many interest groups, political activists, campaign professionals, journalists, and other people also become involved in the process, although the extent of their involvement varies from one election to another and even over the course of a campaign season. Their expectations and capabilities add even more variety and complexity to the process. Some campaigns are further complicated by the entry of minor party candidates who may draw significant support away from one or more of the major party candidates and, consequently, tip the balance of the election from one side to the other, as Ralph Nader may have done in the 2000 election.

As the presidential selection process has grown more complex and especially as it has required the candidates to appeal for the support of tens of millions of people, campaigns have grown longer and longer. In fact, the process now goes on continuously, with candidates spending years seeking the presidency and with the winners continuing to engage in campaign-like activities throughout the course of their presidencies.

At some risk of oversimplification, we can break the presidential selection process down into four phases: the precampaign campaign, the nomination campaign, the general election campaign, and the postcampaign campaign (for the winner). The four phases overlap at times, as in the case of a candidate who has largely clinched the party nomination and begins the general election campaign while contenders in the other party are still battling for the nomination. In addition, even as the nomination or general election phase for one election contest is drawing to a close, candidates who were not successful in that contest or not actively involved in it may be laying plans for a bid for their party's nomination four or more years in the future.

THE PRECAMPAIGN CAMPAIGN

The scope and complexity of the nomination and general election phases of the presidential selection process are enormous, and many potential candidates realize that they cannot possibly succeed during those phases without extensive advance preparation. Building a nationwide organization, developing a national political following, raising enormous sums of money, building an impressive political resume, and other aspects of the quest for the presidency are very time consuming. Moreover, many states now choose their convention delegates early in the nomination schedule, a practice that leaves candidates little time to build support once the nominating season begins. As a result, candidates are now spending years gearing up for the "active" phase of the nomination contest.[1]

Gaining relevant political experience is one important part of the **precampaign campaign.** Although Americans often tend to look down on politicians, most, at least in the modern era, seem to prefer presidential candidates who have some experience in public office. Contrary to some other countries, however, we do not appear to place particular emphasis on national government experience. A number of recent American presidents, including Jimmy Carter, Ronald Reagan, Bill Clinton, and George W. Bush, came to the White House with little or no national government experience but with significant experience in state politics. Compared with national leaders in some other Western democracies, American presidents often come to the job with considerably less experience in foreign policy, national security issues, or national economic or budgetary policy.[2]

Holding public office gives potential presidential candidates the chance to develop a track record on various issues and to gain experience in dealing with other public officials and the media. Holding public office also gives opportunities for becoming better known, although the opportunities vary considerably from one office to another. When large numbers of U.S. senators began to entertain hopes of running for president after World War II, they became active across a wider range of policy issues and became more active earlier in their careers than had been the norm. Involvement in more issues helps a potential candidate gain exposure and expertise in the wider range of issues that are likely to pop up in a presidential campaign.[3]

---

[1] On the importance of front loading and the need to be prepared before the campaign season begins, see Andrew Busch, "New Features of the 2000 Presidential Nominating Process: Republican Reforms, Front-Loading's Second Wind, and Early Voting," in *In Pursuit of the White House 2000,* ed. William Mayer, (New York: Chatham House, 2000), pp. 57–86; William Mayer, "The Presidential Nominations," in Gerald Pomper, et al., *The Election of 2000* (New York: Chatham House, 2001), pp. 12–45; Terry Neal, "By March, It'll All Be Over," *Washington Post National Weekly Edition,* 12 July 1999, p. 12; Stephen Wayne, *The Road to the White House 2000* (Boston: Bedford/St. Martin's, 2000), pp. 24–132.

[2] For comparisons of the backgrounds of U.S. presidents with the backgrounds of presidents and prime ministers in other countries, see Richard Rose, *The Postmodern President,* 2d ed. (Chatham, N.J.: Chatham House, 1991), pp. 94–114.

[3] On the impact of U.S. senators' quest for more media coverage, see Barbara Sinclair, *The Transformation of the U.S. Senate* (Baltimore: Johns Hopkins University, 1989).

Holding elective office also gives potential presidential candidates the opportunity to gain experience in campaigning and to demonstrate their vote-getting ability, both of which can be helpful in convincing party officials, political activists, and campaign contributors that the candidate might be successful in a national campaign. Of course, success in a single state or congressional district does not guarantee success in a national campaign, but some experience is better than none.

Bear in mind that the process of building a track record may at times bring an end to presidential aspirations. A governor may become embroiled in enough controversies to create a legion of political adversaries. Decisions that accommodate the preferences of people in a single state or congressional district may not play well before a national audience in a later campaign. A member of the House of Representatives may launch a bid for the U.S. Senate and suffer a major defeat that undermines future hopes for the presidency. Defeats do not always preclude future success, however; Lyndon Johnson, Richard Nixon, Ronald Reagan, and George H. W. Bush all failed in their first bid for a presidential nomination or in the general election but later made it to the White House.

Note, too, that a potential candidate may, to a significant degree, build a track record in nonelective offices. George H. W. Bush served in a number of appointive positions, including director of the Central Intelligence Agency and national chair of the Republican Party. Franklin Roosevelt worked in the Navy Department, and Dwight Eisenhower served as supreme allied commander during World War II.

Becoming better known is another important part of the precampaign campaign. Part of this effort involves trying to attract the attention of the media, a task that is difficult for many potential candidates. Favorable comments by the so-called **Talent Scout** journalists are particularly helpful. The Talent Scouts are prestigious reporters who sometimes draw attention to someone whom they believe deserves consideration as a possible presidential contender. The Talent Scout's work is noticed by other journalists, who may then give the candidate additional exposure.[4] Candidates may also try to gain the attention of relatively specialized media networks, many of which are linked to specific industries or interest groups and can reach a national audience with a common interest.

Cultivating relationships with the mass media is a time-consuming enterprise and is more likely to succeed when adequate attention is given to the needs and priorities of journalists, who must cope with a variety of deadlines and may lack expertise on many substantive policy issues. As a result, presidential aspirants who occupy an office with staff support, some of which can be used for media relations, have some advantage over aspirants who lack that staff support. Not coincidentally, a large proportion of the more serious presidential contenders since World War II have come from the ranks of governors and U.S. senators—both sets of offices having significant staff assistance.

---

[4]Some sources use the term "Great Mentioner" instead of Talent Scout. See Thomas Patterson, *Out of Order* (New York: Vintage, 1994), p. 35.

Another tactic for becoming better known is writing books or magazine articles (possibly with the help of staff) that may attract the attention of the general public, people who are interested in particular issues, or reporters. Written work can serve to make the candidate's name more familiar, demonstrate expertise in one or more policy areas, convey the candidate's views on one or more issues, or reveal some degree of political skill or at least perceptiveness. One of the best-known presidential books is John Kennedy's *Profiles in Courage,* which was published four years before he won the presidency and earned him the Pulitzer Prize.[5] Bear in mind, however, that potential opponents may look for controversial passages in a candidate's writings in hopes of undermining that candidate's image. Moreover, many struggling authors have found that written work may attract little or no attention. Nonetheless, writing has some appeal for potential candidates, especially given the difficulty of gaining nationwide attention.

Some presidential hopefuls have used other approaches to become better known. Ronald Reagan combined a career in show business, his experience as governor of California, and a considerable number of speaking engagements to become a nationally known figure. Ross Perot and Steve Forbes spent millions of dollars of their personal fortunes to purchase substantial publicity in quest of a national political following. Presidential hopeful Jack Kemp used prominence gained from having played professional football to help him win a seat in Congress, and Senator Bill Bradley gained some of his visibility from having played professional basketball. A number of presidential hopefuls have appeared on entertainment-oriented television shows in order to win the attention of people who try to avoid political news whenever possible. Richard Nixon attracted considerable attention when he appeared on *Laugh-In,* a comedy show, with deliberate uncertainty recited one of the show's regular punch lines saying, "Sock it to me?" More recently, a number of candidates have appeared on television talk shows.

Extensive travel is another important part of the precampaign campaign. Travel gives a potential candidate access to local media in different parts of the country. In addition, face-to-face meetings with political activists may help the presidential hopeful build relationships that are very helpful in a campaign. Meeting with groups in different parts of the country may enable a candidate to demonstrate broad appeal and cultivate ties with blocks of potential supporters, whether they are union members, professionals, party activists, or people with an interest in a specific issue, such as gun control.

Building a campaign organization is critical for anyone seeking the presidency. Candidates cannot campaign everywhere at once, even in the age of television and the Internet, and a campaign requires special skills that many candidates do not possess. Candidates need help with fundraising, dealing with the media, legal issues, public opinion polling, and recruiting campaign workers. Candidates need to develop relationships with party officials and interest group leaders. Building an organization large enough to support a credible presidential bid is

[5]Perhaps the most famous presidential candidate book was John Kennedy's *Profiles in Courage* (New York: Harper Perennial, 1964). It was originally published in 1956.

very time consuming and sometimes risky, for relying on inept or untrustworthy people may greatly reduce a candidate's chances of success.

The precampaign campaign does not always have a clearly defined beginning. Someone may run for a state or local office with no intention of seeking the presidency. A later opportunity may lead to a run for the Senate, and the senator may only gradually develop an interest in running for president. That interest may never develop beyond the level of an occasional daydream, or the senator may eventually have a strong desire to run for president but find initial efforts so discouraging that most Americans never know that he or she wanted to be president. On the other hand, someone may spend years in a conscious effort to win the White House and may be known to any number of people as a presidential hopeful. Many presidential aspirants probably never get beyond the precampaign campaign.

Potential candidates often want to know whether they have any realistic chance of success. In an earlier time, that assessment was relatively difficult. Possible contenders might discuss their chances with party leaders in different parts of the country or other politically knowledgeable people, and their educated guesses were sometimes reasonably accurate. In recent years, however, public opinion polling can give political hopefuls more accurate information on their chances of winning. Polls can give them guidance on a number of considerations: How many people have heard of them? Who are their likely competitors? How popular are the possible contenders? Do the opponents have weaknesses that can be exploited? What strengths do the likely competitors have?

These preliminary estimates of candidate prospects are not always good predictors of election outcomes, especially if the election is some time away. In 1991, President Bush was riding high in the public opinion polls in the wake of the victory of America and its allies in the war with Iraq. By the summer and fall of 1992, however, the public's attention had shifted to the economy, which was not performing very well, and Bush's popularity declined dramatically. If potential candidates believe that their chances of winning a given presidential election are very poor, they may decide to wait until a later election in hopes of having a better chance of victory.

Candidates may launch an apparently hopeless bid for the presidency in some cases. Some place their hopes on dumb luck, with the belief that the front-runner may stumble in the course of the campaign. Others may believe that they will fall short in the current campaign but will emerge from it as better known nationwide, better organized, and more experienced in presidential campaigning—all of which will be helpful in a future campaign. They may also entertain hopes of being chosen to be the vice presidential candidate. Some candidates, such as those nominated by minor parties, may run in order to call attention to a policy problem or a political viewpoint. If the candidate represents a perennially small party, such as most of the socialist parties in the United States, the attention gained may be relatively small, but a candidate running as the head of a splinter movement within one of the major parties may gain considerable exposure, as Theodore Roosevelt found in 1912.

THE NOMINATION CAMPAIGN

Many people might conceivably be presidential contenders, but typically, no more than a dozen people (and often fewer) are serious, active candidates in any given year. The task of narrowing that group down to the two (usually) major candidates falls to the nominating process. When the nominating process works well, the general election will offer voters appealing, well-qualified candidates who are reasonably able to work with other political leaders. When the process works poorly, voters in the general election will have unsatisfactory choices, and the ultimate winner may be poorly prepared to meet the demands of the office and have little ability to work with other leaders.

The presidential nominating process has changed dramatically over the years and in a number of ways. The laws and rules governing presidential nominations have been modified considerably. The groups involved in nomination decisions have also changed, as have the technologies used in the quest for the nomination. Finally, the cost of running for a presidential nomination has risen substantially and has helped draw attention to the role of money in American politics. Moreover, all of these changes are related to one another.[6]

The first nominating system established with the formation of the political parties early in U.S. history was the **congressional caucus,** a meeting of all or most of the party's members in both houses of Congress. The congressional caucus had a number of strengths as a nominating system. First, the decision makers were reasonably knowledgeable regarding the nature of the president's job and the people who were likely to be qualified for it. In addition, nominating by congressional caucuses was relatively inexpensive and simple. The small size of the decision-making group made negotiations and discussions reasonably easy. Members of the congressional caucuses were also likely to pay some attention to whether the nominees appeared to be able to work with Congress, although that consideration was not necessarily decisive in all cases. In a time of primitive communications and transportation systems, nomination by caucuses had a very practical advantage, too: members of Congress had to convene to perform legislative work, anyway. No one needed to make a special trip to a common location just to participate in the nomination decision.[7]

Nomination by congressional caucuses also had a number of shortcomings, at least in the opinion of many critics. Deliberations were often conducted in secret, and outsiders sometimes feared that unfair or corrupt agreements were part of the nomination decisions. Moreover, senators were not elected by the voters in that era, and most adults, including women, African Americans, and Native Americans, were not allowed to vote in House elections. Some members of Congress also declined

---

[6]For overviews of the development of the presidential nominating system, see V. O. Key, *Politics, Parties, and Pressure Groups,* 5th ed. (New York: Crowell, 1964), chap. 15; Paul Beck and Marjorie Hershey, *Party Politics in America,* 9th ed. (New York: Longman, 2001), chap. 10; John Jackson and William Crotty, *The Politics of Presidential Selection* (New York: Harper Collins), chap. 2–3; Wayne, *Road,* pp. 6–13.

[7]Jackson and Crotty, *Politics,* pp. 24–25.

to participate in caucus deliberations. Public influence over the nominating decisions was, therefore, likely to be limited and uneven. Some critics suspected that the congressional caucuses were biased in favor of national officials and against state or local officials, who might be highly capable. Nomination by caucuses might also have reduced presidential independence from Congress and, consequently, weakened the effectiveness of presidential checks on congressional encroachment. Finally, as state and local party organizations developed in the early 1800s, their leaders resented being excluded from presidential nomination decisions.

Pressures for reform grew during the 1820s, and by 1832, the congressional caucus was being replaced by the national nominating convention. Nominating conventions provided for representation of state and local party officers and public officials as well as members of Congress, depending on party rules and state laws for selecting convention delegates. That broader representation might increase sensitivity to public sentiments across the country, for many of the convention delegates wanted nominees who could win and, in the process, boost party fortunes generally. Convention deliberations were ostensibly more open to the press and public; that openness might discourage the use of corrupt or unfair deal making. Important state and local officials, such as governors, might have a better chance of being nominated by conventions than by congressional caucuses. Although the conventions included more participants than the congressional caucuses, they were still small enough to permit discussion and negotiations among the delegates. That capability was important when disagreements erupted over the choice of party nominees, the contents of party platforms, or party rules.[8]

The conventions, which were also adopted at the state level for nominating candidates for statewide offices, came under increasing attack beginning in the late 1800s. Critics complained that the conventions were dominated by party bosses and paid too little attention to public sentiments. Critics also complained that the apparent openness of conventions was largely a sham, for important decisions sometimes appeared to be made away from the convention floor. Some convention delegates were obviously pawns under the control of party leaders. Ordinary citizens and groups that were not closely linked to party officials felt excluded from the process at times.

One other important development cast a shadow over conventions at the state level and had spillover effects on the national conventions. A major **realignment** of the political parties occurred in the 1890s, and one consequence of the realignment was the emergence of many areas where one party was virtually certain to win. In those areas, winning the dominant party's nomination was tantamount to election, for the general election was rarely a contest. Consequently, nominating systems came under increasing scrutiny, and reformers began calling for giving voters a greater voice in nominations. At the state and local level, that meant adopting some form of the direct primary, which enabled voters to decide who would be nominated. In presidential politics, the reformers called for letting voters choose more of the delegates to attend the national nominating conventions.

[8]Jackson and Crotty, *Politics*, pp. 25–30.

Early in the twentieth century, a number of states began using **primaries** to select at least some of their national convention delegates, but enthusiasm for the primary began to decline after 1916, at least in presidential politics. Some states abandoned their presidential primaries, and delegates were chosen through a variety of mechanisms. Many states allotted a number of delegate slots to important public officials and party officers, and other delegates were chosen through state party conventions and other methods. Presidential primaries survived in a number of states, however, and were used to select delegates and as an opportunity to assess the electoral appeal of potential nominees.[9]

The period from the 1950s through the 1970s saw the mobilization of a number of new groups in American politics. The civil rights movement, the women's movement, the environmental movement, the antiwar movement, and other groups brought new demands and new pressures on many facets of the political system, including the presidential nominating process. Because the leaders of these new groups often believed that entrenched party officials were unresponsive to their concerns, pressures for more reforms began to build. Those pressures were more pronounced in the Democratic Party, but both parties adopted major changes in delegate selection processes (sometimes through changes in state laws or state party rules).[10]

The most visible change was the adoption of presidential primaries for selection of convention delegates. Most states adopted primaries, but others chose to select their delegates in multistage processes, beginning with neighborhood meetings to choose representatives to higher-level meetings (such as county conventions, which in turn picked delegates to state conventions, which chose the national delegates). In many states, virtually all delegates were chosen through primaries or the multistage processes, especially in the Democratic Party. As a result, Democratic conventions in the 1970s had relatively few party leaders or public officials attending, a development that was not very helpful in promoting party unity or forging links between the presidential nominees and other members of the party. Later rules changes permitted allocating some convention seats to party leaders and public officials, but most delegates today are chosen by primaries or the multistage meeting and convention system in the year of the campaign. Candidates have, therefore, a powerful incentive to conduct extensive campaigns in order to have their supporters chosen as convention delegates.

The current nominating system has been the subject of considerable criticism since it emerged in the 1960s and 1970s. Critics have charged that primaries tend to attract extremists and produce nominees that are out of step with the average voter. Recent research has cast doubt on that complaint, although primary voters do tend to be somewhat older and more partisan than the average general election voter. They are also interested in nominees who appear likely to win the general election.[11]

[9]Jackson and Crotty, *Politics,* pp. 29–35; Wayne, *Road,* pp. 9–13.

[10]Jackson, and Crotty, *Politics,* pp. 33–35 and chap. 3; Wayne, *Road,* chap. 4.

[11]Barbara Norrander, "Ideological Representativeness of Presidential Primary Voters," *American Journal of Political Science* 33 (1989): 570–87.

Critics in party organizations complain that primaries permit **"raiding,"** in which members of one party vote in the other party's primary in hopes of nominating a weak candidate who will be easy to defeat in the general election. Again, research casts doubt on this criticism; voters who cross party lines during primaries seem to be motivated by a desire to support candidates that they like rather than a desire to support a poor candidate.

A primary-dominated nominating system may also produce the problem of **fratricide,** in which candidates with similar issue positions divide their supporters and, consequently, enable a candidate who has fewer supporters to win the primary. Because candidates who come in first in primaries attract a very large share of the media coverage over the next several days following the primary, fratricide can cause candidates whose views are similar and shared by many voters to fall by the wayside. The process may then yield a nominee who has little chance of winning.

The shift to a primary-dominated nomination process has also increased the cost of seeking the party nomination. Candidates are now spending many millions of dollars in the quest for the nomination, and while high campaign spending does not guarantee victory, low spending pretty nearly guarantees defeat. Ironically, reforms designed to give the average voter more influence over presidential nominations have increased the political importance of campaign contributors, who tend to be wealthier than the average citizen.[12]

A related concern stems from the new campaign technologies (to be discussed in more detail later in this chapter), which have become very important in nomination campaigns, as well as in the general election. Candidates rely on professional fundraisers, pollsters, media consultants, and campaign consultants to provide vital campaign assistance. Most of these professionals are unknown to the public, a circumstance that makes holding them accountable very difficult. The old concerns regarding hidden centers of power still seem to be with us.

Party strategists are also concerned that the current nominating system, with its months of public conflict between contenders for a party's nomination, produces party disunity that is difficult to overcome in time for the general election campaign. Supporters of candidates who lose the nomination contest may be so unhappy over their favorite's defeat that they do not support the party nominee or provide only half-hearted support. A costly nomination battle can leave a party's financial supporters with less money to give during the general election to support party-based campaigning or other party candidates. Disunity at the nominating stage is not always harmful to a party's general election prospects, but battles over policy positions (rather than tactics) that leave moderates unhappy appear to be particularly harmful, for those voters may defect to the other party. Nomination battles in the president's party when an

---

[12]See Anthony Gierzynski, *Money Rules* (Boulder, Colo.: Westview, 2000), pp. 59–64, and chap. 5; Jackson and Crotty, *Politics,* pp. 193–94; Frank Sorauf, *Money in American Elections* (Glenview, Ill.: Scott, Foresman/Little, Brown, 1988), pp. 298–307, 347–53); Wayne, *Road,* pp. 56–58, and the studies they cite.

incumbent president seeks renomination also tend to be harmful in the general election, in part because they are likely to indicate a lack of enthusiasm for the incumbent in a good bit of the party and in the country generally.[13]

Critics also charge that the results in individual states, especially those that hold their primaries or precinct caucuses separately from other states, are sometimes blown out of proportion and may give inordinate attention to candidates with relatively little nationwide support. Some of those critics have called for holding several state primaries and caucuses on the same day rather than allowing some states to hold them on different days. To some degree, this has happened since the mid-1970s, but Iowa and New Hampshire officials have resisted efforts to share their individual dates with other states. The new, shorter primary schedule, with a considerable number of primaries being held early, has placed an even greater premium on being well known, well organized, and well financed before the season begins. That development has led some observers to wonder whether the schedule should be revised to extend over a longer period to give less famous and more poorly financed candidates the chance to develop support gradually.[14]

Some of the recurring dissatisfaction with the presidential nominating system stems from America's conflicting expectations and needs. We appear to want considerable public involvement in presidential nominations, but many Americans do not vote in primaries or precinct caucuses, and many do not want to devote much time or effort to learning about the candidates. We do not seem to want a process dominated by political insiders, yet the president needs to be able to work with other political leaders. We do not appear to trust party leaders with making nomination decisions, but our efforts to reduce their control have enhanced the influence of paid campaign experts. We do not yet know how to hold those experts accountable for the candidates that they help to nominate.

THE NATIONAL CONVENTIONS: CONTINUITY AND CHANGE

The changes in the delegate selection processes across the United States have brought significant changes to the national party nominating conventions. Nevertheless, the conventions continue to play an important, if poorly understood, role in the presidential selection process.

The national conventions serve several purposes, with varying degrees of success. One basic task is the formal designation of the presidential and vice presidential nominees. Before the 1960s, nominees were sometimes not known when the conventions met, and the delegates made relatively independent choices regarding the nomination. Although some nominations were clearly foregone conclusions, especially when incumbents sought renomination, some conventions

---

[13]Lonna Rae Atkeson, "From the Primaries to the General Election: Does a Divisive Nomination Race Affect a Candidate's Fortunes in the Fall?" in *In Pursuit of the White House 2000,* ed. William Mayer (New York: Chatham House, 2000), pp. 285–312; Jeffrey Cohen and David Nice, "Party Unity and Presidential Election Performance, 1936–1980," *Presidential Studies Quarterly* 12 (1982): 317–29.

[14]Andrew Busch, "New Features;" William Mayer, "Presidential Nominations."

TABLE 4-1   NUMBER OF BALLOTS REQUIRED TO SELECT NOMINEE, SELECTED YEARS

Year	Democrats	Republicans
1880	2	36
1912	46	1
1920	43	10
1924	103	1
1940	1	6

Source: Lyn Ragsdale, *Vital Statistics on the Presidency,* rev. ed. (Washington, D.C.: Congressional Quarterly Press, 1998), pp. 38–39.

needed a considerable number of ballots to choose the party nominees (see table 4-1). Since the 1960s, a candidate has clinched the nomination before the convention meets by winning the selection of loyal delegates to the convention.[15]

A second task of the convention is adopting the party platform. Contrary to the conventional wisdom, party platforms are not simply political hot air and campaign slogans, although they usually contain some of both. Platforms usually include discussions of party records and numerous proposals for future policies. Moreover, the presidential candidate winning the White House usually delivers on most of the platform proposals. The platforms might help voters decide which candidates to support, but the typical platform receives very little attention from the news media or the public. The platform is usually written by supporters of the party nominee, but some provisions may be drafted to placate other groups within the party. Platform hearings may also give groups the chance to call attention to issues or proposals that do not appear in the platform but that may appear in some future year.[16]

The conventions may also face proposals to modify procedures and rules, and may encounter disputes regarding their application. Although those discussions are not usually of much interest to the general public, rules and procedures may help some groups gain political leverage or an advantage over their opponents. In some years, there are disputes regarding which set of delegates is entitled to the seats allotted to a particular state. The convention tries to resolve those disputes, preferably without antagonizing too many people.

A long-standing task of the convention is unifying the party, although those efforts are not always successful. A 1948 battle in the Democratic Party convention over civil rights triggered a walkout by several southern state delegations. Some of the southern Democratic Party organizations did not support the official party nominee, Harry Truman, in the general election. Years earlier, Theodore Roosevelt bolted his party and ran as the Progressive/Bull Moose candidate against his former ally, Republican William Taft, and Democrat Woodrow Wilson. Conflicts may

[15]Jackson and Crotty, *Politics,* chap. 4; Wayne, *Road,* chap. 5.

[16]Gerald Pomper and Susan Lederman, *Elections in America,* 2d ed. (New York: Longman, 1980), chap. 7–8.

erupt over policy issues or the nomination. Considerable diplomacy is often needed to bring the contending sides back together, if that can be done.

A final job of the convention is generating support for the presidential ticket and for other party candidates. Part of that task emphasizes firing up the party activists for the fall campaign to increase their campaign efforts. That is particularly difficult when the convention is wracked by policy disputes or when a significant number of delegates are unhappy with an incumbent president's performance, a fate that befell Jimmy Carter in 1980 and George H. W. Bush in 1992.

The convention tries to mobilize support among the general public by presenting the nominee and the party in a positive light and hoping that the mass media cooperate in that effort. The rise of television has complicated the work of convention managers seeking to reach the public. The traditional convention, with some relatively spontaneous activities and occasional disputes, appeared somewhat chaotic on television, and the slowness of proceedings sometimes yielded rather boring viewing. Recent conventions have been less spontaneous and more "stage-managed," with prepackaged videos on the nominees and carefully chosen speakers. Reporters have found the newer format less newsworthy, and television ratings for conventions have slumped, partly due to the rise of cable television systems and their greater variety of viewing options. The networks have responded by cutting back their convention coverage. Nevertheless, pollsters find that the conventions appear to produce a modest rise in support for the party nominees.[17]

Citizens who worry about the influence of party insiders may take some comfort from studies that find high rates of delegate turnover from one party convention to the next, with nearly half to as many as three-fourths of the delegates having never been to a national convention before. At the same time, however, delegates are usually people with a high level of political involvement, especially in party politics, and the typical convention includes a considerable number of people holding party or public office.[18]

CHANGING CAMPAIGN TECHNOLOGIES

The traditional presidential campaign was a labor-intensive enterprise. Party workers campaigned door to door, talking with voters and distributing campaign literature. Those workers helped people register to vote, stuffed envelopes for campaign mailings, and contacted voters to remind them to vote. Presidential campaigning was often linked to campaigns for other candidates, including congressional, state, and local contenders. Where a party's organizations were in good condition, the party ticket was likely to gain several percentage points in the vote.[19]

[17]Wayne, *Road,* pp. 175–83.

[18]Wayne, *Road,* pp. 119–21.

[19]William Wright, ed., *A Comparative Study of Party Organization* (Columbus, Ohio: Merrill, 1971), sec. 6.

During the twentieth century, the traditional approach to campaigning encountered a number of problems. Reforms reduced the availability of political patronage and, consequently, made mobilizing large numbers of party workers increasingly difficult. Presidential and other candidates did not always want to be tied to their party organizations. Some voters became less receptive to the appeals of party workers, in part because of weakening party ties and in part because old-fashioned partisanship fell increasingly out of fashion in many parts of society. People in party organizations were sometimes hesitant to take sides in nomination contests for fear of angering the eventual winner (in the event that the party organization supported a candidate who did not win the nomination). Traditional campaigning did not disappear, but some candidates became increasingly interested in finding other techniques for campaigning.[20]

One of the most dramatic changes in campaign technology is the rise of electronic media. This shift began with radio, which enabled candidates to speak to voters all over the country. With radio, candidates with good speaking voices could appeal directly to voters. Franklin Roosevelt repeatedly used radio to reach out for support, both during the active campaign season and throughout his presidency. The rise of television, especially beginning in the 1950s, gave candidates even more opportunities to communicate with the public directly rather than campaigning through the party organizations. More recently, some candidates have experimented with campaigning on the Internet, with candidate web sites and electronic mail offering voters information and appeals for votes and campaign assistance.

The growing importance of electronic communication, especially television, has greatly contributed to the rising cost of presidential campaigns. Broadcast time during time slots with large audiences is very expensive, and poorly funded candidates cannot afford to purchase much air time. Candidates also try to gain media attention without paying for it. As noted earlier, one strategy is to seek invitations to appear on interview or talk shows or other entertainment-oriented programs. Another approach is staging "media events" in hopes of attracting news coverage. Those events take many forms, from winning an endorsement from a prominent celebrity to riding in a tank or issuing a controversial statement. Candidates who are trailing in the polls often have difficulty in attracting media coverage without paying for it, for reporters may dismiss those candidates as not newsworthy. Successful candidates generally combine paid advertising, which is more fully under the candidate's control but costly, and unpaid coverage, which is easier on the campaign budget but less subject to the candidate's control.[21]

With the exception of the Internet, the growing importance of electronic communication has produced a significant change in presidential campaigns. When party workers handled much of the campaign work, voters could talk as well as

[20]See Beck and Hershey, *Party Politics,* pp. 319–22; Mathew McCubbins, et al., *Under the Watchful Eye* (Washington, D.C.: Congressional Quarterly Press, 1992), chap. 1–2.

[21]Jackson and Crotty, *Politics,* pp. 87–91; McCubbins, et al., *Under the Watchful Eye;* Thomas Patterson, *Out of Order* (New York: Vintage, 1994); Wayne, *Road,* pp. 224–25, 241–45.

listen. Television and radio, by contrast, are fairly good at sending messages from candidates to the public but not very useful in sending messages in the other direction. The Internet offers better capabilities for two-way communication, but it is still being developed as a campaign tool, and assessing its long-term potential is difficult at this point.

Computers have become important tools of presidential campaigning in a number of respects. Computer databases combine information from a variety of sources, including group memberships, magazine subscriptions, and previous campaign contributions, to help candidates target their appeals. A candidate who emphasizes better environmental protection policies can locate people who are likely to have similar views. A candidate who advocates major education reforms can find people who are interested in education issues. A candidate who needs money can find people who have given to similar candidates or political organizations in the past.

Computers can also help to personalize political mailings by putting the recipient's name in the letter in several places to make the mail appear more personal and less like junk mail. Coupled with databases of people's interests, the mailings can be targeted to people who are likely to be interested in the topic addressed in the mailing. Mailings, telephone calls, and e-mail appeals asking for campaign contributions can be sent to people who are relatively likely to give, based on previous contributions to political campaigns or groups sharing the candidate's views. Campaign finance reforms that have increased the value of raising large numbers of small contributions (to be discussed shortly) have encouraged using those computer-assisted fundraising methods.[22]

Another staple of modern campaigning is the use of public opinion polling, which, as noted earlier, can be used to assess a potential candidate's prospects for success. If the preliminary evidence is especially discouraging, the potential candidate may postpone making a full-fledged effort until a later election year or abandon the enterprise entirely. For those contenders who decide to launch an active bid for the White House, polling has a number of vital uses.[23]

Polling can help candidates determine their strengths and weaknesses in the public mind; that information is valuable for guiding campaign decision making. If many people believe that a candidate seems aloof and unfriendly, campaign appearances or commercials showing the candidate acting in a warm and friendly fashion may help. If many people feel uncertain regarding a candidate's position on a major issue, commercials and speeches discussing that issue may help to clarify matters—although being clear and specific is not always a good campaign strategy. Polling is sometimes better at identifying a problem than a solution to it, but identifying the problem is a critical step to resolving it.

[22]Charles Euchner and John Maltese, *Selecting the President* (Washington, D.C.: Congressional Quarterly Press, 1992), pp. 68, 72, 148–49; Wayne, *Road,* pp. 32, 211.

[23]Herbert Asher, *Polling and the Public,* 5th ed. (Washington, D.C.: Congressional Quarterly Press, 2001), chap. 7.

Polls can also help to identify weaknesses in opponents. Perhaps the opponent has made some unpopular decisions in the past or is regarded as being too friendly with an unpopular interest group. Many people might regard the opponent as too abrasive or comparatively inexperienced in foreign policy. Striking at those weaknesses, either directly or through intermediaries, may undercut the opponent's campaign.

Polling enables candidates to learn what kinds of people support them and which ones are undecided. A candidate who learns that many suburbanites are still undecided can target additional campaign efforts at the suburbs in hopes of winning their support. If farmers appear to be very hostile, a candidate may decide to cut back on campaign appearances in farm country and focus efforts elsewhere.

The electoral college (to be discussed shortly) makes the location of support important to presidential candidates. Polling can inform candidates where they have support and where many voters remain undecided. If polling reveals that a candidate is hopelessly behind in one state, campaign efforts may shift away from that state to another where the race is closer and, therefore, where campaign efforts may make a difference in the election's outcome.

The development of jet airliners is another important element in the new approach to campaigning. For much of American history, presidential candidates faced serious limitations on their ability to campaign in many different locations within a brief span of time. With modern jets, candidates can campaign in widely scattered locations on the same day and talk with reporters while in transit.

The new campaign technology is expensive, and candidates who have difficulty raising money are at a severe disadvantage. Television advertising alone costs many millions of dollars, and travel, polling, and computerized mail and phone appeals add further expenses. A generously funded campaign gives a candidate many political options denied to others with smaller budgets.

THE GENERAL ELECTION

After a candidate has secured the party nomination, the campaign for the general election begins. In some cases, it begins much earlier, particularly for presidents who are in their first term. They may begin running for reelection as soon as they have won election to their first term. We will examine that development shortly.

The techniques used in the general election campaign are mostly similar to those used in the nomination campaign, but some important differences exist. A coalition large enough to win a party's nomination will not be large enough to ensure victory in the general election. Media coverage becomes more focused on the two major party candidates (unless there is a strong third-party challenge, such as Ross Perot provided in 1992), and voters must choose from among candidates of different parties, rather than choosing from among nomination candidates of the same party.[24]

[24]Euchner and Maltese, *Selecting*, chap. 4; Jackson and Crotty, *Politics*, chap. 5; Wayne, *Road*, chap. 6–7.

TABLE 4-2   PRESIDENTIAL VOTE BY SELECTED GROUPS, 2000

	Gore (Democrat)	Bush (Republican)
White	42%	54%
Black	90	8
Hispanic	67	31
Married men	38	48
Married women	48	49
Unmarried men	48	46
Unmarried women	63	32
White Protestant	34	63
Catholic	49	47
Jewish	79	19
Family income		
Under $15,000	57	37
Over $100,000	43	54
Union household	59	37
Large city (over 500,000)	71	26
Rural areas	37	59

Source: Gerald Pomper, "The Presidential Election," In Gerald Pomper, et al., *The Election of 2000* (New York: Chatham House, 2001), p. 138.

The coalition-building process involves trying to add new supporters while retaining the support gained during the nomination contest and, if possible, encouraging disunity in the other candidate's coalition. Candidates strive to mobilize their supporters to vote and, if possible, do more than vote in favor of the party ticket while trying to sway undecided people to support the ticket as well. Building coalitions is complicated by the tendency of some groups to lean toward one party or the other. Republican presidential candidates have a somewhat easier time winning the support of wealthier Americans, farmers, born-again Protestants, and conservatives (see table 4-2). Democrats have a somewhat easier time gaining the support of poorer people and blue-collar workers, Jews, African Americans, women, and liberals. Candidates cannot depend on the support of any of these groups, however, and must devote considerable effort to cultivating their support.[25] Most of these groups provide significant support to both parties a good deal of the time.

A coalition large enough to win the general election will invariably contain people with a variety of opinions, and keeping them together is often very difficult. That difficulty may be compounded if the other candidate uses **wedge issues,** which are calculated to encourage disunity. Richard Nixon's campaign used

[25]Beck and Hershey, *Party Politics,* pp. 122–31; Gerald Pomper, "The Presidential Election," in Gerald Pomper, et al., *The Election of 2000* (New York: Chatham House, 2001), pp. 137–40.

TABLE 4-3 PARTY IDENTIFICATION, 1996

Strong Democrats	19%
Weak Democrats	20
Independent, leaning Democratic	14
Independent	8
Independent, leaning Republican	11
Weak Republican	15
Strong Republican	13
Other	1

Source: American National Election Study, Center for Political Studies, University of Michigan; presented in Paul Beck and Marjorie Hershey, *Party Politics in America,* 9th ed. (New York: Longman, 2001), p. 119.

civil rights and law and order as wedge issues; he appealed to white southern Democrats by offering to ease enforcement of civil rights laws in the South. Candidates employ a number of tactics in hopes of keeping their coalitions together. Offering vague positions on issues, trying to change the subject to issues on which coalition members agree, or emphasizing nonissue factors such as personality or experience can sometimes help fend off disunity.

The quest for support in the general election is strongly influenced by party loyalties in the American public. Most Americans have a fairly stable preference for one or the other of the major parties (see table 4-3), and those preferences are a powerful influence on voting decisions.[26] Republican candidates generally have an easy time winning the support of strongly loyal Republicans and a very difficult time winning the support of strongly loyal Democrats. Democratic candidates face the opposite tendencies. Many people's party loyalties are somewhat soft, however, and they may be willing to vote for the other party's nominee on occasion. Nonetheless, even the most appealing major party candidate has generally been unable to gain much more than 61 percent of the popular vote since the 1860s, and even the weakest major party candidate has typically received at least 38 percent of the popular vote unless minor party candidates receive noticeable support.

Party loyalties eroded somewhat from the 1950s through the mid-1970s but have rebounded since then. Strong partisans have given over 90 percent of their votes to their own party's presidential candidates in most recent presidential elections, and weak partisans and independent leaners have usually given two-thirds or more of their votes to their party's nominee. When weak partisans and independent leaners are unhappy with their party's nominee, though, they may defect in large numbers, as happened with Democrats in 1980 and Republicans in 1992.[27] Maintaining some semblance of party loyalty requires a great deal of effort under all but ideal circumstances.

[26]William Flanigan and Nancy Zingale, *The Political Behavior of the American Electorate,* 9th ed. (Washington, D.C.: Congressional Quarterly Press, 1998), chap. 3–5; Warren Miller and J. Merrill Shanks, *The New American Voter* (Cambridge: Harvard University, 1996), part III.

[27]Flanigan and Zingale, *Political Behavior,* chap. 8; Miller and Shanks, *New American,* part IV.

Voters also try to assess the personal characteristics of the candidates. The public traditionally has preferred white males who are at least middle-aged, who belong to mainstream Protestant denominations, and who are not divorced. Those traditional criteria have eroded somewhat over the years, with John Kennedy being the first Catholic president and Ronald Reagan, the first divorced president. Pollsters also find that increasing numbers of voters are willing to consider female and nonwhite candidates, at least in the abstract.

Voters also prefer candidates who appear to be trustworthy, strong leaders (at least in the modern era), and experienced in public life. They may attach particular significance to experience or expertise that is relevant to a particularly salient problem, such as Eisenhower's military experience when the Korean War was underway. Determining whether a candidate is actually trustworthy or capable of providing strong leadership is not an easy task, but voters' assessments of the candidates as people are a powerful influence on their voting decisions. As a result, candidates devote considerable effort to projecting an image that will win support and sometimes try to cast doubts on the personal character or abilities of their opponents. In most presidential elections since the 1950s, the candidate appeal factor has tended to favor the Republican nominee.[28]

Issues are another significant influence on voter decisions, at least in some elections. Issue voting can involve a significant amount of work for voters. They must pay enough attention to be aware of the issues and must decide what positions they favor or oppose. They must also try to determine which candidate appears to share their policy preferences most closely. In many circumstances, that may be very difficult. The presidential candidates may not have different positions on the issues of concern to the voter, or their issue positions may not be communicated with much clarity. Reporters covering the campaign may provide little coverage of the candidates' issue positions, or voters may not be willing to take time to learn about the candidates' views. A voter may find that one candidate is preferable on one issue but that the other candidate is preferable on another issue. Overall, when voters perceive policy differences between the candidates on issues that they (the voters) care about, those policy considerations can be a powerful influence on voter decisions.[29]

Unfortunately for people who want clarity, different people may be interested in different issues. Some people may vote for a candidate because of tax issues, while others vote the same way but because of defense, welfare, or civil rights concerns. Still others may vote for that candidate due to party loyalties, the candidate's personal characteristics, or a strong dislike of the other candidate. When we consider these varying motives, interpreting the meaning of the election is a difficult enterprise. Winners in the general election are often tempted to claim that their victories mean public approval of their policy views, but that is not necessarily true. Candidates sometimes win in spite of their policy views.[30]

---

[28]Flanigan and Zingale, *Political Behavior,* chap. 8; Miller and Shanks, *New American,* chap. 8, 14–15.

[29]Flannigan and Zingale, *Political Behavior,* chap. 6, 8; Miller and Shanks, *New American,* chap. 11–12.

[30]Robert Dahl, "The Myth of Presidential Mandate," *Political Science Quarterly* 105 (1990): 355–66.

A slightly different perspective on voter decision making, the **retrospective model,** emphasizes judgments about the past. When people believe that the country is in good shape, they will tend to keep the party in the White House in charge. When people believe that the country is not doing well, they will tend to vote for changing party control of the White House. Judgments regarding the condition of the country may be based on many things, but the economy is often an important consideration. When the economy is performing poorly, people are more likely to favor throwing out the party in the White House than when the economy is performing well.[31]

According to the retrospective model and other, somewhat similar models, candidates may win elections without many voters knowing very much about them, feeling very positive about them, or agreeing very much with their policy views. If the Republicans control the White House and people are reasonably satisfied with the condition of the country, they will tend to elect another Republican. If they are not satisfied, they will tend to vote for a Democrat.[32] Presidential elections, then, are often more about the past and current conditions than about the future, with many people sometimes voting more against one side than in favor of the other. Once again, deciphering the message that voters are trying to send is a tricky business.

Candidates sometimes try to encourage voters to vote against other candidates or stay home by using **negative campaigning.** A campaign team will look for unflattering information about the opponent: remarks made in speeches, votes on legislation, personal financial dealings, involvement in scandals—practically anything that may help to tarnish the opponent's image. If need be, actions may be taken out of context to make them appear especially bad. If all else fails, accusations may be fabricated out of thin air. Even if the accusations are eventually disproved, they may leave lingering doubts in the minds of many voters. The reporters covering the campaign may make little or no effort to determine whether the accusations are backed up by evidence, as occurred in 1988. In that campaign, Vice President Bush and his allies made a number of false statements regarding Governor Dukakis's record and policy views, but reporters did little to point that out. In such cases, many voters will never learn that the accusations were groundless, and a candidate's vindication, if any, is likely to receive less news coverage than the accusations received. Although research has reached mixed conclusions regarding the impact of negative campaigning, it seems to be fairly common in presidential campaigns and may sometimes succeed in reducing a candidate's electoral support.[33]

---

[31]Miller and Shanks. *New American,* chap. 14.

[32]Michael Gant and Lilliard Richardson, "Presidential Performance, the Expectations Gap, and Negative Voter Support," in *The Presidency Reconsidered,* ed. Richard Waterman (Itasca, Ill.: Peacock,1993), pp. 47–74; V. O. Key, *The Responsible Electorate* (New York: Vintage, 1966); Allan Lichtman, *The Keys to the White House* (Lanham, Md.: Madison, 1996).

[33]See the collection of articles on negative campaigning in *American Political Science Review* 93 (1999): 851–910. See also Kathleen Hall Jamieson, *Dirty Politics* (New York: Oxford, 1992), pp. 254–59.

Even when the voters have cast their ballots, the election is not over. The next stage in the process takes place in one of the more peculiar institutions in the American political system: the electoral college.

THE ELECTORAL COLLEGE

The authors of the Constitution faced a number of divisive issues in designing the presidency. One of the most sensitive issues was presidential selection. Some of the founders favored direct election by the voters, but that proposal faced a number of difficulties. Some of the founders doubted that the average voter had the ability to make a sound choice. Direct election would leave the states out of the selection process, and delegates from states with fewer residents feared that the more populous states would dominate a system of direct election. There was also a practical objection: the country had no nationwide political parties and no well-developed nationwide communication or transportation system. With the vast majority of the population scattered across rural areas and small towns, how could anyone possibly campaign for voter support across the entire country?[34]

Another option was presidential selection by the Congress. This proposal, too, presented a number of problems. Could a president chosen by Congress provide adequate checks and balances against congressional excesses? Would congressional selection lead to corrupt deals, with presidential hopefuls or even foreign powers offering preferential treatment or gifts to members in exchange for their votes? Would congressional selection give the public and the states too little say in presidential selection?[35]

The framers of the Constitution found the electoral college to be a reasonable compromise, with each state having one electoral vote for each member it had in the U.S. House of Representatives and in the U.S. Senate. They added the requirement that the winner would have to gain a majority in the electoral college. If no one received a majority, the final choice would be made by the House of Representatives, with each state having one vote. The state legislatures were to decide how members of the electoral college were to be chosen. Not surprisingly, the state legislatures initially gave themselves the power to select the members of the electoral college.

This compromise proved to be acceptable to many people. Delegates from more populous states liked the fact that their states would have more votes than the less populous states. Some delegates from the less populous states believed that many elections would be decided in the House, where each state would have equal clout. The presidential choice would be somewhat insulated from the whims of public opinion, and the electors would presumably be prominent citizens who were better informed than the average person. No one, however, was very sure how the process would actually work.[36]

[34]Wayne, *Road,* pp. 4–5.

[35]Ibid.

[36]See Richard Ellis, ed., *Founding the American Presidency* (Lanham, Md.: Rowman and Littlefield, 1999), chap. 5.

The electoral college did not function as originally intended (bearing in mind the lack of clarity of the original intentions) for very long. Many political leaders quickly realized that winning elections and passing legislation would be much easier with the large-scale organization of people with similar beliefs. The political parties grew out of that realization. Each of the parties began assembling slates of electors who planned to vote for their party's nominee if chosen to be part of the electoral college. Critics of the new system of government also began agitating for reforms to make the system more democratic. One reform, which spread rapidly across the country in the early 1800s, allowed the voters to choose the state's members of the electoral college. The other reform—expansion of the right to vote—began equally early but lasted much longer, with early reforms focusing on elimination of property requirements and later efforts granting the right to vote to nonwhites, women, people who have moved recently, and young people. Battles over efforts to increase voter turnout continue today, for voting turnout in the United States is among the lowest in Western democracies.[37]

The electoral college remains an important part of presidential elections, partly because forty-eight of the fifty states allot their electoral votes by the **plurality winner-take-all rule.** Under this rule, the candidate who comes in first in the statewide popular vote receives all of the state's electoral votes. Candidates who finish second or worse in the statewide vote receive nothing. The plurality winner-take-all rule strongly encourages candidates to focus attention on politically competitive states, for there is no reward for increasing one's margin of victory or narrowing the margin of defeat in a state. Shifts between first and second place in the state are all that matter.

Among the most competitive states, however, not all are equally valuable. Shifting from second place to first in one of the least populous states will yield only a few electoral votes. By contrast, shifting from second place to first in one of the heavily populated states will yield twenty or more electoral votes (270 are needed to win). California, New York, Texas, and Florida have a combined 144 electoral votes, more than half of the required total. Presidential candidates have a very strong incentive to pay particular attention to the competitive states with large populations and, consequently, large numbers of electoral votes.[38]

The mechanisms for allotting electoral votes create discrepancies between the popular vote and the electoral vote. In many years, the result is that the winner's margin of victory in the electoral college is much larger than the margin of victory in the popular vote. In 1984, Ronald Reagan won 59 percent of the popular vote but 98 percent of the electoral vote. Twelve years later, Bill Clinton won 49 percent of the popular vote but 69 percent of the electoral vote. The same candidate typically places first in both arenas. However, the electoral college has occasionally awarded the victory to the candidate who placed second in the popular vote. The most recent instance occurred in the 2000 election, with Albert Gore winning the popular vote and George W. Bush winning the electoral vote.

[37]Euchner and Maltese, *Selecting*, pp. 5–17; Wayne, *Road*, pp. 13–21.

[38]See David Nice and Patricia Fredericksen, *The Politics of Intergovernmental Relations,* 2d ed. (Chicago: Nelson-Hall, 1995), pp. 42–43; Wayne, *Road*, pp. 17–20.

THE 2000 PRESIDENTIAL ELECTION: "GOVERNING UGLY" AND WINNING THE WHITE HOUSE

An experienced scholar of national politics described the 1990s as the "decade of governing ugly." Party polarization, difficult and complex issues, media cynicism, and an erosion of standards of political courtesy have produced many outbursts of accusations, insults, and denunciations. This phenomenon is not limited to the national government, and some observers believe that these developments reflect, in part, efforts by groups that are unable to achieve their political goals by appealing to the public. Those groups try to shift decision making to arenas where the public has less influence.[39]

The 2000 presidential race was not a pretty sight in the eyes of many observers, in part due to the wrangle over the vote in Florida. After the ballots were cast, George Bush appeared to have won a very narrow victory, which would give him all of Florida's electoral votes and, consequently, the White House. However, Albert Gore's campaign staff called for a recount, particularly in several counties that were predominantly Democratic. Scattered reports suggested that some of the ballots might have been miscounted by tabulating machines, some ballots might have confused voters, and some African Americans had been improperly turned away from voting.[40]

After a recount conducted by tabulation machines narrowed Bush's lead, some local election officials began a manual recount of ballots. However, Florida's top election official, Secretary of State Katherine Harris (who was also co-director of Bush's campaign in Florida), issued a series of rulings that greatly restricted the scope of possible recounts. Both the Bush and Gore campaigns began mobilizing teams of lawyers for legal challenges, and partisans on both sides accused their opponents of trying to steal the election. Republicans in the Florida legislature began to discuss the possibility of directly appointing a slate of pro-Bush electors to the electoral college if the election was not settled to their satisfaction.

Legal battles in a number of federal and state courts followed, with the Gore campaign faring better in Florida state courts and the Bush campaign faring better in federal courts. Finally, on December 9, 2000, the U.S. Supreme Court put a stop to the recounts and effectively awarded the presidency to George W. Bush. Five of the most conservative Supreme Court justices voted as Bush wanted, while the more moderate and liberal justices voted as Gore wanted. Critics complained that the Court's decision seemed inconsistent with several of its recent decisions striking down federal actions as encroaching on state government autonomy.[41] Public and media interest in the dispute seemed to decline fairly rapidly after the Supreme Court's decision, but partisan diehards on both sides remained agitated for months.

---

[39]See Benjamin Ginsberg and Martin Shefter, *Politics by Other Means,* rev. ed. (New York: Norton, 1999); Alan Rosenthal, *The Decline of Representative Democracy* (Washington, D.C.: Congressional Quarterly Press, 1998), chap. 3; Barbara Sinclair, "The Plot Thickens: Congress and the President," in *Great Theatre,* ed. Herbert Weisberg and Samuel Patterson (Cambridge, England: Cambridge University, 1998), pp. 195–96.

[40]See *36 Days* (New York: Times, 2001); Pomper, "Presidential Election," pp. 125–31.

[41]*36 Days;* Pomper, "Presidential Election," pp. 125–31.

In the aftermath of the election, scholars and news organizations began combing through the Florida ballots. They found some evidence suggesting that voters were confused by the ballots in some counties, including hundreds of voters in one county who marked their ballots in favor of a candidate and also wrote in his name. Even though the ballot mark and the name written in were the same, their ballots were excluded from the presidential vote totals. Overall, the inquiries yielded conflicting results: Using some procedures for deciphering the ballots, Bush emerged as the winner; using other procedures produced a victory for Gore. The inquiries also found that the number of ballots that could be found did not match the official number of ballots counted in most Florida counties.[42]

THE POSTCAMPAIGN CAMPAIGN

In recent years, the presidential campaign does not end after the election. Instead, presidents continue to engage in campaign-like activities throughout their presidencies. They give speeches and travel frequently, work hard to raise money for their parties, try to generate favorable media coverage, and cultivate various interest groups in hopes of gaining or retaining their support.[43]

A number of factors have given rise to the **postcampaign campaign.** Presidents often want to keep their campaign teams together to be ready for the campaign for a second term. Improvements in aircraft have made long-distance travel faster and more comfortable. The difficulties of building and maintaining dependable support and of gaining cooperation from Congress, along with the growing number of interest groups active in national politics, have increased the need for presidents to seek support wherever they can find it and to placate potential adversaries when possible. Also, if a president appears vulnerable, strong candidates may be encouraged to challenge the president's bid for a second term.

According to some observers, the postcampaign campaign presents a number of risks. Frequent trips and other campaign activities may divert the president's attention from governing, and presidents may select governing tasks based on whether they have appeal in the campaign. Meeting with a prominent leader from another country or providing public leadership during a crisis may have greater public relations value than improving the routine operations of government programs or learning more about various public policies. Appeals for public support may meet with public indifference or even opposition. Presidents who publicly appear to be "just politicians" may face a loss of respect, especially from members of the opposition party and reporters.[44]

President George W. Bush seemed to avoid campaign-like activities during the first year of his presidency. He maintained a lower profile than other recent

[42]Peter Slevin, "In Florida, the Media's Still Looking at Ballots," *Washington Post National Weekly Edition* (14–20 May 2001), pp. 14–15.

[43]Samuel Kernell, *Going Public,* 3d ed. (Washington, D.C.: Congressional Quarterly Press, 1997).

[44]Ibid., chap. 8.

presidents, a practice that drew some criticism from people in his own party. After the terrorist attacks of September 11, 2001, however, he assumed a much more public leadership role, with more travel and more public appearances.

POLITICAL MONEY

Politics in the modern era is expensive. Television advertising, travel, and skilled public opinion polling are all expensive. Campaign fundraising is also expensive; professional fundraisers usually keep one-fourth to one-third of the money that they raise. The nomination campaign alone can cost tens of millions of dollars for one candidate, and presidents and presidential candidates are often under pressure to raise money for their parties and for other candidates who need funds.

The high cost of presidential and other campaigns worries many observers. Some of them are concerned that candidates may win or lose based on the size of their campaign treasury rather than their abilities. Some critics worry that campaign contributors may receive preferential treatment from presidents and presidential candidates. That preferential treatment might take a number of forms: additional access to the president or candidate, additional attention to issues of concern to contributors, or even policy decisions based on who gave money and who did not.

Research on political money in a variety of offices supports a number of these charges. Candidates with more generously funded campaigns usually have a better chance of winning, especially if they are not very well known before the campaign. In presidential politics, money appears particularly influential at the nomination stage: candidates with small campaign treasuries are pretty certain to lose. Campaign spending appears to make less difference in the general election for president most of the time, perhaps in part because the general election receives considerable media coverage and because the major party candidates are both well known. Public officials are more likely to spend time with people who contribute to their campaigns and to pay attention to issues of concern to campaign contributors. Money appears to have less influence on the decisions that officials make, at least when those decisions are fairly visible to the public.[45]

Revelations of campaign funding abuses in the 1972 presidential campaign, coupled with other scandals of the Nixon administration, led Congress to enact a major reform of presidential campaign finance in 1974. The law, along with earlier reforms and subsequent modifications, establishes a general framework for regulation of presidential campaign funding.[46]

The system provides voluntary public funding for presidential campaigns. Candidates seeking the major party nominations become eligible for the funding by raising a considerable amount of money in small contributions in a number of dif-

[45]Gierzynski, *Money Rules,* 59–64; Jackson and Crotty, *Politics,* pp. 193–94; Wayne, *Road,* pp. 56–59.

[46]Anthony Corrado, "Financing the 2000 Election," in Gerald Pomper, et al., *The Election of 2000* (New York: Chatham House, 2001), pp. 92–124; Wayne, *Road,* chap. 2.

ferent states. No candidate is required to accept the public funds, but any candidate who does accept public money must abide by limits on nomination campaign spending. In 2000, George W. Bush did not accept public funds and raised a record $94 million in his successful quest for the Republican nomination. Nominees of the major parties also receive full public funding for their general election campaigns. If they accept the public funds, they must accept limits on their official campaign spending. Candidates must file reports on the sources of their campaign funds during the nomination contest, and the law limits the size of contributions that people and political action committees can make to an individual candidate. Most of the limits are adjusted each election cycle to allow for inflation, but the contribution limits are not adjusted.

The 1974 reforms were controversial and were challenged in court. In *Buckley v. Valeo,* the U.S. Supreme Court upheld most parts of the law but also opened a large loophole. The Court ruled that spending money to publicize one's personal beliefs was a form of free speech if not formally coordinated with a candidate's campaign. Consequently, that "independent spending" could not be limited. The Court's ruling allows wealthy individuals and interest groups to spend immense sums criticizing or praising presidential candidates as long as that spending is not officially linked to any candidate's campaign. Some skeptics have noted that informal coordination appears to occur at times.[47]

Critics have also complained about the growing importance of **soft money.** A combination of new laws and court rulings has permitted the transfer of large amounts of money among party organizations. Presidents and presidential candidates have worked hard to raise ever-increasing amounts of that soft money, which is supposed to be used for party-based campaigning. The critics charge that some of the money essentially goes to help the presidential campaigns and that the transfers are sometimes used to circumvent either national or state regulations of campaign finance. The amounts of soft money raised have increased dramatically in recent years, with the national party committees raising more than $400 million in soft money in 2000 alone.[48]

Devising an acceptable array of campaign finance policies has proven very difficult, in part because of conflicting priorities. Reforms that make fundraising more difficult may discourage capable people from seeking the presidency and narrow the range of choices offered to voters. Regulations that are too lenient, however, may give wealthy individuals and groups much more political power than other Americans. Many Americans are concerned about the unfair influence of political money, but many of those same Americans will not give any of their own money to a campaign. Republicans sometimes propose limiting contributions that go primarily to Democrats, and Democrats sometimes propose limiting contributions that go primarily to Republicans; as a result, reaching agreement on reforms is often difficult.

---

[47]Sorauf, *Money in American Elections,* pp. 235–41, 360–79.

[48]Corrado, "Financing," pp. 118–19.

CONCLUSION

The presidential selection process is remarkably complex, and winning the presidency is an arduous task. Candidates spend years seeking the office, and many of them are not successful. Even the eventual winners must often overcome major setbacks.

At their best, presidential campaigns enable the public to learn about the candidates and the major issues of the day. In addition, the candidates learn about the needs and wants of the country. Citizens become involved in the selection process and choose from among candidates who are well prepared for the presidency and in step with public sentiments.

At their worst, presidential campaigns provide little meaningful information and even false or deceptive information, with important national issues being ignored or discussed in very vague terms. Candidates try to minimize their contact with the general public and focus most of their attention on loyal partisans. Public involvement is low, and voters feel unhappy with the candidates who emerge.

The presidential selection process has changed in many ways since the adoption of the Constitution. Opportunities for public involvement have expanded dramatically, although many Americans do not make use of those opportunities. The nominating system has grown vastly more complex, with millions of Americans participating. The technologies used in campaigns have also changed, with a growing use of electronic communication, especially television, as well as public opinion polling and computer-assisted appeals for money and votes. Candidates have also begun experimenting with the Internet to communicate with potential supporters.

The new technologies have helped increase the cost of running for president. The ability to raise large sums of money has become a virtual requirement for seeking the presidency; a large campaign treasury does not guarantee success, but a small treasury virtually guarantees failure, at least at the nominating stage. In spite of numerous reform efforts, campaign finance continues to raise troubling questions in presidential politics.

KEY TERMS

congressional caucus 74
fratricide 77
negative campaigning 87
plurality winner-take-all rule 89
postcampaign campaign 91
precampaign campaign 70
primaries 76

raiding 77
realignment 75
retrospective model 87
soft money 93
Talent Scout 71
wedge issues 84

DISCUSSION QUESTIONS

1. What are the important features of the precampaign campaign?
2. How has the presidential nominating process changed over the years? Why did it change? How have the changes affected the presidency?
3. What roles do the national party conventions play in presidential politics?
4. How have campaign technologies changed over the years? How have the changes affected presidential politics?
5. How does the general election campaign differ from the nomination campaign?
6. What factors influence voter decisions in presidential elections?
7. How does the electoral college affect the presidential selection process? How has it changed since its creation?

SUGGESTED READINGS

Rhodes Cook, *Race for the Presidency*. Washington, D.C.: Congressional Quarterly Press, 2000.

William Flanigan and Nancy Zingale, *The Political Behavior of the American Electorate,* 9th ed. Washington. D.C.: Congressional Quarterly Press, 1998.

Warren Miller and J. Merrill Shanks, *The New American Voter.* Cambridge: Harvard University Press, 1996.

Stephen Wayne, *The Road to the White House 2000*. Boston: Bedford/St. Martin's, 2000.

5

THE PERSON IN OFFICE

In this book, in order to understand presidential behavior we emphasize two themes. The first is the constitutional structure. In our system, separation of powers and checks and balances at times restricts presidents, but it also may create opportunities for presidents to take unilateral action under some circumstances. The second factor is public expectations. At least since Franklin Roosevelt's presidency, the public has come to expect the president to provide leadership. A problem for modern presidents is that presidents do not always possess the political authority to fulfill that public expectation for leadership.

Both of these factors strongly affect what presidents can do in office. To some degree, presidents are captives of the constitutional structure and public expectations. More important, however, is that this perspective on the presidency leads us to see the similarities in behavior across presidents. In other words, presidents of the modern era (since FDR) have faced the same basic problem, that of high public expectations but limited political authority. Each has grappled with that context, and as we have suggested and will develop more fully in later chapters, all such presidents seem to use the same approach to dealing with the context of limited authority and high public expectations. Presidents will, among other approaches, take unilateral action when they can and when the chance is small that Congress will overturn their actions. Presidents will also centralize policy making and other decisions as much as possible in the White House and in their own hands. And presidents will strive to ensure that members of their administration are loyal to the president and his goals.

But we must remember that unlike so many political institutions, the presidency is unitary and, from a constitutional perspective, not well defined. This opens the prospect that individual presidents can have impact on the presidency and that the unique attributes of the people who serve as president may be important in understanding the presidency.

For instance, George W. Bush was often seen as uncomfortable before the public, especially in formal settings that required major speeches. In contrast, Bill Clinton seemed to thrive on such public appearances. Would it have made any difference to the nation and the presidency had Bill Clinton been president when the Pentagon and World Trade Center were attacked on September 11, 2001? Would the approach to the public have differed much? Would the policies and governmental response to the terrorist attack have differed if the person in office had been different?

From a longer historical perspective, would any president have lived up to the demands of the nation during the Civil War as Lincoln did? Would any successor to Herbert Hoover have realigned American public policy, altered the relationship between the people and the presidency, and built up the capacity of the institutional presidency as FDR did? Is understanding the presidency just a matter of context, the combination of the constitutional system and public expectations, or do the attributes of individuals come into play? And if attributes do come into play in understanding the behavior of presidents and the development of the office, which attributes should we focus on? Which are the important ones?

These are the types of issues that we will address in this chapter. Much controversy exists among not only scholars of the presidency but also historians, political scientists, and others as to this question of whether great people make history or historical circumstances make some leaders great. Although the major themes of this book focus on the impact of circumstance, the answer to this question is far from settled. We do not attempt to settle the dispute here, either. Instead, we want to bring to your attention some ways of thinking about this question and the kinds of evidence that students of the presidency have used to address it. We begin with a discussion of the conditions under which personal attributes can be expected to influence personal behavior and ask: do these conditions apply to the presidency?

IMPACT OF THE INDIVIDUAL ON THE PRESIDENCY

Political psychologist Fred I. Greenstein some years ago outlined the conditions under which we might expect personal factors to influence behavior (table 5-1). First, Greenstein suggests that personal attributes are likely to have impact to the degree that the environment can be restructured.[1] What does it mean to restructure the environment? By this, Greenstein means that individuals can alter the situations and contexts that they face. Some contexts are hard to alter. Think of the difficulty of amending the Constitution and the fact that presidents as individuals, although they may ask that the document be amended, are virtually powerless to

TABLE 5-1   FACTORS THAT AFFECT THE PERSONAL IMPACT OF PRESIDENTS

1.	Ability to restructure the environment
2.	Location—for example, the ability to mobilize resources
3.	Personal strength and weaknesses—for example, intellectual ability, character, skill
4.	Situational ambiguity—for example, new situations, complex situations, contradictory situations

Source: Adapted from Fred I. Greenstein, *Personality and Politics: Problems of Evidence, Inference, and Conceptualization* (Chicago: Markham, 1969), pp. 42–57.

[1]Fred I. Greenstein, *Personality and Politics: Problems of Evidence, Inference, and Conceptualization* (Chicago: Markham, 1969), pp. 42–44; Margaret G. Hermann, ed., *Political Psychology* (San Francisco: Jossey-Bass Publishers, 1986); and Stanley A. Renshon and John Duckitt, eds., *Political Psychology: Cultural and Crosscultural Foundations* (New York: New York University Press, 2000) provide good overviews of the field of political psychology. Alan C. Elms, *Personality in Politics* (New York: Harcourt, Brace, Janovich, 1976), like Greenstein, is a good, if dated text on the topic.

effect such a change *without the support of others*. Presidents cannot go it alone to amend the constitutional system.

But presidents have some impact on the way that they organize their White House staffs. Presidents can be more or less involved with their staff; they can delegate more or less responsibility to them. Reagan, for instance, often delegated much responsibility to his staff. Carter and Clinton, in contrast, did not. But presidents may even be limited in the degree to which they can mold the White House staffing system to suit their personal needs and predilections. Some of the offices of the White House were legislated by Congress, giving them a permanent and special status. Presidents may not use these congressionally mandated offices as much as others that they can directly reorganize, but such a strategy may incur costs with Congress. And since Jimmy Carter, each president has designated a person to be his chief of staff. No president can now be his own chief of staff, however much he may want to do so. The job of president is now just too big to allow presidents to be their own chief of staff.[2] We will discuss these issues of staff organization in Chapter 9. For now, our main point is that the more malleable the context in which the president finds himself, the more impact his personal attributes may have.

Greenstein's second point is that the location of an actor is also important in whether or not that actor's personal attributes will be important.[3] People in positions that are well defined may have more trouble having an impact than those who are in jobs that are less well defined. Similarly, people who sit atop organizations with resources that can be mobilized will be more personally effectual than those who are the objects of mobilization or who have superiors who can dictate what they are to do.

The president possesses the advantage of sitting at the top of the executive branch. The executive branch provides the president with a vast reservoir of resources that he can tap, including people and their knowledge and experience, as well as money and governmental authority that can be mobilized. But presidents are also constrained in mobilizing the executive branch. The departments and agencies of the executive branch must comply with the statutes that created them and authorize them to take action. Presidents can reprogram some money and people, that is, transfer them from one function to another, but presidents cannot reprogram the entire executive branch. Thus, while the president's position as chief executive provides a vantage point from which he can mobilize resources, restrictions limit the president's flexibility in using these resources exactly as he wants to.

Even in the days following the terrorist attacks on the Pentagon and World Trade towers, President Bush often had to go to Congress for additional resources to address the terrorist threat. He sought and received money to upgrade airport security, the intelligences services (e.g., the FBI and CIA), the armed forces, and economic aid to severely affected industries (e.g., the airlines). On his own, he

---

[2]Samuel Kernell and Samuel L. Popkin, eds., *Chief of Staff: Twenty-five Years of Managing the Presidency* (Berkeley: University of California Press, 1986).

[3]Greenstein, "Personality and Politics," pp. 44–45.

was able to issue orders to the military to mobilize and deploy troops and to expand the discretion of the Immigration and Naturalization Service to detain aliens residing in the United States. But one must ask, given these circumstances, wouldn't any president have done the same?

Greenstein's third point is that the impact of an individual will vary with the strengths and weaknesses of that person and his or her attributes.[4] A vast array of characteristics can come into play here. Surely Bill Clinton's intellectual powers provided him with an asset denied less talented presidents, but his lack of personal integrity may have undermined his ability to accomplish what he set out to do.[5]

Another attribute that is widely discussed with respect to presidents is skill. No clear definition exists as to the nature of **presidential skill.** Neustadt thinks of skill in the sense of a president's ability to understand the power context that he faces and the application of proper resources to that power context. According to Neustadt, then, a skillful president will not waste his resources while trying to acquire power, and a skillful president is one who is able to increase his power or his ability to persuade others to follow his lead.[6]

Often skill is divided into several categories, each based on different activities to which a president must attend. Thus, we can think of being skillful with regard to the public, Congress, foreign nations, or in terms of building public policies or planning political campaigns and strategies. A president may be skillful in one activity but less so in another. Jimmy Carter, for instance, was widely regarded as being inept with Congress. Early in his administration, he alienated the Democratic congressional leadership by opposing water construction projects, which he thought were wasteful pork-barrel programs but which members of Congress thought were vital to their reelection efforts. As a consequence, he got off to a bad start with Congress and was never really able to take advantage of the fact that the Democrats possessed large majorities in Congress. His lack of skill may have undermined what he could have accomplished with respect to Congress.

Fourth, Greenstein suggests that the more ambiguous a situation is, the greater the likelihood that personal attributes will be important.[7] What is meant by an ambiguous situation? First, situations that are new may be ambiguous, because past experience may not serve as a useful guide for action. For example, in the wake of the Pentagon and World Trade Center attacks, the Bush administration fumbled about trying to explain what its response would be. The president and administration leaders variously labeled the policy as a war, a campaign, and a conflict.

[4]Greenstein, "Personality and Politics," pp. 45–46.

[5]Simonton argues that intellectual brilliance is important in understanding whether presidents are thought of as great or not but that integrity does not so strongly come into play. We will discuss presidential greatness later in this chapter. Dean Keith Simonton, *Why Presidents Succeed: A Political Psychology of Leadership* (New Haven: Yale University Press, 1987) and Simonton, "Predicting Presidential Performance in the United States: Equation Replication on Recent Survey Results," *Journal of Social Psychology* 141, no. 3 (2001): 293–307.

[6] Richard E. Neustadt, *Presidential Power and the Modern Presidents* (New York: Free Press, 1990).

[7]Greenstein, "Personality and Politics," pp. 50–51.

Clearly, the terrorist suicide attacks of September 2001 differed from anything previously encountered. They did not constitute a war in the traditional sense because no foreign nation was overtly involved. Moreover, the extent of the destruction and civilian fatalities differentiated these acts from other terrorist actions, which were more modest in size. A wholly new type of foreign policy issue had emerged with these terrorist attacks, requiring a new type of policy as a response, as well as a new vocabulary to communicate to the public and the world what the United States would do. The rhetorical confusion on the part of American and world leaders at the time underscores the ambiguity of the situation.

Ambiguity may also arise when a situation is highly complex. Complexity may require the juggling of many considerations. Deciding which considerations to include or exclude and how to balance those that will be used is harder to do when there are many such considerations as opposed to only a few.

A third type of ambiguity is when different perspectives lead in contradictory directions.[8] Again, take the response to the Pentagon and World Trade Center terrorist attacks. On the one hand, the administration decided to increase security measures, but doing so may restrict freedom, the primary value that the administration aimed to protect. A policy designed to protect freedom may actually undermine it.

Presidents as individuals may have much impact because the situations that they encounter are fraught with ambiguity—many situations are new and lacking precedent, many problems that presidents must confront are complex, and many problems and issues push presidents simultaneously in opposite directions.

When thinking about the impact that individual presidents may have, instead of asking the broad question of whether any president has an impact, we must address the question of whether circumstances are present that allow individual decisions and actions to have an impact. And we must recognize that even if those circumstances are present, presidential actions may not have much impact on the outcome of events. The circumstances that allow for individual impact must be viewed as presenting only the *potential* for individual impact. What presidents and others do will determine if the president was the prime mover or not.

SOCIAL AND POLITICAL BACKGROUNDS OF PRESIDENTS: WHAT DIFFERENCE DO THEY MAKE?

When thinking about which individual traits of presidents may be important, investigators generally look at two different sets: the social and political background of presidents, and their personality and psychological profile. In this section, we address the question of whether the social and political background traits of presidents make any difference for presidential behavior and impact. "The Psychological Presidency" section will address personality-psychological profile impacts.

Even if social and political background characteristics do not greatly affect presidential performance, these traits may tell us something about what the public (and the political system) wants in its presidents and how those preferences may have changed over time.

---

[8]Greenstein's list of factors is much larger than the set provided here. See ibid., pp. 50–57.

Social Class

A myth, dating to the 1820s, contends that American presidents come from humble origins. This **log cabin myth** was first used in political campaigns as the Democrats and Whigs of the period before the Civil War tried to make themselves attractive to voters during an era in which the franchise was being extended and democratized, at least to adult white males.

Andrew Jackson is perhaps the first major political figure to employ the log cabin myth about his origins. He did so to differentiate himself from what he considered a ruling oligarchy in the generation after the Revolution. One of his critiques of the leaders who came out of the revolutionary era—Washington, Jefferson, Madison, the Adamses, and so on—was that they ruled the nation alone and without much input from the people. In other words, according to Jackson, our first generation of leaders was not truly democratic but rather was composed of men of privilege. Jackson wanted to associate himself with the new democratic forces that were challenging the old leaders. These democratic forces were located mainly in the western and frontier states and territories of the era, where family background and social connections were considered less important and relevant than a person's own efforts.

The Whig Party, which emerged in the 1830s as a competitor to Jackson's Democrats, saw the political necessity and value of such a democratic cast. The Whig's first successful candidate for the presidency, William Henry Harrison, in the 1840 campaign used the theme of humble origins despite the fact that he came from an upper-class background. Even Andrew Jackson, who pioneered in exploiting the myth of humble origins, was more well-to-do than his campaigns for the presidency in the 1820s and 1830s portrayed.

The myth that presidents could come from humble backgrounds not only resonated in the nation but became useful politically. For most of the nineteenth century, it became a political liability for presidential candidates to be thought of as coming from privilege. But the log cabin myth is mostly just that, a myth. Table 5-2 lists the social class backgrounds of American presidents. Although one may argue with the exact placement of a president in, say, the middle-upper or lower-upper classes and although one may dispute what distinguishes upper from middle, it is unmistakable that American presidents throughout our entire history are more likely to come from more than less privileged backgrounds.

True to Jackson's critique of the first generation of leaders, each president from Washington to John Quincy Adams came from the upper class. Still, we can see an opening up of recruitment to the presidency in the wake of the Jacksonian critique, as men of the middle class are about as likely to reach the presidency as those from the upper class. Rarely in the nineteenth century is a man of truly humble origins able to reach the presidency. Only one, Andrew Johnson, did so, and his rise to that office is unusual, acceding to the presidency on the assassination of Abraham Lincoln.

In the twentieth century, more men of modest backgrounds rise to the presidency, but men of more than modest means are still chosen to lead the nation. Herbert Hoover was orphaned but still managed to make it to Stanford University.

TABLE 5-2   THE SOCIAL BACKGROUND CHARACTERISTICS OF PRESIDENTS

President	Family social class**	Higher education*	Occupation*	Age upon election*
Washington	Upper-upper	None	Farmer	57
Adams, J.	Lower-upper	Harvard	Farmer/Lawyer	61
Jefferson	Upper-upper	William and Mary	Farmer/Lawyer	58
Madison	Upper-upper	Princeton	Farmer	58
Monroe	Lower-upper	William and Mary	Farmer/Lawyer	59
Adams, J. Q.	Upper-upper	Harvard	Lawyer	58
Jackson	Upper-middle	None	Lawyer	62
Van Buren	Upper-middle	None	Lawyer	55
Harrison, W.	Upper-upper	Hampden	Military	68
Tyler	Upper-upper	William and Mary	Lawyer	51
Polk	Middle-upper	North Carolina	Lawyer	50
Taylor	Upper-upper	None	Military	65
Fillmore	Lower-middle	None	Lawyer	50
Pierce	Lower-upper	Bowdoin	Lawyer	48
Buchanan	Upper-middle	Dickinson	Lawyer	65
Lincoln	Middle	None	Lawyer	52
Johnson, A.	Upper-lower	None	Tailor	57
Grant	Upper-middle	West Point	Military	47
Hayes	Lower-upper	Kenyon	Lawyer	55
Garfield	Lower-middle	Williams	Educator/Lawyer	50
Arthur	Upper-middle	Union	Lawyer	51
Cleveland	Lower-upper	None	Lawyer	48
Harrison, B.	Upper-upper	Miami (Ohio)	Lawyer	56
McKinley	Upper-middle	Allegheny	Lawyer	54
Roosevelt, T.	Upper-upper	Harvard	Lawyer	43
Taft	Upper-upper	Yale	Lawyer	52
Wilson	Lower-upper	Princeton	Educator	56
Harding	Lower-upper	Ohio Central	Newspaper editor	56
Coolidge	Lower-upper	Amherst	Lawyer	51
Hoover	Upper-middle	Stanford	Engineer	55
Roosevelt, F.	Upper-upper	Harvard	Lawyer	49
Truman	Lower-upper	None	Store owner	61
Eisenhower	Middle	West Point	Military	63
Kennedy	Middle-upper	Harvard	Lawyer	43
Johnson, L.	Upper-middle	Southwest Texas	Educator	55
Nixon	Lower-middle	Whittier	Lawyer	56
Ford	Upper-middle	Michigan	Lawyer	61
Carter	Upper-middle	Annapolis	Farmer/Businessman	52

TABLE 5-2 CONTINUED

President	Family social class**	Higher education*	Occupation*	Age upon election*
Reagan	Middle	Eureka	Actor	69
Bush, G. H. W.	Upper-upper	Yale	Businessman	64
Clinton	Middle	Georgetown	Lawyer	46
Bush, G. W.	Upper-upper	Yale	Businessman	54

Sources: *Lyn Ragsdale, *Vital Statistics on the Presidency: Washington to Clinton,* rev. ed. (Washington, D.C.: Congressional Quarterly Press, 1998), pp. 21–23; ** Edward Pessen, *The Log Cabin Myth: The Social Backgrounds of the Presidents.* New Haven: Yale University Press, 1984). Joseph Pika, John Maltese, and Norman Thomas, *The Politics of the Presidency,* 5th ed. (Washington, D.C.: Congressional Quarterly, 2002), p. 130.

Very few received a college education in his day. Similarly, Gerald Ford was also orphaned, but he was adopted and raised by close relatives of some means. Ford, too, went to college and law school.

This leads to a second related point. Even when a president's family was truly humble, most were able to compensate by entering a profession or earning a college degree. This "self-enhancement" often catapulted these men up in social status. Perhaps their drive and ambition to overcome their modest backgrounds account for their rise to the presidency. Even Bill Clinton, whose nuclear family was truly modest in means, made it to Georgetown University and Yale Law School. But as is the case for many with similarly modest backgrounds, extended family members were important bases of support that enabled Clinton and others like him (Ford, Hoover) to realize their ambitions.

Harry Truman may be the most interesting president in this regard, because his background and career path differ so much from the more typical one that we have been describing. Truman came from a farming family of secure, if not wealthy, means, and his wife, Bess, came from a much more well-off family, soundly upper-middle class at least. But Truman fumbled around in his early adulthood for a career. He did not attend college, although he was well read in history. He failed as a businessman but showed talents for leadership during the First World War, when he served in the Army and fought in France. With his business failure in the 1920s, he ventured into politics, more to find a livelihood than because of any burning political ambition. Truman's path into politics truly differed from that of other presidents of modest means because he did not go to college or into a profession. Instead, politics became a way to earn a living.

Truman stands out among presidents of the twentieth century by not attending college. The last man before him to make it to the White House without a college degree was Grover Cleveland in the late 1800s. But Cleveland was a lawyer. Andrew Jackson, Abraham Lincoln, Martin Van Buren, and Millard Fillmore also practiced law but did not attend college. In the nineteenth century, one could become a lawyer by working in a law office, studying for the bar examination, and passing it. It was not until the late nineteenth century that a law degree was required.

For the most part, presidents also have attended the more elite colleges and universities. In the twentieth century alone, from Teddy Roosevelt to George W. Bush, of eighteen presidents, ten attended private elite institutions, one went to a major state university, and two attended the military academies. Only Harding, Johnson, Nixon, and Reagan attended less well-known colleges. But this must be put into perspective—few men of their generation attended college at all. Mass enrollment in higher education began only after the Second World War and attained high levels in the population only in the mid-1960s and after. In this regard, even those presidents who attended less well-known colleges can still be thought of as relatively privileged compared to others of their generation.

Another sign of the relative privilege of presidents is their occupation. The vast bulk of presidents were lawyers (see table 5–2 again). Of the twenty-four presidents who served from Washington to McKinley, nineteen were lawyers and three were primarily military men (Benjamin Harrison, Taylor, and Grant). Washington was a farmer and land surveyor, and Madison was a farmer; Jefferson, Adams, and Monroe were also farmers, but other than with Adams, these were more estates than farms.

Law was considered a route into politics for several reasons. Through a law practice, one could come into contact with many people. Being a self-employed lawyer, one could regulate one's time, giving some to political affairs as the times required. People of other means of livelihood, store ownership and farming, are more constrained in use of their time. Their stores have to remain open during business hours, and farmlands have to be attended to during the agricultural cycle of planting and harvesting. But perhaps more important, in a land that makes policy by legislating, legal training is useful. Lawyers understand the nature and language of the law. Further, much of law is about formalizing contracts between people. This often requires much negotiating and bargaining, skills that may be very useful in political settings. Thus, not only do political hopefuls see the law as a good training ground for an eventual political career, but the political system also sees the value of lawyers in its legislative, judicial, and executive branches.

The dominance of legal training has waned in the twentieth century. Of the eighteen presidents from Theodore Roosevelt to George W. Bush, only eight were lawyers. In part, this spreading of occupational types is a reaction to the increase in the size, complexity, and reach of government programs. Technical skills, such as engineering and business management, may be useful in running a large executive branch. Moreover, people from occupational sectors that once had little direct contact with politics and government may come into more contact and regulation as government has grown. This may have stimulated some people to enter politics who in an earlier era might have been less inclined to do so.

And we should not forget that some of the twentieth-century presidents were being groomed for political careers, irrespective of occupation. Some of these were men of high privilege—the Roosevelts, Bushes, and Kennedys—who possessed a sense of public service much like the first generation of presidents. And there is also Lyndon Johnson, whose eyes were on politics from an early age, despite his more modest background, compared to the Roosevelts, Bushes, and Kennedys. Still, Johnson came from a politically active family, his mother was well educated, and although not wealthy, his family was not poor either.

In terms of social class backgrounds, presidents by and large come from relatively privileged families. They are mostly highly educated and have attended the nation's elite institutions of higher learning. And they are trained in the professions, especially law. That they come so much from the upper reaches of society suggests that they possess resources advantageous to political careers that others of truly modest means lack. But their social backgrounds, while pointing to competitive career building advantages, also suggest that society and the political system prefers some traits more than others. Education and legal training come to mind here. Both may be necessary in a society that makes policy by writing legislation. Thus, those who are educated and trained in the law have some advantages in the eyes of the political system over those lacking these attributes.

Age

By and large, presidents are middle age, neither too young nor too old to serve. Of the forty-three men who have served as president, twenty-five have been in their fifties. Only seven have been in their forties. And of these seven, only Theodore Roosevelt and John F. Kennedy were in their early forties (forty-three). None was elected in their seventies: only William H. Harrison, Zachary Taylor, James Buchanan, and Ronald Reagan were sixty-five or over upon taking office. Notably, Harrison and Taylor were military heroes. What does this tell us about the preferences of the political system and the nature of presidential careers?

In this age distribution, we can see the convergence of two factors. On the one hand, in selecting people of advanced middle age, the political system seems to be exhibiting a preference for experienced people in the White House. Thus, very young men tend not to be elected. But at the same time, this need for experience is moderated by the need for having someone with energy and stamina for the job. Thus, rarely are elderly men selected for the presidency.

The bias against the very old is clearly evident in the 1996 presidential election, in which Senator Robert Dole of Kansas challenged Bill Clinton. Dole was seventy-three in 1996, making him the oldest man to be nominated for the presidency for the first time. Dole's physical vigor may have helped him overcome the fear that he was too old for the presidency. In a March 1996 poll taken by *Time* and CNN, only 26 percent thought that he was too old, compared to 69 percent who thought that he was not too old.[9] Still, it is telling that the public was asked about his age during the campaign, suggesting that age may be an issue for the public in selecting its presidents.

[9]March 6–7, 1996. Detailed information on the poll results was retrieved from the Roper Center archive on Lexis-Nexis. See Herbert L. Abrams and Richard Brody, "Bob Dole's Age and Health in the 1996 Election: Did the Media Let Us Down?" *Political Science Quarterly* 113 (Fall 1998): 471–91 for a detailed discussion of Dole's age as an issue in the 1996 contest.

Political Experience

The discussion of age and presidential selection suggests that experience is an important factor in selecting presidents. Prior political experience is the most important type of experience that a president can have. Table 5-3 lists how many years each president served as either a member of Congress, a governor, or vice

TABLE 5-3   THE POLITICAL EXPERIENCE OF PRESIDENTS

Presidents	Years in Congress	Years as Governor	Years as Vice President
Washington	2	0	0
Adams, J.	5	0	4
Jefferson	5	3	4
Madison	15	0	0
Monroe	7	4	0
Adams, J. Q.	0	0	0
Jackson	4	0	0
Van Buren	8	0	4
Harrison, W.	0	0	0
Tyler	12	2	<1
Polk	14	3	0
Taylor	0	0	0
Fillmore	8	0	1
Pierce	9	0	0
Buchanan	20	0	0
Lincoln	2	0	0
Johnson, A.	14	4	<1
Grant	0	0	0
Hayes	3	6	0
Garfield	18	0	0
Arthur	0	0	1
Cleveland	0	2	0
Harrison, B.	6	0	0
McKinley	14	4	0
Roosevelt, T.	0	2	1
Taft	0	0	0
Wilson	0	2	0
Harding	6	0	0
Coolidge	0	2	3
Hoover	0	0	0
Roosevelt, F.	0	4	0
Truman	10	0	<1

TABLE 5-3   CONTINUED

Presidents	Years in Congress	Years as Governor	Years as Vice President
Eisenhower	0	0	0
Kennedy	14	0	0
Johnson, L.	24	0	3
Nixon	6	0	8
Ford	25	0	<1
Carter	0	4	0
Reagan	0	8	0
Bush, G. H. W.	4	0	8
Clinton	0	12	0
Bush, G. W.	0	8	0

Source: Lyn Ragsdale, *Vital Statistics on the Presidency: Washington to Clinton,* rev. ed. (Washington, D.C.: Congressional Quarterly Press, 1998), pp. 24–25.

president. Only John Quincy Adams, William H. Harrison, Zachary Taylor, Ulysses S. Grant, William H. Taft, Herbert Hoover, and Dwight Eisenhower never held one of these three positions. And of this list, only Harrison, Taylor, and Grant never held a political office. Each of these three, however, was a military officer and war hero. Adams, Taft, and Hoover all held various posts in government before becoming president.

The political path to the presidency has changed over time, though. During the nineteenth century, appointive office, such as being ambassador, a cabinet secretary, or a military officer, was more common than in the twentieth century. Of the twenty-four men who served as president in the eighteenth and nineteenth centuries, nine (27.5%) held such an appointive office immediately before becoming president. In contrast, only three of the eighteen (16.7%) presidents in the twentieth century did so.[10]

The governorship has become a major stepping stone into the presidency in the twentieth century, a role that it did not play so heavily in the nineteenth century. Six of the eighteen (33.3%) twentieth-century presidents moved directly from the governor's mansion to the White House. Only four of twenty-four (16.7%) eighteenth- and nineteenth-century presidents moved directly to the White House from the governorship, although eleven of the twenty-four (45.8%) had some service as governor, compared to eight of eighteen (44.4%) in the twentieth century, an almost identical percentage. Governorships have become a more common stepping stone to the presidency in the last quarter of the twentieth century. Jimmy Carter, Ronald Reagan, Bill Clinton, and George W. Bush were all governors immediately

[10]These figures and the ones for the next several paragraphs come from Lyn Ragsdale, *Vital Statistics on the Presidency: Washington to Clinton,* rev. ed. (Washington, D.C.: Congressional Quarterly Press, 1998), pp. 24–25.

before becoming president. Only George H. W. Bush did not move to the presidency directly from the governorship. In fact, he is the only president of this set who never served as governor.

The vice presidency is another important post that positions one for the presidency, but the importance of the vice presidency has changed over time. Many of the early vice presidents went on to become president, including John Adams, Thomas Jefferson, and Martin Van Buren. Equally commonly in the nineteenth century, the vice president succeeded to office with the death of the president—John Tyler, Andrew Johnson, and Chester A. Arthur. The twentieth century has seen its share of such successor vice presidents—Theodore Roosevelt, Calvin Coolidge, Harry Truman, and Lyndon Johnson. But Richard Nixon and George H. W. Bush earned the presidency after having served as vice president, and Hubert Humphrey (1968), Walter Mondale (1984), and Al Gore (2000) became their party's candidate for president after having been vice president but were defeated in their presidential bids. Unlike in the nineteenth century however, nowadays, almost anyone who becomes vice president is seriously considered as a presidential prospect. Perhaps only Dan Quayle, George H. W. Bush's vice president, and Dick Cheney, George W. Bush's vice president, failed to make it onto this select list. Quayle was generally not regarded as a strong enough prospect, and Cheney's health and age limited his prospects for the Oval Office. In Chapter 9, we discuss the development of the vice presidency in more detail.

THE PSYCHOLOGICAL PRESIDENCY

As we have noted, there are two major approaches to addressing the question of the impact of personal traits on the presidency and presidential behavior. We have discussed the first, social and political background characteristics. Now we turn to a discussion of presidential psychology and personality.

In designing the presidency, the founders gave great attention to the character of the person in office. As Jeffrey Tulis observes, "For the founders, the question of character was a central consideration in the design and selection of the presidential office."[11] The founders thought that men with ambition and a hunger for power would be attracted to politics. Checks and balances was one device to safeguard against extremes of those tendencies. Similarly, it was hoped that unlimited terms of office for the presidency would create an incentive for those in office to convert their selfish aims into more publicly spirited goals in an attempt to remain in office.

Even the electoral college was in part created to ensure that men of character would enter the presidency. The founders did not think that in a nation as large as the United States, the public would be able to determine or learn of the character of the men who were candidates for the office. But the founders did think that an electoral college, composed of local political notables, would have such

---

[11]Jeffrey Tulis, "On Presidential Character," in *The Presidency in the Constitutional Order,* ed. Joseph M. Bessette and Jeffrey Tulis (Baton Rouge: Louisiana State University Press, 1981), p. 286.

knowledge, either because they personally knew the candidates or their networks of political contacts would provide them with reliable knowledge. To the founders, the electoral college would in part act as a screening device to ensure that people of good character would become president.

The Modern Understanding of Presidential Character: James David Barber's Theory

One political scientist, James David Barber, has developed a theory about the psychological underpinnings of presidential character. Barber uses his theory to try to predict the performance of men in office. His theory became quite notable in 1972, when he predicted that Richard Nixon possessed character traits that would lead to a major political disaster in his administration. Barber's theory gained great notoriety as a result of his prediction, which seemed confirmed with the Watergate break-in and eventual impeachment proceedings that were brought against Nixon, forcing Nixon from office.[12]

Barber focuses on two underlying traits—a person's activity level and a person's affect. **Activity** refers to how much energy a person expends, how much a person tries to affect his or her environment, how much a person "acts upon" as opposed to being "acted upon." According to Barber's scheme, a person may be active or passive. **Affect** refers to a person's attitude toward work and others. Does a person find fulfillment in work and other people, does the person enjoy what he or she is doing? According to Barber's scheme, a person may have a positive affect or a negative affect toward work and others.

The combination of these two traits, activity and affect, produce four types:

- **Active-positive**
- **Passive-positive**
- **Active-negative**
- **Passive-negative**

Table 5-4 provides some details about each of the four types. Active-positives are adaptive and self-confident and use power as a means to an end. They tend to be flexible when they encounter resistance and competitors, take criticism well, and are open to advice. Active-negatives, in contrast, are likely to be compulsive and use power as a means to self-realization. They tend to have problems managing aggression and become rigid in the face of resistance, competition, and criticism. Passive-positives tend to be compliant, possess low self-esteem, and seek the approval and love of others. Passive-negatives also suffer from low self-esteem, are withdrawn, avoid power, and serve out of a sense of duty. Both types of passive presidents are likely to let the nation drift, not offering it the leadership required in the presidency, according to Barber.

Barber is most concerned with active-negatives, who he thinks may sometimes do great harm. In 1969, he classified Nixon as an active-negative. Barber, a strong advocate for his approach, feels that voters should take into account the

---

[12]James David Barber, *The Presidential Character* (Englewood Cliffs, N.J.: Prentice-Hall, 1972).

TABLE 5-4   JAMES DAVID BARBER'S CLASSIFICATION OF CHARACTER TYPES

Activity Level	Affect	
	Positive	Negative
Active	Adaptive and self-confident, power as a means to an end	Compulsive, power as a means to self-realization, problem with managing aggression
Passive	Compliant, low self-esteem, seeks approval and love	Withdrawn, duty-bound, avoids power, low self-esteem

Source: James David Barber, *The Presidential Character: Predicting Presidential Performance in the White House,* 4th ed. (Englewood Cliffs, N.J.: Prentice-Hall, 1992); and Joseph Pika, John Maltese, and Norman Thomas, *The Politics of the Presidency,* 5th ed. (Washington, D.C., Congressional Quarterly Press, 2002), p. 139.

TABLE 5-5   CLASSIFYING PRESIDENTS WITH BARBER'S CHARACTER TYPE SCHEME

Activity Level	Positive	Negative
Active	Franklin Roosevelt	Woodrow Wilson
	Harry Truman	Herbert Hoover
	John Kennedy	Lyndon Johnson
	Gerald Ford	Richard Nixon
	Bill Clinton	
	George H. W. Bush	
Passive	William H. Taft	George Washington
	Warren Harding	Calvin Coolidge
	Ronald Reagan	Dwight Eisenhower

Source: James David Barber, *The Presidential Character: Predicting Presidential Performance in the White House,* 4th ed. (Englewood Cliffs, N.J.: Prentice-Hall, 1992).

character profile of those running for the office. Clearly, Barber prefers active-positive presidents.

Table 5-5 presents Barber's classification of a number of presidents. Franklin Roosevelt, Harry Truman, John Kennedy, Gerald Ford, Bill Clinton, and George H. W. Bush have all been classified as active-positives. Woodrow Wilson, Herbert Hoover, Lyndon Johnson, and Richard Nixon have been classified as active-negatives. Barber points to Wilson's losing campaign to get the United States to enter the League of Nations, Hoover's adherence to laissez-faire economic ideas in the Depression, Johnson's continued Vietnam war policies in the face of massive public criticism, and Nixon's Watergate scandal as all resulting, at least in part, from their active-negative character type. In contrast, the active-positives often rebounded from major defeats, changing the course of their administrations and adapting well to changing political contexts; for example, Bill Clinton and his health care package, the Republican takeover of Congress in 1995, and the budget showdown with Congress in 1996.

Notably, Barber has classified George Washington as a passive-negative. In designing the presidency with thoughts that Washington would be its first occupant, did the founders recognize this quality in Washington—that he would serve out of a sense of duty and not use the office to acquire personal power?

Criticisms of the Barber Scheme

Barber's scheme has been highly influential in public discourse as well as scholarship on the presidency. In each election since 1968, Barber or someone else has offered an assessment of the presidential candidates' character profile. In one episode, Jimmy Carter, after having read Barber's book, was reported to have said that an active-positive is "what I would like to be. That's what I hope to prove." Shortly after Carter's election, Barber indeed classified him as an active-positive.[13] As is the case for any highly visible theory, Barber's has come under some criticism.

First, how can we be certain that in an age of media handlers and presidential image makers that a president is not trying to appear what he is not? Carter's preference for being thought of as an active-positive may raise speculation that he would try to create an image of being an active-positive, whether or not he truly was. Barber is much too careful a scholar to be so fooled. He bases his classification on careful research, including biographical materials, not only on the public behaviors of presidents. But others have been glib in using the Barber scheme, in part because of its basic simplicity and intuitive appeal.

Second, factors other than personality or character may lead a president to be active or not. Ronald Reagan is a good example. Barber classifies him as passive-positive. But one must wonder if it was not Reagan's ideology that led him to appear a passive or inactive president, not his character. By the time Reagan became president, he held an ideology of smaller government. The policies that he proposed sought to scale back government. No only did his ideology extend to his policy preferences, but also he decided that he could symbolize his preference for smaller government by being a less active president. Thus, his workdays were short and his vacations away from the White House long.

But Reagan's lower activity level does not mean he was an inactive person. Rather, he seemed to steer his activities in other directions, often toward physical exercise. To create an image of a vigorous, if older, man, news reports of Reagan displayed him horseback riding and chopping firewood. In Reagan's case, ideology, not character, may account for his passive presidency.

Third, Barber's scheme has been criticized for being too simplistic, classifying presidents as being active or passive and positive or negative. But presidents may vary in their degree of activity-passivity and positive-negative affect. Some presidents may be hyperactive; perhaps Bill Clinton is such an example. Other presidents may be merely active, such as Kennedy and FDR, without the frenetic activity level of

---

[13]Quoted in Michael Nelson, "The Psychological Presidency," in *The Presidency and the Political System,* ed. Michael Nelson (Washington, D.C.: Congressional Quarterly Press, 1984), p. 166. The original citation is David S. Broder, "Carter Would Like to Be An Active Positive," *Washington Post,* 16 July 1976, p. A12. Barber classified Carter as an active-positive in James David Barber, "An Active-Positive Character," *Time,* 3 January 1977, p. 17.

Clinton or George H. W. Bush, both of whom seemed always on the move. Calvin Coolidge may be the example of the extreme passive, in contrast to Washington, Eisenhower, and Reagan, whose passivity levels may be less extreme. Coolidge, for instance, napped every day. When he died, one quip is reported to have remarked, "How would one know?", a reference to Coolidge's extreme level of inactivity.

Similarly, a president need not be described as either wholly positive or negative. Some active-positives seem to display negative behavior traits at some times. For example, frustrated by the Supreme Court, which overturned several of his New Deal policies, FDR embarked on a policy to secure Court support. He offered a proposal to reform the Supreme Court. One provision was to increase the size of the Court. Although FDR tried to justify this proposal by citing the increased workload that the Court faced, the nation seemed to see through his ploy, and his plan was dubbed the "Court packing plan." Despite the opposition that FDR encountered, he persisted in pursuing his Court plan, which resulted in the defeat of his proposal and greatly harmed his reputation. In this circumstance, FDR's rigidity, unwillingness to compromise, and his view of his opponents as enemies smack more of the active-negative than the active-positive, even though FDR is often thought to be the model of an active-positive.[14]

It is not entirely clear whether Bill Clinton is a positive or negative type. Although he seemed to relish politics and publicly stated his enjoyment of politics, he also at times appeared frustrated and lashed out at those who opposed or criticized him. His criticisms of the mass media were especially harsh, and he accused a conspiracy of right-wingers of fomenting the charges against him that led to his impeachment. Whatever the truth behind his claims or the justification for being so frustrated, his reactions at times seemed closer to the active-negative, like Lyndon Johnson or Richard Nixon, than the active-positive, like John Kennedy.[15]

A fourth criticism is that whether a president displays negative behavior may be a function of whether he faces situations that cause his negative tendencies to be expressed. If such a situation does not occur, a president who is a negative may be mistaken for being a positive. As Renshon states, "The real test of active-positives is not how they feel when things are going well. . . . The real test is how they respond when things are not going their way."[16] For instance, had Watergate never happened, Nixon in all likelihood may have been thought to be an active-positive. His willingness to go to China and open up diplomatic relations with a then-communist nation, as one example, seems more consistent with someone who is positive than negative, especially when we consider that Nixon built much of his career on staunch anticommunism.

[14]A good account of the Court packing scheme can be found in Michael Nelson, "The President and the Court: Reinterpreting the Court-packing Episode of 1937," *Political Science Quarterly* 103 (Summer 1988): 267–93.

[15]For an account that suggests that Clinton may be an active-negative, see Stanley A. Renshon, "Character, Judgement, and Political Leadership: Promise, Problems, and Prospects of the Clinton Presidency," in *The Clinton Presidency: Campaigning, Governing, and the Psychology of Leadership,* ed. Stanley A. Renshon (Boulder, Colo: Westview Press, 1995), pp. 58–60, and Stanley A. Renshon, *High Hopes: The Clinton Presidency and the Politics of Ambition* (New York: Routledge, 1998).

[16]Renshon, "Character," p. 60.

But Nixon's China policy may have been more a function of strategic goals and needs than personality and character. This raises a fifth point that builds on the discussion at the beginning of this chapter on the impact of the person on the office. How important is personality and character in understanding what a president does in office?

Lastly, Barber asserts that active-positives, because of their character, make the best presidents. The list of active-positives is an impressive one—Franklin Roosevelt, Thomas Jefferson, and Harry Truman—all very highly thought of presidents. But not all active-positives have been stellar presidents—Jimmy Carter, George H. W. Bush, and Bill Clinton easily come to mind. Perhaps more telling, some of our greatest presidents have been active-negatives, the type that Barber argues we should keep out of the White House.

Jeffrey Tulis argues persuasively that Abraham Lincoln, perhaps our greatest president, who served during among the darkest days of the Republic, was a classic active-negative.[17] Although Lincoln had a good sense of humor and was able to make jokes under severe stress, which would suggest that he was a positive, he seems more the negative than the positive. Lincoln often justified his actions by referring to duty and the will of God, which suggests that he often felt that he was forced to act rather than seek opportunities or try to mold his environment to suit his needs. Also consistent with negatives, Lincoln tended to stick to his decisions once he made them, a sign of rigidity. Moreover, Lincoln often appeared depressed and had a dark outlook on the world. He seemed to enjoy neither being president nor his relationships with those in politics and government. Lastly, and perhaps most fundamental, Lincoln was highly self-critical and often doubted his abilities and judgment. In summing up Lincoln, Tulis describes him as "an active-negative president—ambitious, an incessant worker who didn't enjoy his work, but doggedly unwavering in pursuit of objectives he considered to be 'right'."[18]

Although Barber contends that active-positives are preferable to active-negatives, Lincoln's active-negative attributes may have been functional during the Civil War. Trying to hold the nation together under such stresses probably required steadfastness and resolve that might not work well in other circumstances. Quite likely, the nation would have unraveled and the union dissolved had Lincoln not been so resolute in trying to hold the nation together, especially in the face of the years of military defeat that the Union armies in the eastern front suffered at the hands of Robert E. Lee. In other situations, what we might think of as more normal politics, the ability to compromise and forge coalitions are useful skills, while rigidity might alienate potential supporters and undermine coalition formation. The Civil War, however, was not normal politics; the combination of Lincoln's talents and his activity-negative character may actually have helped the nation through that perilous time.

Barber's character theory, despite the criticisms that have been leveled against it, has added to our understanding of presidential behavior. There is an intuitive

[17]Tulis, "On Presidential Character."

[18]Ibid., p. 301

plausibility to his theory, which is one reason that it has been taken so seriously among students of the presidency, as well as the more general public.[19]

GREAT PRESIDENTS

In 1948, historian Arthur Schlesinger, Sr., conducted a survey for *Life* magazine that polled fifty-five experts on American history to rank the presidents.[20] This was the first presidential ranking, although from the beginning of the Republic, Americans have debated whether a president had done a good job in office or not. Since Schlesinger's first expert poll, presidential rankings have become commonplace. His son, Arthur Schelsinger, Jr., conducted another poll in 1962 to update his father's efforts, and more extensive polls of a larger number of experts were conducted in 1970 and 1982.[21] The 1990s witnessed many presidential ranking polls, including an extensive poll by C-SPAN, a poll by the *Wall Street Journal* in 2000, and one by Ridings and McIver in 1997 that has been analyzed in great detail.[22] Table 5-6 presents the results of many of these polls. Table 5-7 presents the

[19]A thoughtful series of articles written over long careers that focuses on the personalities of leaders, especially presidents, and critiques Barber's approach is Alexander L. George and Juliette L. George, *Presidential Personality and Performance* (Boulder, Colo: Westview Press, 1998). Their early study—Alexander L. George and Juliette L. George, *Woodrow Wilson and Colonel House: A Personality Study* (New York: John Day, 1956)—is a seminal classic that relies on psychoanalytic theory. Other important presidential psychology and personality studies include Renshon, *High Hopes*. A few recent studies that build on the political psychology traditions but attempt to move beyond without rejecting Barber's approach include Michael Lyons, "Presidential Character Revisited," *Political Psychology* 18 (December 1997): 791–811; and Robert H. Swansbrough, "A Kohutian Analysis of President Bush's Personality and Style in the Persian Gulf Crisis," *Political Psychology* 15 (June 1994): 227–76. On whether presidential personality makes any difference, see Dean Keith Simonton, "Putting the Best Leaders in the White House: Personality, Policy, and Performance," *Political Psychology* 14 (September 1993): 537–48.

[20]Arthur M. Schlesinger, Sr., "Historians Rate U.S. Presidents," *Life*, 1 November 1948, pp. 65–74.

[21]Arthur M. Schlesinger, Jr., "Our Presidents: A Rating by 75 Historians," *New York Times Magazine*, 29 July 1962, pp. 40–43. Other polls up to the 1990s include Thomas A. Bailey, *Presidential Greatness: The Image and the Man from George Washington to the Present* (New York: Appelton-Century 1966); Steve Neal, "Our Best and Worst Presidents," *Chicago Tribune Magazine*, 10 January 1982, pp. 8–13, 15, 18; and William D. Pederson and Ann M. McLaurin, eds, *The Rating Game in American Politics* (New York: Irving Publishers, 1987), which reproduces the 1981 poll by historian David L. Potter. Among the most extensive and well researched of the earlier rankings is that of Gary M. Maranell and R. Dodder, "Political Orientations and the Evaluation of Presidential Prestige: A Study of American Historians," *Social Science Quarterly* 51 (September 1970): 415–21, and Gary N. Maranell, "The Evaluation of Presidents: An Extension of the Schlesinger Polls," *Journal of American History* 57, no. 1 (1970): 104–13.

[22]Presidential greatness rankings of the 1990s include Robert K. Murray and Tim H. Blessing, *Greatness in the White House: Rating the Presidents from George Washington Through Ronald Reagan*, 2d updated ed. (University Park: Pennsylvania University Press, 1994). The Intercollegiate Studies Institute poll is reported in James Piereson, "Historians and the Reagan Legacy," *Weekly Standard*, 29 September 1997, pp. 22–24, and the *Wall Street Journal* poll is found in James Lindgren and Steven G. Calabresi, "Ranking the Presidents," *Wall Street Journal*, 16 November 2000, p. A26. More information on the *Wall Street Journal* poll, which was co-sponsored by the Federalist Society, can be found at *http://www.Opinion.Journal.com*. Also see William J. Ridings, Jr., and Stuart M. McIver, *Rating the Presidents: A Ranking of U.S. Leaders, from the Great and Honorable to the Dishonest and Incompetent* (Secaucus, N.J.: Citadel Press, 1997). Arthur M. Schlesinger, Jr., returned to the rating game in the 1990s with "The Ultimate Approval Rating," *New York Times Magazine*, 15 December 1996, pp. 46–51, and "Rating the Presidents: Washington to Clinton," *Political Science Quarterly* 112 (Summer 1997): 179–90. The C-SPAN poll results can be found at *http://www.americanpresidents/org/survey*.

TABLE 5-6   PRESIDENTIAL GREATNESS RANKINGS OF EXPERTS

	1	2	3	4	5	6	7	8	9	10
					Year of Ranking					
President	1948	1962	1970	1981	1982	1982	1997	1997	2000	2000
Washington	2	2	3	2	2	3	1	3	3	1
Adams, J.	9	10	11	10	15t	9	9	14	16	13
Jefferson	5	5	4	4	5	4	3	4	7	4
Madison	14	12	15	13	17	14	18	10	18	15
Monroe	12	18	13	17	15t	15	17	13	14	16
Adams, J. Q.	11	13	18	18	19	16	10	18	19	20
Jackson	6	6	8	7	7	7	4	8	13	6
Van Buren	15	17	22	19	18	20	19	21	30	23
Harrison, W.								35	37	
Tyler	22	25	25	28	28	28	26	34	36	34
Polk	10	8	10	9	10	12	16	11	12	10
Taylor	25	24	27	27	26	27		29	28	31
Fillmore	24	26	29	29	31	29	27	36	35	35
Pierce	27	28	31	33	33	31	38	37	39	37
Buchanan	26	29	28	36	34	33	32	40	41	39
Lincoln	1	1	1	1	1	1	2	1	1	2
Johnson, A.	19	23	21	31	30	32	39	39	40	36
Grant	28	28	32	32	32	35	33	38	33	32
Hayes	13	14	24	20	22	22	22	25	26	22
Garfield							23	30	29	
Arthur	17	21	23	24	24	23	24	28	36	26
Cleveland	8	11	14	15	13	17	11	16	17	12
Harrison, B.	21	20	26	25	25	26	21	31	31	27
McKinley	18	15	17	16	11	18	12	17	15	14
Roosevelt, T.	7	7	5	5	4	5	6	5	4	5
Taft	16	16	16	21	20	19	13	20	24	19
Wilson	4	4	7	6	6	6	28	6	6	11
Harding	29	29	33	36	36	36	34	41	38	38
Coolidge	23	27	30	30	29	30	14	33	27	25
Hoover	20	19	19	22	21	21	31	24	34	29
Roosevelt, F.	3	5	2	3	3	2	7	2	2	3
Truman	8	9	6	8	8	8	15	7	5	7
Eisenhower		22	20	12	9	11	8	9	9	9
Kennedy			12	14	14	13	29	15	8	18
Johnson, L.			9	11	12	10	35	12	10	17
Nixon				34	35	34	30	32	25	33

(continued)

TABLE 5-6   CONTINUED

President	1	2	3	4	5	6	7	8	9	10
					Year of Ranking					
	1948	1962	1970	1981	1982	1982	1997	1997	2000	2000
Ford				26	23	24	20	27	23	28
Carter				23	27	25	36	19	22	30
Reagan							5	26	11	8
Bush, G. H. W.							25	22	20	21
Clinton							37		21	24

Sources: 1 = Arthur M Schlesinger, "Historians Rate U.S. Presidents," *Life,* 1 November 1948, pp. 65–74; 2 = Arthur M Schlesinger, Jr., "Our Presidents: A Rating by 75 Historians," *New York Times Magazine,* 29 July 1962, pp. 40–43; 3 = Gary M. Maranell and R. Dodder, "Political Orientations and the Evaluation of Presidential Prestige: A Study of American Historians," *Social Science Quarterly* 51 (September 1970): 415–21; 4 = 1981 poll by historian David L. Potter, reproduced in William D. Pederson and Ann M. McLaurin, eds., *The Rating Game in American Politics* (New York: Irving Publishers, 1987); 5 = Steve Neal, "Our Best and Worst Presidents," *Chicago Tribune Magazine,* 10 January 1982; 6 = Robert K. Murray and Tim H. Blessing, *Greatness in the White House: Rating the Presidents from George Washington Through Ronald Reagan,* 2d updated ed. (University Park: Pennsylvania University Press, 1994); 7 = 1997 Intercollegiate Studies Institute poll in James Piereson, "Historians and the Reagan Legacy," *Weekly Standard,* 29 September 1997, pp. 22–24; 8 = William J. Ridings, Jr., and Stuart M. McIver, *Rating the Presidents: A Ranking of U.S. Leaders, from the Great and Honorable to the Dishonest and Incompetent* (Secaucus, N.J.: Citadel Press, 1997); 9 = C-SPAN, 2000, http://www.americanpresidents/org/survey; 10 = James Lindgren and Steven G. Calabresi, "Ranking the Presidents," *Wall Street Journal,* 16 November 2000, p. A26.

TABLE 5-7   THE C-SPAN PRESIDENTIAL GREATNESS SURVEY OF EXPERTS AND THE PUBLIC

President	Ranking by experts	Ranking by C-SPAN viewers	Difference in rank (expert–viewer)
Washington	3	2	1
Adams, J.	16	14	2
Jefferson	7	5	2
Madison	18	10	8
Monroe	14	9	5
Adams, J. Q.	19	15	4
Jackson	13	14	−1
Van Buren	30	30	0
Harrison, W.	37	35	2
Tyler	36	32	4
Polk	12	17	−5
Taylor	28	25	3
Fillmore	35	37	−2

TABLE 5-7 CONTINUED

President	Ranking by experts	Ranking by C-SPAN viewers	Difference in rank (expert–viewer)
Pierce	39	39	0
Buchanan	41	41	0
Lincoln	1	1	0
Johnson, A.	40	38	2
Grant	33	29	4
Hayes	26	26	0
Garfield	29	27	2
Arthur	36	33	3
Cleveland	17	21	−4
Harrison, B.	31	31	0
McKinley	15	18	−3
Roosevelt, T.	4	3	1
Taft	24	24	0
Wilson	6	13	−7
Harding	38	40	−2
Coolidge	27	22	5
Hoover	34	33	1
Roosevelt, F.	2	4	−2
Truman	5	7	−2
Eisenhower	9	8	1
Kennedy	8	12	−4
Johnson, L.	10	19	−9
Nixon	25	20	5
Ford	23	23	0
Carter	22	27	−5
Reagan	11	6	5
Bush, G. H. W.	20	16	4
Clinton	21	36	−15

Source: C-SPAN, 2000, http://www.americanpresidents/org/survey.

results of the C-SPAN poll, which is unique in that it also surveyed the mass public, along with experts on American history and the presidency.

Although some may consider presidential rankings to be a trivial parlor game, by trying to understand why some presidents are highly ranked and others are not, we can get a sense of the standards that Americans use to judge performance.[23] Moreover, presidents are concerned with their historical reputation.[24] Thus, it is useful to know why we regard some presidents as great and others as failures. Before discussing these standards, let us take a closer look at which presidents are highly rated and which ones are not.

The Great and the Not-So-Great Presidents

Despite the variety of methodologies employed, the different sets of experts surveyed, and the vagueness in instructions given to those asked to rate the presidents, the polls in tables 5-6 and 5-7 show much agreement in presidential rankings. Abraham Lincoln, George Washington, and Franklin Roosevelt are generally ranked in the top three slots, usually in that order. All are considered great presidents. Woodrow Wilson, Thomas Jefferson, and Theodore Roosevelt usually fall just below the top three, but not in any particular order. Listed at the bottom are Grant, Harding, Buchanan, and Pierce. Social psychologist Dean Keith Simonton has statistically compared many of the rankings against each other and found that they are highly similar.[25]

Moreover, most presidential rankings are quite stable over time, although a few presidents have been reassessed, often as more research has been done on their presidencies and new information made available. For example, in recent years, Grant has moved up the rating scales. From the earlier rankings, which tended to place him near the bottom, he moved up seven or so slots in the C-SPAN survey, although he stays quite low in the Ridings-McIver 1997 one. Nixon initially appeared very low in the rankings, which was probably due to fallout from the disgrace of the Watergate episode, the impeachment proceedings, and his resignation. Now, Nixon ranks nearly ten slots higher in the Ridings-McIver survey and fifteen slots higher in the C-SPAN expert survey. In both cases, major new biographies and studies have been published in recent years, leading to their reevaluations.

---

[23]There are several discussions of what makes presidents great besides the studies noted above. See, for instance, T. Kynerd, "An Analysis of Presidential Greatness and 'President Rating'," *Southern Quarterly* 9 (April 1971): 309–29; J. E. Holmes and R. E. Elder, "Our Best and Worst Presidents: Some Possible Reasons for Perceived Presidential Performance," *Presidential Studies Quarterly* 19 (Summer 1989): 529–57; Marc Landy and Sidney M. Milkis, *Presidential Greatness*. (Lawrence: University Press of Kansas, 2000); Fred I. Greenstein, *The Presidential Difference: Leadership Style from FDR to Clinton* (Princeton, N.J.: Princeton University Press, 2000); and Mena Bose, "Presidential Ratings: Lessons and Liabilities," paper presented at the 2001 American Political Science Association meeting, San Francisco, 29 August-2 September 2001. The most thorough study of presidential greatness is Dean Keith Simonton, *Why Presidents Succeed: A Political Psychology of Leadership* (New Haven: Yale University Press 1987). Simonton has replicated and updated his study in "Predicting Presidential Performance in the United States: Equation Replication on Recent Survey Results," *Journal of Social Psychology* 141, no. 3 (2001): 293–307.

[24]Paul C. Light, *The President's Agenda: Domestic Policy Choice from Kennedy to Reagan,* rev. ed. (Baltimore: Johns Hopkins University Press, 1991).

[25]Simonton, *Why Presidents Succeed,* and Simonton, *"Predicting Presidential Performance."*

What Makes a President Great?

Ever since the first Schlesinger ranking in 1948, there has been much debate over why some presidents rate highly and whether these rankings are meaningful. The earlier ratings tended to just ask the experts to rate presidents into categories or to rank them from best to worst. These early surveys of experts rarely offered much instruction to the raters as to standards or guidelines in rating the presidents. As a consequence, there has often been a good deal of ambiguity over what the ratings mean. What aspect of presidential performance did individual raters employ in rating the presidents? Did the raters weigh some aspects of performance more heavily than others? Did personal and political biases, as well as relative level of information about each president, affect how the experts rated the presidents?

Students of presidential ratings have attempted to address these issues in several ways. First of all, more recent polls present the raters with a set of characteristics of the presidents or dimensions of performance. For instance, the Ridings-McIver 1997 survey of experts asked that presidents be rated on five attributes: presidential leadership qualities, presidential accomplishments and crisis management, political skills, the appointments that the president made, and character and integrity [26] The C-SPAN surveys are even more ambitious, asking about ten presidential attributes:[27]

- Public persuasion
- Relations with Congress
- International relations
- Economic management
- Administrative skills
- Moral authority
- Crisis leadership
- Vision and agenda setting
- Performance within the context of the times
- Pursued equal justice for all

Simonton has analyzed the relationships among the five dimensions of the Ridings-McIver ranking. He found that four of the attributes—leadership qualities, accomplishments and crisis management, political skills, and appointments—are all closely related. Presidents who rate high on one tend to rate high on the others. In contrast, presidential character and integrity are not so highly related to the other four categories, nor does presidential character and integrity seem to affect the overall presidential ranking as much as the other four attributes.

A second way to deal with the criticisms of the presidential ranking polls is to ask whether the raters differ in predictable ways. Do Democratic and Republican raters view the presidents similarly or differently, for example? Ratings conducted by the Intercollegiate Studies Institute (ISI) in 1997 and the *Wall Street Journal* in 2000 sought a more balanced group of raters than other surveys.[28] Other ratings had been criticized for being composed mostly of Democrats and liberals, who

---

[26]Ridings and McIver, *Rating the Presidents.*

[27]See more detail at the C-SPAN website, *http://www.americanpresidents/org/survey.*

[28]Piereson, "Historians," and Lindgren and Calabresi, "Ranking the Presidents."

bring their party or ideological understanding to rating the presidents. Still, the results of the ISI and *Wall Street Journal* surveys were generally consistent with those of other ratings of presidents.[29]

In 1970, scholars Maranell and Dodder, who included hundreds of experts in their poll, tackled the political bias question head on.[30] They asked whether the political leanings of individual raters varied by party affiliation. Thus, they looked at the responses of individual raters, not a summary comparison of the ratings of all of the raters. They found that party affiliation had no impact on presidential ratings. Democratic and Republican raters viewed the presidents similarly. Thus, there seems to be something about these presidential ratings that transcends narrow political and ideological perspectives. Perhaps the ratings have something to do with common understandings of presidential performance and governance in office.

A third perspective has been to look at what characteristics of presidents and their time in office affect how they are rated. Simonton has pioneered this approach.[31] He has looked at literally dozens of attributes about the presidents and their time in office. Using sophisticated statistical methods, he has isolated six factors that consistently seem important in understanding how presidents are ranked. He has applied these same six factors to several ratings of presidents with the same results.

Simonton's six factors are:

1. How long a president served in office. Long service is better.

2. Whether a president served while the nation was at war. Service during wartime boosts a president's ranking.

3. Whether the president was assassinated in office. Being assassinated boosts a president's ranking.

4. Whether a major scandal touched the administration. If so, a president's ranking drops.

---

[29]Bose, "Presidential Ratings."

[30]Maranell and Dodder, "Political Orientations."

[31]Simonton, *Why Presidents Succeed,* and Simonton, "Predicting Presidential Performance." Other studies that also look at the factors that determine greatness include R. J. Deluga, "Relationship Among American Presidential Charismatic Leadership, Narcissism, and Related Performance," *Leadership Quarterly* 8, no. 1 (1997): 51–65; R. J. Deluga, "American Presidential Proactivity, Charismatic Leadership, and Rated Performance," *Leadership Quarterly* 9, no. 3 (1998): 265–91; P. J. Kenney and T. W. Rice, "The Contextual Determination of Presidential Greatness," *Presidential Studies Quarterly* 18 (Winter 1998): 161–69, S. J. H. McCann, "Alternative Formulas to Predict the Greatness of U.S. Presidents: Personological, Situational, and Zeitgeist Factors," *Journal of Personality and Social Psychology* 62, no. 3 (1992): 469–79; S. J. H. McCann, "Presidential Candidate Age and Schlesinger's Cycles of American History (1789–1992): When Younger Is Better," *Political Psychology* 16, no. 4 (1995): 749–55; David C. Nice, "The Influence of War and Party System Aging on the Ranking of Presidents," *Western Political Quarterly* 37 (September 1984): 443–55; Dean Keith Simonton, "Predicting Presidential Greatness: An Alternative to the Kenney and Rice Contextual Index," *Presidential Studies Quarterly* 21 (Spring 1991): 301–05; Dean Keith Simonton, "Presidential Greatness and Personality: A Response to McCann," *Journal of Personality and Social Psychology* 63, no. 4 (1992): 676–79; Dean Keith Simonton, "Putting the Best Leaders in the White House: Personality, Policy, and Performance," *Political Psychology* 14 (September 1993): 537–48;. W. D. Spangler and R. J. House, "Presidential Effectiveness and the Leadership Motive Profile," *Journal of Personality and Social Psychology* 60, no. 3 (1991): 439–55.

5.   Whether the president was a war hero. War heroes have higher rankings.
6.   Whether the president displayed what Simonton calls intellectual brilliance. Being smart boosts a president's ranking.

For the most part, these factors that Simonton focuses on relate to the importance of the context and situation in determining presidential greatness. Only intellectual brilliance is truly a personal characteristic, although a president's character may affect whether a scandal touches the president.

The impact of these factors on presidential greatness is obvious in most cases. Long service equates to being reelected. Presidents who do a good job of being president in their first term tend to be reelected. Similarly, wars tend to rally a nation behind the president and often serve as opportunities for major change in the nation, the government, and the presidency. Part of Lincoln's and Franklin Roosevelt's reputations derived from their war leadership. However, some wars cause problems for presidential leadership—Korea for Truman and Vietnam for both Johnson and Nixon come to mind readily. Assassinated leaders are thought of highly, not so much for what they accomplished but for opportunities lost. Being assassinated also creates an historical aura about the president, perhaps turning the fallen president into a martyr. The connection between being a war hero and presidential greatness is not so clear. Perhaps war heroes can lead by positioning themselves above politics and thus not only carry the public along with them but also avoid the squabbles of partisan bickering that may tarnish their reputations. Lastly, being highly intelligent may lend itself to more effective problem solving and generally better job performance. Presidents often encounter intellectually challenging problems and issues to deal with. Perhaps the smarter president is better able to cope with such challenges than one not so well equipped.

Using Simonton's Model to Rank Bill Clinton

Bill Clinton is certainly a controversial president. He served during an era of great prosperity, displayed public leadership qualities rarely seen in any president, and was reelected for a second term. But he seemed to squander his opportunities with the failed health care reform proposal, which some suggest led to the Republican capture of Congress. And of course, there is the Monica Lewinsky scandal and the impeachment. While we may still be too close in time to judge his presidency, we can apply Simonton's six factors to get a sense of how Clinton might fare when later generations and historians attempt to assess him.

Simonton's system grants points to each president for each of the six factors. Each point can be thought of as a rank. Up to and including Clinton, there were forty-two presidents. With 42 as the top possible score, how does Clinton fare? First, each president begins with 5.5 points. Clinton receives no points for three of the items—he was not a war hero, did not serve during a war, and was not assassinated. According to the Simonton system, each president receives about 2.5 points for each year in office. Clinton receives 20 for his eight years of service $(8 \times 2.5 = 20)$. However, he loses 15 points because of the Lewinsky scandal and impeachment. Clinton scores well on intellectual brilliance. Clearly, he is above average in intelligence. The Simonton scheme gives him 2.5 points here. Thus, Clinton accumulates 13 total points ($5.5 + 20 - 15 + 2.5 = 7.5$), which will place him around the twenty-ninth rank, at the top of the bottom third or bottom of the middle third.

This is quite lower than the C-SPAN historian survey, which rated him twenty-first. Without the scandal Clinton would have rated much higher, between the top and middle third of presidents. It seems as if the historians of the C-SPAN survey are discounting the impact of the Lewinsky scandal and impeachment on Clinton's ratings. This may reflect the debate over whether the affair with Lewinsky was truly an impeachable offense, as many supporters of Clinton argued it was not. Still, we are too close in time to judge Clinton's presidency fairly. But if Simonton's idea has any usefulness, we may expect our assessment of Clinton to decline markedly in the future.

Comparing Public and Expert Opinions on Presidential Greatness

Thus far, we have discussed in detail only how experts judge the presidents. In part, this is a function of the lack of information on pubic ratings of the presidents. But with the C-SPAN survey, we now have a public ranking that uses questions similar to those posed to the experts. More useful in comparing public and expert opinions is that C-SPAN asked experts the same questions that it asked the public.

Some might question the value of public assessments of presidential greatness. The public is notoriously ill informed about much of American history and may lack the knowledge to rate the presidents with any validity. Still, the public must rate presidents when election time rolls around, and a comparison of public and expert opinion will tell us much about whether common understandings exist within society about presidential performance.

Recall Table 5–7, which lists the C-SPAN public and expert rankings. The C-SPAN public rankings come from viewers who took the survey online during a ten-day period in late December 1999. C-SPAN reports that 1,145 people took its survey in addition to the fifty-eight experts. We should not consider the C-SPAN viewers to be a representative sample of public opinion and there is some possibility that some people might have expressed their opinions more than once. Clearly, these viewers are more interested and informed than average people, who are unlikely to recognize the names of many presidents. Yet neither are the C-SPAN viewers professional scholars, however much their knowledge of and interest in American history and the presidency.

On the whole, the C-SPAN viewers and experts agree as to the rankings of the presidents. There is only an average difference of three ranks between the viewers and experts. Viewers, however, assess several presidents more positively or negatively than the experts. The experts rate Madison eight ranks lower than the viewers (eighteenth versus tenth place). In contrast, viewers rate three presidents much lower than the experts: Wilson (thirteenth for viewers versus sixth for the experts), Lyndon Johnson (nineteenth for viewers, tenth for experts), and Clinton (thirty-sixth for viewers, twenty-first for the experts). Seemingly, Vietnam (Johnson) and the Lewinsky affair and impeachment (Clinton) weigh more heavily for viewers than for the experts. In fact, the viewers' assessments are more in line with Simonton's predicted Clinton ranking that we have discussed than those of the experts. More important, however, than these discrepancies between the rankings of viewers and experts is the similarity between their rankings.

THE IMPACT OF THE PRESIDENCY ON THE PRESIDENT

Thus far in this chapter, we have looked at the impact of the individual president on the presidency and presidential performance. In the conclusion to this chapter, we turn to the flip side of the relationship between the person and the office of the president. We ask, what impact does serving as president have on the president?

One student of the subject puts the matter quite bluntly, "The presidency is dangerous . . . to the president."[32] Another study sums up a similar point of view, "The position [the presidency], then, surely would seem injurious to the health of those who hold it."[33] These perspectives point to two areas of danger of the presidency to the president—physical and mental health. Together, they raise the issue of what to do if the president is physically or mentally incapable of carrying out his duties. Given the unitary nature of the office and the responsibility placed on the person occupying the post, the issue of the president's health and ability to serve has implications for the proper functioning of the political system. In 1967, the Twenty-fifth Amendment to the Constitution was adopted to deal, in part, with these issues.

The Presidency and the President's Physical and Mental Health

The presidency takes a toll on the president's physical health. First of all, it is literally a dangerous job to hold. Assassins have killed four presidents: Lincoln, Garfield, McKinley, and Kennedy. Numerous other presidents have been the targets of assassins. Ronald Reagan, who was shot in 1981, is the only president to survive being shot in an assassination attempt.[34] About one-half of twentieth-century presidents have been attacked.[35]

Political leaders are often the targets of assassins and attackers. In this respect, the presidency may be no different from other highly visible political leadership

---

[32]Bruce Buchanan, *The Presidential Experience: What the Office Does to the Man* (Englewood Cliffs, N.J.: Prentice-Hall, 1978), p. 7.

[33]Robert E. Gilbert, *The Mortal Presidency: Illness and Anguish in the White House* (New York: Fordham University Press, 1998), p. 1.

[34]David Nice, "Partisan Realignment, the Modern Presidency, and Presidential Assassination," *Social Science Journal* 31(1994): 293–305.

[35]Gilbert, *The Mortal Presidency*, p. 1.

posts. But presidential life expectancy is also short. About two-thirds of those who served as president did not reach their life expectancy, compared to other white males of their era. This trend has become more pronounced since the 1840s. If we exclude the assassinated presidents from calculations, we still find presidents not living to their life expectancy.[36]

The nature of the job is a major factor in the short life expectancy of presidents. The job imposes significant stresses on presidents. Medical scientists have linked stress, especially prolonged stress, to many types of illnesses and shorter life spans.[37]

Buchanan suggests that the presidency is stressful and may at times be frustrating. Furthermore, the office, by its nature, is lonely. Each of these may create psychological issues for presidents, which may also sometimes have negative physical implications.[38]

The presidency is stressful because of the responsibility and demands placed on the president. Many of the decisions that the president is forced to make—for instance, whether or not to go to war—may have profound implications for citizens. Adding to the importance of the decisions that presidents make is the fact that presidents often are faced with numerous such decisions to render, many of which must be made within a short time frame. Clearly, such burdens weigh heavily on the men in office.

But presidents may also find their job frustrating. When presidents are unable to attain their goals, we can say that they are being frustrated. The separation of powers and checks and balances system of the United States is meant to frustrate presidents at least some of the time. Frustration may be a constant of the presidency, rooted to some degree in the constitutional structure but probably also exacerbated in the modern era with the increase in expectations for presidential leadership and responsibility.

Whether the president faces stress or frustration, he is often alone. The unitary nature of the office creates a type of loneliness; only one person can be president. In the end, the president is responsible for what he does and the decisions that he makes. No matter how many advisers a president turns to, he alone makes the final decision about what to do, and he alone is held responsible for the outcome of his decisions and actions. Harry Truman's quip, "The buck stops here," sums up the official type of loneliness that presidents face. The stresses and frustrations of the job may mount, increasing the psychological and physical toll, because presidents really have no one with whom to share their burdens. Given such a job, it is little wonder that presidents mental and physical health may suffer, that the illnesses and conditions that they bring to office are exacerbated, and that their life spans are abbreviated.

---

[36]Ibid., pp. 2–6.

[37]Ibid., pp. 16–17.

[38]Buchanan, *The Presidential Experience.*

The Twenty-fifth Amendment and Presidential Succession and Disability

In the wake of John F. Kennedy's assassination in 1963, reformers sought to address the issues of succession to the presidency, what to do when the vice presidency was vacant, and what to do if the president is incapacitated and incapable of carrying out his duties. The **Twenty-fifth Amendment** to the Constitution, ratified in February 1967, was meant to address these concerns. Table 5-8 lists the provisions of the amendment.

The first provision of the Twenty-fifth Amendment deals with vice presidential succession. The founders were unclear in the Constitution as to whether the vice president, upon the death, removal, or resignation of the president, becomes the acting president or the actual president. With William Henry Harrison's death in 1841, John Tyler, his vice president, took the oath of office of the presidency. No one objected. Subsequently, each president who succeeded to office on the death of the sitting president did the same, but until the Twenty-fifth Amendment, the constitutional right to do so was ambiguous. The Twenty-fifth Amendment makes the succeeding vice president the president in his own right, not just an acting president.

TABLE 5-8   THE PROVISIONS OF THE TWENTY-FIFTH AMENDMENT TO THE U.S. CONSTITUTION (RATIFIED FEBRUARY 10, 1967)

Section 1. In case of the removal of the President from office or of his death or resignation, the Vice President shall become President.

Section 2. Whenever there is a vacancy in the office of the Vice President, the President shall nominate a Vice President who shall take office upon confirmation by a majority vote of both Houses of Congress.

Section 3. Whenever the President transmits to the President pro tempore of the Senate and the Speaker of the House of Representatives his written declaration that he is unable to discharge the powers and duties of his office, and until he transmits to them a written declaration to the contrary, such powers and duties shall be discharged by the Vice President as Acting President.

Section 4. Whenever the Vice President and a majority of either the principal officers of the executive departments or of such other body as Congress may by law provide, transmit to the President pro tempore of the Senate and the Speaker of the House of Representatives their written declaration that the President is unable to discharge the powers and duties of his office, the Vice President shall immediately assume the powers and duties of the office as Acting President.

Thereafter, when the President transmits to the President pro tempore of the Senate and the Speaker of the House of Representatives his written declaration that no inability exists, he shall resume the powers and duties of his office unless the Vice President and a majority of either the principal officers of the executive department or of such other body as Congress may by law provide, transmit within four days to the President pro tempore of the Senate and the Speaker of the House of Representatives their written declaration that the President is unable to discharge the powers and duties of his office. Thereupon Congress shall decide the issue, assembling within forty-eight hours for that purpose if not in session. If the Congress, within twenty-one days after receipt of the latter written declaration, or, if Congress is not in session, within twenty-one days after Congress is required to assemble, determines by two-thirds vote of both Houses that the President is unable to discharge the powers and duties of his office, the Vice President shall continue to discharge the same as Acting President; otherwise, the President shall resume the powers and duties of his office.

The second provision of the Twenty-fifth Amendment clarifies the line of succession to the presidency when the vice presidency is vacant. Through 1967, seven vice presidents have died in office, one resigned, and eight succeeded to the presidency upon the death or assassination of the president.[39] Over the course of U.S. history, the vice presidency has been vacant quite frequently. Section 2 of the Twenty-fifth Amendment provides that the president shall nominate a new vice president, to be approved by a majority vote of both houses of Congress. Since 1967, this provision has been invoked twice. The first time was in 1973, when Vice President Spiro Agnew resigned from office and Richard Nixon nominated Gerald Ford to succeed him. The second time came in 1974, when Nixon resigned the presidency, Ford moved from the vice presidency to the presidency, and Nelson A. Rockefeller was named by Ford to become the vice president.

Provisions 3 and 4 deal with the issue of presidential disability. Section 3 calls on the president to inform Congress in writing that he is unable to perform his duties. The vice president then becomes only the acting president. When the president informs Congress in writing that he is able to resume his duties, the vice president ceases being the acting president. Section 3 has been invoked only once, in 1985, when President Reagan underwent colon surgery, which required that anesthesia be used on him during the operation. Vice President Bush wound up serving as acting president for only eight hours.

Section 4 deals with the most controversial situation: when the president is unable or unwilling to notify Congress of his inability to discharge his duties. That provision allows the vice president and either the cabinet or another formally recognized body designated for the task to inform Congress of the president's inability to carry out his duties. This route is not to replace impeachment for removing a president but is meant to come into effect only when the president is incapable of performing his duties. Although the president's impairment may keep him from doing so for the remainder of his term, the president is never removed from office, and the vice president becomes only the acting president. At any time, the president, upon written notification to Congress, may resume his duties.

Although much of the burden of the process is placed on the vice president, he cannot go it alone. He must have the formal support of the majority of the cabinet or another body that Congress designates to judge the president's fitness to serve. Furthermore, Congress, not the vice president, decides if the vice president will become the acting president. The danger of such a method of removing the president is that members of the president's administration may engage in a power grab to take the presidency away from him. Placing final responsibility in Congress serves as a safeguard against such intra-administration intrigues.

Vice presidential notification, with backup from the cabinet, is clearly useful when the president is physically impaired and unable to notify Congress of his in-

---

[39]Gilbert, *The Mortal Presidency,* p. 270.

tentions to step aside, even for a short period of time. Potentially more dangerous is the situation when a president, through mental incapacity, refuses to relin-
quish his office, if only temporarily.

Although thoughts of a madman in the White House are more the stuff of
thriller fiction, the prospect of a president wanting to retain the office but not being able to carry out his duties may not be merely the stuff of fiction. Calvin
Coolidge is thought by many to have suffered from debilitating depression during his presidency. His frequent napping is offered as one behavioral manifesta-
tion of his depression.[40] Ronald Reagan suffered from Alzheimer's disease not
long after leaving office. What would have happened had the symptoms appeared
while he was president?

In the end, no matter what medical support exists to remove a president from
his duties, the decision to do so is political. Those who support relieving the president of his duties under the Twenty-fifth Amendment must not appear power
hungry. Such appearances would only undermine them and delegitimize their actions. The requirements that a majority of the cabinet or some other body and
Congress's responsibility for taking final action are probably the best safeguards
that can be developed to ensure the legitimacy of forcing a president to step aside,
even if only for a temporary period. Still, given the history of the presidency, the
impact of the job on the health of presidents, and the need for the president to
be physically and mentally capable of carrying out the job, it is important to have
a way of dealing with such emergency situations.

CONCLUSION

In this chapter, we have discussed the impact of individual presidents on the
presidency, as well as the impact of the presidency on individual presidents.
The presidency is a type of institution in which an individual may have a great
impact. It is unitary, and often the president must deal with issues and problems
that are novel. But for us to talk about a president having an individual impact on
the office, that impact must be lasting. That is, it must set a precedent that suc-
cessive presidents will follow. If not, if the impact of a presidential decision or action vanishes when a new president comes to office, then the president really had
little lasting impact on the office. Thus, there is an irony in talking of individual
impact on the presidency. Over time, individual impacts may pile up such that
later presidents have many precedents to follow. In this way, early presidents may
have had the greatest opportunity to impact the office because they were the first
to encounter a problem that required a response or solution. Inasmuch as their
solutions were effective, later presidents would follow suit by using those solutions. We have discussed this type of dynamic in Chapter 3's review of the evolution of the presidency. We will return to this theme in Chapter 9, when we discuss the presidency as an institution.

[40]Ibid., pp. 19–42.

KEY TERMS

active-negative   109
active-positive   109
log cabin myth   101
passive-negative   109

passive-positive   109
presidential activity and affect   109
presidential skill   99
Twenty-fifth Amendment   125

DISCUSSION QUESTIONS

1. What factors affect the impact of the individual president on the presidency? Give some examples of an individual president having an impact on the office. Are there other ways to explain why the office changed or developed as it did other than by focusing on the individual in office?
2. What are the social backgrounds of presidents? What impact does social background have on presidential performance? What does the social background of presidents tell us about what the public wants in its presidents?
3. How does a president's personality affect his behavior in office? Use Barber's types to categorize the personalities of recent and current presidents. What evidence would you need to categorize a president by his personality? How useful is presidential personality in understanding the behavior of presidents?
4. What do the greatness rankings of presidents tell us about the actual performance of presidents? What do they tell us about the standards used to assess presidential administrations? Will Bill Clinton and George W. Bush be thought of as great presidents or not? Why?
5. What impact does the presidency have on the person in office? Should we reform the office to reduce its ill effects on the president? What reforms can you suggest? How effective would they be?

SUGGESTED READINGS

James David Barber, *The Presidential Character: Predicting Presidential Performance in the White House,* 4th ed. Englewood Cliffs, N.J.: Prentice-Hall, 1992.

Bruce Buchanan, *The Presidential Experience: What the Office Does to the Man.* Englewood Cliffs, N.J.: Prentice-Hall, 1978.

Alexander L. George and Juliette L. George, *Woodrow Wilson and Colonel House: A Personality Study.* New York: John Day, 1956.

Robert E. Gilbert, *The Mortal Presidency: Illness and Anguish in the White House.* New York: Fordham University Press, 1998.

Fred I. Greenstein, *The Presidential Difference: Leadership Style from FDR to Clinton.* Princeton, N.J.: Princeton University Press, 2000.

Robert K. Murray and Tim H. Blessing, *Greatness in the White House: Rating the Presidents from George Washington Through Ronald Reagan.* 2d updated ed. University Park: Pennsylvania University Press, 1994.

Stanley A. Renshon, *High Hopes: The Clinton Presidency and the Politics of Ambition*. New York: Routledge, 1998.

William J. Ridings, Jr., and Stuart M. McIver, *Rating the Presidents: A Ranking of U.S. Leaders, from the Great and Honorable to the Dishonest and Incompetent*. Secaucus, N.J.: Citadel Press, 1997.

Dean Keith Simonton, *Why Presidents Succeed: A Political Psychology of Leadership*. New Haven: Yale University Press, 1987.

Jeffrey Tulis, "On Presidential Character," in *The Presidency in the Constitutional Order*, ed. Joseph M. Bessette and Jeffrey Tulis. Baton Rouge: Louisiana State University Press, 1981.

6

PRESIDENTS, POLITICAL PARTIES, AND INTEREST GROUPS

PRESIDENTIAL LEADERSHIP, PARTIES, AND INTEREST GROUPS

Successful presidential leadership depends heavily on whether a president can build support for his policies.[1] Although presidents may build coalitions of support one voter or one member of Congress at a time, building support this way is difficult, time-consuming, and highly inefficient. Presidents, thus, often look for more efficient ways of building support coalitions. They often rely on ready-made organizations of people, such as political parties or interest groups, to provide a base of support. After having established that base of support, presidents will then seek the additional support necessary to ensure that their preferences prevail. In this way, political parties and interest groups are important for successful presidential leadership.

By looking at presidential candidate behavior in election campaigns, we can see the role that parties play in providing a base of support. Candidates usually begin by assuming that members of their party are highly likely to vote for them. To win the election, the candidate must expand that base of support to include a majority of voters in a two-way race and a plurality in a multi-candidate race. The candidate may seek the support of independents or members of the opposition party in addition to his or her party base. Similarly, in seeking congressional passage of their programs, presidents often begin with the assumption that representatives and senators of their party are more likely to support his proposals than opposition party members. After having established that base, a president may seek support from opposition party members as needed to put his proposals over the top. In both of these examples, while the party provides the president with a base of support, party support alone is not enough for presidents to prevail, because either the party does not command a majority or some members of the party are not supporting the president. Still, the first step in building support for his candidacy or programs usually entails mobilizing the president's (or candidate's) party behind him.

We should not, however, assume that party *always* provides a base of support for presidents. Sometimes, for example, the president's party is divided

---

[1]George C. Edwards, III, "Building Coalitions," *Presidential Studies Quarterly* 30 (March 2000): 47–78.

over an issue. When a party is severely divided, it may be hard for a president to use the party as a base on which to build a support coalition. Free trade is an issue that has divided the Democrats in recent years. In his attempt to secure congressional passage of the North Atlantic Free Trade Agreement (NAFTA) in 1994, President Clinton had to seek support from Republicans, who on average were more hospitable to free trade than Democrats. Some key Democrats, including some party leaders, actively opposed Clinton's efforts in behalf of NAFTA.[2]

When presidents cannot count on their party acting as a base of support, they must find supporters from other quarters. Sometimes, as in the NAFTA example, this means seeking the support of opposition party members. Such a strategy may lead to ruptured relations between the president and his own party and undermine later efforts to rally his party behind him on other issues. In lieu of relying on parties as a base of support, presidents may turn to interest groups. As interest groups have become more important in American politics, as we will see later in this chapter, presidents have increasingly turned to them as a base in building coalitions of support behind their policies.

Political parties and interest groups are often the raw material that makes up presidential support coalitions. A president can use parties and interest groups, however, only when they are already organized around the issues that the president is concerned with. When he is concerned about an issue that is not of concern to the parties and no interest group exists to represent opinion on that issue, then the president must organize people himself. Doing so may be a difficult task. Presidents who are able to organize people around new and emerging issues often may have great impact on the political system.

In a sense, President George W. Bush's efforts to enlist faith-based organizations to deliver welfare programs to the needy may be viewed as an attempt to organize a previously politically unorganized people into a new coalition of support behind his initiatives in this realm of public policy. At this point, we do not know how successful Bush will be in that endeavor, but if he succeeds in mobilizing these people behind his efforts, he may reshape the way we think about and deliver welfare services to the needy.

Political parties and interest groups also may impede presidential leadership efforts when they view issues from a different perspective than the president. For example, Bill Clinton, in proposing health care reform in 1994, saw the issue as one of providing affordable health care to people who did not have health insurance. In contrast, opponents, who included Republicans and many interest groups, saw the Clinton proposal in terms of big government. At the time, the political system was better organized to defeat a big government proposal than enact an expansion of the health care system.[3]

[2]Jeffrey E. Cohen, *Politics and Economic Policy in the United States,* 2d ed. Boston: Houghton-Mifflin, 2000), pp. 325–27.

[3]Darrell M. West and Burdette Loomis, *The Sound of Money: How Political Interests Get What They Want* (New York: W. W. Norton, 1999), pp. 75–108.

As this introduction points out, parties and interest groups are important to presidential leadership. Sometimes political parties and interest groups help presidents build support coalitions; other times they may frustrate presidents. No matter whether parties and interests help or frustrate presidents, they are important to presidential leadership.

THE EMERGENCE OF POLITICAL PARTIES
AND INTEREST GROUPS IN AMERICAN POLITICS

From the days of the framing of the Constitution to the present, Americans have harbored ambivalent attitudes toward political parties and interest groups. This ambivalence has important implications for presidential association with political parties and interest groups. While both are important to presidential leadership, as we have already pointed out, presidents have also tried to seem above partisan and interest group politics in order not to appear as captives of either type of political organization. And at times some presidents have even attacked both parties and interest groups, usually in the name of the public interest. Using parties and interests as bases of support in building coalitions, while at the same time trying to appear independent of parties and interest groups and sometimes attacking them, often requires deftness and skill on the part of the president.

Political parties, as we now understand them, did not exist in the late eighteenth century, and the framers made no provision for them in the Constitution. Shortly after George Washington organized his cabinet, disputes over policy broke out between Alexander Hamilton and Thomas Jefferson. From these policy disputes, two camps of political opponents formed, the Federalists of Hamilton and the Republicans of Jefferson. Although not yet political parties in the modern sense, the Federalists and Republicans portended what politics would be like when full-fledged parties finally emerged.

When the vote franchise expanded in the early 1800s to include almost all free, white males, modern political parties finally became a reality and a mainstay of American politics. By the 1820s, the Federalists had vanished from the political world. From the Jeffersonian Republicans, a political party called the Democrats emerged. Shortly thereafter, the Whig Party developed to oppose the Democrats. Two major, national competitive parties have been the norm for American politics ever since, although at times third parties have tried to challenge the dominance of the two major parties. Rarely have third parties been so successful, but in the several years before the Civil War, the Republicans transformed from a third party into one of the two major parties, replacing the Whigs, which ceased to exist by the early 1860s.

Although political parties did not exist when the Constitution was being forged, the framers and the nation's early leaders were worried that organizations like parties would emerge and that they would divide the nation. In his farewell address to the nation after having served two terms as president, George Washington cautioned Americans about the dangers of political parties, which were just beginning to form. At this early stage in the nation's history, Washington thought it important that the nation build a political system that all could support. His fear was that division between Hamilton's Federalists and Jefferson's Republicans might imperil the nation's future.

With the expansion of voting rights in the early decades of the 1800s, modern political parties developed, and with this came a sense of disillusionment and distrust. While Washington's fear that parties would divide the nation waned, a view that parties were fundamentally corrupt took its place. Rather than serving the public interest, political parties came to be seen as a group of politicians out to get from government as much benefit as possible—such as patronage, power, and money. Parties began to serve the interests of the parties rather than act as vehicles for popular expression and democratic accountability, or so critics charged.

Interest groups, in contrast to political parties, indirectly possess constitutional protections, mostly through some of the amendments in the Bill of Rights that guarantee freedom of expression, association, and religion. Allowing people to associate with whomever they desire, without government restriction, fostered an atmosphere in which people would form and join groups. As early as the 1820s and 1830s, when the French nobleman Alexis de Tocqueville visited the United States, he noted how prevalent the tendency was for Americans to participate in groups and associations.[4] Although some argue that we do not join as many groups, political or otherwise, as we once did, compared to most other nations we are still a nation of group joiners.[5]

But interest groups, while allowing for diverse expression, also have been viewed from a more suspicious angle, especially with regard to their role in politics. Many feel that interest groups seek benefits from government at the expense of the public interest. Moreover, interest groups are more likely to exist to represent the positions of the rich, powerful, and well-connected sectors of society than the less fortunate. Such critics as Senator John McCain charge that the power of interest groups, especially their capacity to finance political campaigns, has created a barrier to major reform, such as of health care and other policies.

Thus, both parties and interest groups are seen not as expressions of broad opinion or as organizations that promote democracy but rather as narrow-minded organizations out for their own self-interest and often impeding the public interest. With such a view of parties and interest groups ingrained in our political culture, the presidential relationship to these two types of political organization becomes complex. While parties and interest groups are important in helping presidents build support coalitions, too close an association between them and the president may undermine the president's ability to lead the public. The importance of parties and

---

[4]Alexis De Tocqueville, *Democracy in America* (New York: Mentor, 1956).

[5] On U.S. group participation in comparative perspective, see Sidney Verba, Norman H. Nie, and Jae-on Kim, *Participation and Political Equality: A Seven Nation Comparison* (New York: Cambridge University Press, 1978). On the decline of group participation and social capital, see Robert D. Putnam, *Bowling Alone: The Collapse and Revival of American Community* (New York: Simon and Schuster, 2000).

interest groups for coalition building and the costs of tight association with these two types of organization are the themes of this chapter. We begin by discussing presidents and the parties, and then turn to interest groups and the president.

THE PRESIDENT AS PARTY LEADER

Presidents are often thought to be the leaders of their parties. But what do we mean when we say that the president leads his party? On the one hand, the president does not occupy a formal party leader position, unlike prime ministers in parliamentary systems, who are formally chosen by the party membership in the parliament to lead their party. In fact, each party has a person named to head the national party organizations. But the occupants of these posts play more the role of spokesperson for their parties than leader of the Democrats or Republicans.

Still, in the United States the president comes closest to being his party's leader, even though he may not occupy a formal position, other than the presidency, to claim such a role. We can think of the **president as party leader** because his party nominated him to run for the presidency, the most highly prized office in government that a party can hold. Similarly, the president is the most visible official in government. The public views the president, when he takes a policy position, as speaking not only for himself and his administration but also for his party (and sometimes for the country). Whether other politicians in the president's party like it or not, the public thinks of the president as leader of his party. Thus, in constructing the party's platform for the presidential election, usually the candidate who is nominated determines the content of that platform.[6] Also, presidents are allowed to name the person who will head the national party organizations.

It is more difficult to speak of a party leader when that party does not occupy the White House. Under those circumstances, many people may vie to be viewed as their party's leader. For example, with the election of George W. Bush in 2000, the Democrats were somewhat in disarray as to their party's leader. Several people aimed for that role, including Tom Daschle (South Dakota), leader of the Senate Democrats, and Richard Gephardt (Missouri), leader of the House Democrats. Other people felt that outgoing President Bill Clinton should speak for the party or that former Vice President Al Gore, who lost to Bush in 2000, should be the party leader. The Democrats will go without a single party leader, in contrast to the Republicans, until 2004, when they nominate a new candidate for the presidency. In the United States, the presidency is crucial in this regard.[7]

But in recognizing that the president may be the only person who can assume the role of party leader, we should not also assume that presidents have an easy

---

[6]Sometimes nominees for the presidency will allow losing candidates to place planks into the platform as a way of bringing the losing candidate's supporters into the fold and healing divisions formed during the primary season. Jimmy Carter allowed Ted Kennedy's supporters in 1980 to have some say over the platform after the bitter contest, but the thrust of the platform remained Carter's.

[7]Paul Beck and Marjorie Hershey, *Party Politics in America,* 9th ed. (New York: Addison Wesley Longman, 2001), p. 284.

time leading their parties. While it is true that presidents possess some assets in leading their parties, they cannot *command* their parties to follow. Important tensions exist between presidents and their parties, and presidents do not possess the tools to command loyalty. Much as presidents must build coalitions in support of their policies, as we have discussed, they must also build coalitions of support within their parties. We begin the next section by discussing some of the obstacles to presidential leadership of their parties. After that discussion, we will consider the resources that presidents possess to influence and lead their parties.

Obstacles to Presidential Party Leadership

Being a party leader can be a difficult and frustrating task for presidents and may entail serious risks in some circumstances. For starters, much of the organizational apparatus of the American parties is insulated from presidential influence to a considerable degree. Members of Congress choose their congressional leaders; generally, the president's wishes are secondary to congressional politics in determining who will occupy those leadership posts. After Newt Gingrich, the Republican whip in the House, helped lead opposition to a budget agreement negotiated by President George H. W. Bush, Gingrich retained his leadership position and later went on to become Speaker of the House. Most other party leaders in the United States are chosen at the state or local level, and presidents have no formal control over their selection.

A related obstacle to presidential leadership of the party is the fact that the White House has, at most, limited influence over the political careers of other elected officials who bear the party's label. Nominations of senators, representatives, governors, and other party candidates are made at the state or local level, usually in primaries that are governed by state or local laws. Presidents rarely intervene in party nominations, and attempted interventions are rarely completed. If the party nominates large numbers of candidates who do not share the president's political beliefs, the prospects for party unity are likely to be poor.[8]

General election campaigns are also beyond presidential control much of the time. Candidates for Congress and for state and local offices are largely on their own in the campaign, and much of the party-based help they receive comes from the congressional party campaign organizations or from state or local parties. Presidential assistance is sometimes helpful for candidates, but with hundreds of thousands of elected officials in the United States, many of them will be chosen with little or no presidential involvement.

Presidents may indirectly influence the outcomes of other elections by generating strong **coattails** in presidential election years. An appealing presidential candidate at the top of the party ticket may help to stimulate higher turnout among party loyalists and sway some independents and even voters of the other party to support party candidates for other offices. Unfortunately for presidents,

[8]Beck and Hershey, *Party Politics,* chap. 9; John Bibby, *Politics, Parties, and Elections in America,* 4th ed. (Belmont, Calif.: Wadsworth, 2000), chap. 5.

the coattail effect has weakened considerably since World War II, partly because of declining party loyalties. Even a strong coattail will shift the vote by only a few percentage points, which will make a difference only in competitive races. Many officials are chosen in elections held separately from presidential elections and so are insulated from presidential coattails. In a similar vein, if a president is able to win high approval ratings from the public and keep the economy performing well, the party's candidates may do better in midterm elections, although the effect is modest at best and very weak some years. Note, too, that presidents cannot ensure that they will have high approval ratings or a healthy economy.[9]

Another obstacle to party leadership is that it is a laborious and time-consuming task. In the modern era, presidents have a very wide range of responsibilities, and many of the decisions that presidents face are complex and difficult. Taking large blocks of time to be a party leader is often impossible in view of the many other demands on the president's time and attention.

Tensions Between Presidents and Their Parties

On top of these obstacles to presidential leadership of their parties, tensions between presidents and their parties may exist. The stronger these tensions, the harder for presidents to lead their parties.

First of all, the parties are quite diverse. People of different viewpoints may call themselves Democrats (or Republicans). It may be difficult for presidents to rally support from sectors of the party that hold opposing policy viewpoints. For example, from the 1940s until about the 1970s, the Democrats were divided into two major wings, northern and southern. The major division between these two wings was over civil rights and racial policies. In 1948, many southern Democrats walked out of the Democratic Party convention, and a number of them did not support President Truman, the party's official nominee, in the fall campaign, mostly because of Truman's supportive stance on civil rights.[10] In 1860, the Democratic Party also split into two regional wings, northern and southern, and each wing nominated its own candidate for the presidency. Slavery and related issues that exploded into the Civil War were the sources of the Democratic split back then.

In recent years, intraparty division has ebbed. Most Republicans are conservative on most issues, while most Democrats are liberal. Even in this environment where differences between the parties strongly overwhelm the differences within the parties, members of the same party may strongly disagree on some issues. We mentioned at the outset of this chapter that despite President Clinton's support for free trade and the NAFTA agreement, many members of his party opposed it.

[9]Gary Jacobson, *The Politics of Congressional Elections,* 5th ed. (New York: Addison Wesley Longman, 2001), chap. 6.

[10]Samuel Eldersveld and Hanes Walton, *Political Parties in American Society,* 2d ed. (Boston: Bedford/St. Martin's, 2000), chap. 6-7; Louis Koenig, *The Chief Executive,* 6th ed. (Fort Worth, Texas: Harcourt Brace, 1996), pp. 121–22.

The sources of intraparty division are many and complex. In part, they reflect the great diversity of the United States and the attempt by each party to include as many potential voters as possible. With only two major parties to gravitate toward, it should not be a surprise that fellow co-partisans would sometimes disagree over major policies and issues. The fact that not all opinions may comfortably fit within the confines of a two-party system also explains in part the existence of third parties in the United States.[11]

Secondly, presidents and their parties may possess different time horizons. These different time horizons may lead presidents and their parties to think differently about issues, electoral campaigns, and party building activities. A president has at most eight years to stay in office. To reach a second term, the president must demonstrate some policy success in the first term. Thus, presidents have basically a short or medium-length time horizon. Parties, in contrast, are organizations that aim to exist long after the sitting president has lost office. With a longer time perspective, parties and their leaders may be more concerned than the president about the implications of policies farther into the future.

Because of their limited time perspective, presidents possess few incentives to build the party organization. Whatever party building activities a president engages in will in most cases be geared to molding the party of today in support of the president, not in ensuring that the party will be strong into the future. Thus, presidents can be expected to emphasize, for example, expending party resources on current issues, candidates, and campaigns, rather than investing party resources into training a cadre of future candidates or developing future sources of support. Bill Brock, the Republican national chair in the 1970s, was instrumental in revitalizing the resources of the Republican National Committee and in recruiting people to run for office. His efforts only began to tangibly and measurably pay off many years later, in the 1980s and after. Although his work was applauded by Republican Presidents Nixon and Ford, those presidents offered little in the way of help for Brock's program, putting more of their efforts into their own reelection campaigns.

Presidents and their parties also possess different organizational needs. Presidents seek loyalty to themselves and their policy goals. Thus, presidents have a desire to concentrate policy control and its benefits in the administration. Parties, in contrast, want to disperse the benefits of policies to the many constituents who comprise the parties, as well as use those benefits to attract new members into the parties. Similarly, parties want to be involved in constructing policy. Thus, where presidents want to control the policy process and its fruits, parties want involvement in the policy-making process. In a sense, parties are decentralizing forces in the policy-making process, at least in terms of opposing presidential dominance of policy making and implementation.

We see this tension in the New Deal programs of Franklin Roosevelt. A well-developed network of Democratic Party bosses and leaders at the local level existed in the United States at the time. Roosevelt could have relied on them to implement

[11]Steven J. Rosenstone, Roy L. Behr, and Edward H. Lazarus, *Third Parties in America: Citizen Response to Major Party Failure,* 2d ed., rev. and expanded. (Princeton, N.J.: Princeton University Press, 1996).

the many programs of the New Deal. These leaders, however, were not always friendly to the Roosevelt administration and sometimes contained elements that challenged Roosevelt's party leadership. Thus, instead of using these local party organizations to deliver the New Deal programs to the nation, the president built federal bureaucracies, which he could more tightly control. Most scholars agree that this action of Roosevelt actually weakened the local party machines by taking away one of the functions of local parties—providing tangible services to constituents—and using federal bureaucrats to deliver those services instead.[12]

The current nomination system also breeds tension between the president and his party. We have already discussed the nomination system in Chapter 4. In the era from the 1830s until about 1972, state delegations, under the control of local party leaders, would select the party's nominee for the presidency. This often entailed negotiation among the important local party bosses. The influence of these bosses in anointing a person as the party's nominee, plus their ability to deliver votes on election day, meant that local party leaders were powerful members of the party. To some extent, presidents were the creatures of these local party leaders and owed these leaders much.

In the modern era of primary campaigns, local leaders are less useful to those seeking the nomination. To win the nomination, candidates must build personal organizations in each state in which they enter the primary. Although party organizations may help, they generally refrain from doing so in order not to alienate whoever becomes the party's nominee. Furthermore, the local organizations are often too weak to help. Primary voters are not activated so much by loyalty or attachment to local party organizations as by the image or issue positions of the candidates for the office.[13]

Thus, candidates for the presidential nomination build personal organizations. These organizations often are constructed on issues and groups that transcend state and local borders, and become the foundation of the presidential support coalition once the president has been elected. Presidents need the parties less now than they needed them in the past. This has caused another tension between the parties and the presidents, as the parties have become less relevant to presidents. But as we discuss in the "Factors That Discourage Presidential Party Leadership" section, not only have parties become less relevant to presidents, in an atmosphere in which many hold ambivalent attitudes toward the parties, there may exist high costs for presidents to act as party leaders.

Factors That Discourage Presidential Party Leadership

Even if party leadership were easy, which it is not, trying to be an effective party leader entails some serious risks for presidents. One major risk centers on the president's relationship with Congress. Because members of the president's party

---

[12]Sidney M. Milkis, *The President and the Parties: The Transformation of the American Party System Since the New Deal* (New York: Oxford University Press, 1993).

[13]Paul Allen Beck and M. Kent Jennings, "Political Periods and Political Participation," *American Political Science Review* 73 (September 1979): 737–50.

in Congress do not always provide dependable support for presidential proposals and because the opposition party may have a majority in at least one house
of Congress, particularly since the late 1960s presidents often need at least some
votes from members of the opposition party. Those votes may also be needed to
end a Senate filibuster or take other actions that require more than a simple majority. Presidents who appear to be too partisan may have difficulty in gaining
those opposition party votes. Even if a president is able to garner enough votes
from his own party to win passage of a bill, a policy adopted with bipartisan support may be more secure against future changes in party control in Washington.[14]

Being too partisan may also create difficulties with state and local officials,
many of whom belong to the opposition party. Given the important role that state
and local governments play in implementing virtually all of the federal government's domestic programs, a president who places too much emphasis on being
a party leader may encounter more resistance from governors, state legislators,
and other state and local officials belonging to the other party.

The electorate provides additional incentives for presidents to downplay their
role as a party leader. Neither party has been able to command a stable majority
of the electorate for many years. The president's own partisans are not always
loyal, and some of them may not vote at all. The large numbers of political independents and adherents to the opposition party may be crucial to a presidential
candidate's election or reelection prospects. Presenting a relatively nonpartisan
image may make garnering votes from independents and members of the other
party considerably easier. When President Nixon sought reelection in 1972, his
campaign organization was named the Committee to Reelect the President, and a
number of his campaign appeals made little or no mention of his party affiliation.

Some observers believe that reforms of the presidential nominating process since
World War II have further discouraged party leadership by presidents. Candidates
who want to win the presidency must create a nationwide, personal campaign organization to win the nomination, and that organization will remain crucial to the
general election campaign. The support of members of the party organizations can
be helpful but is not always necessary. Candidates for other offices often follow the
presidential candidates' example and set up their own personal organizations as
well. Elected officials (including presidents) who look to the next election try to
keep their personal organizations intact and engage in continuous campaignlike activities. These changes may have encouraged many officials to emphasize their personal image and career rather than presenting themselves as members of a party
team. Party leadership is very difficult in that environment.[15]

Recent evidence, however, indicates that party-based campaigning is making a
comeback. Improvements in fundraising and policies giving the parties more flexibility in funding campaigns have increased the help that the parties can provide

[14]R. Douglas Arnold, *Congress and the Bureaucracy* (New Haven: Yale University Press, 1979),
pp. 53, 68.

[15]See Austin Ranney, "Political Parties: Reform and Decline," in *The New American Political System,* ed. Anthony King (Washington, D.C.: American Enterprise Institute, 1978), pp. 236–47.

to candidates. Party strategists have also realized that party support can help to produce stronger candidates and help them to do better in their campaigns. Party assistance alone is rarely enough to produce an adequate campaign, but the assistance is sometimes enough to tip the balance between a hopeless campaign and a serious challenge. That assistance is provided from a number of party sources, such as the parties' congressional campaign committees, most of which have considerable autonomy.[16] Even so, a shift to somewhat more party-oriented campaigning is likely to make assembling blocks of support a bit easier.

One other risk associated with trying to be a party leader is the lackluster image of the political parties in the eyes of the public and many journalists. Many Americans do not believe that the parties stand for anything or make any positive contributions to the operation of government. Many believe that the parties create unnecessary conflicts and blow minor disputes all out of proportion. Some research also indicates that a considerable number of Americans are not hostile to the parties but appear to regard them with indifference or neutrality, a viewpoint that is better than hostility but not a very good basis for mobilizing a political following.[17]

Assets for Presidential Party Leadership

We have been discussing the difficulties that presidents have with their parties. But parties are important to organizing the political world, and as we stated at the outset of this chapter, they may be important building blocks in the presidential effort to construct support coalitions. While party leadership is difficult, presidents are not without resources to influence their parties.

Presidential Visibility   Presidents have several resources that they may use in hopes of leading their parties, but the resources are not always very effective. One important resource is visibility; the president is the most visible political figure in the United States, at least in the modern era. Presidents usually have good access to the mass media and are often in a better position to convey a message to the public than any other political figure. Presidential initiatives may influence the party's image for years to come, and presidential accomplishments (or the lack of them) may have the same effect. Moreover, the president's public image, for better or worse, may affect the image of the party and the people in it. For example, for decades the Democrats were able to point to Franklin Roosevelt, and in more recent times, the Republicans continually extol the successes and leadership of Ronald Reagan. Clearly, both of these presidents had a major impact on their parties' images that lasted long after their administrations came to an end.

[16]See Paul Herrnson, *Congressional Elections,* 3d ed. (Washington, D.C.: Congressional Quarterly Press, 2000), esp. chap. 4; Alan Rosenthal, *The Decline of Representative Democracy* (Washington, D.C.: Congressional Quarterly Press, 1998), chap. 5.

[17]See Martin Wattenberg, *The Decline of American Political Parties 1952–1984* (Cambridge: Harvard University Press, 1986), chap. 4; for a somewhat more positive assessment, see Eldersveld and Walton, *Political Parties,* chap. 5.

The president's influence over the party's image gives other people in the party an incentive to work with their president. If the president appears to be ineffective, that failing may affect the image of others in the party. The president's fellow partisans in Congress, therefore, may suffer, as the Democrats did in 1994. Many attributed the Democratic loss of Congress to the defeat of Bill Clinton's health care reform proposal. The defeat not only made the president look ineffectual in dealing with Congress, but the health care reform initiative also branded the party as the party of big government, a position that was out of step with public opinion, which favored less government.

As many presidents have found, however, visibility is not necessarily an asset. The presidency's visibility can make it a magnet for all manner of anger and resentment, including matters that do not involve the president. When a president's performance is regarded as unsatisfactory, that unfortunate image may cloud the party's image for years, as Herbert Hoover's did for the Republican Party with the Great Depression and Lyndon Johnson's did for the Democrats with Vietnam. Ronald Reagan blamed Jimmy Carter for the sad state of the economy, a situation that persisted for several years into the Reagan administration, until the economy turned around in 1983. Not surprisingly, many Democrats distanced themselves from Carter during his term of office, as well as after, not wanting to be associated with that administration. And in his run for the presidency in 2000, Al Gore distanced himself from Bill Clinton because of the Monica Lewinsky affair and the impeachment process that followed. In fact, relations between the once-close Gore and Clinton became strained in the aftermath of Gore's defeat, with each blaming the other for the loss. Not until the terrorist attack on New York and the Pentagon in September 2001 did the two even speak to each other.[18]

In addition, presidents do not always want to use their visibility for partisan purposes. Some presidents have not had very strong ties to some elements of their parties and have sometimes tried to use their visibility to further their own personal goals rather than working on behalf of the party. Nixon, for example, achieved some major public relations triumphs, including his much-publicized trip to the People's Republic of China, but seemed to keep much of the Republican Party at arm's length for most of his presidency.

Party Loyalty   Party loyalties are another important resource for presidential leadership of the parties. The party loyalties of the public influence many of their voting decisions and their evaluations of presidents, with Democrats tending to give more positive evaluations to Democratic presidents and Republicans tending to give more positive evaluations to Republican presidents. Party differences in presidential approval ratings vary over time, with some presidents showing relatively modest differences in how they are viewed by Republicans and Democrats and others showing large differences (see table 6-1). During Reagan's second term, he averaged an 83 percent approval rating

---

[18]Katherine Q. Seelye, "Tragedy Reunites Clinton and Gore," *New York Times,* 15 September 2001, p. A14.

TABLE 6-1   PARTY LOYALTIES OF THE PUBLIC AND PRESIDENTIAL APPROVAL

	Republicans	Democrats	Difference
Lyndon Johnson	40%	69%	−29%
Jimmy Carter	29%	55%	−26%
Ronald Reagan, second term	83%	32%	51%
Bill Clinton, first term	22%	79%	−57%

Source: Lyn Ragsdale, *Vital Statistics on the Presidency,* rev. ed. (Washington, D.C.: Congressional Quarterly Press, 1998), p. 226.

from Republicans but only a 32-point approval rating from Democrats. The gap for Clinton's first term was even larger, with an average approval rating from Democrats that was 57 percentage points higher than his approval rating from Republicans. We will discuss this point in more detail in Chapter 8 on public opinion and the presidency.[19]

Party loyalties are also important for public officials. Many Americans doubt that our political parties stand for anything, but party affiliations are often a good predictor of how members of Congress are likely to vote, a point to which we will return in greater detail in Chapter 10 on the president and Congress. Party ties affect the decisions of many other public officials as well, including state and local officials and even federal judges.

Party loyalties are not always very reliable, however. At some points in history, the party loyalties of the public have been comparatively weak, with the result that presidents have had considerable difficulty in winning reelection or gaining election of many like-minded members of Congress. Many factors besides party loyalties influence the actions of members of Congress and other public officials. More than one president has been disappointed by fellow partisans in Congress or elsewhere who opposed presidential initiatives, criticized presidential decisions, and even tried to deny renomination to a sitting president, as Ronald Reagan tried in 1976 with President Ford and as Ted Kennedy did four years later with President Carter.

Even when party loyalties hold sway, that result may require laborious negotiation, consultation, and compromise. Party loyalty can almost never be taken for granted. President George W. Bush received a dramatic reminder of that point in 2001 when Senator James Jeffords of Vermont announced that he was leaving the

---

[19]The literature on the relationship between party loyalties and behavior includes a number of controversies. For overviews and evidence, see William Flanigan and Nancy Zingale, *Political Behavior of the American Electorate,* 9th ed. (Washington, D.C.: Congressional Quarterly Press, 1998), chap. 3, 4, and 8; Warren Miller and J. Merrill Shanks, *The New American Voter* (Cambridge: Harvard University Press, 1996), parts III and IV; Wattenberg, *The Decline of American Political Parties;* Beck and Hershey, *Party Politics,* chap. 13–14; Jon Bond and Richard Fleisher, eds., *Polarized Politics* (Washington, D.C.: Congressional Quarterly Press, 2000).

Republican Party. Jeffords' decision shifted party control of the Senate from the Republican Party to the Democrats, and some observers blamed the White House for Jeffords' defection.[20]

Shared Policy Beliefs   Presidential leadership of the party is also based on shared beliefs among fellow partisans, particularly at the level of party activists and public officials. Although the American parties do not communicate clear policy positions to the public very often, many studies find evidence of broad agreement (though not perfect unity) within each of the major parties on a number of issues. The depth and breadth of agreement appear to vary over time and from issue to issue, but shared beliefs often help presidents gain cooperation from other political actors in the same party.[21] Bear in mind, however, that those shared beliefs may also limit a president's options at times. Going against what most party activists and officeholders believe may unleash a barrage of criticism and active opposition from within the party. For example, Jimmy Carter stirred up much trouble with congressional Democrats because he was often more fiscally conservative than the mainstream of his party in Congress. Similarly, Bill Clinton's support for welfare reform, including limiting the duration that a person may receive welfare assistance, found much resistance within the more liberal wing of the Democratic Party. Not only did several members of his administration resign in protest, but several liberal members of Congress criticized him publicly.

Party Organizations   Presidents also have some influence over their party organizations. Much of that leverage is informal; the best-known example is the president's (or presidential candidate's) influence over the selection of the party's national chair and over the national chair's approach to the job. Presidential candidates and presidents also have considerable influence over their national party conventions, largely through their control of the delegates to the convention—the nominated candidate has the support of the majority of convention delegates. That influence is used to shape the party platforms and party rules, as well as the selection of the vice-presidential nominee. A president may help to mobilize like-minded activists who can affect party organizations across the country.

The capabilities of party organizations in the United States have varied considerably over the years and from one part of the country to another. Some analysts believe that many of the party organizations began a long-term decline some time around 1900. Rising levels of education, reforms that lessened the availability of political patronage and party control over nominations, changing cultural values,

---

[20]See Mike Allen and Ruth Marcus, "GOP Missteps Helped Prompt Jefford to Leave the Party," *Washington Post National Weekly Edition* (May 28–June 3, 2001), p. 7; Flanigan and Zingale, *Political Behavior;* Miller and Shanks, *New American Voter;* David Nice, "Party Realignment and Presidential Tenure: Some Implications for the Six-Year Term Proposal," *Policy Studies Journal* 13 (1984): 295–302; Wattenberg, *Decline of American Political Parties.*

[21]Bibby, *Politics, Parties,* p. 409; John Kingdon, *Congressmen's Voting Decisions,* 3d ed. (Ann Arbor: University of Michigan, 1989), pp. 75–81; Thomas Flinn and Frederick Wirt, "Local Party Leaders: Groups of Like-Minded Men," *Midwest Journal of Political Science* 9 (1965): 77–98.

party sectionalism, and new technologies reduced the party organizations' role in all aspects of politics. Candidates for public office became increasingly able to reach the public directly through radio and television.

Gradually, however, party organizations adapted to the changed environment and began providing more services to candidates. Party finances improved, and the parties began to play a more active role in politics again. Presidential influence over the parties may well be worth considerably more today than in the 1950s and 1960s.[22]

In recent years, presidents have also exercised party leadership by assisting their party and its candidates in raising money. Campaigns for major offices are very expensive, and candidates who are not well known often have considerable difficulty in raising money unless they are independently wealthy and can fund their own campaigns. A presidential appearance at a fundraising event can greatly boost attendance and encourage potential contributors to open their checkbooks. Both Ronald Reagan and Bill Clinton devoted considerable time and energy during their presidencies to helping their parties and their parties' candidates in this way, appearing at many fundraisers, which generated millions of dollars.

Presidents have also become very active in raising so-called **soft money** for party-based campaigning. Soft money allows parties to spend money on advertising and other party activities during election campaigns. Such spending is not restricted as long as it is not funneled directly through candidate campaigns. Thus, some critics complain that soft money is sometimes used to circumvent campaign finance regulations. But soft money also helps to encourage party unity. Because poorly financed candidates who are not well known win few elections, they may have a better chance with this type of party assistance. Raising money can help the party's candidates win elections and may give some of them a sense of obligation to support the president in return.[23]

Patronage and Nominations   Lastly, we should not forget the **patronage** and control over nominations and policies that presidents possess, each of which may be used to build support for the president within his party. For instance, on taking office, presidents appoint approximately five thousand people to administration posts, from cabinet secretaries to lower-level political appointees in the bureaucracy to diplomatic posts and ambassadorships to presidential aides in the Executive Office of the President. Such appointments may be made to repay those who helped the president win election. These appointees may also help bind the different wings of the party together behind the president.

[22]Bibby, *Politics, Parties,* chap. 4 and pp. 381–86; Beck and Hershey, *Party Politics,* chap. 3–4 and p. 282. Also, Jeffrey E. Cohen, Richard Fleisher, and Paul Kantor, *American Political Parties: Decline or Resurgence?* (Washington, D.C.: Congressional Quarterly Press, 2001).

[23]Anthony Gierzynski, *Money Rules* (Boulder, Colo.: Westview, 2000), chap. 4; Jacobson, *Politics of Congressional Elections,* chap. 4 and pp. 121–22; Louis Koenig, *The Chief Executive,* 6th ed. (Fort Worth, Texas: Harcourt Brace, 1996), pp. 119–20; Norman Thomas and Joseph Pika, *The Politics of the Presidency,* rev. 4th ed. (Washington, D.C.: Congressional Quarterly Press, 1997), p. 132.

For instance, in 1981, President Reagan named James Baker to be his chief of staff, dividing duties with Edwin Meese at the highest level of the administration. Unlike Meese, who was a long-time loyalist of Reagan but lacked Washington experience, James Baker came from Vice President Bush's camp and had some Washington political experience. Nancy Reagan, in particular, urged the president to use Baker in this way, not only for his talents but also as a way to salve the wounds that had been created between Reagan and Bush during the primary season.[24]

Research finds that even during the Depression, President Roosevelt's administration boosted federal support to localities that were highly supportive of the president, while those areas that showed less support received lower levels of federal support. Need was not the only criterion in determining where federal money was to be spent, even in a time as dire at the Great Depression of the 1930s.[25]

While administrative appointments are political plums that the president can dispense in building party loyalty, so too are the many judicial appointments that range from justice of the Supreme Court to federal circuit and district judges.

Presidents have other tangible ways to build party support. They can support the programs and projects that members of Congress desire, programs and projects that may affect members' districts, with little or no national implications. These may include construction projects, placement of military installations, granting of government contracts, as well as honoring or meeting with citizens and friends of members of Congress.

All in all, as our discussion indicates, presidents possess many resources that they may employ in gathering the support of members of their party. These resources vary from the symbolic and less tangible, such as image and visibility, to the highly tangible, such as appointments and contracts. Withholding some of these benefits may be a way of punishing a member who fails to support the president, of raising the cost of not supporting the president, and of providing an inducement to support the president. But most important, in talking of the costs and benefits of supporting the president, we must emphasize that the president is not in the position to command support or loyalty. Most other members of the party have power that is independent of the president, such as members of Congress and state and local officials who are elected by their own constituencies. Thus, the task of building party support is not a simple one for presidents. Moreover, many observers disagree regarding what role parties should play in politics.

Presidential Leadership and the Responsible Party Model

Some academic critics of the American parties share the skepticism held by many other Americans. Some of those critics have called on the parties to do a better job of providing a clear, consistent set of policy proposals and of fielding a team of

[24]James P. Pfiffner, *The Modern Presidency*, 3d ed. (Boston: Bedford/St. Martin's, 2000), pp. 66–69.

[25]Don C. Reading, "New Deal Activity and the States, 1933 to 1939," *Journal of Economic History* 33 (December 1973):792–810; Garvin Wright, "The Political Economy of New Deal Spending: An Econometric Analysis," *Review of Economics and Statistics* 56 (February 1974):30–38; John Joseph Wallis, "Employment, Politics, and Economic Recovery During the Great Depression," *Review of Economics and Statistics* 69 (August 1987): 516–20.

candidates who all support those proposals. The parties and their candidates also need to communicate those policy positions to the public. The voters, in turn, should pay close attention to the party programs and select the party that most closely reflects their views. The party winning the election should be cohesive and disciplined enough to deliver on the policies that it has proposed, and the losing party should monitor the performance of the party in power and criticize its failings but also offer constructive alternatives. These critics contend that the parties have often failed to take clear stands on major issues, failed to communicate their positions to the public, fielded candidates bearing the same party label but standing for different policies, and failed to deliver on promises when they have made them. More **responsible parties** would do a better job of linking majority preferences with government policy decisions and would promote greater accountability.[26]

The responsible party model has generated its own critics, some of whom contend that the American parties do a better job than is often believed. The parties and their presidential candidates often take stands on major issues, although they may not always communicate those stands very effectively. Some responsibility for the communication problems also rests with journalists who neglect covering issues and with an inattentive public. Moreover, the party winning the White House usually does much of what has been proposed in its party platform and by its presidential candidate. When the voters perceive reasonably clear choices on issues they care about, issues are likely to be a strong influence on voter decisions.[27]

Other criticisms of the responsible party model emphasize its practical difficulties in the United States in view of its size, diversity, and structure of government. A coalition large enough to win the presidency or a majority of the seats in Congress is virtually certain to contain a range of opinions on many issues. A party that takes clear stands on a number of controversial issues is highly likely to alienate many people and, therefore, lose elections and possibly even disintegrate. The many important officials chosen at the state and substate levels give the parties a strong incentive to adapt to the local political environment rather than trying to enforce strict party discipline, for failing to adapt is likely to bring defeat. Moreover, parties that contain a range of opinions and have the flexibility to compromise may help keep political conflicts from becoming too intense and erupting into violence. Finally, with large numbers of offices, officials who are elected for different terms of office, and shifts in voter turnout and salient issues from one election to the next, a president may face a Congress with at least one house controlled by the opposition party. Without some compromise, little is likely to be accomplished.[28]

From a presidential standpoint, party politics presents some difficult choices. Historical ratings of presidents reveal that the presidents regarded as greatest tended to serve during or shortly after party realignments, when each party is

[26]For some classic assessments, see Pendleton Herring, *The Politics of Democracy* (New York: Norton, 1940); V. O. Key, *Politics, Parties, and Pressure Groups*, 5th ed. (New York: Crowell, 1964), chap. 24; E. E. Schattschneider, *Party Government* (New York: Holt, Rinehart, and Winston, 1942).

[27]Gerald Pomper and Susan Lederman, *Elections in America*, 2d ed. (New York: Longman, 1980).

[28]Herring, *Politics of Democracy*.

likely to have a reasonably clear position on the major issues of the day, party loyalties are reasonably strong, the White House and Congress are controlled by the same party, and voter participation is high. The political environment, then, is conducive to making major policy decisions and supporting them for some years. When the parties are relatively weak, presidents are more likely to face a Congress controlled by the opposition party, both parties are likely to have significant internal conflicts, and winning reelection is more difficult. A president in that environment is not very likely to amass a major record of accomplishment.[29]

At first glance, those findings suggest that presidents would benefit from having stronger parties, perhaps along the lines of the responsible party model, for presidents acting alone have only limited ability to bring about major policy changes. Even if a president does succeed in bringing about some policy change unilaterally, that change is more likely to survive if it has some organized support that will sustain it after the president is gone from office. However, a party that is strong enough to provide that kind of support is likely to be strong enough to make demands on the president as well as provide support. The history of presidential relations with their parties indicates that a number of our presidents have not wanted their parties to make very many demands on them and have been wary of relying too much on their parties. Control over political appointments, for example, has gradually shifted away from the national party organizations to the White House, and serious presidential candidates create their own personal campaign organizations rather than relying totally on their party.[30] Nor is it clear that very many other elected officials in the United States want to have parties exerting significant pressure on them.

Presidents and Their Parties: A Conclusion

The American political system has a very large number of elected officials. The political parties help to simplify the range of choices offered to voters and to coordinate the actions of many of the elected officials, although critics do not think the parties do either job consistently well. Presidents have sometimes found the parties to be fairly helpful in mobilizing political support, but they also may help mobilize political opposition, and party support is not always reliable or easily achieved.

As a result, some political tasks have shifted from the parties to organizations under more direct presidential control, including the White House staff, personal campaign organizations, and political appointees in the bureaucracy. These organizations are less likely to challenge the president, but they are also of limited value in linking the president to other public officials, such as members of Congress.

[29]David Nice, "The Influence of War and Party System Aging on the Ranking of Presidents," *Western Political Quarterly* 37 (1984): 443–55.

[30]Sidney Milkis, *The President and the Parties* (New York: Oxford, 1993); Richard Waterman, "Combining Political Resources: The Internalization of the President's Appointment Power," in *The President Reconsidered*, ed. Richard Waterman (Itasca, Ill.: Peacock, 1993), pp. 195–214.

PRESIDENTS AND INTEREST GROUPS

Interest groups have been important in American politics since the founding of the Republic, but from then until about the 1960s, interest groups mainly represented the core sectors of the economy, such as agriculture, big business and industry, small business, and labor. In recent decades, however, the interest group system has transformed, with increases in both the number and types of interest groups. And while the older interest group system contained many influential groups, political activity by interest groups today is much greater and more intense than in earlier times. In short, interest groups have become a more important part of the political process.

The relationship between interest groups and the presidency has also undergone a transformation. Interaction between interest groups and the president is greater than before, and it is more systematized and routinized. And presidents now are more important to interest groups than ever before, while interest groups too have increased in importance to presidents. We begin this section of this chapter by detailing some of the changes in the world of interest groups, which is followed by a discussion of the interactions between presidents and interest groups, and the consequences of these changes on the political system and the presidency.[31]

The New Interest Group Environment

Recent years have witnessed a remarkable transformation of the interest group side of the political system. More social and political resources have poured into interest groups during the past thirty or forty years than before. This has meant more interest groups, more resourceful interest groups, and more types of interest groups.

For instance, as to size, one study estimates that around five hundred lobbies were based in Washington in 1929, but by 1977 the number had increased to about thirteen hundred, and the estimate for 1980 is seventeen hundred.[32] Another study, based on interest groups surveyed in 1981, found that 40 percent with Washington offices were founded since 1960, while 25 percent appeared since 1970. These newer groups seemed concentrated among citizen, civil rights, and welfare groups, whereas trade associations and business groups seem to have a longer Washington history.[33] Thus, not only are there more groups, but there are new types of groups as well. Where the interest group world was once composed of groups that mainly represented the major economic sectors and activities, many

[31]Benjamin I. Page and Mark P. Petracca, *The American Presidency* (New York: McGraw-Hill, 1983), pp. 140–68.

[32]Jack L. Walker, "The Origins and Maintenance of Interest Groups in America," *American Political Science Review* 77 (June 1983):390–406. The cited figures are found on p. 394.

[33]Kay Lehman Schlozman and John T. Tierney, *Organized Interests and American Democracy* (New York: Harper and Row, 1986), pp. 75–82.

other types of interest groups now exist, including citizen and public interest groups and ideologically motivated groups.

Interest group forms of political activity have also altered. Before this transformation, the classic strategy of interest groups was the **inside game.** The inside game is built on established relationships between interest groups, usually their lobbyists, and legislators and other governmental policy makers. Interactions between lobbyists and policy makers, while not private, were out of public view. The style of interaction often involved negotiating, bargaining, trading favors, and passing along information.

This close, personal interaction style differs markedly from the **outside game,** which has become more prevalent, especially among the newer types of interest groups. The inside game assumes interest group access to government officials; the outside game does not. Instead, one objective of interests is to garner access, which an outside strategy may facilitate. The outside game often involves bringing public pressure to bear on policy makers. Publicity campaigns attracting media attention and pubic support and sympathy are some of the techniques of the outside game. Where the inside game is one of negotiation among parties, the outside game is often one of the application of pressure by interest groups to policy makers. The seemingly cordial relationships of the inside game have given way to more combative, antagonistic relationships of the outside game. It is important to note that not all interest group behavior is of the outside type nowadays; insider games still exist in large number. What has changed is the presence of outsider-type behavior by some interest groups and the effects of that behavior on the relationships between interest groups and policy makers.

Besides the rise of outsider behavior, interest group political activity has also changed with regard to campaign activities. It was once the case that corporations could not donate money to candidates while labor unions could, but in 1974 the federal law regulating campaign finance was reformed. That reform allowed corporations and other groups to establish independent bodies that could donate money to candidates. These organizations are called **political action committees (PACs).** PACs have become among the most important elements of the interest group presence in politics and have opened a whole new avenue of contact between interest groups and candidates for office, including candidates who vie for their party's presidential nomination.[34]

This new interest group system has several important implications for politics. First, policy making has become more complex as more groups, representing more types of people, participate and compete. Second, the political system has been taxed by the multitude of interests seeking government policies.

---

[34]PACs admittedly are a bigger influence in congressional than presidential races because of public funding of presidential campaigns. Still, as of 1996, there were estimated to be more than four thousand PACs, a four-fold increase since the mid-1970s, and in 1995–1996, PACs contributed $430 million to candidates for office, about one-half going to congressional races and most of the rest to local races. See Harold W. Stanley and Richard G. Niemi, *Vital Statistics on American Politics, 1997–1998* (Washington, D.C.: Congressional Quarterly Press, 1998), pp. 94–95. Up-to-date figures can be found on the Federal Election Commission website, http://www.fec.gov.

Third, the rise of ideologically and cause-motivated groups has increased political conflict and reduced the ability to resolve disputes and differences by compromising. The older groups tended to seek economic benefits. When they tangled with each other, a compromise, often splitting the difference, could resolve the issue. Ideology and deeply felt causes are not so easily compromised. Instead, resolution can occur only if one side decisively defeats the other, and as decisive defeats are rare, deadlock and political acrimony are the results.

Fourth, it is now harder to build coalitions than in earlier times.[35] The presence of so many groups with narrow interests means that it is difficult to build lasting alliances across issues. Today's allies may be tomorrow's adversaries. Coalition building is also hampered by the fact that each additional interest adds only a small number of supporters. Coalition builders must now attract a larger number of groups to their side. When not so many interest groups existed, it took fewer of them to create a winning coalition.

Thus, the effects of the new interest group system are not so benign. Although the transformation of the interest group world has mobilized a large number of people into politics who previously were not participants, the political system has become more complex, less stable and predictable, and more acrimonious and prone to deadlock. As we will discuss later in this chapter, these changes have important implications for presidential leadership.

Increasing Presidential Attention to Interest Groups

One implication for the president of this new interest group system is that as interest groups have become more important to politics, presidents have had to spend more time interacting and dealing with them. We can gain a glimpse of this increased presidential attention by looking at who the president talks to when giving speeches.[36] We divide the modern presidency into three subperiods, 1945–57, 1958–70, and 1971–82. This helps smooth out any bumps associated with individual presidents and years, and allows us to see the longer-term trend, if it exists.

Across these years, the percentage of speeches that presidents give before interest groups has steadily increased. Thus, from 1945 to 1957, 18.3 percent of all speeches were presented to special interest groups; during the middle period from 1958 to 1970, the total climbed to 26.5 percent; and during the most recent period, from 1971 to 1982, the percentage inched up a little more to 27.1 percent. And this percentage increase has occurred while the total number of presidential speeches has grown.[37] Thus, in both relative and absolute terms, presidential attention to interest groups has expanded.

---

[35]Anthony King, "The American Polity in the Late 1970s: Building Coalitions in the Sand," in *The New American Political System,* ed. Anthony King (Washington, D.C.: American Enterprise Institute, 1978), pp. 371–95.

[36] Roderick Hart, *The Sound of Leadership* (Chicago: University of Chicago Press, 1987).

[37] Ibid.

In comparison, earlier presidents were not so attentive to interest groups. One study looked at presidential speeches across the nineteenth century. Not one was directed toward interest groups.[38] That approximately one-quarter of presidential speeches are now directed toward interests and innumerable passages in other speeches are also relevant to the policy positions of special interest groups highlights just how radically the relationship between interest groups and the presidency has been transformed.

Why Presidents Have Turned to Interest Groups

Presidential interaction with interest groups has increased because of a series of fundamental changes in the political system. These include evolution of the presidency into the modern presidency, the weakening of the political parties, the changes in the interest group world already noted, the new presidential nomination system, and presidential desire to control the bureaucracy.

The modern presidency is characterized by heightened expectations for presidential leadership, especially with regard to making public policy, but the constitutional foundation of the office was not amended to reflect this new environment of high expectations. The office is still located in a separation of powers system. To help narrow the gap between expectations and presidential power, presidents must seek additional resources that they can apply to the task of policy leadership. In Chapter 7, we will discuss in more detail how presidents seek public support. We can think of public support as one of these additional resources. Interest groups may be thought of as another resource that presidents try to mobilize in their behalf when trying to provide policy leadership for the nation. Both public opinion and interests groups may be considered potential allies of the president in the task of trying to get other policy makers, such as members of Congress, to follow the president's lead. Thus, as interest groups have become a larger and more important presence in the political system, it makes sense that a president would try to rally them in his behalf.

The decline of political parties provides another rationale for presidents to seek interest group support and for increased presidential attention and interaction to interests. Political parties provide several functions that may be useful to presidents. First, parties help structure political debate. With the president standing as titular head of one party, he is assured a prominent role in setting and structuring debate on policies and issues. Second, in part through this structuring function, parties help to mobilize people behind certain efforts, whether it be the election of candidates or the passage of legislation. Within Congress, parties have historically been important in building coalitions of support for or against policies in the legislative process. In a sense, parties have historically been the fundamental building blocks of creating and maintaining coalitions in the legislature.

[38]Jeffrey K. Tulis, *The Rhetorical Presidency* (Princeton, N.J.: Princeton University Press, 1987), p. 138.

But the decline of parties has reduced their effectiveness and efficiency in structuring political debate and mobilizing supporters and opponents of policies. Presidents, thus, have had to look elsewhere to supplement or replace parties. Interest groups present one such supplement. For one, they organize people into politically relevant units. Presidents may find it helpful if they can use these organizations that are already in place rather than build from the ground up new organizations each time a new issue comes to the fore. Moreover, interest groups may have become indispensable to members of Congress seeking reelection, due to their political action committees, which make important financial contributions to election campaigns. Again, presidents may find it helpful to use interest groups with this kind of sway in Congress as they lobby the legislature to pass their policies.

Another factor that leads presidents to interact more frequently and intensely with interest groups arises from the new nomination system.[39] In Chapter 4, we saw that the process of nominating presidents had changed from one in which state party bosses controlled blocks of delegates to one of primaries. Without strong party organizations to rely on, prospective candidates for the nomination would have to construct their own organizations in each state where they entered the primary. Interest groups often provide ready-made organizations, transcending state boundaries, that candidates may use as foundations for or adjuncts to their campaigns.

Moreover, interest groups provide other needed resources for primary contesting. They may contribute financing, through their PACs, as noted; they may endorse a candidate; they may mobilize and donate campaign workers; and they may provide needed political understanding and knowledge of key issues, localities, and personalities. Members of interest groups may be more involved in the primary campaign than people in general, and at conventions they may provide blocks of delegates, which may be important when writing planks of the party's platform.

Candidates for the presidency understand the importance of interest groups to their winning the nomination and the general election. Through the campaign, prospective candidates must offer interest groups something for their campaign support. These may be pledges to pursue certain policies, creating access to government for the interest, and the like.

The process of seeking and winning the presidential nomination, thus, involves the support and participation of interest groups. Candidates find interest groups invaluable in winning the nomination. Moreover, through this primary campaign process, involvement with interest groups carries over into the general election and the administration, once elected. By the time they are elected, presidents are used to dealing with interest groups and understand the politics of interest groups and their political uses.

And as in election campaigns, presidents use their speeches to tie interests to the presidency. Thus, presidents tailor their speeches to the audience, telling the

[39]Jack L. Walker, "The Presidency and the Nominating System," in *The Presidency and the Political System,* ed. Michael Nelson (Washington, D.C.: Congressional Quarterly Press, 1984), pp. 183–203.

interest group audience what it wants to hear. And presidential positions may shift as presidents speak before different groups.[40] Inasmuch as governing now comes to resemble campaigning, presidents will use interest groups.

Another rationale for increasing interaction with interest groups is to weaken the alliances of interests, bureaucrats, and legislatures, known as **policy subsystems.**[41] This motivation grows out of the policy leadership expectations associated with the modern presidency, but it also has some constitutional roots in the clause that the president must ensure that the laws are faithfully executed. For the most part, the bureaucracy carries out policy execution, what political scientists like to term "policy implementation." It is generally understood that policy making and policy implementation are linked. Those who have a say in policy making may influence policy implementation; those without such a say in policy making will in all likelihood also lack influence over implementation.

Many policies are forged in policy subsystems, which are informal alliances of interest groups, members of relevant congressional committees, and bureaucrats in germane agencies. Notable is the absence of the president from most policy subsystems. The relatively narrow scope of policy subsystems and their great number inhibit much presidential participation across most policy-making subsystems.

Presidents often look askance at policy subsystems. Subsystems may provide bureaucrats with allies, who may be able to stymie presidential efforts to direct or control specific agencies. Subsystems may push in a policy direction that runs counter to the direction that the president wants to take. In general, they undermine presidential ability to control the bureaucracy, his arm for carrying out his policies.

By pulling interests into the White House, by making interest groups somewhat reliant on the presidency, the president may be able to weaken the bonds among the participants within the policy-making subsystems. Presidents may gain greater control over the bureaucracy this way and may even centralize some subsystem policy making in the White House, which will enhance presidential influence over public policy. However, the number and resilience of policy subsystems may easily overwhelm presidents.

To keep from being swamped by the sheer multitude of policy subsystems and interest groups and to deal more effectively and efficiently with the complex world of interests, presidents must organize the White House appropriately. Interest groups, by their nature, will mobilize only on issues of interest and concern to them. Any interest group will, thus, be active on only a few issues during any given legislative session, unlike parties, which activate across a

---

[40]Lawrence Miller and Lee Sigelman, "Is the Audience the Message? A Note on LBJ's Viet Nam Statements," *Public Opinion Quarterly* 42 (Spring 1978):71–80, and Malcom L. Goggin, "The Ideological Content of Presidential Communications: The Message Tailoring Hypothesis Revisited," *American Politics Quarterly* 12 (July 1984):361–84.

[41]Thomas L. Gais, Mark A. Peterson, and Jack L. Walker, "Interest Groups, Iron Triangles and Representative Institutions in American National Government," *British Journal of Political Science* 14 (1984):161–85; and Hugh Heclo, "Issue Networks and the Executive Establishment," in *The New American Political System,* ed. Anthony King (Washington, D.C.: American Enterprise Institute, 1978), pp. 87–124.

wide span of issues. For each new issue that must be dealt with, the configura-
tion of interest groups that the president needs to collect will change. It helps
if the presidency has an organizational presence, with a memory and historical
sense about the positions of interest groups, their effectiveness and helpfulness,
and the like. Knowledge and understanding of each interest group of relevance,
as well as of the nature of the interest group side of the political system, facilitate presidential mobilization of interests in his behalf. Thus, the Office of Public Liaison was created, which we will discuss in "The Creation and Rise of the
Office of Public Liaison" section in this chapter.

Why Interest Groups Seek Access to the Presidency

Just as presidents now find interest groups important to their policy and public
leadership, interest groups find the president increasingly important to the attainment of their goals. Interest groups have several goals that the president may help
them achieve, including social and political legitimacy and influence in the policy-
making process.

Presidents can confer a special status on issues, groups, and people. When a
president gets involved in an issue, even if that involvement is limited and superficial, it still connotes that the president deemed the issue worthy of some attention. Presidential acknowledgment signifies to the public and the political
world that the issue is of national importance. An issue that cannot gain such presidential acknowledgment cannot claim such national importance. Moreover, presidential acknowledgment is a very scarce resource, given limits on the president's
time, his own agenda, and the multitude of pressing problems. Add to this mix
the vast number of groups that seek presidential attention, and the value of a president acknowledging a group's issue increases. Once having secured presidential
acknowledgment, a group's political stock goes up; it has secured a place in the
nation's policy agenda and debates. While this does not ensure that the group will
attain the policy ends that it seeks, failure to gain presidential support may often
doom a group's efforts.

This is especially the case for groups that are outside of the system and are trying to break in and establish a sense that their issue is a legitimate one for the political system to address. The situation of AIDS activists in the 1980s is illustrative.
By the mid-1980s, the devastation caused by the AIDS epidemic was becoming evident. However, the epidemic was also viewed by many in the public as an issue
affecting only gays and, because of their lifestyle choice, not worthy of public attention or support. As of mid-1987, six years after the discovery of the AIDS virus,
President Reagan had delivered only two major speeches on the topic and, to the
last days of his presidency, would resist action concerning AIDS.

In part, Reagan was caught between two interest groups. On the one hand, the
conservative and religious right, who helped Reagan win the presidency, opposed
almost all policy, except mandatory testing for the AIDS virus, believing that AIDS
was fundamentally a gay issue. In contrast, AIDS activists and many public health
officials called for increased funding for research and education, sex education in

the schools, distribution of condoms, and greater presidential activism. Reagan walked a fine line between the two groups but usually leaned more toward his conservative allies. He stalled the distribution of the educational pamphlet developed by C. Everett Koop, his surgeon general, for nearly two years and rejected a large number of recommendations issued by the special commission on AIDS that was chaired by retired Admiral James D. Watkins. However, he did call for *routine* but not *mandatory* testing for the AIDS virus, and after a slow start, funding for AIDS research did grow to $1.3 billion by the end of his term in office, making it among the most heavily funded diseases. Still, by the end of Reagan's administration, most AIDS activists felt that he offered too little too late. As one journalist summed up the Reagan approach to AIDS, "Instead of providing presidential leadership, Reagan largely finessed the issue."[42]

A second reason for interest groups to seek greater interaction with the presidency is because of the prominent role the president plays in the policy-making process. Much policy making has centralized in the White House. The budget process begins in the White House, where the Office of Management and Budget (OMB) prepares a budget under presidential direction that is then submitted to Congress. The OMB even has the power of legislative clearance, which means that before an agency can send a proposal for new legislation to Congress, it must meet with the approval of the president. The Office of Information and Regulatory Affairs has the power of regulatory clearance, which means that it can review most new regulations before they can take effect. Similarly, appointment to the federal judiciary and many important posts in the federal bureaucracy are reviewed at the presidential level. Thus, the president has influence or control over a large number of policy-making devices.

Many interest groups cannot get what they want without the use of one or more of the policy-making devices. Thus, interest groups now find the president to be more important to the attainment of their policy goals than used to be the case. This is not to suggest that all interest groups can be helped or blocked by the president, but given the increase in the scope of the policy-making devices, the president is likely to be able to affect the policy fates of many more groups than was once the case. In such a situation, it is not unreasonable that interest groups will seek presidential support and access to policy making in the White House and top levels of the administration more than they did in the past.

Thus, from the perspective of both the president and interest groups, each has strong motivations and incentives to increase their interaction with the other. This increased interaction takes many forms. One is electoral, as we have already discussed. The other major form is institutional. As we have noted, within the White House an office has been created to manage relations between the president and the world of interest groups, the Office of Public Liaison.

---

[42]The quote is from Abigail Trafford and Larry Thompson, "The Muddled State of AIDS Policy," *Washington Post,* 23 August 1988, p. T16. Also useful is Lynn Simross, "AIDS, Politics: Seeking a Safe Stand," *Los Angeles Times,* 3 June 1987, part 5, p. 1.

The Institutionalization of Presidential–Interest Group Ties

From Roosevelt to Johnson Presidents have had to deal with interest groups and their representatives since the beginning of the Republic, but the limitations of president staff and presidential policy-making activity meant that presidential interactions with interest groups were intermittent and unsystematic.[43] Relations with interest groups began to formalize and routinize only as presidents acquired staff to whom they could assign the task of handling interest group relations and as presidents became more active participants in the policy-making process, which made interaction with interest groups an important part of their policy leadership.

Franklin Roosevelt was the first president with a large enough staff to assign any to interest group affairs.[44] Through the creation of the Executive Office of the President in 1939, Roosevelt was not only able to expand the size of his staff, but he also could assign them to specific tasks that he deemed necessary. Interest groups were important to Roosevelt because he built a majority Democratic Party on a loose coalition of groups that he helped mobilize into the political process. He needed these groups because they composed his power base, yet he did not want to be cowed by them either. Thus, he assigned staffers to liaise with specific important groups, such as small farmers, labor unions, and ethnic groups, especially Jews. Still, such liaison work was ad hoc, with specific staffers assigned to particular interests based on the ties the staffer held with the interest. No organizational apparatus yet existed for interest group affairs in the White House, but the number of interests was still small and manageable, and the role of interest groups in the political process had not yet become as significant as it would, although interests in Roosevelt's day were important. This ad hoc liaison system, where the staffer who acted as liaison between the group and the White House tended to possess the characteristic of the interest group or come from it, remained in effect throughout the Truman era.

The Eisenhower years of the 1950s saw a few modest developments, which were built on the basic Roosevelt ad hoc liaison model. First, the groups with whom the administration liaised changed because of the shift in party control of the White House. More business groups were brought in, and labor, of course, was shunted aside, but Jewish groups were retained, in part because of U.S. relations with Israel and Middle East policy.

[43]A good overview of presidents and interest groups is found in Joseph A. Pika, "Reaching Out to Organized Interests: Public Liaison in the Modern White House," in *The Presidency Reconsidered,* ed. Richard W. Waterman (Itasca, Ill.: F. E. Peacock, 1993), pp. 45–168; Joseph A. Pika, "Opening Doors for Kindred Souls: The White House Office of Public Liaison," in *Interest Group Politics,* 3d ed., ed. Allan J. Cigler and Burdett A. Loomis (Washington, D.C.: Congressional Quarterly Press, 1991), pp. 277–98; Martha Joynt Kumar and Michael Baruch Grossman, "The Presidency and Interest Groups," in *The Presidency and the Political System,* ed. Michael Nelson (Washington, D.C.: Congressional Quarterly Press, 1984), pp. 282–312; Benjamin Ginsberg and Martin Shefter, "The Presidency and the Organization of Interests," in *The Presidency and the Political System,* 2d ed., ed. Michael Nelson (Washington, D.C.: Congressional Quarterly Press, 1988), pp. 311–30.

[44]Joseph Pika, "Interest Groups and the White House Under Roosevelt and Truman," *Political Science Quarterly* 102 (Winter 1987/88): 647–68.

More important, however, was that Eisenhower saw a role for interests that neither Roosevelt nor Truman had made much use of. Both Roosevelt and Truman were activist presidents who did not hesitate to lobby Congress directly for policies that they believed in. Eisenhower held a less active view of the presidency. He wanted to scale back public expectations of the office and of government itself. Thus, he thought it important that he not overtly intercede in all policy matters that he agreed with, but instead, he used agents to carry his cause, feeling that the presidency could be harmed and diminished as an object of national leadership and respect by too much activity and lobbying of Congress. Eisenhower's restrained, behind-the-scenes type of presidential leadership has been termed **hidden-hand presidential leadership.**[45]

Thus, Eisenhower found in interest groups people who could lobby Congress for him without necessarily using his name but pushing for the policies that he believed in because they did, too. Thus, on occasion, he or an aide would instruct an interest (or several) to lobby Congress. This practice was continued by all subsequent administrations, whether they followed Eisenhower's hidden-hand leadership model or the more active models of Roosevelt and Truman.

The same basic system continued under Kennedy and Johnson, except that with the shift in party control of the White House came a new set of interest groups. Again, we see the basic alignment between interests and parties that existed from Roosevelt to Eisenhower, but the list of groups to include was growing larger. To the old New Deal groups (farmers, labor, Jews), Kennedy and Johnson added women, consumers, Greeks, the elderly, academics, blacks, and business. Only in the case of business did the party-interest group alignment break down, but business may have been too important for Democrats in the 1960s to ignore.

The interests under Kennedy and Johnson have several notable characteristics. Not all interests began with well-organized groups. Some, like women and consumers, got some of their organizational impetus from being invited to the White House. Second, Kennedy, and especially Johnson, used the White House conference to bring together interests under White House sponsorship. This was done to mobilize interests in behalf of the president, keep them and their issues under presidential control, and inspire them to organize, thereby creating new allies for the president. But White House conferences were also used to keep a lid on the issues that interests and others might be pushing. White House conferences allowed presidents to point to their support, activity, and attention to an issue without necessarily following through with policy or legislative proposals. In fact, it has been argued that Johnson invited civil rights groups to the White House before the great march on Washington in 1963 to lessen the likelihood of violence, to scale back their expectations, and to interpose himself into a leadership role in the movement.[46] Thus, while interest group interactions ratcheted up during the Kennedy-Johnson years, no office was officially designated to deal with interest group affairs.

---

[45]Fred I. Greenstein. *The Hidden-Hand Presidency* (New York: Basic Books, 1981).

[46]Bruce Miroff, "Presidential Leverage over Social Movements: The Johnson White House and Civil Rights," *Journal of Politics* 43 (February 1981): 2–23; and Mark Stern, *Calculating Visions: Kennedy, Johnson, and Civil Rights* (New Brunswick, N.J.: Rutgers University Press, 1992).

The Creation and Rise of the Office of Public Liaison   Richard Nixon was the first president consciously aware of a need for an interest group coordinating mechanism in the White House. In 1970, under the direction of Charles Colson, public liaison functions began to be consolidated and coordinated. However, the Watergate scandals that drove Nixon from office stalled any further development until Gerald Ford assumed office.

Thus, in 1974, the **Office of Public Liaison (OPL)** was created. Not only was a formal office created and staff with particular duties assigned, but the OPL was accorded similar status to the office that lobbied Congress, the Office of Congressional Liaison. Such status recognized the growing importance of interest groups and the people in the White House who liaise with such groups.[47]

Whereas Ford needed interests and other types of support to legitimize his presidency since he came to office without the benefit of being elected even to the vice presidency, Carter initially saw interest groups as a problem for presidents to overcome. But with his activist agenda, Carter found that he could not do without strong liaison efforts with interest groups. Midway into his term, Carter enhanced group access to the White House when he titled aides who liaised with women, blacks, Jews, labor, white ethnics, consumers, and Hispanics as "special assistants to the president."[48]

The Ups and Downs of OPL   The high point of interest group access to the White House through OPL came during the late Carter years. Under Reagan, OPL was demoted from an independent unit that reported to the chief of staff to a unit of the Office of Communications, which we discussed in Chapter 6. By so moving OPL, interest group affairs were coordinated with overall presidential publicity operations and made a part of this larger effort.

Why did Reagan demote OPL? One reason is that with the budget deficit of the 1980s and early 1990s, Reagan had a smaller legislative agenda and thus had less need for interests to lobby and pressure Congress.[49] More important, however,

[47]On the creation of OPL see Martha Joynt Kumar and Michael Baruch Grossman, "Political Communication from the White House: The Interest Group Connection," *Presidential Studies Quarterly* 16 (Winter 1986):96–99; Mark A. Peterson, "Interest Groups and the Reagan White House: For Whom the Door Bell Tolls," paper presented at the 1986 American Political Science Association, pp. 6–7; Joseph Pika, "Interest Groups and the Executive: Presidential Intervention," in *Interest Group Politics,* ed. Alan J. Cigler and Burdett A. Loomis (Washington, D.C.: Congressional Quarterly Press, 1983), pp. 317–19; and Mark A. Peterson, "Interest Mobilization and the Presidency," in *The Politics of Interests: Interest Groups Transformed,* ed. Mark P. Petracca (Boulder, Colo.: Westview Press, 1992), pp. 21–241; and Mark A. Peterson, "The Presidency and Organized Interests: White House Patterns of Interest Group Liaison," *American Political Science Review* 86 (September 1992): 612–25.

[48]Kenneth E. Collier, *Between the Branches: The White House Office of Legislative Affairs* (Pittsburgh: University of Pittsburgh Press, 1997), pp. 189–96.

[49]Harold Wolman and Fred Teitelbaum, "Interest Groups and the Reagan Presidency," in *The Reagan Presidency and the Governing of America,* ed. Lester M. Salamon and Michael S. Lund (Washington, D.C.: The Urban Institute, 1984), pp. 297–329; and Benjamin Ginsberg and Martin Shefter, "The Presidency, Interest Groups, and Social Forces: Creating a Republican Coalition," in *The Presidency and the Political System,* 3d ed., ed. Michael Nelson (Washington, D.C.: Congressional Quarterly Press, 1990), pp. 335–52.

was that OPL personnel had a tendency to identify too closely with the interests with whom they liaised, especially ideological and interest groups that often took politically extreme positions. As Reagan's administrative philosophy emphasized loyalty to the president over all else, the demotion of OPL cut down on the prestige of staff who might deviate from the president's line and signaled to others the costs of disloyalty to the president.[50]

George H. W. Bush also kept OPL in its subservient position, mostly because of his limited agenda and attempts to scale back public expectations about the presidency. Clinton, however, with his more activist agenda, saw greater need to mobilize interests in his behalf. Moreover, Clinton aimed to reshape the Democratic Party and the groups that supported it, moving the party away from the left and toward the center, consistent with his "New Democrat" theme. This would require an activist interest group liaison effort, bringing new groups into the fold and mobilizing them behind the president's program. Thus, OPL was upgraded back to its former status as an independent unit of equal status with the Office of Legislative Affairs and the Office of Communications.[51]

The Importance of an Institutional Office for Interest Group Affairs
Whether OPL is a stand-alone unit of prestige or a unit of the Office of Communications, the fact that an office responsible for interest group affairs exists is important to the modern presidency and our understanding of the office. OPL rationalizes relations with interest groups, coordinates those relationships, relates them to congressional liaison and presidential publicity, and, of equal importance, provides the president a mechanism to control and manage interest groups to his own advantage.

By rationalization, we mean to organize and make sense of the interest group world. Thus, interest groups are categorized; the identification of those categories gives a sense of the contour of the major interest groups' political fault lines and divisions. Rationalization is apparent in the organizational structure of OPL. OPL "represents" eight identifiable interests through a staff assistant acting as liaison: business, labor, Jews, consumers, blacks, women, Hispanics, and the elderly.[52] These liaison personnel carry information back and forth between the interest groups and the White House, help brief the interests, perform casework for them, and sometimes run interference for them with the bureaucracy.

---

[50]Mark A. Peterson and Jack L. Walker, "Interest Group Responses to Partisan Change: The Impact of the Reagan Administration upon the National Interest Group System," in *Interest Group Politics,* ed. Allan J. Cigler and Burdett A. Loomis (Washington, D.C.: Congressional Quarterly Press, 1986), pp. 162–82.

[51]Mark A. Peterson, "Clinton and Organized Interests: Splitting Friends, Unifying Enemies," in *The Clinton Legacy,* ed. Colin Campbell and Bert A. Rockman (Chappaqua, N.Y.: Chatham House of Seven Bridges Press, 1999), pp. 163–96; Ronald G. Shaiko, "Reverse Lobbying: Interest Group Mobilization from the White House and the Hill," in *Interest Group Politics,* 5th ed., ed. Allan J. Cigler and Burdett A. Loomis (Washington, D.C.: Congressional Quarterly Press, 1998), pp. 255–82; and Graham K. Wilson, "The Clinton Administration and Interest Groups," in *The Clinton Presidency: First Appraisals,* ed. Colin Campbell and Bert A. Rockman (Chatham, N.J.: Chatham House, 1996), pp. 212–33.

[52]Pika, "Interest Groups and the Executive," p. 318.

TABLE 6-2   A TYPOLOGY OF WHITE HOUSE–INTEREST GROUP RELATIONS

		Breadth of Group Interactions	
		Inclusive	Exclusive
Purpose of Group Interactions	Representational	Legitimation	Outreach
	Programmatic	Consensus Building	Governing Party

Source: Mark A. Peterson, "Clinton and Organized Interests: Splitting Friends, Unifying Enemies," in *The Clinton Legacy,* ed. Colin Campbell and Bert A. Rockman (Chappaqua, N.Y.: Chatham House of Seven Bridges Press, 1999), pp. 177–78.

However, naming a staff assistant as liaison to a specific interest may also create interest expectations about access and influence to the White House. By managing interest relations through OPL, presidents keep interests from overwhelming the administration.

Varieties of Presidential Relationships with Interest Groups   All modern presidents need interest groups. Thus, the level of interaction between interest groups and the president has increased, and those relationships have been routinized with the creation of the OPL. Still, the manner of presidential interaction with interest groups may vary, depending on the president's style, his political circumstances, and his policy agenda.

One study suggests that there are four possible ways for presidents to use their liaison office in conducting affairs with interest groups: 1) clearinghouse, 2) consensus building, 3) outreach, and 4) governing party.[53] These four types are based on the joining of two dimensions, whether the president has programmatic or representational concerns vis-à-vis interests and how exclusive or inclusive presidential-interest group interactions should be. Table 6-2 diagrams these possibilities.

"Inclusive" means that presidents will bring all interests into the fold; "exclusive" suggests that presidents will work with only some interests, those that are more compatible with his goal. "Programmatic" refers to presidents who wish to employ interests in pursuit of policy goals. "Representational" refers to presidents who give interests a place to be heard, who try to bestow on interests a sense of being represented in the White House. The representation here is more symbolic than policy-focused. Thus, liaison with interest groups as clearinghouse is inclusive and representational; outreach is exclusive and representational; consensus building is inclusive and programmatic; and governing party is exclusive and programmatic.

The logic of the modern presidency seems to push presidents toward the governing party style. Policy leadership is one expectation placed on modern presidents; thus, the modern president's programmatic orientation. Second, exclusivity restricts access to those groups supportive of or in agreement with the president's program. Exclusivity may help presidents manage their relations with interest groups, reducing the demands of the interest group system on the president and directing specific interest groups toward the president's programmatic

[53]Peterson, "Interest Groups and the Reagan White House," pp. 8–16.

goals. By being exclusive in their relations with interests, presidents may be better able to stick to their policy agenda and presidential program, that is, to control the definition of their administration.

Still, not all modern presidents follow the dictates of the governing model. Some may not be able to, depending on their political circumstances. For instance, Carter came to office with an outreach orientation, wanting to keep interests at bay and alter the image of the Democratic Party as being controlled by liberal interest groups. But over time, as his program faltered in Congress, he put greater effort into mobilizing interests in behalf of his policy goals.[54]

Ford's approach was essentially of the clearinghouse type. Ford did not choose the governing approach because, unlike every other incumbent, he did not benefit from the legitimacy that election to office confers. Ford's administration took on the tones of a campaign for election—hence, the clearinghouse approach. The inclusive, representational quality of a clearinghouse approach intersected with his election needs quite well.

Reagan's relations with interest groups fit the pattern of governing party and the logic of the modern presidency most clearly. Reagan had clear programmatic designs. Of that there is no doubt. One of his concerns, however, was that interest group dominance of the political system had led to increases in the federal budget, leading to governmental overload.[55] Reagan was also concerned about the policy subsystems discussed in the section on "Why Presidents Have Turned to Interest Groups," especially his sense that liberal elements controlled many of these policy subsystems. To help break that liberal hold, Reagan treated interest groups differently, depending on how well they fit with his more conservative policy objectives.[56]

The Dangers of Bringing Interest Groups into the White House   Presidents and interest groups need each other, and their need for each other has increased with changes in the political system in recent decades. Consequently, presidents and interest groups are interacting with each other more than in earlier times, and more systematically and routinely, because of the creation of the OPL in 1970. However, this increased presence of interest groups in the White House poses some issues for the political system and the presidency.[57]

[54]Ibid, p. 14.

[55] See Wolman and Teitlebaum, "Interest Groups."

[56]On the politicization of interest group relations under Reagan and the changing reactions of interests in the Carter to Reagan transition, see Peterson, "Interest Groups and the Reagan White House;" Gais, Peterson, and Walker, "Interest Groups;" Peterson and Walker, "Interest Group Responses," and Wolman and Teitelbaum, "Interest Groups."

[57] Nelson Polsby, "Interest Groups and the Presidency: Trends in Political Intermediation in America," in *American Politics and Public Policy,* ed. Walter Dean Burnham and Martha Wagner (Cambridge: MIT Press, 1978), pp. 41–52; and Benjamin Ginsberg, Walter R. Mebane, Jr., and Martin Shefter, "The Presidency and Interest Groups: Why Presidents Cannot Govern," in *The Presidency and the Political System,* 4th ed., ed. Michael Nelson (Washington, D.C.: Congressional Quarterly Press, 1995), pp. 331–47; and Benjamin Ginsberg, Walter R. Mebane, Jr., and Martin Shefter, "The Presidency, Social Forces, and Interest Groups: Why Presidents Can No Longer Govern," in *The Presidency and the Political System,* 5th ed., ed. Michael Nelson (Washington, D.C.: Congressional Quarterly Press, 1998), pp. 358–73.

The establishment of the office for interest group affairs, the OPL, may create tensions between the president and his staffers who work in that office. First, OPL staffers straddle two tasks. Are they presidential emissaries to interests or interest group emissaries in the White House? Interest groups may view OPL staffers as "their people" in the White House, much as journalists view the presidential press secretary as their representative. To effectively bridge the gap between the interest and the White House, the OPL staffer must be respected by the interest group. The staffer must be viewed as one who understands the interest's point of view, is sympathetic to that position, and who will honestly report that position within the White House. To maintain the trust, cooperation, and line of communication to an interest, the OPL staffer must be viewed as someone who will advocate the interest's position within the White House, as well as someone who is respected and influential within White House circles.

That influence and respect, however, derives from being thought of by the president as a loyal member of his administration. An OPL staffer cannot appear to be too closely tied or sympathetic to the interest, lest the president begin to suspect or view the staffer as more the interest group's advocate than a member of his administration. Thus, questions of staff loyalty and issues of staff management arise with the establishment of OPL. In part because of these types of issues, Reagan demoted OPL, feeling that OPL staffers were too likely to turn into interest advocates.

A second staff management issue arises, not from the establishment of OPL itself, but from the multiple interests that are represented in the White House through OPL: inasmuch as these interests may disagree on policy priorities or directions, conflict among staffers with ties to these different interests may erupt. The political debates and conflicts among interests may get played out within the White House. And the closer such conflicts come to the president, the greater the need for the president to intercede in the squabble. If such fights are kept out of the White House, the president can sit on the sidelines if he so chooses. But once an interest group conflict engages presidential staffers, the conflict is transformed from one of interest group rivalry to that of presidential management of his administration, presidential priorities, and who controls the White House. Under such conditions, presidents may not be able to avoid entering the fray, and depending on the course of action that they take, they may alienate one or both sides in the conflict.

But bringing interest groups formally into the White House, as is done through OPL, may also have consequences beyond staff management issues. First, the formal establishment of an interest group affairs office may signal to the world that for an interest to be taken seriously, it must have entry and access to the White House. Presidential acknowledgment of an interest may become part of the process of politically legitimating that interest. More and more issues may become "presidentialized" if such an expectation takes root.

Following from this point, if interests feel the need for White House access and presidential acknowledgment of them and their positions, the presidency may become overloaded with supplicants and others seeking such presidential attention. The sheer multitude of interests in American politics and their competitiveness practically foreordain such an overloading of the White House.

Still, presidents possess some techniques that may lighten the interest group demands on them. For one, as it is groups that generally seek out the president, the president can pick and choose among them when deciding which ones he will support or acknowledge. Such a strategy may be politically risky, however; presidents may create as many enemies as friends by being so choosy.[58] Perhaps a better route for the president is to insulate himself from the interest group world in general by attending to "higher" issues of state, such as foreign affairs, or issues that command broader public concern, such as the state of the economy. Still, some slack may exist in the president's schedule, which opens the door for interest groups to make their demands on him.

Among the greatest resources that an interest can use in politics is to remind politicians of the electoral resources that they command, such as campaign finance support. Here is where presidents may actually be blessed insofar as they accept federal funds to finance their general election campaigns. Although interest group support is critical in financing the primary election campaign, most presidential candidates, even those who could easily have raised more money than the federal system provides, have eschewed private money for public. One motivation for doing so is appearances; another may be to help keep interests at arm's length by reducing the power of their argument that they helped him secure the presidency.

Perhaps the most perilous consequence of the establishment of interest groups in the White House is its potential impact on public regard for the presidency. People expect the president to represent the body politic at large. With that expectation comes the attendant one that presidents especially must resist the demands of interest groups when those demands run counter to the public interest or majority opinion. If a president appears captured by certain interests, even on singular issues, his leadership and reputation may be threatened. Among the president's greatest advantages is his ability to speak to the entire nation and appear as the spokesperson for the nation. Too close an association with an interest (or set of interests) may undermine the ability of the president to speak for the nation and to rally the public behind his efforts. Rather than seeing the president as a guardian of the public interest, the public may come to suspect the motives behind his actions and his words.

CONCLUSION

Presidents must build coalitions of support if they are to gain approval of their policies. Presidents may try to build coalitions separately for each issue that

---

[58]Jeffrey M. Berry and Kent E. Portney, "Centralizing Regulatory Control and Interest Group Access: The Quayle Council on Competitiveness," in *Interest Group Politics,* 4th ed., ed. Allan J. Cigler and Burdett A. Loomis (Washington, D.C.: Congressional Quarterly Press, 1995), pp. 319–48.

arises, with different supporters in each of these distinct coalitions. Building support coalitions this way would not only be time-consuming but also would necessarilyinvolve recruiting opponents from one issue as allies on a second issue. Parties and interest groups offer presidents a more efficient way to begin building these coalitions of support. Not only do political parties and interest groups offer presidents ready-made organizations that they can use, but they may provide a stable core of support across issues. However, as we have discussed throughout this chapter, it is not always easy for presidents to use parties or interest groups as coalition supporters. In some instances, presidents may have to distance themselves from these organizations in the name of acting as a representative of the nation and the more general public interest. Much of the character of an administration can be understood by looking at how that president relates to the parties and interest groups. Because parties and interest groups are important elements of American politics, presidents cannot avoid dealing with either of them.

KEY TERMS

coattails   135

hidden-hand presidential
　leadership   157

inside game and interest groups   149

Office of Public Liaison (OPL)   158

outside game and
　interest groups   149

party loyalty   141

patronage   144

policy subsystems   153

political action committees (PACs)   149

president as party leader   134

responsible parties   146

soft money   144

DISCUSSION QUESTIONS

1. In what way have U.S. citizens' attitudes toward parties and interest groups changed over time? What are the implications of these attitudes for presidential use of and association with parties and interest groups?
2. In what sense can we think of the president as leader of his party? Who leads the party when it does not occupy the presidency? What obstacles exist to presidential leadership of his party? What does this tell us about the relationship between the president and his party and the nature of parties in the United States?
3. How has the environment of interest groups changed over the past several decades? How have presidents responded to this changing interest group environment? What implication does this changing interest group environment have for presidential leadership and presidential–interest group relationships?
4. Why was the Office of Public Liaison established? What is the office responsible for and where it is located in the Executive Office of the president? Why have its fortunes risen and fallen over the course of its existence? What do these changing fortunes tell us about presidents and interest groups?

SUGGESTED READINGS

Jon Bond and Richard Fleisher, eds., *Polarized Politics*. Washington, D.C.: Congressional Quarterly Press, 2000.

Jeffrey E. Cohen, Richard Fleisher, and Paul Kantor, *American Political Parties: Decline or Resurgence?* Washington, D.C.: Congressional Quarterly Press, 2001.

Hugh Heclo, "Issue Networks and the Executive Establishment," in *The New American Political System,* ed. Anthony King. Washington, D.C.: American Enterprise Institute, 1978.

Sidney M. Milkis, *The President and the Parties: The Transformation of the American Party System Since the New Deal.* New York: Oxford University Press, 1993.

Steven J. Rosenstone, Roy L. Behr, and Edward H. Lazarus, *Third Parties in America: Citizen Response to Major Party Failure,* 2d ed., rev. and expanded. Princeton, N.J.: Princeton University Press, 1996.

Martin Wattenberg, *The Decline of American Political Parties 1952–1984.* Cambridge: Harvard University Press, 1986.

Darrell M. West and Burdette Loomis, *The Sound of Money: How Political Interests Get What They Want.* New York: W. W. Norton, 1999.

7

THE MASS MEDIA AND
THE PRESIDENCY

Shortly after being sworn in as president in 1993, Bill Clinton began to deliver on some of the promises that he made to voters during the presidential election campaign. Congress, controlled by the Democrats, quickly enacted a number of his campaign pledges early in the legislative session, including his budget, the Family and Medical Leave Act, and Motor Voter legislation. Clinton also used his executive order power to implement several other campaign pledges. He lifted the "gag rule" that prohibited abortion counseling at federally funded clinics, eliminated the prohibition on funding of medical research that used fetuses from elective abortions, and reversed U.S. policy that barred aid to international organizations that promoted abortions.[1]

Moving forward so quickly and decisively on many of his campaign pledges, however controversial, should have resulted in Clinton establishing an image of an active president accomplishing much of what he set out to do. However, the early image of the Clinton administration was that of a floundering administration, besieged by opponents and beleaguered by policy and political fiascos. Rather than concentrate on Clinton's early accomplishments, the news media focused on the administration's early problems, controversies, and missteps.

Two news stories that highlighted Clinton's troubles received abundant media attention and helped create his poor image—the issue of allowing gays to serve in the military and the difficulty Clinton was having staffing top-level administrative posts. These crowded his positive accomplishments off of the pages of newspapers and broadcasts of the evening news. At least in terms of public relations, Clinton's presidency was not getting off to a good start.

In the modern era, the news media have become important to presidential leadership and the president's ability to govern. Through news media reports, the image of a president is established. A positive image may enable presidential leadership, while a poor image may frustrate presidents in their desire to provide policy and political leadership for the nation. Consequently, presidents go to great lengths to try to ensure a positive image. One study goes so far as to argue that in the modern era, image has become so important to the presidency that policy is used to serve a president's image needs, rather than presidents using image to help secure policy.[2]

---

[1] See Barbara Sinclair, "The President as Legislative Leader," in *The Clinton Legacy,* ed. Colin Campbell and Bert A. Rockman (Chatham, N.J.: Chatham House, 1999), pp. 89–90.

[2] Richard W. Waterman, Robert Wright, and Gilbert St. Clair, *The Image-Is-Everything Presidency: Dilemmas in American Leadership* (Boulder, Colo.: Westview Press, 1999).

This emphasis on image management catapults the news media into the forefront of presidential concerns. Without positive news coverage, a president's image is bound to suffer, and the news media, especially television, provide perhaps the most important channel of communication to the mass public. Presidents need the news media to reach the mass public and to govern; consequently, relations with the news media are important to presidents as they try to ensure that they are covered in a favorable light. As we will see, this is not an easy task, despite the fact that a large proportion of the people working for the president in the White House are there to help in the task of securing favorable media coverage. In this chapter, we will discuss the interactions between the president and the mass media.

THE PRESIDENT–NEWS MEDIA RELATIONSHIP

The president and the news media are intertwined in a complex relationship. At times, they appear quite cooperative. This is especially the case where their interests converge. But just as likely, their relationship may turn conflictual and antagonistic when their interests diverge, as they do at times.[3]

We can characterize the presidential–news media relationship as one of exchanges or trades.[4] An **exchange relationship** exists when two parties each need something that the other party possesses. Each party will enter into an exchange or trade as long as the benefits from the exchange exceed the costs. The cost is what each party gives up to the other to obtain what it wants. Thus, as the costs of the exchange exceed the benefits, the exchange relationship may terminate.

The problem for the president and the news media is that they cannot permanently terminate their exchange relationship: each possesses something that the other wants but cannot get without entering into an exchange with the other. Thus, as the costs of their relationship go up or the benefits decline, the president and the news media may seek advantages over the other in their exchange relationship to tilt the balance of benefits and costs in their direction. However,

---

[3]That presidential–media relations are not always adversarial, see Robert Locander, "The Adversarial Relationship: A New Look at an Old Idea," *Presidential Studies Quarterly* 9 (Summer 1979): 266–74; David L. Paletz and Robert M. Entman, "Presidents, Power, and the Press," *Presidential Studies Quarterly* 10 (Summer 1980): 416–26; and Elmer E. Cornwell, Jr., "The President and the Press: Phases in the Relationship," *Annals of the American Academy* 427 (September 1976): 53–64. However, journalist David Broder contends that the relationship between the president and the media is naturally and mostly adversarial. See David Broder, "The Presidency and the Press," in *The Future of the American Presidency,* ed. Charles W. Dunn (Morristown, N.J.: General Learning Press, 1975), pp. 255–67.

[4]On the relationship between journalists and government officials in general, see Leon V. Sigal, *Reporters and Officials: The Organization and Politics of Newsmaking.* (Lexington, Mass.: D. C. Heath, 1973). The specific relationship between the president and the news media is developed in Michael Baruch Grossman and Francis E. Rourke, "The Media and the Presidency: An Exchange Analysis," *Political Science Quarterly* 91 (Fall 1976): 455–70; Michael Baruch Grossman and Martha Joynt Kumar, "The White House and the News Media: The Phases of Their Relationship," *Political Science Quarterly* 94 (Spring 1979): 37–53; and Michael Baruch Grossman and Martha Joynt Kumar, *Portraying the President: The White House and the News Media* (Baltimore: Johns Hopkins University Press, 1981).

when such advantages cannot be acquired or when they have been acquired but the result is a lopsided relationship such that one party is severely disadvantaged, their exchange relationship may break down, and interactions between the president and the news media may diminish. But as their long-term interests require that they reestablish a relationship, neither can do without the other for long.

Presidential–News Media Exchanges

Presidents cannot command the news media to cover them the way that they would like because the news media are formally independent, privately owned organizations and are protected from formal government control by the Bill of Rights. But both the president and the news media value what the other party can do for them. The president wants to be favorably covered in news reports about him and sometimes wants to convey a substantive message, for example, about a policy or issue. The news media view the president as someone whom the public wants to know about; hence, the public will buy media that report on the president. In other words, the news media need the president to sell their product to consumers. Thus, both the president and the media need each other.

The news media, however, do not always write stories the way the president wants them written. Nor does the president always offer the news media the access and kind of material that make for good news copy. This creates a layer of complexity to their relationship. Sometimes the president or the news media will try to gain bargaining advantages over the other. The president seeks advantages that would ensure that the media write positive stories about him. The media seek advantages so that they can produce stories that they think will be of interest to their audiences. As long as each views the other as necessary but less than satisfying, each may seek advantages over the other in their exchange relationship.

But sometimes the exchange relationship between the president and the news media may break down. This tends to occur when either the president or the news media or both view their relationship as unsatisfying and counterproductive. In such circumstances, presidents may seek access to the mass public without having to rely on the news media, especially the media located in Washington, D.C. And the news media may try to cultivate news sources other than the president and the White House, so that they will not be totally dependent on the president and his White House publicity offices for news.

But over the long haul, neither the president nor the news media seem to be able to do without the other. Broken relationships have to be rebuilt and some cooperation reestablished. Thus, we cannot simply characterize the relationship between the president and the news media as cooperative or conflictual. It can vary from cooperative to competitive to antagonistic, depending on a host of factors, from the president's news management style, to news reporting routines, story emphases, and styles, to available technologies, to the times. The relationship between the president and the news media is complex and multifaceted, can easily change, and is ever evolving due to the host of factors that affect it.

PRESIDENTIAL NEEDS FOR THE NEWS MEDIA

Presidents have several uses for the news media besides just good coverage. One, they learn about what is going on in the world through the media. For instance, they may get a sense of what is of concern to the public, what their political opponents and allies are up to, and what is happening in other countries that may have consequence for the United States. Media communications channels may often be faster in reporting information to the president than the chains of command in the federal bureaucracy and the presidential staff. And the president, fearing that reports from the federal bureaucracy or his staff may be self-serving and not highly objective, may use news media stories as an alternate source of information to check the validity of those reports.

Two, the news media help the president convey his messages and actions to other political leaders and decision makers, such as members of Congress and bureaucratic officials. With a far-flung bureaucracy, the president is able, through the news media, to communicate to the members of his administration, both White House staff and career bureaucracy, what his priorities are, what policy actions he is taking or will take, and what their role will be.

Three, the news media help the president communicate to the mass public. In the modern age, presidents cannot govern effectively without public support. To get that support, presidents need to be able to inform the public about what they are doing. The news media, especially television, are the primary source of information and news for most people. Thus, on just an informational level, the president needs the news media to report on his activities. But the president also needs favorable reporting to mobilize the public behind his efforts. One of the more difficult tasks modern presidents have had is ensuring favorable reporting. As news reporting has become less favorable, presidents often have sought other ways to communicate to the public.

Four, the news media also keep the president in full view of the public, often at the expense of other political elites who are also trying to acquire public attention. The more the president is in the news, the less his opponents and competitors are because there is only so much time on a news broadcast or space in a newspaper. Such an imbalance of news coverage makes the president appear the dominant figure in American politics, an image that presidents want to maintain because it eases the tasks of cultivating public support. But such an emphasis on the president also raises the costs of negative reporting and can present other dangers as well, such as attracting blame.

Thus, in communicating through the news media, the president has several objectives. Considering the many and important uses of news coverage to the president, ensuring that what the president deems as appropriate news coverage is one of the important tasks of the modern presidency.

NEWS MEDIA NEEDS

The president is the most visible and important political personality to the mass public. As a consequence, people in the news media feel that they need to cover the president to secure newspaper readers and broadcast audiences. But the president may not always receive the type of coverage that he desires. At least four factors may affect news media coverage of the president: 1) the profit-making nature of news organizations, 2) the professional norms of journalists, 3) the structure of news organizations, in particular the division between editors and reporters, and 4) the career needs of individual journalists.[5]

Profit-Making Organizations

First and foremost, whether we are talking of newspapers, news magazines, radio, or television, the news media in the United States are overwhelmingly profit-making enterprises.[6] Only public radio and television and a few special interest news outlets are not profit-making organizations, but they comprise a small proportion of the news media in the United States. Thus, the first order of business of all news organizations is to make a profit. This profit motivation decidedly colors the decisions of journalists about what they deem is newsworthy and how to present their news stories.

Making a profit requires selling a product to the public. Acquiring these news consumers requires stories that will interest them. In the competition for the consumer's time and money, news is generally disadvantaged compared with entertainment and sports. During prime time, when television audiences are at their peak, entertainment and sports dominate programming. Public interest and news programming is less frequent and when aired tends to attract smaller audiences. Even the weekly television news magazines (60 Minutes, 20/20) are more oriented toward human interest stories and entertainment than hard news.

Adding to the monetary pressures of news organizations is the fact that they are also in competition with each other. Not only must the news media direct consumers away from entertainment to the news, but each news organization also must direct consumers away from competitive news organizations.

To attract audiences, then, news must be interesting. Journalists have used two devices, among many, to attract audiences to the news—focus on the president and present news items as drama. The president is inherently of interest to most Americans. In a sense, the modern president shares much of the *celebrity* of movie stars and sports figures but on a grander stage. The news media use curiosity about celebrities to attract audiences.

For many in the public, the president is also the only figure of politics. In a world that may be threatening, people will often turn to the president for reassurance and guidance. This attribute adds to the public's interest about the president.

Furthermore, the unitary nature of the presidency lends itself to the dramatic codes of news reporting more easily than the other institutions of government,

[5]Herbert Gans, *Deciding What's News* (New York: Pantheon Books, 1979), and Michael Schudson, *Discovering the News*. (New York: Basic Books, 1978).

[6]A good review of the impact of business needs on the news media is found in Bartholomew H. Sparrow, *Uncertain Guardians: The News Media as a Political Institution* (Baltimore: Johns Hopkins University Press, 1999), esp. pp. 73–104.

such as Congress. By covering the presidency, the world of politics can be simplified to a single actor, a type of story that is less taxing for a relatively disinterested and underinformed public than one that covers the complications of politics and policy making in our separation of powers system. Moreover, journalists believe that the public may identify or react more easily to a person, such as a president, than to an institution, such as Congress. This focus on the person of the president is used, then, as a vehicle to bring people into the world of politics and get them to consume news.

But dramatic stories contain other elements, as well. Among the most important of such elements is conflict, with protagonists confronting antagonists. Consequently, the president is often portrayed in the context of political conflict, being confronted by opponents. A common device for a news story is to interview a member of Congress, an opposition party spokesperson, or a major interest group representative who has something critical to say about the president's proposal or action.

The profit-making dictate of news organizations also steers them to sensationalism in news reporting. Sensationalist stories are those that focus on scandal and corruption, interpersonal conflicts, and the like. Rather than being informative, they often appeal to our baser instincts.

Although very apparent in the modern news media, sensationalism was also notable during the last third of the nineteenth century. Two varieties of sensational stories were common then, **yellow journalism** and **muckraking.** Yellow journalism's roots were found in newspapers that tried to attract large mass audiences, especially among immigrants, whose command of English was often limited. Such papers were often led by strong editors and publishers, for example, William Randolph Hearst and Joseph Pulitzer. Their newspapers experimented with features, pictures, color printing, comics, and human interest stories. In fact, the "yellow" in yellow journalism derives from those newspapers printing comics in color. However, the core of yellow journalism is rooted in the strong editorial stands and crusades that these papers would take, often on page one.

Muckraking is much the same as what we now call investigative journalism, but it often was presented with a strong point of view, in contrast to today's somewhat more balanced, objective style of reporting. The excesses and power of big business were typical topics of muckraking stories, as was governmental corruption, and while more subdued than its yellow journalism contemporary, muckraking was also used to attract readers. Thus, sensationalism has a long history in the American news media.

In more recent years, sensationalism in news reporting has ratcheted up a notch with what are now recognized as **media feeding frenzies.**[7] The core style of a feeding frenzy is attack journalism, where stories are reported that are quite critical of their subjects, accompanied by intense news media attention. News

[7]Larry J. Sabato, *Feeding Frenzy: How Attack Journalism Has Transformed Politics* (New York: Free Press, 1991), and Paul J. Maurer, "Media Feeding Frenzies: Press Behavior During Two Clinton Scandals," *Presidential Studies Quarterly* 29 (March 1999): 65–79.

organizations expend massive resources to cover such a story as they compete with other news organizations to get the next item in the story out before the competition. As a consequence, some time-honored journalistic practices, such as relying on multiple sources in an effort to confirm all information, are dispensed with. Instead, the rush to print or broadcast first dominates decision making.

Professionalism

The press in the United States was highly partisan through the late nineteenth century, but as the century neared its end, sensationalism became more apparent in news stories because of the growing commercialism of the press. In response to these two reporting styles, partisanship and sensationalism, **professionalism,** with its emphasis on objectivity in news reporting, began to develop late in the nineteenth century.

Another related impetus for professionalism in the news was the Progressive movement, which emphasized greater public involvement in political affairs. This required a well-informed public. A press that fed the public with objective information about the world of politics could help in that regard. Such a professional press would also see its status and social power increase as it aligned with the forces of progressivism and helped to reform society and political institutions.

Professional norms affect the news-gathering enterprise by instructing journalists about the nature of newsworthiness and how a story is to be constructed. Obviously, the new and the novel, the "man bites dog" story is newsworthy. But in the world of hard news, importance may be a more fundamental criterion.

What makes a story important? First, a story about something that affects many people is more likely to be important than one about something that affects fewer people. Second, matters that strongly and profoundly affect people's lives are more likely to receive news coverage. And the combination of widespread and profound impacts is nearly irresistible to journalists. Thus, stories about war and peace, major economic events and trends, natural disasters and major accidents (such as airplane crashes) will find their way into the news. As government is involved in many important events, government and its chief player, the president, will become a focus of many newsworthy stories.

Moreover, the president himself may be newsworthy because of his position as head of government in the most powerful nation in the world. What presidents decide to do, what policies to address or ignore, and how to address them may affect many people and touch their lives in important ways. The position of the president in the governmental system ensures that many of the things that presidents do are important, and thus, perhaps more than any other policy maker, the president and his actions will be covered by the news media. The news media will cover the president because he helps define the news for professionally oriented journalists. But professional norms will also affect how a story on the president, or any story for that matter, is presented or constructed.

Objectivity is perhaps the most important standard by which stories are constructed. Rather than reporters interposing their judgments and interpretations into the news, as the partisan and sensational press was wont to do, professional norms of objectivity dictated that reporters present the facts, which readers would then interpret for themselves.

The facts in politics are not often obvious or self-explanatory. People may have different opinions about how the facts should be interpreted, and journalists may not feel that they can judge among these differing interpretations. Thus, instead of filtering what is important to the news consumer, professional reporters tend to present multiple sides in political stories. By presenting the opinions and statements of politicians and others on opposite sides, journalists may remove themselves from direct engagement in the controversy, thereby securing their role as objective presenters of the news.

Thus, objectively presented stories present debaters and their debates. For the president, this is consequential. Rather than reporting only what the president is doing and deciding, news stories may also present others who comment, usually negatively or critically, about the president's decisions and policies. *Balanced news* is less than wholly positive to presidents. Presidents prefer that all news about them be uncritical, feeling that criticism undermines their ability to govern and to rally public support behind their policies and initiatives. As we will see, this has been a constant source of tension between the president and the news media.

But also notice that objective, balanced reporting is consistent with the commercial needs of the media to present interesting, dramatic, and sensationalistic stories to the news-consuming public. Journalists may defend their reporting decisions, even when being sensationalistic, by suggesting that they are being objective. Objective professionalism becomes a strong defense against charges by presidents and others about how they are treated in the media.

The Structure of News Organizations

News organizations are also complex. Different people who are in a position to affect how the news is reported may hold different ideas about any news story. Among the most important of such divisions is that between news editors and reporters.[8]

Editors and news management, such as publishers, often hold different journalistic and political views from those of reporters. First, the perspectives and jobs of editors and reporters may lead them to have different ideas about what stories to print or broadcast. The editorial perspective encompasses the entire range of potential news items. Editors must prioritize among all potential news stories, deciding which ones will be lead stories, which ones will not be run, and how much time or space each story will receive. Complicating the editorial decision is that there is finite space or time for news stories. Newspapers have budgets that limit how many pages can be printed, and television is constrained by broadcast time.

In contrast, reporters have a narrower focus than editors, one that emphasizes the importance of the story that they have written and the beat that they cover. Each reporter sees his or her story as the most important. Moreover, the reporter's

---

[8]On the complex structure of news organizations, see Sparrow, *Uncertain Guardians,* pp. 105–37.

career depends on getting into print or on the air. Thus, for personal reasons, reporters become advocates of their own stories. Although editors must juggle the
competitive demands of journalists and their stories within the confines of finite
room for them, each reporter advocates his or her story above all others.

Editors, thus, determine in the end what is printed or broadcast and have employment and assignment power over reporters, but they cannot easily dictate to
reporters. First, editors need talented and resourceful journalists to fill their news
holes. Second, news organizations compete with each other for the most well-
known, prominent, and talented reporters, using their reporters at times to attract
readers and viewers. In this sense, some reporters become stars or celebrities, bringing readers and viewers with them. The celebrity status of some journalists, the need
that editors have for news stories, and the threat that a star reporter might go elsewhere mitigate the power of editors over reporters. Consequently, editors and reporters often enter into bargains and negotiations over what will be reported.

Aside from different institutional and career perspectives, editors and reporters
also seem to hold different political views. Generally, editors and others near the
top of news management (such as publishers and owners) tend to be Republican,
while rank-and-file reporters are more likely to be Democrats.[9] While partisan attitudes do not seem to overly color news stories and do not appear to be able to
override news judgments that are rooted in professional norms, partisanship may
marginally affect how journalists see a story and how to play that story. For example, a Republican editor may want to hit hard a presidential policy initiative,
where a Democratic reporter may prefer a softer touch. The compromise between
them is likely to be the *balanced* story. Again, the negotiation between editor and
reporter may reinforce the commercial and professional imperatives to produce
dramatic, conflict-laden, but objectively balanced stories.

The Career Needs of Journalists

A fourth consideration is the competition among journalists, who have an individual interest in furthering their careers. Competition leads journalists to be first
with the story, to get exclusives, and to be the most sensational. However, competition also ensures that for each story reported, there will be a winner and losers, the winner being the journalist who got the story first. Over time, however,
all journalists will be losers; they can win only a small fraction of the time, given
the number of reporters. Thus, reporters would like to decrease the likelihood of
being a loser, so that they can further their careers. This means creating structures
that will help overcome the natural tendency of reporters to compete with each
other and it means enforcing rules that inhibit reportorial competition.

This is most likely to happen on **beats** that are covered by more than one journalist. Beats are subjects that reporters are assigned to on an ongoing and con-

[9]Robert S. Lichter, Stanley Rothman, and Linda S. Lichter, *The Media Elite: America's New Power-
brokers* (Bethesda, Md.: Adler & Adler, 1986), and G. Cleveland Wilhoit and David H. Weaver, *The
American Journalist in the 1990s* (Mahwah, N.J.: Lawrence Erlbaum, 1996).

sistent basis. For instance, in localities, there is the crime beat, covered by reporters who often hang out at police headquarters and precincts stations. In modern times, the White House has become a beat; the same reporters collect there
each day to cover the president. Beats are most likely to center around official
governmental institutions that routinely produce news, such as the White House
and the Pentagon.

In such situations, journalists will develop mechanisms to ensure that all on the
beat have access to the news story so none of them gets the story first or exclusively. Journalists may informally share with each other, but more likely they will
create a mechanism through which the press secretary distributes news items to all
at the same time. If a press secretary violates that process, representatives of the
beat reporters, acting on behalf of the beat reporters, will issue a complaint and try
to rectify the situation so that it does not happen again. The White House press
corps acts as the official representative of those whose job is to cover the president.
It is easy to see why beat reporters like news conferences, and as we will see, the
creation of the news conference partly came about through pressure from reporters.

Still, journalists understand that the timely scoop can further a career, and they
will seek out the exclusive interview, the leak, and whatever else may give them
an edge on their competition. The contract among reporters to squelch competition may break down in at least two circumstances.

First, journalists at the top and bottom of the reporter hierarchy may not play
by the rules of the beat reporters. Celebrity journalists have access to government
officials and powerful people, access often denied the rank-and-file reporter.
Their status as celebrity and opinion maker opens these doors for them, and this
combination of celebrity and access makes them powerful players in the political
world. Consequently, they are sometimes able to negotiate with news makers, like
the president, for the exclusive interview or leak.

Journalists at the bottom of the hierarchy, especially those who are independents and who work for smaller and nontraditional news outlets, may also attempt
to secure the exclusive and the leak. For many, acquiring the news story first will
help them build a career. Acquiring a scoop demonstrates their resourcefulness and
separates them from the pack or mass of reporters. Another motivation may be ideological, with the journalist viewing him or herself as a critic of people in power.

Second, when journalists on the beat do not feel that they are being fed enough
material to run good stories and thus may be feeling pressure from their editors,
they may violate the pact among themselves to put a lid on their competitive behaviors. Presidents, thus, may have a considerable impact on reporters' behavior.
By feeding the press corps usable material, they can quiet journalistic competitive
drives. And it may be in the president's interest to do that. When journalistic competition rears its head, presidents can expect an increase in leaks and in news reports critical of the president. Franklin Roosevelt seemed to understand this point
and fed his White House press corps a tidbit very frequently. Consequently, he
and the press that covered him daily were on generally good terms.[10]

[10]Betty Houchen Winfield, *FDR and the News Media* (Urbana: University of Illinois Press, 1990).

THE EVOLUTION OF PRESIDENTIAL–NEWS MEDIA RELATIONS

Presidents and the news media have always had some type of relationship, but the nature of that relationship has changed over time with political changes in the presidency and the wider political system, in mass communication technology, and in the economy of news production.[11] We can roughly divide presidential–news media relationships into five periods: 1) the partisan period of roughly the late 1700s to the early post–Civil War era; 2) the detached period of the weak presidency, from the end of the Civil War until about the turn of the century; 3) the rebuilding period, from the turn of the century until Franklin Roosevelt came to office; 4) the institutionalized era, spanning the presidencies from FDR through Eisenhower; and 5) the electronic era, which dates from the presidency of John Kennedy to the present. The rise of new media, such as cable television, talk radio, and the Internet, may mean we are entering into a new, sixth era of presidential–news media relations. Table 7-1 lists the eras and their major characteristics.

The Partisan Era

The Constitution laid the basic framework for presidential–media relations by providing for a free press. Such freedom insulates the press from direct control by the president. Thus, censorship is prohibited and news editors decide on the quantity and quality of the coverage afforded the president and government overall. Rather than being able to dictate their preferences, government officials must

TABLE 7-1   MAJOR ERAS OF PRESIDENTIAL-NEWS MEDIA RELATIONS AND THE CHARACTERISTICS

Period	Characteristic
1. Partisan era (1789–1865)	Partisan press, subsidies from political patrons and parties to newspapers and printers
2. Weak presidency era (1865–1900)	Weak presidency, little news coverage of president, beginning of commercial press
3. Rebuilding era (1900–1932)	Increased coverage of president, expanding political role of president, experimentation in forms of interaction
4. Institutionalized era (1932–1960)	Frequent interactions, organized relations, reliance on news conferences
5. Electronic era (1961–now)	Multiple channels of presidential communications to the public, rise of television, assertive Washington press
6. New media era? (Now?)	Splintered presidential audience, uncertainty

[11]An overview of presidential use of newspapers across the nineteenth century can be found in Mel Laracey, "The Presidential Newspaper: The Forgotten Way of Going Public," in *Speaking to the People: The Rhetorical Presidency in Historical Perspective,* ed. Richard J. Ellis. (Amherst: University of Massachusetts Press, 1998), pp. 66–86.

negotiate their relationship with a formally independent, albeit politically interested, press. A free press also ensured that no one politician or clique of politicians could gain ultimate power. Their competitors would have access to a free press, something that incumbents in control of government agencies could not choke off.

Early in U.S. history, political leaders saw the value of the press and exploited what it had to offer for their personal, political, and policy needs. As we learned in Chapter 2, Hamilton, Madison, and Jay published their *Federalists Papers* in the press to publicize and rally public support in their campaign for ratification of the Constitution. Their Antifederalist opponents did the same.

As early as the Washington administration, politicians of competing beliefs and policies took their viewpoints to the public in the press.[12] More important, politicians learned to divert needed resources to friendly press outlets, while keeping such resources away from unfriendly, opposition press outlets. During the first several decades of the Republic, the major device used in this strategy was the issuance of contracts to publishers to print government documents. Such printing assignments provided the bulk of revenues of publishers, as paper was expensive and production costs high, while the literate reading population was modest in size. These subsidies kept many establishments alive. In repayment for these contracts, publishers had to be friendly to their governmental patrons. Criticism was thus constrained, and access to the press was freely given to friendly politicians.

With the development of mass-based parties and more well-established party organizations in the 1820s, the parties themselves began to subsidize press outlets, such as newspapers. Even as government printing contracts dried up, being taken over by government itself through the Government Printing Office, these partisan presses were assured of sufficient revenue from their partisan benefactors.

Thus, until the Civil War, the press had a decidedly partisan flavor, often denoted in the names of newspapers, such as the *Democrat* or *Republican*. Objectivity was rarely found in news reports; partisan positions and "propaganda" were closer to the norm. Consequently, while politicians could not control the entire news media, the press mirrored the competition between the parties, and politicians dominated the outlets that they funded, ensuring control over content at least in these organs. During the partisan press era, presidents could usually depend on receiving some friendly coverage from their own party's press and some unfriendly coverage from the opposition party's press. This system provided some predictability for presidents.

[12]Carol Sue Humphrey, *The Press of the Young Republic, 1785–1833* (Westport, Conn.: Greenwood Press, 1996); Culver H. Smith, *The Press, Politics and Patronage: The American Government's Use of Newspapers* (Athens: University of Georgia Press, 1977); John Tebbel and Sarah Miles Watts, *The Press and the Presidency* (New York: Oxford University Press, 1985); William David Sloan, "The Early Party Press: The Newspapers in American Politics, 1789–1812," *Journalism History* 9, no. 1 (1982): 18–24; Walt Brown, *John Adams and the American Press: Politics and Journalism at the Birth of the Republic.* (Jefferson, N.C.: McFarland & Co, 1995).

From the Civil War to the Turn of the Century

During most of the nineteenth century, little interaction occurred between the president and the press and consequently little coverage. One study that counted the number of stories about the president and the Congress in a nineteenth-century newspaper found that the bulk of coverage concentrated on Congress.[13] The only exception to this emphasis occurred in presidential election years, where news about the president took center stage. In contrast, coverage of midterm Congress elections was slight. Rather, when reporting on Congress in the nineteenth century, the focus of attention was policy making. About the only time that presidents were connected to policy in nineteenth-century press reports was in conjunction with issue positions that they took in their election campaigns. Capturing the presidency was an important affair in the nineteenth-century, as it is today, but presidents were less likely to be viewed as important policy makers, unlike today. Thus, presidents were not covered much in the news.

The dependency of the press on political patrons gave way in the second half of the nineteenth century because of changes in both the press and the government. A new relationship based on bargaining and exchange began to develop during the late 1800s.

The rise of the commercial press and the diminishing of the presidency in the decades after the Civil War decreased press attention to the presidency and shifted focus to Congress, the government institution that was thought to be more important.[14] Andrew Johnson's impeachment and the rampant corruption scandals of the Grant administration diminished the presidency in the eyes of the public. The president became a less important actor in politics, while strong party leaders in Congress assumed the more prominent governing role. Thus, Congress in the late nineteenth century was where the action—and consequently, press coverage—was.

At the same time, other forces—technological, social, and economic—were stimulating the press's transformation from partisan to commercial.[15] First, technological innovations, especially with regard to the cheap manufacture of paper, drove down the costs of production and hence the price of newspapers. Profits could now be made by selling a **one-penny newspaper,** which was in economic reach of almost everyone. But large mass circulations were necessary to collect the revenues needed to run the newspapers. At the same time, greater circulation made newspapers attractive to advertisers, who became another source of newspaper revenue.

---

[13]Samuel Kernell and Gary C. Jacobson, "Congress and the Presidency as News in the Nineteenth Century," *Journal of Politics* 49 (November 1987): 1016–35.

[14]Mark Wahlgren Summers, *The Press Gang: Newspapers and Politics, 1865–1878* (Chapel Hill: University of North Carolina Press, 1994), and Harry J. Maihafer, *The General and the Journalists: Ulysses S. Grant, Horace Greeley, and Charles Dana* (Washington, D.C.: Brassey's, 1998).

[15]Jeffrey Rutenbeck, "Newspaper Trends in the 1870s: Proliferation, Popularization, and Political Independence," *Journalism Quarterly* 72 (Summer 1995): 361–75.

To reach a mass audience required publication of material that the mass readership desired. As a consequence, not only were features such as comics added to the newspapers, but the style of reporting became less overtly partisan. Still, most papers remained affiliated or aligned with either the Democrats or Republicans, though not economically beholden, as was the case before the Civil War. In the wake of that war, two sometimes conflicting styles of news reporting emerged—professional, objective reporting and sensationalism, which included muckraking and yellow journalism.

The Civil War had a great impact on the press. It stimulated professionalism but also increased the commercial prospects of newspapers. Interest in the Civil War was high because of the massive mobilization of men into the armed forces on both sides and the extreme rate of casualties. People were concerned because of what might happen to loved ones who were serving in the two armies. To feed this interest, journalists reported in a relatively straightforward manner what was happening, where armies had fought, and who was killed or injured. The telegraph was also used to transmit stories from the battle front to the editorial and publishing offices in a timely manner. Norms that we now recognize as professionalism in news reporting, such as objectivity and speed, got their start in the Civil War.

The war also served the commercial interests of news organizations. Large numbers of papers could be sold if the news was of interest to readers. Some of the sensationalism of the post–Civil War era can be traced in part to newspapers' efforts to recapture the attention of the public that existed during the war. Moreover, the prospects of large mass circulation papers drove innovations to cut the costs of news production.

Rebuilding Interest in the Presidency

By the end of the century, presidents and journalists took some tentative steps to reestablish press coverage of the presidency. Several factors encouraged presidential courting of the press, with presidential–press interaction increasing as the twentieth century neared.[16] The Progressive movement, with its emphasis on executive-centered government and well-informed public opinion, motivated presidents at the end of the nineteenth century to begin to expand the power of the office.[17] Some of the first stirrings of the modern presidency can be located during this period. Too, the increasing role of government, especially regulation, enhanced the prominence of the president in the political system and thus his newsworthiness. Changes in news gathering, especially the beginning of professionalism among journalists who covered the White House, also helped the trends

[16]General historical treatments of the development of presidential press relations can be found in Elmer C. Cornwell, Jr., *Presidential Leadership of Public Opinion* (Bloomington: Indiana University Press, 1965); James E. Pollard, *The Presidents and the Press* (New York: MacMillan, 1947); and Richard L. Rubin, *Press, Party, and Presidency* (New York: Norton, 1981).

[17]George Juergens, *News from the White House: The Presidential–Press Relationship in the Progressive Era*. Chicago: University of Chicago Press.

of greater interaction between the press and the president and greater news coverage of the presidency. Thus, by the early 1900s, presidents began to acquire a growing share of news coverage, at the expense of coverage of Congress. As the century progressed, the president would dominate news coverage, relegating Congress to a minor and supporting role.[18]

Grover Cleveland was one president bent on asserting himself vis-à-vis Congress, unlike many of his predecessors, but he did little to stimulate press coverage. First, Cleveland was a Democrat, and most of the press was partial to the Republicans. Consequently, Cleveland could not be assured of favorable coverage. Further, Cleveland may have fathered a child out of wedlock before becoming president, a child he financially supported. This became common knowledge, and Republicans used it as a campaign weapon against Cleveland. News coverage of the scandal led him to dislike the press. Still, aware of the growing importance of public opinion to the presidency at the close of the century, Cleveland did install tables in the White House for journalists to use.[19]

It was Cleveland's Republican successors, William McKinley and Theodore Roosevelt, who took the first major steps in establishing press coverage of the presidency.[20] Both encouraged press coverage to stimulate public opinion and create an image of presidential leadership, but both, as well as all subsequent presidents, were concerned to ensure that press reports were faithful to presidential intentions. McKinley expanded the working area for reporters and met personally with some. He also lobbied reporters by inviting them to social functions at the White House and attended their functions, such as the Gridiron Club dinners.

The Spanish–American War, which occurred while McKinley was president, required greater efforts by the administration to control press coverage.[21] To stem leaks, the White House made McKinley's statements available to the press shortly after they were prepared but before he publicly issued them. To ensure that his messages reached the entire nation, McKinley supplied the wire services and newspaper syndicates with statements before making them available to individual newspapers. Procedures to ensure that these advance copies of presidential statements would not be leaked were also instituted. This suggests that McKinley wanted to control the news flow, while at the same time trying to make it easier for journalists to report on the presidency.

McKinley also instituted the practice of following cabinet meetings with press briefings, again to stem leaks and rumors by his secretaries. When the president traveled outside of Washington, a small entourage of reporters accompanied him,

[18]Elmer E. Cornwell, Jr., "Presidential News: The Expanding Public Image," *Journalism Quarterly* 36 (1959):275–83.

[19]Martha Joynt Kumar, "The White House Beat at the Century Mark," *Harvard International Journal of Press/Politics* 2 (Summer 1997): 10–30.

[20]Stephen Ponder, *Managing the Press: Origins of the Media Presidency, 1897–1933* (New York: St. Martin's Press, 1998).

[21]Robert C. Hilderbrand, *Power and the People: Executive Management of Public Opinion in Foreign Affairs, 1897–1921* (Chapel Hill: University of North Carolina Press, 1981).

providing him with even more coverage. The administration even supplied a stenographer on these trips to record McKinley's brief comments so that they could be reported.

Theodore Roosevelt was even more attuned to the press than McKinley, being more personally available to them for comments and questions. Roosevelt even encouraged the press to cover him as a personality and made his active family available to the press, as well. Whereas McKinley's main driving force in increasing and centralizing news coverage revolved around the Spanish–American War, Roosevelt had a more expansive view of presidential leadership that extended to all matters of policy in which the president was engaged. Thus, he used the presidency as a "bully pulpit" to activate and lead public opinion. Press coverage was an important element of that view.

The presidents between the two Roosevelts were not as adept at press relations, but all begrudgingly recognized the importance of good press to presidential governance. Uncomfortable with the press, Taft withdrew from them and was roundly criticized for doing so. Criticism of presidential detachment indicated a growing demand in the body politic for such leadership by the early 1900s.

Presidential–press relations got a major boost from the Wilson administration. The Progressive presidents, such as McKinley and Roosevelt, believed that a well-informed public was important for policy making and thus reached out to the public through the press. Woodrow Wilson went a further step in establishing a political theory of presidential leadership that focused on public opinion as an important source of presidential power. Uplifting the presidency was necessary to overcome Congress, which Wilson thought was more attuned to servicing the local political needs of its members than the national interest. Only the president, the sole nationally elected official, had incentives to meet the national interest, according to Wilson. But the president needed support to overcome the institutional and interest group power located in and associated with Congress. Here was a role for public opinion. Thus, Wilson laid the intellectual foundations for the modern presidency to come some twenty years later with Franklin Roosevelt.

To implement his ideas, Wilson needed to increase the presidential presence before the public and to control how the public viewed that presence. Thus, the quantity of news coverage had to be increased and the content of that coverage controlled. Increased coverage came about with the creation of the presidential news conference.[22] Control of content came about through centralization of news coverage. Table 7-2 presents the frequency of press conferences across the twentieth century.

[22]Blaire Atherton French, *The Presidential Press Conference: Its History and Role in the American Political System* (Washington, D.C.: University Press of America, 1982); Elmer C. Cornwell, Jr., "The Press Conferences of Woodrow Wilson," *Journalism Quarterly* 39 (Summer 1962): 292–300; Jarol B. Mannheim, "Presidential Leadership of Public Opinion: Does the Tail Wag the Dog?", paper presented at the American Political Science Association, 1979; Jarol B. Mannheim, "The Honeymoon's Over: The News Conference and the Development of Presidential Style," *Journal of Politics* 41 (February 1979): 55–74; and William W. Lammers, "Presidential Press Conference Schedules: Who Hides and When?" *Political Science Quarterly* 96 (Summer 1979): 261–78.

TABLE 7-2   PRESIDENTIAL PRESS CONFERENCES FROM COOLIDGE TO CLINTON

President	Total number of press conferences	Yearly average	Monthly average
Coolidge	407	81	6.8
Hoover	268	67	5.6
Roosevelt I	280	70	5.8
Roosevelt II	332	83	6.9
Roosevelt III	256	64	5.3
Truman I	142	36	3.0
Truman II	160	40	3.3
Eisenhower I	99	25	2.1
Eisenhower II	94	24	2.0
Kennedy	65	22	1.9
Johnson	132	26	2.1
Nixon I	30	8	.6
Nixon II	9	5	.5
Ford	41	19	1.4
Carter	59	15	1.2
Reagan I	23	6	.5
Reagan II	19	5	.4
Bush	131	30	2.7
Clinton I	118	30	2.5

Source: Lyn Ragsdale, *Vital Statistics on the Presidency: Washington to Clinton* (Washington, D.C.: Congressional Quarterly Press, 1998), pp. 170–71.

From March 1913 through July 1915, Wilson gave twice-weekly news conferences to reporters. Although finding the news conference useful in garnering news coverage, Wilson disliked the exchanges with reporters and discontinued them. The White House press group reacted strongly to their cessation. Realizing the journalists' need, Wilson assigned his secretary Joseph P. Tumulty to act as spokesperson in his place. Tumulty would hold informal meetings each day at 10 A.M., answering questions, informing the press about Wilson's activities, and providing them with handouts. While not officially designated as the president's press secretary,[23] Tumulty's activities established the pattern for later, formally recognized presidential press secretaries.

The onset of the First World War gave Wilson the excuse that he needed to centralize news operations in the White House and control its content. Part of Wilson's motivation was to prevent cabinet secretaries and others in government from making public statements that might undercut his policies or upstage him in

[23]See Samuel Kernell, *Going Public,* 3rd ed. (Washington, D.C.: Congressional Quarterly, 1997), pp. 76–79.

the public. He justified his actions with his wartime emergency powers and other war powers that Congress delegated to him.

His major news control arm was the **Committee on Public Information (CPI),** which he established through an executive order in 1917.[24] The CPI engaged in extensive publicity campaigns to rally public support for the war, but more controversially, it censored news about the war. It even had a Censorship Board to coordinate suppression of news. Government announcements emanating from any agency had to pass through the CPI before being released to the public. To further control the content of news, the CPI published a news sheet, the *Official Bulletin,* which contained presidential statements and announcements. The bulletin was distributed to news organizations and others through the nation; the press complained that it had become a governmentally sanctioned and financed newspaper. Not unexpectedly, the CPI proved very unpopular, and one of the Congress's first actions after the war was to dismantle the agency. Still, the CPI was the first attempt by an administration to organize its news-related activities and set a model, however extreme, for future administrations.

By the end of Wilson's term, the press had also transformed. This transformation gave the president an avenue to reach the public, but it also increased press resources in dealing with the president. As the press became a more equal partner in its transactions with the president, conflict between the two, who naturally possessed divergent incentives, became a frequent, if not constant, part of their interactions.

The presidency contributed to the transformation of the press. By Wilson's time, the White House had become a beat that offered regular news for journalists covering it. As a result, the White House beat attracted more professionalized and ambitious journalists. These journalists even conspired with the White House to restrict access to their beat. The White House initially asked for such restrictions to regulate the advance notifications of presidential speeches, thereby preventing leaks before the president officially made the announcement.

White House journalists also had an interest in restricting entry to the White House beat because of the prestige that now came with covering the presidency. Fewer reporters increased the prestige value of the White House beat, allowing the White House press corps to act as a journalistic gatekeeper of news about the president. From these roots, the organization of reporters covering the White House began; that organization eventually would limit presidential manipulation of journalists and become a resource that journalists tried to use to force the president to be more responsive to their needs. These developments were still decades away, however.

Wilson's Republican successors, Harding, Coolidge, and Hoover, continued his basic policies by offering relatively frequent press conferences, work space in the White House, advance copies of speeches, and the like.[25] Harding experimented with "photo opportunities" and Coolidge with radio, but in the main, the 1920s and early 1930s was a period of continuity from precedents

[24]Ponder, *Managing the Press,* pp. 91–107, and Hilderbrand, *Power and the People.*

[25]Louis Liebovich, *Bylines in Despair: Herbert Hoover, the Great Depression, and the U.S. News Media* (Westport, Conn.: Praeger, 1994).

established under Wilson, without the extreme efforts at centralizing news in the White House and controlling its content.

The first third of the twentieth century saw the establishment of president–press relations, the routinization of those relations, the accumulation of resources by both the president and journalists covering the president, and the intellectual rationale for a relationship between the president, the press, and the mass public. Despite advantages that presidents held in their relationship with the press during this era, presidents were still dependent on journalist mediation of their message to the public. Presidents throughout this period were more successful in increasing news coverage than controlling the content of that coverage.

The Institutionalization of the Press Conference System: FDR to Eisenhower

With the presidency of Franklin Roosevelt, the relationship between the president and the press that had been developing for the past thirty years became fully realized and institutionalized.[26] By FDR's time, it had become apparent to presidents that they needed good press coverage if they were to lead effectively. Such coverage was even more important to a president like Roosevelt, one who possessed an ambitious policy agenda to deal with the necessities of the Great Depression. Through press coverage, Roosevelt hoped to rally support for his policy efforts. Press coverage not only allowed Roosevelt to communicate his policies but also increased the presidency's power in the political system, making it the focal point of Washington-based news. Other politicians were pushed off the pages of the newspapers because of the dominating presence of the president. Consequently, the locus of political power in Washington shifted from Congress to the White House.

To gain favorable coverage, Franklin Roosevelt needed to offer the Washington press corps something that they could report and that would satisfy their growing professional needs. This turned out to be "hard news, openly conveyed." [27] The presidential press conference was to be the forum through which newsworthy items were to be disseminated to the press.

Both presidential needs and the growing professionalism of the press pushed for press conferences, which presidents before FDR had used, but not so systematically or exclusively. The news-gathering business is inherently competitive. Newspapers and other news outlets try to increase sales by offering exclusive stories and news scoops, and by being first to report on important events. Presidents could play on this natural competitiveness among reporters by feeding stories to favored reporters. The difficulty this situation creates for reporters is that any one reporter is likely to be left out, with the consequence that his or her career will suffer. Also, the favored reporter may lose his or her status if the story is not re-

[26]On FDR's relations with the press, see Richard W. Steele, *Propaganda in an Open Society: The Roosevelt Administration and the Media, 1933–41.* (Westport, Conn.: Greenwood Press, 1985); Gary Dean Best, *The Critical Press and the New Deal: The Press and Presidential Power, 1933–1938* (Westport, Conn.: Praeger, 1993); and Betty Houchen Winfield, *FDR and the News Media* (Urbana: University of Illinois Press, 1990).

[27]This is Samuel Kernell's term. See Samuel Kernell, *Going Public: New Strategies of Presidential Leadership* (Washington, D.C.: Congressional Quarterly Press, 1986), p. 63.

ported as the president wants. Thus, presidents can gain a measure of control by playing reporters off against each other.

To guard against this tendency, reporters banded together, creating professional norms of behavior. They also sought a news-gathering system that would limit the president's ability to manipulate individual members of the press corps. The solution that they arrived at was the presidential press conference. Through the press conference, each working member of the press would receive the news at the same time. Thus, no reporter had a competitive edge over any other reporter.

For this system to satisfactorily serve both the president's and the reporters' interests, the president would have to give the press something to report, a newsworthy story. The several presidents who preceded FDR were not always so compliant. Coolidge, for instance, would answer only questions that were presented to him before the press conference. He refused to address many questions. Hoover, Harding, and Wilson were similarly evasive.

FDR understood the press's needs and used the biweekly press conference to feed the reporters something that they could write about. He also dropped the requirement for written questions. Instead, he categorized news from the press conferences into four sets: "(1) occasional direct quotations permitted only through written authorization from the White House; (2) press conference comments attributed to the president 'without direct quotation'; (3) background stories to be used in stories without a reference to the White House; and (4) 'off the record' remarks not to be repeated to absent reporters." FDR designated Stephen Early as press secretary, the first person so formally titled, to administer the press conferences and authorize the direct quotations.[28]

As a consequence, the press conference became the primary method that FDR relied on in dealing with the press. Members of the press who covered FDR were pleased because they had access to frequent stories of value. Their status also rose as the presidency became a more important center of the political system. In effect, FDR drove a wedge between reporters and their editors and news managers, who tended to be steadfastly Republican, by serving needs of reporters so well. The tone of the stories that they wrote, as a result, were more favorable to the president than one would expect, given the Republican and conservative tendency of news editors and publishers.

In the main, the press conference system of FDR remained in effect until John Kennedy assumed the presidency in 1961. Although Truman and Eisenhower did not enjoy the same degree of cordiality in their relations with the press that FDR had, the institutionalized press conference was the centerpiece for conducting business between the president and the press.[29]

---

[28]Ibid., pp. 63–64.

[29]On Truman and the media, see Franklin D. Mitchell, *Harry S. Truman and the News Media: Contentious Relations, Belated Respect* (Columbia: University of Missouri Press, 1998), and Herbert Lee Williams, *The Newspaperman's President: Harry S. Truman* (Chicago: Nelson-Hall, 1984). One study contends that Truman's personality made relations with journalists difficult. In particular, Truman boiled at press criticism and at times would shout down journalists in face-to-face meetings. See Louis William Liebovich, "Failed White House Relations in the Early Months of the Truman Administration," *Presidential Studies Quarterly* 19 (Summer 1989): 583–91.

The Electronic Media Presidency

Relations between the president and the press fundamentally altered with the presidency of John Kennedy. While Kennedy's personality clearly has something to do with this transformation, the development of the electronic media is perhaps more important in understanding why and how the presidential–press relationship transformed. Basically, under this system of presidential–press relations, the press conference declined as a vehicle for the dissemination of presidential news, replaced primarily by direct appeals by the president to the public. Furthermore, as presidents bypassed the Washington press, relations between the president and the Washington press corps shifted from cooperation, notable in the FDR system, to competition.[30]

Kennedy's major innovation was the live televised broadcast of his press conferences. He was not the first to realize the potential significance of the electronic mass media for the presidency. Coolidge experimented with radio, and FDR used radio for his famous fireside chats. However, compared to modern use of the electronic media, FDR's use of radio was restrained. Despite their memorableness, he delivered only thirty fireside chats in his twelve years as president.[31] Moreover, FDR tended to use the fireside chats to build public support and confidence in himself more than to rally the public behind his policy initiatives. Truman and Eisenhower also made tentative and modest steps to incorporate the electronic media into their dealings with the press. Truman allowed radio to broadcast excerpts of his news conferences, and Eisenhower admitted television crews to press conferences in 1955.[32]

But Kennedy's live telecast decision had broad implications for the relationship between the president and the press and presidential news management. First, it put everything that the president said on the public record. Gone were the days when presidents, like FDR, could use a press conference to feed news to the press but not have it directly attributed to him.

The live telecast also made the press conference a public spectacle, where presidential and journalist performance rose in importance as news content declined. Journalists had an incentive to ask questions. In so doing, they would become celebrities themselves, which would distinguish them from the rest of the pack of journalists. As a result, the collective interests of journalists to cooperate in the gathering of news eroded, while competition among them reemerged. Print journalists also began to lose out to journalists from the electronic media. By the time their stories appeared in their newspapers, usually the next morning, the news was already old, having been broadcast the previous evening. Understandably, print journalists became disgruntled with the new press conference system.

[30]Kenneth T. Walsh, *Feeding the Beast: The White House Versus the Press* (New York: Random House, 1996).

[31]John Tebbel and Sarah Miles Watts, *The Press and the Presidency: From George Washington to Ronald Reagan* (New York: Oxford University Press, 1985), p. 478.

[32]Kernell, *Going Public,* p. 68.

Kennedy further eroded the value of the press conference as a hard news source by decreasing its frequency, which was done to maintain public interest in the press conference. Too frequent press conferences would lessen their public appeal and impact. Kennedy exacerbated the competition among journalists when he decided to grant private interviews to select journalists. This and the effort to cultivate relations with the local as well as the Washington-based press were instituted in an attempt to control the content of news.

Being cut off from hard news and being somewhat cut out of the presidential news system, the Washington-based press, especially the White House Press corps, became increasingly antagonistic to the president. Questions at news conferences became more challenging, as did news reporting from these Washington-based sources. The cooperation that had characterized the FDR press conference system had transformed into antagonism between the president and the press in the electronic media system.[33]

CONTROLLING THE NEWS IN THE ELECTRONIC MEDIA ERA

In the electronic media era, the major drive of presidents is to control the content of news coverage, and the importance of the president in the political system compels news media coverage. Several studies have tried to estimate how much of the "news hole" the modern president occupies. One study calculated that 20 percent of stories on the network nightly news is about the president, and National Public Radio gives about 10 percent of its coverage to the president.[34] In the periodical press, the weekly news magazines such as *Time* and *Newsweek* show increases in coverage of the president over the twentieth century.[35] Presidents are now copiously covered in the news media.[36] To help control this voluminous news content,

---

[33]Ibid. One study argues that personal factors of presidents determine their media strategies, in opposition to the more standard view that the relationship has developed in patterned ways over the years, especially with the advent of electronic communications. See Robert Locander, "Modern Presidential In-Office Communications: The National, Direct, Local, and Latent Strategies," *Presidential Studies Quarterly* 13 (Spring 1983): 242–54. There is also a large number of studies of the press relations of individual presidents since Kennedy. See Joseph C. Spear, *Presidents and the Press: The Nixon Legacy* (Cambridge, Mass.: MIT Press, 1984); Mark J. Rozell, *The Press and the Ford Presidency* (Ann Arbor: University of Michigan Press, 1992); Mark J. Rozell, *The Press and the Carter Presidency* (Boulder, Colo.: Westview Press, 1989); Mark Hertsgaard, *On Bended Knee: The Press and the Reagan Presidency*, rev. ed. (New York: Schocken Books, 1989); Mark J. Rozell, *The Press and the Bush Presidency* (Westport, Conn.: Praeger, 1996). More general treatments include Grossman and Kumar, *Portraying the President;* and Louis Liebovich, *The Press and the Modern Presidency: Myths and Mindsets from Kennedy to Clinton* (Westport, Conn : Praeger, 1998).

[34]Fred Smoller, "The Six O'Clock Presidency: Patterns of Network News Coverage of the President," *Presidential Studies Quarterly* 16 (Winter 1986): 31–49; on NPR, see Mary S. Larson, "Presidential News Coverage and 'All Things Considered': National Public Radio and News Bias," *Presidential Studies Quarterly* 19 (Summer 1989): 347–53.

[35]John Orman, "Covering the American Presidency: Valence Reporting in the Periodical Press, 1900–1982," *Presidential Studies Quarterly* 14 (Summer 1984): 381–90. These data are updated to 1992 in John Orman, "Images of the Presidency in the Periodical Press," *Presidential Studies Quarterly* 25 (Fall 1995): 683–95.

[36]Other studies that report on either the frequency or the growth of news media coverage of the presidency include Elmer C. Cornwell, Jr, "Presidential News: The Expanding Public Image," *Journalism Quarterly* 36 (Summer 1959): 275–83; Todd Shields and Robert K. Goidel, "The President and Congress as Sources in Television News Coverage of the National Debt," *Polity* 18 (Spring 1996): 401–10.

presidents build a large staff to help in presidential "publicity" efforts. Presidents also have sought out devices and ways to circumvent the increasingly assertive, and often hostile, Washington-based press.

The Presidential Public Relations Machine

Two major staff offices in the White House help the president in his relations with the news media—the **White House Press Office** and the **Office of Communications.**[37]

Press Secretary   The major functions of the White House Press Office and the **press secretary** are to 1) serve the needs of the White House press corps, that specialized group of reporters and journalists whose beat is the White House; 2) create and manage the flow of news from the White House; and 3) disseminate the news daily and field queries from reporters.[38]

Press secretaries are in a difficult position. On the one hand, they are spokespeople for the president. On the other hand, they are viewed by journalists as their source and gateway into the inner workings of the White House. To be believed by the news media, the press secretary must be credible but also thought of as friendly to the press and understanding of press needs. However, becoming too closely associated with the news media may undermine the press secretary in the eyes of the president. Thus, the press secretary has the difficult task of balancing the needs of both the press and the president in order to be effective.[39]

Office of Communications   Where the press secretary's position dates back officially to the administration of Franklin Roosevelt, the Office of Communications did not become a formal body until 1969, when Richard Nixon created it with an executive order. But as with the press secretary's office, Office of Communications' activities were around long before its creation. The development of the "going public"-style of political communications of Kennedy, plus the problems of relations with the news media that Lyndon Johnson experienced, led Nixon to create the Office of Communications.

Across its history, the Office of Communications has been periodically reorganized by presidents to meet their own needs, but the need for such an office and its basic functions have remained constant. The major functions of the Office of Communications include 1) coordinate the flow of news from the entire exec-

[37]On the presidential press secretary, see W. Dale Nelson, *Who Speaks for the President? The White House Press Secretary from Cleveland to Clinton* (Syracuse: Syracuse University Press, 1998), and Colin Seymour-Ure, "Presidential Power, Press Secretaries and Communication," *Political Studies* 28, no. 2 (1981): 253–70. The White House Office of Communications is covered in John Anthony Maltese, *Spin Control: The White House Office of Communications and the Management of Presidential News,* 2d ed. (Chapel Hill: University of North Carolina Press, 1994).

[38]On these functions, see Maltese, *Spin Control,* p. 5, and Grossman and Kumar, *Portraying the President.*

[39]Michael J. Towle, "On Behalf of the President: Four Factors Affecting the Success of the Presidential Press Secretary," *Presidential Studies Quarterly* 27 (Spring 1997): 297–319.

utive branch, 2) target local, non-Washington-based media outlets, and 3) develop a long-term news management plan for the administration.[40]

As for local, non-Washington news media, the Office of Communications sends out mailings, briefs local journalists on the presidential activities and other newsworthy events and items, and schedules presidential trips and appearances with these news outlets. In general, the Office of Communications maintains contact with the non-Washington-based news media, which presidents tend to feel will be less hostile than the White House press corps and other Washington-based journalists.

The Office of Communications also tries to control the flow of news of the departments and agencies of the executive branch and the activities of these units' public information officers (PIOs) and press secretaries. At times, regular meetings are held between Office of Communications personnel and the PIOs, fact sheets about presidential activities are circulated to the departments, and departmental personnel are enlisted to serve as presidential spokespersons, often being provided with speeches to deliver. Also, most public statements by departmental personnel have to be cleared by the Office of Communication before being issued. This clearance process in effect controls the access of the news media to the departments, as well as departmental access to the news media.[41]

The Office of Communications and the Press Office serve as the two principal organizations within the White House that are specifically charged with presidential public relations duties. Generally, the two have been kept separate, and since the Carter administration the Office of Communications has also held higher status in the White House structure than the Press Office.[42] Yet, other White House personnel may be enlisted for public relations activity, and it may not be too far a stretch to contend that the major activity of most White House personnel is geared toward presidential public relations.[43]

Presidential Channels of Communication

In the electronic age, presidents have numerous channels of communication to the public.[44] We can characterize those channels as being more or less subject to presidential control.[45] Obviously, presidents prefer those channels over which they have greater control, which should increase the likelihood that presidents will get their message out as they intend. But the importance of the other, less controlled

---

[40]Maltese, *Spin Control,* pp. 5–6.

[41]Ibid., pp. 110–13, 118–19.

[42]Ibid., pp. 240–41.

[43]On this point, see Grossman and Kumar, *Portraying the President.*

[44]William W. Lammers, "Presidential Attention-Focusing Activities," in *The President and the Public,* ed. Doris Graber (Philadelphia: Institute for the Study of Human Affairs, 1982), pp. 145–71.

[45]Fred T. Smoller, *The Six O'Clock Presidency: A Theory of Presidential Press Relations in the Age of Television* (New York: Praeger, 1990).

channels, such as network television, means that presidents cannot avoid their use. Major presidential addresses, presidential Saturday radio addresses, meetings with local news media, photo opportunities, leaks, and exclusive interviews tend to be the most easily controlled channels of communication. Evening news broadcasts and newspaper stories of the major press tend to be least under presidential control. Press conferences and press secretary briefings are somewhere in the middle. Over the years, presidents have developed the channels of communication more under their control but have also tried to control or influence news content of the other, less controllable channels of communication.

More Controllable Channels of Communication

Major Speeches   In the modern media era, major presidential addresses tend to be defined as those that are presented during prime-time hours and broadcast by the major networks. Some of these are expected or required speeches, such as inaugural and State of the Union addresses. They are usually preceded by efforts on the part of the White House to drum up interest in the pending speech, highlighting its importance. As a consequence, public anticipation and interest in such speeches are higher than for more routine speeches.

Major presidential addresses to the nation present the president with several distinct advantages over other forms of communication. First, presidents completely control the content. Unlike during press conferences, questions may not be asked of the president. Second, these speeches tend to attract the largest audiences for the president. Third, they help focus attention on the president, especially in his role as president and leader of the nation.

Still, there are limitations to this type of communication. First, presidents cannot use major speeches too frequently. Doing so undercuts their interest value for the public. From Coolidge through the Clinton presidency, presidents gave only 4.5 major speeches on average per year. If we subtract the nondiscretionary ones, such as inaugural and State of the Union addresses, the average drops to 3.6.[46]

Second, three developments may limit their impact as presidential leadership devices. The first of these developments is the use of opposition party speeches, aired by the networks, that follow the presidential one. Such rebuttal speeches may undercut the ability of the president to get his message across uncontested. Research suggests that these rebuttal speeches may undermine presidential leadership of public opinion. Even the instant analyses of presidential speeches by news commentators, which are also quite common after major presidential speeches, seem to weaken the effect of the presidential speech on public opinion.[47] The second development has been resistance on the part of the networks to grant presidential access to prime time. On several occasions, such presidential requests have

[46]These figures come from Lyn Ragsdale, *Vital Statistics on the Presidency: Washington to Clinton* (Washington, D.C.: Congressional Quarterly Press, 1998), p. 167.

[47]Shanto Iyengar and Donald R. Kinder, *News That Matters: Television and American Opinion* (Chicago: University of Chicago Press, 1987).

been refused. On several others, not all major networks have broadcast the speech. When one or a few networks broadcast the speech, the presidential audience is limited because of competition from other programming.[48] Lastly, the rise of cable television and other media, such as the Internet, seems to be eroding the presidential audience. Comparison of television ratings for major presidential speeches across the past several decades indicates a decline of the percentage of households tuned to the presidential speech from about 50 percent during the Nixon years of the early 1970s to about 30 percent for Clinton.[49]

Courting the Local Press   In part because of some of the limitations of major speeches noted above and in part because of the increasing independence and perceived antagonism of the White House press corps and the Washington press in general, presidents have sought other media channels to communicate with the public. One channel has been through the local and specialized media. Nixon began this practice with more systematic efforts than previous presidents to court and use the local media. He traveled around the nation, meeting with local press and thus avoiding the White House press corps. Ford built on Nixon's model by inviting local media people to the White House. Succeeding presidents have continued and refined these efforts, with the Office of Communications taking the lead in establishing and maintaining ties to local media outlets.[50]

The advantage of the local media for the president is that they tend to be less critical of the president, feeling flattered by presidential attention. They also tend to be less well versed in the ways of Washington politics or the nuance of policy; thus, they tend to accept the presidential lead less critically than the White House press corps. But there is a downside, too. The local media cannot always attract the large audience that the networks can, and the White House press corps may feel neglected if the local news media are used too heavily. The press corps strongly criticized Clinton early in his term for such practices, which they felt neglected them, and the volume and stridency of this criticism surely hurt Clinton's image, as we discussed at the start of this chapter.

Media Events   Over the past few decades, presidents have developed a wide repertoire of staged media events, such as photo opportunities, town hall meetings, talk show appearances, and the like. In the main, these events try to present the president in a ceremonial role, as head of state, and in other symbolic roles. During classic photo opportunities, such as allowing cameras to shoot pictures and film of the president crossing the White House Rose Garden, journalists cannot ask questions of the president; if they do, it is understood that

[48]On this point, see Joe S. Foote, *Television Access and Presidential Power: The Networks, the Presidency, and the "Loyal Opposition"* (New York: Praeger, 1990).

[49]Matthew A. Baum and Samuel Kernell, "Has Cable Ended the Golden Age of Presidential Television?" *American Political Science Review* 93 (March 1999): 99–114, figures from p. 100.

[50]Robert Locander, "Carter and the Press: The First Two Years," *Presidential Studies Quarterly* 10 (Winter 1980): 106–20.

he will not answer. Because Ronald Reagan had a habit of answering reporters' queries, to the consternation of his media handlers, a band would play music or the president's helicopter would begin spinning its rotors in an attempt to make enough noise so that Reagan could not hear the question.

The main problem with staged events is that we have become so accustomed to them; we all know they are staged events and, thus, a subtle public cynicism exists about their use. Still, ceremonial activities, especially in events of high drama, such as Reagan's speech for mourners after the *Challenger* space shuttle accident or Clinton's after the Oklahoma City bombing, can put a president in good light with the public. These ceremonial appearances, however, have a meaning because of the event that inspired them, unlike the staged event.

Radio Broadcasts   Presidents have experimented with radio as a form of communication since its development and dissemination. FDR made the most effective use of radio in its early years, and after the advent of television in the 1950s, presidential use of radio declined. But Ronald Reagan reinstituted radio with his Saturday afternoon radio address, a practice that both Bushes and Clinton followed.

Despite the fact that in the age of television, radio audiences are meager, presidents find the Saturday radio speech useful. First, there is often little news on the weekend. The radio speech allows the president to be a news maker in an otherwise slow news period. Also, the president's speech may set the agenda for the Sunday morning television talk shows. Again, while these Sunday morning shows attract small audiences, the audiences are often composed of relatively well-informed people, Washington political types, and other opinion leaders. Still, in recent years, the opposition has been granted air time to respond to the president. The impact of these responses is less well understood than the rebuttals that attend major presidential speeches. More important probably than the president winning the policy argument with these radio speeches is the fact that they keep the president in the news during the weekend, and they help set the terms of public debate, which limits the opportunity for others to capture the public and political agenda.

Less Controllable Channels of Communications

Network Nightly News   Perhaps the most important channel of communication for the president is the network nightly news. These broadcasts are the major source of most people's news in the modern era, which makes them indispensable to the president. The most important reporters here are those in the White House press corps who work for the major networks, but the cynical attitude of this group to presidents has been persistent presidential thorn since the days of Lyndon Johnson. And presidents may have cause to worry about the way they are portrayed in the nightly news. One study shows, for example, that presidential approval poll levels decline when the news turns in a negative direction.[51] Not surprisingly, presidents complain about their treatment in the nightly news.[52]

However, bad news may be justified, because, for instance, the president is doing a poor job of leading the nation or the nation and government may have many difficult problems to deal with. Just because the news about the president is bad does not mean that the news media are biased against the president, that they are out to get him.

Many studies have tried to assess just how negative the news about the president is.[53] Doing so is a daunting task, as it requires collecting a huge number of news stories, reading them, and finally judging each story's tone, that is, whether the president is being portrayed in a negative or positive light. In general, these studies present evidence that presidential news may not be as negative as presidents assert, but over time, especially since the late 1960s, the tone of presidential news has turned more negative. Still, neutral stories are far more common than either positive or negative stories.[54]

How do we know, though, if this trend of increasingly negative presidential news reflects reality—that is, a trend of bad events and conditions—or the biases of the news media? As we mentioned earlier, some bad news about the president is rooted in reality. When the administration issues reports that the economy has slid, which the White House does frequently because of the large number of economic statistics that government collects, it is bad news. But the news media cannot report on every event that one might construe as news. The population of potential news stories is greater than the available news slots. Consequently,

[51]Richard A. Brody, *Assessing the President: The Media, Elite Opinion, and Public Support* (Stanford, Calif.: Stanford University Press, 1991). In general, the public seems more receptive to presidential leadership when the president is popular. Also see Benjamin Page, Robert Shapiro, and Glenn R. Dempsey, "What Moves Public Opinion," *American Political Science Review* 81 (September 1987): 815–31; Lee Sigelman and Alan Rosenblatt, "Methodological Considerations in the Analysis of Presidential Persuasion," in *Political Persuasion and Attitude Change*, ed. Diana C. Mutz, Paul M. Sniderman, and Richard A. Brody (Ann Arbor: University of Michigan Press, 1996), pp. 171–92; and John Zaller, "A Model of Communication Effects at the Outbreak of the Gulf War," in *Do the Media Govern? Politicians, Voters, and Reporters in America*, ed. Shanto Iyengar and Richard Reeves (Thousand Oaks, Calif.: Sage, 1997), pp. 296–313.

[52]Harvey G. Zeidenstein, "White House Perceptions of News Media Bias," *Presidential Studies Quarterly* 13 (Summer 1983): 345–56.

[53]For instance, see F. M. Fedler, M. Meerske, and J. Hall, "*Time* Magazine Revisited: Presidential Stereotypes Persist," *Journalism Quarterly* 56 (Summer 1979): 353–59; Roderick P. Hart, Deborah Smith-Howell, and John Llewellyn, "Evolution of Presidential News Coverage," *Political Communication and Persuasion* 7, no. 1 (1990): 213–30; Roderick P. Hart, Patrick Jerome, and Karen McComb, "Rhetorical Features of Newscasts About the President," *Critical Studies in Mass Communications* 1, (no. 1 (1984): 260–86; Roderick P. Hart, Deborah Smith-Howell, and John Llewellyn, "The Mindscape of the Presidency: *Time* Magazine, 1945–1985," *Journal of Communication* 41 (Summer 1991): 6–25; J. C. Merrill, "How *Time* Stereotypes Three U.S. Presidents," *Journalism Quarterly* 42 (Autumn 1965): 563–70.

[54]Grossman and Kumar, op. cit., pp. 253–72; Brody, *Assessing the President,* pp. 137–39; Smoller, *Six O'Clock Presidency;* Larson, "Presidential News Coverage." For a study of lame-duck presidents in the news, see Karen S. Johnson, "The Portrayal of Lame-Duck Presidents by the National Print Media," *Presidential Studies Quarterly* 16 (Winter 1986): 50–65. Lame-duck presidents tend to receive poor and spotty news coverage, especially if they were unable to gain reelection.

journalists select some to report but not others. If they tend to select bad presidential news in greater proportion than it exists in the population of presidential news stories, we can suggest that the news media are biased against the president.

For instance, we can all agree that when the president's polls are on the rise, it is good news for the president, but it is bad news when his polls are sliding. One study found that the three television networks are more likely to report that the president's polls have dropped than that they have gone up or remained stable.[55] Thus, an antipresidential bias may be said to exist. These results suggest that presidential complaints are not merely unreasonable tirades, but the fact that most news is neutral suggests that perhaps presidents are too strident in their criticisms of the press.

Another related issue that presidents encounter in trying to get their message across to the mass public through the news media is that presidents often want to convey substantive information, but news media coverage tends to be superficial and content tends to be played down, especially on television. Moreover, the length of news stories has been shrinking, and use of clips from presidential speeches have gotten much shorter, while journalist narration has taken up a greater proportion of the news report. For instance, the average **sound bite,** that is, the "block of uninterrupted speech by a candidate on the television news" decreased from forty-two seconds in 1968 to ten seconds by 1988. At the same time, more air time is given to the reporters covering the presidential candidates. In 1988 and 1992, for each one minute showing the candidates speaking, six minutes were given to the journalist reporting the story.[56] Probably the same is true of coverage of the presidency in nonelection campaign periods. In all, these developments and journalistic practices make it increasingly difficult for presidents to convey substantive information to the public through the electronic news media.

Presidents have sought ways to lessen the likelihood of bad news or otherwise blunt its effects. The overall approach crystalized with Ronald Reagan under what has been termed the "**Reagan treatment.**"[57] The Reagan treatment contained several elements. The first was aimed at controlling daily news reporting of the president. This was accomplished by focusing attention on a single story or theme. This approach limited the ability of others to set the political agenda, kept the president in the public eye, and made the administration appear to be united behind the president. The "item of the day" also presented the opportunity for the president to turn attention away from issues and problems that he was not able or willing to address or that had been causing him problems.

The other elements of the Reagan treatment involved physically helping the news media cover the president, offering photo opportunities, limiting impromptu and unscheduled news media access to the president, and maintaining presidential

[55]Tim Groeling and Samuel Kernell, "Is Network News Coverage of the President Biased?" *Journal of Politics* 60 (November 1998): 1063–87.

[56]Thomas Patterson, *Out of Order* (New York: Vintage Press, 1994), pp. 74–75, 160.

[57]See Robert E. DiClerico, "The Role of Media in Heightened Expectations and Diminished Leadership Capacity," in *The Presidency Reconsidered,* ed. Richard W. Waterman (Itasca, Ill.: F. E. Peacock, 1993), pp. 115–43.

restraint when it came to publicly criticizing the news media. The objective of all these elements of the "treatment" was to limit news media opportunity to criticize the president and to provide the news media with a story about the president.[58]

Press Conference   The press conference during the FDR-to-Eisenhower era was the dominant channel of communication that the president employed. After FDR, the press conference became more a more formal and routinized event. Presidents created a formal distance between themselves and reporters, trying to emphasize their stature and position as president. Thus, the idiosyncracies of presidential personality and style become less pronounced at press conferences. In part, this was a function of the expectation that press conferences must be held, the growth in the number of reporters on the White House beat, and presidential attempts to control press behavior.[59]

Journalists tend to view the president as having the upper hand in press conferences.[60] Presidents can determine the timing and do not always provide journalists with much time to prepare. Lyndon Johnson, for instance, often called impromptu press conferences.[61] Presidents also decide which reporters to call on to ask a question; friendly ones may be given preference. And presidents decide when the press conference is over.

Despite these presidential control mechanisms, press conferences have declined in use, in part because of the attractions of other, more easily controlled channels of communications and in part because of the potential risks of press conferences. The major risk of the press conference is that a journalist will ask the president a hard or challenging question or one that the president is not prepared to answer. Either type of question may prove damaging to a president. In the first instance, a hard question may appear to challenge presidential leadership and may suggest opposition to the president and the direction that he wants to take. In the second case, a president who cannot effectively deal with a question, who appears unprepared, may not look like a leader who knows what is going on, thus undermining public confidence in his leadership ability. Because of these two risks, presidents have steered away from press conferences since the advent of television, using channels of communication that they are better able to control and spending more time being briefed and prepared before press conferences.

---

[58]For more detail on the "Reagan treatment," see Hertsgaard, op. cit., who argues that the news media was unduly easy on and uncritical of Reagan. Mark Hertsgaard, *On Bended Knee* (New York: Farrar, Straus, & Giroux, 1988).

[59]Jill McMillan and Sandra Ragan, "The Presidential Press Conference: A Study in Escalating Institutionalization," *Presidential Studies Quarterly* 13 (Spring 1983): 231–41.

[60]On journalists' attitudes toward presidential press conferences, see Delbert McQuire, "Democracy's Confrontation: The Presidential Press Conference II," *Journalism Quarterly* 45 (Spring 1968): 31–41. For a more general overview of media perceptions, see Harvey G. Zeidenstein, "News Media Perceptions of White House News Management," *Presidential Studies Quarterly* 14 (Summer 1984): 391–98.

[61]David L. Paletz and Robert M. Entman, "Presidents, Power, and the Press," *Presidential Studies Quarterly* 10 (Summer 1980): 416–26

ASSESSING PRESIDENTIAL COMMUNICATIONS IN THE ELECTRONIC AGE

Who has the upper hand, the president or the news media? The answer to this question has several components. We have addressed one element, the fact that news may be biased against the president, with the caution that the modal type of news coverage of the president is neither positive nor negative but neutral. A more complete answer would also look at the resources and advantages that the president and the news media bring to their relationship, as well as who is more important in affecting the other's agenda. In other words, does the president respond to the news media, or does the news media respond to the president in terms of what is reported in the news?

Relative Advantages of the President and the News Media

Several studies contend that despite the resources that the news media possess, the president is inherently advantaged over the news media.[62] One study contends that presidents are advantaged because they "benefit from prevailing news definitions and practices; the large staff of media manipulators they call on; presidents and their staffs grant, limit, and deny access to reporters; their exploitation of secrecy; their control over the timing of information releases; and their ability to dominate press conferences."[63]

Presidents control access. This is especially the case in granting interviews. As we have argued, presidents will extend access to the media when it is in their interest to do so. One study of the Ford administration found that the president's electoral need outstripped all other reasons in his decision to grant interviews. Thus, the rate of acceptance of interview requests went up during the primary and general election season. And during the primary season, media that represented localities in which primaries were held were more likely to receive interviews than those not so positioned, and those interviews tended to be held within a month before the primary. Otherwise, Ford granted only a minority of requests for interviews, which tended to go mostly to the major media.[64]

Presidents sometimes try to reduce or alter media coverage of an event or activity by using a group of techniques that affect the availability of information. One technique withholds information altogether, sometimes by placing it under national security classifications, citing executive privilege, or simply keeping quiet.

[62]Robert E. Gilbert, "Television and Presidential Power," *Journal of Social, Political, and Economic Studies* 6, no. 1 (1981): 75–93; Grossman and Rourke, "The Media and the Presidency"; Grossman and Kumar, *Portraying the President;* C. Don Livingston, "The Televised Presidency," *Presidential Studies Quarterly* 16 (Winter 1986): 22–30.

[63]Paletz and Entman, "Presidents, Power."

[64]Matthew R. Kerbel, "Against the Odds: Media Access in the Administration of President Gerald Ford," *Presidential Studies Quarterly* 16 (Winter 1986): 76–91. Kerbel also found that during Ford's short term of office, there were 1,647 media interview requests; only 42 percent were granted, but 64 percent were granted during the primary season. Primary-season requests also accounted for nearly one-half of all requests. In comparison, outside of the primary season, only about 22 percent of requests were granted.

The White House may also speed up or delay the release of information to reduce its impact, sometimes waiting for another event or distraction to occur, with the hopes that the other event will divert attention. Another technique employs vague wording, technical jargon, and other devices to make the information difficult for journalists and others to understand. Similarly, a released report may be voluminous in the hopes that it will not be read carefully in its entirety or even at all.

Other devices may be used to modify the meaning of the information being released. For instance, the basis of comparison may be changed (such as from raw to inflation-adjusted dollars), assumptions may be revised (such as changing projections of future growth rates), or definitions may be modified (such as what constitutes social programs).[65] In recent years, the shrinking budgets of network news divisions have reduced their ability to gather much information on their own, as well as independently analyze it, a development that probably has strengthened presidential leverage in this area.

Despite these advantages and resources, however, presidents may not always be able to manage the news. Rozell argues that there are three factors that affect the quality of news coverage of the president: context, the personal skills of the president, and the president's media strategy.[66] Context refers to the times, the public mood and issues of the day, the state of the economy, the party composition of Congress, and the like. Many contextual factors may be out of a president's control. It is important to note that the context may set limits on the president's ability to lead and thus on the kind of news coverage that he is likely to receive. When the context is favorable, a president may be better able to create a favorable image that is reported as such in the media. However, an unfavorable context may lead to critical and unflattering news of the president, despite his efforts to create a positive image.

But Rozell argues further that even given a good context, if a president lacks the personal inclination and media skills, he may squander the opportunity provided him. A media strategy also may be important. Perhaps the most important aspect of a media strategy is to deliver a clear and consistent message from the White House. The way that this is done can be tailored to each president based on his own needs and requirements. Thus, the image of the president that gets conveyed in the news is a function not merely of the resources that presidents possess but also of the times, the president's media skills, and the strategy the president employs.

While the above account is theoretical and abstract, one study presents information on the behavior and decisions of news editors. That study, based on a 1969 survey of newspaper editors, found that editorial practices may be affected when the president criticizes the press. However, more financially secure and independent newspapers seemed less affected by the president.[67]

[65]See George C. Edwards, III, and Stephen Wayne, *Presidential Leadership: Politics and Policy Making,* 5th ed. (Boston: Bedford/St. Martin's, 1999), pp. 126–30.

[66]Mark J. Rozell, "Presidential Image-Makers on the Limits of Spin Control," *Presidential Studies Quarterly* 25 (Winter 1995): 67–90.

[67]Richard Senter, Jr., Larry T. Reynolds, and David Gruenenfelder, "The Presidency and the Print Media: Who Controls the News," *Sociological Quarterly* 27, no. 1 (1986): 91–105.

Presidential–Media Agenda Influences: Who Influences Whom?

Another critical question is whether the president can set the news agenda or whether the news affects the president's agenda. Control over the agenda is important and is often considered among the greatest sources of influence that presidents in the modern age of mass communications possess. Moreover, the theory of the modern presidency is built in part on the assumption that presidents can affect the agenda of others, including Congress, the public, and the mass media. Here, we have begun to amass a large number of studies. They show a complex relationship between the news media and presidential agendas.

The results of these studies find that sometimes the president leads or affects the news media agenda. Other studies find the president following the lead of the news media.[68] What are we to make of these studies? First, presidential ability to affect the news seems to vary by issue type, presidential concern, and public interest. When multiple news sources exist or when the issue has a long history of media and public attention, presidential influence over media agendas drops off. But when presidents have a special interest or their party owns an issue (that is, the issue is strongly associated with a party, like tax cuts are associated with Republicans), the president may greatly affect the news media agenda. Presidential influence on the news media agenda also seems to increase when it is easier for the president to mobilize public attention.[69] The multiplicity of issues and the complexity of the relationships between the president, the news media, and the mass public means that sometimes the president will affect the news media's agenda and sometimes the news media will affect the president's agenda.

[68]The number of relevant studies is large. See Sheldon Gilberg, Chaim Eyal, Maxwell E. McCombs, and David Nicholas, "The State of the Union Address and the Press Agenda," *Journalism Quarterly* 57 (Winter 1980): 584–88; Ronald E. Ostman and William A. Babcock, "Three Major U.S. Newspapers' Content and President Kennedy's Press Conference Statements Regarding Space Exploration and Technology," *Presidential Studies Quarterly* 13 (Winter 1983): 111–20; Tsan-Kuo Chang, "The Impact of Presidential Statements on Press Editorials Regarding U.S. China Policy, 1950–1984," *Communication Research* 16 (August 1989): 486–509; Wayne Wanta, Mary Ann Stephenson, Judy Van Slyke Turk, and Maxwell E. McCombs, "How President's State of Union Talks Influenced News Media Agendas," *Journalism Quarterly* 66 (Autumn 1989): 537–41; William J. Gonzenbach, "A Time-Series Analysis of the Drug Issue, 1985–1990: The Press, the President, and Public Opinion," *International Journal of Public Opinion Research* 4, no. 2 (1992): 126–46; Wayne Wanta, "The Influence of the President on the News Media and Public Agendas," *Mass Communication Review* 19, no. 3 (1992): 14–21; Wayne Wanta and Joe Foote, "The President–News Media Relationship: A Time Series Analysis of Agenda-Setting," *Journal of Broadcasting and Electronic Media* 38 (Fall 1994): 437–48; Thomas J. Johnson and Wayne Wanta, with Timothy Boudreau, Janet Blank-Libra, Killian Schaffer, and Sally Turner, "Influence Dealers: A Path Analysis Model of Agenda Building During Richard Nixon's War on Drugs," *Journalism and Mass Communication Quarterly* 73 (Spring 1996): 181–94; B. Dan Wood and Jeffrey S. Peake, "The Dynamics of Foreign Policy Agenda Setting," *American Political Science Review* 92 (March 1998): 173–84. George C. Edwards, III, and B. Dan Wood, "Who Influences Whom? The President, Congress, and the Media," *American Political Science Review* 93 (June 1999): 327–44; David B. Holian, "Follow the Leader? Issue Ownership, the President, and the Press," paper presented at the Midwest Political Science Association, 1999.

[69]However, Wood and Peake, "Dynamics of Foreign Policy," and Edwards and Wood, "Who Influences Whom?" do use television in their studies.

THE NEW MEDIA, THE PRESIDENT, AND THE FUTURE
OF PRESIDENTIAL COMMUNICATIONS

In recent years, the mass media have undergone a major transformation with potential implications for the president and for his ability to get out his message to the public in the way that he wants. Consider the number of new media that have come on line in the past decade or two: cable television, VCRs, fax machines, and the Internet. Moreover, there has been a revolution in use of old technology with the development of talk radio and the proliferation of television talk shows, television news magazines, and electronic town meetings, many aimed at politically interested audiences. There also has been a convergence between entertainment and news and politics, such as the "Rock the Vote" campaigns on MTV, and the rise of tabloids and tabloid-type television shows that often report political news (e.g., *Hard Copy*). Even among the traditional news media, entertainment has affected the style and substance of news reporting.[70]

What are the implications of these new media and the transformation of old technology for the presidency, communications, and the relationship between the president and the news media? On the one hand, these new media represent opportunities for presidents and other politicians to exploit, but they also present their own problems for presidents and other politicians to overcome.

First, and perhaps most obvious, consider the impact of the speed of communication possible with the new media, especially faxes and the Interent. Through these media, people may be mobilized quickly and public pressure brought to bear on political leaders almost instantaneously. Interest groups and others may monitor policy debates and other events in real time, communicate to their constituents and supporters through these new media, and request that they use the same media to contact politicians immediately. Just as presidents may take advantage of this mobilization capacity of the new media to bring public pressure to bear, say, on members of Congress, so too can the president's opponents. Most critical, however, is that the speed of communication and mobilization possible through the new media, especially those media that rely on new technology, may undercut deliberation and debate, shoving the political system to swift resolution rather than reasoned debate. Inasmuch as presidential leadership relies on reiterating the president's message and following through on initiatives,[71] the faster pace of politics may undercut presidential leadership potential.

Second, the new media may have splintered the audience. Just two decades ago, the three major networks held a virtual monopoly of public attention when it came to disseminating the news electronically. Since then, the hold of the major networks on the news audience has dropped precipitously. One report estimates that in 1975, nearly half of all households watched the evening news every

---

[70]On the new media, see Richard Davis and Diana Owen, *New Media and American Politics* (New York: Oxford University Press, 1998).

[71]Jeffrey E. Cohen, "Presidential Rhetoric and the Public Agenda," *American Journal of Political Science* 39 (February 1995): 87–107, argues that presidents, to lead public opinion, must persist in speaking out on a particular issue over an extended period of time.

night. That figure dropped to about one-fourth by 1997. The greatest decline in network audiences occurred in the 1990s, the period of the most rapid expansion and penetration of the new media into American life.[72] Rather than a national, mass audience, as was the case in the era of network television's dominance (roughly 1950 to 1980), the television audience has specialized, as particular tastes are catered to by the multitude of channels on cable, while others seek out other forms of media with which to engage (VCRs, Internet, etc.). This new environment has been characterized as "narrow casting" to distinguish it from "broadcasting" of old.[73]

One implication of this new media environment is the declining audience for major presidential speeches, which we noted in the section on "More Controllable Channels of Communication."[74] Such an environment makes the president's task of leadership of the public writ large more difficult. But this new environment also provides presidents with different leadership opportunities. Presidents may be better able to target specialized audiences, whose members may be more politically interested, at least in the particular policy or question that he is addressing. Thus, in 1992, President Clinton appeared on MTV in an attempt to attract younger voters, and he gathered talk radio hosts for a mass broadcast from the White House during 1993.[75] But just as presidents may use these new media, so too may their competitors and policy opponents, perhaps leveling the playing field between the president and his opponents compared to the days when network broadcasting was king and presidents almost alone had access to the airwaves.

A third aspect of the new media, especially talk radio, is the jettisoning of traditional journalistic conventions, such as objectivity. Radio talk shows tend to be extremely one-sided. While this may help a president when such programs are on the president's side, they may damage him when they oppose the president. Bill Clinton has been a special target of radio talk shows, owing to their conservative tilt,[76] and they even attacked George H. W. Bush on occasion for not being sufficiently conservative.[77]

Lastly, consider the interactivity of the new media, especially talk radio and the Interent. The old media did not have such a capability. Perhaps viewing interactivity as a way to secure public support, the Clinton administration built a web page on the Internet. People may also contact the president via e-mail. Estimates

---

[72]Davis and Owen, *New Media*, p. 136.

[73]Austin Ranney, "Broadcasting, Narrowcasting, and Politics," in *The New American Political System*, 2d ver., ed. Anthony King (Washington, D.C.: American Enterprise Institute Press, 1990), pp. 175–203.

[74]Baum and Kernell, "Has Cable Ended?"

[75]Davis and Owen, *New Media*, p. 242.

[76]Ibid., pp. 234–36.

[77]We need to note, however, that talk radio and many other of the new media are not primarily news but rather entertainment media. Thus, they tend to have different orientations about programming than traditional news outlets. See David and Owen, *New Media*, on this point.

are that by 1996, the White House home page was receiving nine hundred thousand "hits" a month, and by summer 1993, the president was receiving eight hundred e-mail messages a month.[78] But the White House is not alone in its presence on the Internet. Congress maintains a website, and all members have either web pages, e-mail, or both, as do government agencies and interest groups. In fact, the administration job of coordinating communications from the agencies may become much more complicated due to the proliferation and decentralization of web pages.

Interactivity carries with it expectations of responsiveness by those who bother to call a talk show or e-mail the president. Considering the volume of such communications, the task of responding to all is indeed daunting, and cynicism with government may increase if political leaders are not able to respond to messages. Such an environment would surely undermine presidential leadership efforts and the president's ability to connect with the public.

Still, these media are new and the shape they will take in the future is unknown; thus, we can only speculate, as we have, about their potential impact on the president, political leadership, and presidential–news media relationships. What we can say is that these new media are likely to have an impact, for better or worse, and that they represent other channels of communications than the traditional news media for the president to exploit. In that sense, their presence is but part of the trend of presidents to circumvent the Washington-based media in the hopes of controlling their message and securing more positive treatment in the media.

KEY TERMS

Committee on Public
  Information (CPI)   183
exchange relationship   167
journalistic professionalism   172
media feeding frenzies   171
muckraking   171
news beats   174
objective news reporting   172

Office of Communications   188
one-penny newspaper   178
presidential press secretary   188
Reagan treatment   194
sound bite   194
White House Press Office   188
yellow journalism   171

DISCUSSION QUESTIONS

What are the major reasons that the president needs news coverage? Why is the president so important to the news media? How does this mutual need for each other affect the relationship between the president and the news media?

How has the evolution of the news media and the presidency affected the relationship between them? Who seemed to hold the upper hand at different points in history?

[78]David and Owen, *New Media,* pp. 116–17, 125.

How did late nineteenth- and early twentieth-century presidents rekindle news media interest in the presidency? Why was news interest in the presidency so much lower earlier in the nineteenth century? In what ways have modern presidents followed the news attention practices of early twentieth-century presidents? In what ways have they changed the news attention practices of early twentieth-century presidents?

What impact did television have on news media–presidential relationships? How have more recent technological innovations, such as cable television and the Internet, affected presidential–media relationships? What are the implications of these modern forms of mass communication for the presidency?

How able is the president to influence the news about him and his activities? For instance, can he set the news media agenda and ensure that news about him is positive? What are the major devices and techniques that he possesses to influence the news? How effective are they?

Compare the Office of Communications with the White House Press Office. Why are there two such offices in the White House? How and why has their influence waxed and waned over the years?

SUGGESTED READINGS

Michael Baruch Grossman and Martha Joynt Kumar, *Portraying the President: The White House and the News Media*. Baltimore: Johns Hopkins University Press, 1981.

Richard A. Brody, *Assessing the President: The Media, Elite Opinion, and Public Support*. Stanford, Calif.: Stanford University Press, 1991.

Elmer C. Cornwell, Jr., *Presidential Leadership of Public Opinion*. Bloomington: Indiana University Press, 1965.

Richard Davis and Diana Owen, *New Media and American Politics*. New York: Oxford University Press, 1998.

Joe S. Foote, *Television Access and Presidential Power: The Networks, the Presidency, and the "Loyal Opposition."* New York: Praeger, 1990.

John Anthony Maltese, *Spin Control: The White House Office of Communications and the Management of Presidential News,* 2d ed. Chapel Hill: University of North Carolina Press, 1994.

Thomas Patterson, *Out of Order*. New York: Vintage Press, 1994.

Stephen Ponder, *Managing the Press: Origins of the Media Presidency, 1897–1933*. New York: St. Martin's Press, 1994.

Larry J. Sabato, *Feeding Frenzy: How Attack Journalism Has Transformed Politics*. New York: Free Press, 1991.

Bartholomew H. Sparrow, *Uncertain Guardians: The News Media as a Political Institution*. Baltimore: Johns Hopkins University Press, 1999.

John Tebbel and Sarah Miles Watts, *The Press and the Presidency: From George Washington to Ronald Reagan*. New York: Oxford University Press, 1995.

Richard W. Waterman, Robert Wright, and Gilbert St. Clair, *The Image-Is-Everything Presidency: Dilemmas in American Leadership*. Boulder, Colo.: Westview Press, 1999.

8

THE PRESIDENT AND
THE MASS PUBLIC

IMPORTANCE OF THE PRESIDENT TO THE MASS PUBLIC AND OF THE MASS PUBLIC TO THE PRESIDENT

One of the defining characteristics of the modern presidency is the relationship between the president and the mass public. The development of the electronic mass media, especially television, coupled with the president's publicity apparatus in the White House staffing system, has tightened and strengthened that relationship. But even before the modern presidency existed, the president was probably the central figure in the political lives of ordinary people due to the constitutional position and structure of the office. As a consequence, no other politician can claim such a close and intense relationship with the mass public. That is, no other political leader can claim legitimately to be *the public's leader* as the president can. But this ability to claim that he is the sole national spokesperson and representative of the nation also has a high price—the public places high expectations on the president, and other political leaders closely observe how successful the president is in leading the public.

The relationship between the president and the average person has several important aspects. First, most people are likely to focus their political attention on the president. Other political leaders are, as a consequence, slighted by the public. For example, the president is the most visible political actor in people's minds. Nearly the entire adult population can correctly identify the president, but knowledge of other political leaders quickly falls off. Only one-third can name both home-state U.S. senators, and slightly less than half are able to identify their representative.[1] As one study concludes about the public's view of the political world, "[T]he President is . . . the best-known American political leader. For some people he is the only known political leader, and for others one of the few."[2]

Several reasons exist for the primacy of the president in the public's mind. First, the unitary nature of the office makes it easier for people to follow and identify with the president than with a collective body like Congress. In watching the action of the president, the public has to focus only on a single person. Interpreting politics and government from such a viewpoint is easier than trying to make

---

[1]Michael X. Delli Carpini and Scott Keeter, *What Americans Know About Politics and Why It Matters* (New Haven: Yale University Press, 1996), pp. 74–75; and Fred I. Greenstein, "What the President Means to Americans: Presidential 'Choice' Between Elections," in *Choosing the President,* ed. James David Barber. (Englewood Cliffs, N.J : Prentice-Hall, 1974), pp. 121–47.

[2]Greenstein, "What the President Means," p. 124.

sense of the many personalities of Congress, the different positions that they hold (majority versus minority, party leader versus committee chair), and the rule governing the legislature (committee jurisdiction, debate, voting, etc.).

Second, school textbooks on history, government, and civics are often organized around presidents and their accomplishments. Early in life, children come to see the president as the central figure in the political system. Similarly, the media spend more time covering the president than any other leader, presenting another president-centric portrait of American politics and government.

Beyond this informational centrality, the president also offers a psychological center for the ordinary citizen. We see this in the reactions of people to the sudden death or assassination of presidents in office. Upon learning of the assassination of John F. Kennedy, many people reported feeling distressed and suffered from psychosomatic symptoms, such as stress, unease, sleeplessness, and so on. Similar reactions seemed to follow each time a president died in office.[3]

How do we account for such reactions? First, with so many people relying so heavily on the president, his death naturally should lead people to feel uncertain about the future. Who will replace him? What will the new president be like? How will foreign powers, many of which are unfriendly to the United States, react? One of the crucial functions of the president for the average citizen is to provide a sense of security in a hostile and complex political world, to indicate to people that someone is in charge and that critical matters are being taken care of.[4]

The president also serves as the average person's gateway to involvement and participation in the political system. People, for instance, may root for or against the president and therefore psychologically invest themselves in politics. Rather than partisanship or ideology, the structure of the average person's political world is composed of teams of politicians who support and oppose the president. Moreover, people may take a more active role in politics by voicing their approval or disapproval for the way the president is handling his job and by voting for candidates for the office.

The president also serves as a cue about matters political. Normally, most people are little involved and concerned with the political world. The president can change all of that by making a major announcement, preempting prime-time television programming to give a speech about a topic that he considers important. In this way, the president helps to set the public agenda, informing the public when to pay attention to politics and identifying what issues people should be concerned with.

Thus, the president is important to the political world of the average person. He is the central figure in that world, provides a sense of security and leadership, identifies when politics is worth attending to and which issues are important, and supplies a figure around whom the debates of politics and issues are structured. But all of this comes with a price: people's expectations of the president are high and seem to have grown over recent decades.

[3]Ibid., pp. 123–24.

[4]Murray Edelman, "The Politics of Persuasion," in *Choosing the President,* ed. James David Barber (Englewood Cliffs, N.J.: Prentice-Hall, 1974), pp. 149–73.

DEVELOPMENTS IN THE RELATIONSHIP BETWEEN THE PRESIDENT AND THE MASS PUBLIC

The Early Presidency and the Mass Public

As he did in so many regards, George Washington set a standard for the relationship between the president and the mass public. Washington limited the "public" presidency to matters of symbolism, ceremony, and democratic education, and generally refrained from using the office to rouse the public for political and policy reasons. To Washington, the presidency was an important symbol that could help bind the nation together and establish an identity for the new republic. Thus, Washington acted as a symbolic representative of the both the people and the nation, tying both concepts together. He similarly surrounded the office with a public dignity, using ceremonial occasions to create a tie with the public and to establish how future presidents should behave in office. Washington aimed to downgrade the person who occupies the office and tried instead to make the office itself the object of people's attentions. While it was a public presidency, Washington did not intend it to become a personal presidency, as is the case in the twentieth century.

At the same time, Washington was attempting to forge a relationship with the mass public that would shore up the political foundations of the office, asserting its constitutional independence from the other branches, while also securing for it a base of public support. In all of this, Washington was helping to establish and secure the institutional strength of the office as a constitutional branch of government rather than as an office that factions, parties, or the occupant would use for political gain. Thus, just as Washington relied on Alexander Hamilton, his Treasury secretary, to spearhead his policies in Congress, Washington did not use the presidency as a position from which to rally the public behind his political or policy causes. Like many of the founders, who were leery of demagoguery. Washington wanted to establish customs and practices that would protect the office from potential demagogues. Overall, then, Washington was engaging not only in presidential institution building but also in nation building.

With modifications, Washington's model of the public presidency set the standard until the close of the nineteenth century. Still, nineteenth-century presidents, while not eschewing the democratic educative role of the presidency, did imbue it with more of a political and policy cast. John Adams, who was often beleaguered in office, used the press to appeal to public opinion in an attempt to overcome opposition to his policies, especially his foreign policies. Still, little indication exists that Adams publicly spoke out to rally the public behind him.[5] Jefferson, too, sought support, but he used the political parties, especially their membership in Congress, to organize and mobilize that support. Like Washington and Adams, Jefferson did not directly seek public support for his policies.

[5]Karen S. Hoffman, "Public Opinion Before the 20th Century: Measuring the President's Relationship with the Public," paper presented at the annual meeting of the American Political Science Association, 1999.

Probably the first president to seek public support openly and explicitly was Andrew Jackson. He sought public support for his economic policies, especially those associated with the Second National Bank. The economic policies of Jackson and the Democratic Party emphasized the role of the states, instead of the national government, in internal improvement and development. Those policies also favored small farmers and entrepreneurs over monied, elitist, and industrial interests. The Whigs, in contrast, supported greater federal involvement in economic development, spurred on by the Second National Bank, which funneled national development through just those interests that Jackson and the Democrats opposed. Thus, when Nicholas Biddle, head of the bank, sought its rechartering in 1832, Jackson vetoed the bill, raising one of the critical controversies and political battles of his administration. For present purposes, it is noteworthy that in his veto message, Jackson dragged the public into the fray by making his veto a basis for his reelection campaign. He merely asked that if the public opposed his policies, they should not reelect him to office. Unlike modern presidents, he did not stump for public support to pressure Congress to support his policies. But he opened a role for the public, through voting, in policy debates. Congress sustained his veto.[6]

The bank veto episode was a singular event and did not mark the onset of sustained presidential efforts to curry or mobilize public favor. Yet Jackson represents a turning point in the presidency, conceptualizing the presidency for the first time as a policy representative of the people. And while not aiming to replace Congress as a representative institution, he argued that Congress represented special interests and, thus, the presidency should represent the entire nation.[7] Moreover, he expanded the meaning of presidential elections, viewing them as policy mandates, whereas the founders' conception of the election of the president focused on the character of the person elected, not on policies or issues.[8]

Across the nineteenth century, on occasion presidents would follow Jackson's lead and go public on select policies and issues of critical concern to their administrations. However, several factors limited how much presidents would overtly seek public support in the nineteenth century. Modern mass communications and a transportation system capable of delivering people back and forth and messages between politicians and the public in a timely manner did not yet exist. The technology to measure public opinion precisely, the modern poll, did not exist either. Public opinion was narrowly defined in the nineteenth century to either the voting public, which would be activated only during election campaigns, or to those who wrote letters to politicians and newspapers and magazines, surely an unrepresentative slice of the American mass public. These factors, plus the cus-

---

[6]Sidney M. Milkis and Michael Nelson, *The American Presidency: Origins and Development, 1776–1990* (Washington, D.C.: Congressional Quarterly Press, 1990), pp. 121–23.

[7]Patricia Lee Sykes, "President as Legislator: A 'Superepresenator,'" *Presidential Studies Quarterly* 19 (Spring 1989): 301–15.

[8]Richard J. Ellis and Stephen Kirk, "Presidential Mandates in the Nineteenth Century: Conceptual Change and Institutional Development," *Studies in American Political Development* 9 (Spring 1995): 117–86.

tom that presidential candidates would not personally run for office a custom that lasted until the early twentieth century, lent some brakes to the popular foundations of the office in the nineteenth century. While public opinion had a role to play in the nineteenth-century presidency, it was limited compared to its modern role. Public opinion defined as the opinion of the entire adult population did not become a meaningful concept until the twentieth century.

The Rhetorical Presidency

As the nineteenth century drew to a close, the relationship between the president and the mass public began to alter. Presidents began more and more to seek public support for policies that they cared about, and in time, "popular or mass rhetoric . . . [became] a principal tool of presidential governance."[9]

Before the twentieth century, presidents involved themselves in policy making, but they communicated their positions on policy mostly by sending written messages to Congress. The public was not a prime audience of such presidential communications. Also, presidents would rely on the press, which tended to be highly partisan, to express their policy preferences, but generally, surrogates were used to write such articles, and presidents never personally identified themselves.[10]

Presidents of the nineteenth century also toured the nation, a practice begun by George Washington. But rarely did they use such tours to make direct policy appeals to the public. Even when a policy agenda motivated a tour, presidents were often indirect and oblique about pressing their issue before the public. For instance, in 1877, Rutherford B. Hayes toured New England, the Midwest, and the South to promote his policy of withdrawing federal troops from the South and allowing local civilian control of government in that region. "But he assiduously avoided explicit references to politics and specific policies" and often told audiences that he was not there to make a "political speech."[11] Together, presidential use of the partisan press, rarity of public rhetoric on policy issues, and presidential tours of the nation give a strong sense of the cultural norm of the nineteenth century that proscribed direct presidential appeals to the public about pressing issues.

Theodore Roosevelt (1901–1908) ushered in the **rhetorical presidency.** By the administration of Woodrow Wilson (1912–1920), a new norm that emphasized presidential leadership of the public in pursuit of policy had taken root in the political system. Changes in the press and the political parties, and new ideas about the linkage between the president and the public transformed the presidency and how it would relate to the broad public.

[9]Jeffrey K. Tulis, *The Rhetorical Presidency* (Princeton: Princeton University Press, 1987).

[10]Mel Laracey, "The Presidential Newspaper: The Forgotten Way of Going Public," in *Speaking to the People: The Rhetorical Presidency in Historical Perspective,* ed. Richard J. Ellis (Amherst: University of Massachusetts Press, 1998), pp. 66–86.

[11]Gerald Gamm and Renee M. Smith, "Presidents, Parties, and the Public: Evolving Patterns of Interaction, 1877–1929," in *Speaking to the People: The Rhetorical Presidency in Historical Perspective,* ed. Richard J. Ellis (Amherst: University of Massachusetts Press, 1998), pp. 87–111.

First, the press, as described in Chapter 7, became less partisan and more professional and objective in reporting the news. The partisan press was instrumental in educating the public about political issues and thus in helping to mobilize voters behind candidates. The rise of the professional press and the decline of the partisan press forced the parties to find some other forum to educate voters about why they should support the party's candidates. Campaigns became one such forum, as did other public events, which campaign managers hoped would generate press coverage. Thus, presidential candidates began to campaign and to make public appearances, even if most of such activity took place on their front porches.

By the turn of the century, the public began to expect popular leadership from the president not only during presidential election campaign periods but throughout his term of office.[12] An indication of the development of this new, more public presidency, is Theodore Roosevelt's colorful description of the presidency as a "bully pulpit."

Although Roosevelt may have been the first rhetorical president, Woodrow Wilson provided the intellectual foundation and justification for such a presidency. Wilson was closely associated with the Progressive movement of the late nineteenth and early twentieth centuries. Progressives were not all of one mind, but in general, they thought that parties were corrupt and that the bosses that ran them had too much power. They preferred more direct forms of democracy, such as primaries to nominate candidates.[13]

Wilson identified the separation of powers as a fundamental defect in the structure of government.[14] To Wilson, the separation of powers enabled Congress to dominate policy making. But in *Congressional Government,* his most famous book, he argued that special interests, through their hold on congressional committees, would make most policy decisions. As a consequence, national issues or the public interest were not adequately addressed, national leadership from the nation's capital was not forthcoming, nor was there much policy coordination. Perhaps even more important, the public had little or no role to play in the governing process.

Wilson, like many Progressives, had great faith in the public, especially if it was informed and led. Leadership, to Wilson, was a process whereby the leader would "interpret" the people's desires.[15] Thus, unlike the founders, who viewed public opinion as something that leaders instilled in the mass public, Wilson reversed the process, arguing that public opinion began in the hearts and minds of ordinary people. It was the job of political leadership to give such opinion political and policy meaning and shape. In this process of interpreting, the pres-

---

[12]Ibid., pp. 90–92.

[13]On the Progressives and their political views, see Richard J. Hofstadter, *The Age of Reform* (New York: Alfred Knopf, 1977). On the impact of Progressives on the presidency, see Lester G. Seligman and Cary R. Covington, *The Coalitional Presidency* (Chicago: Dorsey, 1989), pp. 27–45.

[14]On Wilson and the rhetorical presidency, see Tulis, *Rhetorical Presidency,* pp. 118–32. Much of the following discussion comes from that source.

[15]Ibid., p. 125.

ident became the people's representative, with the process involving a "discussion" or "conversation" between the people and its leaders. To Wilson, only the president could effectively lead the public because only the presidency held national perspective.

The founders limited popular democracy in part out of a fear of demagoguery. Wilson answered this charge, too. He felt that political norms could be established that steered leaders away from the pursuit of personal power and toward serving the public. Wilson also felt that the public could judge character and would shun demagogues. And finally, Wilson argued that the difficulty of changing and moving public opinion would provide a bulwark against demagoguery. Wilson's ideas provided an important justification for a presidency based on popular leadership. His ideas are still important to our understanding of the operation of the modern presidency and the functioning of our political system.

Public Relations and the Presidency

The change from a president who rarely sought public support for policies to one who did so often required the establishment of an apparatus in the White House to help publicize the president's policy aims. The process of institutionalizing these offices began in the early 1900s and continued across the century. Now a very sophisticated publicity operation exists in the White House. The major components of this operation include the presidential press secretary, the Office of Communications, the Office of Public Liaison, and presidential use of polls.

Much of this material was covered in Chapter 7 on the president and the news media, but some points bear mention here. First, the institutional development of the staffs and offices began at the turn of the century with a person who became the president's press secretary. By the 1930s, that position was officially recognized. The press secretary's office expanded slowly, but its main task was to deal with the day-to-day needs of the press that covered the president.

The invention of television altered presidential relations with the public. Now, rather than needing press coverage, the president could speak before the public directly. This began in earnest in the early 1960s under John F. Kennedy. As a consequence, the press was being downgraded, along with the press secretary, while people with television skills and knowledge were being upgraded within the White House.

Presidential publicity operations were becoming more specialized, with experts about different aspects of those operations being hired to work in the White House. The press secretary's office was not geared to handle the many and diverse publicity tasks of the presidency in the television age, as the press secretary saw his role as one of facilitating the job of reporting on the president. Albeit important, this was only one part of presidential publicity efforts aimed at reaching the mass public. Further, one could argue that the audience for news reports, especially written journalism, was tilted in an elitist, opinion-maker direction. Reaching the mass public required a different medium of communication, and television fit that bill especially well.

To deal with the growing differentiation of tasks associated with reaching the mass public, the Nixon administration established the Office of Communications.[16] That office was concerned more with developing a public strategy for the president than with day-to-day service activities, like that of the press secretary's office. As a result, tension between the press secretary and the Office of Communications developed, although both recognized that the other was part of the puzzle of publicizing the president and developing a positive public face for the administration.[17]

The two offices have been constantly reorganized—sometimes the press secretary's office has been placed within the Office of Communications, sometimes it has been separated and placed on an equal footing. The complexity and multifaceted nature of presidential public relations plus the qualities of the staffers and the preferences and styles of each president have determined how the two offices are used and how they relate to each other.

The third office, the Office of Public Liaison, which we discussed in detail in Chapter 5, was created to handle relations with interest groups. Coordinating relationships with interest groups is considered another vital aspect of presidential public relations and outreach efforts. Lastly, presidents began to make greater use of polls for information on public attitudes and opinion, and in some cases to develop public relations and governing strategies.

The important point is that a large and complex staffing structure has been developed in the White House to deal with the task of presidential public relations. A differentiated staff populated by experts with different skills, backgrounds, and perspectives now works in the White House. Perhaps more people now in the White House work in this capacity than in any other.

Polling and the White House

Politicians in democracies, in part because of the need to get elected, are often intensely curious about what is going on in the public's mind. This was as true of nineteenth-century presidents as it is of today's, although it is safe to say that modern presidents are more highly interested in public opinion because of changes in both the political system and the technology of monitoring public opinion.

The apparatus for monitoring public opinion in the nineteenth and early twentieth centuries was crude. Presidents and other politicians of that era would learn of public preferences and opinions from reading letters that people would write to them and to newspapers, by reading articles in the print media (newspapers and magazines), by talking with people, by judging the size and enthusiasm of crowds, by conducting straw polls, and by analyzing and interpreting election results. The party organizations, with their ties to local committees, were also important sources of information about public opinion.

---

[16]John Anthony Maltese, *Spin Control: The White House Office of Communications and the Management of Presidential News,* 2d ed. rev. (Chapel Hill: University of North Carolina Press, 1994).

[17]Charles E. Walcott and Karen M. Hult, *Governing the White House: From Hoover Through LBJ* (Lawrence: University Press of Kansas, 1995), pp. 52–73.

Each of these methods was severely limited in gauging mass opinion. Neither letter writers, people with whom politicians talked, nor straw poll results are representative of the nation at large. Crowds and rallies are often manufactured, and again, those who attend such gatherings are not representative either, generally being more politically active than the average person. And election results indicate only who won the election, not the reasons people voted for one candidate over another. As a result, the quality of information about public opinion in the nineteenth and early twentieth centuries was limited. When people of that time used the term *public opinion,* they were inclined to mean journalists and others whose voice was heard in the news outlets of the day.[18]

The creation of the scientific survey changed not only how information about public opinion was collected but the meaning of the term *public opinion* as well.[19] Now, *public opinion* had come to mean the opinion of the broad mass of people, not a select segment or slice of the population.

The scientific survey enabled politicians and social scientists to be more precise in describing the opinions that people hold on an issue or toward a candidate or leader. The science of survey research began in the 1930s under the direction of George Gallup, Hadley Cantril, Louis Harris, and a few others.[20] Gallup made a national name for himself by predicting the outcome of the 1936 presidential election. The *Literary Digest,* an important magazine of the day, also ran a poll, but it was way off the mark, predicting a massive defeat for Franklin Roosevelt. Gallup, using sampling techniques to ensure representativeness among the people whom he polled, predicted an FDR victory. While the *Literary Digest* episode undermined public confidence in polling, some politicians, especially FDR, became interested in using polls.

FDR, the first president to use polls, received them from private sources and employed them in various ways.[21] First, he used Emil Hurja's polls, which were conducted for the Democratic National Committee, to decide which congressional districts and localities would receive federal patronage. In this way, FDR was building the administrative presidency and distancing the presidency from the political parties and Congress. FDR often found that party bosses were too locally preoccupied and thus not wholly loyal to his administration. Further, his New Deal program encountered trouble from members of Congress, even some from his own party. Using polls this way enabled the president to begin building a presidency that was more independent of these other power centers.

[18]See Susan Herbst, *Reading Public Opinion: How Political Actors View the Democratic Process* (Chicago: University of Chicago Press, 1998).

[19]Susan Herbst, *Numbered Voices: How Opinion Polling Has Shaped American Politics* (Chicago: University of Chicago Press, 1993).

[20]On the history of survey research and polling, see Jean M. Converse, *Survey Research in the United States: Roots and Emergence* (Berkeley: University of California Press, 1987).

[21]Robert M. Eisinger and Jeremy Brown, "Polling as a Means Toward Presidential Autonomy: Emil Hurja, Hadley Cantril and the Roosevelt Administration," *International Journal of Public Opinion Research* 10, no.3 (1998): 237–56, and Robert M. Eisinger, *The Illusion of Certainty: Explaining the Evolution of Presidential Polling (Public Opinion).* Ph.D. dissertation, University of Chicago, 1996.

But FDR also relied on polls to learn about public opinion. Cantril, who supplied the president with much of his polling information, also offered advice to the president on how to sell his ideas to the public. Also, FDR was very interested in polls on the 1944 presidential election contest. Lastly, FDR kept his polls secret, in part to have at hand information not available to others but also to keep others from charging that he was using polls to manipulate public opinion. Until recent years, all presidents have kept their polls secret and for the same reasons.[22]

FDR's successor, Truman, disdained polls and thus made little use of them, while Eisenhower, like FDR, saw some utility in polls. But the institutionalization of polling operations in the White House began with the Kennedy administration, developed more under Johnson, and became a fixture under Nixon.[23]

Kennedy used polls mostly in his 1960 campaign for the presidency. Polls seemed to affect the positions that he took on issues and they also helped him devise a campaign strategy that would emphasize certain aspects of his character, like being bold, and differentiate him from his opponent, Nixon.[24] While he was interested in polls, once he was in office Kennedy's attention to them dropped off.[25] Johnson, like Kennedy, was keenly interested in polls but, unlike Kennedy, made greater use of them for governing purposes, especially to direct his publicity efforts on the Vietnam War,[26] as well as his 1964 reelection race. And LBJ used polls to shore up his public image. He loved to wave in front of journalists the latest polls reporting his popularity, especially as journalists became more antagonistic toward him because of Vietnam.[27]

Compared to Nixon and subsequent presidents, the polling operations of the Kennedy and Johnson administrations were quite crude. While Johnson commissioned some private polls, incorporation of poll information into the presidency was informal. Nixon built a more well-developed and well-defined polling operation in his White House.[28]

First, Nixon increased the White House's capacity to track public opinion by hiring up to seven people to design and analyze polls, where Johnson had at most only one junior staffer. Moreover, the Nixon pollsters and other staff possessed the technical skills, such as an understanding of statistics, to interpret poll results, and

---

[22]Lawrence R. Jacobs and Robert Y. Shapiro, "The Rise of Presidential Polling: The Nixon White House in Historical Perspective," *Public Opinion Quarterly* 59, no. 1 (1995): 163–95.

[23]Ibid.

[24]Lawrence R. Jacobs and Robert Y. Shapiro, "Issues, Candidates, and Priming: The Use of Private Polls in Kennedy's 1960 Presidential Campaign, *American Political Science Review* 88 (September 1994): 527–40.

[25]Jacobs and Shapiro, "Rise of Presidential Polling," p. 167.

[26]Lawrence R. Jacobs and Robert Y. Shapiro, "Lyndon Johnson, Vietnam, and Public Opinion: Rethinking Realist Theory of Leadership," *Presidential Studies Quarterly* 29 (September 1999): 592–616.

[27]On LBJ's use of polls, see Bruce E. Altschuler, *LBJ and the Polls* (Gainesville: University of Florida Press, 1990).

[28]The next several paragraphs are based on Jacobs and Shapiro, "Rise of Presidential Polling."

Nixon insisted on detailed reports of the latest polls. Nixon's pollsters also innovated by developing tracking polls to monitor public opinion over time and by using telephone interviewing so that polls could be conducted and reported back to the president within two days. By privately purchasing polls, Nixon and his staff had great input into the time and content of the polls, making them even more useful.

Second, Nixon tightly organized his polling staff, making it unlike the looser informal arrangements under previous presidents. Polling staff were assigned to an office that reported directly to Nixon's chief of staff, Robert Haldeman. It was located outside of the government and was paid for with private donations and contributions. Nixon kept a tight rein on his polling information, not making it generally available, even to other staffers or managers of his 1972 reelection campaign. Nixon kept tight control in part to help build an image of a political genius and also to deflect charges of political manipulation or pandering to the public.

But Nixon used polls not only to help his reelection but to run his presidency. Polls helped inform Nixon's public relations efforts and, on select occasions, affected some policy choices. Nixon even at times tried to get the firms that secretly polled for him to publicize results when they were favorable about the administration and its policy stands. He thought that such results would be thought more true if they were not associated with the White House but appeared independent. In all, the Nixon administration represents a turning point in presidential use of polls.

Subsequent presidents have elaborated on the system built by Nixon, with differences to suit their own personal tastes, but no president since then has shunned polls in running for election or reelection, or in governing.[29] Rather, these most recent presidents are interested in polls. They receive memos about poll results and, more important, send memos or other queries asking about poll numbers. For most of these administrations, the Chief of Staff's Office has been the central clearinghouse for polls. Through that office, polls are deposited and organized as well as transmitted to other staff throughout the White House.

Lower in the staff ranks of the White House, offices that are concerned with outreach, such as the Office of Communications, the Office of Public Liaison (which works with interest groups), and the Political Liaison Office (which works with the parties and other political groups and is most concerned with presidential reelection efforts), are also avid users of polls. So is the domestic policy staff, which helps build domestic policy proposals for the president. But the Office of Congressional Liaison is not, suggesting that presidents and those in the White House who lobby Congress for the president do not find polls very useful in bargaining with Congress.[30]

Two last changes in presidential poll use since Nixon are noteworthy. First, unlike the Nixon administration, which tightly restricted access to polls, subsequent presidential administrations have disseminated poll results more widely and more

[29]Diane J. Heith, "Staffing the White House Public Opinion Apparatus, 1969–1988," *Public Opinion Quarterly* 62 (Summer 1998): 165–89.

[30]Ibid., p. 176.

systematically among staffers. Second, these administrations have become more open about the fact that they collect poll data, something that Nixon and his predecessors desired to keep secret. This provides a sense of not only how useful polls have become to presidents but also how accepted they have become within the political system.

An important issue is whether polls have affected presidential behavior—especially whether polls make presidents more sensitive to public opinion or whether they increase the ability of presidents to manipulate public opinion. We will return to this question later in this chapter, after we have more completely discussed the relationship between the president and the public.

PUBLIC EXPECTATIONS OF THE PRESIDENT

High Expectations

The president's prominent place in the minds of ordinary citizens comes at a price: the public holds high expectations of the president. Sometimes, those expectations are unrealistic and misread our constitutional system. At other times, those expectations are contradictory. The combination of the public's concentration of attention on the president, reliance on the president for leadership, and high expectations also leads the public to blame the president for bad times.

First, the public has high expectations about presidential policy making and leadership. As we have noted, the public views the president as the center of the political system, and although many understand the constitutional status and role of Congress and the Supreme Court, they often view the president as the chief policy maker. It is the president more than either Congress or the Court to whom the public looks to solve pressing problems and issues of the day. Moreover, these expectations for policy performance reach to problems that the president may have neither responsibility for nor the tools to deal with.

Second, the public also maintains high expectations about the qualities that it wants in a president. Table 8-1 lists public responses to eleven qualities, in October 1995, at about the midpoint of Clinton's first term in office. Among the traits that the public views as being most essential in a president are sound judgment in a crisis; high ethical standards; compassion for the average citizen; saying what one believes, even if unpopular; forcefulness and decisiveness; and having consistent positions on issues. The public prefers a president who provides strong leadership and can also relate to average people. Rather than a compromiser, the public wants a president who will take the lead, who is decisive, and who knows what he wants to do. Interestingly, the public does not view party loyalty as being important, nor is political or Washington experience comparatively important.

Third, high public expectations of the president also extend to personal behavior, although this may be moderating in the wake of the Clinton administration. A survey taken in the late 1970s reported that the public objected to a president who "smoked marijuana occasionally; told ethnic jokes in private; was not a member of a church; used tranquilizers occasionally; wore blue jeans occa-

TABLE 8-1   QUALITIES THE PUBLIC LOOKS FOR IN A PRESIDENT

Quality	Essential quality (5)	Important quality (4)	Less important to not important quality (1-3)	Don't know
1. Sound judgment in crisis	76%	12	10	2
2. High ethical standards	67	18	13	2
3. Compassion for the average citizen	64	19	16	1
4. Willingness to compromise	34	29	35	2
5. Experience in public office	30	23	46	1
6. Experience in Washington	21	23	54	2
7. Saying what one believes, even if unpopular	59	21	18	2
8. Forcefulness and decisiveness	50	30	18	2
9. Political savvy and know-how	31	26	41	2
10. Having consistent positions on issues	51	28	19	2
11. Loyalty to one's party	25	15	58	2

Source: Princeton Survey Research Associates, 25–30 October, 1995, National Adult Population, n = 2000

"Question: I'm going to read you a list of personal characteristics or qualities. If '5' represents an absolutely essential quality in a President and '1' a quality that is not too important, where on the scale of 5 to 1 would you rate. . . ? (5 = Absolutely essential, 4 = Important, 1–3 = Not important)"

sionally in the Oval Office; was divorced; had a cocktail before dinner each night."[31] Thus, the public disapproves of the president behaving, even in private, as many Americans do in their own homes. Rather, the public wants a president who is not only better than the average citizen but who also lives up to a higher standard of comportment both public and private.

We must, however, be careful about generalizing all of these specific behaviors and traits to all times. Social norms change, allowing or disallowing certain behaviors. Take divorce as a case in point. In 1964, Nelson Rockefeller's campaign for the Republican presidential nomination was hurt because he was divorced. Antidivorce sentiments continued, as is evident from the results of the survey mentioned in the previous paragraph, which was taken in 1979, before Ronald Reagan became president. However, it is probably the case that after Reagan's term of office, the public is more tolerant of having a divorced person in the White House. Robert Dole, also divorced, easily secured the Republican presidential nomination in 1996.

[31]Stephen J. Wayne, "Great Expectations: What People Want from Presidents," in *Rethinking the Presidency,* ed. Thomas E. Cronin (Boston: Little, Brown, 1982), pp. 185–99.

TABLE 8-2   COMPARING PUBLIC ASSESSMENTS OF BILL CLINTON'S HONESTY AND
INTEGRITY WITH JOB APPROVAL, 1994–1998

Date	Clinton's honesty		Clinton's job performance	
	Yes*	No*	Job approval**	Job disapproval**
May 6, 1994	46	46	46	42
August 22-23, 1996	45	49	53	36
August 28-29, 1996	53	42	57	32
January 1998	40	52	70	26
August 13, 1998	40	55	59	33

Source: Princeton Survey Research Associates

*"Question: From everything you know about (President) Bill Clinton, does he have the honesty and integrity you expect in a president, or not?"

**"Question: Do you approve or disapprove of the way Bill Clinton is handling his job as president?"

It is also likely that Bill Clinton's personal behavior in office has affected public thinking about presidential behavior and the possible trade-off between having a good president versus a good person as president, although ideally, the public probably wants both qualities in a president. At least in the late 1990s, the public seemed to prefer the good president to the good person. A February 1998 poll asked respondents this question: "President (Bill) Clinton's personal character has been questioned throughout his presidency. Yet the public continues to approve of the job he is doing. I am going to ask if you agree or disagree with each of the following statements about this situation. People expect that powerful government officials are not perfect and mostly judge them by how well they do their jobs." The poll found that 77 percent agree with the statement, while 19 percent disagreed and 4 percent had no response.[32] Table 8-2 compares how much honesty and integrity survey respondents thought Bill Clinton had with whether or not they approved of the way he was handling his job as president from 1994 through 1998, the last year being the one in which the Monica Lewinsky scandal was made public. As the public increasingly saw Clinton lacking honesty and integrity, they were also more likely to approve of his job performance as president.

Contradictory Expectations

Not only are public expectations of the president high, they are also sometimes contradictory. For instance, Thomas Cronin has assembled this list of what he calls paradoxes of the president.[33]

[32]Zogby International, February 1998. A survey of national likely voters (948 respondents).

[33]This is but a selection from a much longer list that Cronin assembled. Thomas E. Cronin, *The State of the Presidency,* 2d ed. (Boston: Little, Brown, 1980), pp. 1–26. For a more updated discussion, see Thomas E. Cronin and Michael A. Genovese, *The Paradoxes of the American Presidency* (New York: Oxford University Press, 1998), pp. 1–28.

1. *The president should be decent and just but also decisive and guileful.* We want a president who is good and decent, a role model for the nation about matters both private and public. But we also require a person of action who can accomplish his goals in a political world. Especially in the dangerous world of international politics, to protect the national interest may require deceit with one's adversaries. At the same time, Americans express lofty idealistic goals for international politics, such as the spread of democracy and political rights.

2. *The president should be programmatic but also pragmatic.* This point is similar to the previous one, but here, we desire a president who stakes out a policy program for action, who sticks by it, and who is guided by a set of principles. At the same time, Americans are pragmatic in the sense that they desire policies that can work over ideological or other types of principled commitments. In other words, the public prefers that a president be flexible and adaptive, rather than rigid.

3. *The president should be an innovative and inventive leader but also a majoritarian who is responsive to the public.* Here, we confront the fundamental tension in the American executive—the need for leadership, coupled with sensitivity to the public, its preferences, and its needs. To the public, the president must be both leader and follower, something a president cannot do simultaneously.[34]

4. *The president should be a common man who gives an uncommon performance.* Reflecting much of the poll results reported earlier in the chapter, we want a president who is better than ourselves, who will provide a role model of how we should act. But at the same time, the public views the office and its occupant in democratic terms, preferring "one of the people" as president, not someone out of an elite class who is detached from the concerns of ordinary people. For instance, George H. W. Bush came under public fire for having been astonished at price scanners at checkout counters of retail establishments many years after their introduction into the marketplace. This was taken as a sign that he was out of touch with the lives of average people. Yet the fact that Jimmy Carter was criticized for seeming to be too ordinary also speaks to the public desire for a president who will serve as a role model, one who is better than the average person.

PUBLIC EVALUATIONS OF THE PRESIDENT

One consequence of public expectations of the president is that those in and out of Washington scrutinize how well the president is doing with the public. Since the Gallup Poll began asking people to assess the job performance of the president in the late 1930s, it has become almost a national political pastime to scrutinize the president's latest poll results to see if his approval is high or low and whether it has gone up or down. Due to the popularity of presidential poll watching, a number of other agencies and firms also query the public on its attitude toward the president, and polling about the president and specific issues and events of the day has become commonplace in news reporting. Poll results have become much of the stuff of the modern presidency.

[34]On this dilemma, see Cohen, *Presidential Responsiveness.*

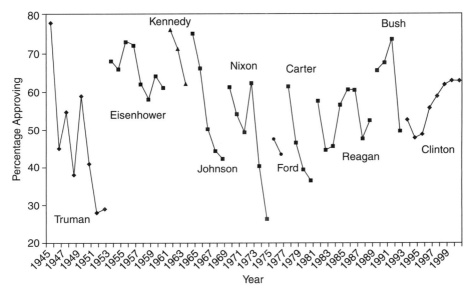

FIGURE 8-1
Annual Presidential Job Approval, 1945–2000

However, we can scrutinize these polls for more than immediate curiosity about the president's standings. We can use these poll results over the course that they have been asked as a historical barometer of public regard of the president. And by looking at the ups and downs in presidential poll standings, we can also begin to understand what moves the public to sometimes approve of or sometimes disapprove of the president's job in office.

Popularity and Job Approval

The poll question on the president that has been used most frequently and for the longest time is the Gallup job approval question: "Do you approve or disapprove of the way [president's name] is handling his job as president?"[35] While often called popularity, this question is probably better referred to as presidential job approval to distinguish it from more recent poll questions that ask people whether they have a favorable or unfavorable impression of the president. Figure 8–1 presents the average annual **presidential job approval ratings** from 1945 to 2000.

Clearly, presidential job approval has its ups and downs. What accounts for the highs and lows in presidential job approval? Is the president able to influence these poll results? Three sets of factors seem important in answering this question: **honeymoon effects,** policy effects, and symbolic activity effects.

---

[35]This question has been asked at least monthly, if not more frequently, since the early 1950s.

TABLE 8-3   PRESIDENTIAL HONEYMOON EFFECTS: COMPARISON BETWEEN
PRESIDENTIAL ELECTION RESULTS AND FIRST JOB APPROVAL RATING

President	First poll rating*	Percentage of the popular vote for the president	Difference (poll rating − vote percentage)
Eisenhower	68	55.1	12.9
Kennedy	73	49.7	23.3
Nixon	59	43.4	15.6
Carter	71	50.1	19.9
Reagan	51	50.7	0.3
Bush	57	53.4	3.6
Clinton	58	43.0	15.0

Source: Gallup Poll

Honeymoon Effects   Presidents tend to come to office with a surge of public support over and above the vote that they received in the general election. Many Americans, it seems, set aside partisan differences once a new president enters office. They seemingly root for the new president, indicating perhaps that Americans feel that a successful presidency and all of the positive effects that such a presidency brings to the nation are more important than their party or whether they voted for the winner or not. Thus, presidents generally enter office on a high note.

But as Table 8-3 also shows, this is not the case for all presidents. Ronald Reagan, for instance, entered office with public support barely higher than his vote total. One explanation for this exception to the general rule of initial surges in public support for new administrations is that Reagan was a polarizing president. He came to office with a specific and ideologically coherent policy program that was decidedly conservative, and early in his term he did not play to the broad middle. Rather than trying to accommodate to the moderate policy preferences of mainstream Americans, Reagan attempted to pull public opinion to his point of view, often with forceful rhetoric.

Policy Effects   People also seem to grade the president on the state of the nation and on issues that they care about. One study finds, for instance, that the importance that the public attributes to an issue affects its impact on presidential job approval. Thus, when an issue is thought to be important, it weighs heavily in people's assessment of the president.[36]

People also seem to hold the president responsible for the state of the economy and international relations almost all of the time. Thus, when the economy is strong, presidential approval tends to be high. International conditions are not so simply reduced, as we discuss in the section on "International and Foreign Policy Effects."

[36]George C. Edwards, III, William L. Mitchell, and Reed Welch, "Explaining Presidential Approval: The Significance of Issue Salience," *American Journal of Political Science* 39 (February 1995): 108–34.

Economic Policy Effects   The impact of the economy on presidential job approval presents a good example of how the public blames or rewards presidents even for events and conditions that the president may be little able to affect. Despite the policy tools that presidents can use to influence the economy, it is not clear how much impact government policies have over the economy in the short run or whether the president's economic policy making tools are as potent as those possessed by other policy making bodies.

For instance, implementation of new economic policies often requires legislation, and this means bringing Congress into the picture. Perhaps the most important legislation that can be used to affect the economy is the budget, and in recent years it is not clear that budgetary manipulation has much impact on the economy, a topic that we will discuss more fully in Chapter 14. Further, no president is assured that Congress will pass his economic policies or that Congress will do so in a timely enough fashion for the policies to take effect to the president's benefit. In fact, since the late 1960s, Congress has often been unable to finish work on the budget by the start of the fiscal year in which that budget is to go into effect.

Moreover, economists tend to believe the monetary policy has greater impact on economic performance. But monetary policy is controlled by the independent body, the Federal Reserve Board, and not the president. We will discuss the Fed in more detail in Chapter 14. Lastly, foreign nations may take actions that harm (or help) the U.S. economy, but presidents have, at best, limited influence on the policies of foreign nations. Still, all of the evidence points to the fact that when the economy is doing poorly or when people think it is doing poorly, presidential job approval drops.

Thus, the public holds the president accountable for the state of the economy no matter what effort the president has put into economic policy making or the limited ability of the president to affect the economy. Consequently, it is easy to see why presidents care so much about the economy. But what is it about the economy that influences public thinking about the president?[37]

[37]The literature on the impact of the economy and economic perceptions on presidential job approval is vast and quite technical. Recent studies include John R. Freeman and Daniel Houser, "A Computable Equilibrium Model for the Study of Political Economy," *American Journal of Political Science* 42 (April 1998): 628–60; Paul Brace and Barbara Hinckley, "George Bush and the Costs of High Popularity: A General Model with a Current Application," *PS: Political Science and Politics* 26 (September 1993): 501–06; Michael B. MacKuen, Robert S. Erikson, and James A. Stimson, "Peasants or Bankers? The American Electorate and the U.S. Economy," *American Political Science Review* 86 (September 1992): 597–611; Helmut Norpoth, "Presidents and the Prospective Voter," *Journal of Politics* 58 (August 1996): 776–92; Harold D. Clarke and Marianne C. Stewart, "Prospections, Retrospections, and Rationality: The 'Bankers' Model of Presidential Approval Reconsidered," *American Journal of Political Science* 38 (November 1994): 1104–23; Harold D. Clarke, Jonathan Rapkin, and Marianne C. Stewart, "A President Out of Work: A Note on the Political Economy of Presidential Approval in the Bush Years," *British Journal of Political Science* 24 (October 1994): 535–48; Paul Brace and Barbara Hinckley, "The Structure of Presidential Approval: Constraints Within and Across Presidencies," *Journal of Politics* 53 (November 1993): 993–1017; Henry W. Chappell, Jr., "Economic Performance, Voting, and Political Support: A Unified Approach," *Review of Economics and Statistics* 72 (May 1990): 313–20; John T. Williams, "The Political Manipulation of Macroeconomic Policy," *American Political Science Review* 84 (September 1990): 767–95; Charles W. Ostrom and Dennis M. Simon, "Promise and Performance: A Dynamic Model of Presidential Popularity," *American Political Science Review* 79 (June 1985): 334–58; Paul Brace and Barbara Hinckley, *Follow the Leader: Opinion Polls and the Modern Presidents* (New York: HarperCollins, 1994).

Early research looked at how economic conditions influence attitudes toward the president by focusing on two economic conditions that most directly affect people's lives, unemployment and inflation. This **pocketbook theory** asserted that people who were feeling ill effects from the economy would be the most negative toward the president. Thus, studies found that when unemployment and inflation were on the rise, presidential popularity would drop.[38] These studies, however, did not make a direct link between a person's economic circumstances and his or her attitude toward the president. They found only that aggregate tides in economic conditions were related to trends in presidential job approval.

With this critique in mind, attention shifted to survey data, where one could look at the direct link between an individual's economic circumstances and attitudes toward the president. These survey studies found that the unemployed, for instance, were no more negative toward the president than were other people. Rather than personal economic circumstances affecting attitudes toward the president, it seemed that people of all economic circumstances looked at the state of the economy overall and rated the president accordingly. This has been termed the sociotropic effect.[39]

The **sociotropic theory** has led research on presidential job approval away from trying to isolate which economic condition, either inflation or unemployment, has the more meaningful effect and toward an understanding of economic attitudes and their political implications. This perspective raises the question, Do people judge the president on how well the economy has performed (the retrospective theory) or on how well they expect the economy to perform in the future (the prospective theory)?

It is natural to turn to future expectations when discussing economic behavior. Much economic activity is based on calculations about future payoffs and profits. If economic thinking greatly affects political attitudes, might future orientations also govern people's assessments of presidential job performance? Evidence has been found for the prospective idea, but it is controversial, and not all agree that the public is prospectively oriented when it comes to presidential evaluations, arguing instead that retrospective judgments better describe how the public thinks about the president.[40]

The issue of the nature of economic attitudes and their linkage to presidential evaluations also raises the question of where people's economic attitudes come from. Clearly, people's economic attitudes in part come from their own personal experiences, as well as those of friends and family and others with whom they

[38]Early studies include John E. Mueller, "Presidential Popularity from Truman to Johnson," *American Political Science Review* 64 (March 1970): 18–34; and Samuel Kernell, "Explaining Presidential Popularity," *American Political Science Review* 72 (June 1978): 506–22. For a review of the early literature, see Kristen R. Monroe, *Presidential Popularity and the Economy* (New York: Praeger, 1982).

[39]Donald R. Kinder and D. Roderick Kiewiet, "Sociotropic Politics: The American Case," *British Journal of Political Science* 11 (April 1981): 129–61.

[40]The classic statement of the prospective theory is found in MacKuen, Erikson, and Stimson, "Peasants or Bankers." Norpoth, "Presidents and the Prospective Voter," favors the retrospective theory.

come into contact. But as the critique of the pocketbook theory suggests, people may feel economically threatened even if their own circumstances are currently strong, because they see so many others in distress. People learn about the wider economy, the economy beyond their own personal experience, from the mass media. Thus, economic news, its pessimism or optimism, may add into people's calculations about the nature of the economy and its prospects, and, consequently, their attitudes about the president.[41]

We come back to presidential concern with the news media. By affecting the tone of news reports on the economy, the president may be able, through this route, to influence his own job approval ratings. But here, presidential ability to alter reporters' perceptions is limited. A president cannot make journalists believe that a bad economy is in good shape. He can, perhaps, convey a sense that he is on the right track to solving the economy's ills and thus soften the way journalists think about the economy's prospects. This might also lower media criticism of the way the president is handling the economy, which may lead to somewhat stronger approval levels.

International and Foreign Policy Effects   Besides the economy, the international situation also affects presidential job approval ratings, but unlike the economy with its relatively simple equation that good times lead to high job approval, the relationship between the international situation and presidential approval is more complex. While the public has a general preference for peace and quiet times, under some conditions hostilities can help boost a president's job approval rating.[42]

It seems to be the case that in an international crisis or the initial stages of hostilities between the United States and another nation, the public rallies behind the president in a show of national unity, with the effect of lifting the president's approval rating. Presidents cannot be assured, however, that their approval levels will stay high if the hostility persists. Sometimes, as was the case in the Second World War, presidents can maintain public support despite high casualty levels and a long conflict. It seems that FDR's ability to instill a clear sense of purpose was instrumental in maintaining public support for the war and his presidential leadership. At other times, presidents do not seem able to articulate a clear reason for hostile engagement with another nation that results in American casualties. When this happens, support for the military effort, as well as the president,

---

[41]Richard Nadeau, Richard G. Niemi, David Fan, and Timothy Amato, "Elite Economic Forecasts, Economic News, Mass Economic Judgments, and Presidential Approval," *Journal of Politics* 61 (February 1999): 109–35; Deborah J. Blood and Peter C. B. Phillips, "Recession Headline News, Consumer Sentiment, the State of the Economy and Presidential Popularity: A Time Series Analysis, 1989–1993," *International Journal of Public Opinion Research* 7 (Spring 1995):2-22; Darrell M. West, "Television and Presidential Popularity in America," *British Journal of Political Science* 21 (April 1991): 199–214; Thomas Holbrook and James C. Garand, "Homo Economus? Economic Information and Economic Voting," *Political Research Quarterly* 49 (June 1996): 331–75.

[42]Studies that look at the impact of international affairs on presidential approval include Bradley Lian and John R. Oneal, "Presidents, the Use of Military Force, and Public Opinion," *Journal of Conflict Resolution* 37 (June 1993):277–300; and Robin F. Marra, Charles W. Simon, Jr., and Dennis M. Simon, "Foreign Policy and Presidential Popularity: Creating Windows of Opportunity in the Perpetual Election," *Journal of Conflict Resolution* 34 (December 1990): 588–623.

drops off. Lastly, sometimes even when the president has articulated a clear goal, the public disagrees or comes to disagree with it. The Vietnam War is a case in point. After several years, thousands of battle casualties on both sides, and no apparent end in sight, the American public, after initially supporting the war effort, shifted, feeling that the cost was just too high or that the goal of containing communism in Southeast Asia was not worth the effort.

Rally Effects   The time trends in presidential approval are not smooth but sometimes are interrupted by short-term upward spikes in presidential job approval, what we can call **rallies.** Sometimes international events and crises become rally events. Also, major presidential speeches, as well as other special presidential actions, such as a public appearance or statement associated with a major event like a natural disaster or tragedy, tend to evoke short-term upward spikes in presidential job approval. Why do some of these events become rally points, and who rallies in support of the president?

One study suggests that major media coverage is necessary for an event to become a rally point. In comparing international events in which the United States was a participant, when the event was reported on page one of the *New York Times,* presidential approval jumped by eight percentage points. Without such coverage, no movement in public approval was noticed.[43] This finding is important because another study reports that those who are more attentive to the news media are more likely to rally in support of the president. Moreover, rallying behind the president is not a generalized phenomenon but is particular among select groups within the mass public. People already disposed to support the president are more likely to rally, while critics of the president seem immune.[44] These findings help us understand why all deployments of U.S. troops do not lead to higher presidential approval levels. Except in the most extraordinary events and crises, such as the Second World War, the presidential use of troops is not viewed from a patriotic viewpoint but instead from a political or partisan one.

Still, U.S. military action is the most studied type of rally. At the onset of a military action ranging from the activation of military units to the deployment of troops to their actual engagement in battle, the public tends to rally behind the president and his efforts.[45] But not all U.S. military engagements or international

---

[43]John R. Oneal and Anna Lilliar Bryan, "The Rally 'Round the Flag Effect in U.S. Foreign Policy Crises, 1950–1985," *Political Behavior* 17 (December 1995): 379–401.

[44]George C. Edwards, III, and Tami Swenson, "Who Rallies? The Anatomy of a Rally Event," *Journal of Politics* 59 (February 1997): 200–12.

[45]There is a large literature on rally effects. See, for instance, Edwards and Swenson, "Who Rallies?" and Suzanne L. Parker, "Toward an Understanding of 'Rally' Effects: Public Opinion in the Persian Gulf War," *Public Opinion Quarterly* 59 (Winter 1995): 526–46; Oneal and Bryan, "The Rally 'Round the Flag Effect"; Barbara Norrander and Clyde Wilcox, "Rallying Around the Flag and Partisan Change: The Case of the Persian Gulf War," *Political Research Quarterly* 46 (December 1993): 759–70; Karen J. Callaghan and Simo Virtanen, "Revised Models of the 'Rally Phenomenon': The Case of the Carter Presidency," *Journal of Politics* 55 (August 1993): 756–64; Gordon L. Bowen, "Presidential Action and Public Opinion about U.S. Nicaraguan Policy: Limits to the 'Rally Round the Flag' Syndrome," *PS: Political Science and Politics* 22 (December 1989): 793–800.

crises stimulate rallies.[46] It appears that for public opinion rallies to occur, the public has to think that the hostility will lead to measurable U.S. casualties or has the potential to turn into a major military effort (possibly even war), or opinion elites have to spend considerable time discussing the issue before the public. Consequently, the September 11, 2001, terrorist attacks, which killed many people, quickly led to talk of war, and generated considerable media coverage, yielded a dramatic increase in President Bush's approval rating.

Some people are quite cynical about the presidential use of the military and argue that if by committing troops, presidents can boost their job approval levels, then presidents will commit troops to build their job approval, especially when their polls are in the dumps. Thus, rather than for international policy or national security reasons, presidents commit troops for domestic political reasons. This cynical theory was the premise of a motion picture, *Wag the Dog,* and has crept into our public discourse about presidential behavior.

For instance, in August 1998, just as Monica Lewinsky was to appear before the grand jury to give testimony relating to her affair with the president, President Clinton ordered missile strikes against cities in Afghanistan and Sudan that were reportedly locations of terrorists groups that had bombed U.S. embassies. Some cynics argued that the president's action was a cynical attempt to divert public attention from the Lewinsky affair, which at the time was hurting his presidency.[47] And one national poll reported by the *Buffalo News* found that Clinton's approval rating dropped ten percentage points from just before the bombing announcement to just shortly after it. That story credited the drop to public cynicism about the president's motivation for the bombing missions.[48]

In spite of public acceptance of the **Wag the Dog theory,** however, few studies find that presidents use American military forces this way. In fact, studies do not find that presidents low in the polls are more prone to use troops than presidents riding high in the polls. Nor do studies find that the deployment of troops actually boosts presidential approval to a measurable or sustainable degree. Moreover, groups involved in the embassy bombings were also involved in the September 11 attacks, a fact that may justify the 1998 strikes (or enhance their credibility).

Symbolic Activity Effects Throughout the course of their administrations, presidents give speeches, travel around the nation and to other countries, and engage in a host of daily activities aimed at building and presenting an image for public consumption. Although many of these activities will have policy making implications, many will not, focusing instead on the image of the president in the public's mind. But whether such public activities are policy related or not, all have implica-

[46]George C. Edwards, III, *The Public Presidency: The Pursuit of Popular Support* (New York: St. Martin's Press, 1983).

[47]David M. Shribman, "A Hectic Period That Left a Lasting Skepticism; U.S. Strikes Back/ Reaction and Fallout/ The Week That Was/ News Analysis," *Boston Globe,* 22 August 1998, p. A9.

[48]Jerry Zremski, "President's Popularity Falls Nearly 10 Percent, Poll Finds," *Buffalo News,* 22 August 1998, p. 1A.

tions for the image of the president in the public consciousness. In this sense, we can talk about such activities as being image-making or symbolic activities.

Presidents aim to project a public image that will, among other things, build public support and elevate job approval ratings. This is one reason presidents engage in so many of these public activities and invest so many White House resources, such as staff and planning, in them. Several studies have documented that when presidential polls are low or sliding, presidents will be more likely to give major speeches or travel to foreign nations. They do so presumably to avert a further slide in their polls or to try to boost their ratings.[49]

Despite this huge investment, however, the public support payoff may not be as great as the effort. For instance, the most comprehensive study on the topic finds that while major speeches may improve presidential job approval by as much as six percentage points during the first term of office, trips to foreign nations have no impact on job approval ratings during the first term and trips around the nation during the first term actually depress job approval by about one percentage point. During the second term, none of these three activities (major speeches, and foreign and domestic trips) has any effect on approval levels.[50] All indications are that the effects of these activities on job approval are quite fleeting. Within a month or two, whatever effect a major speech or trip had on presidential approval has vanished.

Still, presidents may find even such short-lived effects strategically important. Upward movements in presidential approval may indicate public momentum toward the president, or at least presidents may be able to sell such an explanation for any uptick in job approval ratings.

Elite Discourse and Job Approval

So far, our discussion has focused on the impact of policy and nonpolicy-related events on presidential job approval. At times, such events, like the ups and downs in the economy, had easily predicted and wholly expected impacts. At other times, as with international events, major speeches, and trips, the relationship between the event and public opinion was quite complex.

As we have discussed public evaluations of the president thus far, we have implied that average people make sense out of these real-world events and use the event to help make a judgment about the president's performance. For many

[49]See Paul Brace and Barbara Hinckley, "Presidential Activities from Truman Through Reagan: Timing and Impact," *Journal of Politics* 55 (May 1993): 382–93; Lyn Ragsdale, "The Politics of Presidential Speechmaking, 1949–1980," *American Political Science Review* 79 (December 1984): 971–84; Lyn Ragsdale, "Presidential Speechmaking and the Public Audience: Individual Presidents and Group Attitudes," *Journal of Politics* 49 (August 1987): 704–27; Dennis M. Simon and Charles W. Ostrom, "The Impact of Televised Speeches and Foreign Travel on Presidential Approval," *Public Opinion Quarterly* 53 (Spring 1989): 58–82.

[50]Brace and Hinckley, "Presidential Activities," pp. 392–96; also see Michael B. MacKuen, "Political Drama, Economic Conditions, and the Dynamics of Presidential Popularity," *American Journal of Political Science* 27 (May 1983): 165–92.

events, such a personal translation process from event to presidential approval is reasonable. But other events are more confusing to the average person, who may need help in interpreting their meaning. When confronted with an event or context that is not easily interpretable or obviously meaningful, many people may take cues from what political elites and opinion makers say about the event. These political elites may be news commentators and pundits, members of Congress, or representatives of interest groups who fill the ranks of those interviewed for news stories or who appear on the political talk shows, such as those that are aired on Sunday mornings.

Especially in our electronic media-saturated world, with its myriad of television and other commentators on politics and instant analyses of political events, the average person may pick up either directly from these media or indirectly from conversations with friends and relatives what these elites are saying. One intriguing study has found that the nature and the distribution of such elite opinion affect public perceptions of the event and the president. Thus, when elites are united in support of the president, the public takes the positive cue, and presidential job approval ratings go up. However, if elite discourse is negative, job approval ratings are likely to go down, while split opinion in this political elite is also mirrored in the public.[51]

Given such an impact, one can see in part why presidents spend so much time on public activities and spin control when the public actually pays little attention to politics or the minutia of day-to-day political maneuvering by the president and other politicians. The president's strategy seems to be to mold opinion within the opinion-leading elite with the hope that the broad mass will follow. From such a perspective, one can appreciate why presidents do not want to be criticized in the media. It gives voice to his opponents and indicates to the mass public less than total support for the president by the nation's political elite.

Favorability Versus Job Approval

The public evaluates not only the job that the president is doing but also the person in office. And presidents may seek not only public support for their policies but also public support for themselves. Thus, it is possible that the public may like a president as a person but not approve of his performance in office or vice versa. This second pattern of approving but disliking seems to be how the public related to Bill Clinton. Ideally, a president would prefer to be both liked and approved of, while the worst of all possible situations would be to be both disliked and disapproved of. Without having much strong evidence at hand, it may be the case that Nixon was both disliked and disapproved of during the last two years of his term in office, when the Watergate scandals and a poor economy plagued him.

[51]Richard A. Brody, *Assessing the President: The Media, Elite Opinion, and Public Support*. Stanford: Stanford University Press, 1991. John Zaller, *The Nature and Origins of Mass Opinion*. Cambridge, England: Cambridge University Press. 1997. On the impact of elite discourse on public opinion more generally, see John Zaller.

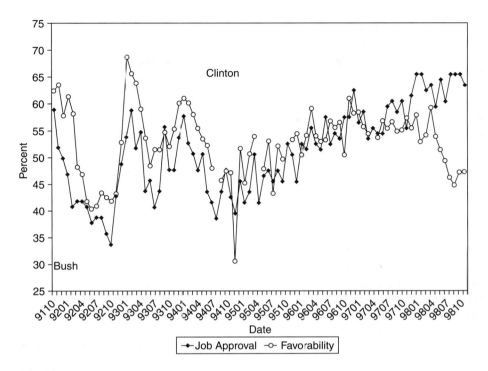

FIGURE 8-2
Presidential Job Approval and Favorability, October 1991–December 1998

In recent years, polling firms have been asking people their "impressions" of the president as a supplement to the job approval question. A typical such question is Gallup's, which reads this way: "We'd like to get your overall opinion of some people in the news. As I read each name, please say if you have a favorable or unfavorable opinion of this person—or if you have never heard of him or her. How about . . . Bill Clinton?" Quite frequently in the news, reporters make comments about a president's "likability" or **favorability** with the public. Questions such as Gallup's are used to generate these results.[52]

Much overlap exists within the mass public between favorability and job approval. Many people who approve of the president also like him, while those who disapprove also tend to dislike. But the correspondence between the two is far from perfect. Figure 8–2 presents the time line of Bill Clinton's favorability and job approval from 1993 through 1999. Across much of his tenure, the two move together, but in 1998, they begin to separate, with Clinton's job approval ratings inching up, while his favorability ratings turn downward.

---

[52]On favorability ratings of presidents, see Jeffrey E. Cohen, "The Polls: Favorability Ratings of Presidents," *Presidential Studies Quarterly* 29 (September 1999): 689–95; Jeffrey E. Cohen, "The Polls: The Dynamics of Presidential Favorability, 1991–1998," *Presidential Studies Quarterly* 29 (December 1999): 896–902; and Jeffrey E. Cohen, "The Polls: The Components of Presidential Favorability," *Presidential Studies Quarterly* 30 (March 2000): 169–177.

In 1998, the Monica Lewinsky scandal broke. One would expect that such an event, accompanied by massive news media interest, would undermine public regard for the president. This is what we find when inspecting public favorability toward Clinton. But across the period of the Lewinsky scandal and the impeachment trial that followed, Bill Clinton's job approval ratings seemed to go up. The source of the boost in Clinton's job approval did not come from the scandal but from the improving economy and the public's increased sense of economic well-being.[53] That public opinion about the president moved in two directions during scandal-plagued 1998 suggests the ability of the public to discriminate in its opinions about the president. We have hinted at such discrimination in public attitudes toward the president, and from this evidence, we may make a case that the public is separating the public presidency, and his job as president, from the private behaviors of the president. In effect, the public holds two evaluations of the president, job performance and personal demeanor and attributes.

It is hard to say which of the two is more important for presidential leadership. Some thinkers suggest that both sides of the presidency are important. The president is not only a policy making figure but also a symbol for the nation, a person for citizens to identify with and react to. As such, his personal attributes and behavior become important. Furthermore, in creating the presidency and deciding how presidents were to be selected, the founders gave great weight to the person who was to be selected and made little mention of the president as a policy leader. From such a perspective, the personal president may be more important than the public policy president.

During the Clinton impeachment debates, the central argument was whether we should judge a president by his policy actions, or his personal actions, or both. For now, the public seems to have answered the question by stressing public policy over personal behavior. The public may or may not hold that view in the future; and as the office, our political institutions, and public opinion evolve, standards for judging presidents may change.

Still, there are some ironies in all of this. Some have argued that we are now in an age of the "image is everything" presidency and that policy choice by presidents is secondary to image building. This does not seem to be the way that the public reacted to Bill Clinton and the Lewinsky impeachment scandal. This might mean that the "image first" strategy of presidential public relations is misguided or will not be successful under all circumstances.

Lastly, why did Clinton's job approval ratings remain high despite the scandal and the downward slope of his favorability ratings? First, on one level, the nation and the government were in good shape, especially the economy. But Clinton may have also done something to steer public attention away from his favorabil-

[53]See Molly W. Andolina and Clyde Wilcox, "Public Opinion: The Paradoxes of Clinton's Popularity," in *The Clinton Scandal and the Future of American Government,* ed. Mark J. Rozell and Clyde Wilcox (Washington, D.C.: Georgetown University Press, 2000), pp. 171–94; John Zaller, "Monica Lewinsky's Contribution to Political Science," *PS: Political Science and Politics* 31 (June 2000): 182–89; Molly W. Sonner and Clyde Wilcox, "Forgiving and Forgetting: Public Support for Bill Clinton During the Lewinsky Scandal," *Political Science and Politics* 32 (September 1999): 554–57.

ity ratings (and his personal misbehaviors) and toward his job performance. Rather than spend time throughout 1998 and early 1999 defending himself from the scandal charges, Clinton tried to look more presidential, speaking frequently on policy issues and otherwise emphasizing his performance as president. From this perspective, it is not foreordained that the public will always hold job performance in higher regard than favorability or that disliking the president will so weakly influence public assessments of job approval. In other words, presidents may to some degree be able to manage their public relations and influence public assessments of them.

PRESIDENTIAL LEADERSHIP VERSUS FOLLOWERSHIP OF PUBLIC OPINION

As we have pointed out, the question of presidential leadership of public opinion is complex and has no simple answer. Under some conditions and at some times, presidents are able to lead public opinion. A similar point can be made about presidential responsiveness or followership of public opinion. Sometimes presidents are responsive to public opinion and thus follow it, but not always. In this conclusion, we sort out some of these issues.

Presidential Leadership of Public Opinion

In discussing presidential leadership of public opinion, we must distinguish among types of public opinions that the president would like to influence. Naturally, presidents want to affect how the public views them and the job that they are doing in office, and we spent much time on this topic in this chapter. Much of the public's evaluation of presidential job performance is a function of what is happening in the real world, such as with the economy and the international situation, and presidents will be able to influence public perceptions of job performance only insofar as they can affect these real-world conditions, something that is very difficult to do. Presidents can take specific actions, such as making speeches and traveling, that might improve public assessments, but such actions tend to have at best modest and short-lived effects on public opinion.

Still, as the case of Clinton and the Lewinsky scandal illustrated, presidents can help their case before the public through public relations campaigns, although such campaigns must be rooted in reality. A president cannot make a failed administration look successful from public relations activities alone. Thus, while greatly affected by the real world, presidents are not total captives of their times, but generally, presidents are able to affect public opinion about their job performance only marginally.

Presidents want to influence not only public assessments of the job that they are doing but also how the public thinks about public policies and issues. Here, we need to distinguish what the public sees as important problems, the public's agenda, from the position that the public takes on issues of the day, policy and issue preferences. It is easier for the president to affect the public agenda than to affect policy preferences.

One study, for instance, found that the more a president emphasized an issue in his State of the Union address, the more important that issue became to the mass public.[54] Other studies have also found that when the president makes a major speech, especially one delivered during prime time on television and that preempts normal programming, the issue covered in the speech becomes a more important concern to the mass public. In contrast, presidents are not always able to affect public preferences on an issue. One study concluded that only popular presidents were able to move public preferences and that unpopular presidents had either no effect or, by speaking, might even stimulate the public to move in the opposite direction from that which the president wanted.[55]

What accounts for these differences in presidential ability to affect public thinking on issues? As far as the public agenda is concerned, people seem to use the president as a cue about what is important. Often people are not very attentive to politics, but when the president takes time out of his normally busy routine to deliver a major speech, it is a signal to the public that the president considers the topic to be important and worthy of attention. Thus, presidents can activate public opinion.

But presidents have a harder time influencing policy preferences because that often involves converting people from one opinion to another. Conversion is a difficult process, and people with preexisting opinions are not highly likely to change them just because the president asked them to. To make a comparison, a Republican might see an issue as more important when a Democratic president speaks about it, but that same person might not agree with the president's proposal to deal with it because so many other factors, such as partisanship, ideology, and past preferences, lead the person to hold policy views different from the president.

Barriers to Presidential Leadership of Public Opinion   Thus, barriers exist to easy presidential influence over public opinion. The lower those barriers, the easier time the president will have in influencing public thought. In general, the barrier around the public's agenda is lower than it is for policy preferences. Presidents have to contend with several major barriers. The first is getting the public's attention. The second is the strength of opinion among people. A third is the nature of elite discourse on politics and policy.

Gaining Attention   Gaining public attention is an important barrier to presidential leadership of public opinion. If the public is not paying attention to the president and what he says and does, the president will not be able to lead the public. Although one might think that someone as important as the president would have an easy time gaining public attention, this is not the case.

---

[54]See Jeffrey E. Cohen, "Presidential Rhetoric and the Public Agenda," *American Journal of Political Science* 39 (February 1995): 87–107; and Kim Quaile Hill, "The Policy Agendas of the President and the Mass Public: A Research Validation and Extension," *American Journal of Political Science* 42 (October 1998): 1328–34.

[55]Benjamin Page and Robert Y. Shapiro, *The Rational Public* (Chicago: University of Chicago Press, 1992).

One, much of the public in the United States is notoriously disinterested in pol-itics, and the percentage of people who show little interest in politics has been growing in recent decades. Furthermore, disinterest is increasingly prevalent among younger adults. Thus, for the population at large, not only have voting turnout rates declined but so has newspaper readership, and in Chapter 7, we re-marked on the decline in the audience for major presidential speeches.

Several factors may account for this disinterest in politics. First, many people are turned off by the bickering among the nation's political leadership, feeling that politicians spend more time trying to outmaneuver rivals than attending to the na-tion's problems. A second factor is that there is now much competition for peo-ple's attention. Cable television, offering dozens of entertainment alternatives, has siphoned off the audience that the three major networks once commanded. The VCR and, to a lesser degree, computers and the Internet have also captured the time and attention of many. Compounding the competition from other sources for people's attention is the increasing resistance of the major networks to allowing the president to preempt their prime-time programs with major speeches.[56] As a consequence of these factors, the audience for presidential leadership has shrunk.

Overcoming Existing Opinion   The second barrier to presidential leadership is overcoming the opinions about politics and issues that people already hold. The stronger one's beliefs, the harder it is to change those beliefs. Strongly held beliefs take time to take root and are usually based in a person's life experiences. Many are associated with a whole host of reinforcing attitudes. Because opinions have such a strong foundation, a president is not likely to make a huge dent in public opinion by delivering one speech. A whole, well-thought-out opinion campaign is necessary, and even then it may fail when pitted against deeply held beliefs.

Making matters worse for a president bent on altering the public's mind about deeply held beliefs is that people tend to ignore new information, like a presi-dent's arguments, that fly against beliefs already held. New information that is consistent will be filtered in, but new information that is inconsistent will often be filtered out. A last irony is that people who pay attention to politics, the potential presidential audience, are more likely to hold strong beliefs about politics and is-sues than those who do not pay attention to politics.

Now we can understand why presidents might have an easier time altering the public's agenda than redirecting attitudes on issues. Altering the agenda involves more the activation of opinion about political matters. Few people have deeply felt views about the most important problems that the nation is facing, although some do. Moreover, as people are often disinterested in politics but not uncon-cerned, when the president takes the time to tell the public that a problem is pressing and should be dealt with, many people will go along.

However, getting people to adopt a president's solution to problems often in-volves converting people's opinions. Attitudes about the proper role of govern-ment may come into play here, as well as attitudes on similar and related policy

[56]Matthew A. Baum and Samuel Kernell, "Has Cable Ended the Golden Age of Presidential Tele-vision?" *American Political Science Review* 93 (March 1999): 99–114.

issues. These may act as a barrier to easy acceptance of the president's solution. Thus, presidents are likely to have greater luck activating opinions and creating new ones than altering opinions already in place.

Elite Discourse   The third major barrier to presidential leadership relates to the way that the nation's political elite and opinion makers react to the president. People in general are more likely to alter their thinking when several sources of new information all reinforce each other and point them in a new direction. One can view the nation's political elite and opinion makers as information sources that compete with the president for the public's attention. When that elite is united in support of the president's position, then a person is confronted with a political environment in which new information is self-reinforcing. If that elite is united in opposition to the president, then not only is a person receiving contradictory information from the political environment, but the president's leadership position is literally being challenged. And even if that opinion elite is divided, people will be receiving new information that is argumentative, and the president's leadership position is still being challenged.

Clearly, a president will be better able to lead when the political elite of the nation is behind him. Thus, much of what we see as presidential publicity campaigns, spin control, and the like is aimed at corralling the nation's political elite behind the president or cutting the volume of opposition voices in public debate and discourse. As we have noted, this is not a easy task in an open and decentralized political system like that of the United States. All of this indicates that presidential leadership of public opinion is not ensured. Because public support is not certain, presidents have poured much energy and resources into public leadership, believing that leadership of public opinion is critical for presidential leadership overall in the age of the modern presidency.

Education Versus Manipulation   Educating the public about issues and policies is an important function for leadership in a democracy. But where does the attempt to lead the public stop being educational and become manipulative? Clearly, we elect people to office in part so they will provide us with guidance on issues of the day and all other political matters. Public officials spend more time on issues than the average citizen and possess more knowledge and information on such topics. They are "experts" in this sense and in the fact that they are often involved in the policies, issues, and controversies of the day. But the access of leaders to information not readily available to the public also makes the public dependent on the quality of information that the leadership transmits to the public. This opens the potential for leader manipulation of the mass public.

How would we know if leaders are trying to manipulate rather than educate? What distinguishes political leadership from manipulation? First, we can think of political education as a process in which leaders provide the public with the information that it needs to make up its own mind about what policy action to take, if any. Thus, manipulation would occur if leaders did not provide the public with all of the relevant information. Further, when leaders engage in disinformation campaigns, that is, when they provide erroneous or misleading information, manipulation is going on.

The timing of information dissemination is also a factor. The public needs time to digest and make sense of information provided. If information is released too near a deadline, such that public debate is not possible, we can argue that the public is being manipulated. Plus, if the information is released along with an abundance of other types of information so that the key information is obscured or lost in a crowd of information, manipulation is likely the intention. Further, manipulation is likely the case when leaders try to rouse public support through emotional or nonrational appeals. Such appeals may be noble, such as patriotism; others may be more base, such as racism. However packaged, nonrational appeals involve manipulation. Lastly, manipulation is likely when the leadership tries to cut off debate and opposing voices. They may do this in nondemocratic situations through control of the media or jailing of opponents. In our democracy, such types of manipulation may be accomplished by feeding stories to select journalists while avoiding others, pressuring news outlets to restrict information flow for, say, national security reasons, or not allowing time for debate before a decision must be made.

How manipulative are presidents? It is hard to say. There have been instances of public manipulation by presidents. And in some circumstances that truly involve national security, hiding information from the public and otherwise manipulating it are possibly justifiable. But the multiplicity of political voices in the nation, the many institutional vantage points from which one can speak, such as Congress or the news media, and the decentralization of political power, all help to cut down on the incidence of manipulative attempts and the success of manipulation or propaganda campaigns. Further, the support of politicians for democratic processes probably creates norms that inhibit the most overt attempts at manipulating the public. Also, the fact that presidents are not uniformly successful in leading public opinion or even in being able to enjoy high popularity and job approval probably means that there is less manipulation than severe critics assume or at least that presidents on the average are not very good manipulators.[57]

Presidential Responsiveness to Public Opinion

Just as the answer to the question of presidential leadership of public opinion is complex, so is the answer to whether presidents are responsive to public opinion. Sometimes presidents are responsive, but at other times they are not, and the answer to the question must seek the conditions under which presidents will respond to public opinion and when they will not. Let us simply define responsiveness as presidential followership of public opinion.

---

[57]For an opposed view that argues that in recent decades, politicians, including the president, have actively and frequently tried to manipulate public opinion, see Larry R. Jacobs and Robert Y. Shapiro, *Politicians Don't Pander: Political Manipulation and the Loss of Democratic Responsiveness* (Chicago: University of Chicago Press, 2000).

First, the growing use of polls has probably increased the degree to which presidents are responsive to public opinion. For one thing, polls provide presidents with better and more accurate information about public opinion. Thus, we may surmise that presidents who make use of polls will make fewer mistakes in trying to interpret and understand the public's opinion on an issue. Also, the presence and use of polls, even if they were intended as tools to help the president manage public opinion, will sensitize the administration to public opinion in its decision making. Thus, we might suggest that presidents of the past two decades or so have been more responsive to public opinion than earlier presidents because of the greater use of polls within and without the White House during this time frame.[58]

However, one study contends that polls do not make presidents more responsive to public opinion but instead increase the potential for presidential manipulation of public opinion by providing presidents with better information about public thinking. Presidents, thus, have commissioned polls to find out which political terms, symbols, and arguments resonate with the public and which do not. From this, presidents may tailor their public speaking to avoid certain rhetorical approaches and to use others.[59]

Second, presidents who interpret their role of president as a representative of the people, perhaps in competition with Congress, are likely to be more responsive to public opinion as well. Such a view began with Theodore Roosevelt and the presidents of the turn of the twentieth century. As we discussed in the section on "The Rhetorical Presidency" in this chapter, the writings of Woodrow Wilson laid a firm intellectual foundation for viewing the presidency in policy representational terms. Lastly, the rise of public expectations about the presidency by the middle third of the century, the development and use of public opinion polls, and the new nomination process with its emphasis on primaries helped to reinforce the view of the presidency as a representational office. Thus, modern presidents will probably be more likely to view the office in representational terms, which may translate to greater responsiveness to public opinion.

We are also likely to see presidential responsiveness to public opinion increasing as a president's need for public support increases. Thus, presidents in their first term of office should be more responsive than in their second term because of their greater need for public support, if for nothing else than to get reelected. Similarly, presidents who are not popular may feel that they need to do something to increase their levels of public support. This may entail greater responsiveness, perhaps by taking the "popular" position on issues as a demonstration of being in step with prevailing public thought. Conversely, second-term and popular presidents may feel less need to curry public favor, and their degree of responsiveness to public opinion is likely to drop.

Lastly, presidential responsiveness is likely to peak when public opinion on an issue is strong and clear, that is, when large majorities hold a reasonably firm position on an issue. It is hard to resist public opinion under such circumstances. Pres-

[58]See John G. Geer, *From Tea Leaves to Opinion Polls* (New York: Columbia University Press, 1996).

[59]See Jacobs and Shapiro, "Rise of Presidential Polling."

idents who do are likely to find themselves in a situation in which political rivals have assumed the mantle of public leadership, and presidents running against both strong public opinion and announced rivals will in all likelihood find themselves on the losing side. The public, however, rarely speaks with a strong, clear voice about public matters, but when it does, it is often on issues of great consequence. The rarity and weight of such events makes presidential resistance to public opinion even riskier. Thus, few presidents are likely to resist public opinion.

Still, there are several important barriers to presidential responsiveness that we must take into account. First of all, presidents come to office with prior commitments. Many of these commitments were generated in the primary and general election campaigns for the presidency, as presidential aspirants promised to groups and to voters at large what they would do on particular policy fronts. Once in office, it is hard for presidents to change course and do something different from what they promised in the campaign. Acting so unreliably can harm a president's reputation with the public, who might come to view him more as an opportunist than a leader. George H. W. Bush, for example, was soundly criticized when he altered course on his "no new taxes" pledge. Democrats had boxed Bush into a corner because of another of his policies, which was to keep a lid on new government spending by requiring any new program to pay for itself by either adding government revenues or cutting other programs. That Bush had spoken so vehemently about "no new taxes" and that he compromised with the demands of congressional Democrats harmed Bush's leadership image with the public.

In contrast, Bill Clinton changed his early economic policies from focusing on the recession, which he promised to do something about, to focusing on reducing the budget deficit.[60] While Clinton incurred some political cost for this course change, he tried to justify it with the argument that the economy was pulling out of the recession and that the budget deficit problem was graver than he had thought. Thus, unlike Bush, Clinton did not appear to be caving in to political circumstances, and also unlike Bush, he was not as wedded to his antirecession package as Bush was to his "no new taxes" pledge. Instead, he based his change of course on changing conditions and responsible leadership.

Presidents may also come to office with personal beliefs that will lead them to resist public opinion. Ronald Reagan presents a good case in point. Reagan generally held conservative positions across almost all of the issues for which he had articulated a policy position. This was especially true of his economic views and program, which were labeled "supply side economics." However, a little over a year into his administration, the economy took a nosedive. As the recession deepened and lengthened, public criticism of his program heightened, and Reagan's approval ratings plummeted. Still, Reagan tried to convince the public to "stay the course" with his policies, that matters would improve, which they did about a year later. Because of his beliefs about economic policy, Reagan stood his ground in the face of growing public opposition.

[60]Bob Woodward, *The Agenda: Inside the Clinton White House* (New York: Simon and Shuster, 1994).

This leads to another point about presidential resistance to public opinion. When the president's program and policies are working or he feels they are working, the president will likely resist public opinion and instead try to convince the public to view the program and policies in the positive light that he thinks they deserve.

The political context may also affect presidential responsiveness to the public. One study argues that currently, the context undermines incentives for presidential responsiveness to public opinion.[61] This context is defined in part by the control over nomination- and election-based resources that political activists and interest groups possess, making them potentially more important than the public or the average voter to political careers. Added to the power of activists and interest groups is the high degree of polarization between the parties, which in part is a function of the scarcity of moderates in political office. There are few moderates because elected politicians owe their posts to the efforts of political activists and interest groups, which tend to have extreme political views, when compared to average people. Thus, the structure of incentives for presidents leads them to activists and interest groups, and away from being responsive to public opinion. Ironically, democratizing the nomination system, which was intended to increase the public's control over its leaders, may have actually undermined public influence, because activists and interest groups have such disproportionate influence in nomination politics. Thus, because of this context, presidents aim more to move, lead, or, more cynically, manipulate public opinion than to follow it.

Lastly, presidents seem to be more responsive to the public agenda than to the public's policy preferences. Quite often the public wants political leaders to address their problems of concern but at the same time allows its leaders to develop solutions and policies to deal with these problems. Thus, presidents, like other politicians, may find themselves under pressure to address particular issues but not under much public pressure about what type of policy should be used. Presidents may feel comfortable with such a public opinion context because it allows them to be responsive to public opinion and to maintain control of the design and implementation of policies. In this way, presidents may be able to fulfill the public's contradictory expectations of responsiveness and leadership.

KEY TERMS

favorability 227	rallies 223
honeymoon effects 218	rhetorical presidency 207
pocketbook theory 221	sociotropic theory 221
presidential job approval rating 218	*Wag the Dog* theory 224

---

[61]Jacobs and Shapiro, "Rise of Presidential Polling."

DISCUSSION QUESTIONS

1. Why is the president important to the mass public, and why is the public important to the president? In what ways is the president–public relationship unique? In what ways does the relationship between the president and the public present the president with opportunities as well as constraints?
2. How has the relationship between the president and the public evolved over time? What does this evolution tell us about the changing nature of the American democracy and the role of the presidency in our political system?
3. What is Woodrow Wilson's theory of the government and the role of public opinion in the governmental process? In what ways were Wilson's ideas a departure from previous thinking? How have Wilson's ideas affected current thinking and presidential behavior?
4. How has the office of the presidency evolved to mobilize public support in behalf of the president? What are the major offices that have been established for that end?
5. In what ways has polling affected the presidency? Are presidents attentive to polls? Do polls increase presidential responsiveness to public opinion or merely enable presidents to manipulate public opinion more effectively?
6. What devices and strategies do presidents use to generate public attention and support? How successful are presidents in influencing public opinion? What are the implications of presidential attempts to influence public thinking on the quality of governing in the modern United States?
7. What is the nature of public opinion toward the president? What influences a president's standing with the public? What can the president do to improve his public standing? Which presidents seem to be most successful in generating a strong public standing?

SUGGESTED READINGS

Richard A. Brody, *Assessing the President: The Media, Elite Opinion, and Public Support*. Stanford: Stanford University Press, 1991.

Jeffrey E. Cohen, *Presidential Responsiveness and Public Policy-Making: The Public and the Policies That Presidents Choose*. Ann Arbor: University of Michigan Press, 1997.

George C. Edwards, III, *The Public Presidency: The Pursuit of Popular Support*. New York: St. Martin's Press, 1983.

Richard J. Ellis, ed., *Speaking to the People: The Rhetorical Presidency in Historical Perspective*. Amherst: University of Massachusetts Press, 1998.

John G. Geer, *From Tea Leaves to Opinion Polls*. New York: Columbia University Press, 1996.

Susan Herbst, *Reading Public Opinion: How Political Actors View the Democratic Process*. Chicago: University of Chicago Press, 1998.

Larry R. Jacobs and Robert Y. Shapiro, *Politicians Don't Pander: Political Manipulation and the Loss of Democratic Responsiveness*. Chicago: University of Chicago Press, 2000.

9

THE PRESIDENCY
AS AN INSTITUTION

The election of a new president is momentous not only because it brings a new person to office but also because a large cadre of people will accompany that new incumbent to office. These people will comprise the presidential staff and will fulfill many formally recognized functions and responsibilities in government. Some will even become household names and identifiable political personalities in their own right. Many more, when they speak in public, will be speaking for the president, as surrogates for the president and in the president's name.

Despite the fact that so many new faces come to government service with each newly elected president, the president does not organize these new people without guidance from past presidents. Posts carry over from one administration to the next. Some of these are legislatively mandated, and others are considered politically necessary.

The large number of presidential assistants who occupy formal posts in government is what we call the institutional presidency. The institutional presidency officially began in 1939, when Franklin Roosevelt issued Executive Order 8248, which established the **Executive Office of the President (EOP).** This is one of the watershed events in the development of the modern presidency. With the establishment of the EOP, the once small entourage of assistants to the president increased in size and formalized, as specific positions and offices were created. In the process of building the EOP, the presidency was fundamentally altered.

For instance, now presidents would have to spend more time on staff management issues, such as ensuring that this large cadre of staffers would work for the president rather than pursue their own agendas. Much presidential time also would be spent dealing with issues of staff conflict, disagreement, intrigue, and competition.

But this new staffing structure, while it presented challenges to presidents, also offered important opportunities. With enhanced staff support, the president could begin to participate across a wider range of policy concerns and could better manage and coordinate the growing government bureaucracy and its myriad of programs. In this respect, the institutional enrichment of the presidency helped catapult the office into the nation's leading political institution.

In this chapter, we will discuss the development of the institutional presidency, how it affects the president, how presidents make use of the institutional presidency to heighten their role in American politics and policy making, and the problems and issues of having a large, complex staffing structure.

CREATING THE INSTITUTIONAL PRESIDENCY

The Constitution explicitly recognizes that the executive branch will include more than the president and the vice president. By requiring "the Opinion, in writing, of the principal Officer in each of the executive Departments, upon any Subject relating to the Duties of their respective Offices" (Article II, Section 2), the Constitution assumes that the executive branch will include advisers for the president. Furthermore, the Constitution grants the president the power to nominate "other public Ministers and Consuls" and "all other Officers of the United States, whose Appointments are not herein otherwise provided for, and which shall be established by Law" (Article II, Section 2). This too suggests that the founders intended that the executive establishment would extend beyond the offices of the presidency and vice presidency. Lastly, the constitutional duty to "take Care that the Laws be faithfully executed" (Article II, Section 3) makes the president responsible for the conduct of government, including its departments and agencies. In other words, the founders expected that the president would rely on others to help him discharge his duties of office. Who those others would be and the shape of the offices that they would occupy were not formally specified in the Constitution. Those decisions were left for Congress to decide at a later date, after ratification of the Constitution.

Staffing Patterns and Issues from Washington to FDR

Beginning with George Washington, presidents hired assistants and aides to help them. From 1787 until 1857, the president's staff was small, the appointees usually friends or family members, and presidents paid them directly out of their own pocket. No public funds were authorized to pay for presidential staff, owing in part to the constitutional language that the president "shall not receive within that Period (his tenure in office) any other Emolument from the United States" (Article II, Section 1). Staff assistance was taken as a possible emolument or payment. But in 1857, Congress passed a law that appropriated funds for a private secretary to the president, a White House steward, and a messenger.[1] From then on, presidents could seek funds from the national treasury to pay for staff aid.

During these early years, presidential staffers were essentially clerks. Their main tasks centered on correspondence, a laborious task in the days before typewriters, computers, and word processors, when everything had to be handwritten. The introduction of office technologies in the late 1800s, such as the typewriter and telephone, increased the professional competence of presidential staffers, who now had to possess these new office skills. When the telephone was first installed, Grover Cleveland answered it himself. As late as the 1910s, Woodrow Wilson typed his own letters.[2] This gives a sense of the paucity of staff help for presidents before FDR.

[1]John Hart, *The Presidential Branch: From Washington to Clinton,* 2d ed. (Chatham, N.J.: Chatham House, 1995), p. 17.

[2]John P. Burke, *The Institutional Presidency* (Baltimore: Johns Hopkins University Press, 1992), p. 6.

Because the pay they could offer was low, presidents were frequently turned down when they asked someone to serve as an assistant working in the White House. To rectify this situation, late nineteenth-century presidents sought to increase the prestige and pay for White House service. During McKinley's term, the post of private secretary was retitled "secretary to the president."

By the turn of the century, the job duties of presidential secretaries expanded to drafting speeches, regulating access to the president, liaising with party leaders and journalists, and on occasion providing political and policy advice to the president.[3] Thus, many of the staff functions that are now performed began during the early twentieth century. Still, as late as 1922 the official staff of the presidency totaled only thirty-one. This included a secretary to the president, an executive clerk, an appointments clerk, a record clerk, two stenographers, an accounting and dispersing clerk, two correspondents, and twenty-one other, mostly lower-level, clerks. In 1929, the number of secretaries to the president was increased to three.[4]

When Franklin Roosevelt came to office in 1933, a recognizable, albeit small, presidential staff existed. It was slowly growing in size and beginning to show signs of specialization and a division of labor among staffers. More and more tasks were being performed by assistants to the president, and for some, especially at the highest level of secretary to the president, the distinction between administrative and political advice was blurring. With the multiplicity of staff and the specialization of their duties, power struggles among staffers also began to occur.

Despite the growth of the White House staff, Roosevelt still felt overwhelmed due to the growth in the size of government and the addition of new agencies and programs, many of which were created to deal with the demands of the Great Depression. FDR tried to increase the staffing capability of the White House by "detailing" or borrowing staff from the departments and agencies.[5] He felt, however, that this strategy was a stopgap measure and sought, instead, a permanent solution to the problem of the managerial overload of the presidency. In 1936, he called together Louis Brownlow, Charles Merriam, and Luther Gulick, three of the most respected scholars of government and public administration, to study the organization of the government and the issues of administrative management. They reported back to the president in January 1937 with the **Brownlow report,** among the most important documents of the presidency and public administration in U.S. history.

The Brownlow Report

Characteristic of FDR, he gave little in the way of specific guidelines when he asked Brownlow, Merriam, and Gulick to study issues of presidential management and administration. Yet the Brownlow committee went on to produce a wide-

[3]Hart, *Presidential Branch,* p. 22.

[4]Ibid, p. 23. A comprehensive history of presidential management issues is found in Peri E. Arnold, *Making the Managerial Presidency: Comprehensive Reorganization Planning, 1905–1996,* 2d ed. (Lawrence: University Press of Kansas, 1998).

[5]Burke, *Institutional Presidency,* p. 7.

ranging and thoughtful study and offered a number of major recommendations for change, many of which met with FDR's approval.

The Brownlow report argued that administration in the presidency was important to the functioning of democracy, because administration facilitates carrying out the will of the people. In the opinion of the Brownlow committee, presidential administration must concern itself with helping the president execute his duties, manage his staff, organize the presidency, recruit people to government, and oversee fiscal matters, such as budgeting and expenditures. In particular, the report made five major recommendations that dealt with 1) the increased executive management duties falling on the president; 2) the major managerial functions of government, including budgeting, efficiency research, personnel, and government planning; 3) the extension of the merit civil service system; 4) the reorganization of the entire structure of the executive branch of the federal government; and 5) the revision of the fiscal system of government, especially with regard to record keeping, auditing, and financial accountability.[6]

From the outset, the Brownlow report came under severe criticism. The most strident attacks viewed the Brownlow report as one element of a strategy by FDR to grab political power and expand the presidency at the expense of the other branches of government, especially Congress. But these criticisms aimed more at the proposals to reorganize government than at those to upgrade presidential staff.

In the late 1930s, FDR's political position with Congress had weakened, due to his court packing scheme, which we discuss more fully in Chapter 13 on the president and the judiciary. FDR's proposal to reform the White House staff system, sent to Congress in 1937, languished there. It was not until April 1939 that Congress enacted a much watered-down version. Although most of FDR's government reorganization proposals were scrapped, the reforms dealing with staff assistance for the president were retained.[7]

The Brownlow report envisioned a narrow but well-specified role for presidential staff. Only six new staffers were requested, all to be executive assistants, enhancing the small number of such aides already present. Their duties would be limited to helping the president obtain necessary information for decision making, especially from the executive branch departments and agencies. Also, once the president made a decision, the staffers were to inform the affected agencies and departments. In no way were these staffers to become assistant presidents, to interpose themselves between the president and others in and out of government. Nor were they to possess any decision-making authority or policy making role.

[6]Hart, *Presidential Branch*, pp. 27–28; also see the Brownlow report itself: President's Committee on Administrative Management, *Administrative Management in the Government of the United States* (Washington, D.C.: Government Printing Office, 1937). On FDR executive reform efforts in general, see Barry Karl, *Executive Reorganization and Reform in the New Deal* (Cambridge: Harvard University Press, 1963).

[7]The legislative history is detailed in Richard Polenberg, *Reorganizing Roosevelt's Government, 1936–1939* (Cambridge: Harvard University Press, 1966).

The Brownlow report modeled the roles and duties of these proposed presidential assistants on the British staffing system and argued that the people serving in these posts should be ones whom the president could trust and who had little in the way of personal political ambitions other than serving the president. The Brownlow report's position on these new staff was summed up in the pithy phrase that these aides should have a "passion for anonymity."

Roosevelt found the notion that aides to the president would lack political ambitions and settle for anonymity amusing and ridiculous. He jettisoned the Brownlow report's proposal that the six staffers should be organized into an administrative secretariat, with one serving as executive director, or chief of staff. Roosevelt did not trust having someone in such a capacity, preferring to act as his own chief of staff.[8]

The Executive Office of the President in 1939

The Reorganization Act of 1939 gave the president, subject to congressional veto, the authority to reorganize the executive branch. Under that authority, Roosevelt's Reorganization Plan No. 1 of 1939 established the Executive Office of the President and transferred the National Resources Planning Board and the Bureau of the Budget to the EOP. Further details on the organization and structure of the EOP were spelled out in his Executive Order 8248 of that same year.

FDR's 1939 EOP consisted of five divisions. Two of these, the White House Office (WHO) and the Bureau of the Budget (BOB) (which was transformed into the Office of Management and Budget [OMB] in 1970), became important and lasting parts of the EOP. The other three, the National Resources Planning Board, the Liaison for Personnel Management, and the Office of Government Reports, were of lesser importance as the EOP developed. Now eleven units exist in the EOP. We will discuss the more important ones in more detail later in this chapter.

The EOP has undergone remarkable change during its sixty-year history.[9] New units have been added, existing units deleted, and a handful of units have persisted from their creation until the present. Overall, since 1939, a total of forty-five different units have existed within the EOP. Table 9-1 lists those units and their dates of existence and method of creation. Despite this growth and the seemingly ever-present change in the units that comprise the EOP, it has remained a mainstay of the presidency for the sixty-plus years of its existence.

IS THE EXECUTIVE OFFICE OF THE PRESIDENT AN INSTITUTION?

The EOP has undergone remarkable change since its creation in 1939. It is now larger in both people and units than when it was established. It performs more functions for the president than the early EOP did for FDR. How are we to make sense

---

[8]Hart, *Presidential Branch,* pp. 29–30.

[9]See Charles E. Walcott and Karen M. Hult, *Governing the White House: From Hoover through LBJ* (Lawrence: University Press of Kansas, 1995); and Phillip G. Henderson, *Managing the Presidency: The Eisenhower Legacy—From Kennedy to Reagan* (Boulder, Colo.: Westview Press, 1988).

TABLE 9-1   UNITS IN THE EXECUTIVE OFFICE OF THE PRESIDENT, 1939–2000

Unit	Date of existence	Method of creation***
White House Office	1939–	EO
Bureau of the Budget	1939–1970	RP
National Resources Planning Board	1939–1943	RP
Office of Government Reports	1939–1948	RP
Liaison Office for Personnel Management	1939–1953	RP
Office of Emergency Management	1940–1953	EO
Office of War Mobilization	1943–1944	EO
Office of War Mobilization and Reconversion	1944–1946	PL
Council of Economic Advisers	1946–	PL
National Security Council	1949–	RP
National Security Resources Board	1949–1953	RP
Office of Defense Mobilization	1950–1958	EO
Office of the Director for Mutual Security	1951–1953	PL
Telecommunications Adviser to the President	1951–1953	EO
President's Advisory Committee on Government Organization	1953–1961	EO
National Aeronautics and Space Administration	1958–1973	PL
Office of Civil and Defense Mobilization	1958–1961	RP
Office of Science and Technology	1962–1973	RP
Office of Special Representative for Trade Negotiations	1963–1975	EO
Office of Economic Opportunity	1964–1975	PL
National Council on Marine Resources and Engineering	1966–1971	PL
Office of Emergency Preparedness	1968–1973	PL
Council on Urban Affairs	1969–1970	EO
President's Foreign Intelligence Advisory Board	1969–1977	EO
Council on Environmental Quality	1969–	PL
Office of Telecommunications Policy	1970–1978	RP
Office of Management and Budget	1970–	RP
Domestic Council	1970–1977	RP
Council on International Economic Policy	1971–1977	PL
Office of Consumer Affairs	1971–1973	EO
Special Action Office for Drug Abuse Prevention	1971–1975	EO
Federal Property Council	1973–1977	EO
Energy Policy Office	1973–1974	EO
Council on Wage and Price Stability	1974–1981	PL
Presidential Clemency Board	1974–1977	EO

(continued)

TABLE 9-1   CONTINUED

Unit	Date of existence	Method of creation***
Office of the Special Representative for Trade Negotiations*	1975–	PL
Office of Drug Abuse Policy	1976–1978	PL
Office of Science and Technology Policy	1976–	PL
Domestic Policy Staff**	1977–1993	RP
Office of Administration	1977–	RP
National Critical Materials Council	1984–1993	PL
National Space Council	1988–1993	PL
Office of National Drug Control Policy	1988–	PL
National Economic Council	1993–	EO
Domestic Policy Council	1993–	EO

*Renamed the Office of the U.S. Trade Representative in 1979.

**Renamed the Office of Policy Development in 1981 and replaced by the Domestic Policy Council in 1993.

***EO = executive order, RP = reorganization plan, PL = public law

Source: Adapted from John Hart, *The Presidential Branch: From Washington to Clinton,* 2d ed. (Chatham, N.J.: Chatham House, 1995), pp. 242–44.

of the changes in the EOP? What is the nature of the EOP? To help sort through these questions, we will ask whether the EOP is an institution. As we will see, the EOP has acquired some characteristics of a matured institution, but it is also highly malleable. Presidents and others have altered the EOP to suit their needs; the EOP seems, in this sense, highly adaptable. One irony is that the EOP can be altered so readily by others yet retains its identity as the president's staff organization.

One might argue that it would be best if the EOP were not heavily institutionalized. Then presidents could reshape and use their staffs as they see fit, adapting to an ever-changing political environment. However, despite the changeability of the political world in which the president operates, many issues with which the president must deal are recurring. For instance, each year a budget must be prepared. People must be appointed to the established offices of government, both in the executive branch and the judiciary. Presidents must be aware of their level of popularity and how the media cover and treat them. First-term presidents must gear up for a reelection campaign. Presidents must also find ways of generating support in Congress for policies that they want enacted, as well as devise methods to ensure that the bureaucracy implements the policies in the ways intended by the president and Congress. The list could easily go on, but the main point is that no matter who is president, the same basic sets of problems, issues, and tasks recur.

An institution helps decision makers cope with recurring problems and tasks by applying time-tested routines and decision rules, by avoiding mistakes that have been made in the past, and by enabling decision makers to learn how best to do their jobs. In this sense, institutions help decision makers like the president behave both more efficiently and effectively. But institutions are also better able at handling issues that have come up before or that have precedents or analogs. Institutions are less well suited to dealing with the unique, the unexpected, the untried. It is clear that presidents are also confronted with such unprecedented events and circumstances. Thus, it might be best if the institutional presidency were not so rigid that it tied the president down, restricting his span of choice and making him less capable of responding to new situations.

What Is an Institution?

An **institution** is a type of complex organization. Students of organizations point to four major characteristics of institutions. They possess identifiable boundaries, they are internally complex, they employ universalistic criteria, and they are continuous in the sense of being able to persist over time, withstanding threats to their existence.[10]

The Boundedness of the EOP

First, an institution is well **bounded.** That means that one can distinguish the institution from its environment and from other institutions. The EOP is well bounded. The mere fact of its name gives a sense of the ability to identify the Executive Office. Furthermore, the official actions that created the EOP, such a legislative statute or presidential executive order, describe the nature and extent of the office and its units. Lastly, we see the boundedness of the EOP in the fact that it liaises with other organizations, such as Congress, interest groups, and so on, through such units as the Office of Congressional Liaison and Office of Public Liaison. Thus, the EOP resembles other institutions in the fact that it is well bounded.

The Complexity of the EOP

Institutions are also internally **complex.** Complexity implies that a division of labor exists within the institution. This division of labor allows the institution to deal with many tasks at the same time. The two major sets of tasks involve internal

[10]On theories of institutionalization and their application to the presidency, see Burke, *Institutional Presidency;* Robert S. Gilmour, "The Institutionalization of the Presidency: A Conceptual Clarification," in *The Presidency in Contemporary Context,* ed. Norman G. Thomas (New York: Dodd, Mead, 1975), pp. 147–159; Samuel P. Huntington, *Political Order in Changing Societies* (New Haven: Yale University Press, 1968); Joseph A. Pika and Norman C. Thomas, "Institutions and Personality in Presidency Research," paper presented at the American Political Science Association, San Francisco, August 29-September 1, 1996; Nelson Polsby, "The Institutionalization of the U.S. House of Representatives," *American Political Science Review* 62 (March 1968): 144–68; Lyn Ragsdale and John J. Theis, III, "The Institutionalization of the American Presidency, 1924–1992," *American Journal of Political Science* 41 (October 1997): 1280–1318; Lester G. Seligman, "Presidential Leadership: The Inner Circle and Institutionalization," in *The Presidency,* ed. Aaron Wildavsky (Boston: Little, Brown, 1969), pp. 632–46; and Charles E. Walcott and Karen M. Hult, *Organizing the White House: The Presidency as an Organization, 1929–1969* (Lawrence: University Press of Kansas, 1995); Jeffrey E. Cohen, *The Politics of the U.S. Cabinet: Representation in the Executive Branch, 1789–1984* (Pittsburgh: University of Pittsburgh Press, 1988), pp. 22–43.

management and external relations. The EOP is relatively complex. We can see the complexity of the EOP in the number of units and people within it, and in the fact that the EOP has developed units whose main task is to coordinate the people and offices of the EOP. Also, the internal complexity of the EOP has led to status differentiation among its units and people who work there. Some people and units are more important than others.

The Size of the EOP   We can chart the growth of the EOP through the number of organizational units, the number of employees, and the size of the budget. Although the EOP is larger now than it was in 1939, its peak size came in the early 1970s.

It is difficult to estimate the precise number of employees who work in the EOP. First, the president may borrow or detail employees from the federal agencies to the White House and EOP. FDR did much of this, especially during the Second World War, when he detailed a large number of military officers to serve as advisers during the war. Also, presidential staff may be paid for out of special funds that began to be allocated to the presidency in the 1940s and 1950s, and continue to this day.[11] Using these two devices enabled presidents to hide the true number of people working in the EOP.

Still, we can get a ballpark idea of the size of the EOP staff and the trend in growth over time. From FDR through Nixon, the EOP experienced consistent staff growth, especially during the Johnson and Nixon years. As a result of the Watergate scandals, critics charged that the EOP had grown too large, and the political mood required presidents to attempt to reduce staffing levels. In the wake of Watergate, during the Ford and Carter administrations, staff levels declined, especially in units other than the WHO and the OMB. Official data for 1994 indicate nearly seventeen hundred professionals working across all of the units of the EOP.[12] The 1994 budget for the EOP stood at almost $173 million, and it shows a time path similar to that of staff levels, when corrected for inflation. Thus, while we cannot be entirely precise about the size of the EOP, it has grown since 1939, and it has grown much larger than the Brownlow committee envisioned.

Adding Functions to the EOP   The Brownlow committee conceived the EOP as a small administrative staff to assist the president in his managerial duties. While the EOP plays that role, over time it has added other functions to which the Brownlow committee would have objected, including policy advice, outreach (communications and liaison), and political functions.[13]

Currently, the entire scope of public policy is represented by an office in the EOP. Economic advice is offered the president by the Council of Economic Advisers (CEA). In 1993, President Clinton created the National Economic Council (NEC) to coordinate among the many economic policy advisers to the president,

[11]Hart, *Presidential Branch,* p. 44.

[12]Ibid., p. 46.

[13]Burke, *Institutional Presidency,* p. 15.

in and out of the EOP. The NEC seems to be eclipsing the CEA in economic policy advice to the president. Foreign policy advice comes through the National Security Council (NSC). Domestic policy advice is the realm of the Domestic Policy Council, which was created by Clinton in 1993 but has roots dating to the Domestic Council that President Nixon set up in 1970.[14]

Environmental policy comes under the auspices of the Council on Environmental Quality, and drug policy is coordinated by the Office of National Drug Control Policy, which also had predecessors, such as the Domestic Policy Council (Special Action Office for Drug Abuse Prevention, 1971–1975; Office of Drug Abuse, 1976–1978). The Office of the Special Representative for Trade Negotiations and the Office of Science and Technology Policy offer policy advice for trade and science and technology policy, respectively. Perhaps most important is the OMB, which not only helps the president prepare the budget but offers advice on economic and other policies that affect the budget; it also possesses instruments, such as legislative and regulatory clearance, to control the bureaucracy. These offices do more than design policy. They may also monitor policy implementation and coordinate agencies responsible for different aspects of the policy.

The EOP, especially units within the White House Office, has also become important in presidential outreach to interest groups (Office of Public Liaison), Congress (Office of Congressional Liaison), the mass media (Office of Communications and the Office of the Press Secretary), and local governments (Office of Intergovernmental Relations). Many of these units have political functions—to help show the president in a good light, to mobilize support for presidential initiatives, to enhance president popularity, and even to aid the president in his renomination quest.

The Office of Political Affairs (OPA) performs this political function. President Reagan created the OPA to deal with the presidential nomination process and regulation of campaign finances. The current nomination system requires presidential aspirants, including presidents seeking a second term, to enter a large number of primaries and to collect large sums of money to run in those primaries. Consequently, first-term presidents seeking a second term spend considerable time near the end of their first term running for reelection. To comply with existing regulations, to ensure a professional campaign staff and ready election organization, and to separate these political activities from other White House and governing duties and responsibilities, Reagan created the office. Presidents since Reagan have found it to be especially useful in this regard, and the OPA has been in existence ever since.[15]

[14]In 1978, the Domestic Council was succeeded by the Domestic Policy Staff, which Clinton's Domestic Policy Council replaced. The history and politics of the domestic policy staff are found in Shirley Anne Warshaw, *The Domestic Presidency: Policy Making in the White House* (Boston: Allyn and Bacon, 1997).

[15]Hart, *Presidential Branch*, p. 128; and Kathryn Dunn Tenpas, "Institutionalized Politics: The White House Office of Political Affairs," *Presidential Studies Quarterly* 26, no. 1 (1996): 511–22.

Coordinating Units   With the growth in size and the addition of functions to the EOP came units to coordinate them into a coherent whole. The most important of these coordinating units is the **chief of staff.** In 1939, FDR objected to a chief of staff position, even though the Brownlow report recommended such an office. FDR preferred to be his own chief of staff. Many subsequent presidents tried to be their own chief of staff. The last to have tried this was Jimmy Carter in the late 1970s. The number of staffers and the multitude of offices within the WHO and EOP make it impossible for the president to both make policy decisions and run his staffing operations in any detailed manner.[16] The creation in 1993 of the National Economic Council by Clinton is another example of a coordinating body, but here the aim is to coordinate economic policy advice to the president. As one last example, Reagan pulled together all units that would work on different aspects of campaigns to win congressional approval of his policy initiatives. This included not only the legislative liaison office but also the media offices (Office of Communications and Press Secretary) and the Office of Public Liaison, which would reach out to interest groups, among others. George H. W. Bush and Bill Clinton followed this multipronged approach to winning congressional support.

Status Differentiation and the EOP   Another implication of the growing complexity of the EOP is the establishment of a hierarchical structure among units and personnel working for the president. We can observe this status hierarchy at work by noticing how close one's office is to the president's, how large of an office one has, and how many aides work for the staffer. But perhaps most critical here is how often and in what capacity the staffer comes into contact with the president. The vast number of people who work in the White House have no face-to-face contact with the president and may rarely even glimpse him. In fact, speechwriters for the president, who author messages that the president airs daily, have had little or no personal contact with the president since the Johnson and Nixon years. While presidents and top aides write the president's major speeches, such as the State of the Union address, the mass of routine but still official presidential messages might not see his eyes until just before he is to deliver them.[17]

Universalistic Criteria and the EOP

The third characteristic of institutions is the use and application of **universalistic criteria.** This means that institutions use precedent, routines and rules, and merit, rather than fiat, favoritism, or cronyism, in processing their workload.[18] This can be seen at work in the recruitment, advancement, and retention of personnel

---

[16]Samuel Kernell and Samule L. Popkin, *Chief of Staff: Twenty-Five Years of Managing the Presidency* (Berkeley: University of California Press, 1986).

[17]Karen M. Hult and Charles E. Walcott, "Policymakers and Wordsmiths: Writing for the President Under Johnson and Nixon," *Polity* 30 (Spring 1998): 465–87.

[18]Burke, *Institutional Presidency,* p. 28.

working for the president, and here we find tensions between the president's need for knowledgeable people with his often contradictory need for loyal aides.

Each president brings with him to office a large number of political associates, those people who helped him win the office. Thus, there was the Irish-Boston "mafia" of John Kennedy, the Georgians who served with Carter, the Californians of Reagan, the staffers with Arkansas roots of Clinton. But the political skills that these staffers bring are not always useful in the Washington arena, where presidential concerns also must turn to policy, staff management, and presidential public relations, all of which may require sharply different skills than needed for the combative politics of electoral campaigns.[19] For instance, James Baker, an associate of George H. W. Bush, was originally appointed by Ronald Reagan, in part as a concession to Bush. Baker, along with two long-time Reagan associates, Ed Meese and Michael Deaver, served as top-level advisers to the president in a troika arrangement in which each would have equal status but divide responsibilities. In time, Baker emerged to become the president's chief of staff because he possessed more Washington experience than the other two, having served in the Ford administration, as well as possessing national political experience on the Ford and Bush campaigns.[20] Even Bill Clinton pushed out of the top levels of his staff long-time friends in favor of aides with more Washington political experience. A case in point is Leon Panetta, a former member of Congress from California who served as Clinton's second chief of staff beginning in July 1994, replacing long-time friend Thomas McClarty, who served in that position from the onset of the administration.[21]

An equally important trend is the placement of presidential loyalists in the policy offices of the EOP, as in the CEA and OMB. It was originally hoped with the establishment of offices such as these that they would be staffed by long-time civil servants who would continue in those positions for several administrations, serving the presidency more than the president. Presidents, nonetheless, have found greater utility in having loyalists in these sensitive policy positions, people who would better understand than civil servants the politics of policy making, who are more likely to employ other criteria in developing policy, such as effectiveness or efficiency. We return to this issue of "politicizing" the presidential staff and the EOP in the section on "Has the EOP Been Deinstitutionalizing?"

The Persistence of the EOP

Lastly, institutions are continuous bodies that **persist** for long periods of time, often for many generations. Institutions have staying power. The EOP overall has had great staying power, existing for over six decades now, even though the particular units and subunits within the EOP have been less durable. Recall table 9-1, which listed the many units of the EOP that have come and gone over the

---

[19]On the differences between campaigning and governing, see Charles O. Jones, *Passages to the Presidency: From Campaigning to Governing* (Washington, D.C.: Brookings Institution, 1998).

[20]Burke, *Institutional Presidency*, p. 33.

[21]Panetta served until 1997, when he was replaced by Erskine Bowles.

years or the fact that the WHO has been constantly reshuffled and reorganized by each succeeding president to meet his own needs and preferences. This may indicate lack of institution presence of the EOP, but it might also indicate the great adaptability of the EOP to its very dynamic environment, the most important dynamic element being the arrival of a new president every four to eight years. This remarkable responsiveness to each new president also signals the overall utility and value of the EOP to the president. No president has sought to do away with the EOP. Instead, they have sought to mold it to their own special and personal requirements.

Still, presidents have not been able to fully mold the EOP. Congress has insisted on certain offices, such as the CEA and NSC. And presidents have not been able to rid themselves of units that they no longer feel they want or need when Congress feels that those units should continue. Thus, President Clinton was unsuccessful in his efforts to terminate the Council on Environmental Quality (CEQ) because of resistance in Congress to such a move. It is more in the WHO that presidents have greatest ability to configure their staff as they see fit. The other units of the EOP, those outside of the WHO complex, are much less subject to his control. Still, Congress cannot make a president use or heavily rely on a unit that he is disinclined to heed or interact with.

Phases in the Institutional Development of the EOP

The EOP did not arrive on the scene as a full-blown and mature institution. The institutional properties of the EOP developed over time. Some argue that in recent decades, the EOP has been deinstitutionalizing as well, which we hinted in the section on "Universalistic Criteria and the EOP," when we mentioned the political criteria used to appoint staffers in the EOP. Understanding the institutional development of the EOP over time will help us grasp some of the implications of an institutionalized office for presidential behavior and why presidents have both resisted and promoted the institutional development of the Executive Office.

We can suggest three phases to the institutional development of the EOP: the preinstitutional phase, the institutionalizing phase, and the institutionalized phase.[22] The degree of institutionalization is important for presidential behavior and choice. Institutionalization increases presidential capacity and ability to act across a wide span of activities and policy concerns. Presidents can do more when supported by an institutional staff. But as the EOP institutionalizes, more and more of that increased presidential activity is prescribed for the president. His freedom to decide what to do declines as he must attend to the responsibilities associated with the offices and duties of the units of the EOP. Thus, institutionalization has implications for the president—it increases his capacity for action but also tells him what to do with much of his time.

[22]See George A. Krause and Jeffrey E. Cohen, "Opportunities, Constraints, and the Development of the Institutional Presidency: The Issuance of Executive Orders, 1939–1996," *Journal of Politics* 62 (2000): 88–114.

The preinstitutional phase spans the years from the founding of the presidency until the creation of the EOP in 1939. During this period, as described in the "Creating the Institutional Presidency" section of this chapter, the presidential staff was small and composed of generalists. As a consequence, presidential activity, such as policy making and lobbying of Congress, was necessarily limited. Still, with the growth of government that commenced in the late nineteenth century and accelerated in the twentieth century, demands on the president for policy leadership and management of the bureaucracy mounted beyond that which this informal staffing structure could handle.

Beginning in 1939, the process of institutionalization took off with the creation of the EOP. For the next thirty years, the process of institutionalizing continued. By the time that Richard Nixon came to office in 1969, the EOP could be characterized as a relatively well-developed institution.[23] Several of Nixon's reforms helped cement the institutional character of the EOP, the most important being the reorganization of the Bureau of the Budget into the Office of Management and Budget, the massive growth in size of staff, and the creation of the Domestic Council.

The change from the BOB to OMB, with the word *management* in the title being placed before *budget,* indicates the importance to Nixon of management for both policy making and presidential control of the bureaucracy. The Domestic Council, designed to coordinate all domestic policy, would downgrade the cabinet in policy making but would also boost the capacity of the EOP with regard to developing domestic policy.

The period of institutionalizing increased presidential capacity to act across a wider array of fronts than was true in the preceding period. But the period of institutionalizing was also a time of experimentation. Presidents could shuffle and reshuffle units in the EOP relatively freely. No one was quite sure what the newly created units would turn into or what their place would end up being in the EOP structure. This may have been the best of all possible worlds for the president—increasing capacity to act while also possessing a staffing system that was highly responsive to his needs.

By the early 1970s, the EOP looked like an institution. It possessed rules and routines. Many of the offices in place were there to fulfill the agendas of interests outside of the White House, such as Congress, the media, and interest groups. The combination of routines and offices to serve outside interests, while increasing presidential capacity, also structured the president's agenda and limited his freedom of action. Naturally, presidents liked the enhanced capacity that the stronger EOP presented to them, but they also resisted the structure that a fully institutionalized EOP heaped on them. Presidents have tried to break free of the straitjacket of the institutionalized EOP. They did so by attempting to politicize or deinstitutionalize the EOP.

[23]Hult and Walcott "Policymakers and Wordsmiths"; and Ragsdale and Theis "Institutionalization of the American Presidency."

Has the EOP Been Deinstitutionalizing?

Deinstitutionalization can be thought of as a process to make the EOP responsive to the needs and demands of each new president. Feeling confined by the expectations and routines of an institutionalized EOP, presidents began to search for ways to make the EOP responsive to their needs. The major routes to deinstitutionalize the EOP involve **politicization** of the staff and reduction of the capacity of units that the president could not control or preferred not to deal with.[24]

Thus, beginning in the 1970s, many units of the EOP had their staff levels cut. In contrast, the unit most amenable to the president and the one least affected by outside interests, the WHO, was not cut in size but tended to grow. Similarly, the analytical capacity of several offices was reduced, in part through staff reductions but also through replacement of experts with people loyal to the president. This is especially apparent in the CEA and CEQ, two congressionally mandated units.[25] And to ensure that people loyal to the president were recruited and hired, the White House Personnel Office was created. Although it dates to 1948, it was most active and influential after 1974.[26] In these ways, then, presidents have tried to balance the greater capacity of an institutionalized EOP with the limits that an institutionalized EOP places on a president.

THE EOP TODAY

Currently, there are eleven major organizational units in the EOP: White House Office, Council of Economic Advisers, National Security Council, Council on Environmental Quality, Office of Management and Budget, Office of the Special Representative for Trade Negotiations, Office of Science and Technology Policy, Office of Administration, Office of National Drug Control Policy, National Economic Council, and the Domestic Policy Council. This is a far cry from the original EOP, which housed only five units.[27] In this section, we briefly discuss the history and tasks of the more visible and important of these units—the White House Office, Office of Management and Budget, Council of Economic Advisers, and National Security Council.

---

[24]Terry M. Moe, "The Politicized Presidency," in *New Directions in American Politics,* ed. John E. Chubb and Paul E. Peterson (Washington, D.C.: Brookings Institution, 1985), pp. 235–72; Margaret Wyszomirski, "The De-institutionalization of Presidential Staff Agencies," *Public Administration Review* 42, no. 5 (1982):448–58; and Margaret Wyszomirski, "The Discontinuous Institutional Presidency," in *Executive Leadership in Anglo-American Systems,* ed. Colin Campbell and Margaret Wyszomirski (Pittsburgh: University of Pittsburgh Press, 1991).

[25] Walter Williams, *Mismanaging America: The Rise of the Anti-analytic Presidency* (Lawrence: University Press of Kansas, 1990).

[26]Thomas J. Weko, *The Politicizing Presidency: The White House Personnel Office, 1948–1994* (Lawrence: University of Kansas Press, 1995).

[27]All of the units of the EOP and WHO are described in Bradley H. Patterson, *The Ring of Power: The White House Staff and Its Expanding Role in Government* (New York: Basic Books, 1988).

TABLE 9-2   THE WHITE HOUSE OFFICE, 1998–1999

Chief of Staff

Cabinet Secretary

Counsel to the President

Office of Communications

Office of Intergovernmental Affairs

Office of Legislative Affairs

Office of Political Affairs

Office of Presidential Personnel

Office of Public Liaison

Office of Scheduling

Office of Special Projects

Office of Speechwriting

Press Secretary

Staff Secretary

Director of the Domestic Policy Council*

Director of the National Economic Council*

National Security Adviser*

Office of Administration*

Special Envoy to the Americas

Advance Office

Senior Adviser to the President for Policy and Strategy

Senior Adviser to the President for Policy Development

---

*Also direct units in the Executive Office of the President that are located outside of the White House Office.

Source: Office of the Federal Register, National Archives and Records Administration, *United States Government Organization Manual,* (Washington, D.C.: Government Printing Office, 1999).

The White House Office

The **White House Office (WHO)** manages the daily affairs of the president, including scheduling, speechwriting, liaising with Congress, and the like. It has become the most important of the units of the EOP, except perhaps for the budget office (OMB). Table 9-2 lists the major offices of the WHO. Other parts of the EOP have been described as satellite offices of the EOP,[28] with the WHO as the central unit. The power of the WHO derives in part from the addition over the years of political, policy making, and advising functions to its basic managerial function. But the WHO is also the most controversial unit in the EOP, in part because of its power and in part because members of the WHO have been central figures in many of the great presidential scandals of the past thirty years, including Watergate and the Iran-Contra affair.

---

[28]Hart, *Presidential Branch,* p. 125.

The most important office within the WHO is the chief of staff. The chief of staff sits atop the organizational structure of the WHO and reports directly to the president. Chiefs of staff have two major functions: to manage the White House and to advise the president. Management includes selecting other key staffers and structuring the offices of the WHO to meet the president's needs to control the flow of paper and people to the president. Like this managing, advising includes several tasks, including providing advice to the president on all major concerns of the president, from political to policy to personnel matters. Other advising responsibilities include protecting the interests of the president and the presidency, and negotiating with major actors in the external environment, such as members of Congress, the news media, and so forth. Overall, the span of duties of the chief of staff is quite wide, and in many respects, the chief of staff has turned into the most important person working for the president. The chief of staff is in daily contact with the president and deals with the broadest range of presidential concerns.

The Brownlow report envisioned a chief of staff who would sit in the background, an almost invisible presence who would possess no real political power or influence. But modern chiefs of staff have become important figures in their own right, often highly visible and powerful. This is a far cry from the Brownlow committee's conception. In part, the Brownlow group was probably naïve about a chief of staff in the American political context remaining merely a servant to the president, without any political ambition or agenda. FDR understood that a chief of staff would wield great political influence, and thus, he refused to create a chief of staff position.

Other presidents, like FDR, tried to be their own chief of staff but found it too difficult to carry on the duties of the president and the chief of staff at the same time. Bill Clinton came to office with the idea of being his own chief of staff. Although Clinton named someone to that position, his first chief of staff remained a weak figure. But policy and other problems led Clinton to ask Leon Panetta, a member of Congress, to serve as his chief of staff and to be a strong chief. The problems of modern government and the presidency—the many programs; the size and complexity of the EOP; the many demands that outside interests, such as Congress, the media, and the public, place on the presidency—all lead a president away from being his own chief of staff and to hiring someone whom he can trust to fulfill that role. That a president now needs a chief of staff gives some sense of the constraints of the institutionalized presidency on the president.

Bureau of the Budget/Office of Management and Budget

The **Bureau of the Budget/Office of Management and Budget** has taken on special importance for the president, converting from a budget and accounting office to a general staff agency for the president. BOB was created in 1921 under the Budget and Accounting Act of that year.[29] Its primary responsibilities under that act were to deal with helping the president prepare the annual budget that had to be submitted to Congress annually. Even though the BOB was located initially in the Department of the Treasury, the director and assistant director were appointed by the president, without requiring senatorial confirmation, and they reported directly to the president.

Under the 1939 executive order creating the EOP, the duties of the BOB were expanded. Perhaps the most important additions concerned legislative clearance. **Legislative clearance** required that before an agency could submit legislation to Congress, it had to be approved by the Office of Legislative Affairs of the BOB, which was to determine if the proposal was in accord with the president's program. With this authority, the president began to centralize and control policy development and the federal bureaucracy. Soon after, BOB began to review legislation passed by Congress to determine if the president should sign or veto it. In a short time, the quality and quantity of personnel at BOB improved, making it a major support office for the president and among the most powerful units of the EOP.

In 1970, Nixon reformed the BOB, creating the OMB. As we have mentioned, management of policy and the bureaucracy rose in prominence as a task of the reformed agency. In the early 1980s, the authority of the OMB was expanded yet further. Under several executive orders, Reagan authorized OMB to review regulations, much as it reviews legislation. Thus, OMB took on **regulatory clearance** duties, which entail determining whether regulations that federal bureaucrats are contemplating should be allowed to proceed. Many federal agencies have the power to implement regulations; the power to do so derives from their legislative mandates. Complex procedures exist for the writing and implementing of new regulations, but until Reagan's actions, the president was not directly involved. Given the large number of agencies with the power to write regulations, the large number of regulations, and the supposed effect on the economy and society, however, presidents felt that they should have a greater say in the implementation of new regulations. Thus, we can understand Reagan's motivation to involve OMB in the regulatory rule writing process.

From this quick review, we can see the policy sweep of OMB. (We will discuss BOB/OMB in more detail in Chapter 14 on the president and economic policy making.) Although the OMB was originally designed to focus on budget making, its duties expanded to include legislative and regulatory clearance. Combined, these powers of budget making, legislative clearance, and regulatory clearance give the president an agency that can help him as he tries to manage and control the far-flung federal bureaucracy.

---

[29]The history of BOB and OMB until 1979 is recorded in Larry Berman, *The Office of Management and Budget and the Presidency, 1921–1979* (Princeton: Princeton University Press, 1979). For a more recent assessment, see Shelley Lynne Tomkin, *Inside OMB: Politics and Process in the President's Budget Office* (Armonk, N.Y.: M. E. Sharpe, 1998). OMB is compared with the Government Accounting Office, an arm of Congress with similar oversight duties, in Frederick C. Mosher, *A Tale of Two Agencies: A Comparative Analysis of the General Accounting Office and the Office of Management and Budget* (Baton Rouge: Louisiana State University Press, 1984).

The Council of Economic Advisers

In 1946, Congress passed a major piece of legislation, the Full Employment Act. That act solidified the role of the federal government in managing the economy. The Full Employment Act also piled new economic responsibilities onto the president. Most important, he was required to report to Congress each year on the state of the nation's economy. To help him prepare that report, as well as to more generally advise him on economic policy matters, the **Council of Economic Advisers (CEA)** was created. Like BOB/OMB, we will discuss the CEA more fully in Chapter 14 on economic policy making, but some general comments about the CEA are useful here.

Congress was quite specific about the duties of the CEA in the enabling legislation. The statutory duties of the CEA are to 1) assist the president in the annual economic report of the president, which was to be presented to Congress—a new presidential responsibility under the Full Employment Act; 2) collect and analyze economic data; 3) monitor federal government programs to determine their impact and consistency with the goals of the Full Employment Act; 4) recommend economic policies to the president; and 5) provide the president with whatever economic advice he requires.

Congress was also quite specific about the training, experience, and attainments qualifications of who could serve in the CEA. In practice, this has meant that people from academia and those with Ph.D.s were more likely to be appointed to CEA positions, either on the council itself or its staff. Here, Congress's intention seems to have been to broaden the economic advice to the president.

CEA has had a checkered history in terms of influence with the president, with its high point coming during the Kennedy-Johnson years. The fact that Congress created and forced the CEA on the president, that almost every policy issue that the president deals with has economic implications, and that economic effects of policies have political implications has meant that presidents are in control of how much access and influence they want to give the CEA. This has varied tremendously across presidents, and as we will discuss in more detail in Chapter 14, many other economic policy advising bodies in the EOP have been created and reorganized by presidents to get a handle on economic policies and their implications for the presidency.

The National Security Council

Like the CEA, the **National Security Council (NSC)** was created by congressional legislation shortly after the end of the Second World War. Part of the impetus for the creation of the NSC came from congressional frustration with FDR's management of the war, which was often thought confusing and chaotic and too highly controlled personally by FDR. But presidents have been less resistant to using the NSC than the CEA because the NSC structure allows them to centralize their control over foreign policy making. In 1949, the NSC was moved into the EOP by President Truman.

The mandate of the NSC is to "advise the president with respect to the integration of domestic, foreign, and military policies relating to national security." Roughly [the size has varied over the years] a dozen people serve on the NSC: the president and the vice president; the secretaries of State, Defense, and Treasury; the ambassador to the United Nations; the director of the Central Intelligence Agency (CIA); the chair of the Joint Chiefs of Staff; the assistant to the president for national security affairs; the assistant to the president for economic affairs; and the White House chief of staff (several of these members were added after the creation of the NSC). Also, under the direction of the assistant to the president for national security affairs, also called the national security adviser, is a small staff located in the National Security Agency.

Due to the establishment of the NSC, the national security adviser has turned out generally to be the most important presidential adviser on national security matters. A consequence of this has been the lowering of the status of the secretary of State and the downgrading in many instances of policy advice coming from the department. As a result, presidents sometimes lose the expertise of the State Department in making foreign policy. But presidents and White House advisers are often suspicious of departmental bureaucrats, irrespective of the department. They often think that departmental personnel do not always have the president's interests in mind but instead are pursing what is best for their department, which sometimes is in conflict with the president's interests. We will pick up on these points in more depth in Chapter 15, when we discuss presidential foreign policy decision making.

The CEA and NSC examples illustrate how Congress can make its demands felt on the organizational structure of the EOP. But these examples also show how functions have been added to the EOP and how the EOP has expanded from the Brownlow committee's original conception. The Brownlow committee intended the EOP to be little more than a centralized administrative management office. With the CEA and NSC, policy advising, policy making, and policy implementation were added to the functions of the EOP. As the EOP took on these policy duties, the cabinet and executives agencies lost influence within the presidency. Also, with the accumulation of added functions, such as policy advising, critics began to claim that the EOP was gaining too much power.[30]

THE OUTWARD EXPANSION OF THE INSTITUTIONAL PRESIDENCY: THE VICE PRESIDENCY AND OFFICE OF THE FIRST LADY

The institutional development of the White House has not stopped with the EOP. It has reached out to include the vice presidency and the Office of the First Lady. Like the presidency, a complex set of factors from both outside and inside the executive establishment have pushed for the institutional enhancement of these two units.

---

[30]On the conflict between the White House staff and the cabinet and the loss of influence of the cabinet to White House staff policy advisers in general, see Shirley Anne Warshaw, *Powersharing: White House–Cabinet Relations in the Modern Presidency* (Albany: State University of New York Press, 1996).

The Vice Presidency

The constitutional duties of the vice president are quite minimal. Other than serving as the president of the Senate, that is, the presiding officer, who can vote only to break a tie, the main role of the vice president is to succeed to the presidency upon the death or incapacity of the president.[31] Consequently, until relatively recent times, vice presidents had little good to say about the office. John Adams, the first vice president, said this about the vice presidency: "My country has in its wisdom contrived for me the most insignificant office that ever the invention of man contrived or his imagination has conceived."[32] Perhaps the most colorful comment criticizing the office came from John Nance Garner, FDR's first vice president, who said that the office was "hardly worth a pitcher of spit."[33] However, beginning slowly during the Eisenhower years and picking up pace in the late 1970s, the vice presidency has developed into an institution, paralleling the developments that we have discussed concerning the presidency. No longer can we so easily deride the office.

During the Eisenhower years, Vice President Richard Nixon was invited by the president to sit in on cabinet, NSC, and legislative strategy meetings.[34] Lyndon Johnson, owing to his great stature as a leader of the Democrats in the Senate, was often involved in legislative affairs by John Kennedy and was given much responsibility for civil rights and space policy in that administration. Kennedy also moved Johnson's vice presidential offices from Capitol Hill to the Executive Compound. Still, presidential use of the vice president in the 1960s and 1970s was subject entirely to the desires and needs of the sitting president. Neither Lyndon Johnson nor Richard Nixon made much use of their respective vice presidents, Hubert Humphrey and Spiro Agnew.

Beginning in the late 1960s, the vice presidency began to acquire an institutional identity that was linked more to the presidency than to the legislative branch. In 1969, the vice presidency was given a line item in the budget; most of the funding for the office was now to come from the EOP rather than the legislative branch. This allowed the staff of the vice presidency to begin to grow. It numbered about twenty in 1960; by the mid-1970s, it was between sixty and seventy. Furthermore, the organization of personnel attached to the vice president's office began to parallel the structure of staff working for the president. Another impor-

[31]These duties are spelled out in Article II and the Twentieth and Twenty-fifth Amendments to the Constitution.

[32]John Adams, *The Works of John Adams,* vol. 1, ed. C. F. Adams (Boston: Little, Brown, 1850), p. 289.

[33]Cited in George C. Edwards, III, and Stephen J. Wayne, *Presidential Leadership: Politics and Policy Making,* 5th ed. (New York: St. Martin's/Worth, 1999), p. 208.

[34]Much of the rest of this section is based on Joel K. Goldstein, *The Modern American Vice Presidency* (Princeton: Princeton University Press, 1982); Paul C. Light, "The Institutional Vice Presidency," *Presidential Studies Quarterly* 13 (Spring 1983): 198–211; Paul C. Light, *Vice-presidential Power: Advice and Influence in the White House* (Baltimore: Johns Hopkins University Press, 1984); Timothy Walch, ed., *At the President's Side: The Vice Presidency in the Twentieth Century* (Columbia: University of Missouri Press, 1997).

tant event occurred in 1972, when the vice presidency was for the first time listed as a unit in the *United States Government Organization Manual*. This designation was more than merely symbolic. It helped to define the boundaries of the office, an important step in the office's institutional development.

By the mid-1970s, the office was also developing some internal independence from the presidency. The vice president, by then, could hire and fire his own staff. This fostered loyalty to and identification with the vice president among his staff and helped differentiate the vice president's staff from the president's. Also, at about this time, the organization of the vice presidency began to take a well-defined shape. Rather than a loose collection of staffers, somewhat reminiscent of the president's staff before 1939, the vice president's staff by the mid-to-late 1970s had a formal cast and a hierarchical structure. This fostered better communication between the presidential and vice presidential staffs, as people of the same rank and job communicated with each other. And the arrival of administrative staff freed up the vice president to spend more time on advising the president on policy. Having policy specialists on the vice president's staff also upgraded the quality of vice presidential advising to the president. By the late 1970s, Walter Mondale, Jimmy Carter's vice president, was among the most influential advisers in the administration. Subsequent vice presidents would also carry a important advising role in later administrations, even in foreign policy, an area that presidents often reserved to themselves.[35]

The growing importance of the vice president's office to the president, as well as its growing prestige, is indicated by the improvements in perks for vice presidential staff and, maybe even more important, by the location of the vice president's staff in the West Wing of the White House. Interaction between the two staffs consequently increased and the staffs began to further integrate, although the vice president's staff retained its separate identity.

Presidents have found the enhanced modern vice presidency useful, especially with regard to certain symbolic functions and activities. For instance, vice presidents often become presidential emissaries to other nations, attending meetings and functions that the president cannot or does not want to attend. Table 9-3 lists the number of foreign trips by modern vice presidents. With the realization of the institutional vice presidency that began with the Mondale vice presidency, we see a steplike increase in the number of vice presidential trips, an indication that the vice president can "stand in" for the president and the host nation need not feel snubbed, as it might have in the days when the vice presidency was so disparaged.

Varieties of Modern Vice Presidential Behavior   Modern vice presidents have pursued two strategies in office. The first strategy is modeled on Walter Mondale's, in which the vice president assumes a relatively high profile within the

[35]On the foreign policy advice by Vice Presidents Bush and Gore, see Paul. G. Kengor, "The Role of the Vice President During the Crisis in the Persian Gulf," *Presidential Studies Quarterly* 24 (Fall 1994): 783–807; and Paul G. Kengor, "The Foreign Policy Role of Vice President Al Gore," *Presidential Studies Quarterly* 27 (Winter 1997): 14–38.

TABLE 9-3   FOREIGN TRIPS OF VICE PRESIDENTS, NIXON TO GORE

Vice president	Number of foreign trips
Nixon	7
Johnson	10
Humphrey	12
Agnew	7
Ford	1
Rockefeller	6
Mondale	14
Bush I*	23
Bush II**	18
Quayle	19
Gore I*	25

*First term. **Second term.

Source: Joseph A. Pika, "The Vice Presidency: New Opportunities, Old Constraints," in *The Presidency and the Political System,* 5th ed., ed. Michael Nelson (Washington, D.C.: Congressional Quarterly Press, 1998), p. 535.

administration and with the mass media. The vice president may involve himself in policy disputes and controversies within the administration, sometimes becoming an advocate of a particular policy course. In contrast is the strategy that George H. W. Bush pursued. While still aiming to maintain access to the president, the Bush model is more modest and emphasizes being a loyalist to the president, a team player, and reluctant to enter policy disputes.[36]

Presidential and vice presidential preferences and styles, plus how well the two individuals work together, will determine which style is adopted. Some presidents demand great loyalty and prefer a hierarchical staff management style. Such presidents probably will not be highly tolerant of a Mondale-styled, activist vice president. Other presidents prefer a more open staffing system and like the give and take of policy debate. Those presidents may entertain greater policy activism and advocacy by their vice presidents, especially when the two work well together and when the vice president is not viewed as a rival.

Ronald Reagan organized his staff in a hierarchical manner, demanded loyalty to the president and his program, and delegated much responsibility, especially of an administrative nature, to staffers, although he retained final decision making for himself. Thus, he probably would not have tolerated a Mondale-styled vice presidency very well. Added to the fact that George H. W. Bush challenged Reagan for the presidential nomination in 1980, often rather caustically, and that Bush was not viewed initially as a member of the Reagan team, Bush probably had no option if he wanted to become important in the administration other than to cultivate a less visible, loyalist approach.

[36]On these two models, see Joseph A. Pika, "The Vice Presidency: New Opportunities, Old Constraints," in *The Presidency and the Political System,* 4th ed., ed. Michael Nelson (Washington, D.C.: Congressional Quarterly Press, 1995), pp. 496–528.

Dan Quayle entered the vice presidency under a different set of circumstances.[37] Bush was more open to input and alternative views than Reagan, being less ideologically predisposed. But Quayle also entered the office under the suspicion that he was not qualified for the job. Quayle had to prove himself. One way of doing this was by engaging in policy disputes, advocating policy directions, showing his knowledge and ability to learn, and demonstrating the soundness of his advice. Quayle was most active on the regulatory front, chairing the Council on Competitiveness in the White House, a forum from which he could attack regulations. He was persistent enough to even move President Bush to call a moratorium on new regulations when some began to criticize Bush for allowing growth in government regulations and undoing the policies of Reagan, who curtailed them.[38]

Luckily, Bush allowed Quayle to take an activist approach, but then, Bush was also questioned for naming Quayle and thus had incentives to enhance the public stature of his vice president. While Quayle's reputation did improve during his tenure as vice president, there were still calls to dump him from the ticket in 1992, and Quayle was still not taken seriously as a presidential contender in the 2000 election contest.

Al Gore pursued an activist vice presidential role, becoming possibly the most influential and visible vice president in U.S. history up to then. Unlike previous presidents, Bill Clinton employed a thorough process in selecting his running mate. William Christopher, a secretary of State under Carter, initially screened many prospective vice presidential candidates. Six names were forwarded to Clinton, who interviewed each. It was in these interviews that Clinton discovered himself at ease with Gore, realizing their potential compatibility.

Gore did not start out as a major presidential adviser but in time grew to be one of the leading advisers in the Clinton administration.[39] Several policy topics were given to Gore, including the governmental reform program, called Reinventing Government, as well as immigration policy reform, telecommunications and technology reforms, the environment, and some foreign policy issues. Gore's stature rose, however, when the administration called upon him to publicly debate H. Ross Perot over passage of the North American Free Trade Agreement. The vice president seemed more knowledgeable than Perot, commanding facts and arguments well, and is credited with creating some momentum for the treaty in the final days of the congressional debates. Gore's star was so high as a result that he became a major fundraiser for the administration in the reelection contest of 1996. An indication of the regard that Clinton held for Gore was that Clinton named Gore as his choice to succeed him as president.

[37]On the Quayle vice presidency, see Ibid., esp. pp. 512–20.

[38]Jeffrey M. Berry and Kent E. Portnoy, "Centralizing Regulatory Control and Interest Group Access: The Quayle Council on Competitiveness," in *Interest Group Politics,* 4th ed., ed. Allan J. Cigler and Burdett A. Loomis (Washington, D.C.: Congressional Quarterly Press, 1995), pp. 319–38.

[39]On Gore, see Joseph A. Pika, "The Vice Presidency: New Opportunities, Old Constraints," in *The Presidency and the Political System* 5th ed., ed. Michael Nelson (Washington, D.C.: Congressional Quarterly Press, 1998); pp. 547–60.

Dick Cheney, vice president under George W. Bush, also displayed an activist style but seemed to upgrade the office from the heights seen under Gore. Reputedly, Bush selected Cheney because of Cheney's long experience in Washington, having served in Congress for twelve years, as Gerald Ford's chief of staff, and as secretary of Defense under George H. W. Bush. Cheney has spearheaded many legislative initiatives for the Bush administration and seems to be much relied upon by the president, perhaps more even than Gore was relied upon by Clinton.

How Institutionalized Is the Vice Presidency?   Several forces have pushed for the institutional enhancement and role of the vice presidency. First are societal and political system pressures. The combination of the Cold War and the specter of nuclear war put some pressure on the president to upgrade the vice presidency to prepare the vice president to assume the presidency in case of emergency. FDR's failure to prepare Harry Truman for office, especially his failure to inform Truman of the atom bomb project during the Second World War, illustrates that such a concern may not be merely academic. The assassination of John Kennedy in 1963 further fueled arguments for a stronger, more prepared vice president, as did Richard Nixon's resignation from office in 1974. The stakes had become just too great for the vice presidency to be the worthless office that its occupants had complained about from Adams to Garner.

Moreover, presidents have found some utility in an enhanced vice presidency. As noted, the vice president can stand in for the president on some occasions. For presidents who seek multiple sources of advice, an enhanced vice presidency can help fulfill that role. For presidents who prefer greater centralized control over policy and government, a loyal vice president can help in that way also. Further, a competent vice president may complement a president's reputation, indicating the soundness of perhaps his most consequential single decision. And a president may be able to continue his programs and policies to some degree beyond his two-term limit by having his vice president succeed him. While successor vice presidents have some reason to distinguish themselves from their predecessor, they cannot wholly disregard the policies of the former incumbent if they had something to do with their generation and implementation.

Perhaps most important, an institutionally vibrant vice presidency is just another resource that a president can employ as he sees fit. While possessing increased institutional supports, the vice presidency, like the rest of the EOP and WHO, is not so firmly institutionalized that presidents are completely at the beck and call of these offices. Thus, presidents may find it is useful to have a stronger vice presidency.

The Office of the First Lady

While not a constitutional office like the vice presidency or even one with a statutory foundation, a First Lady's Office has been established and developed, although not to the degree of the vice presidency. Social and political system pressures, as well as presidential incentives, have pushed for the development of an institutional first lady, but the personal style of the first lady also has a great impact on how much of a public figure and adviser to the president she will be.[40]

George Washington recognized the symbolic importance of the first lady. Early in his administration, he had his wife, Martha, arrive in New York, then the capital city, on the presidential barge. He then escorted her from the barge amid fanfare and crowds.[41] The president's wife has been a source of public interest since, although the term *first lady* was not used until it appeared in a newspaper column in 1870.[42]

Presidential wives have played numerous roles, including running the domestic side of the White House and performing the standard ceremonial role. But the president's spouse has at times also been a political and policy adviser and confidant to the president. There does not appear to be a linear development of the First Lady's Office, but the development and prestige of the presidency, the public notions of acceptable first lady activity, and the personal preferences of the first lady all seem to affect the role that the first lady will take.

Early first ladies performed mostly ceremonial and domestic management roles, although some, such as Abigail Adams, John Adams's wife, seem to have had special influence with their husbands, and Dolly Madison saw the political uses of White House entertaining. As the presidency waned in political power and public prestige in the mid-to-late 1800s, public interest in and the activity of first ladies also declined. The development of more activist presidents by the turn of the century, however, also brought new, more assertive and active partners.[43] By the turn of the century, long before the vice president acquired executive staff and offices, the first lady had a staff and office space allocated to her to assist in running the increasingly demanding domestic and entertainment chores of the White House.[44]

Public interest in the first lady blossomed in the early years of the twentieth century, as well. By then, the first lady had become a topic of numerous newspaper articles, more, in fact, than the vice president, and as the media developed, the volume of media reports on the first lady continued to grow (see table 9-4). By the 1980s, polls began to regularly ask the public its opinion of the first lady,

[40]Most of the work on the first lady consists of biographies of particular first ladies. Eleanor Roosevelt and Jacqueline Kennedy are perhaps the most studied, the first with important scholarship, the second of the more popular and gossipy variety. Some general and useful works include Carl Sferrazza Anthony, *First Ladies: The Saga of the Presidents' Wives and Their Power, 1961–1990* (New York: William Morrow, 1991); Betty Boyd Caroli, *First Ladies* (New York: Oxford University Press, 1987); Lewis L. Gould, ed., *American First Ladies: Their Lives and Their Legacy* (New York: Garland Publishing, 1996); Gil Troy, *Affairs of State: The Rise and Rejection of the Presidential Couple Since World War II* (New York: Free Press, 1997).

[41]Caroli, *First Ladies,* pp. 3–4.

[42]Ibid., p. xv.

[43]Robert P. Watson, "The First Lady Reconsidered: Presidential Partner and Political Institution," *Presidential Studies Quarterly* 27 (Fall 1997): 805–18.

[44]Karen O'Connor, Bernadette Nye, and Laura Van Assendelft, "Wives in the White House: The Political Influence of First Ladies," *Presidential Studies Quarterly* 26 (Summer 1996): 835–53.

TABLE 9-4   MENTIONS OF THE VICE PRESIDENT AND FIRST LADY IN THE *NEW YORK TIMES* INDEX, 1853–1993

Year	Vice president mentions	First lady mentions
1853	5	2
1861	9	1
1869	6	1
1877	6	1
1889	14	0
1897	10	4
1909	35	38
1913	55	50
1921	89	47
1929	73	67
1933	40	244
1945	98	51
1953	133	88
1961	376	213
1969	473	130
1977	373	410
1981	199	29
1989	113	67
1993	133	232

Source: Karen O'Connor, Bernadette Nye, and Laura Van Assendelft, "Wives in the White House: The Political Influence of First Ladies," *Presidential Studies Quarterly* 26 (Summer 1996): p. 841.

and commentators began to talk of the first lady as being a political liability or asset to the president. For instance, Hillary Clinton's activism and leadership over the failed health care reform package of 1995 was thought to have hurt Bill Clinton's poll ratings, but her support of her husband during the Monica Lewinsky affair and the subsequent impeachment proceedings not only improved her stock with the public but seems to have buoyed the president's poll ratings, too.[45]

Staff support for the first lady improved as well. Of the seventy or so professional staff positions for the WHO that are listed in the *United States Government Organization Manual,* five are assigned to the first lady, including a chief of staff and a deputy chief of staff, an assistant to the president and adviser to the first lady for the Millennium Program, a director for scheduling, and a director for advance.

First Lady as Political and Policy Adviser to President   By the middle of the twentieth century, it had become commonplace for first ladies to campaign for their husband's reelection. But some first ladies also began to be more as-

[45]On public attitudes toward Hillary Clinton before the Lewinsky/impeachment period, see Barbara Burrell, *Public Opinion, the First Ladyship, and Hillary Rodham Clinton* (New York: Garland Publishing, 1997).

sertive in acting as a political and policy adviser to the president. The most visible pioneer in this regard is Eleanor Roosevelt, who had a newspaper column even while FDR was president and at times would criticize him in print. She heartily advocated liberal policies during FDR's long tenure as president and toured the nation and the world for FDR, whose physical limitations prohibited much travel.[46] (Even earlier, Edith Wilson managed many of the day-to-day affairs of the White House and presidency in 1920, after Woodrow Wilson suffered his stroke).[47]

Still, many of Eleanor Roosevelt's successors adopted a less active, more limited role, including Bess Truman, who preferred to live in Missouri rather than Washington, D.C., and Mamie Eisenhower and Jacqueline Kennedy, who restricted themselves mostly to ceremonial duties, despite the latter's high public visibility. Lady Bird Johnson reinaugurated a policy role for the first lady with her advocacy of the highway beautification program, and her successors tended to follow suit with interests that focused on topics considered "suitable" for women.

With Rosalyn Carter, matters took another step, as she attended cabinet meetings, and both she and her successor, Nancy Reagan, were considered to be very influential advisers to the president across a whole host of issues, however private they kept their advising. While Barbara Bush styled herself in the more private role as first lady, Hillary Clinton seems to have added another dimension. On assuming office, Bill Clinton avowed that he and his wife would offer a "presidential partnership," and as already mentioned, Hillary Clinton was given responsibility for the major health care reform initiative in 1995. The failure of the reform to receive congressional support and public criticism of her role shifted her activities toward more traditional women's issues, such as children's policies, but she reemerged as an important political, if not policy, adviser during the scandals of 1998. And while Laura Bush, George W. Bush's wife, has taken a less visible role than Hillary Clinton, she still has been active in several policy fronts, especially with regard to education.

Social norms of what is acceptable for women affect strongly the role the first lady can take publicly. Hillary Clinton set out a model of a first lady that was in tune with the more independent and career-oriented woman's role of the last several decades of the twentieth century. That not all women subscribe to that role has made her somewhat controversial. Moreover, the fact that the first lady is not really accountable raises other important questions about the legitimate scope and role of the first lady. She cannot be impeached or fired from office, which distinguishes her from all other public figures in government. But her proximity to the president opens up an avenue of influence that no one else can duplicate. Such complications mean that we have not yet, as a political culture, sorted out what role we want the first lady to assume.

[46]Doris Kearns Godwin, *No Ordinary Time: Franklin and Eleanor Roosevelt: The Home Front in World War II* (New York: Simon & Schuster, 1994).

[47]Caroli, *First Ladies,* pp. 143–52.

IS THE EOP TOO POWERFUL?

The institutionalization of the presidency has fundamentally altered the character of the office.[48] On the one hand, presidential capacity has remarkably increased. The large staff of the EOP has enabled the president to become active across a wider variety of issues than had been the case. At the same time, this increased capacity has fueled public expectations about the president. Presidents are now not only expected to be engaged across a larger number and variety of issues, but they also are expected to provide leadership for the nation. In other words, the president is now held responsible for the state of the nation, the government, and the government's policies and programs.

But the institutionalization of the office has had other impacts. Although it gives the president resources that allow him to be active across many concerns, the institutionalized office also limits presidential discretion. Some tasks, such as preparing and submitting a budget or an economic report, must be performed. The president must be attentive to the demands of others on his time. Thus, the institutionalized presidency brings with it trade-offs, costs, and benefits.

One important issue is whether the EOP has grown too powerful. The addition of functions to the EOP—besides management of the executive establishment—has heightened the power of the EOP. Also, the EOP is important in politics and policy making because it has become a location where important political and policy decisions are made.

Several factors account for the increased power of the EOP.[49] First, the political system has changed in response to social and economic changes. This, in turn, has affected public expectations and views of government. Beginning in the late 1800s, the economy transformed from a primarily agrarian and locally based economy to one that was industrial and nationally organized. Economic and related social problems that were once local in scope now began to have national effects and implications. Among the most important transformations of this period was the invention of the corporation, which organized business operations on a national scale and acquired extensive economic and political power. During this period, Progressives began to argue that only government was potentially strong enough to counter the power of big business in the name of the public interest.

It was not until the onset of the Great Depression in the 1930s, however, that the public mood with respect to increasing the responsibilities of government began to take hold. The depth and longevity of the Depression undermined public confidence in the ability of unregulated market capitalism to pull itself out of the Depression. The public began to look to government to solve the crisis of the De-

---

[48]Peri Arnold, "The Institutionalized Presidency and the American Regime," in *The Presidency Reconsidered,* ed. Richard W. Waterman (Itasca, Ill.: F. E. Peacock, 1993), pp. 215–45.

[49]Hart, *Presidential Branch,* pp. 43–49; Thomas Cronin, *The State of the Presidency* (Boston: Little Brown, 1975), pp. 121–24; Stephen Hess, *Organizing the Presidency* (Washington, D.C.: Brookings Institution, 1976); John Helmer, "The Presidential Office: Velvet Fist in an Iron Glove," in *The Illusion of Presidential Government,* ed. Hugh Heclo and Lester M. Salamon (Boulder, Colo.: Westview Press, 1981), pp. 60–62.

pression. In particular, the public began to look to the president. Thus, we have the foundations of high public expectations and responsibilities being placed on the president. The twin foreign policy crises that followed—the Second World War and the Cold War—added to public expectations and ensured that the public would focus on the presidency long after the Depression had ended.

Congress also felt a need for a strengthened presidency. Legislators understood the necessity of implementing policies that could deal with national problems. Careers depended on the ability of Congress to discharge such responsibilities. But congressional careers and perspectives are aimed at localities. Congress needed someone to point out what the national problems were and to help set congressional legislative priorities. The presidency, with its national perspective, was seen as an ideal place to fulfill this congressional need.[50] Thus, Congress began to heap responsibilities and duties onto the president, such as the preparation of the budget, the issuance of the annual economic report, and later the issuance of the annual report on the state of the environment.[51]

But interest groups also felt a need to be represented in the growing White House in order to influence policy and to legitimate and secure their positions in the political system. Similarly, the news media, which needed the modern president because of his newsworthiness, also required services and help from the White House in doing its job of covering the president. Thus, part of the rise of the EOP can be explained as a response to forces outside of the White House attempting to gain access, representation, and influence in the White House and to ensure that the presidency serves their needs.

But presidents and their staffs were not merely pushed by outside forces in creating a powerful and large EOP. Presidents and their staffs also pushed to augment the power of the EOP. In other words, presidents were ambitious to increase their political power and presence in the political system and saw the building up of the EOP as one way to do this.

First of all, the growing responsibilities of government, which presidents seemed to readily accept, if not actually seek, led them to seek more staff assistance. At the same time, presidents also sought to control the substance of policy making and implementation. This is in part the reason for the proliferation of policy advising in the EOP. Presidents often feel that bureaucracies cannot be trusted, that they are resistant to presidents, and that they have their own agendas that may deviate from the president's. Thus, presidents find some utility in having a loyal staff, with a presidential perspective, for policy advice.

The increased public and political attention placed on the president also required that the president serve the needs of the public and the news media to ensure his visibility and support. Thus came the establishment of the office of the press secretary, of communications, and of public liaison. Moreover, ambitious men and women saw the rise of the EOP as a way to build a political career, do

---

[50]Samuel P. Huntington, "Congressional Responses to the Twentieth Century," in *Congress and America's Future,* 2d ed., ed. David B. Truman (Englewood Cliffs, N.J.: Prentice-Hall, 1973), pp. 6–38.

[51]Some view this as congressional abdication of responsibility. See Cronin, *State of the Presidency.*

good work, and be at the center of the action. Thus, they would also fight to add a function to the EOP, enlarge their office and staff, in the process becoming more influential.

In a sense, then, the development of the EOP is in part a response to political forces outside of the presidency—forces that may be beyond the control of the president—mixed together with presidential needs in the areas of policy advice and political support. A complex of factors came together, giving rise to the EOP. Scaling the EOP back to its more modest roots, as the Brownlow committee desired, might thus require more than simplistic reforms such as reducing the size of the staff. A full-scale reorientation of public expectations about government, the reduction of the activities of government, and the redirection of political ambitions to other outlets may be required.

KEY TERMS

Brownlow report   240
Bureau of the Budget/Office of Management and Budget (BOB/OMB)   254
chief of staff   248
Council of Economic Advisers (CEA)   256
deinstitutionalization   252
Executive Office of the President (EOP)   238

institution   245
institutional boundedness   245
institutional complexity   245
institutional persistence   249
legislative clearance   255
National Security Council (NSC)   256
politicization   252
regulatory clearance   255
universalistic criteria in institutions   248
White House Office (WHO)   253

DISCUSSION QUESTIONS

1. Compare the presidential staff system before and after the establishment of the EOP. In what ways has the presidential staffing system changed with the creation of the EOP?
2. In what ways was the Brownlow report a blueprint for the development of the EOP and the modern presidential staff? In what ways was it not a blueprint? What accounts for why some of the ideas and recommendations of the Brownlow report were not implemented or had little impact on the development of the president's staff?
3. What is an institution? In what ways is the EOP institutionalized? In what ways is it not well institutionalized? What accounts for the lack of institutionalization of the EOP?
4. What role does the chief of staff play in the modern White House? Why do all presidents now need a chief of staff? Why can presidents no longer assume that role for themselves?

5. How has the vice presidency evolved in recent decades? Why has the office taken on more responsibility? How has the greater role of the vice presidency affected the relationship between the president and vice president?
6. How and why is the first lady's role different now from what it had been in the past? Which first ladies have had the greatest impact on the role of the first lady? In what ways can we say that an Office of the First Lady now exists? Is that office becoming an institution? What do these developments tell us about modern American politics?
7. Is the EOP too powerful? What are the implications for government and representative democracy of having a strong Executive Office of the President? What, if anything, can and should we do about the EOP?

SUGGESTED READINGS

Peri E. Arnold, *Making the Managerial Presidency: Comprehensive Reorganization Planning, 1905–1996,* 2d ed. Lawrence: University Press of Kansas, 1998.

John P. Burke, *The Institutional Presidency.* Baltimore: Johns Hopkins University Press, 1992.

Betty Boyd Caroli, *First Ladies.* New York: Oxford University Press, 1987.

Jeffrey E. Cohen, *The Politics of the U.S. Cabinet: Representation in the Executive Branch, 1789–1984.* Pittsburgh: University of Pittsburgh Press, 1988.

John Hart, *The Presidential Branch: From Washington to Clinton,* 2d ed. Chatham, N.J.: Chatham House, 1995.

Samuel Kernell and Samuel L. Popkin, *Chief of Staff: Twenty-Five Years of Managing the Presidency.* Berkeley: University of California Press, 1986.

Paul C. Light, *Vice-Presidential Power: Advice and Influence in the White House.* Baltimore: Johns Hopkins University Press, 1984.

Charles E. Walcott and Karen M. Hult, *Governing the White House: From Hoover through LBJ.* Lawrence: University Press of Kansas, 1995.

Shirley Anne Warshaw, *The Domestic Presidency: Policy Making in the White House.* Boston: Allyn and Bacon, 1997.

Thomas J. Weko, *The Politicizing Presidency: The White House Personnel Office, 1948–1994.* Lawrence: University of Kansas Press, 1995.

10

THE PRESIDENT AND CONGRESS

Presidents possess several avenues for making policy. For instance, they can employ executive orders, which direct the bureaucracy to initiate or refrain from taking action. Executive orders are attractive to presidents because Congress rarely overturns them. Yet presidents cannot do everything that they want through executive orders. Sometimes legislation must be enacted. For example, only through legislation could George W. Bush have gotten the tax cuts that he wanted. Thus, in the modern era, presidents have focused much of their policy-making attention on getting legislation passed by Congress. Presidents do this even though Congress fails to enact a large percentage of presidents' legislative proposals and many others are heavily compromised or altered.

Presidents spend so much time on legislation for several reasons. First, it is hard to change policies that are legislated. Thus, a president's policies may survive long after the end of his administration. The long life of legislatively enacted policies is in part a function of the difficulty of passing legislation to begin with. Once in place, it may be difficult for Congress to mobilize the support needed to overturn or fundamentally alter a policy that was enacted through legislative statute.

Second, the public regards presidents who get Congress to enact their proposals as successful leaders. A legislatively successful president may project an image that he can and has gained congressional support, that Congress is willing to follow his lead. Furthermore, a legislatively successful president may build a reputation as a keen negotiator and bargainer with Congress. Thus, early legislative successes may pave the road for later ones.

Still, despite these benefits, legislating poses challenges for presidents. One, the president cannot coerce or force Congress to support his proposals. Because of this, the failure rate of presidential proposals to Congress may be quite high. Two, the legislative process tends to take a long time. Plus, considerable presidential and staff energy and diligence are required to see a proposal to enactment.

In this chapter, we will discuss the president's legislative role and his relations with Congress. We will begin with a discussion of the constitutional relationship between the president and Congress, focusing on the impact of checks and balances. Then we will discuss the president's role in setting the congressional agenda and presidential success with Congress. A discussion of the presidential veto will follow, where we will raise the issue of whether the veto is a sign of presidential weakness with Congress. Lastly, we will turn to congressional curbs on the president, especially impeachment.

THE CONSTITUTION ON PRESIDENTIAL-CONGRESSIONAL RELATIONS

As we discussed in Chapter 2, a strict understanding of separation of powers would allocate legislative duties to Congress, executive duties to the president, and judicial duties to the courts. But our constitutional framework mixes separation of powers arrangements along with checks and balances. Thus, the president holds some important legislative and judicial duties in addition to his executive ones, and both Congress and the courts hold important executive duties. When looking at presidential relations with Congress, we must therefore recognize the legislative powers of the president, as well as the executive powers of Congress.

Two constitutional provisions outline the bulk of the president's legislative powers. The first is the constitutional requirement that the president "[S]hall from time to time give to Congress Information of the State of the Union, and recommend to their Consideration such Measures as he shall judge necessary and expedient . . ." (Article II, Section 3). It is from this provision that the annual State of the Union address developed. The second major legislative power of the president is the power to sign or veto legislation (Article I, Section 7). Through the act of signing or vetoing legislation, the president becomes formally involved in the legislative policy-making process. Of lesser importance, the president may also convene Congress on "extraordinary Occasions" (Article II, Section 3).

Congress also holds several constitutionally based executive powers. For instance, the Senate must confirm presidential nominees to certain executive branch posts, including department secretaries and ambassadors, as well as the judiciary (Article II, Section 2). Here, Congress is assuming an executive function, involving itself with the personnel decisions of government.

Moreover, the president's veto power is not absolute; Congress can override a veto if two-thirds of the membership of both chambers vote to do so (Article I, Section 7). Similarly, although the president is granted the power to make treaties, acceptance of a treaty requires a two-thirds vote of approval in the Senate (Article II, Section 2). Lastly, and perhaps most critical, Congress can impeach and remove a president from office "on Impeachment for, and Conviction of, Treason, Bribery, or other high Crimes and Misdemeanors" (Article II, Section 4).

Congress may also be acting as an executive when it is making legislation and when it is investigating, both of which derive from constitutional powers granted to it. For instance, when Congress makes legislation, it may decide on the structure of executive units, whether they will be located in a cabinet department or be an independent regulatory commission. It may outline in such legislation detailed job duties, responsibilities, and requirements for bureaucrats. The budget, which is legislated, may direct how much money is to be spent in what ways. Moreover, when Congress investigates or oversees the executive branch, it may ask whether bureaucrats are carrying out their duties as Congress intended. Such actions are usually thought of as executive in nature. We will discuss these executive actions of Congress in more detail in Chapter 11, when we discuss presidential relations with the bureaucracy. The important point here is that our system of checks and balances sometimes gives presidents legislative powers and duties and gives Congress executive powers and duties.

SOURCES OF CONFLICT BETWEEN THE PRESIDENT AND CONGRESS

Allowing the president to have some legislative powers and duties and Congress to have some executive ones might be benign and lacking in any implications except that the Constitution also builds in differences between the two branches. These differences may sometimes lead to conflict. When conflict between the branches exists, these constitutional checks and balances may allow one branch to stop the other from taking action.

In fact, the founders intended there to be conflict between the policy-making branches of government. Each branch was to represent different elements of society. As each branch represented its constituency, conflict over policy was likely to erupt. For policy to emerge from this brew, politicians of the two separate branches would have to find some way of accommodating or compromising. This system would ensure that no branch would be able to concentrate and command all of the power of government and would thus safeguard liberty. But such a system would also be more likely to produce incremental changes in public policy, as opposed to sweeping or radical departures from the status quo.

Different Time Perspectives

Congress and the president differ in their time perspectives, career potential, constituencies, and internal organization. The election cycle structures presidential and congressional time perspectives.[1] The four-year term of office compels presidents to move quickly on their policies. Presidents want policy accomplishments in place to establish a record that they can then run on for reelection. Presidents also need the policies in place for a while to demonstrate that they are working. This means getting Congress to pass legislation in the first year or so of the president's term, which allows years two and three to show how effective the policy is. In year four, the president will possess a record on which he can run for reelection.

The congressional election cycle differs. On the one hand, presidents face representatives whose electoral cycle is fast moving, counted in two-year terms. At the same time, they face senators, whose electoral cycle is much slower than the president's, measured in six-year terms. Thus, while members of the House may be willing to move fast, as a president might like, senators may be less willing to speedily address the president's legislative proposals.

---

[1]Nelson W. Polsby, *Congress and the Presidency,* 3d ed. (Englewood Cliffs, N.J.: Prentice-Hall, 1976), pp.–180–81.

Different Career Potential

The career potential of the president compared to that of members of Congress also contributes to conflict between the branches. In the modern age, presidents have been limited to two terms of office, but members of Congress are not restricted. The two-term limitation often means that presidents look beyond a career as president, casting their ambitions toward the history books. Presidents, in other words, want to go down in history as great presidents. To be great, a president must leave a distinctive mark on the nation. He must be able to point to policies that dramatically altered the nation for the better. Presidents with such historical ambitions often propose large, sweeping, and innovative policies.

Lyndon Johnson is a good case in point. Johnson was a great admirer of Franklin Roosevelt. He felt that the Roosevelt's New Deal restructured life in the United States in profound ways. But Johnson was also an intensely competitive person and wanted to outdo his hero, FDR. Thus, he labeled his program the "Great Society" and encompassed within it proposals to expand social programs to the less fortunate, medical coverage for older Americans (the Medicare program), regulation of corporations, and civil rights for minorities. One may understand Bill Clinton similarly. Clinton's health care reform proposal can be seen as intended to produce a large-scale social accomplishment for him, on the scale of New Deal and Great Society programs. In this way, he might be compared to FDR. Unfortunately for Clinton's historical ambitions, Congress defeated his health care package.

In contrast, the potential for a long-term career leads members of Congress to think differently about policy. Drastic change is a great threat to a political career. Each new policy or change in existing policy may in some small or large way alter the balance of support for a member in his or her district. Policy change may mobilize opponents into the political arena, change party loyalties, and the like. For example, when the voting rights and civil rights laws of the 1960s were passed, black Americans had greater access to the ballot, especially in the South. Many southern politicians now had to balance the claims of black voters in addition to their traditional white constituents. In the process, some southern political leaders who were once staunch opponents of civil rights policies began to moderate their views and positions on civil rights issues.

Policy change may take benefits away from interest groups and constituents who may resent the loss of their benefit and blame their representative in Congress for the loss. Again referring to the civil rights example, some whites resented or felt threatened by the rise of black voting rights. Some of these voters even began to cast their ballots for Republicans. By the 1990s, Republicans were representing a large number of southern districts. Thirty years earlier, it was almost unheard of to have Republicans elected to Congress from the South. The important point about policy change is that its implications are to some degree unpredictable. No member of Congress can truly know whether changing a policy or creating a new one will in the end harm or help him or her.

Moreover, members of Congress are never totally sure why they win office. All that they can bank on is that if they won one time, they will likely be reelected, *if nothing in their political environment changes.* Thus, members of Congress who are interested in maintaining a long career in that body will try to control their political environment as much as possible. This, and the unpredictable impact of policies, might leave members of Congress resistant to much policy change. But legislators also realize that they must produce some legislation to show to their constituents.

On average, then, members of Congress will support incremental changes rather than innovative or sweeping changes in policy.[2] Incremental or small policy changes still allow members to show a record of legislative accomplishments to voters and electoral supporters. And it is generally easier to predict the outcome of incremental change than innovative change. Further, incremental change in policy will likely produce less change in a member's political environment than innovative change.

Thus, we are likely to find Congress often at odds with the president, with legislators generally preferring small policy change and the president wanting big, innovative change. We should not imply, however, that Congress always opposes large-scale, innovative change.

Congress is more likely to support major change in policy when large numbers of new members enter Congress, especially when they have defeated incumbents for reelection. New members will be less beholden to the status quo than long-serving members, and new members will be keen on building a political environment that is to their career advantage. Often new members win office because of voter discontent with the status quo. In reacting to this disaffected political climate, new members will often seek policies that are responsive to such voter discontent. Sometimes this leads legislators to promote or support big, sweeping, innovative policies.[3]

We see an example of the impact of an influx of new members on congressional support for innovative policy change with the election of 1980. Democrats suffered a major loss in the 1980 election. The large majority that they held in the House shrunk considerably, and for the first time in a quarter century the Republicans took control of the Senate. Strong support existed for major reductions in federal spending, taxes, and regulation of business, as well as for increased defense spending. It just happened that these were also the major policy planks of the newly elected president, Ronald Reagan. In fact, many of the first-term Republicans thought that they owed their election to the popularity of their presidential candidate and the positions that he took in the campaign. Thus, support for major policy change that was the same as the president's existed in Congress in 1981.

[2]See R. Douglas Arnold, *The Logic of Congressional Action.* (New Haven: Yale University Press, 1990); and David R. Mayhew, *Congress: The Electoral Connection* (New Haven: Yale University Press, 1974).

[3]On the impact of member change on support for new policies in Congress, see Herbert B. Asher and Herbert F. Weisberg, "Vote Change in Congress: Some Dynamic Perspectives on an Evolutionary Process," *American Journal of Political Science* 22 (May 1978): 391–425; and Keith T. Poole and Howard Rosenthal, *Congress: A Political-Economic History of Roll Call Voting* (New York: Oxford University Press, 1997), esp. chap. 4 and 5.

The same can be said about the tax reforms that Congress passed early in George W. Bush's term in 2001. Although not many new members came to Congress that year, the Republicans recaptured the White House, making it the first time since the 1920s that the Republicans held all three branches of government. Seeing an opportunity to enact policy because of united control of the branches, Republicans pushed through the Bush proposal, although it was compromised. In particular, a group of moderate Republican senators thought that Bush's tax cut was too large. Thus, they forced the administration to accept a scaled-back tax cut of about 75 to 80 percent of what the president wanted. Thus, sentiment in Congress existed to moderate the president's proposal.

It is not always the case that when Congress supports major policy change, such support will so closely align with the president's preferences. In 1994, Republicans took control of the House for the first time since Eisenhower was president. However, Bill Clinton was still president. Republicans, under the leadership of House Speaker Newt Gingrich, proposed a set of sweeping policy reforms, the "Contract with America." These proposals plainly opposed many of Clinton's policies. Although the House passed most of these proposals, few made it into law because of opposition by Senate Democrats and the president.

Different Constituencies

Congress and the president also represent different constituencies. This difference in representation may also lead to conflict between the two branches. Presidential and congressional constituencies differ in two ways—geographically and temporally.

Geographic Differences   Tip O'Neill, the speaker of the House from 1977 to 1987, was famous for his quip that "all politics is local." While this might be true for members of Congress, presidents have a different perspective, a national one. The president is elected from and represents a national constituency, while each member of Congress represents a locality. This difference in perspective may lead to policy conflict between the president and Congress.

For example, Jimmy Carter believed that government should be run as efficiently as possible. Consequently, he opposed what he thought was waste, including pork-barrel bills that were important to members in Congress. In one famous incident, Carter threatened to veto a water projects bill in 1978. Water projects include building dams, deepening harbors, and making rivers more navigable. Such projects are especially popular in the western half of the nation, where water resources are relatively scarce and improvements in water-based infrastructure and facilities are often a boon to local economies. Carter, however, thought that the water projects bill winding its way through Congress was too costly, totaling over $10 billion, and that many of the proposed projects were unnecessary. He threatened to veto the bill, only to face stiff resistance in Congress. Finally, a compromise between the president and Congress was struck, with Congress getting more of what it wanted and the president backing down from his veto threat.[4]

By definition, a national constituency is going to be more heterogenous and diverse than local constituencies. In smaller constituencies, such as House districts, there is a chance that one interest will be the most important, that it might dominate local politics. For instance, in some rural districts, agricultural interests, often based on a single crop (e.g., cotton, corn, hogs), dominate the local economy and thus may be unrivaled in political power. In southeastern Michigan, the automobile industry often holds a similar political status. In larger constituencies, such as that of the nation, no one interest is likely to be so big as to dominate politically. It is more likely that in large constituencies, many rival interests exist and compete with each other.

This pattern has important implications for presidential and congressional policy making preferences. First, compared to any individual member of Congress, the president is more likely to encounter the demands of numerous interests. In contrast, members of the House are likely to face the demands of only one or a few interests, with senators facing a larger number of interest demands, although not nearly as many as the president. Second, the president has incentives to pay attention only to a subset of the numerous interests that may be making demands on him. Only the largest interests, those with national memberships or very large regional memberships, are likely to receive the attention of the president. Thus, the president and Congress are likely to respond to a different mix of interests.

Moreover, the intensity of interest demands or "pressure" is likely to vary. Members of Congress representing districts dominated by one or a few interests are likely to feel intense pressure from them. If that interest withdraws its support from a member, that member's reelection prospects will fade. However, rarely is an interest so important to a president. Those that are tend to be major elements of the national parties, such as minorities and labor in the Democratic Party and anti-abortion groups in the Republican Party. The multiplicity of interests that presidents face, compared to members of Congress, enables the president to sometimes balance off one interest against another, such as environmental versus development groups.

Furthermore, the national constituency of the president often leads him to reflect on the national implications of a policy. In contrast, members of Congress often focus more attention on the local implications of a policy. This may lead to disagreement between the president and Congress over policy. For instance, in 1992, when Bill Clinton came to office, his first objective was to produce a budget that would help reduce the ballooning budget deficit. To that end, he sought tax

---

[4]On this incident, see Mary Russell, "Carter Loses Key Vote on Funding Bill; House Shrugs Off Veto Threat, Kills Move Against Eight Water Projects; House Shrugs Off Veto Threat, Keeps All Water Projects," *Washington Post,* 16 June 1978, p. A1; Richard Kirschten, "Back in Hot Water over Water Projects," *National Journal,* 1 July 1978, p. 1052. On Carter's theory of good government, see Erwin C. Hargrove, *Jimmy Carter as President: Leadership and the Politics of the Public Good.* (Baton Rouge: Louisiana State University Press, 1988); and Charles O. Jones, *The Trusteeship Presidency: Jimmy Carter and the United States Congress* (Baton Rouge: Louisiana State University Press, 1988).

increases, including one on energy consumption. However, members of energy-producing regions opposed the energy, or BTU, tax because of they thought it would hurt their local economies. Side deals and compromises had to be made to pacify these critics, and these passed Congress by the narrowest of margins.[5]

Election Timing   Members of Congress and the president are often elected at different times. Thus, they possess different temporal constituencies. This is important because public opinion can change from one time point to another.[6] Politicians elected at one point in time may be responsive to a different opinion set from politicians elected at another point in time. Thus, representatives coming off of the midterm election may feel a need to be responsive to voters who cast ballots in that election, while the president may not feel so inclined because he was elected two years before. Inasmuch as opinion changes from the presidential election year to the midterm, the gap in the policy preferences of members of Congress and the president may widen, as legislators respond to preferences of voters expressed during the midterm contest.

Not only may the opinion of voters change from one election to the next, but the voters may change. Turnout drops off considerably from the presidential to the midterm election. This dropoff may alter the mix of opinion of voters from the presidential to the midterm election, even if overall public opinion did not change. For instance, let's assume that moderates vote only in presidential elections, but liberals and conservatives vote in both presidential and midterm elections. A member running for Congress in a presidential election year might find his or her supporters to be a mix of moderates and liberals (or conservatives). However, in the midterm year, the representative might find his or her supporters to be decidedly liberal (or conservative). This might lead the member to move to the left (or right) and away from the middle. The same basic dynamic holds for the Senate, except that only one-third of that chamber is elected during presidential election years.

One of the dangers of the election cycle to the president is that the composition of Congress may change from the first to the second half of the president's term. This, in fact, happened to Clinton during his first term of office. The House of Representatives, which was narrowly Democratic in 1993 and 1994, turned over to Republicans in 1995 and 1996. As a consequence, the policy differences between the president and Congress widened from the first two years of his first term to his second two years.

More generally, the difference in timing of presidential and congressional elections increases the prospect of **divided government,** especially in the second half of the president's term.[7] When divided control exists, the gap between pres-

---

[5]On this, see Richard E. Cohen, *Changing Course in Washington: Clinton and the New Congress.* (New York: Macmillan, 1994).

[6]On changes in public opinion over time, see James A. Stimson, *Public Opinion in America: Moods, Cycles, and Swings,* 2d ed. (Boulder, Colo.: Westview Press, 1999).

[7]On this point, see Poole and Rosenthal, *Congress.*

idential and policy preferences is likely to spread because of party differences on many policies. Divided control tends to be more common during midterm sessions than during the first two years of a president's term. From 1860 to 2001, split control of the House and presidency existed only 25 percent of the time for the first two years of the president's term but 49 percent for midterm sessions. For the Senate, the figures are 18 percent and 37 percent, respectively.[8]

Different Internal Organization

Also, the internal organizational structure of Congress and the executive may lead to conflict between the branches.[9] While the presidency is organized hierarchically, the Congress is decentralized. Due to their perch atop the large, hierarchically structured executive branch, presidents are likely to manage by command, and they may get to use issuing commands and directives to subordinates, who then carry them out.[10] In contrast, each member of Congress is equal in the sense that all share voting rights when roll calls are taken. Congressional leaders are unable to command how members vote, and each member may legitimately claim that serving his or her constituents and district take priority over following the dictates of congressional leaders. Conflict may ensue between the president and Congress if a president tries to command members of Congress, even those in his own party, who may balk at being told what to do.

Moreover, their structural differences lead the executive and legislature to acquire and use information differently. Presidents may, if they desire, receive information from the expanse of the federal bureaucracy. The amount of information that potentially is available to presidents may become overwhelming. Thus, information is likely to be filtered before it gets to the president. More important, presidents may receive information that allows them to compare policies, programs, and government agencies. From such a comparative perspective, presidents may balance the demands of competing interests and agencies for priority status in the president's program.

In contrast, both houses of Congress assign members to serve on committees. Committees deal with specific and distinct policy areas. Through their service on these specialized bodies, members become specialists and experts on only a handful of issues. This division of labor within Congress means that few members

---

[8]Over the period, two Senates (1881 to 1882 and 2001 to 2002) contained equal numbers of Democrats and Republicans. These two sessions were not included in these calculations. For figures on the party breakdowns for each congressional session, see Harold W. Stanley and Richard G. Niemi, *Vital Statistics on American Politics, 1997–1998.* (Washington, D.C.: Congressional Quarterly Press, 1998), pp. 32–36.

[9]George C. Edwards, III, and Stephen J. Wayne, *Presidential Leadership: Politics and Policy Making,* 5th ed. (New York: St. Martin's/Worth, 1999), pp. 326–28.

[10]We should note that however much presidents may act this way, they are not assured that their command will be obeyed or carried out with the enthusiasm and dispatch that they want. We discuss the issue of presidential relations with staffers and subordinates in Chapter 9 on the institutional presidency and Chapter 11 on the president and the bureaucracy.

will be in a position to make the comparisons across policies that a president can make. Compared to the president, members of Congress are likely to be knowledgeable about only a narrow slice of the nation's policy issues.

Although policy comparison can be made when Congress as a whole is in session, such as during floor debates, these types of government-wide comparisons are still not as likely for Congress as for the president. The power that an individual member of Congress possesses, whether he or she is a party leader, a senior member, a chair of a committee, or a member of the majority party, may affect the ability of a member to see his or her issues of concern get to the floor of Congress. Thus, many comparisons across policies that a president may make are not open to Congress as a whole because many issues do not rise to the level of floor consideration. When convening as a "committee of the whole," Congress is less likely than the president to consider as many policy areas. Perhaps the only occasion when the Congress matches the president in comparing policies is when it is preparing the annual budget. In Chapter 14, we will discuss budget making in more detail.

Summary

The potential for conflict between the president and Congress is ever present. Conflict derives from the constitutional structure of the two branches, as well as their differing executive and legislative natures. To build policy through the legislative route requires some degree of agreement between the two branches. Finding such bases of agreement is never easy. But creative politicians have been able to do so. Much of the rest of this chapter discusses how the two branches arrive at policy agreement. The first step is for the president and Congress to be thinking and talking about the same policies. In other words, their agendas must overlap.

SETTING THE CONGRESSIONAL AGENDA

If there is no overlap between the presidential and the congressional agenda, the president's ability to influence policy making is severely restricted. Without agenda overlap, presidents will help shape only issues that Congress wants to deal with but not policies that are on his agenda but not on Congress's. His legislative role will be reactive, which limits his leadership role in policy making.

Fortunately for presidents, Congress seems quite willing to at least consider presidential legislative proposals, even if it is less likely to enact the president's proposals. One recent study reports that of 865 significant pieces of legislation that presidents submitted to Congress from 1953 through 1996, all but eight received a congressional committee hearing.[11] In other words, almost every important proposal that the president submits to Congress in the modern age gets onto

---

[11]George C. Edwards, III, and Andrew Barrett, "Presidential Agenda Setting in Congress," in *Polarized Politics: Congress and the President in a Partisan Era,* ed. Jon R. Bond and Richard Fleisher, (Washington, D.C.: Congressional Quarterly Press, 2000), pp. 109–33.

the congressional agenda. But Congress enacted only about one-half of those proposals. Presidents, it seems, have a greater ability to influence the congressional
agenda than to shape the outcome of public policy.

Presidential access to the Congress developed over time. It began with the
constitutional power to report to the Congress on the state of the union, which
developed into the State of the Union address. From George Washington on,
presidents have offered in their State of the Union addresses topics that they
would like to see Congress work on. With the budget process that began in the
1920s, the presidential ability to set the congressional agenda increased. By mid-
century, presidents were expected to help shape the congressional agenda. Now
it is routine and commonplace for important presidential agenda items to get
onto the congressional agenda.

Presidents and the Congressional Agenda: Establishing a Relationship

The president's agenda-setting role developed in three phases. The first stretched
from George Washington until Theodore Roosevelt. During that phase, presidents
might suggest legislation to Congress, but Congress jealously guarded its legislative turf. Senator George Hoar, writing about practices during the mid-nineteenth
century, said that when senators would visit "the White House, it was to give, not
to receive advice."[12]

Early in the twentieth century, a second phase began, a phase in which presidents
would become more assertive in suggesting legislation to Congress and trying to promote their legislative initiatives.[13] Theodore Roosevelt took some of the first steps
here, cajoling Congress to take action on issues that he deemed important. But he
did not submit drafts of legislation for congressional consideration. He did, however,
supply allies with legislative drafts. Roosevelt's successor, William Howard Taft, began the practice of sending draft legislation to Congress, and Woodrow Wilson
worked closely with congressional party leaders on drafting legislation.[14] Wilson also
began the practice of appearing before Congress to demand legislation.

The demands on presidents for legislative leadership escalated with Franklin
Roosevelt in the 1930s. FDR sought legislation to deal with the problems of the
Great Depression. In the famous first hundred days of his presidency in 1933, he
submitted a stream of proposals to Congress. The large Democratic majorities in
Congress were eager to act and swiftly enacted the vast bulk of FDR's proposals.
Some proposals were passed with little debate and often before fully drafted leg-
islation was available to members of Congress. For example, FDR sent emergency

[12]Cited in Sidney Milkis and Michael Nelson, *The American Presidency: Origins and Development,
1776–1998* (Washington, D.C.: Congressional Quarterly Press, 1999), p. 171.

[13]Much of these next several paragraphs follow the discussion found in Andrew C. Rudalevige,
"The President's Program: Centralization and Legislative Policy Formulation, 1949–1996," Ph.D. diss.,
Harvard University, especially chap. 3.

[14]Arthur W. Macmahon, "Woodrow Wilson as Legislative Leader and Administrator," *American Political Science Review* 50 (September 1956): 641–75.

banking legislation to Congress in a special session shortly after his inauguration. The House debated the bill for a mere forty minutes before voting on it. It was passed. Still, FDR was mindful of Congress, often consulting and bargaining with key members before submitting his legislative proposals.

The Presidential Program and the Congressional Agenda

By FDR's time, the president had become an active participant in the legislative process. FDR tended to participate in policies one at a time as issues arose that he cared about. He did not put together a package of ideas that he wanted Congress to work on nor did he try to set legislative priorities. Such a package, a **presidential program**, would come in the 1940s and 1950s, with Harry Truman and Dwight Eisenhower.

The president's legislative program has two major elements. First, it is an overview of all of the president's legislative concerns and priorities. These are discussed in the major presidential addresses, such as the State of the Union address, the budget message, and the economic message. Later, detailed draft legislation from the White House and the departments is submitted to Congress. The second major element of the president's program is that it comes early in the congressional session. Its early arrival is meant to structure the congressional session, to steer Congress to give presidential proposals high priority. Thus, the presidential program is both comprehensive in scope and timely in appearance.

The first president to possess a formal legislative program was Harry Truman. Running for reelection in 1948, Truman criticized the Republican-controlled Congress for failing to enact important legislation and for trying to scale back much of the New Deal. He claimed that the Eightieth Congress (1947 to 1948) was a "do-nothing" Congress, his campaign theme. His legislative program was intended to point out to voters what Congress had failed to do.[15]

But Congress found the idea of a formal legislative program attractive. It helped the legislature organize its workload. In 1953, President Dwight Eisenhower was slow to submit a legislative program to Congress. A House committee chair, also a Republican, publicly chided, "Don't expect us to start from scratch on what you people want. That's not the way we do things here—you draft the bills and we work them over."[16]

The Foundations of Presidential Agenda-Setting Influence

Both Congress and the president found the legislative program useful. Presidents found that not only did the legislative program increase their influence over the congressional agenda, but presidential policy success also rose. A study

[15]On Truman and the Eightieth Congress, see Susan M. Hartmann, *Truman and the 80th Congress* (Columbia: University of Missouri Press, 1971).

[16]Richard Neustadt, "Presidency and Legislation: Planning the President's Program," *American Political Science Review* 49 (1955): 980–1021.

by Covington, Wrighton, and Kinney found that presidents are more successful on roll calls when the issues come from their program than when they are not parts of the president's program.[17] This makes sense. By the time a bill has come to the floor, it has had to go over a number of important hurdles. For it to get to the floor, it must pick up some support from members. It may be hard for a president to stop or alter a bill that has built such support among members. Perhaps all that he can do in such situations is veto or threaten to veto a bill.

Congress also found the program useful, and this is the key to why presidents are so able to influence the congressional agenda. First, as Samuel Huntington has argued, in the late nineteenth and early twentieth centuries, several political, social, and economic trends came together, leading Congress to need a presidential program and to view the president as an important agenda setter.[18]

By the late nineteenth century, members of Congress could build a long-term career in Congress. Those members who were able to do this tended to come from districts that were somewhat insulated from the shifting tides of national politics. In other words, some Republicans represented districts that could withstand tides in favor of the Democrats and be reelected, and the same held for some Democrats. These members would build power in Congress by acquiring seniority. The most senior member of the majority party on a committee would become its chair, and the committee chairmanship evolved into an important institutional base of power in Congress by the 1910s. But this also meant that the congressional leadership became increasingly parochial. Those who could serve their districts well would be the most likely to be returned to Congress year in and year out.

The nation was also undergoing a process of nationalization, especially the economy. Corporations, with nationwide operations, became a basic unit of the economy by the start of the twentieth century. Economic sectors and regions were integrating into a national whole. Many problems and issues became national ones, requiring national responses.

Thus, a gap between congressional careers and policy concerns developed, as successful and influential members of Congress looked toward their districts while issues increasingly became national in scope. The Depression in the 1930s starkly exposed Congress's inability to respond effectively to national problems. The presidency, however, was also transforming in these years, becoming a more capable institution. Moreover, the presidency possessed a national perspective, thus leading the president to focus on national problems. And the public began to look to the president for leadership.

Congress, fearing that it would become irrelevant, turned to the president to identify problems of national scope, that is, to set its agenda. The legislature would use the president's identification of problems as the raw material for or-

[17]Cary R. Covington, J. Mark Wrighton, and Rhonda Kinney, "A 'Presidency-Augmented' Model of Presidential Success on Roll Calls," *American Journal of Political Science* 39 (November 1995): 1001–24. Also see Wayne P. Steger, "Presidential Policy Initiation and the Politics of Agenda Control," *Congress and the Presidency* 24 (Spring 1997): 17–36.

[18]Samuel P. Huntington, "Congressional Responses to the Twentieth Century," in *The Congress and America's Future*, 2d ed., ed. David B. Truman (Englewood Cliffs, N.J.: Prentice-Hall, 1973), pp. 6–38.

ganizing itself and deciding what to work on. In this way, the legislature would play a role in national policy making. It would work on relevant problems that the president identified but put a congressional stamp on the policies that emerged. Thus, while Congress might accept the president's opinion about what was important to work on, Congress reserved for itself the power to shape policy. Quite often, the president would find Congress altering the policy solutions that he offered.

A second factor that enhances presidential influence over the legislative agenda is that many, in and out of Congress, view the president as the nation's representative or spokesperson. Research has demonstrated that major public concerns almost always get onto the president's agenda.[19] In this sense, the president's program may reflect the concerns of the public. By incorporating the president's program into the congressional agenda, legislators may feel that they are representing the nation, too.

Third, Congress may feel political retribution from the public if it does not at least address concerns that the president has identified. If the public looks to the president for leadership, then it may be politically dangerous for Congress to ignore the president. Members of Congress may find it more defensible to say that the president's proposal was ill-considered, that the policy solution that he offered would not work, or that other issues are more important to work on. But each such political defense is couched as a response to the president's program. Members cannot make such arguments to the public if they ignore the president's legislative program. Only by placing the president's proposals on the table can members then disagree with them.

PRESIDENTIAL POLICY-MAKING INFLUENCE IN CONGRESS

Presidents have several motivations for becoming involved in the legislative process and trying to shape legislation. First, the public expects presidential leadership of the policy-making process. Second, presidents believe that legislative accomplishments provide a record that they can run on for reelection. Third, presidents built a historical legacy primarily by establishing a record of legislative accomplishment. Finally a president may come to office with definite ideas about how he wants to shape and direct the nation. Enacting policy may be one way to achieve that vision.[20]

But a president needs help in dealing with Congress. He needs information about congressional preferences. He needs help to convince Congress that his policies are sound. And he needs others to act and speak in his name because he tends to have a large number of proposals wending their way through Congress. The president cannot be everywhere at the same time.

---

[19]Jeffrey E. Cohen, *Presidential Responsiveness and Public Policy Making: The Public and the Policies That Presidents Choose* (Ann Arbor: University of Michigan Press, 1997); and Paul C. Light, *The President's Agenda: Domestic Policy Choice from Kennedy to Carter* (Baltimore: Johns Hopkins University Press, 1982).

[20]On presidential motivations for policy accomplishment, see Light, *President's Agenda.*

For these reasons, the president needs loyal and competent people in his administration. The Senate must confirm many of these appointees before they can assume office. Thus, the president's legislative task involves not only moving his proposals through the legislative process and stopping those that he opposes but also seeing that he fills administration posts with the people he wants. We begin this discussion of the president in the legislative process by focusing on the people who help him in dealing with Congress. That discussion is divided into two parts—confirmation processes and the Office of Legislative Affairs. Then, we move on to the sources of presidential policy success in Congress.

The Politics of Confirmation

In general, presidents are likely to be more successful on confirmation votes than on policy roll calls. We can define success as how often the president is on the winning side. For example, of 1,464 nominations to major posts from 1965 to 1994, the Senate failed to confirm only seventy-one (4.8 percent).[21] In contrast, only about one-fourth of a president's legislative proposals eventually make it into law.[22] The congressional orientation toward each type of roll call is the major reason for this difference in presidential success. For confirmation votes, there exists a *presumption of success*. There is no presumption of presidential success for policy votes. Rather, there seems to be a *presumption of failure*.[23]

Senators are likely to confirm a presidential nominee for several reasons. First, the Senate is likely to defer to the president on staffing his administration, allowing him to create his own administration. The constitutional provision making the president responsible to see that the laws are faithfully executed reinforces senatorial deference over appointments. For example, some in Congress objected to John Ashcroft becoming George W. Bush's attorney general because they thought Ashcroft's views on abortion and civil rights were too conservative and rigid. Many Democrats voted against Ashcroft, but their aim seemed to be more to send a signal to the administration that they wanted a moderate course at the Justice Department than to bar Ashcroft from assuming the post.

Another factor leading to confirmation of appointees is that government posts must be filled. This contrasts with legislation, most of which is not required. Moreover, members of Congress may more closely guard legislation than appointments because of the greater electoral implications of policy. And Congress may direct the behavior of appointees in the administration, in some instances requiring them to take action and in others prohibiting them from acting in certain ways. Thus, a president is highly likely to get who he wants in his administration but much less likely to get what he wants in terms of policy.

---

[21]These figures come from Glen S. Krutz, Richard Fleisher, and Jon R. Bond, "From Abe Fortas to Zoe Baird: Why Some Presidential Nominations Fail in the Senate," *American Political Science Review* 92 (December 1998): 871–81.

[22]Mark A. Peterson, *Legislating Together: The White House and Capitol Hill from Eisenhower to Reagan* (Cambridge: Harvard University Press, 1990).

[23]This terminology comes from Krutz, Fleisher, and Bond, "From Abe Fortas."

The Office of Legislative Affairs

In 1953, President Eisenhower created the **Office of Legislative Affairs.**[24] As is the case with many White House offices, it has undergone several name changes. It was called the Office of Congressional Relations under Kennedy and Johnson and the Office of Congressional Liaison under Carter. Despite these name changes, the basic tasks of the office have remained the same. Under George W. Bush, it is called the Office of Legislative Affairs.

The primary responsibilities of the legislative affairs office are to maintain a presence on Capitol Hill, informing and negotiating with members of Congress about the president's legislative proposals. Some of the legislative affairs office staffers work on Capitol Hill, often with a larger number assigned to working with the House than with the Senate. The office also coordinates the administration's legislative activities. Staffers located at the White House are primarily responsible for such coordination activities. Finally, the office collects information for the president about congressional policy preferences, competing bills, potential problems, and the like. From such information, presidents and top aides develop legislative strategies.

The information that the staff of the legislative affairs office collect about Congress is especially important to the president. Such information may help the president craft legislation that will find greater support in Congress, and it may help the administration avoid making mistakes in negotiating and bargaining with Congress. That the office has remained a White House fixture for nearly fifty years attests to the value presidents see in liaison operations.

But it is not clear that the legislative affairs office is important to a president's legislative success in Congress. A clumsy office may harm the administration's relations with Congress. Carter's legislative affairs team, under the direction of Frank Moore, was sorely criticized. Some of that criticism focused on the lack of Washington experience of many of the legislative affairs staffers. But even legislative affairs offices with experienced personnel have been criticized for heavy-handedness, as was the case with George H. W. Bush's.

But more important, members of Congress are not likely to respond to the appeals of staffers unless the president is actively involved in the issue at hand. When the president is not actively involved, the issue is not considered a top presidential policy, and legislators do not consider staffers to be particularly important in administration decision making.

In part, presidents caused the loss of influence of the legislative affairs staff on Capitol Hill. Much of the office's operations were moved to Capitol Hill. Since

---

[24]There are several important studies of the Office of Legislative Affairs. For a recent study, see Kenneth E. Collier, *Between the Branches: The White House Office of Legislative Affairs* (Pittsburgh: University of Pittsburgh Press, 1997). Older studies include Abraham Holtzman, *Legislative Liaison: Executive Leadership of Congress* (Skokie, Ill.: Rand McNally, 1970); John Manley, "Presidential Power and White House Lobbying," *Political Science Quarterly* 93 (Summer 1978): 253–66; Eric L. Davis, "Legislative Liaison in the Carter Administration," *Political Science Quarterly* 94 (Summer 1979): 287–302; and Eric L. Davis, "Congressional Liaison: The People and the Institution," in *Both Ends of the Avenue: The Presidency, the Executive Branch, and Congress in the 1980s,* ed. Anthony King (Washington, D.C.: American Enterprise Institute, 1983), pp. 59–95.

the location of one's office is often taken as a sign of the influence of a politician, that the Office of Legislative Affairs is mostly located outside of the White House suggests its lack of influence within the administration. Similarly, the Office of Legislative Affairs has been shrunk in size, another indication of lessened presidential attention and reliance on that office and thus a decline in its prestige and influence. In 1981, Reagan had thirty-nine people working in that office. By 1994, Clinton's legislative affairs staff had declined to eighteen.[25]

Equally as important, presidents have often taken on the task of lobbying Congress themselves. For instance, on major legislative efforts, the Clinton White House would organize a "war room," modeled after their election campaign headquarters.[26] Clinton relied on these intensive personal efforts rather than building a staff in the legislative affairs office to push his program in Congress. By organizing his legislative efforts in this way, Clinton helped create expectations of his active involvement. When he was not actively pushing a policy, members of Congress felt that the issue was just not a high enough priority to take seriously either. Thus, rather than being seen as an important lobbying arm of the presidency, as it was during the Kennedy days, the legislative affairs office is now mostly an information-gathering arm of the president's legislative team.

PRESIDENTIAL POLICY SUCCESS AND SUPPORT IN CONGRESS

Staffing the administration with competent and loyal people is important to any administration. The hoped-for result of staffing the administration with loyal and competent people is the enactment of the president's legislative proposals. However, several methods exist for determining, or calculating, presidential success with Congress. Before discussing why some presidents are more successful than others, let us consider the many ways of calculating a president's success with Congress.

One method, mentioned in the "Politics of Confirmation" section, is to count how many of a president's legislative proposals get enacted. By that method, only about one-fourth are successes.[27] Another method is to count how many times a president was on the winning side of a roll call in Congress. This method mixes together proposals that the president submitted to Congress as well as those that members of Congress submitted. By this method, **presidential success** is higher because the least popular proposals are unlikely to reach the floor of the House and Senate for a vote. Lastly, we can also look at **support for the president,** that is, whether a member of Congress votes on the same side as the president. This last method gives us a sense of the basis and nature of congressional support for the president.

---

[25]These numbers come from Lyn Ragsdale, *Vital Statistics on the Presidency: Washington to Clinton* (Washington, D.C.: Congressional Quarterly Press, 1996), p. 373.

[26]Adriel Bettelheim, "State of the Presidency: What Bush Inherits," *CQ Weekly Report,* 20 January 2001, p. 162; and Collier, *Between the Branches.*

[27]Peterson, *Legislating Together.*

All of the methods of calculating presidential success weigh each bill or roll call equally. However, bills and roll calls may differ in their importance and policy impact, and the comparative importance of bills may affect whether we think a president was a success or not. For instance, a president may look successful if he won on a large number of small bills but lost on a few key ones. In contrast, a president who won on a few key bills with big impact but lost on many smaller and less important ones might not look as successful if we count each vote or bill equally. Most, however, would probably agree that the second type of president was the more successful in terms of affecting the nation.

Thus, we might want to distinguish important and unimportant bills and roll calls when tallying presidential success. Yet doing so is not easy because people may reasonably differ as to the importance of a bill. And a bill that today looks modest may in hindsight have far greater impact than previously imagined. We need to bear these points in mind when comparing presidential success with Congress.[28]

Keeping in mind the points just laid out regarding the comparative importance of roll calls, consider figure 10-1, which plots presidential support in the House and Senate since the early 1950s. Several things are apparent from inspecting the figure. One, some presidents claim more support in Congress than others, and presidential support may even vary across a president's term. For example, Clinton registered among the highest levels of congressional success of any president during his first two years in office, 1993 and 1994, with 86 percent success in both years. (LBJ received the highest success level, 93 percent, in 1965). In contrast, Clinton's success dived to 36 percent in 1995 and 55 percent in 1996.

Two, when the president's party controls the legislative chamber, presidential support almost invariably surpasses the support that minority presidents can enjoy. The solid diamonds (success) and circles (support) in figure 10–1 denote periods of united government, while the white-centered diamonds and circles indicate divided government. Almost all of the time, the solid diamonds and circles are higher than the white-centered ones. For example, during periods of united government, presidents average an 82 percent success rate and a 65 percent support rate. Their success and support rates drop to 65 and 53 percent, respectively, under divided government. In other words, presidents succeed over 20 percent more often under united than divided government, and they receive the support of over 10 percent more members of Congress under united than divided government (see table 10-1). More than any other factor, party control of Congress conditions presidential support and success.[29]

[28]For a review of these points and the literature on presidential relations with Congress, see Jon R. Bond, Richard Fleisher, and Glen S. Krutz, "An Overview of the Empirical Findings on Presidential-Congressional Relations," in *Rivals for Power: Presidential–Congressional Relations,* ed. James A. Thurber (Washington, D.C.: Congressional Quarterly Press, 1976), pp. 103–39.

[29]Martha L. Gibson, "Issues, Coalitions, and Divided Government," *Congress and the Presidency* 22 (Fall 1995): 155–66; and Brad Lockerbie, Stephen Borrelli, and Scott Hedger, "An Integrative Approach to Modeling Presidential Success in Congress," *Political Research Quarterly* 51 (March 1998): 155–72.

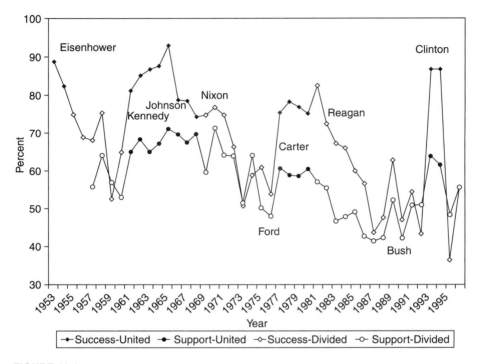

FIGURE 10-1
President Success and Support in Congress, 1953–1996

TABLE 10-1 PRESIDENTIAL SUCCESS AND SUPPORT, 1953 TO 1996

	Success (%)	Support (%)
All years	68.9	57.3
United government	82.3	64.9
Divided government	61.3	53.2

Source: Lyn Ragsdale, *Vital Statistics on the Presidency: Washington to Clinton.* (Washington, D.C.: Congressional Quarterly Press, 1996), pp. 383–84, 387–89.

Party Control of Congress and Presidential Success and Support

The fundamental reason that party control so strongly affects presidential support and success is that members of the president's party are more likely than opposition party members to agree with him on policy. Figure 10-2 plots presidential and House support for liberal issues, as judged by the liberal Americans for Democratic Action (ADA), from 1947 through 1999. The ADA creates an index of support by selecting roll calls before Congress that it considers to divide

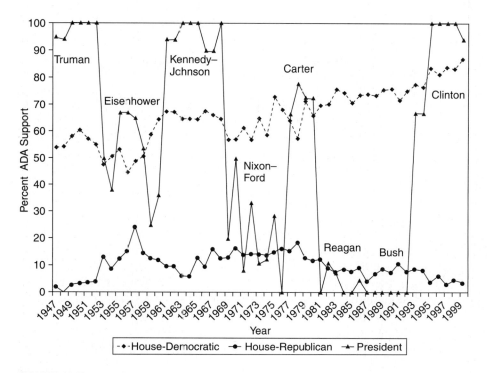

FIGURE 10-2
Presidential and House ADA Support Scores, 1947–1999

liberals from conservatives. In its calculations, the higher the percentage of these supported, the more liberal the president or member of Congress. As the figure shows, Democrats in the House are invariably more liberal than Republicans. The dotted line denoting Democrats is always higher on the figure than the solid line that denotes Republicans.

We can also see trends in the liberalism or conservatism of the two parties. During the 1950s and early 1960s, Democrats hovered around the 50 percent mark. The two wings of the party differed quite markedly, with the southern Democrats often quite conservative and northern Democrats liberal. This began to change in the late 1960s, as the Democrats became increasingly liberal. By the 1990s, Democrats posted an 80 percent liberalism score, about a 30 percent increase from the 1950s. The source of this trend is that southern Democrats became less conservative. Also the proportion of southerners in the party declined, as Republicans began to represent large numbers of southern districts.

The Republicans too display a trend, although it is not as pronounced as the Democrats'. Republicans in the late 1940s were very conservative, hugging the bottom of the figure, but in the mid-1950s they moderated, hovering in the 10 to 20 percent area until the late 1970s. Then the Republicans began to get more conservative again. We also notice from this figure that the gap between the Democrats and Republicans changed from the 1970s, when it was comparatively small, to the 1990s, when it was very wide.

Almost always, the president's ADA score falls closer to his party's than the opposition's. In many cases, the president is actually more extreme than his party. Thus, Truman, Kennedy, Johnson, and Clinton were almost always more liberal than the Democrats in Congress. In each case, these presidents scored nearly 100 percent on the ADA liberalism scale. Reagan and Bush were more conservative than their party, also almost always scoring nearly zero. In a few instances, presidents were closer to the opposition party. This is the case with Eisenhower several times and with Nixon in 1970. In fact, Eisenhower was more liberal than the Democrats from 1955 through 1959.[30]

There are several sources of policy agreement among members of the same party.[31] First, members of the same party tend to share fundamental values about politics and policy, what we might term ideology. In general, Democrats have leaned in a liberal direction and Republicans in a conservative direction, as figure 10-2 demonstrates. When presidents are not ideologically close to their parties, it is often because of splits within their parties. This helps explain the difference between Eisenhower and the Republicans noted on figure 10-2. On foreign policy, Eisenhower took a strong internationalist position. Many Republicans, especially those from the Midwest, held to a more isolationist ideal, while Democrats, like Eisenhower, tended to be internationalist in foreign policy.[32]

Second, members of Congress have electoral incentives to agree with a president of their party and oppose an opposition party president. The public tends to associate all members of the president's party with the president. Inasmuch as the public views the administration as a failure, the public might also blame members of the president's party in Congress. On the other hand, members of the president's party in Congress may also expect to bask in the glow of public accord when the president is popular or thought of highly. Come election day, voters may cast ballots against members of the president's party when he is unpopular as a way of voicing their disapproval of the president, or they may vote for members of the president's party when he is popular. In this fashion, the electoral fate of members of Congress may be tied to the fortunes of the administration, and we

[30]Why Eisenhower is so often closer to the Democrats than the Republicans is a mystery. Part of the answer is that Democrats and Republicans were closer together during the Eisenhower years than in any others during the time frame depicted in the figure. Also, Eisenhower took internationalist positions on foreign policy to which Democrats were also more favorable than Republicans during this time era. Lastly, other research suggests that Eisenhower and the Democrats were closer together on civil rights issues; see Cohen, *Presidential Responsiveness*.

[31]Helmut Norpoth, "Explaining Party Cohesion in Congress: The Case of Shared Policy Attitudes," *American Political Science Review* 70 (December 1976): 1156–71.

[32]On Eisenhower, Congress, and foreign policy, see George L. Grassmuck, *Sectional Biases in Congress on Foreign Policy* (Baltimore, Johns Hopkins Press, 1951); and Cohen, *Presidential Responsiveness*, pp. 105–8.

might expect that members of the president's party would want to help the president look good to the public. One way of doing this would be to support him and his policies.

For instance, Democrats in Congress strongly supported Bill Clinton during the impeachment process in 1998 and 1999. In one photo opportunity, a large number of Democrats gathered with Clinton on the grounds of the White House in support of their president. At the time, Clinton was popular, and many Democrats in Congress wanted to be associated with their popular president. At the same time, many of these same Democrats publicly criticized Clinton for having an affair with a White House intern. During the midterm elections of 1998, the Democrats actually took several seats from the Republicans. Some commentators suggested that this was because of public support for Clinton and public opposition to the Republican impeachment moves against him.[33]

In a related vein, **presidential coattails** may also affect a member's reelection prospects. A president is said to have coattails when people who vote for the president also vote for the congressional candidate of the president's party just because that candidate comes from the president's party. Thus, some votes go to the candidate for Congress because of voter support for the president. In tight congressional races, a coattail that is long enough may help the candidate win the election. Members who come to office because of coattail effects may feel beholden to the president, who they feel helped them get elected. Members may also view coattails as a sign that the president is popular in the district, in fact, that the president is more popular in the district than the member. Such members might want the public to associate them with the president. By supporting the president's program, members may be able to claim their loyalty to the president and his program.

In recent decades, however, for a number of reasons presidential coattails have shrunk. First, the advantages of congressional incumbency have increased, insulating members running for reelection from political tides and ensuring their reelection efforts. Now many members run ahead of the president in their districts. At times, members may even view the president as a drag on their reelection prospects. Presidents, such as Jimmy Carter, who won very narrow election victories may have been viewed this way by members of their party. This may create incentives for members of the president's party to distance themselves, a point to which we will return shortly. Still, while coattail effects may not be as potent a source of support for the president as they once were, shared policy views still lead members of the president's party to support his policies.

Party control of Congress also presents presidents with key institutional advantages that minority-party presidents lack—the majority party controls the institutional leadership positions. In turn, these leaders control Congress's workload, agenda, scheduling, and committees. The workload may be organized to help a president's proposals, for instance, by giving the president's proposals

---

[33]Gary C. Jacobson, "Impeachment Politics in the 1998 Congressional Elections," *Political Science Quarterly* 114 (Spring 1999): 31–51.

priority over other legislation or by providing the president's proposals with favorable schedules and rules of debate. Perhaps more important than the help that congressional leaders may give to the president's program is the harm that they might do, for instance, by killing a proposal in committee, bringing the proposal up for consideration under a tight or unfavorable schedule, sending it to a hostile committee, and so on. Manipulation of these institutional levers may be important in whether a president is successful with Congress or not. Studies indicate that without such leader support, presidents cannot expect much success with Congress,[34] and minority-party presidents are much less likely to receive the help and cooperation of opposition party leaders in control of Congress than majority-party presidents.

George W. Bush had to contend with a shift in party control of the Senate midway into the congressional term, when Senator James Jeffords of New Hampshire dropped out of the Republican Party in May 2001.[35] The 2000 elections produced a Senate equally split between Democrats and Republicans. Republicans were able to organize the Senate because Vice President Dick Cheney possessed the constitutional role to cast tie-breaking votes. When Jeffords became an independent, Democrats held a one-seat majority (fifty to forty-nine) and took over the Senate.

Jeffords' midsession bolt from the Republican Party does not affect the distribution of preferences in the Senate—the legislators remain the same. But by shifting control from the Republicans to the Democrats, the Senate's agenda also shifted. For instance, the newly organized Democratic Senate made the patients' bill of rights its first order of business. Republicans had not scheduled that legislation for floor consideration when they were in control. Democratic Senate leaders also put minimum wage and hate crimes legislation on the legislative agenda, again legislation that was not on the Senate Republicans' or President Bush's agenda. Losing party control lessened the president's ability to manage the Senate's agenda.[36]

Possessing a majority in Congress, however, does not guarantee that the president will be able to accumulate enough support to move his proposals through the legislative process. The party may, for instance, be internally divided. Often the larger the congressional majority, the greater the potential for intraparty policy splits. The main reason that very large congressional majorities may fracture is that under such conditions, the party becomes home to an increasingly diverse set of opinions.

For instance, in the early 1930s, congressional Democrats stood behind Franklin Roosevelt and his New Deal policies with a rare voice or vote of opposition. However, the Democratic majority grew to massive proportions after the 1936 elections, holding 333 of 435 (77 percent) seats in the House and seventy-

[34]Jon R. Bond and Richard Fleisher, *The President in the Legislative Arena* (Chicago: University of Chicago Press, 1990).

[35]Mark Allen and Ruth Marcus, "GOP Missteps, Jeffords' Feelings About Agenda Led Toward Exit," *Washington Post,* 24 May 2001, A26.

[36]Alison Mitchell, "Rough Ride in the House: Bush and G. O. P. Leaders Are Scrambling to Forge Deal on Patients' Bill of Rights," *New York Times,* 27 July 2001, p. A1; and Dana Milbank, "Bush Lacks the Ability to Force Action on Hill," *Washington Post,* 25 July 2001, p. A1.

five of ninety-six (78 percent) in the Senate.[37] The issues of race and support for labor had long divided Democrats, with northern Democrats favoring civil rights and labor legislation and southern Democrats opposing them. Southerners, who comprised a large segment of the party in Congress, were able to keep such issues off the congressional agenda. By 1937, however, northern Democrats commanded enough seats and support to bring such votes to the floor and win, and they did so with FDR's support and encouragement. As a consequence, southern Democratic opposition to the New Deal increased, fracturing the party into two wings, a fracture that would persist for the next forty years or so.[38]

FDR was fortunate, however, in the fact that he still commanded a large enough following to move his policies through Congress. Ninety-nine representatives and twenty-two senators came from the South. Even if all southern Democrats defected, FDR still had 234 Democratic representatives and fifty-three Democratic senators. While FDR could not afford too many defections in the Senate, he still had a cushion of sixteen votes in the House, and he could often count on several of the third-party legislators to vote with him.

In contrast, the split between northern and southern Democrats plagued Presidents Kennedy and Johnson. This split limited their ability to succeed with Congress and forced them to work with Republicans, often to the consternation of liberal Democrats. Only in 1965 to 1966, when Democrats held 295 House and sixty-eight Senate seats was Johnson able to get most of his liberal legislative program enacted with little southern support. But with nearly one hundred representatives and twenty senators coming from the South, Johnson had to secure some Republican support to win. He was able often to muster a handful of liberal Republicans to his side on such issues as civil rights.

By the time Jimmy Carter became president in 1977, the north-south split in the Democratic Party had mostly healed, but loyalty among all Democrats to the party had waned. In 1977, Democratic unity stood at 74 percent, and in 1978, it was 71 percent. Democrats held 292 seats, but with these party loyalty levels, Carter could count on only 216 votes in 1977 and 207 in 1978 if only Democrats supported him.[39] Even with about two-thirds of congressional seats held by his party, lack

[37]Because of third parties holding some seats in Congress, Republican totals were even smaller. In 1936, Republicans held just eighty-nine seats in the House and seventeen in the Senate, or 20 and 18 percent, respectively.

[38]Poole and Rosenthal, *Congress*.

[39]Democratic Party unity stood at 80 percent in 1965, giving Johnson a potential of about 236 Democratic votes. In fact, in 1965 to 1966, Democrats supported Johnson about 84 percent of the time, for an average of 248 votes. In comparison, 68 percent of Democrats supported Carter in 1977 to 1978, giving him an average of 199 Democratic votes that he could count on, nineteen short of the 218 necessary for victory in the House. The party unity and congressional support figures come from Norman J. Ornstein, Thomas E. Mann, and Michael J. Malbin, *Vital Statistics on Congress, 1997–1998* (Washington, D.C.: Congressional Quarterly Press, 1998), pp. 208–10. Party unity is defined as the percentage of party members siding with their party on party unity votes. Party unity votes are those in which a majority of voting Democrats oppose a majority of voting Republicans. Congressional support for the president is defined as the total number of votes supporting the president divided by the total number of votes cast on roll calls on which the president took a position.

of party unity doomed much of Carter's legislative program. The Johnson and Carter cases clearly demonstrate the fragility of presidential success in Congress. Even when the president's party possesses a commanding majority, lack of party cohesion may doom the president's program.

Thus, it is not enough that a president command a large majority in Congress. To succeed, he requires a cohesive majority, one that is united behind his program.[40] Very large congressional majorities may allow some defection and still produce presidential victories, as was the case during the 1937-to-1938 Congress. But defection rates cannot be so high as to undermine the party's working majority. When majorities are not so large, smaller defection rates may doom a president's program, making party cohesion behind the president all the more important. Large, cohesive majorities are rare in American history. This means that even majority-party presidents have to work hard if they are to see their program enacted.

Thus, presidents must collect a handful of votes on each individual bill that comes up, knowing that those supporters will change with each bill. In the words of George Edwards, most presidents must work "at the margins" if they are going to see their proposals enacted by Congress.[41] Working at the margins becomes a time-consuming challenge, considering the number of presidential proposals and the shifting bases of support for each bill, once the president's partisan base of support is taken into account. What resources and strategies do presidents employ in drawing those last holdouts to their side?

Presidential Popularity and Presidential Success with Congress

Presidents commit considerable White House resources in the pursuit of public support. They believe that public support will enhance their ability to bargain with other political elites, especially members of Congress. This will lead, in their estimation, to greater success with Congress.

Members of Congress might be sensitive to a president's standing or popularity with the public for two major reasons.[42] The first pertains to a member's desire to be reelected. Members search for clues about their reelection chances and build their reelection strategies on the information that they acquire and their anticipation of the electoral environment at the next election. One factor in that electoral environment might be the president's standing with the public. As we have stated, some people may vote for a member of Congress of the president's party just because the president is popular. Likewise, someone may vote against a member of the president's party when the president is not popular.[43] If some voters

---

[40]Jeffrey E. Cohen, *Legislative Studies Quarterly*.

[41]The phrase "at the margins" comes from George C. Edwards, III, *At the Margins* (New Haven: Yale University Press, 1989).

[42]George C. Edwards, III, "Presidential Influence in the House: Presidential Prestige as a Source of Presidential Power," *American Political Science Review* 70 (March 1976): 101–13; and George C. Edwards, III, "Aligning Tests with Theory: Presidential Approval as a Source of Influence in Congress," *Congress and the Presidency* 24 (Autumn 1997): 113–30.

[43]The obverse may also hold, that people will vote for an opposition party candidate when the president is unpopular and against an opposition party candidate when the president is popular.

behave this way, then members running for reelection may have an incentive to associate themselves with the president when he is popular and distance themselves when he is not.

Second, legislators may feel that part of their job is to reflect public opinion, to be responsive to the preferences and opinions of their constituents. To fulfill that role, members must discover or learn about their constituents' preferences. The president's standing with the public may be one piece of information about public thinking. Insofar as members desire to faithfully represent their constituents, they may be inclined to support the president when he is popular but oppose him when he is not.

A mountain of research exists that looks at the linkage between presidential popularity and congressional support for the president. The evidence, however, is quite mixed. Several early studies found that presidents receive more support in Congress when they are popular,[44] but recent research has not uncovered a strong relationship between presidential popularity and congressional support for the president.[45]

One reason that presidential popularity does not seem to affect congressional support very strongly is that most studies employ national-level indicators of presidential popularity. However, members of Congress are concerned about opinion within their districts, not the nation. National approval readings may inaccurately reflect district opinion. Congressional districts are clearly more homogeneous than the nation, and many may be more strongly opposed or favorable to the president than the nation as a whole. One study, however, used statewide presidential popularity polls in an investigation of the support of senators for the president's program. Even here, with opinion matched to districts—in this case, states—presidential popularity failed to affect support for the president.[46]

Second, presidential approval tends to display short-terms peaks and valleys. It sometimes changes dramatically in a short period of time. Members of Congress may be well aware of the short-run variability in presidential approval and thus discount the president's level of approval when deciding whether or not to support a presidential legislative proposal. Rather than focus on the popularity

[44]Edwards, "Presidential Influence"; Charles W. Ostrom and Dennis M. Simon, "Promise and Performance: A Dynamic Model of Presidential Popularity," *American Political Science Review* 79 (June 1985): 334–58; Douglas Rivers and Nancy Rose, "Passing the President's Program: Public Opinion and Presidential Influence in Congress," *American Journal of Political Science* 29 (May 1985): 183–96; Paul Brace and Barbara Hinckley, *Follow the Leader: Opinion Polls and the Modern Presidency* (New York: Basic Books, 1992). This literature is reviewed extensively in Jon R. Bond, Richard Fleisher, and Michael Northrup, "Public Opinion and Presidential Support," *Annals of the American Academy of Political and Social Science* 499 (September 1988): 47–63.

[45]The studies include Jon R. Bond and Richard Fleisher, "Presidential Popularity and Congressional Voting: A Reexamination of Public Opinion as a Source of Influence in Congress," *Western Political Quarterly*, 37 (1984): 291–306; Bond, Fleisher, and Northrup, "Public Opinion"; Jeffrey E. Cohen, Jon R. Bond, Richard Fleisher, and John A. Hamman, "State-Level Presidential Approval and Senatorial Support," *Legislative Studies Quarterly*, 25 (November 2000): 577–90; Kenneth Collier and Terry Sullivan, "New Evidence Undercutting the Linkage of Approval with Presidential Support and Influence," *Journal of Politics* 57 (1995): 197–209; and Peterson, *Legislating Together*.

[46]Cohen, Bond, Fleisher, and Hamman, "State-Level Presidential Approval."

reading of the day or week, members of Congress might focus instead on public approval for the president as a general environmental factor that helps set the tone of the times.[47] Thus, they might ask themselves, in general, does the public approve of the president? Does he appear to have considerable public backing? Can the president rally the public to his side if he needs to?

From such a vantage point, members of Congress might have viewed Reagan as more popular with the public than George H. W. Bush, despite the fact that Bush's polls reached levels much higher than Reagan's ever did. Reagan seemed to possess a deep tie with a segment of the American public, a tie that was resistant to change no matter the problems of the day. This provided Reagan with a firm foundation of unwavering public support. In contrast, Bush's support seemed more superficial. Even people who approved of Bush's performance in office were quick to abandon him when times deteriorated. Thus, Bush's polls fell rapidly from the highs recorded during the Gulf War in 1991.

In a similar vein, what may be important to members of Congress is not current presidential popularity but future popularity, especially how popular the president might be come the next election. Current popularity readings might not be accurate predictors of presidential popularity into the future, especially given that presidential popularity swings up and down, as we already discussed.

Several developments in recent decades may have insulated members of Congress from presidential popularity pressures. First, the advantage of incumbency has increased markedly over the past several decades. This bigger incumbency advantage gives members of Congress a larger electoral cushion, allowing them to resist all kinds of political pressures. As a consequence, they may fear the impact of a popular or unpopular president on their reelection less than was once the case. The effect of an increased advantage of incumbency can cut both for and against the president. Members of the president's party may have less to fear from aligning with an unpopular leader, just as member of the opposition may have less to fear from opposing a popular leader.

Also, the increasing ideological polarization in Congress might insulate members from many political pressures, including presidential popularity. As we discussed in the "Party Control of Congress and Presidential Success and Support" section and displayed on figure 10-2, Congress has, in recent years, polarized into two camps of ideologically opposed partisans, liberal Democrats and conservative Republicans. There are many sources of this increasing polarization,[48] but for our purposes, it is important to point out that more members are ideologically predisposed than was the case several decades ago. Many members are now strongly committed to liberal or conservative policies. As a result, they are less inclined to compromise and are more resistant to political pressures that

[47]For an argument along these lines, see Edwards, "Aligning Tests with Theory."

[48]See Jon R. Bond and Richard Fleisher, eds., *Polarized Politics: Congress and the President in a Partisan Era* (Washington, D.C.: Congressional Quarterly Press, 2000) on this point. Also Richard Fleisher and Jon R. Bond, "The President in a More Partisan Legislative Arena," *Political Research Quarterly* 49 (December 1996): 729–48.

might push them in directions opposed to their ideological moorings. To such hardened ideologues, it might not mean much that a president is popular or not. Such reasoning has been used to explain the Republican insistence in Congress on impeaching Bill Clinton in 1998, despite his high popularity levels with the public at that time.

Presidential Skills and Bargaining

In Chapter 3, we discussed Richard Neustadt's theory of presidential bargaining. Neustadt is the major proponent of the view that to be successful with Congress, presidents must be accomplished bargainers. The separation of powers framework denies the president the right to command Congress as he might command the bureaucracy. And although party support may go a long way toward ensuring presidential success in Congress, even presidents blessed with majority-party control of Congress may lack enough votes to carry the day. To win on the floors of the House and Senate, presidents may need to supplement their party support base from the remaining members, many of whom may not be inclined to go along with the president.

According to accounts such as Neustadt's, **skillful presidents** are those who can mobilize these recalcitrant members to support their proposals. Presidents who bring bargaining advantages may be more able to sway such members than presidents who lack sufficient bargaining advantages. What kinds of bargaining advantages might a president possess?

Fundamentally, Neustadt argues that successful bargaining requires that a president convince members of Congress that it is in their best interests to support the president's policy proposals. Well-crafted arguments such as that his policy is superior to any alternative or that it is best for the nation may sometimes convince a member to support the president's proposal. But as we discussed in Chapter 3, Neustadt suggests that prestige and reputation are the major sources of presidential bargaining advantages.

Prestige refers to the president's standing with the public—for instance, popularity. But we already suggested in Chapter 3 that public standing may not be such a strong asset. That discussion focused on the ability of popularity to affect the average or typical member of Congress. The bargaining model that we are now discussing applies to situations in which presidents bargain with only a small number of members of Congress. Thus, presidents may bring public pressures on those members who are most susceptible to such influences, such as members of the president's party who come from districts where the president is popular. A president may be able to make a convincing argument to such a member that opposition may come to haunt that member when the next election is held.

Reputation, the second source of presidential bargaining advantages, refers more to the way that political elites or the Washington political community see the president. Is he viewed as a tough leader or someone who easily caves into the demands of others? Will the president carry out his threats? How does the president deal with those who oppose him? These are the types of considerations that politicians may weigh when bargaining with a president. Still, like the use of prestige to bargain with members of Congress, bargaining that employs reputational assets will be highly situation-specific, a mixture of the president's reputation with the members of Congress and how the president's reputation resonates with the members.

Presidents may gather votes by other techniques, such as by negotiating or compromising with members of Congress. Negotiating and compromising essentially involve the president giving up something to a member of Congress in order to acquire that member's support on a particular policy. For example, a president may compromise by softening a provision in the bill, perhaps by lowering the budget or reducing the authority of the bureaucrats who will oversee implementation. Negotiating may involve vote trading, in which a president promises to support a member's preferences on another bill if the member will support the bill in question. Especially in the case of bargaining, it may be hard to discern if the president is successful or not with Congress. That assessment may depend on how much the president had to give up to acquire the member's support. Presidents might like to claim victory even though they conceded much of what they originally desired.

Presidents may also try to acquire support by doing favors for or withholding favors from members of Congress. Unlike with compromising and negotiating, favors need not be policy-specific. For instance, the president may support a member's choice for an appointment to a governmental post. Or a president may help a member running for reelection by campaigning for that member or appearing at fundraising events.[49] Invitations to the White House, meeting with important constituents from the member's district, and the like are other kinds of favors that presidents may do for members of Congress.

There are, however, several limitations on employing favors when trying to secure a member's support. First, the favor may not be significant enough when the president is faced with a member who has strong policy objections to the president's proposal. Second, presidents possess a limited reserve of favors, such as appointments or time to meet with constituents. Third, giving some favors, such as appointments, to one member may deny the president the ability to employ that favor with another member. And lastly, a president who uses favors indiscriminately or often may create an expectation among members of Congress that he will bestow favors on them to get their votes. If the president develops such a reputation, he may induce normally supportive members of Congress to withhold their support for his proposals until they too receive some kind of favor from him.

Thus, presidents must be very sensitive to the context in which they are bargaining, compromising, negotiating, and doing favors for members of Congress. What works with one member may not work with another, and what

---

[49]Jeffrey E. Cohen, Michael A. Krassa, and John A. Hamman, "The Impact of Presidential Campaigning on Midterm U.S. Senate Elections," *American Political Science Review* 85 (March 1991): 165–79.

works at one time may not work at another time. All of this underscores the complexity and difficulty of building coalitions of support for the president's program in Congress.

Some presidents, however, have developed reputations as being skillful in their dealings with Congress, while others have been blasted for their lack of legislative skill. Lyndon Johnson, for instance, is often reputed to be among the most skillful presidents in dealing with Congress. Johnson's long tenure in Congress and as a majority leader in the Senate supposedly provided him with a working knowledge of Congress, which he employed skillfully as president. In contrast, Jimmy Carter was not thought to be so adept in his dealings with Congress, which some attribute to his lack of Washington experience. But Ronald Reagan, like Carter, lacked Washington experience before becoming president, although most considered Reagan to be very adroit in dealing with Congress.

It is not clear, then, what makes a president skillful. Experience, political savvy, and good advisers may all contribute to legislative skill. Skill may be so highly idiosyncratic that it may be hard to predict if a person will become a legislatively skillful president or not. But does legislative skill really make any difference?

Several studies have investigated this question. One study compares the degree of success in Congress of presidents considered to be skillful with those not considered to be skillful. That study concluded that skillful presidents were no more successful than reputedly less skillful presidents.[50] Another study, by George Edwards, also compares reputedly skilled and unskilled presidents but argues that skilled presidents should win on more close votes than unskilled presidents. Presidential skill, Edwards argues, is about collecting that last small batch of votes needed for victory on the floor. But Edwards, too, finds that reputedly skilled presidents fare no better with Congress than reputedly less skilled presidents.

Both of these studies use the historical reputation to assess presidential-legislative relations. Another study argues that one must look at president reputation at the time in order to assess whether reputation for skill indeed affects congressional support for the president. That study uses editorial comment from the *New York Times* to assess the then-current president's reputation. The study concludes that reputation for being legislatively skillful does affect presidential success with Congress,[51] but it may also be the case that presidents build a reputation for legislative skill because they were successful to begin with. Thus, it may be difficult to untangle reputation from success, because success helps build a reputation as being skilled and a reputation for being skillful may increase the likelihood of success with Congress.

---

[50]Bond and Fleisher, *President in the Legislative Arena*.

[51]Brad Lockerbie and Stephen Borelli, "Getting Inside the Beltway: Perceptions of Presidential Skill and Success in Congress," *British Journal of Political Science* 19 (January 1989): 97–106. Also see Dennis W. Gleiber, Steven A. Shull, and Colleen A. Waligora, "Measuring the President's Professional Reputation," *American Politics Quarterly* 26 (July 1998): 366–86.

THE PRESIDENTIAL VETO

Perhaps the most formidable constitutional tool that a president possesses in dealing with Congress is the **veto.** By using the veto, a president may keep Congress from enacting legislation that the president opposes. Furthermore, Congress is unlikely to override a veto because doing so takes a two-thirds vote in each chamber. Rarely can Congress muster the two-thirds needed to override a veto. The threat of a presidential veto may also improve a president's bargaining situation with Congress. Under certain circumstances, a veto threat may lead Congress to produce a bill that is more to the president's liking than if he did not threaten to use the veto. In this section, we discuss the presidential veto, how it developed, factors that give rise to vetoes, and the impact of veto threats on presidential policy success with Congress.

The Mechanics of the Veto

The Constitution grants the president a limited or qualified veto (Article I, Section 7). We consider the veto power to be limited or qualified because under certain conditions, Congress may override the veto. In contrast, an absolute veto denies the legislature the right to override a veto.[52]

The veto is also limited in that a president must veto the entire bill under question. In some states, governors possess what is called a line-item veto, in which they may veto specific provisions of a bill to which they object. Through line-item veto power, governors may shape legislation without dispensing with entire bills. In contrast, when deciding to veto or not, presidents sometimes encounter situations where they agree with most of the bill but object to only one or several provisions. Presidents must then determine whether their objections outweigh what they like in the bill in deciding whether or not to veto the bill.[53]

Presidents possess two ways of vetoing a bill. In one, the president may return the bill to the chamber of origin unsigned and with reasons for his objections. However, if two-thirds of those present in both chambers vote to override the president's veto, the bill will become law. In the second way, the president may **pocket-veto** a bill. Pocket vetoes are complicated despite the fact that the president takes no action on the bill. If the bill languishes on the president's desk for ten days without the president either signing or vetoing the bill, it becomes law. However, if the congressional session ends before the ten days are up, the bill is pocket-vetoed. Unlike a regular veto, Congress has no opportunity to override a pocket veto.

---

[52]Absolute vetoes exist outside of the United States. For a discussion of absolute vetoes in a comparative perspective, see Matthew Shugart and John Carey, *Presidents and Assemblies: Constitutional Design and Electoral Dynamics* (New York: Cambridge University Press, 1992).

[53]For a short period of time, the president possessed a power resembling the line-item veto. Although Congress passed a law granting the president that power, the Supreme Court struck down the law as unconstitutional. See Michael Nelson, ed., *The Evolving Presidency* (Washington, D.C.: Congressional Quarterly, 1999), pp. 247–252; David Nice, *Public Budgeting* (Belmont, CA: Wadsworth, 2002), p. 185.

The Development of the Veto

Presidents employed the veto sparingly in the nineteenth century, mostly because they adhered to a restricted conception of the presidency and presidential-congressional relations.[54] Most presidents in the nineteenth century embraced a strict version of separation of powers. By adhering to such a view, they limited their activity in the legislative process. While they might voice preferences about policy under debate in Congress, rarely would they become active in that process. This perspective also restricted their use of the veto to bills that they deemed unconstitutional. Thus, they would often sign into law bills to which they objected on policy grounds.[55]

Although Andrew Jackson was the first president to veto a bill on policy grounds, such a rationale of the veto did not become common until the latter part of the nineteenth century. A change in the conception of the presidency from that of the "clerk" to that of the "steward" stimulated the shift for vetoing from constitutionality to policy. By the turn of the century, presidents wanted—and were expected—to provide policy leadership. That applied to the veto as much as it did to other policy-making activities, such as developing policy alternatives and rallying public and congressional support behind those alternatives. By the onset of the twentieth century, the veto had become a fixture of presidential-congressional relations.

Vetoes and Overrides

Presidents vary in their use of the veto. Consistent with the policy leadership conception of the presidency, policy differences between the president and Congress have become the most important reason that some presidents veto more than others. In particular, we find that presidents who face an opposition-party Congress are more likely to veto bills than when the same party controls both Congress and the presidency. For instance, in 1993 to 1994, when the Democrats held Congress, Bill Clinton did not use the veto even once. In contrast, during the remainder of his term in office, when the Republicans held Congress, Clinton vetoed some thirty-seven bills and was overridden only twice.[56] Consistent with the idea that presidents veto more when they are in a weak bargaining situation in Congress,

---

[54]For a historical discussion of the development of the veto, see Carlton Jackson, *Presidential Vetoes, 1792–1945* (Athens: University of Georgia Press, 1967). General treatments of the rise and use of the veto are found in Robert J. Spitzer, *The Presidential Veto: Touchstone of the American Presidency* (Albany: State University of New York Press, 1988); and Richard A. Watson, *Presidential Vetoes and Public Policy* (Lawrence: University Press of Kansas, 1993).

[55]For an analysis of the reasons that presidents give in their veto messages for using the veto, see Albert C. Ringelstein, "Presidential Vetoes: Motivations and Classification," *Congress and the Presidency* 12 (Spring 1985):43–55. Also, Dennis W. Gleiber and Steven A. Shull, "Justifying Presidential Decisions: The Scope of Veto Messages," *Congress and the Presidency* 26 (Spring 1999): 41–60.

[56]These figures come from Victoria Allred, "Versatility with the Veto," *CQ Weekly Report,* 20 January 2001, p. 175.

TABLE 10-2   PRESIDENTIAL VETOES FROM WASHINGTON TO CLINTON

President	Years in office	Total vetoes	Regular vetoes	Pocket vetoes	Vetoes overridden
Washington	1789–1797	2	2	0	0
J. Adams	1797–1801	0	0	0	0
Jefferson	1801–1809	0	0	0	0
Madison	1809–1817	7	5	2	0
Monroe	1817–1825	1	1	0	0
J. Q. Adams	1825–1829	0	0	0	0
Jackson	1829–1837	12	5	7	0
Van Buren	1837–1841	1	0	1	0
W. Harrison	1841–1841	0	0	0	0
Tyler	1841–1845	10	6	4	1
Polk	1845–1849	3	2	1	0
Taylor	1849–1850	0	0	0	0
Fillmore	1850–1853	0	0	0	0
Pierce	1853–1857	9	9	0	5
Buchanan	1857–1861	7	4	3	0
Lincoln	1861–1865	7	2	5	0
A. Johnson	1865–1869	29	21	8	15
Grant	1869–1877	93	45	48	4
Hayes	1877–1881	13	12	1	1
Garfield	1881–1881	0	0	0	0

studies also find that when presidential popularity is on the decline, the president's propensity to veto increases.[57]

Presidential vetoes are rarely overridden because of the two-thirds vote rule discussed at the start of "The Presidential Veto" section. From Washington through Clinton, presidents have vetoed some 1,482 bills, not counting pocket vetoes (see table 10-2). Of these, only 106, or 7.2 percent, have been overridden. However, some vetoes are more vulnerable to overrides than others. Just as minority-party status may lead presidents to veto more, when the opposition party controls Congress with sufficient strength, veto override attempts may be more successful. For

[57]Todd Shields and Chi Huang, "Presidential Vetoes: An Event Count Model," *Political Research Quarterly* 48 (September 1995): 559–72; Todd Shields and Chi Huang, "Executive Vetoes: Testing Presidency- versus President-Centered Perspectives of Presidential Behavior," *American Politics Quarterly* 25 (October 1997): 431–57; Samuel B. Hoff, "Saying No: Presidential Support and Veto Use, 1889–1989," *American Politics Quarterly* 19 (July 1991): 310–23; Gary W. Copeland, "When Congress and the President Collide: Why Presidents Veto Legislation," *Journal of Politics* 45 (August 1983): 696–710; David Rohde and Dennis Simon, "Presidential Vetoes and Congressional Response: A Study of Institutional Conflict," *American Journal of Political Science* 29 (1985):397–427; and John T. Woolley, "Institutions, the Election Cycle, and the Presidential Veto," *American Journal of Political Science,* 35 (May 1991): 279–304.

TABLE 10–2   CONTINUED

President	Years in office	Total vetoes	Regular vetoes	Pocket vetoes	Vetoes overridden
Arthur	188*–1885	12	4	8	1
Cleveland I	1885–1889	414	304	110	2
B. Harrison	1889–1893	44	19	25	1
Cleveland II	1893–1897	170	42	128	5
McKinley	1897–1901	42	6	36	0
T. Roosevelt	1901–1909	82	42	40	1
Taft	1909–1913	39	30	9	1
Wilson	1913–1921	44	33	11	6
Harding	1921–1923	6	5	1	0
Coolidge	1923–1929	50	20	30	4
Hoover	1929–1933	37	21	16	3
F. Roosevelt	1933–1945	635	372	263	9
Truman	1945–1953	250	180	70	12
Eisenhower	1953–1961	181	73	108	2
Kennedy	1961–1963	21	12	9	0
L. Johnson	1963–1969	30	16	14	0
Nixon	1969–1974	43	26	17	7
Ford	1974–1977	66	48	18	12
Carter	1977–1981	31	13	18	2
Reagan	1981–1989	78	39	39	9
Bush	1989–1993	46	27	19	1
Clinton	1993–2000	37	37	0	2

Sources: Presidential Vetoes, 1789–1976 (Washington, D.C.: Government Printing Office, 1978); *Presidential Vetoes, 1977–1984* (Washington, D.C.: Government Printing Office, 1985); and various issues of *Congressional Quarterly Almanac* (Washington, D.C.: Congressional Quarterly Press).

instance, Gerald Ford, who faced large Democratic majorities, saw twelve of forty-eight, or 25 percent, of his regular vetoes overridden. Ronald Reagan and Richard Nixon had override rates similar to Ford. In contrast, John Kennedy, Lyndon Johnson, and Bill Clinton, in his first two years when the Democrats controlled Congress, did not have a single veto overridden, and Jimmy Carter had only two of thirteen regular vetoes overridden.[58]

Veto Bargaining and Presidential Influence

The veto seems a double-edged legislative weapon. On the one hand, the resort to vetoing a bill indicates that a president is incapable of keeping Congress from passing a bill that he dislikes. In other words, a veto may indicate a lack

[58]These figures come from Lyn Ragsdale, *Vital Statistics on the Presidency* (Washington, D.C.: Congressional Quarterly Press, 2000), p. 402.

of presidential influence with Congress. On the other hand, the fact that so few vetoes are overridden may suggest the power of the veto. Still, when Congress sus-
tains or does not challenge a presidential veto, no legislation is forthcoming. It is
hard to talk about presidential influence over public policy when none is produced.

The power to veto may shape policy under two circumstances: when Congress
must enact legislation or when a president threatens to veto a bill. Sooner or later,
Congress must enact a budget. Usually presidents can get Congress to trim spending on certain areas, but Clinton was able to get Congress to increase spending in
certain areas by vetoing or threatening to veto budget and appropriations bills.[59]

Clinton gained a reputation for standing firm, a result of the government shutdown in 1995 that occurred when Clinton refused to sign the budget until Congress produced one to his liking. The public stood behind Clinton in this episode
or at least blamed Congress for the government shutdown. Some observers felt
this episode of Clinton standing up to Congress rehabilitated Clinton's image with
the public and paved the way for his reelection in 1996. As a consequence, Congress, fearing another public backlash, became timid in challenging Clinton on
spending issues when he threatened to use or did use the veto.

Clinton used the veto on spending legislation to extract policy concessions
from Congress. Other presidents have used the threat of a veto to do the same
thing.[60] However, veto threats will not be effective in all encounters with Congress. Primarily, two situations must hold for a veto threat to be effective. First,
presidents must not be forthright about whether they will veto or not or what their
true preferences are on a bill. In other words, Congress must be somewhat uncertain as to the president's intentions and preferences. By not knowing for certain what the president's preferences are, Congress may overcompensate to avoid
a veto showdown. Second, Congress must prefer new policy to the existing status quo and must think that the president prefers new policy to the status quo. In
other words, both the president and Congress must desire a change in policy.

The patients' bill of rights issue of 2001 illustrates both the limits and the potential of a veto threat strategy. Under existing law, patients could not sue health
maintenance organizations (HMOs). Thus, if an HMO denied a treatment and
some harm came to a patient because of the treatment denial, a patient could not
sue the HMO to seek redress. By the 1990s, HMOs had become one of the most
common forms of health care insurance for Americans. Many began to feel that
HMOs, under their legal protections, had placed profit above patient regard. Calls
for reform of the patient-HMO relationship got onto the agenda and became a
very popular issue in the late 1990s.

[59]Allred, "Versatility with the Veto."

[60]On the impact of veto threats, see Charles M. Cameron, *Veto Bargaining: Presidents and the Politics of Negative Power* (New York: Cambridge University Press, 2000). Also see Daniel E. Ingberman
and Dennis A. Yao, "Presidential Commitment and the Veto," *American Journal of Political Science* 35
(May 1991): 357–89; D. Roderick Kiewiet and Mathew D. McCubbins, "Presidential Influence on Congressional Appropriations Decisions," *American Journal of Political Science* 32 (August 1988): 713–36;
and Nolan M. McCarty, "Presidential Pork: Executive Veto Power and Distributive Politics," *American
Political Science Review* 94 (March 2000): 117–29.

Once Senator Jeffords left the Republican Party in late spring 2001, as we mentioned in the "Party Control of Congress and Presidential Success and Support" section of this chapter, Senate Democrats produced a bill that permitted patients to sue HMOs in both the state and federal courts. The bill also placed no limit on damages that suing patients could seek in federal courts, but damages were capped in state courts when state laws imposed caps on awards.

George W. Bush opposed the Senate bill and threatened to veto it before the Senate passed it. He felt that expensive lawsuits against HMOs would raise the costs of health care and that would lead many to lose their health care coverage or have it severely reduced. Still, the Senate passed the bill because Senate Democrats felt that they had nothing to lose in challenging the president. There was strong public pressure on Bush to sign a patients' bill of rights. If he vetoed a patients' rights bill, he might create an issue that the Democrats could use against him. The Senate Democrats also pushed their legislation because the House, under Republican control, displayed less sentiment to allow easy access to suits against HMOs.

Still, several leading sponsors of the patients' bill of rights in the House supported the idea of allowing patients to sue HMOs. One of those leaders was Republican Charlie Norwood of Georgia, who was a practicing dentist before becoming a member of Congress. Most members of Congress who, like Norwood, practiced in some field of medicine supported more expansive patients' rights because of the difficult dealings that they had had with HMOs. It appeared that enough votes existed in the House to produce a bill similar to the one that the Senate passed. House leaders decided to put off a vote until they could gather enough votes to support the president's less expansive position. If that failed, they might keep a bill from even being considered to keep Bush from having to issue the veto and creating an issue for the Democrats against the president.

With such high stakes and with pressure to produce patients' rights legislation, Bush and Norwood negotiated a compromise. Bush moved a little, allowing patients to sue in state courts and raising the limits on caps for pain and suffering and punitive damages from $500,000 to $1.5 million. This satisfied Norwood, although the compromise barred suits in federal courts. Most congressional Democrats remained dissatisfied with the compromise. Norwood accepted the compromise in order to produce legislation and to help his party's president, despite the fact that he seemed to give up more than the president. The House passed the Norwood-Bush patients' rights bill with support from all Republican members and a handful of Democrats. At least in the House, Bush's veto threat forced a compromise.[61]

In another example, Bush's veto threat compelled Senate Democrats to cave in. Just days after the vote on the patients' bill of rights in the House, the Senate accepted emergency farm subsidy legislation budgeted at $5.5 billion, although Senate Democrats originally sought $7.5 billion. In this case, there was little public pressure on the issue. Thus, unlike the patients' rights bill, Democrats had no

[61]Most of the details of this story come from Robert Pear, "Measure Defining Patients' Rights Passes House," *New York Times,* 3 August 2001, p. A1.

way of turning it into a public issue to use against the president. The president stood his ground and was probably helped by his resoluteness on patients' rights, which made his threat to veto credible. To get any legislation and help farm constituents, Democrats in the Senate acceded to the president's position, which the House had already endorsed.[62]

From these cases, we can see that veto threat politics is complicated, but if used deftly, a president can extract policy concessions from Congress by threatening to veto. As Cameron shows in his book on veto bargaining with Congress, even minority presidents can employ veto threats to their policy advantage.[63]

From the veto threat perspective, we see the multifaceted nature of the presidential veto. On the one hand, the resort to a veto is an indication of a president who lacks sufficient influence with Congress to motivate it to produce the policies that he wants. But the threat of a veto, under the circumstances outlined above, may motivate Congress to compromise with the president to produce policy that they can both live with. Thus, not only can the veto stop Congress from taking action that the president does not like, but the threat of a veto also may encourage Congress to produce legislation that the president likes. In this latter sense, veto threats may be an important part of the president's bargaining arsenal with Congress.

IMPEACHING THE PRESIDENT

Thus far in this chapter we have been discussing presidential-congressional relations from the perspective of presidential activity in the legislative process. But we can also look at the relations between the two branches through the lens of legislative controls over the executive. In Chapter 11 on the presidency and the bureaucracy, we will look at congressional oversight of the executive and the bureaucracy. There, we will consider the issue of congressional micromanagement of the executive. Now we turn to the issue of impeachment, the most dire form of congressional control over the personnel in the executive branch.

Impeachment can be viewed as a complement to the Senate's confirmation power. Where the confirmation power gives the Senate some influence over who is chosen to serve as appointees to the highest levels in executive (see our discussion in the section on "The Politics of Confirmation" in this chapter), impeachment allows the Senate to remove officials from office, including the president. In this chapter, we limit our discussion to impeachment of the president, noting that high-level bureaucrats and federal judges have also been impeached and removed from office.

The Impeachment Process

The Constitution lays out the impeachment process in detail, although grounds for impeachment have been open to debate. The impeachment process begins when the House of Representatives brings impeachment charges against the pres-

[62]Philip Shenon, "Senate Approves Farm Subsidy Bill President Backed," *New York Times,* 4 August 2001, p. A1.

[63]Cameron, *Veto Bargaining.*

ident. Then the process moves to the Senate, which sits in judgment of the president, much like a jury. The chief justice of the Supreme Court acts as presiding officer, similar to a trial court judge. To remove a president from office through impeachment requires a two-thirds vote of the Senate.

The only penalties that impeachment can mete out are removal from office and denial of ever holding public office again. However, removal does not guarantee that the president cannot be brought up on criminal charges after being removed from office.

The constitutional standard for impeachment is "treason, bribery, or other high crimes and misdemeanors" (Article II, Section 4). Although the treason and bribery standards are self-evident, controversy exists over the meaning of "high crimes and misdemeanors." Part of this ambiguity stems from a compromise at the Constitutional Convention over the nature of the presidency and impeachment.[64]

On one side were opponents of a strong presidency. They viewed impeachment as a way of controlling the presidency. Proponents of this view wanted to include such offenses as maladministration and corruption. However, advocates of a stronger presidency opposed such low standards, fearing that they would be easily used against presidents. For instance, a corruption standard might stand in the way of presidents using patronage, which could easily be construed as corruption. They preferred limiting impeachment to treason and bribery, although most advocates of a strong presidency also realized that the nation must be protected against other types of political crimes that were not indictable offenses, as treason and bribery were. These might include abuse of power or injuries to the Republic that could be made only by those serving in official governmental posts. Thus, many constitutional scholars suggest that the phrase *high crimes and misdemeanors* is meant to refer to such political crimes. Still, the founders supposedly kept the definition of *high crimes and misdemeanors* ambiguous because they thought that it would have to be defined on a case-by-case basis and that each generation would have to decide if specific acts so harmed the nation.[65]

The Politics of Impeachment

The ambiguity over the meaning of "high crimes and misdemeanors" has opened the process of impeachment to politics. Political opponents of the president have often applied a broader conception of what is impeachable than defenders of the president. Yet, in spite of political motivations that often animate impeachment moves against a president, only three presidents have seen impeachment proceedings commence against them—Andrew Johnson in 1868, Richard Nixon in 1973, and Bill Clinton in 1999. Both Johnson and Clinton survived the impeachment processes against them, while Nixon resigned from office before a vote to remove could be taken in the Senate.

[64]Richard M. Pious, "Impeaching the President: The Intersection of Constitutional and Popular Law," *Saint Louis University Law Journal* 43 (Summer 1999): 859–904.

[65]Michael J. Gerhardt, "Putting the Law of Impeachment in Perspective," *Saint Louis University Law Journal* 43 (Summer 1999): 905–30.

Andrew Johnson's troubles with Congress stemmed over reconstruction policy. Reconstruction policy concerned how the South should be treated in the aftermath of the Civil War. Johnson supported a liberal policy that would bring southern states back into the Union and end Union military occupation and governing of the South as fast as possible. Many Republicans in Congress held that the South should be punished severely. However, this policy debate merely served as the backdrop to understanding why Congress impeached Johnson. Congress could not remove Johnson from office for such naked policy reasons. It found what was thought to be a more legitimate excuse for proceeding with impeachment in the Tenure of Office Act.

We will discuss the Tenure of Office Act in more detail in Chapter 11, on presidential relations with the bureaucracy. For now, all that is important is that the act limited the president's ability to name an appointee to an office requiring Senate confirmation until the Senate had confirmed the successor. Until then, the departing member of the executive branch would stay in office. Johnson tried to remove from office Edward Stanton, his secretary of the Treasury, but Stanton refused to leave, in part because he was aligned with the forces that opposed Johnson's reconstruction policies. Conflict boiled over between the two as Johnson tried to keep Stanton from assuming his duties, in violation of the Tenure of Office Act. Then Congress took action against the president, citing his violation of the law as the rationale for the impeaching him. But Johnson survived conviction and removal from office by a one-vote margin in the Senate.

Richard Nixon, like Andrew Johnson, was embroiled in bitter policy conflict with Congress. But policy differences between Nixon and Congress were not the major source of the impeachment proceedings against him. The Watergate break-in and the White House's attempts to interfere with Congress's investigations of the break-in triggered Congress to impeach the president. The impeachment charges against the president accused him of obstructing justice and tampering with the Watergate investigations. Specifically, he was accused of making false statements to official investigators; withholding relevant information and evidence; "approving, condoning, acquiescing in, and counseling witnesses to give false statements to investigators"; interfering with the conduct of the investigation; and paying money to witnesses and potential witnesses to remain silent or offer false testimony.[66] Unlike Johnson, Nixon was accused of indictable and criminal charges.

And although partisan divisions were clearly evident, many Republicans joined with the Democratic majority in the House and voted for the impeachment charges.[67] The nature of the charges against Nixon may have led many of these Republicans to defect from their party's president and support impeachment. But polls also showed that public support for Nixon had eroded as well. Supporting him could be politically costly. In fact, one study found that those members of Congress who stood by Nixon were more likely to be defeated for reelection in

---

[66]Pious, "Impeaching the President," p. 869.

[67]Terry Sullivan, "Impeachment Practice in the Era of Lethal Conflict," *Congress and the Presidency* 25 (Autumn 1998): 117–28.

1974 than Republicans who supported impeachment.[68] However, the impeachment process never got far in the Senate, as Nixon resigned from office before a removal vote could be taken. Accounts indicate that Nixon thought that the Senate would vote to remove him from office and he resigned to save himself from such embarrassment. Later on, when Gerald Ford assumed the presidency, Ford pardoned Nixon of any indictable offenses.

In 1998, Congress also impeached Bill Clinton. As with Johnson, the impeachment process made it to the Senate, which voted on removal. And like Johnson, Clinton survived the removal vote but by a wider margin as Democrats stood by him in lock-step fashion.

Clinton, similar to Johnson and Nixon, had policy disputes with Congress, which the Republican opposition controlled. While policy differences may have set context for the Republican challenge, however, the airing of Clinton's affair with the White House intern Monica Lewinsky launched the process. Impeachment supporters claimed that Clinton, like Nixon, had obstructed justice, falsely testified under oath, and tampered with witness testimony in the Paula Jones sexual harassment case against Clinton.

Democratic defenders argued that while Clinton's behavior was abhorrent and possibly criminal, it constituted a low crime and not a high crime; that is, Clinton's troubles stemmed from a civil case, not a criminal one, and impeaching and removing a president must have a higher bar than Clinton's accusers leveled against him. The public seemed to agree with Clinton's defenders; at least, polls indicated that the president enjoy high support among the public. This public supported probably provided a bulwark for congressional Democrats, who steadfastly supported the president, although many expressed public disapproval of his personal behavior.[69]

What do these three cases tell us about the impeachment process? First of all, in each case, the president and Congress were at loggerheads over policy. Partisan politics, thus, entered into the process. These cases also tell us that it is easier to impeach than to remove a president. Impeachment only requires a simple majority in the House, while removal requires a two-thirds vote in the Senate. To form the two-thirds majority requires strong public backing. A comparison of the Nixon and Clinton episodes, where public opinion data exist, suggests that the public will support the president unless the public thinks that the president's actions profoundly harm the nation and the constitutional regime. Neither personal transgressions, policy differences with Congress, nor even indictable offenses, as in the Clinton case, are enough to push the public in the direction of removing a president.

 Lastly, impeachment may have had an unintended consequence—that of expanding presidential power.[70] As presidents sought to increase the range of

[68]Eric Uslaner and Margaret Conway, "The Responsible Electorate: Watergate, the Economy, and Vote Choice in 1974," *American Political Science Review* 79 (1985): 788–803.

[69]Pious, "Impeaching the President"; David J. Lanoue and Craig F. Emmert, "Voting in the Glare of the Spotlight: Representatives' Votes on the Impeachment of President Clinton," *Polity* 32 (Winter 1999): 253–69; and Lawrence S. Rothenberg and Mitchell S. Sanders, "Lame-Duck Politics: Impending Departure and the Votes on Impeachment," *Political Research Quarterly* 53 (September 2000): 523–36.

[70]Pious, "Impeaching the President," p. 864.

their powers—for instance, with regard to removing lower-level appointed officials from office and using the veto—they challenged Congress to use the impeachment weapon against them if Congress wanted to disallow such actions. Impeachment also worked for presidents as they sought to increase their control
over the bureaucracy: They argued that because they would be held responsible
for abuse of power, they needed to be able to control the entirety of the bureaucracy to ensure that other executive branch personnel did not abuse power. Thus,
in an ironic twist, a mechanism meant to curb the presidency may actually have
been used to expand its powers as expansionist presidents could argue that the
presence of the impeachment mechanism would safeguard the nation from excessive presidential power.

KEY TERMS

divided government   277
impeachment   306
Office of Legislative Affairs   285
pocket-veto   300
presidential coattails   291
presidential program   281

presidential success
   with Congress   286
presidential support in Congress   286
presidential skill with Congress   297
presidential veto   300

DISCUSSION QUESTIONS

1. What are the major sources of conflict and cooperation between the president
   and Congress? How much of this conflict and cooperation is a function of our
   constitutional design, and how much comes from other sources?
2. In what ways can we think of the president as helping to set the congressional
   agenda? How successful is the president in helping to set the congressional
   agenda? How has the president's role as congressional agenda setter evolved over
   time? Why is agenda setting so important for presidential legislative success with
   Congress?
3. Compare the legislative politics of confirmation with that of passing legislation.
   In which is the president more successful? Why? What does the difference in presidential success between confirmations and passing legislation tell us about the
   nature of presidential-congressional relations?
4. Describe the role of the Office of Legislative Affairs and the congressional liaison
   operations of the White House. How have the Office of Legislative Affairs and the
   congressional liaison operations evolved over time? How important are these to
   presidential success in Congress?
5. Compare the different ways of calculating how successful a president is in Congress and how much support he receives from members of Congress. What are
   the major sources of high levels of presidential success and support in Congress?
   What, if anything, can presidents do to enhance their success with, and support
   from, Congress?

6. What makes a president skillful in his dealings with Congress? How important is such skill in building support for the president in Congress? Can you think of examples of presidents who were considered skillful yet were not very successful with Congress? Are there examples of presidents who were not thought to be very skillful with Congress but were very successful in getting much of what they wanted from Congress?

7. How important to the president is the veto? Is use of a veto a sign of a weak or a strong presidency? How can the threat of a veto affect the president's success with Congress?

8. What were the founders' intentions with regard to presidential impeachment? How often has Congress used impeachment against the president? When has it been used successfully? Is impeachment a useful device to curb the presidency?

SUGGESTED READINGS

Jon R. Bond and Richard Fleisher, *The President in the Legislative Arena*. Chicago: University of Chicago Press, 1990.

Jon R. Bond and Richard Fleisher, eds., *Polarized Politics: Congress and the President in a Partisan Era*. Washington, D.C.: Congressional Quarterly Press, 2000.

Charles M. Cameron, *Veto Bargaining: Presidents and the Politics of Negative Power*. New York: Cambridge University Press, 2000.

Kenneth E. Collier, *Between the Branches: The White House Office of Legislative Affairs*. Pittsburgh: University of Pittsburgh Press, 1997.

Paul C. Light, *The President's Agenda: Domestic Policy Choice from Kennedy to Carter*. Baltimore: Johns Hopkins University Press, 1982.

Mark A. Peterson, *Legislating Together: The White House and Capitol Hill from Eisenhower to Reagan*. Cambridge: Harvard University Press, 1990.

Richard M. Pious, "Impeaching the President: The Intersection of Constitutional and Popular Law," *Saint Louis University Law Journal* 43 (Summer 1999): 859–904.

Robert J. Spitzer, *The Presidential Veto: Touchstone of the American Presidency*. Albany: State University of New York Press, 1998.

11

THE PRESIDENT AND THE BUREAUCRACY

Although the president's constitutional duty to see "that the laws are faithfully executed" gives the president immense, if not very clear, authority over the federal bureaucracy, the president does not manage the bureaucracy alone. Congress, through its powers to confirm nominations, create departments, legislate, appropriate, investigate, and impeach, also has much input into the design, direction, and operation of the nation's bureaucracy. And inasmuch as separation of powers and checks and balances produce tensions between the presidency and Congress, the bureaucracy becomes an arena of presidential-congressional conflict.

The Constitution makes no formal provision for a bureaucracy, but there are suggestions in the Constitution that the framers presumed the necessity of having bureaucratic agencies that would carry out the policies and programs of government. For instance, the president and Congress are given the power to nominate and confirm appointees to the offices of government. Also, the president is authorized to "require in writing, of the principal Officer in each of the executive Departments, upon any Subject relating to the Duties of their respective Offices." (Article II, Section 2). And during the Revolutionary War and Articles of Confederation periods, federal offices, which would become the State and Treasury departments, existed. Thus, the founders, in drafting the Constitution, acknowledged that some type of executive establishment and bureaucracy would exist, but they gave little guidance as to the form or structure of the bureaucracy and its relationship to the constitutional branches.

The Constitution fails to answer many questions regarding the bureaucracy. Neither the duties of the bureaucracy nor its structure were outlined. Most important, nothing was said about lines of authority to the bureaucracy. Who should run the bureaucracy—the president, as head of the executive branch, or Congress, as it had done under the Articles of Confederation? This ambiguity over whether the bureaucracy is responsible to the president or Congress has left a legacy to this day, with both branches claiming authority over the bureaucracy.

THE DEVELOPMENT AND STRUCTURE OF THE BUREAUCRACY

While the seeds of the U.S. bureaucracy dated to the Revolutionary War period, most of the development of the bureaucracy came afterward, in a series of major enactments and reforms. These episodes of bureaucratic development would greatly influence the role that the bureaucracy would play in policy making and implementation, as well as the relationship between the bureaucracy and its constitutional masters—the president, Congress, and the courts. Thus, the bureaucracy has been shaped indirectly by the Constitution, as the needs and preferences of those within the constitutional branches determine the direction, duties, and structures of the bureaucracy.

The Revolutionary War was fought in part as a backlash against what was felt to be excessive and unaccountable government. Thus, Americans historically have held mistrusting attitudes toward government, especially the bureaucracy. Whereas most of the other European democracies grew out of established governmental systems, often with strong bureaucracies already in place, the reverse is the case for the United States. No strong tradition of bureaucratic service to the nation existed in the United States. The democracy was in place before the bureaucracy; thus, there is a heavy imprint of our democratic government on the bureaucracy. This imprint entails distrust of bureaucrats and mechanisms to control the actions and activities of bureaucrats.

Combining these ingredients—the natural competition between the president and Congress, the historical mistrust of bureaucracy, and mechanisms to control the behavior of bureaucrats—often makes the bureaucracy into a political football that the president and Congress try to use for their own ends. The outcome of these forces on the bureaucracy often results in both branches limiting each other's influence and control over the bureaucracy, as well as sometimes leading to ineffectual and inefficient bureaucracy.

The Structure of the Federal Bureaucracy

The current structure of the federal bureaucracy is quite complex.[1] A variety of different types of bureaucratic agencies exist, with different relationships to the president and the Congress. The major agencies are the cabinet departments, independent agencies, and government corporations. In addition, there are different types of bureaucrats, the most important distinction being that between politically appointed bureaucrats and civil service (or career) bureaucrats. Presidents tend to prefer cabinet departments and politically appointed bureaucrats because a president's control or influence tends to be higher with these than with other types of agencies and career bureaucrats.

Cabinet departments are organized hierarchically in a pyramid. At the top of the pyramid are the politically appointed offices, such as the secretary, undersecretary, and the like. Presidents nominate people to these posts. The nominations are subject to senatorial confirmation. Rarely does Congress refuse to confirm such appointees. Furthermore, these appointees serve at the pleasure of the president—he can remove, that is, fire, any of the political appointees at

---

[1] A good, concise description of the structure of the federal government can be found in Kenneth J. Meier, *Politics and the Bureaucracy: Policymaking in the Fourth Branch of Government,* 3d ed. (Pacific Grove, Calif: Brooks/Cole, 1993), pp. 17–27; and Harold Seidman and Robert Gilmour, *Politics, Position, and Power: From the Positive to the Regulatory State,* 3d ed. (New York: Oxford University Press, 1986).

will. Lastly, the cabinet departments are placed within the executive branch, which makes the president clearly responsible for them.

Still, there are limits to presidential control of the cabinet departments. Lower-level bureaucrats are mostly civil servants who earn their job through merit and other formulas not easily subject to presidential manipulation. Also, unlike with political appointees, presidents cannot easily remove civil service bureaucrats from their posts, as they have job protections. To remove a career bureaucrat from office requires a lengthy process that is intended to insulate these government employees from political manipulation and intimidation.

Another factor that may lessen president influence over a cabinet department is lack of attention and interest in that department and its programs. There are many reasons a president may not pay much attention to any one department. Other departments may be dealing with issues and problems that the president considers of higher priority. Or the president may consider the issues and problems that the department deals with as too costly or not easily solvable. Three, the department may not offer enough political or policy benefits for a president to spend his time on. For whatever reason, lack of presidential interest and involvement in a department may result in less presidential influence over the department than over one in which the president takes a more active interest.

Also, presidents may not be able to direct a department easily because of the relationship between the department and Congress. Congress has easy access to cabinet departments because they were created to mirror the congressional committee system. In fact, one may argue that Congress created the parallel structure between its committees and the departments to ensure that Congress could build expertise that would enable it to oversee what the agencies do.

Nevertheless, presidents are more able to control the departmental bureaucracy than the independent agencies or government corporations. First, as to the **independent agencies,** presidents command much less control over top-level appointees. Generally, a multimember panel, called a commission or board, heads an independent commission. These agency executives hold staggered terms, which generally last longer than the president's four-year term of office. Thus, presidents will inherit independent agency commissioners from the previous administration, and it may take years before each "seat's" term comes up for reappointment. Moreover, such bodies tend to be governed under bipartisan rules that stipulate that the president's party can hold no more than a majority of one. This limits the president's freedom in selecting new appointees. Nor can the president remove an independent agency commissioner from office for political reasons, such as their policy preferences. Lastly, many independent agencies are not considered to be formally part of the executive branch but rather arms of Congress. One can easily see the severe limitations put on the president with regard to these types of agencies compared to cabinet departments. Taken together, these various features of independent agencies make presidential influence difficult but not impossible, especially if the president serves two full terms and thus has greater opportunities to nominate a larger number of commissioners that are to his liking.

Government corporations pose another set of barriers to easy presidential control. Like independent agencies, most government corporations are somewhat insulated from partisan and political influences through use of bipartisan commissions, which run them. Moreover, government corporations are created to operate in a more businesslike fashion than other government bureaucracies and even to make a profit, if possible. Lastly, some have their own personnel systems that are outside of the government personnel systems. For instance, the workers in the Postal Service, which became a government corporation in 1970, belong to a union and not the civil service.

The Development of the Federal Bureaucracy

By tracing the historical development of the bureaucracy, we can understand the modern tug-of-war between the president and Congress over the bureaucracy. The major developments and reforms centered on the recruitment of bureaucratic personnel and the placement and structure of bureaucratic offices and agencies within the federal establishment.

From Washington to Jackson: A Bureaucracy of Notables   Among the earliest actions that George Washington took was to appoint people to run the departments and agencies that the first Congress had established. Washington was careful in making these major appointments, knowing that these people would become important advisers to him, as well as be responsible for important duties of the new constitutional government. Three people were selected to head the newly created departments: Thomas Jefferson was named secretary of State; Alexander Hamilton became head of the Treasury Department; and Henry Knox, who already was running the War Department, continued in that capacity. Two other major posts that did not hold departmental status were created: Edmund Randolph became attorney general, and Samuel Osgood was appointed postmaster general. In addition, Washington made about one thousand other appointments.[2]

Washington set the tone for early administrations. First, he did not use his appointments as a form of patronage, except to place in office people who were committed to the Constitution. Thus, he could have in his cabinet both Alexander Hamilton and Thomas Jefferson, who opposed each other in their vision of the United States and on most major policies. Moreover, Washington viewed the executive authority as the president's alone, not to be shared with the Senate beyond the upper house's confirmation power. His executive branch appointees were to be responsible to him directly.[3]

The nonpartisan nature of the executive establishment broke down during the presidencies that followed Washington because of the development of the Federalist and Jeffersonian factions, both of which were to develop into political parties. Thus, partisanship was added to Washington's executive-centered model of administration.

[2]Forrest McDonald, *The Presidency of George Washington* (New York: Norton, 1974), p. 38.

[3]Ibid., p. 39.

Despite the growing partisanship of executive appointments, another aspect implanted by Washington continued until Andrew Jackson became president in 1828—the fact that a small circle of notables, known to each other and coming from the higher strata of society, filled the ranks of the bureaucracy. Thus, the early bureaucracy was far from democratic or popular in its personnel makeup.

Bureaucracy as Party Spoils   With Andrew Jackson's presidency came two major developments in the bureaucracy and its relationship to the presidency. First, appointments became consciously partisan, and they were used to help build the political party. Second, the personnel ranks were opened up. No longer were only men of note appointed to office. Loyalty to the party and merit or ability to do the job became the standards by which one acquired a job in the federal bureaucracy. And given that most posts, such as mail delivery or simple office clerking, did not require much skill beyond literacy, the bureaucracy began to more closely resemble the population, although with a partisan coloration.

Using the bureaucracy for party building also led to pressure to increase the number of bureaucratic offices and agencies. Thus, in the nineteenth century, several cabinet departments were added (Interior in 1849, Agriculture in 1862, and Justice in 1870), as well as numerous bureaus. Overall, however, the national establishment stayed small; more government service was provided at the state and local levels.

Protecting Bureaucracy from Politics: Civil Service and Independence In the late nineteenth century, the pressures of urbanization and industrialization led to greater demand for governmental services, which would mean more bureaucracy. These pressures were felt first in the states and localities but percolated up to the national level. Important in this movement were the Progressives, who argued that government could apply the newly developed techniques of business management and science to the operation of public agencies and programs. Thus, the Progressives attacked the patronage-partisanship model of government administration that had been in place since Andrew Jackson.

This led to two important changes in administration at the federal level in the last third of the nineteenth century. First, most bureaucrats were pulled out of the politically appointed ranks and moved into the civil service, which was to be protected from politics by the merit system. The second major innovation was the creation of the independent regulatory commission as a bureaucratic form, as was described in the section on "The Structure of the Federal Bureaucracy."

Both of these changes led to a decrease in presidential control over the executive branch. Several factors promoted this diminishing of the presidency in the late nineteenth century. First, the impeachment of Andrew Johnson in 1866 led many in Congress to feel that a strong presidency would hurt Congress as well as the parties. Second, while the Republican Party held a slight edge over the Democrats during this era, both parties were highly competitive in national politics. The Democrats dominated in the South and were very competitive in rural regions throughout much of the Midwest and West. Although unable to win the presidency very often (the Democrats did so only twice from 1860 to 1912, with the elections of Grover Cleveland), Democrats were often in a position to control Congress, and rarely were Republican majorities large. With a strong prospect of divided government, both parties felt it advantageous to weaken the presidency, especially its hold over the bureaucracy. Moreover, given the prevailing Progressive mood of this era, doing so made for good politics. Not wanting to be too cynical, we should also mention that the capability of government did increase during this era, with many more skilled people entering government service, as government took on more complicated and technical tasks.

The Positive State, the Presidency, and Congress   By the early twentieth century, many of the elements of the modern bureaucracy were in place. Despite the fact that two ideas of the Progressives—civil service and independent commission styles of bureaucratic organization—limited presidential control over the bureaucracy, the Progressives did believe in executive control of the bureaucracy. With the rise of the modern presidency in the early twentieth century, presidents began to collect some tools to increase their ability to manage and direct the bureaucracy.

The first of these was the **executive budget,** which was instituted at the federal level in 1921. This new budget process made the president responsible for developing a budget that was then to be submitted to Congress. We will examine this process in more detail in Chapter 14. For now, it is important to note that during each budgetary cycle, each agency submits its budgetary request to the Office of Management and Budget (formerly the Bureau of the Budget), which advises the president on preparation of the budget. The president can then modify the agency request before submitting the budget to Congress. From this process, presidential control over the bureaucracy is enhanced, as he helps set agency budgets, but Congress may, upon receiving the budget, amend the president's recommendation.

In the 1930s, presidents began to acquire and develop other tools of bureaucratic control, especially legislative clearance. Legislative clearance required each agency to clear proposals for legislation with the president (actually an office within the Budget Bureau) before the agency can submit the legislative proposal to Congress. Furthermore, all agency testimony before Congress has to be cleared.

In addition to these presidential tools to control the bureaucracy, the bureaucracy grew at a rate unprecedented in American history. Although the number of bureaucratic offices increased in the first two decades of the twentieth century, the first great surge in the federal bureaucratic establishment came in the 1930s with Franklin Roosevelt's New Deal. Most of these agencies aimed at either stabilizing or helping the economy to expand, or providing welfare and social services to citizens who were suffering as a result of the Depression. Some of the agencies were declared unconstitutional by the Supreme Court, which argued that they interfered too much in the economy. However, by the end of the 1930s, the idea of federal government involvement in managing and regulating the economy had become a fixture and was accepted by most Americans.

A second major surge in the size of the bureaucracy came with the Second World War. Where the United States had a small military establishment for its size compared to other nations in the prewar years, it emerged from the war with a large military. Notably, the military was not drastically reduced in size after the war because of the Cold War with the Soviet Union. In the past, the United States had scaled back its military during peacetime. Another surge in bureaucratic growth came with Lyndon Johnson's Great Society of the 1960s. The Great Society programs extended the reach of federal regulation and expanded welfare and social services to citizens.

Members of Congress found the large federal bureaucracy that was built over the twentieth century an asset that could help their careers. Agencies delivered programs to constituents that members could claim credit for. Federal agencies spent money in districts, either because they were located there or because they administered projects such as school, highway, or dam construction. Such federal spending, in turn, helped local economies, which members could also claim credit for.[4]

Thus, both the president and Congress had uses for the bureaucracy, although their perspectives might differ. Presidents tended to be concerned how the bureaucracy could be used to address national problems or how the size of the bureaucracy might affect the budget. The public also holds presidents responsible for the state of the government; thus, presidents deem to control the bureaucracy. Members of Congress see their individual careers tied to the bureaucracy—what programs are established, which constituents are served, and the like. Thus, the president and Congress may disagree over the structure and uses of the bureaucracy. The bureaucracy is another arena in which competition between these two branches gets played out. We will come back to this theme in "The Issue of Micromanagement" section of this chapter when we discuss congressional micromanagement of the bureaucracy.

THE PRESIDENT'S CABINET

The most visible "bureaucrats" who work for the president are the secretaries of the departments that comprise the president's cabinet. The idea of a cabinet to advise the executive and head the major departments of government originated in late eighteenth-century Britain. It became an early fixture in U.S. government, notwithstanding the fact that the Constitution makes no provision for a cabinet and Congress has never legislatively created such a body.[5]

George Washington found the cabinet useful in supplying a forum to coordinate his administration and as a source of advice. In part because of Washington's initiation of the cabinet, it has become a fixture of the presidency, although different presidents have used their cabinet officers differently. Some, like Eisenhower, approximated cabinet government by holding frequent cabinet meetings.

---

[4]A concise review since FDR can be found in James A. Gazell and Darrel L. Pugh, "Expansion of Centralized Presidential Control," *Bureaucrat* 17, no. 3 (1988): 30–36.

[5]On the history of the cabinet, see Richard F. Fenno, Jr., *The President's Cabinet* (New York: Vintage, 1959).

TABLE 11-1   DATE OF CREATION AND YEARS OF EXISTENCE OF CABINET DEPARTMENTS

Department	Period of existence	President when created
State	1789–present	Washington
War*	1789–1946	Washington
Navy*	1789–1946	Washington
Treasury	1789–present	Washington
Interior	1849–present	Polk
Agriculture	1862–present	Lincoln
Justice**	1870–present	Grant
Commerce and Labor***	1903–1913	T. Roosevelt
Commerce	1913–present	Wilson
Labor	1913–present	Wilson
Defense	1946–present	Truman
Health, Education, and Welfare****	1953–1965	Eisenhower
Housing and Urban Development	1965–present	Johnson
Transportation	1966–present	Johnson
Energy	1977–present	Carter
Health and Human Services	1980–present	Carter
Education	1980–present	Carter
Veterans Affairs	1988–present	Reagan

*War and Navy were combined to form Defense in 1946.

**Justice existed as the Attorney General's Office from 1789 until it was elevated to cabinet status in 1870.

***In 1903, the Commerce and Labor Department was split into the Department of Commerce and the Department of Labor.

****In 1980, Health, Education, and Welfare was split into the Department of Health and Human Services and the Department of Education.

In contrast, John Kennedy rarely held cabinet meetings, preferring to deal one on one with his coterie of White House-based advisers or cabinet secretaries.

Most presidents have felt compelled to at least meet with their cabinets on occasion, and most attach some importance to their cabinet appointments. And while new presidents tend to publicly proclaim their desire for something like cabinet government, one in which their cabinet secretaries will have access to the president, no president has gone so far as to feel that a vote of cabinet secretaries would bind him to a course of action.

Waves of Cabinet Creation

Currently, sixteen departments make up the president's cabinet, while several officials, such as the director of the Central Intelligence Agency (CIA) and the U.S. trade representative, also hold secretarial-level status. Departments have come into the cabinet in three waves (see table 11-1). The first wave came early in

George Washington's administration as Congress created the first departments and Washington appointed their heads. These first departments were State, Treasury, War, and Navy. Justice and the Post Office were also created at this time but did not receive cabinet rank until later. The Post Office was removed from the cabinet when it was converted into a government corporation in 1971, and in 1947, War and Navy were combined into the current Department of Defense. The earliest departments can be thought of as providing the basic functions that all governments must furnish: defense, foreign relations, a revenue system, and a justice system.

A second "wave" of cabinet departments was created across the nineteenth and early twentieth centuries. They include Interior (1849), Agriculture (1862), Commerce (1913), and Labor (1913).[6] Each of these departments represents an important economic interest. Interior represents the interests concerned with developing the West, Agriculture with the farming interests, Commerce with big business, and Labor with unions. We can view the creation of each as in part a governmental response to these powerful economic interests seeking representation in government.

Another wave of cabinet departments came in the mid-to-late twentieth century. A few of these departments resemble the economic-based departments of the nineteenth century, such as Transportation. But in the main, the newer departments are more socially focused in what they do, and each department seems to have a very complex environment, composed of many different, often competing and antagonistic interests.

Presidential Uses for Cabinet Departments

Presidents have three major uses for cabinet departments. One is to provide advice to the president, but this is done more by individual cabinet secretaries whom the president trusts and interacts with than by the cabinet as a whole. Second, cabinet secretaries are the chief executives in charge of running the major departments of government. Thus, they become the lead figures in trying to bend the bureaucracy to the president's will and policy outlook. Third, the cabinet is fundamentally a symbolically representative group, where the president can bring into his administration certain constituencies with whom he wants to build and/or maintain good relations.

A Cabinet of Advisers While presidents have often sought the advice of individual cabinet secretaries, they tend to rely on some secretaries more than others. Those who are more heavily used in this capacity have been termed "inner cabinet" secretaries. Those whom the president seeks out less for advice have

---

[6]Actually, a Department of Commerce and Labor was created in 1903. In 1913, it was split into two departments, a signal of the growing power and role of labor in American politics. See Jeffrey E. Cohen, *The Politics and Economic Policy in the United States,* 2d ed. (Boston: Houghton-Mifflin, 2000), pp. 47–48, 109, 127–129.

been called "outer cabinet" secretaries.[7] Inner cabinet secretaries are in relatively frequent contact with the president and may offer the president advice across a host of topics, from policy to political. Moreover, presidents may seek out the advice of inner cabinet secretaries. The nature of the cabinet post, the talents of the secretary, and the relationship between the president and the secretary often determine if the secretary will enter the "inner circle" or stay in the outer ring.

First, secretaries who head wave I departments (State, Treasury, Defense, and Justice) often occupy the ranks of the inner cabinet because of the jurisdictions of their departments. These departments often are involved in the most important issues of the day or in issues that have great consequences for the nation, such as war or peace, the state of the economy, justice, and civil rights. By their nature, these types of issues tend to involve the president.

But sometimes other issues will rise to national prominence and urgency. When this happens, that department's secretary may step from the outer to the inner ring. For example, in the 1970s, the energy crisis became perhaps the most critical domestic issue, save for the economy. As a consequence, James Schlesinger, Carter's Energy secretary, moved into the select rank of inner cabinet.

Sometimes cabinet secretaries are so talented, possessing keen political or policy insight, that presidents will rely on them no matter what department they head. A good example is Drew Lewis, who directed the Transportation Department under Reagan. Their interaction grew because of the strike of the air traffic controllers (the air traffic control system is under the jurisdiction of the Transportation Department). Lewis helped Reagan politically navigate through this rough period, in which Reagan fired all of the striking workers and received much public criticism for doing so. Lewis's advice proved so valuable to Reagan that Lewis remained a trusted adviser throughout his tenure as Transportation secretary.

In contrast, even talented secretaries can alienate presidents because they push policies at odds with what the president wants to do. Some, for instance, will try to promote a pet policy to high-priority status.[8] Other times, talented secretaries will be out of step with the basic tone of the administration. For example, Robert Reich, Clinton's first secretary of Labor, was a well-respected Harvard University economist and even knew Clinton when both were students at Oxford University. But Reich was a determined liberal, and Clinton's policies, especially in the economic realm, were more centrist. This caused friction between the two, and Reich was publicly outspoken about their disagreements. Finally, Reich had to leave the administration.[9]

---

[7]On the distinction between inner and outer cabinet secretaries, see Thomas E. Cronin, *The State of the Presidency* (Boston: Little, Brown, 1980); and Jeffrey E. Cohen, *The Politics of the U.S. Cabinet: Representation in the Executive Branch, 1789–1984* (Pittsburgh: University of Pittsburgh Press, 1988).

[8]Carolyn Rinkus Thompson, "The Cabinet Member as Policy Entrepreneur," *Administration and Society* 25 (February 1994): 395–409.

[9]See the memoir of Clinton's Labor Secretary: Robert B. Reich, *Locked in the Cabinet* (New York: Knopf, 1997).

Other secretaries may have long and well-established associations with the president, in some cases dating to years before the president came to office. Griffin Bell was the Carter family lawyer and served as Jimmy Carter's attorney general. Frequently, presidents will rely heavily on these old friends. Other times, presidents may appoint family members to cabinet posts. Robert Kennedy, John Kennedy's younger brother, served as attorney general.

A Cabinet of Managers The task of managing the department is one of the primary tasks of the cabinet secretary, as well as that of the other political appointees who occupy the subsecretarial posts.[10] Several factors have increased the importance of management. First of all, the departments have grown in size. As of the late 1990s, the smallest cabinet department was Education, with about five thousand employees, the size of a major corporation. The Defense Department has more than eight hundred thousand civilian employees, and Treasury, Justice, and Veterans Affairs each have more than one hundred thousand, with Veterans Affairs totaling nearer to a quarter million.[11]

Departments are managerially complex not only because of their size but also because of the myriad of programs that they implement and for which they have responsibility. In addition, a department may house agencies and bureaus that do not always get along. The task of implementation becomes more complex when programs require the joint efforts of federal, state, and local government officials, and often private contractors, interest groups, and program clients. Furthermore, the task of wave III cabinet department secretaries can be especially intense, given the competitive and often antagonistic relationships of the many interests that these departments have as clients.

It is little wonder, then, that presidents seek people who have managerial background in either government or the private sector. In fact, several studies argue that managerial skill and competence become the most important factors in selecting replacement cabinet appointees, that is, those who come to office after the president's first appointee has left office.[12] Very few cabinet secretaries (or other politically appointed administrators) serve for the full four years of the president's term.[13]

A Cabinet of Representatives The main function of the cabinet for the president is to represent different social and political interests within the administration.[14] Through his appointees to the cabinet, the president signals to the public

[10]Matthew Holden, Jr., "Bargaining and Command by Heads of U.S. Government Departments," *Social Science Journal* 25, no. 3 (1988): 255–76.

[11]For figures, see Harold W. Stanley and Richard G. Niemi, *Vital Statistics on American Politics, 1997–1998* (Washington, D.C.: Congressional Quarterly Press, 1998), pp. 244–45.

[12]Nelson W. Polsby, "Presidential Cabinet Making," *Political Science Quarterly* 43, no. 1 (1978): 15–26.

[13]Cohen, *Politics of the U.S. Cabinet*, pp. 146–68; and Keith Nicholls, "To Leave or Not to Leave: A Logit Model of Turnover in the Presidential Cabinet," *Congress and the Presidency* 20 (Spring 1993): 39–52.

[14]Cohen, *Politics of the U.S. Cabinet, pp. 44–88;* Keith Nicholls, "*The Dynamics of National Executive Service: Ambition Theory and the Careers of Presidential Cabinet Members,*" *Western Political Quarterly* 44 (March 1991): 149–60; and Janet M. Martin, "The Recruitment of Women to Cabinet and Subcabinet Posts," *Western Political Quarterly* 44 (March 1989): 161–72.

important information about the nature of his administration, such as which groups and issues have access to the president and the likely direction that presidential policies will take.

The most important factor in the appointment of a cabinet secretary is partisan status. Presidents overwhelmingly appoint members of their own party to their cabinets. One study has calculated that from 1789 to 1984, 75 percent of cabinet appointees were of the president's party. When we exclude the earlier parties, such as the Federalists and Democratic-Republicans, which existed before mass-based, modern parties, the percentage rises to 80 percent.[15] Clearly, presidents use cabinet posts to help their parties, but also by selecting secretaries from their parties, presidents will cut down on policy disagreement within their administrations.

Still, occasions arise when presidents violate the party rule in selecting cabinet secretaries. Sometimes social or economic interests are powerful enough that the president cannot ignore them. For example, economic interests, such as big business, are often leery of Democrats, whom they fear will follow liberal, redistributive, or antibusiness policies that they feel will hurt business. To reassure big business, Democrats have often been compelled to select a Treasury secretary with a background in business or close ties to big business. Often this means that the Treasury secretary will be a Republican, such as John Kennedy's secretary of the Treasury, Douglas Dillon. The main point here is that cabinet selection can be a way of representing political and other interests in the administration.

The Decline of the Cabinet

In Chapter 9, we discussed the rise of the Executive Office of the President and the accumulation of policy-based capacity there; for instance, in the Council of Economic Advisers, the National Security Council, and the Domestic Policy Council. Housing such policy expertise within the EOP has served to transform cabinet secretaries from being general advisers to the president to managers of a department. For most recent presidents, cabinet secretaries have input only on policy implementation.[16] Policy development and political advice have become the tasks of other advisers, those located within the EOP and the WHO. The role of the cabinet secretary, as such, has been narrowed and, in some respects, has diminished. Overall, the cabinet has become less important to presidents. This is but one indication of the centralization of policy control within the White House.

IMPORTANCE OF THE BUREAUCRACY TO THE PRESIDENT

In his State of the Union address on January 28, 1992, George H. W. Bush announced that he had directed the secretary of the Treasury to change the federal tax withholding tables so that taxpayers could elect to have the government withhold less

[15]Cohen, *Politics of the U.S. Cabinet,* p. 92; and James D. King and James W. Riddlesperger, Jr., "Presidential Cabinet Appointments: The Partisan Factor," *Presidential Studies Quarterly* 14 (Spring 1984): 231–37.

[16]Cohen, *Politics of the U.S. Cabinet,* pp. 22–41; and Shirley Anne Warshaw, *Powersharing: White House–Cabinet Relations in the Modern Presidency* (Albany: State University of New York Press, 1996).

money from their paychecks, giving them more money to spend. President Bush was prompted to take this action because the economy was in a recession. His polls were suffering, and he was concerned about his reelection prospects in November. Bush hoped that this policy would help stimulate the economy without increasing the large budget deficit that then existed, make him appear responsive to public concerns about the faltering economy, and help his reelection chances.

This episode illustrates the importance of the bureaucracy to the president. The bureaucracy holds the major responsibility for the day-to-day implementation of the government's policies. Through the bureaucracy, the president can have a significant impact on the way the nation's policies are implemented. And to a significant degree, this can be done without the need for congressional consent or action. Especially in an era of divided government, when the likelihood declines that presidents will get the kind of legislation that they want out of Congress, presidents view direction of the bureaucracy as a major means of affecting the policies and actions of government. In this section, we address the two major presidential policy-making strategies—the legislative and the administrative.

The Legislative Versus the Administrative Presidencies

Affecting the policies of government is important to presidents because they are judged and held responsible for the state of the nation. As one scholar boldly puts it: "Above all else, the public wants presidents to be strong leaders, and presidents know that their success in office and place in history hinge on the extent to which citizens, political leaders, academics, and journalists see them as fulfilling these lofty expectations."[17] Living up to these expectations and securing the success of their administrations and place in history require the implementation of public policies that deal with problems of concern to people.

Presidents may generate government policies through legislative or administrative means or both. The legislative strategy involves the passage of legislation, which requires the active participation and cooperation of Congress. As we have discussed, the constitutional positions of Congress and the presidency—their different time horizons, constituencies, and institutional perspectives—will often lead to rivalry and friction between the two branches. During the past thirty years, however, the friction between the two branches has increased because of the high incidence of divided government—twenty-six of the thirty-two years (81 percent) from 1968 to 2000. Moreover, the growing polarization of the parties makes gaining cooperation from the opposition party increasingly difficult.[18]

Even under the best of circumstances, when the president's party controls Congress and Congress is in a cooperative mood, producing new legislation is a difficult and time-consuming task. The congressional agenda easily can be diverted

[17]Terry Moe, "Presidents, Institutions, and Theory," in *Researching the Presidency: Vital Questions, New Approaches,* ed. George C. Edwards, III; John H. Kessel; and Bert A. Rockman (Pittsburgh: University of Pittsburgh Press, 1993), pp. 337–85.

[18]Jon R. Bond and Richard Fleisher, eds. *The President in a More Partisan Era* (Washington, D.C.: Congressional Quarterly Press, 2000).

as new problems crop up or as intense minorities try to stymie legislative efforts. Thus, it is not always likely that presidents can get the kinds of policies that they want from Congress.

The advantage of the legislative approach is that the policy that comes out of such a process is firmly set into the fabric of government, holding the status of law. Policy built through legislation tends to remain in place after the president's term of office has expired. To undo legislated policies generally requires another legislative process to revoke the existing policy. Such is arduous to do not only because of the difficulty of the legislative process, as mentioned, but also because agencies and programs may be created and certain constituencies served. In other words, stakeholders with reasons to protect and preserve the policy are created. Thus, inasmuch as anything is permanent in American government and policy, creation through the legislative process lends policy an air of permanence. When we speak of a president's legacy, much of what we mention is the legislation passed during his term of office, another reinforcing reason for presidents to pursue a legislative strategy.

However, a legislative strategy is not always possible. Congress will not enact all of a legislative program for even the most successful or most highly regarded president. And the legislative process is generally slow. It may take years for a policy to finally emerge as legislation, and presidents might want to take action more quickly. In addition, winning passage may require a variety of compromises that might significantly alter the president's original plan. Thus, even presidents who are likely to see Congress enact a large percentage of their initiatives may still look for other means to implement policy in a more timely fashion.

One option is an administrative approach to policy making. The administrative approach focuses on presidential control of policy making without the necessity of formal congressional action. Presidents have developed two major forms of **administrative strategy**—getting bureaucrats to implement the policy directives that they issue and attempting to control policy making within the Executive Office of the President. Both approaches bypass Congress and the established civil service bureaucracy. This has been called **politicizing the bureaucracy** and **centralizing government** in the executive.

The major tools that presidents employ to effect this administrative strategy include appointing people to office who will carry out the president's policies, issuing executive orders and other types of "presidential" legislation, and closely overseeing the actions of bureaucracies. The major limitation of this strategy is that once the president has left office and another has replaced him, all of these actions may be undone with the same tools. New people can be appointed, new executive orders issued, and close oversight of bureaucracies can be used to steer them in new directions.

Sources of Conflict and Cooperation Between the President and the Bureaucracy

Presidents turn to an administrative policy-making approach because of the problems of the legislative approach, as mentioned. This does not mean, however, that the administrative approach is easy to employ. As we will discuss in the section on "The President, Congress, and Control of the Bureaucracy," many problems are associated with centralizing too much policy-making authority in the White House and EOP. For now, we turn to a related point, the sources of conflict and cooperation between the president and the bureaucracy.

Perhaps the president's greatest advantage with regard to directing the bureaucracy is his constitutional and structural position. He is constitutionally recognized as head of the executive establishment, and he is constitutionally empowered and required to see that the laws are faithfully executed. This gives him great leverage and prestige over the bureaucracy. Moreover, as the sole leader elected by the national electorate, he possesses a special kind of legitimacy as representative of the people, the nation as a whole. When he speaks to the bureaucracy, he speaks not only as a constitutional officer and as a manager of the bureaucratic establishment but also as a popularly elected national leader. It is hard for any bureaucrat with a sense of public service and constitutional ethos to resist calls from such a leader, whoever the president may be.

Furthermore, his perch at the top of the executive hierarchy gives him a governmentwide perspective, unlike bureaucrats, who tend to view problems more narrowly, often being restricted to the scope of their department's operations or an even narrower specialty within the department. The president's broader perspective allows him to compare the operation and behavior of different agencies, and gives him access to information that bureaucratic agencies might not possess. Despite these presidential advantages, the bureaucracy possesses several advantages in dealing with the president.

First, whereas the president's information base is wide, the bureaucracy possesses a deeper and more detailed information and knowledge base. Sometimes that information is quite technical and requires special expertise to digest and make sense of. Neither presidents nor their top advisers may hold the expertise to understand or critique such technical information.

Second, bureaucrats tend to serve for a long time; for many, bureaucratic service is a career. Thus, they bring to the table very long time-horizons that stretch into both the future and the past. In contrast, presidents can serve but a comparatively short time, and the dictates of the presidential election calendar do not allow the president the luxury of time. Presidents are in a hurry to make changes, achieve their goals, and show what they have accomplished. With a longer time frame, bureaucrats are less rushed, and when motivated to alter the status quo, they are likely to support smaller changes than the president would prefer. In this time perspective sense, bureaucrats are likely to find more in common with members of Congress, who also possess careerist orientations.

Third, because of their different vantage points, presidents and bureaucrats are likely to have different policy and agenda priorities. The president's agenda is wider and more national in scope than that of any career administrator. The career bureaucrat is likely to view what his or her agency does as the most important problem to deal with. Some of this derives from self-interest—no one wants to denigrate what he or she does. And in the competition for scarce government resources, such as budgets and the president's time, bureaucrats will naturally try to make their own best case.

Fourth, bureaucrats, while they operate in a highly politicized environment, do not confront the same kinds of political problems that presidents do. Bureaucrats do not consider themselves to be politicians. In contrast, while presidents probably do not want to use the term, all recognize the highly political aspects of the presidency. Presidents need the backing of the public. As elected officers, presidents cannot neglect the public, the popular foundation of the office, lest they be defeated. Bureaucrats, in contrast, are less conscious of the electoral implications of the choices they make, though they may be very sensitive to the segments of the public with whom they regularly interact, such as their program clientele groups. Instead, bureaucrats tend to think of themselves as professionals who work in the public sector. They bring their expertise and sense of professionalism to public service, while they may also believe that the political process maligns their special knowledge and learning, substituting popular passions for sound, technically exacting reasoning.

As a consequence of these differences—breadth of perspective, time horizons, priorities, and expertise—presidents may encounter resistance from bureaucrats. Still, bureaucratic resistance to the president will be balanced against the advantages that the president possesses in dealing with the bureaucracy—the constitutional and electoral status of the president, and his seat atop the bureaucratic structure. Thus, presidents will not face resistance from bureaucrats all of the time but only when the president's advantages do not outweigh the impact of the position and perspectives of the bureaucracy. All of this means, however, that the administrative strategy, like the legislative one, will be problematic. In recent decades, presidents have enhanced the tools at their disposal to employ the administrative policy-making strategy.

TOOLS OF PRESIDENTIAL CONTROL OVER THE BUREAUCRACY

Presidents have developed and enhanced a number of tools that they employ in their attempts to control and direct the bureaucracy and to make policy without having to resort to the legislative process. These presidential tools include personnel decisions, influence over the structure of bureaucratic agencies, the use of executive orders and other forms of "presidential legislation," as well as White House budgetary and clearance mechanisms.

Personnel

One way to increase bureaucratic compliance with presidential directives is to ensure that loyal and responsive people fill the bureaucracy. Obviously, when career bureaucrats are protected by civil service and merit regulations or when they are members of a union, like postal workers, presidential control diminishes. For the most part, presidential personnel control is now restricted to the numerous political appointments that he makes, mostly into the higher levels of the bureaucracy.

Still, there are practical problems in finding people to serve who will be loyal to the president. It may be difficult to locate a person who is both loyal and possesses adequate skills for the post. Another problem is convincing people to serve for salaries that are much lower than they could earn in the private sector. Furthermore, the intense scrutiny that nominees must undergo in the confirmation process and the combative Washington climate heighten barriers to finding people to serve in the administration.

Removal   Presidential appointment control is also enhanced when the president can fire an appointee who displeases him. Such removal powers exist for people appointed to positions in the cabinet departments, but most high-level appointments to the independent agencies, government corporations, and special prosecutors' posts are not subject to presidential removal, except for specified grounds.

Although presidents now enjoy removal powers for most of their bureaucratic appointments, this was not always the case, and it was not a power easily gained. Very early in the nation's history, some felt that an official should be removed from office only through impeachment.[19] Until the presidency of Andrew Johnson, however, a tradition developed that allowed the president to remove an official from office unilaterally. While much debated, the issue of presidential versus congressional power to remove did not come to a full head until the presidency of Andrew Johnson.

In 1867, Congress passed the **Tenure of Office Act** over the objections and veto of Johnson. The act stipulated that appointees to office would remain in their posts until the Senate had confirmed a replacement. President Johnson and Secretary of War Edwin M. Stanton disagreed strongly over reconstruction policy toward the South, and Stanton refused to implement Johnson's policy. Johnson suspended him, but Stanton stood his ground. Congress strongly supported Stanton, while opposing Johnson's conciliatory reconstruction policies. Finally, Johnson removed Stanton from office, but Stanton refused to vacate the office. This standoff between Johnson and Stanton precipitated impeachment proceedings against the president. Congress, however, failed to convict Johnson by the slim margin of one vote in the Senate.

For the next twenty years, all presidents called for repeal of the act. Finally, in 1887 in another confrontation, between Congress and Democratic President Grover Cleveland, Congress finally repealed the act.[20] The repeal secured presidential removal of most appointees but, at about the same time, civil service regulations effectively protected most of the federal service from removal by either the president or Congress.

Another removal controversy arose in 1935, when Franklin Roosevelt tried to remove a commissioner of the Federal Trade Commission (FTC), William Humphrey, who was originally appointed by Coolidge and reappointed by

[19]Louis Fisher, *The Politics of Shared Power: Congress and the Executive,* 3d ed. (Washington, D.C.: Congressional Quarterly Press, 1993), pp. 99–101.

[20]Ibid., p. 101.

Hoover. FDR's action was predicated on policy disagreement, not performance in office, and his administration argued that the president possessed discretion to remove officials from independent commissions. While the enabling statute granted the president the power to remove commissioners for specified reasons, FDR read the statute more broadly and expansively. The dispute found its way to the Supreme Court, which overruled FDR. The Court reasoned that an FTC commissioner could be removed from office only for reasons explicitly mentioned in statute. Some legal and constitutional disputes still exist over the president's power to remove independent agency personnel, but subsequent presidents have preferred to pressure such personnel to step down.[21]

The last major office insulated from presidential removal power is the **Special Prosecutor's Office** of the Justice Department. In 1973, President Nixon agreed to the creation of such an office within the Justice Department. This decision came to haunt him in 1974, when he fired Archibald Cox, the special prosecutor investigating the Watergate break-in and related events. This action caused intense controversy, even within Nixon's administration. Since Cox was an employee of the Justice Department, his removal had to go through the chain-of-command structure of the department. Attorney General Elliott Richardson resigned rather than carry out the president's directive. Next, Deputy Attorney General William Ruckelshaus also refused to carry out the order and was fired by the president. Finally, Acting Attorney General (actually Solicitor General, the third-ranking official at Justice) Robert Bork carried out the directive. The mass firings of the "Saturday Night Massacre," as it came to be called, had major consequences for Nixon, including the commencement of impeachment proceedings. Finally, Nixon resigned from office under pressure from supporters in Congress.[22]

In 1978, the Special Prosecutor's Act was amended so that a court would appoint the prosecutor, whose office would have jurisdiction to investigate the president, vice president, and high-level employees in the EOP, Justice Department, CIA, and Internal Revenue Service. Furthermore, only the attorney general could remove the special prosecutor—for reasons of extraordinary impropriety, physical disability, mental incapacity, and the like. Since 1978, special prosecutors have investigated charges against Jimmy Carter's chief of staff, Hamilton Jordan, that he had used cocaine (he was subsequently cleared of those charges), against numerous other executives, and most famously in the 1990s against President Clinton, leading to his impeachment, and acquittal, in 1999. Congress allowed the Special Prosecutor's Act to lapse in 1999, in part because of the controversy over the Clinton impeachment.[23]

[21]Ibid., pp. 131–32.

[22]Ibid., pp. 112–14.

[23]Ongoing investigations were allowed to proceed, however. For a good review of the act and its use, see Louis Fisher, "The Independent Counsel Statute," in *The Clinton Scandal and the Future of American Government,* ed. Mark J. Rozell and Clyde Wilcox (Washington, D.C.: Georgetown University Press, 2000), pp. 60–80.

Ensuring Loyalty   Just because a president appoints someone to an office does not mean that that person will be loyal to the president. First, presidents are often under intense pressure by interest groups to appoint someone from their ranks into important bureaucratic posts. For instance, farmer groups often seek one of their own to serve in the Agriculture Department. The danger for a president in selecting an "interest group representative" is that the appointee might be more concerned with furthering the agenda of the interest than in supporting the president's program and policies.

But even if a president appoints someone with no ties to an interest group, that person may still not exhibit strong loyalty to the president. Top-level bureaucrats spend their working day in the department, not the White House. Most of their contact, consequently, is with agency personnel, whom they may grow to like, understand, respect, and even identify with. In time, the presidential appointee may become more of a spokesperson for the department than the president's point person while in the department. The Nixon people had a colorful phrase to capture this process of building loyalty to the department over the White House: "going off and marrying the natives."

Beginning with the Nixon administration, presidents sought a way to minimize the **going native** effect. The Reagan team seemed to have developed an effective approach to ensure the loyalty of its appointees to high bureaucratic posts. First, the Reagan administration was very careful in who was appointed to office, even at the subcabinet level. The administration conducted detailed background checks and interviews to ensure that appointees were ideologically committed to the Reagan program. Second, before each appointee assumed his or her duties, each was briefed at the White House. The first set of appointees was massed together in the White House in a kind of prejob indoctrination or socialization process. These briefings stressed the primacy of the president to their job and that each member of the administration was part of the president's team.

Third, to lessen potential tensions between White House and cabinet (and subcabinet) personnel, as well as to maintain White House leadership over political appointees in the departments, the Reagan administration established cabinet councils and other working groups. These councils and groups were composed of people in the White House and each department that had some jurisdiction or authority over a policy area. Policy initiatives were worked out in these groups. It is important to note that department people worked on policy with White House personnel and not exclusively in their respective departments and agencies, as had been past practice. The White House was able to centralize policy making by using these councils and working groups, as well as control, direct, and coordinate department people on policy fronts that were deemed important.[24]

Even these careful safeguards, however, did not prevent the appointment of high-ranking officials who later embarrassed the administration in some fashion,

[24]On the Reagan administrative presidency, see Richard P. Nathan, *The Administrative Presidency* (New York: John Wiley and Sons, 1983); and Bert A. Rockman, "Tightening the Reins: The Federal Executive and the Management Philosophy of the Reagan Presidency," *Presidential Studies Quarterly* 23, no. 1 (1993): 103–14.

such as David Stockman, Reagan's director of the Office of Management and Budget, who publicly stated that some of the administration's budget assumptions were unrealistic. Ever since Reagan, presidents have used some variant of personnel control, although subsequent administrations seemed more tolerant of diversity among their appointees.

Getting Rid of Civil Service Bureaucrats   Another important tack has been to try to remove civil service bureaucrats. Nixon, for instance, thought that the career bureaucracy was hostile to him and his policies because it was composed overwhelmingly, at least in the domestic agencies, of Democrats and liberals. But removing a protected civil servant from office for political reasons was not only illegal, it was a politically costly strategy if publicly exposed.

Thus, the Nixon people developed other, less overt approaches. Sometimes they would see to it that the targeted bureaucrat would be kept out of the information and decision-making loop, basically allowing the person to stay in his or her job but not giving that person anything to do. Another tack was to promote or transfer the person out of the job. Often such promotions would entail physical transfers from Washington, D.C., to a field office position that administration personnel knew would be objectionable or impossible for the civil servant to take. Many bureaucrats left the civil service rather than accept jobs under these new conditions.

The Reagan administration used the budget axe to prune the bureaucracy of people whom they wanted out of office. Rather than focus on specific people, the administration slotted agencies for massive budget cuts in the first few years of Reagan's term of office. Personnel levels at many domestic agencies, which the Reagan administration felt were pursuing policies antithetical to the president's program, were the ones most keenly affected by these reductions in force (RIFs). One irony, however, is that while domestic agencies were being scaled back, the Defense Department was being built up; many "riffed" bureaucrats from domestic agencies found new jobs in the Defense Department.

The Senior Executive Service   The major problem that presidents see with the career bureaucracy is that it is not responsive enough to the president and pursues departmental and agency goals over the president's. Presidents of both parties have complained that the career bureaucracy resists, delays, and even undercuts presidential policy directions. With the growth of government across the 1960s and 1970s, the number of programs being delivered by government to its citizens increased markedly. At the same time, public outcry against large government began to mount, while pubic expectations for the president to control government costs and bureaucratic intrusiveness also grew. All presidents since Nixon have campaigned on platforms that emphasized reform to rein in bureaucracy, making it more accountable and responsive. Clearly, some of these campaign promises were mere symbolism, issued to ride the wave of public opinion. But at times major reform proposals also emerged. The one with the most relevance for the topic of control of bureaucratic personnel is the 1978 Civil Service Reform Act.

That act was far ranging. It reorganized the civil service system and established the **Senior Executive Service (SES).** The intention of the act was to increase presidential influence over the bureaucracy. With regard to the civil service system, the former Civil Service Commission, which governed civil service employees, was broken into two components. One component, the Office of Personnel Management (OPM), was to be headed by a single executive appointed by the president and located in the EOP. This office was to bring some presidential control over hiring and firing employees covered under the civil service. Termination processes were modestly streamlined, although the process of employee termination was still difficult and time consuming. A second office, the Merit Systems Protection Board (MSPB), was charged with the authority to investigate alleged abuses of the civil service system and employee grievances. Under the old system, the Civil Service Commission was responsible for personnel decisions, including hiring, firing, disciplining, as well as protecting civil servants. Needless to say, that old body served more to protect than discipline or control.

Perhaps more consequential than the creation of OPM and MSPB for presidential influence over the bureaucracy was the creation of the Senior Executive Service. The intention of the SES was to provide the president with a pool of highly talented and skilled professionals who were still part of the career service, modeled somewhat on the top echelons of the British bureaucracy. The tradition of the British civil service is to serve the government and party in power, no matter the political or policy inclinations of the civil service or the government.

The SES was considered to be a new category of bureaucrat, fitting in a gray area between the political and career bureaucracy. Congress established seven thousand SES positions, the holders of which would be drawn from the highest ranks of the career bureaucracy, while the president was authorized to appoint up to another eight hundred of these executives. Unlike standard career bureaucrats whose tenure is accumulated within departments, the SES executives were to be positioned outside of the agencies and could be transferred from post to post around the bureaucracy at the discretion of the president. It was hoped that this would undermine any identification with the interests of any particular agency, the "going native" syndrome.

Moreover, rather than earning pay increases through civil service performance and step scales, SES bureaucrats were to be rewarded with increases at the discretion of their political superiors, such as department secretaries. Bonuses for outstanding job performance were also allowed, something often found in the private sector but not in merit-protected public bureaucracies. Control of pay by political superiors and the bonus system were intended to create incentives for SES responsiveness to political heads and their chief, the president. Lastly, poor performers could be severed from the SES and sent back to the standard civil service ranks, giving political overseers another lever to control SES personnel. In combination, job rotation, the payment system, and removal were supposed to supply the president with a cadre of high-level bureaucrats to carry out his management and policy directives to the bureaucracy.

The size of the SES grew from just shy of seven thousand in 1980 to eighty-one hundred in 1992, an indication that presidents seem to like the service. At the same time, the total number of SES bureaucrats who come from noncareer ranks, that is, political appointees, has also grown. This suggests that presidents prefer a politicized bureaucracy that they can control to a professional one that may be harder to control.[25]

It is not clear, however, that the SES has been all that useful for presidents. First, the tenure of the political appointees to the SES, the ranks on which presidents seem to rely most heavily, is very short, estimated by one study to be only 1.7 years.[26] Two reasons given for the short time that political appointees stay in office are 1) poor relations with the civil service bureaucrats with whom they must work, and 2) more lucrative job offers from the private sector.[27] Underfunding of bonuses may have exacerbated the problem of retention. And presumably, the antibureaucratic tone of the Reagan administration also strained relations between the political and career bureaucracy.

Bureaucratic Structure

Presidents attempt to structure the bureaucracy to strengthen their ability to influence it. By structure, we mean both the position of the agency with regard to the presidency and its internal organization. Presidents prefer a body that directly reports to them and a structure that minimizes both the independence of the agency and congressional control over the agency. Thus, presidents prefer agencies that are situated within the executive structure and are located in the executive branch; that is, agencies that are units of the cabinet departments as opposed to independent agencies and government corporations. Presidents also tend to prefer internal organizational structures that maximize their penetration into the agency. As noted in the "Personnel" section, appointing loyal people to agencies is among the most effective methods of presidential influence over an agency, and this is done more easily with the single-headed, hierarchically organized bodies, such as cabinet departments, than the multiheaded, collectively run bodies, such as independent regulatory commissions or boards.

Beginning in 1932, Congress gave the president, then Herbert Hoover, reorganization authority. **Reorganization authority** allowed the president (or in certain cases, top-level agency executives, such as the department secretary) to move agencies around, elevating or demoting them in status, consolidating or splitting them apart, as well as transferring functions. However, Congress did not give the president unfettered rights to reorganize agencies. The legislature maintained a

[25]Richard Stillman, II, *The American Bureaucracy: The Core of Modern Government,* 2d ed. (Chicago: Nelson Hall, 1996); pp. 147, 153–54.

[26]Carolyn Ban and Patricia W. Ingraham, "Short-Timers. Political Appointee Mobility and Its Impact on Political-Career Relations in the Reagan Administration," *Administration and Society* 22, no. 1 (1990): 106–24.

[27]Philip G. Joyce, "An Analysis of the Factors Affecting the Employment Tenure of Federal Political Executives," *Administration and Society* 22, no. 1 (1990): 127–45.

legislative veto. Legislative vetoes are devices to stop the executive from taking action if Congress disapproves of the action. For instance, the 1932 act specified that within a sixty-day period after the president issued the reorganization executive order, either house of Congress could disapprove of the reorganization by a simple vote. Congress, overwhelmingly controlled by the Democrats during Hoover's last two years in office, disapproved of all eleven of the executive orders that Hoover issued with his reorganization authority.

Congress renewed the president's reorganization authority in 1933 but this time without the legislative veto provision, in part because Franklin Roosevelt was elected president. Objections from members of Congress to granting the president such broad powers led to the veto provision being allowed to lapse, but Roosevelt insisted that he be regranted the power. In 1938, Congress renewed presidential reorganization authority but added a **legislative veto** provision; now a simple majority of both houses was required to stop the reorganization from taking effect. In the ensuing years, Congress kept amending the president's reorganization authority, basically by prohibiting the president from reorganizing certain favored agencies. The list of exemptions had grown long by 1949. In a compromise with the president, many agencies were removed from the protected list, but Congress's ability to disapprove was eased as the original one-house vote replaced the two-house concurrent resolution of the 1938 legislation.

This system stayed intact until the 1980s. In 1983, the Supreme Court issued its famous *Chadha* **decision,** which declared legislative vetoes, such the ones used in the president's reorganization authority, unconstitutional. To comply with the *Chadha* decision, Congress rewrote the legislation, which now required the president to submit the reorganization plan to Congress. Congress was given ninety days to approve the plan, or it would not take effect. Because of the time period limitation, President Reagan decided not to seek reorganization authority, nor has any succeeding president. Reorganizations now must travel through the normal legislative process.[28]

The combination of protected agencies and legislative veto provisions effectively limited the utility of reorganization authority for the president. Still, research indicates that presidents are relatively successful in getting the types of agency structures they prefer. While it is not the case that presidents always succeed in structuring or restructuring agencies to their desires, one study finds that when presidents are popular and when their party commands strong majorities in Congress, they are more able to get Congress to agree to structure agencies that enhance presidential control over them. Also, presidents are more likely to get the type of agencies that they want when those agencies deal with issues of defense and foreign policy rather than domestic policy.[29]

Presidents also have tried to reorganize the way bureaucrats go about their work. For instance, in the late 1970s, with the urging of President Carter, Congress

---

[28]Fisher, *Politics of Shared Power,* pp. 95–97.

[29]David E. Lewis, "The Presidential Advantage in the Design of Bureaucratic Agencies," paper presented at the 1998 American Political Science Association Meeting.

passed the Paperwork Reduction Act. This act streamlined many of the forms that people and businesses had to fill out as they dealt with the bureaucracy. People were also given greater access to the information of bureaucracy with the passage of the Freedom of Information Act of 1974.

Perhaps the most sweeping effort of a president to change the way that bureaucrats do their work was President Clinton's **National Performance Review** (NPR) effort.[30] The NPR was announced amid great fanfare, and Vice President Albert Gore was slated to head it, a signal that reform of the bureaucracy was a high administration priority. The vice president pulled together an NPR task force, composed of personnel across agencies as well as consultants from the private sector, to study the issue and make recommendations.

Drawing heavily on a book, *Reinventing Government* by David Osborne and Ted Gaebler, the task force produced a document that emphasized four types of principles. These were 1) to make the bureaucracy "customer" friendly, 2) to empower federal employees to put the customer first, 3) to cut red tape, and 4) to cut the government back to its basic and core mission. Other recommendations included implementing Clinton's campaign promise to cut the number of federal employees, to make the bureaucracy more responsive to elected officials, and to sensitize bureaucrats to markets and their possible use in delivering programs.

Clearly, the NPR effort was not completely coherent: making the bureaucracy customer friendly and putting the customer first seemingly would contradict making it more responsive to the president. Implementing NPR was hampered by the Republican takeover of Congress in 1995, but still many aspects were implemented. For the most part, NPR was tailored by each agency to suit its own needs. NPR probably aided Clinton's efforts to reduce the federal workforce, although Congress, through budget cuts, probably had a hand in this reduction. Overall, the federal workforce shrunk by three hundred thousand by the time of Clinton's reelection. That figure may be overstated, however, as much work was farmed out to state and local governments and private and not-for-profit sector consultants and contractors.

Many commentators have criticized the NPR for being internally contradictory, for offering more than could reasonably be expected, for not necessarily producing a bureaucracy more responsive to either customers or the president, and for perhaps inappropriately applying business logic and practices to nonbusiness settings.[31] Yet the effort did alter, if only at the margins, the behavior and operation of many bureaucrats and agencies, and in some select instances has even been termed a "success."[32] It is also questionable whether NPR really helped Clinton

---

[30] A very good discussion of the NPR is Peri E. Arnold, "The Managerial Presidency's Changing Focus: Theodore Roosevelt to Bill Clinton," in *The Managerial Presidency* 2d ed., ed. James P. Pfiffner (College Station: Texas A and M University Press, 1999), pp. 217–38.

[31] Patricia W. Ingraham, James R. Thompson, and Ronald P. Sanders, eds. *Transforming Government: Lessons from the Reinvention Laboratories* (San Francisco: Jossey-Bass, 1998).

[32] Beryl A. Radin, "Varieties of Reinvention: Six NPR 'Success' Stories," in *Inside the Reinvention Machine,* ed. Donald Keel and John Dilulio, Jr. (Washington, D.C.: Brookings Institution, 1995).

tighten the presidential grip on the bureaucracy, but it seems to have aided him in his efforts with the public, helping make him appear to be an effective manager of the bureaucracy.[33]

Executive Orders and "Presidential Legislation"

Presidents have also used written statements, decrees, proclamations, and executive orders, to make public policy and direct the bureaucracy.[34] Of the two formal decrees—proclamations and executive orders—proclamations are the older but now are not used as much. The theory behind **presidential decree powers** is that presidents cannot make new law by use of these actions but can use them only to make existing law operative. For instance, presidents are often given certain types of emergency powers, such as the declaration that a locality is to be named a disaster area and thus is eligible for federal disaster relief. Here, legislation has granted the president the right to name which locality is eligible, based on criteria specified in legislation.

Executive orders, the more common form of "presidential legislation," are also supposed to be restricted and carry the force of law only when they can be justified on constitutional or legislative grounds—in the latter instance, when Congress has delegated authority or discretion to the president. In practice, presidents may have "pushed the envelope" to its limits in many circumstances, created new law and even new agencies, by issuing an executive order. For example, Franklin Roosevelt closed the banks in the banking emergency of 1933, Harry S. Truman desegregated the military, Richard Nixon prohibited racial discrimination in the awarding of federal contracts, John F. Kennedy temporarily established the Peace Corps, and Ronald Reagan imposed a "gag" rule against informing clients of abortion options by family planning clinics that received federal money. Presidents have pushed the use of executive orders to such limits, because so few have been challenged by Congress or overturned by the courts.[35]

Executive orders are numerous. No comprehensive list of all executive orders exists, in part because of unsystematic record keeping and numbering in the first half of the 1800s, but compilations have counted over thirteen thousand numbered executive orders as of January 2001. Given the historical frequency of executive orders, several studies have attempted to catalog why presidents issue more or fewer executive orders. Results of these studies find that presidents tend to issue more executive orders when they are not popular, more during their last month in office if

---

[33]Arnold, "Managerial Presidency's," p. 234.

[34]Kenneth R. Mayer, *With the Stroke of a Pen: Executive Orders and Presidential Power* (Princeton, N.J.: Princeton University Press, 2001).

[35]Forrest McDonald, *The American Presidency: An Intellectual History* (Lawrence: University Press of Kansas, 1994), pp. 295–97; and Terry Moe and William Howell, "Unilateral Actions and Presidential Power: A Theory," *Presidential Studies Quarterly* 29 (December 1999): 850–73.

a new party is going to take over the White House, and more when the economy is in bad shape.[36]

As lower popularity may decrease the ability of presidents to influence Congress, the first finding suggests that presidents increase their use of executive orders when the prospects diminish of finding support in Congress for their policies. The second finding suggests that outgoing presidents will use executive orders to implement some last-minute policy directives as a last chance before the opposition party assumes the presidency. Upon entering office in 2001, George W. Bush complained that Bill Clinton perhaps used this device too often to effect policy in the last days of his presidency, and Bush asserted that he would review the many executive orders issued late in the Clinton administration. The third finding suggests that as the policy environment gets more difficult or when action seems more urgent, presidents will use executive orders as a speedy way to implement new, corrective policies. In each circumstance, presidents use executive orders when Congress seems resistant to presidential policies and when time seems to be of the essence, much as we have suggested motivates presidents to nonlegislative types of policy making and bureaucratic control behaviors.

Another type of presidential legislation—signing statements—was developed in the Reagan administration but exploited most heavily by George H. W. Bush. Signing statements accompany presidential signatures to legislation; in these, presidents declare that certain portions of a bill violate the Constitution, and thus, the president is not bound to carry them out. In effect, signing statements allow presidents to avoid a costly veto battle with Congress, which would open up their risk of being overridden.[37]

Lastly, there are the little studied National Security Decision Directives, the overwhelming majority of which are not made public and thus are not subject to any governmental or public review.[38] These directives focus on national security concerns, usually holding "top secret" and other types of restricted clearances. In Chapter 15, we will say more about these and their implications for presidential informational advantages in the making of foreign policy and the directing of the foreign policy bureaucracy.

Clearance Procedures

Clearance procedures have been instrumental in presidents centralizing their executive authority over the bureaucracy. Three clearance procedures stand out: budgetary, legislative, and regulatory.

---

[36]Christopher J. Deering and Forrest Maltzmann, "The Politics of Executive Orders: Legislative Constraints on Presidential Power," *Political Research Quarterly* 52 (December 1999): George A. Krause and David B. Cohen, "Presidential Use of Executive Orders, 1953–1994," *American Politics Quarterly* 25 (October 1997): 458–81; George A. Krause and Jeffrey E. Cohen, "Opportunity, Constraints, and the Development of the Institutional Presidency: The Issuance of Executive Orders, 1939–1998." *Journal of Politics* 62 (February 2000): 88–114; and Kenneth R. Mayer, "Executive Orders and Presidential Power," *Journal of Politics* 61 (May 1999): 445–61.

[37]Charles Tiefer, *The Semi-Sovereign Presidency: The Bush Administration's Strategy for Governing Without Congress* (Boulder, Colo.: Westview Press, 1994).

[38]McDonald, *American Presidency,* p. 297, and Tiefer, *Semi-Sovereign Presidency,* pp. 89–118.

Budgetary clearance was developed in accord with the requirement of the 1921 Budget and Accounting Act that the president annually prepare and submit a proposed budget to Congress. Rather than follow older practice, in which each agency submitted budget requests to Congress when either their money or authorization to spend was coming to an end, the 1921 act formalized and centralized budgetary decisions. Important for our discussion here, this budget process, by laying responsibility for budget preparation with the president, forced the president to develop a system to collect, collate, and oversee agency budget requests. Thus, each year, each agency would submit to the Bureau of the Budget its budget request for the next fiscal year. (BOB became the Office of Management and Budget in 1970.) The BOB/OMB would review each request to ensure that it was in accord with the president's program and priorities. Then the BOB/OMB would make its recommendations to the president for cuts or additions to each agency's request.

It is important to note that other than for specified agencies, such as the independent agencies, Congress did not receive agency budget requests directly but only as the requests filtered through these executive-control mechanisms. Even at congressional hearings, agency representatives had to toe the administration's line, lest they cause trouble for the agency with the administration. Still, creative friends in Congress could pry out of agencies their true preferences by asking whether or not they could make use of more money for a specific program or operation. Few agency representatives would refuse the prospect of more money, especially if it replaced money that the BOB/OMB and the president had cut during their budget preparation process.

Legislative clearance mechanisms were fully in place by the Truman years. Those procedures required that before an agency could submit a proposal for legislation to Congress, the agency had to submit the proposal to the BOB/OMB for review. The BOB/OMB would determine if the proposed legislation was in accord with the president's program and if it should be sent to Congress, as well as make any suggestions to amend or change the legislative proposal. This legislative clearance process eventually extended to bills already before Congress. The BOB/OMB would review all enrolled bills and recommend that the president either sign or veto them.[39]

It was not until Ronald Reagan had become president that **regulatory clearance** procedures were established. Reagan issued two executive orders that radically revamped regulatory policy making and the role of the presidency in a process that had for the most part been left up to the discretion of bureaucrats. In 1981, less than a month after he took office, Reagan issued Executive Order 12291, which required that proposed regulations be submitted to the **Office of Information and Regulatory Affairs** (OIRA) of the OMB. The OIRA would then employ a cost-benefit analysis to determine whether the regulation should go through or not. In 1984, Reagan issued his second key executive order in this area, Executive Order 12498. That order required that agencies disclose any regulations

[39]Stephen J. Wayne, *The Legislative Presidency* (New York: Harper and Row, 1978), pp. 71–81.

that were being planned, to determine whether they were consistent with the president's program.[40]

Strong opposition to the Reagan regulatory clearance procedures was voiced in Congress, by many of the affected agencies, and among some interest groups. Hearings were held as to whether the administration had the authority to oversee regulation in such a manner. Critics charged that the cost-benefit standard could not be used unless Congress specified its use. Few, if any, statutes required cost-benefit standards to allow regulations to be implemented. Still, despite the vocal opposition, Reagan's centralized regulatory clearance procedures stayed intact. Regulatory clearance remained in use after Reagan because of widespread agreement that government should be more conscious of the cost of regulation.

Presidential centralized control of regulation took another step in the George H. W. Bush administration with the establishment of the **Council on Competitiveness,** which was headed by Bush's vice president, Dan Quayle. The council used White House staff to intervene in the regulatory process, but the special status of the council personnel as advisers to the president, which allowed them to use executive privilege arguments, limited congressional ability to oversee the council personnel and their activities. While many may have agreed with the policy mission of the council, the lack of congressional oversight and the prospect that special interests could gain access to the regulatory process through the council were of special concern. Administration opponents charged that groups important to the Republican Party, including those that had contributed large sums to election campaigns, were in contact with council staff about regulations that the Council was reviewing. This raised the specter of political payoffs by the council to special interests, which critics felt might politicize the regulatory process. Historically, Congress had gone through great pains to try to insulate regulation from politics by using such devices as independent agency status.[41] The council then, to many, seemed to turn the clock back to days when political and interest group pressure on regulation was more intense.[42]

Clinton abolished of the controversial Council on Competitiveness on his first full day in office, in part because of its association with the previous Republican administration but also because the Clinton administration was less hostile to regulation. Next, Clinton reformed the centralized regulatory review process, opening it up to greater governmental and public accountability. Through Executive Order 12866, the OIRA was limited in how long it could review a proposed regulation, and the order established OIRA-agency work groups to coordinate their efforts. Also established was a regulatory planning cycle in which each agency would inform the OIRA of the regulatory actions that it was intending to submit to the OIRA. In the hope of reducing conflict between agencies and the White

----

[40]Barry D. Friedman, *Regulation and the Reagan-Bush Era: The Eruption of Presidential Influence* (Pittsburgh: University of Pittsburgh Press, 1995).

[41]Tiefer, *Semi-Sovereign Presidency,* pp. 61–88.

[42]However, we should note that many political scientists and other students of regulation still see politics in making and implementing regulation.

House, the Regulatory Working Group (RWG) was created in the White House to meet each quarter to analyze regulations that involved more than one agency. Thus, while jettisoning some aspects of the Reagan-Bush approach to centralized regulatory review, the Clinton administration did not abandon the concept. In fact, its reforms could be read as positioning the administration earlier into the regulatory process—through the planning cycle and the RWG.[43]

CONGRESSIONAL LIMITS ON PRESIDENTIAL INFLUENCE OVER THE BUREAUCRACY

Two major stumbling blocks exist to presidential control of the bureaucracy. One is the bureaucracy, which we have already discussed. The other is Congress, to which we now turn. Presidents tend to operate under a theory of executive control of the bureaucracy, focusing on the Constitution's "take care" clause to justify that viewpoint. However, the Constitution leaves much room for interpretation over which branch possesses ultimate responsibility for the bureaucracy. An alternative to an executive control theory of bureaucracy management is one that emphasizes the constitutional powers and duties of Congress.

Congress, for instance, creates each agency and department, and, through legislation, authorizes bureaucrats to take certain actions and prohibits them from engaging in others. Congress also appropriates money to the bureaucracy, directing agency personnel how to spend the money, for what purposes, under specified guidelines, and often naming the recipients. Furthermore, Congress has very broad powers to investigate, and bureaucratic action is often a legitimate topic of such congressional inquiry.

In our separation of powers system, neither the president nor Congress has the exclusive right to direct and control the bureaucracy. They both have such a duty and obligation. We have seen thus far in this chapter how the president has attempted to gain increased leverage over the bureaucracy, often with Congress's consent. But Congress has also sought greater influence over the bureaucracy, sometimes to the consternation of the president.

Bureaucratic Structure

We have discussed presidential efforts to determine the structure of the bureaucracy to afford greater presidential ability to control and influence bureaucratic behavior. At best, presidents can reorganize the bureaucracy only around the margins. The core structure of the bureaucracy is determined by Congress through its power to create agencies and departments, as well as to fund them through the appropriations process. As a consequence, the bureaucracy is structured better to meet congressional than presidential needs.

---

[43]William F. West and Andrew W. Barrett, "Administrative Clearance Under Clinton," *Presidential Studies Quarterly* 26 (Spring 1996): 523–38; and Robert J. Duffy, "Regulatory Oversight in the Clinton Administration," *Presidential Studies Quarterly* 27 (Winter 1997): 71–90.

For instance, the departmental arrangement resembles the congressional committee system. By running the departmental and congressional committee systems in parallel, Congress is better able to develop the expertise to oversee the bureaucracy and to create lasting relationships with that part of the executive. Congress has stymied presidential efforts to reorganize the bureaucracy in a fashion that violates this basic organizing principle. For example, in perhaps the most far-reaching attempt to reorganize the bureaucracy in a rational, comprehensive fashion, President Nixon proposed the creation of four supercabinet departments in domestic policy: community development, natural resources, human resources, and economic affairs. Existing departments would be combined or abolished. Nixon's model envisioned a cabinet structure reflecting broad national problems and issues and not special interest ones, which he saw as the preoccupation of the existing cabinet structure. From a national and presidential perspective, Nixon's proposal possessed a reasonable logic, but it would destroy, or at least jeopardize, relationships among Congress, bureaucratic agencies, and important interest groups, relationships that Congress found valuable and wanted to preserve.[44] For these reasons, Nixon's proposal was not approved.

Congressional Oversight

Congressional oversight of the bureaucracy and the executive, which derives from Congress's power to investigate, focuses congressional attention on bureaucratic implementation of policies and programs. Congress relies on several devices to oversee the bureaucracy and the executive, devices which include requiring agencies to submit annual reports to Congress on their activities and performance, as well as congressional hearings.

Supposedly, the rationale for congressional oversight is to ensure that bureaucrats have performed as Congress expected and wanted.[45] In this sense, oversight is an attempt by the legislature to influence the behavior of the bureaucracy and as such may conflict with presidential control. But rather than being used to control a bureaucracy that might be veering away from congressional intent, most oversight seems more friendly, a way of furthering the ties between Congress and the agencies.[46] However, even this friendly version of oversight may still amount to curtailing presidential control of the bureaucracy.

---

[44]Lawrence C. Dodd and Richard L. Schott, *Congress and the Administrative State* (New York: John Wiley, 1979), pp. 340–48.

[45]On congressional motives for oversight, see Joel D. Aberbach, *Keeping a Watchful Eye: The Politics of Congressional Oversight* (Washington, D.C.: Brookings Institution, 1990); and Diana Evans, "Congressional Oversight and the Diversity of Members' Goals," *Political Science Quarterly* 109 (Fall 1994): 669–87.

[46]Aberbach. *Keeping a Watchful Eye,* esp. pp. 162–86. On congressional delegation to the executive, see David Epstein and Sharyn O'Halloran, *Delegating Powers: A Transaction Cost Politics Approach to Policymaking Under Separate Powers* (New York: Cambridge University Press, 1999).

Congressional oversight activities have increased since the early 1970s.[47] Some reasons for this increase are internal to Congress, such as the reforms of the congressional committee system and the creation of designated oversight subcommittees on each committee. Also, the increasing complexity of policy has motivated more oversight. But conflict with the president, as we have been discussing, is also an important stimulant for the greater occurrence of oversight.[48] Committees hold oversight hearings to protect or advocate for select agencies and programs. Some of these hearings are held to counter presidential attempts to control agencies. And like presidents, members of Congress have also found that passing legislation has grown more difficult since the early 1970s. Increased oversight enables Congress to influence agencies and programs without having to pass new legislation. This raises the issue of micromanagement.

The Issue of Micromanagement

Although the volume of congressional oversight of the executive has increased in recent decades, it is not clear that oversight is very effective. In an attempt to counterbalance the increasing concentration of power collected by the president since the New Deal, much of it bestowed by Congress, Congress has begun to micromanage the executive. **Micromanagement** comes in many forms, but essentially it occurs when Congress specifies in great detail what bureaucrats, and even the president, are allowed and supposed to do.

One form of micromanagement is the greater specification and attention to the details of administration in statutes. One can glean a sense of this by noting that the average length of legislation increased about sevenfold from the late 1940s until the late 1990s. In 1947 to 1948, the average public bill was 2.5 pages long; in 1995 to 1996, it was 19.1 pages.[49] Major pieces of legislation may now run to several hundred pages.

Added to the increase in detail embodied in legislation is the greater use of committee reports written by congressional staff. Committee reports have been used to further specify congressional intent about legislation and thus are to be used as a guide for executive and bureaucratic action. The reasoning behind using committee reports as a guide about congressional intent is that language in enabling statutes may be vague. Committee reports help flesh out statutory language to provide bureaucrats and other policy implementers with more detailed instructions about the meaning of a law.[50]

[47]On the increased volume of oversight activity, see Aberbach, *Keeping a Watchful Eye,* pp. 34–46.

[48]Frederick M. Kaiser, "Congressional Oversight of the Presidency," *Annals of the American Academy of Political and Social Science* 499 (September 1988): 75–89.

[49]Figures are from Norman J. Ornstein, Thomas E. Mann, and Michael J. Malbin, *Vital Statistics on Congress, 1997–1998* (Washington, D.C.: Congressional Quarterly Press, 1998), p. 167.

[50]James Q. Wilson, *Bureaucracy: What Government Agencies Do and Why They Do It* (New York: Basic Books, 1989), p. 243.

Still another method of limiting executive branch discretion has the been the shift away from open-ended to annual authorization. It was once the practice of Congress to authorize a project or program, that is, allow it to operate, until it was completed or at least for a number of years. For instance, defense weapons systems often require several years, if not a decade or more, to go from inception to being ready for combat use. Whereas Congress once allowed such programs to run for as long as needed or expected, since the 1970s it has limited such programs to operating for only one year at a time. Each year, a new authorization from Congress is required to continue the program. This annual authorization process increased the opportunities for Congress to amend or direct the program or project as it developed, as well as offered greater opportunity for foes to kill it before it was completed.[51]

Another method of micromanaging the bureaucracy entails specifying the creation of a particular post within an agency and detailing qualifications for it. Such specification reduces the ability of agency executives and the president to use personnel as they wish, and it limits their discretion in hiring whom they want for a specific job.[52]

Clearly, presidents do not like micromanagement. Presidents argue that such congressional involvement in the details of administration interferes with their ability not only to control the bureaucracy but also to coordinate the many agencies and programs of the executive branch, as well as fulfill their constitutional duties. Presidents also argue that micromanagement may undermine the flexibility needed to deal with changing circumstances. Instead, accountability for running the executive branch and the bureaucracy is diffused, and confusion may erupt as different policy directions are pursued by different agencies. For example, foreign nations may be uncertain as to the nature of U.S. policy toward them when they see Congress forcing an agency to do one thing while the president directs another agency to do something entirely different.

The sources of congressional micromanagement are complex.[53] Micromanagement is in part a reaction to the accumulation of centralized power in the presidency and the executive that began with the New Deal and continued for decades, often not only with Congress's consent but with its prodding. Added to this trend is the feeling in Congress that some presidents usurped too much power over government and lied to Congress.

---

[51]On the shift to annual authorizations, see ibid., pp. 243–44. Annual authorization of the Defense Department is discussed in Thomas Owens-Mackubin, "Congressional Micromanagement. III. Micromanaging the Defense Budget," *Public Interest* 100 (Summer 1990): 131–46; and Kenneth R. Mayer, "Policy Disputes as a Source of Administration Controls: Congressional Micromanagement of the Department of Defense," *Public Administration Review* 53 (July-August 1993): 293–302. Annual authorization of other agencies is the topic of L. Gordon Crovitz, "Congressional Micromanagement. I. Micromanaging Foreign Policy," *Public Interest* 100 (Summer 1990): 102–15; and Jeremy Rabkin, "Congressional Micromanagement. II. Micromanaging the Administrative Agencies," *Public Interest* 100 (Summer 1990): 116–30.

[52]Paul C. Light, *Thickening Government: Federal Hierarchy and the Diffusion of Accountability* (Washington, D.C.: Brookings Institution, 1995).

[53]A good discussion of the sources of micromanagement as well as other tensions between the president and Congress with respect to the bureaucracy can be found in Joel D. Aberbach, "Sharing Isn't Easy: When Separate Institutions Clash," *Governance* 11 (April 1998): 137–52.

Another source of micromanagement is greater congressional responsiveness to constituencies important to congressional careers, along with the reforms of the committee system in Congress in the 1970s. Consequent to reforms of the mid-1970s, power within Congress was dispersed to subcommittee chairs. In the House, this amounts to some 120 or so subcommittee leaders, who have their own constituencies and interests to support and look after, although there has been some loss of subcommittee autonomy since the Republicans took over the House in 1995.

Still another source of micromanagement is the greater complexity of the problems at which government programs are aimed. More interests must be balanced, and many new policies have large costs to some segments of society. This policy environment creates incentives for greater congressional attention to problems of policy implementation. Moreover, the *Chadha* decision, which we mentioned in the "Bureaucratic structure" section and which rendered legislative vetoes unconstitutional, left a void in Congress's ability to control the actions of the executive and bureaucrats. To some extent, micromanagment devices have been used to fill that void, to replace the now-defunct legislative veto.

The final source of congressional micromanagement of the executive is very much an outgrowth of policy differences between the two branches. We have spent much time detailing the different time perspectives and constituencies that lead Congress and the president to prefer different policies. And the high incidence of divided government and the growing polarization between the political parties since the late 1960s heighten the policy differences between the branches. As we discussed in the "Importance of the Bureaucracy to the President" section of this chapter, this situation creates incentives for presidents to try to increase their control over the bureaucracy and public policy. Congressional micromanagement can be viewed as a response by Congress to similar pressures and political demands and as a way to counter the trend of growing presidential control.

THE PRESIDENT, CONGRESS, AND CONTROL OF THE BUREAUCRACY

Despite the complaints of presidents and top White House personnel that the bureaucracy is resistant to the president,[54] most research on the issue now finds that bureaucrats seem to be responsive to the president, although in many cases they attempt to balance the demands of both the president and Congress.[55]

Still, there are costs to presidents who pursue an administrative strategy that emphasizes centralization of policy making in the White House and politicization of both the White House and the bureaucracy. A major cost of centralization is that

---

[54]Thomas E. Cronin, *The State of the Presidency,* 2d ed. (Boston: Little Brown, 1980), pp. 223–52.

[55]Studies that find bureaucrats responsive to the president include Tony Caporale and Kevin B. Grier, "A Political Model of Monetary Policy with Application to the Real Fed Funds Rate," *Journal of Law and Economics* 41 (October 1998): 409–28; Scott R. Furlong, "Political Influence on the Bureaucracy: The Bureaucracy Speaks," *Journal of Public Administration Research and Theory* 8 (January 1998): 39–65; and B. Dan Wood and Richard W. Waterman, "The Dynamics of Political Control of the Bureaucracy," *American Political Science Review* 85 (September 1991): 801–28. However, a study that detects weaker presidential influence over the bureaucracy is Steven A. Shull, "Presidential Influence Versus Bureaucratic Discretion: President-Agency Relations in Civil Rights Policy," *American Review of Public Administration* 19 (September 1989): 197–215.

issues that may not really be important enough for the president to treat find their way to the White House. Time and energy needed for big issues may be spent on minor matters. In addition, moving more and more decisions to the White House may overload the president, requiring larger White House staffs to meet this greater workload, with all the problems that such staff increases entail, as we discussed in Chapter 9, and expectations of presidential involvement in all aspects of policy making and implementation may be heightened. In addition, more centralized White House control may bring more criticism of the president when poor results follow. Thus, centralization is not a costless strategy for a president.

The costs of politicization may be even more crucial. Politicizing, that is, creating a staff and bureaucracy that is loyal to the president, may cut the president off from the expertise that the career bureaucracy has to offer. A tendency to overemphasize the politics of a policy over its effectiveness may also arise when staffs are overly politicized. There is considerable debate among political scientists and those in government about "overpoliticization" of the bureaucracy and even staff agencies attached to the White House, such as the Office of Management and Budget. The difficulty is finding a balance between bureaucratic expertise and responsiveness, what has been termed "responsive competence."[56] Our separation of powers system complicates finding that balance.

KEY TERMS

administrative strategy   325
budgetary clearance   338
cabinet departments   313
centralizing government   325
Chadha decision   334
congressional oversight   341
Council on Competitiveness   339
executive budget   317
executive orders   336
going native   330
government corporations   315
independent agencies   314
legislative clearance   338

legislative veto   334
micromanagement   342
National Performance Review   335
Office of Information and
   Regulatory Affairs   338
politicizing the bureaucracy   325
presidential decree powers   336
regulatory clearance   338
reorganization authority   333
Senior Executive Service   332
Special Prosecutor's Office   329
Tenure of Office Act   328

---

[56]See, for instance, Terry Moe, "The Politicized Presidency," in *The New American Political System,* ed. John E. Chubb and Paul E. Peterson (Washington, D.C.: Brookings Institution, 1985), pp. 235–71, for the best statement in support of the politicized presidency. "Responsive competence" is the term coined by Colin Campbell, *Managing the Presidency: Carter, Reagan, and the Search for Executive Harmony* (Pittsburgh: University of Pittsburgh Press, 1986), pp. 18–19. Thoughtful overviews are found in Joel D. Aberbach and Bert A. Rockman, "Civil Servants and Policymakers: Neutral or Responsive Competence?" *Governance* 7 (October 1994): 461–69; and Joel D. Aberbach and Bert A. Rockman, "Mandates or Mandarins? Control and Discretion in the Modern Administrative State," in *The Managerial Presidency* 2d ed., ed. James P. Pfiffner (College Station: Texas A and M University Press, 1999), pp. 162–74.

DISCUSSION QUESTIONS

1. What are the major forms of bureaucratic organization in the United States? Which types of bureaucracies are more amenable to presidential influence and which ones less so? Why does Congress sometimes create bureaucracies over which presidential control is limited?

2. How has the federal bureaucracy evolved over time? What does this evolution tell us about the role of the president in our government as well as relations between the president and the bureaucracy?

3. How has recruitment for the bureaucracy changed over time? How do the different styles of recruiting bureaucrats affect presidential ability to control the bureaucracy?

4. How useful for the president is the cabinet? What are the major distinctions across cabinet departments? Why have the number of cabinet departments increased over time? What do these cabinet-related developments tell us about the changing nature of the executive and the presidency?

5. Compare the administrative and legislative strategies of presidential policy making. What are the advantages and disadvantages of each? Why would presidents use one over the other? What are the major techniques of the administrative strategy? How effective are they in controlling the bureaucracy and affecting public policy?

6. What are the major sources of conflict and cooperation between the president and the bureaucracy? How easily can the president overcome the conflict between himself and the bureaucracy? What is Congress's role in creating conflict between the president and the bureaucracy? How much of the conflict between the president and the bureaucracy is a function of the nature of bureaucracy?

7. How does Congress oversee the bureaucracy? In what sense are congressional oversight and micromanagement of the bureaucracy similar? What are the implications of congressional oversight for presidential control of the bureaucracy? How effective is congressional oversight in increasing congressional influence over the bureaucracy and limiting presidential influence?

SUGGESTED READINGS

Joel D. Aberbach, *Keeping a Watchful Eye: The Politics of Congressional Oversight.* Washington, D.C.: Brookings Institution, 1990.

Colin Campbell, *Managing the Presidency: Carter, Reagan, and the Search for Executive Harmony.* Pittsburgh: University of Pittsburgh Press, 1986.

Jeffrey E. Cohen, *The Politics of the U.S. Cabinet: Representation in the Executive Branch, 1789–1984.* Pittsburgh: University of Pittsburgh Press, 1988.

Lawrence C. Dodd and Richard L. Schott, *Congress and the Administrative State.* New York: John Wiley, 1979.

Richard F. Fenno, Jr., *The President's Cabinet.* New York: Vintage, 1959.

Louis Fisher, *The Politics of Shared Power: Congress and the Executive,* 3d ed. Washington, D.C.: Congressional Quarterly Press, 1993.

Kenneth R. Mayer, *With the Stroke of a Pen: Executive Orders and Presidential Power.* Princeton: Princeton University Press, 2001.

Kenneth J. Meier, *Politics and the Bureaucracy: Policymaking in the Fourth Branch of Government,* 3d ed. Pacific Grove, Calif.: Brooks/Cole, 1993.

Richard P. Nathan, *The Administrative Presidency.* New York: John Wiley and Sons, 1983.

James P. Pfiffner, ed., *The Managerial Presidency,* 2d ed. College Station, TX: Texas A and M University Press, 1999.

James Q. Wilson, *Bureaucracy: What Government Agencies Do and Why They Do It.* New York: Basic Books, 1989.

Harold Seidman and Robert Gilmour, *Politics, Position, and Power: From the Positive to the Regulatory State,* 3d ed. New York: Oxford University Press, 1986.

Charles Tiefer, *The Semi-Sovereign Presidency: The Bush Administration's Strategy for Governing Without Congress.* Boulder, Colo.: Westview Press, 1994.

Shirley Anne Warshaw, *Powersharing: White House–Cabinet Relations in the Modern Presidency.* Albany: State University of New York Press, 1996.

12

THE PRESIDENCY AND
THE JUDICIAL SYSTEM

Courts play a number of important roles in the American political system. Much of what they do is relatively routine and uninteresting, except perhaps to the people who are directly involved in the case at hand. At times, however, a court case may generate considerable interest and controversy. During the investigation of the Watergate scandal in Richard Nixon's presidency, investigators learned of tape recordings that might cast light on the president's involvement in the matter. President Nixon tried to prevent investigators from gaining access to the tapes, but the U.S. Supreme Court ruled that the president could not conceal them. When members of Congress heard the tapes, Nixon's support eroded greatly. He resigned soon afterward.

In this chapter, we will explore the president's relationship with the federal court system. We will begin with a discussion of the reasons presidents are interested in the federal courts and the methods that presidents use to influence the actions of federal courts. We will discuss several landmark court cases affecting the presidency and conclude with examinations of executive privilege and impeachment.

THE IMPORTANCE OF FEDERAL COURTS
AND JUDGES FOR THE PRESIDENCY

The federal courts and federal judges can affect a president in a number of ways that may overlap at times. Perhaps the least dramatic method is court use of discretion that is written into laws. A statute may provide that someone convicted of a specific crime may be sentenced to between five and ten years in prison or that monetary damages may range from $1 million to $10 million in a particular type of civil suit. If the courts impose the most severe sentences allowed or award the highest possible financial damages, the results for people will be considerably different than if the courts impose lighter sentences or award smaller financial damages. Consequently, a president's policy initiatives may be blunted or accentuated by court discretion, especially if those initiatives leave the courts much flexibility.

A second way in which the courts may affect presidents is the interpretation of laws, including the Constitution. Many laws include words and passages that are somewhat unclear—"due process of law," "good faith," "reasonable," and so forth. Laws are sometimes silent regarding important matters. For example, the Constitution discusses the president's power to appoint people but says nothing regarding the power to fire people. What does that mean? Court interpretation of the vague passages may make obtaining convictions in criminal cases more or less difficult, may affect the likelihood that disputes will reach the courts, and may influence which people and organizations are more likely to win in civil cases. A court's exercise of discretion in deciding whether to hear a case can also be significant. Even if the side dragged into court ultimately wins, the victory may be accompanied by embarrassing publicity, enormous legal fees, and delays in projects while court battles are underway, especially if the initial court decision is appealed one or more times. President Clinton found this out when he was sued for sexual harassment, and George H. W. Bush's Vice President, Richard Cheney, was later sued by groups seeking information about his energy task force meetings.

The federal courts may also affect presidents by exercising the power of **judicial review,** which often involves interpretation and the use of discretion.[1] Judicial review is not mentioned in the Constitution but was asserted by the Supreme Court regarding the national government in the case of *Marbury v. Madison* in 1803. William Marbury was one of a number of last-minute appointees selected by President John Adams, who belonged to the Federalist Party. Some of the appointment letters were apparently not sent before Adams left office. When Thomas Jefferson, a leader of the Democratic-Republican Party, became president, he felt little inclination to send out Adams' appointment letters. Like generations of grumpy Americans to come, Marbury turned to the courts for help.

Marbury's case presented the Supreme Court with an awkward problem. The Supreme Court did not have a very clearly defined role in its early years, and the case pitted members of the two major parties against one another. Moreover, Chief Justice John Marshall was a cousin of President Jefferson, although they did not get along very well. Some of the justices felt unsure whether Jefferson would comply with a court order to give Marbury the job; a public display of the Court's weakness would not add to its stature. The Court seemed likely to anger a considerable number of people, regardless of what it decided.

The Court ruled that, in principle, Marbury deserved the job to which Adams had appointed him. However the Court declined to compel Jefferson to give Marbury the job. The Court declared that the section of the law that brought the case to the Supreme Court was unconstitutional and, therefore, null and void. In effect, the Supreme Court granted itself the power to rule on the constitutionality of federal laws. The Court's assertion of that power generated a storm of criticism, but the furor eventually subsided, in part because the Court did not use the power very much for a number of years.

The federal courts gradually expanded the power of judicial review in a number of directions. Today, that power covers the actions of all levels of government and all branches of government. The exercise of judicial review can affect a president

---

[1]Raoul Berger, *Executive Privilege* (New York: Bantam, 1974), chap. 11; David O'Brien, *Constitutional Law and Politics,* 3d ed., vol. 1 (New York: Norton, 1991), chap. 1; C. Herman Pritchett, *The American Constitution,* 3d ed. (New York: McGraw-Hill, 1977), chap. 8; and Charles Sheldon, *Essentials of the American Constitution* (Boulder, Colo.: Westview, 2002), chap. 2.

TABLE 12-1   SUPREME COURT DEFEATS BY AMERICAN PRESIDENTS, 1789–1997

	Early presidents*	Later presidents
0 or 1 defeats	81% (21)	21% (3)
2 or more defeats	19% (5)	79% (11)
	100%	100%

Source: Lyn Ragsdale, *Vital Statistics on the Presidency,* rev. ed. (Washington, D.C.: Congressional Quarterly Press, 1998), p. 444.

*Early presidents are those who served before Woodrow Wilson. Later presidents are Wilson through Clinton up to 1997.

in a number of ways. A president's use of executive authority or a law enacted at the president's request may be declared unconstitutional, an action that rarely occurs but may undercut a presidential program. A federal court decision may strike down a policy adopted at the state or local level or at the national level during a previous administration and, in the process, create a controversy that may engulf the presidency. When the Supreme Court struck down death penalty laws in 1972, a number of presidents found themselves struggling with conflicts over capital punishment. When the Supreme Court declared a qualified right to abortion services in the following year, the abortion issue became a recurring fixture in presidential politics.

The Supreme Court does not rule against the president very often in most administrations. If we exclude the Nixon administration, presidents have lost only fifty-one cases before the Supreme Court from the adoption of the Constitution through 1997. That amounts to an average of approximately one defeat every four years. Adding Nixon into the calculations raises the average to slightly more than one defeat every three years.

A considerable number of presidents never lost a case before the Supreme Court or, at most, lost a single case (bear in mind that determining whether a president regarded a ruling as a defeat is somewhat of a judgment call). Presidential defeats were especially rare in the early years of American history (before Woodrow Wilson). Only 19 percent of the early presidents suffered more than one defeat in the Supreme Court, but 79 percent of the more recent presidents lost more than once there (see table 12-1). The expanded powers of the national government in more recent years and the greater responsibilities of presidents have apparently increased the risk of presidential rebuffs by the nation's highest court.

A tendency also exists for Supreme Court defeats to be more common during periods of heightened political conflict. The early shift in power from the Federalists to the Democratic-Republican Party may help to account for the total of five defeats suffered by the Jefferson (two defeats) and Madison (three defeats) administrations. The tensions arising from the Civil War and its aftermath help explain the cluster of defeats suffered by Lincoln (five) and Andrew Johnson (two). Similarly, the conflicts erupting from the Depression, battles over New Deal initiatives, and two wars contributed to the eight defeats suffered by Franklin Roosevelt and the three by Harry Truman. The Nixon administration's twenty-five defeats, however, are in a class by themselves and seem to reflect a frequent pattern of disregarding laws in that administration.[2]

If we consider Supreme Court cases in which the U.S. government (rather than the president) is a party, defeats in the Supreme Court are considerably more common, with more than six hundred between 1946 and 1994. Many of those defeats do not constitute defeats for the presidency, however, for the totals include cases arising from acts of Congress and actions taken by the federal bureaucracy. Even for this broader group of cases, victories for the federal government are far more common than defeats.[3]

A much less visible type of judicial influence on the presidency occurs when individual justices offer informal advice to the president. The practice dates as far back as Justice John Jay, who sometimes advised George Washington. Several justices advised Franklin Roosevelt, and Chief Justice Fred Vinson was a member of Harry Truman's inner circle. Justice Abe Fortas, who had known Lyndon Johnson for a number of years before his presidency, gave him guidance on a wide variety of issues. Not all judicial advice is welcomed at the White House, but some presidents have found it very useful.[4]

PRESIDENTIAL INFLUENCE ON THE FEDERAL COURTS

Presidents can influence the federal courts or affect the impact of their decisions in a number of ways. One of the most important methods of influence, particularly in the long run, is the appointment power.[5] Presidents are able to appoint a new justice to the Supreme Court about once every twenty-two months, on average. If all of the current justices disagree with the president's political views, the appointment power will not provide a quick remedy, but new appointments can eventually produce major changes in the Supreme Court's actions.

Presidents normally try to appoint judges whose political beliefs are similar to their own. Most contenders for the Supreme Court have considerable experience in public office, and determining their political leanings is usually not terribly difficult. White House staffers and the Justice Department interview the potential nominees and examine their records. Presidents are occasionally surprised by the

---

[2]Lyn Ragsdale, *Vital Statistics on the Presidency,* rev. ed. (Washington, D.C.: Congressional Quarterly Press, 1998), p. 444.

[3]Ibid., pp. 441–42.

[4]Robert Scigliano, *The Supreme Court and the Presidency* (New York: Free Press, 1971), pp. 68–78.

[5]Henry Abraham, *Justices and Presidents,* 3d ed. (New York: Oxford, 1992); Sheldon Goldman and Thomas Jahnige, *The Federal Courts as a Political System,* 3d ed. (New York: Harper and Row, 1985), pp. 39–59; Glen Krutz, Richard Fleischer, and John Bond, "From Abe Fortas to Zoe Baird: Why Some Presidential Nominations Fail in the Senate," *American Political Science Review* 92 (1998): 871–81; Bryon Moraski and Charles Shipan, 'The Politics of Supreme Court Nominations: A Theory of Institutional Constraints and Choices," *American Journal of Political Science* 43 (1999): 1069–95; Scigliano, *Supreme Court,* chap. 4–5; and George Watson and John Stookey, *Shaping America: The Politics of Supreme Court Appointments* (New York: Harper Collins, 1995).

actions of their appointees, but most of the time, a new justice will act approximately as the president expects. Presidents often seem to feel a need to deny that they attach any significance to a nominee's political beliefs, but the evidence indicates that they do.

Presidents also tend to appoint justices who share their party affiliation. The emphasis on party affiliation reflects, in part, the tendency for party activists and officials to share a common philosophy (with some variation, admittedly). In addition, judicial positions were often a source of political patronage earlier in American history, especially in the case of lower court positions. Here, again, presidents rarely admit that they consider the party affiliations of potential nominees, but the appointments very often follow party lines.

Presidents usually try to appoint judges with fairly impressive qualifications, including some experience working in the legal system, often as a judge in a lower court or as a prosecutor. Not all presidents place a high emphasis on legal credentials, however, and disputes have sometimes erupted regarding what constitutes impressive qualifications. How important is a degree from a prestigious law school? Years spent hearing relatively routine cases in a local court may have little bearing on being a successful Supreme Court justice. Moreover, a president may prefer a judge who agrees with the president's political beliefs to one with stronger qualifications but different political values.

Presidents sometimes consider the issue of representation when nominating justices. That usually meant regional balance in the early years of American history. In more recent years, representational concerns have shifted to religion, race, and gender, but not all presidents are equally interested in demographic representation in the federal courts.

Presidential nominations to the federal bench must be approved by the Senate, and presidents have usually been pretty successful in winning approval of their Supreme Court nominations. The Senate approves roughly 80 percent of the nominees, with most of the defeats occurring during the 1800s, when the Senate was particularly inclined to exercise an independent judgment. Some of the approvals have involved bruising battles in the Senate, the most recent case being the wrangle over Clarence Thomas' appointment during George H. W. Bush's administration. Generally speaking, Supreme Court nominations are particularly likely to encounter Senate opposition when the White House and Senate are controlled by different parties, near the end of a president's term, when nominees have weaker credentials, and when nominees have a history of involvement in controversial political issues.

Lower court nominations are similar to Supreme Court nominations in some respects but have some important differences. Presidents try to appoint district and appellate court justices who share their political beliefs and party affiliation. Presidents also consider expertise and, to varying degrees, representation. Among recent presidents, Carter and Clinton were particularly likely to appoint nonwhites and women to the federal bench.

Lower court appointments differ from Supreme Court appointments in that there are far more to be made; several dozen district and appellate judges have been appointed each year in recent administrations. Presidents must, therefore, rely more heavily on White House staff and the Justice Department in screening nominees.

Lower court appointments are also subject to the traditional practice of **senatorial courtesy,** which gives senators of the president's party a virtual veto over district and appellate court nominations from their respective states. In practice, this often means that senators take the initiative in recommending nominees to the president. If the party of the senators in that state is dominated by a different political philosophy than the president's, senatorial courtesy can produce some nominees that differ from the president's views. During the Reagan years, the White House attempted to exert more control over lower court nominations in order to produce nominees who more closely followed the president's beliefs.

Interest groups have been increasingly active in federal court appointment and confirmation decisions in recent years, a pattern that is also found in the selection of state judges.[6] That increased activity has helped to slow action on judicial appointments as presidents and senators try to sound out, accommodate, or outmaneuver various groups seeking to influence judicial selection. Action was further slowed during the Clinton years by some Senate Republicans after they gained majority control of the Senate in 1995. Some of them apparently wanted to minimize Clinton's influence on lower federal courts by delaying action on a number of his nominations for a year or more, a practice that effectively preserved a number of judicial vacancies for the next president.[7] After President Bush took office in 2001, Republicans charged that Senate Democrats were delaying action on his federal court appointments as well.

From the president's standpoint, the great shortcoming of the appointment power is that it will only gradually change the actions of federal courts. At the beginning of a new president's term, virtually all of the judges will have been appointed by previous administrations. During times of rapid political change, the federal courts may lag behind the other branches, and replacing large numbers of federal judges will take a considerable amount of time. Fortunately for presidents, they can also influence the federal courts and the impact of their decisions in a number of other ways.

A second important method for influencing the federal courts is by changing the laws that they apply and interpret. If an executive order or statute is declared unconstitutional or is being interpreted in a way that the president opposes, a new executive order or statute may help to alter the courts' actions. In extreme cases, that may require a constitutional amendment, as in the case of the federal income tax, which was declared unconstitutional by the Supreme Court in 1895 but later reinstated by the Sixteenth Amendment.[8]

[6]Henry Glick, "Courts: Politics and the Judicial Process," in *Politics in the American States,* 7th ed., ed. Virginia Gray, Russell Hanson, and Herbert Jacob (Washington, D.C.: Congressional Quarterly Press, 1999), pp. 242–43 250–51.

[7]John Maltese, "The Presidency and the Judiciary," in *The Presidency and the Political System,* 6th ed., ed. Michael Nelson (Washington, D.C.: Congressional Quarterly Press, 2000), pp. 505–6; and Elliott Slotnick and Sheldon Goldman, "Congress and the Courts: A Case of Casting," in *Great Theatre,* ed. Herbert Weisberg and Samuel Patterson (Cambridge, England: Cambridge University Press, 1998), pp. 197–99.

[8]O'Brien, *Constitutional Law,* p. 184.

This remedy is easiest for presidents to apply in the case of executive orders, which require only presidential approval; more difficult to apply if legislation must be enacted by Congress, and much more difficult if a constitutional amendment is needed. If the president's relationship with Congress is poor, passing legislation is usually very difficult, and winning approval of a constitutional amendment is virtually impossible under all but ideal circumstances.

Influencing the flow of cases is another method of affecting court decisions. The federal courts cannot make a decision until they have a relevant case before them. Presidents may, therefore, encourage the Justice Department, some other federal agency, or possibly even a private group to institute legal action in order to bring an issue to the federal courts or, conversely, to resolve a dispute informally and keep the issue away from the federal courts.[9]

Influence over a court's agenda is particularly important in the case of the Supreme Court, which can handle only a limited number of cases each year. The **solicitor general,** who oversees the federal government's litigation activity, may encourage the Supreme Court to take up a case or may try to keep an issue off the Court's docket. Partly by virtue of working with the Supreme Court on a regular basis, the solicitor general is often successful in influencing the Court's decisions regarding which cases deserve attention.[10]

Presidents sometimes try to influence federal court decisions by pressing the Justice Department or some other federal agency to file *amicus curiae* (friend of the court) briefs in cases that do not directly involve the federal government. An *amicus* brief contains arguments and evidence that judges may consider in deciding a case. The brief may contain a review of previous court cases of a similar nature, economic arguments, or a variety of other information. Other groups may also file *amicus* briefs from time to time.[11] The briefs serve some of the same functions as lobbying in the legislative or executive branch.

The federal courts rarely have the ability to enforce their rulings directly. If the president strongly disagrees with a court decision, presidential influence over enforcement of the decision may help to determine whether the ruling has any practical influence. Outright defiance of a federal court ruling is relatively rare, but half-hearted enforcement can occur when the president dislikes a decision. Some presidents, for example, have made genuine efforts to enforce court rulings and laws against racial discrimination, but other presidents have made little effort or have even acted to undercut antidiscrimination efforts. If the president reduces funding for enforcement agencies and appoints people who will do little enforcement activity (or even leaves positions vacant), a court decision may be significantly undercut.[12]

[9]Goldman and Jahnige, *Federal Courts,* pp. 59–65; Scigliano, *Supreme Court,* pp. 173–77.

[10]Scigliano, *Supreme Court,* pp. 161–73.

[11]Ibid., pp. 167, 193–95.

[12]O'Brien, *Constitutional Law,* pp. 172–86; Scigliano, *Supreme Court,* pp. 36, 56–58; and Joseph Stewart, "Between 'Yes' and 'But': Presidents and the Politics of Civil Rights Policy-Making," in *The Presidency Reconsidered,* ed. Richard Waterman (Itasca, Ill.: Peacock, 1993), pp. 327–46.

If all else fails, presidents have occasionally confronted federal judges who seem considerably out of line with presidential preferences.[13] The first major wrangle of this type occurred during Thomas Jefferson's presidency. Jefferson and his allies disagreed with some of the decisions made by Federalist judges and felt that Democratic-Republican judges would be much more cooperative. Jefferson encouraged Congress to impeach some of the more troublesome judges, beginning with John Pickering, who was also suffering from mental illness. Supreme Court Justice Samuel Chase was the second target, in part because of his public criticisms of the Democratic-Republicans. Although the Senate voted to remove Pickering from office, Jefferson's allies could not muster enough votes to remove Chase, and the impeachment effort ran out of steam. Jefferson later explored other avenues, included constitutional amendments to limit judicial tenure or make federal judges easier to remove, but those efforts did not succeed.

President Lincoln also clashed with federal (and state) courts during the Civil War. His administration's suspension of the writ of habeas corpus, an action that enabled federal officials to hold in custody people suspected of disloyalty without civilian trial, was maintained in part by directing federal officials to ignore court-issued writs. After Lincoln's death, the tensions continued, with the Radical Republicans in Congress pressuring federal and state courts to let Reconstruction proceed as directed by Congress.

The best-known confrontation between the White House and Congress occurred during Franklin Roosevelt's presidency. Before FDR's election, the White House had been controlled by Republicans for most of the preceding seventy years. As a result, the Supreme Court was dominated by conservative justices who did not approve of Roosevelt's efforts to revive the economy. They expressed their disapproval by striking down a number of his New Deal programs as unconstitutional, along with numerous state laws dealing with social welfare and business regulation.

Roosevelt eventually struck back with what became known as the **court packing plan**.[14] The Constitution did not specify the number of judges on the Supreme Court, and its size had fluctuated over the years. Roosevelt proposed a bill to reform the federal courts; the bill included a provision permitting the president to appoint additional judges to courts that had elderly, infirm judges, ostensibly to help with their heavy workload. The bill would have enabled FDR to appoint six new justices to the Supreme Court and, in the process, tipped the balance of power on the Court in favor of the New Deal (assuming Roosevelt's appointments voted as he hoped).

The court packing plan raised a storm of controversy. Critics saw it as a threat to the principle of checks and balances, and Roosevelt apparently caught some of his political allies off guard by failing to consult with them before announcing the proposal. After the Supreme Court shifted its position somewhat to being less hostile to the New Deal programs and one of the older justices

[13]Scigliano, *Supreme Court,* chap. 2.

[14]Abraham, *Justices and Presidents,* pp. 210–12; and Scigliano, *Supreme Court,* pp. 44–51.

announced his retirement, support for Roosevelt's proposal eroded. He did not gain the chance to appoint six new justices all at once, but the Supreme Court became more friendly to the president's efforts to revive the economy.

SOME LANDMARK CASES INVOLVING THE PRESIDENCY

The Constitution's sketchy description of the presidency and the controversial nature of many political issues have combined to produce a number of legal challenges to presidential actions. These challenges are generally brought by people who oppose a particular policy or action, for people rarely challenge the authority of an official who is doing what they want.[15] Some of these cases were not, in the immediate sense, a challenge to the president; some were directed at other officials who were acting under presidential guidance.

The Executive Power

A number of important cases have involved the president's executive authority, which is left virtually undefined in the Constitution, and the related obligation of the president to "take care" that the laws are faithfully executed. Do these provisions amount to a broad grant of authority, along the lines of the stewardship theory, or must presidential authority be specified somewhere else?[16]

One early Supreme Court decision regarding the president's executive power was *In re Neagle* (1890). The *Neagle* case began with a federal judge whose life had been threatened. The attorney general of the United States assigned a federal marshal to protect the judge. When the man who had made the threat appeared ready to act on his sentiments, the federal marshal killed him. Due to some local sentiment in favor of the dead man, the federal marshal was arrested and charged with murder under state law.

In the course of subsequent legal maneuvering, in which the federal government sought the marshal's release, the Supreme Court faced the question of whether the president, acting through the attorney general, had the authority to order a federal marshal to act as a judge's bodyguard in the absence of any clear federal law on the matter. A cynic might have predicted that the Supreme Court would look favorably on an action to protect the life of a federal judge, and it did. The Court ruled that the president's executive powers are to be interpreted broadly and extend beyond what is clearly granted in legislation. The Court's ruling seems consistent with the concerns expressed at the Constitutional Convention regarding the safety of the country and the need for a vigorous executive, but the ruling also left unclear how broad the interpretation might be.

The broad interpretation of the president's executive powers was reaffirmed a few years later when President Cleveland directed his attorney general to seek a federal court injunction against a railroad strike. The Supreme Court

[15]E. E. Schattschneider, *The Semisovereign People* (New York: Holt, Rinehart, and Winston, 1960).

[16]Berger, *Executive Privilege,* chap. 3; and Pritchett, *American Constitution,* chap. 15.

ruled (in ***In re Debs,*** 1895) that although there was no clear federal statute providing for injunctions in that type of situation, the injunction was valid. A government has inherent powers to meet fundamental needs, even if those powers are not specified in laws. Although this ruling upheld a presidential action, note that it was an action taken in conjunction with the federal courts. Once again, the decision did not provide very clear guidance regarding the limits of the executive power.

During Harry Truman's presidency, the Supreme Court provided some guidance on the limits. A labor-management dispute threatened to shut down the steel industry in 1952, a development that would not be very helpful while the war in Korea was underway. Truman ordered his secretary of Commerce to seize the affected steel mills and keep them operating while negotiations continued. Steel industry executives complied reluctantly with the order, but they also began legal action against it. In ***Youngstown Sheet and Tube*** v. ***Sawyer*** (1952—sometimes referred to as the steel seizure cases), the Supreme Court ruled in favor of the steel companies and against President Truman.

At first glance, Truman's actions appeared similar to Cleveland's actions in the railway strike, but there were two important differences. First, Cleveland's decision to seek a court injunction against the strike amounted to a joint action with the federal court system. Truman's action, by contrast, was unilateral. Second, a few years before the steel dispute, Congress had passed an important but controversial bill, the Taft-Hartley Act. Part of the Taft-Hartley Act dealt with strikes affecting vital industries, and when members of Congress addressed that section of the bill they considered but rejected giving the president power to seize and operate vital industries hit by labor disputes. Instead, they established a less drastic mechanism: a presidential power to order workers back to work for sixty to ninety days while negotiations continued.

The Supreme Court's decision in the *Youngstown* case was rather fragmented, with three justices upholding the president's action and two justices denying (contrary to the earlier *Neagle* and *Debs* rulings) that presidents had any powers other than those specifically granted in laws. The remaining judges, however, seemed to accept the principle of implied or inherent presidential powers but contended that in Truman's case, Congress had indicated a fairly clear preference against a seizure power in labor-management disputes (though it had not prohibited such an action). In addition, the law provided for a clear mechanism for dealing with strikes in vital industries: the presidential back-to-work order. In that context, Truman was not on firm ground, legally speaking. He abided by the Supreme Court's decision.

THE PRESIDENT'S REMOVAL POWER

From a contemporary standpoint, one of the stranger controversies in the American presidency centers on a fairly simple question: does the president have any power to fire people that he (or she, one day) appoints to the executive branch? This seemingly simple question produced legal disputes more than 150 years after the Constitution's adoption and led to the impeachment of President Andrew Johnson.[17]

The dispute grew from the fact that although the Constitution mentions a presidential power to appoint people, it says nothing regarding the power to fire them, apart from the congressional power to impeach and remove people. If presidents can fire people, does the Senate have a voice in firing appointees whom it has confirmed? In practice, presidents asserted and exercised a power to fire executive branch appointees unilaterally for the first seventy-eight years of the presidency. At that point, tensions erupted.

President Lincoln was dead, and Andrew Johnson occupied the White House. The Radical Republicans did not trust him to be as strict with the South as they wanted. They passed the **Tenure of Office Act** in 1867 to prevent the president from removing federal department heads without Senate approval. They evidently hoped this requirement would reduce presidential control and increase congressional control over the bureaucracy.

Johnson responded by ousting a member of his cabinet, apparently in hopes of creating a test case to take to the Supreme Court. There, he hoped, the Tenure of Office Act would be declared unconstitutional. Instead, Congress made Johnson's action a major point of the impeachment effort against him. He survived the effort, and Congress later repealed the law in 1887.

The issue persisted, however. Congress enacted legislation in 1876 to require that some postmasters could be removed only with Senate approval (postal appointments were an important source of patronage in those days). Years later, President Wilson removed a postmaster covered by the law and did not seek Senate approval. The irate postmaster filed suit, and the case eventually made its way to the Supreme Court.

In *Myers* v. *United States* (1926), the Supreme Court placed considerable emphasis on presidential practice before the Tenure of Office Act and on inferences from the "executive power" and "take care" passages in the Constitution. The presidential frame of reference was possibly reinforced because the chief justice, William Howard Taft, had occupied the White House before Wilson. The Court's majority ruled that presidents had a broad power to remove executive appointments without congressional approval and struck down the 1876 law. However, the Court's opinion also indicated that some executive branch positions might be less subject to presidential removal. Those *quasi-judicial* positions, in which individual officials or boards hand down rulings on specific cases after hearings, often regarding regulatory issues, might be less vulnerable to presidential removal except for specific causes, particularly failing to apply the relevant laws appropriately.

This doctrine was addressed directly during Franklin Roosevelt's presidency after he removed a member of the Federal Trade Commission. The removed commissioner, William Humphrey, was a holdover from the previous Republican administrations, and his policy views did not match Roosevelt's views very well.

[17]Louis Fisher, *Constitutional Conflicts Between Congress and the President*, 4th ed., rev. (Lawrence: University of Kansas Press, 1997), chap. 2–3; O'Brien, *Constitutional Law* pp. 308–59; and Pritchett, *American Constitution*, pp. 245–48.

Humphrey filed suit but did not live long enough to see the Supreme Court's ruling. The executor for his estate continued the suit and won Humphrey a measure of vindication.

In *Humphrey's Executor v. United States* (1935), the Supreme Court ruled that President Roosevelt had exceeded his authority in removing Humphrey. Congress had created the Federal Trade Commission to perform the quasi-judicial function of applying legislative standards in specific cases, and the commission's structure was evidently an effort to provide some insulation from presidential dominance. Humphrey should not have been removed simply for having policy beliefs different from the president's.

The Supreme Court reaffirmed and clarified this position after President Eisenhower removed a member of the War Claims Commission to make room for a Republican appointee. The Supreme Court ruled in *Wiener v. United States* (1958) that members of quasi-judicial agencies can be dismissed only for cause (that is, incompetence or failing to do their jobs properly), not for political disagreements. This limitation applies even if the law creating a particular quasi-judicial agency does not state the limitation explicitly.

Overall, these and other court decisions regarding the president's power to remove executive branch officials provide a reasonably consistent set of guidelines. First, presidents may unilaterally remove "political appointees," primarily heads of the regular cabinet departments, a limited number of other high-ranking appointees in the major federal departments, and noncareer members of the White House staff, even if some of those appointees required Senate confirmation. Second, Congress may limit the president's removal authority. The limitation may be explicit, as in the case of civil service coverage for large majority of the federal civilian bureaucracy; those employees can be fired only for cause, primarily incompetence or failure to comply with departmental policies. However, the limitation may also be implicit, since the *Wiener* decision, in the case of quasi-judicial appointees, primarily in the independent regulatory agencies.

FOREIGN RELATIONS

The federal courts have traditionally treated the president's powers in foreign policy and national security policy with considerable deference. The federal courts at all levels have often refused to hear cases challenging presidential actions involving foreign affairs and defense policy. In addition, when the courts have agreed to hear those cases, they are often inclined to support presidential actions—more so than in the case of domestic policy issues.[18]

One of the most important cases in this arena is *United States v. Curtiss-Wright Export Corporation* (1936). In this case, the Supreme Court indicated that the federal government has very broad authority in the conduct of foreign

[18]Robert Dudley, "Judicial Control of the Presidency: Stability and Change," in *Understanding the Presidency*, 2d ed., ed. James Pfiffner and Roger Fisher (New York: Addison Wesley Longman, 2000), pp. 305–6; Fisher, *Constitutional Conflicts*, chap. 8–9; O'Brien, *Constitutional Law*, chap. 3; and Pritchett, *American Constitution*, chap. 8–9.

policy and that that authority goes beyond what is specified in the Constitution. In addition, the bulk of that authority is lodged in the presidency. Presidents serve as the primary channel for communicating with the governments of other countries, the main authority for conducting negotiations with other countries, and the commander of the armed forces. Note that, in practice, members of Congress sometimes meet with officials of other countries, as do governors and other state and local officials, and the heads of major businesses with overseas concerns. In addition, Congress sometimes exerts considerable influence on defense issues, such as weapons procurement.

The rather expansive doctrine expressed in the *Curtiss-Wright* decision has been hedged a bit by several Supreme Court decisions holding that treaties are subject to the Constitution. A president cannot, therefore, use the treaty power to circumvent the Constitution. However, a treaty may sometimes have the effect of expanding national government authority when constitutional provisions are not very clear. The president's powers in treaty making are also limited by the constitutional requirement that treaties must be ratified by the Senate (which it may decline to do), by Senate amendments to a treaty (which may trigger new negotiations with the other countries involved), and by Senate reservations to a treaty. Reservations do not amend the treaty, strictly speaking, but may limit or qualify U.S. obligations arising from the treaty.

The federal courts have been reluctant to intervene in presidential-congressional disputes that arise after a treaty has been ratified. For example, the Constitution says nothing regarding the termination of treaties. When President Carter announced that he was ending a treaty with Nationalist China (Taiwan), some members of the Senate were very upset. They introduced a number of proposals in response to Carter's action, but none of the proposals passed. Several senators also sought help from the Supreme Court. The Court's response was unclear due to differing opinions among the justices, but a number of the justices indicated that the Senate has the primary responsibility for dealing with this type of problem, not the federal courts. If the Senate fails to act, senators are not likely to receive much sympathy from the courts.

The difficulties that may arise when presidents seek Senate approval of treaties have led many presidents to avoid or minimize the use of treaties when dealing with international issues. Instead, presidents have increasingly relied on executive agreements (and similar instruments, such as memoranda of understanding), which do not require Senate approval. Executive agreements date back to the first few presidents but have vastly outnumbered treaties in the modern era.[19]

The use of executive agreements has sometimes provoked conflict, partly because senators resent having no role in their approval and partly because presidents have sometimes failed to inform Congress of the existence of specific agreements or of their complete contents. The federal courts have generally treated executive agreements as legally binding, even though the president is the only U.S. official to approve them. The courts have not, however, regarded executive

[19]Ragsdale, *Vital Statistics,* pp. 309–20.

agreements (or treaties, for that matter) as requiring Congress to appropriate funds to carry out obligations incurred under those agreements.

Although the federal courts have often supported or at least not opposed giving presidents considerable latitude in foreign policy, they do not appear to be able to give presidents very much political protection if the presidential decisions fail to produce desired results. The courts were not willing to challenge Lyndon Johnson's handling of the Vietnam War or Jimmy Carter's management of the Iranian hostage issue, but that acquiescence did little, if anything, to soothe public anger at Johnson and Carter.

THE PARDON POWER

The power of the president to grant pardons is one of the less visible aspects of the presidency, although last-minute pardons by President Clinton attracted considerable attention, at least for a short time. Like many other presidential powers, the pardon authority is not very clearly defined in the Constitution, and a number of major court rulings have helped to clarify matters somewhat.[20]

The Supreme Court has ruled that pardons may be granted after a person has been convicted, after indictment but before conviction, or even before indictment (but probably not before an offence has been committed). Moreover, the pardon essentially wipes out the conviction (assuming a conviction has occurred) and all of the legal effects of the conviction. Presidents may also grant a pardon or commutation (a reduction in punishment, such as changing a death sentence to a life term in prison), with restrictions or conditions attached.

The Court has also ruled that pardons must be accepted in order for them to take effect. An individual has the right to refuse a pardon, although that has not been a particularly common occurrence. A pardon may create an image of guilt if a person has not been convicted of a crime. A pardon will also reduce a person's ability to decline to testify on the grounds that the testimony might be self-incriminating. This consideration apparently lay behind a pardon refusal during Woodrow Wilson's presidency.

PRESIDENTIAL IMMUNITY

A sensitive issue in presidential-judicial relations is the extent, if any, of presidential immunity from various legal processes. This issue is part of the much larger question of public officials' immunity from legal action, whether those officials are mayors, career administrators, or presidents. Court rulings on this issue are not altogether consistent, but some basic patterns can be discerned.[21]

Traditionally, the courts were usually reluctant to hear legal challenges to the official conduct of public officials. There were some early exceptions, such as the Supreme Court's willingness to issue a subpoena to President Jefferson, although

---

[20]Pritchett, *American Constitution* pp. 252–53.

[21]O'Brien, *Constitutional Law,* pp. 385–401; and David Rosenbloom, with the assistance of Deborah Goldman, *Public Administration,* 3d ed. (New York: McGraw-Hill, 1993), pp. 78–80.

the subpoena was not enforced. The Court later refused to issue an injunction against President Andrew Johnson, at least in part because the justices felt that they would not be able to enforce the injunction if the president declined to obey it.

Since the 1960s, the legal immunity of public officials at all levels has declined considerably. Some of the decline is due to legislative acts that have created various categories of rights and, in some instances, given individuals who believe that their rights have been violated greater access to the courts. Changing legal thinking within the court system has also reduced the legal immunity of public officials, including the president.

President Nixon learned a painful lesson regarding the new legal environment when Justice John Sirica subpoenaed White House tape recordings for the grand jury investigating the Watergate scandal. In the course of resolving legal appeals, the Supreme Court ruled that the president was obligated to hand over the tapes. The Court later ruled that new legislation giving the federal government unprecedented long-term control over Nixon's presidential papers and recordings was constitutional, in spite of Nixon's legal opposition.

President Clinton learned a similarly painful lesson when the Supreme Court ruled that he was not immune to a civil lawsuit alleging sexual harassment committed before he became president. Although he won some degree of vindication in the case, at least in a legal sense, the legal maneuvering produced extremely embarrassing publicity. In addition, accusations that he lied in responding to questions raised in the case became a major part of the impeachment case against him. We will return to that issue shortly.

The declining legal immunity of presidents (and other public officials) since the 1960s has helped encourage the use of legal attacks as a method for diverting the president's time, energy, and attention from presidential initiatives and undercutting the president's ability to accomplish very much while in office. People who oppose a president's policies may use legal challenges in the same manner that election campaigns, lobbying, and other more traditional tactics are used to influence government. The average citizen, however, has relatively little influence over the federal court system. At least some observers suspect that groups may prefer legal challenges for precisely that reason.[22]

EXECUTIVE PRIVILEGE

One of the early arguments in favor of having a single president (or some other form of executive) rather than having a committee in charge of executive responsibilities was that a single executive would be better able to keep secrets.[23] During sensitive diplomatic negotiations, the conduct of war, or the development of a new military weapon, secrecy is often vitally important. It is equally impor-

[22]Benjamin Ginsberg and Martin Shefter, *Politics by Other Means,* rev. ed. (New York: Norton, 1999).

[23]Berger *Executive Privilege;* Fisher, *Constitutional Conflicts,* pp. 181–95; Alexander Hamilton, James Madison, and John Jay, *The Federalist Papers* (New York: Bantam, 1982), p. 356; and Mark Rozell, *Executive Privilege* (Baltimore: Johns Hopkins University, 1994).

tant when intelligence services have broken an unfriendly nation's communications codes or have succeeded in placing an agent in that country's military or intelligence services. Leaks of information can endanger the lives of military personnel, intelligence agents, hostages, undercover investigators, or informants who know of criminal activity within the United States. Premature disclosure of a criminal investigation may lead to the destruction of evidence or suspects fleeing the country. Presidential advisors may hesitate to give the president candid advice if they fear that their words will appear on the evening news that day.

Because of these concerns, as well as a few other considerations we will examine shortly, presidents have sometimes declined to make information available to other people, including members of Congress, judges and prosecutors, journalists, and the public. The practice of withholding information, a practice sometimes called **executive privilege,** began in George Washington's presidency.[24] When the House of Representatives requested information on a treaty negotiation, Washington declined to provide it. He contended that the Constitution gives the Senate but not the House a role in approving treaties, and the Senate had the information already.

Washington's action did not meet with universal approval, perhaps in part because the House was working on a spending bill that included funding related to the treaty—and the Constitution clearly gives the House a role to play in funding governmental activities. One observer who did not agree with Washington's action was his own vice president, John Adams. When Adams became president, he was more willing to share diplomatic information with the House.

Executive privilege of a sort also appeared during Thomas Jefferson's presidency, although in a less clear form. When the House of Representatives was investigating the antics of former Vice President Aaron Burr, who was implicated in a plan to found a new country west of the Appalachian Mountains and various other schemes, the House requested information from Jefferson. The House request, however, included a provision that the president could withhold information if the "public welfare" required it.[25] Jefferson did hold back some information. Note that in this case, the House took the initiative in giving Jefferson the right to conceal facts of a sensitive nature.

Andrew Jackson also denied congressional access to information at times. One case occurred when the Senate requested information regarding problems in the sale of public lands. Jackson refused the request in the apparent belief that the Senate inquiry would be conducted unfairly. Unlike Washington, Jackson could not claim in this case that the Senate had no constitutional interest in the operation of a domestic program, and part of the Senate's interest arose from its constitutional role in approving a new appointee who would be involved in public land sales. Later Presidents Polk and Buchanan did not agree with Jackson's action and were more willing to share information with Congress.[26]

[24]Berger, *Executive Privilege,* pp. 187–201.

[25]Ibid., pp. 201–3.

[26]Ibid., pp. 203–5.

Over the years, many other presidents have concealed all sorts of information from other people in the American political system. Some of that concealment is regulated by rules and procedures for handling sensitive information in the national security arena. Very few Americans, for example, knew that America was trying to develop an atomic bomb during World War II. This type of concealment is not usually treated as executive privilege, although critics have sometimes complained that too much information is concealed unnecessarily and for reasons that have little to do with national security.

Critics complain that concealment is too often used to hide mistakes, misconduct, and failures, whether they directly involve the president or various presidential aides, political appointees, or the president's political supporters. In a related vein, how can the president or other executive officials be held accountable to Congress, the courts, or the public if large amounts of information regarding executive branch activities are concealed on a recurring basis? Checks and balances and democratic accountability require information; we cannot judge the appropriateness of actions that we know nothing about. In addition, the executive branch contains more information than the other branches of government. If the president has broad discretion in concealing and releasing information, Congress and the courts may be misled into making decisions that they would not have made if they were more fully informed. They will be unable to tell whether the president and his appointees are complying with the law.[27]

Conflict over executive privilege reached a high point during the Nixon administration, which tried to withhold information on a variety of matters, from impoundment of funds appropriated by Congress to evidence related to the Watergate scandal. When a federal district court sought tape recordings and documents that might cast light on the Watergate scandal, the administration resisted handing over the information. Eventually, the dispute reached the Supreme Court in the case of *United States* v. *Richard Nixon* (1974).[28]

The Supreme Court concluded that an overly broad or absolute power of executive privilege would place an excessive burden on the legal system. How could anyone receive a fair trial if the president has sweeping power to decide what information will be made available to the courts and what information will be concealed? In effect, that would amount to presidential exercise of judicial power, a situation that the Supreme Court found unacceptable.

The Court did admit that some information might be too sensitive to reveal in court but concluded that a judge should normally decide when that was the case. A judge could examine the information in chambers (rather than in open court) and determine if it would jeopardize national security, an ongoing investigation, or innocent lives. Some information might be too sensitive to disclose even to a judge, but the administration had a responsibility to make a case regarding the sensitivity of the information rather than simply asserting a blanket right to conceal.

[27]See ibid.; Rozell, *Executive Privilege,* chap. 1.

[28]Rozell, *Executive Privilege,* chap. 3.

The Court also noted that the legal system must take care not to place an undue burden on the presidency by continually demanding large amounts of information. The Court insisted that the Nixon administration turn over the evidence needed by the district court. The administration complied, with the result that a number of people involved in the Watergate scandal and other wrongdoing were either convicted of or pleaded guilty to various violations of the law. When Congress and the public learned what the evidence revealed, particularly regarding President Nixon's efforts to obstruct the Watergate investigation, his support eroded, and he soon resigned from office.

Nixon's successors, Ford and Carter, ran more open administrations and were more willing to share information with Congress, the courts, and the news media. However, Reagan, George H. W. Bush, Clinton, and George W. Bush all made a number of efforts to withhold information from other political actors.[29] The most dramatic of those efforts are probably the Iran-Contra affair during the Reagan years and Paula Jones's lawsuit against President Clinton. Those efforts at concealment were ultimately not very successful.

Concealing information is a common tactic among leaders, both in and out of the political arena. Some concealment results from commendable motives, but leaders also conceal information to limit the influence of other branches of government, outmaneuver opponents, hide problems, and bolster their popularity.[30] Other people may not try to find the information, which remains hidden by default. When leaders are most successful at keeping something a secret, other people will not even ask about the information because they do not know that it exists.

Keeping secrets for a considerable length of time is frequently very difficult, however. People (including those in the White House) leak information for a host of reasons, from bruised egos and a desire for attention to policy disagreements and a failure to realize that the information needs to be hidden (from the White House's perspective). Outsiders may guess or determine from small clues that the information exists and demand its release. While some presidents, such as Eisenhower, were relatively successful at concealment while they were in office,[31] others have struggled but failed to keep things confidential. When presidents try to conceal failures or scandals and fail in the attempt, the efforts at secrecy may anger members of Congress, judges, and the public—as Reagan and Clinton both found. Striking a balance between legitimate needs for secrecy and the free circulation of information required for accountability is exceptionally difficult in many cases.[32]

[29]Ibid., chap. 4–5.

[30]David Nice, "The Warrior Model of Leadership: Classic Perspectives and Contemporary Relevance," *Leadership Quarterly* 9 (1998): 321–32.

[31]Fred Greenstein, *The Hidden Hand Presidency* (New York: Basic, 1982).

[32]Rozell, *Executive Privilege,* pp. 1–7.

IMPEACHMENT

The Constitution provides that the "President, Vice President, and all civil officers of the United States . . ." are subject to the power of **impeachment.** The House of Representatives is responsible for impeachment, a term that essentially means to accuse or indict. When an official is impeached, the Senate is responsible for trying indictments, and when the president is impeached, the chief justice of the Supreme Court presides at the trial. All three branches are further entangled because most of the impeachments in American history have targeted federal judges, sometimes with encouragement from the president or other executive branch officials. In addition, the three most important presidential impeachment efforts included two that were related to civil or criminal court proceedings (Clinton and Nixon, respectively) and an anticipated court case (Andrew Johnson).[33]

Although only three presidents were impeached by the House, a number of other presidents have worried about possible impeachment efforts. John Tyler and Herbert Hoover were targets of impeachment inquiries that did not receive enough votes in the House to trigger a trial in the Senate. John Kennedy apparently worried about possible impeachment during the Cuban missile crisis, and some of Ronald Reagan's advisors feared that the Iran-Contra affair might lead to impeachment. Ulysses Grant's secretary of War, William Belknap, was also impeached.[34] All of the convictions in impeachment proceedings have involved federal judges, although Nixon resigned when impeachment and removal appeared to be inevitable.

The impeachment power is not defined very clearly in the Constitution, and a number of impeachment proceedings have included considerable disagreement regarding various aspects of the power. One recurrently controversial question is: what constitutes an impeachable offense? The Constitution provides that impeachment is limited to cases of "treason, bribery, or other high crimes and misdemeanors." Treason and bribery are fairly clear-cut, at least in principle. The phrase "crimes and misdemeanors," however, has triggered much of the controversy.[35]

According to one school of thought, that phrase limits the impeachment power to cases of indictable crimes. President Nixon's defenders during the Watergate hearings advocated that viewpoint; unless investigators could find convincing proof that Nixon had broken criminal laws, he should not be impeached. Congress might use different standards of proof than a court would require, but there should be a close correspondence between legal definitions of crime and congressional definitions, in this view. Even here, there may be slippage, for an

[33]Raoul Berger, *Impeachment* (New York: Bantam, 1974); Charles Black, *Impeachment: A Handbook* (New Haven: Yale University, 1998); and Eleanore Bushnell, *Crimes, Follies, and Misfortunes: The Federal Impeachment Trials* (Urbana: University of Illinois, 1992).

[34]Bushnell, *Crimes, Follies;* Lance Gay, "Fear of Impeachment Has a Long History Among U.S. Presidents," *Moscow Pullman (Idaho) Daily News,* 12–13 September 1998, p. 5B.

[35]Berger, *Impeachment,* chap. II, IV-V; Black, *Impeachment,* chap. 3; and Bushnell, *Crimes, Follies,* pp. 10–11, 18–20, 320–23.

offense might be illegal but not seem sufficiently important to justify impeaching and removing the president. Conversely, an offense might seem minor if committed by an ordinary citizen but appear much more troubling if committed by the president.

At the other extreme, some participants in impeachment efforts have advocated a very broad view of impeachable offenses. According to this perspective, determining what constitutes an impeachable offense is a political question. If an impeachment resolution receives the needed number of votes in the House and Senate, then the offense is considered impeachable, regardless of what it was. Advocates of this perspective are often trying to impeach someone because of partisan or policy differences.

A more middle-of-the road perspective rejects both of these extremes. In this view, if Congress can impeach the president for virtually any reason, Congress will overwhelmingly dominate the presidency, and checks and balances will suffer. Presidents might be afraid to veto legislation or speak out on a controversial issue from fear of being impeached. Conversely, limiting impeachment to indictable crimes might leave Congress unable to remove a president who is unable or unwilling to perform the duties of the office or who has committed acts that are technically legal but harmful to the country. The historical record seems to confirm this more moderate view of impeachable offenses (that is, a definition that is broader than just indictable crimes but narrower than everything). Some judges have been removed for conduct that did not constitute an indictable crime but did raise questions regarding their abilities to do their jobs. However, impeachment efforts that appear to be predominantly political disputes have not removed officials from office.

When congressional Republicans impeached Andrew Johnson, their primary motive appears to have been a belief that he was too conciliatory toward the southern states and unwilling to punish them. Partisan and ideological motives also loomed large in Clinton's impeachment, as indicated by the long-running efforts of conservative groups to accuse him of one offense after another, the stark party differences in Congress on the impeachment votes, and the outcome in the Senate. Although Clinton's conduct was far from admirable, the accusations that were proven appear less serious in terms of official conduct than the actions of some other presidents who were not impeached,[36] although that is admittedly a judgment call.

Another issue regarding impeachment centers on the question of whether an impeachment conviction can be appealed to the courts.[37] None of the people who were convicted were successful in mounting a court challenge, but a number of those convictions were in the 1800s, when the federal courts were reluctant to

[36]See Joe Conason and Gene Lyons, *The Hunting of the President* (New York: St. Martin's, 2000); and James Pfiffner, "President Clinton's Impeachment and Senate Trial," in *Understanding the Presidency*, 2d ed., ed. James Pfiffner and Roger Davidson (New York: Addison Wesley Longman, 2000), pp. 466–67.

[37]Berger, *Impeachment*, chap. 3; and Black, *Impeachment*, chap. 4.

hear cases challenging the decisions of the other branches. Some observers believe that, in theory, a convicted person might be able to challenge the decision in court, perhaps on the grounds that his or her conduct did not constitute an impeachable offense. The Constitution does not mention the possibility of an appeal, but it does not prohibit one, either. If the impeachment power is not a blank check for Congress to remove a president for any reason at all, a court review might be appropriate in some cases.

Other observers reject the possibility of an appeal to the courts, at least in the case of presidential impeachments. Spending months or even years of court maneuvering after a president has been convicted by the Senate would virtually paralyze the national government. The prospects for presidential-congressional cooperation would be extremely poor, and the president's ability to deal with the federal bureaucracy or the heads of government in other countries would be little better. Bear in mind that the Supreme Court is sometimes able to handle important cases fairly quickly, as it did during the dispute over the 2000 presidential election in Florida.

Another, less contentious issue regarding impeachment is whether an official can be impeached and convicted after resigning. The impeachment of Secretary of War Belknap in 1876 led to his resignation, but the Senate proceeded with his impeachment trial anyway. Senators may need to explore a case to determine whether actions against other people still in office are needed or whether administrative or legal reforms might be required to prevent similar problems in the future. Moreover, the punishment for conviction in the Senate can include barring the person from holding an office in the future. Because the impeachment process is so unpleasant and stressful for most of the participants and may be upsetting to the public, members of Congress are likely to prefer terminating the process after the person resigns.[38] That was precisely what happened after President Nixon resigned.

CONCLUSIONS

The president's relationship with the legal system is complex but usually fairly harmonious. During many eras in history, the federal courts have been reluctant to confront the president, although most presidents generally seem to comply with federal laws, a practice that reduces the likelihood of confrontations. When party control of the White House shifts after an extended period of control by one party or when levels of political conflict escalate, confrontations between the White House and the federal courts may grow more common. Even then, however, the federal courts are generally reluctant to challenge presidential actions in the national security and foreign policy realms. Note, too, that presidents and their political appointees are involved in a very wide range of actions in the modern era, and the federal courts have an enormous number of cases to process in a typical year. As a result, the courts are not likely to be able to review more than a small fraction of the administration's actions.

[38]Bushnell, *Crimes, Follies,* p. 320.

Presidents and their advisors recognize the importance of the courts and have a number of ways to influence the actions and impact of the courts. One of the most important modes of influence is through the appointment of federal judges. If the administration does a thorough job of screening potential appointees and has a reasonably good relationship with the Senate, a considerable number of new judges may significantly affect the actions of the federal courts. In recent years, the appointment and confirmation processes have grown more contentious, partly because of frequent divided party control between the presidency and the Senate and partly because many interest groups mobilize to influence judicial appointments.

Presidents also try to influence the courts by issuing executive orders, pushing for new legislation, and occasionally trying to amend the Constitution, although amendments are extremely difficult to pass. The president, acting through the solicitor general or other intermediaries, may try to influence the courts' dockets, bringing some cases to the courts' attention and trying to keep other cases out of court. Many other groups try to do the same things, although they are usually less successful than the solicitor general.

The president and other administration officials may submit *amicus curiae* briefs in hopes of influencing court cases in which the administration is not a party, and presidential influence over the implementation of federal court decisions may affect the impact of the ruling considerably. Presidents do not usually defy federal court rulings openly, but some decisions have been implemented with a distinct lack of energy. If all else fails, presidents have sometimes confronted the federal courts (especially the Supreme Court). When those confrontations find the president, Congress, and the public on one side and the Supreme Court on the other, the Court has sometimes appeared to back down.

Over the years, the Supreme Court has decided a number of important cases that greatly affected presidents and the presidency. Some of those rulings have helped clarify the executive powers of the president and the related issue of removing executive appointees from office. Others have dealt with foreign policy, the president's power to pardon people, and presidential immunity (or lack of immunity) from normal legal proceedings while in office. Rulings on foreign policy issues have generally given presidents considerable leeway, as have rulings on the pardon power. Decisions regarding the president's executive powers and removal powers have also given presidents a good deal of discretion, with some exceptions. Presidential immunity from legal action while in office declined noticeably during the Clinton administration, a development that parallels greater court willingness to hear challenges to public officials at all levels of government in recent years.

Bear in mind that the federal courts can, for all practical purposes, uphold a presidential action without hearing a case. If someone files a legal challenge to a presidential or administration action, the federal courts may simply decline to hear the case. In that event, the administration is relatively free to proceed—although in some circumstances, the party seeking to file the challenge may proceed to look for another judge.

The doctrine of executive privilege holds that presidents have the right to conceal information from the other branches of government, the public, and the news media. Executive privilege is not mentioned in the Constitution, but concealment may be needed at times, especially in national security policy. Critics worry that executive privilege may be used to conceal failures, misconduct, and other information that may be embarrassing to the president or stimulate opposition to presidential policies. Withholding information risks antagonizing Congress, the courts, and the news media, but many presidents have done it, though to varying degrees.

The impeachment power enables Congress to indict and remove presidents and judges. Full-blown impeachment proceedings are relatively rare; only two have occurred involving presidents, and neither was removed from office. President Nixon resigned in the face of imminent impeachment and conviction, however, and a number of other presidents expressed concern over the possibility of impeachment. Presidents have also been involved in impeachment efforts directed at federal judges, although that has been rare. According to one count, more than sixty impeachment efforts have occurred in the House since 1789. Fewer than twenty received enough votes to trigger a trial in the Senate, however.[39]

KEY TERMS

amicus curiae   354
court packing plan   355
executive privilege   363
Humphrey's Executor v.
   United States   359
impeachment   366
In re Debs   357
In re Neagle   356
judicial review   349
Marbury v. *Madison*   349

Myers v. *United States*   358
senatorial courtesy   353
solicitor general   354
Tenure of Office Act   358
United States v. *Curtiss-Wright*
   Export Corporation   359
United States v. *Richard Nixon*   364
Wiener v. *United States*   359
Youngstown Sheet and Tube v.
   Sawyer   357

DISCUSSION QUESTIONS

1. How do the federal courts influence presidents and presidential programs?
2. How do presidents try to influence the federal courts?
3. What criteria do presidents use in selecting judicial nominees? When are nominees most likely to encounter Senate opposition?
4. What are some of the landmark court decisions regarding presidential power, and how have the decisions affected the presidency?
5. In what ways may executive privilege be helpful to the country? In what ways may executive privilege be harmful?

[39]Gay, "Fear of Impeachment," p. 5B.

SUGGESTED READINGS

Henry Abraham, *Justices and Presidents,* 3d ed. New York: Oxford, 1992.

Louis Fisher, *Constitutional Conflicts Between Congress and the President,* 4th ed., rev. Lawrence: University Press of Kansas, 1997.

Benjamin Gisberg and Martin Shefter, *Politics by Other Means,* rev. ed. New York: Norton, 1999.

Robert Scigliano, *The Supreme Court and the Presidency.* New York: Free Press, 1971.

13

PRESIDENTIAL
POLICY CHOICE

The world is full of problems, but presidents and government can attend to only a fraction of them. In this chapter, we will discuss why presidents decide to work on some problems and issues and not others. This is the problem of presidential agenda setting. We will also discuss the policy solutions that presidents select. Lastly, we will discuss some cycles and trends in presidential policy making.

SETTING THE PRESIDENT'S AGENDA: THE PROBLEM CONTEXT

Policy making can in part be understood as a process of problem solving, that is, applying policy solutions to problems.[1] We can view the **president's agenda** as those problems and issues that he is working on, that he is attempting to find and apply policy solutions to. Naturally, presidents want to spend time on problems that they consider important, their own policy agenda. Some of the president's personal policy agenda was important in the election campaign, as he might have promised to attend to certain problems and issues if elected. But other problems also vie for presidential attention, and these other problems might divert presidential attention away from his pet concerns.

There are two sources of problems for presidents to deal with other than those he would like to spend his time on: the ongoing activities of government and unanticipated events. Both of these sources of problems may attract presidential attention, forcing him to spend some of his time on them, and consequently lessen the attention he can pay to his own policy agenda.

The Ongoing Activities of Government

Ongoing governmental activities are important because they create routines and expectations about what the president is to do with his time. As government has grown and taken on more responsibilities, more and more presidential time is structured by what government is already doing.[2]

For instance, each year the president must submit a budget to Congress. The process of budget building begins with a review of each agency's budgetary needs; thus, it is broad in scope. Moreover, the needs of each agency must be bal-

---

[1] John W. Kingdon, *Agendas, Alternatives, and Public Policies* (Boston: Little, Brown, 1984).

[2] Charles O. Jones, *The Presidency in a Separated System* (Washington, D.C.: Brookings Institution, 1994).

anced against the revenues that government has at its disposal to spend, as well as the needs of the economy. Presidents now find that they spend a considerable amount of their time on budgetary issues.

Similarly, many programs come up for scheduled review and new people must be appointed to office, as other officials' terms have ended or they have voluntarily left office. The larger government is, the more programs it operates that may need to be reviewed and the more people the president may need to appoint. In other words, the larger government is, the more decisions the president must make about what government is already doing and who should be doing those things. Managing the existing government has become a major preoccupation of presidents as government has grown. This larger government may curtail the time that presidents can give to other decisions and activities, such as working on their own policy agenda.

Unanticipated Events

Unanticipated events come as a surprise or a shock and may turn into crises. If they are upsetting to the public or appear to be of crisis proportion, presidents may be compelled to attend to them, often to the disregard of other activities, such as pursuing their own policy agenda.

Unanticipated events come in many varieties. Most commonly, one thinks of international crises in this regard, but natural disasters, outbreaks of public disorder and violence, and scandals may all force presidential attention. Not all unanticipated events will necessitate a presidential response. Presidents may feel that they must elevate the event onto their agenda when the public is distressed and concerned about the event and when the event seems to have important consequences for policy and society. The September 11, 2001, terrorist attacks, which killed many people, injured many more, and received massive media coverage, altered President George W. Bush's agenda dramatically.

Sometimes the dictates of the situation will force the president to attend to the event. Clearly, when the national security is at stake, the president needs little public prodding to focus attention on an event. And presidents, through their greater access to information, may deem an event as having national security implications, while the public may not be so inclined. Then it becomes the president's task to lead the public so that it views the event the same way that he does.[3]

A good example of a president taking a lead over the public was the crisis in Kosovo in early 1999. Most of the public probably could not have named Kosovo or found it on a map before President Bill Clinton began his public campaign to convince Congress and the nation, as well as U.S. allies in Europe, that military action needed to be taken. And the president seemingly felt that such action needed to be taken not only for humanitarian reasons but also for the sake of NATO.

[3]Sometimes presidents will make a problem appear to be a crisis in order to lead the public. See Denise M. Bostdorff and Daniel J. O'Rourke, "The Presidency and the Promotion of Domestic Crisis: John Kennedy's Management of the 1962 Steel Crisis," *Presidential Studies Quarterly* 27 (Spring 1997): 343–61; and Denise M. Bostdorff, "The Presidency and Promoted Crisis: Reagan, Grenada, and Issue Management," *Presidential Studies Quarterly* 21 (Fall 1991): 737–50.

The North Atlantic Treaty Organization (NATO) is the alliance of European nations that, along with the United States, stood together in opposition to the Soviet Union and its allied nations during the Cold War. With the fall of the Soviet Union, many questioned the need for an alliance such as NATO. But others like President Clinton felt that NATO would still be important for European security. If NATO could not contain the violence in Serbia and Kosovo from spreading to other nations and if NATO could not help find a solution to the crisis in Kosovo, should NATO continue and should the United States continue to support and participate in NATO? Thus, the issue of Kosovo, at least to the president, might have been bigger than the public realized, which is why Clinton made such a case to the public.

In 1990, President George H. W. Bush was confronted with a similar situation when Iraq invaded Kuwait. Bush, like Clinton in 1999, had to rally public support, but this time for a large military intervention and ground war in the Middle East. And Bush was able to gather a large group of other nations, including many Middle Eastern Arab nations, to support the military campaign against Iraq.

But smaller events may also upset the public, calling for a presidential response. For example, in 1993 at Waco, Texas, some eighty Branch Davidian cult followers of David Koresh died after a fifty-one-day siege by federal agents from the FBI and Alcohol, Tobacco, and Firearms (ATF) unit of the Department of the Treasury. The incident, while not attached to any substantive policy in particular, raised issues of the quality of the judgment of President Clinton, his Attorney General Janet Reno, and federal law enforcement officials. A public outcry ensued, and charges that the federal government had covered up improper and illegal behavior by federal law enforcement officers dogged the administration. Finally, six years later, in September 1999, a former Republican senator from Missouri, John Danforth, was appointed by Attorney General Reno as a special counsel to investigate what really happened at Waco and whether federal officials had withheld materials from Congress when it investigated the Waco incident in 1995.[4] In this case, the administration was slow to respond to criticism, but after years of seemingly endless criticism, the Clinton administration decided it had to appoint the special counsel to end charges that it had mishandled the Waco incident and its aftermath.

And lastly, unanticipated events may create windows of opportunity for the president to pursue a policy course that was not then being acted on. For instance, on April 21, 1999, several students massacred fellow classmates at Columbine High School in Colorado. The nation was outraged, and this incident, combined with several other highly publicized school shootings during the past several years, left parents fearful for their children's safety at school. After expressing his sympathies and addressing the nation, President Clinton renewed his effort on gun control legislation, which had been languishing in Congress for several years.[5] This effort generated a short burst of momentum in favor of gun control,

[4]Associated Press, "G.O.P. Plans Broader Look at Waco Fire," *New York Times,* 13 September 1999, p. A14.

[5]Jennifer Day. "School Rampage; Speaking at School, Clinton Pushes for More Gun-Control Legislation," *Houston Chronicle,* 23 April 1999, p. A19.

but the bill stalled by midsummer. Then Clinton took another tack. He announced a gun buy-back program in late summer 1999, partially in hope of pressuring Republicans, who controlled Congress, to produce gun control legislation.[6] Notably, in this case, the Columbine High School incident boosted gun control to the top of the president's agenda, but despite intense effort by the president, little concrete policy resulted other than a small $15 million gun buy-back program.

Unanticipated events are important in that they can upset the normal routines of government and the plans that presidents have made regarding what to do. They are a surprise element, but as the Columbine example demonstrates, sometimes they can reinvigorate policies that were going nowhere or appeared dead. While sometimes pressing presidents to take actions that were not planned, unanticipated events can also become opportunities for presidents to lead and to accomplish a policy goal.

The President's Personal Policy Agenda

Presidents may bring with them to office problems that they want to handle. These agenda items have several important sources. First, presidents as individuals have their own sense of the world, what they deem is important. For example, Ronald Reagan felt that the federal government had grown too large, which was hurting the economy, and that the U.S. military had been severely weakened by previous administrations. He was insistent on doing something about these two problems and refused to let himself be diverted from them. In fact, in 1982, when the economy soured and headed into a deep recession, Reagan resisted calls to change his economic policy course despite the fact that his polls were plummeting. Instead, he asked the American public to "stay the course" because his policies would produce a stronger economy and the economic recession was necessary to correct the ills then present in the economy. The economy finally pulled out of the recession in 1983, and its strength in 1984 is credited with Reagan's large reelection victory that year.

George W. Bush, like Ronald Reagan before him, had a strong desire for major tax reform and, like Reagan, was tenacious in holding to such a policy. Cutting taxes and scaling back government have been important policies within the Republican Party historically. Bush saw an opportunity to cut taxes as reports indicated that the government would be running a budget surplus of large proportions for years to come. Budget surpluses exist when government revenue from sources such as taxes is larger than what government spends on programs and on operating the government itself. Bush argued that in the context of large, sustainable surpluses, the public was being overtaxed.

Not everyone agreed with Bush, however, that taxes should be cut. Some felt that the surplus would be better used to pay down the national debt, which had piled up from large deficits that the government ran throughout the 1980s and

---

[6]Chris Mondics. "Clinton Reveals Gun Buy-Back; Urges Tightening of Sales at Shows," *Arizona Republic,* 10 September 1999, p. A8.

most of the 1990s. Deficits are the opposite of surpluses, with government spend-ing outpacing government revenues. Government finances the shortfall by bor-rowing money. This borrowed money is the national debt.

Others felt that the surplus would be better applied to shoring up Social Se-curity or expanding other government programs, such as instituting a drug ben-efit program within Medicare, the medical insurance program for seniors. Polls indicated more support for the debt payment and enhanced government spending options than for the tax cut that Bush favored, and most polls indi-cated that the public favored a tax cut of much smaller proportions than that which Bush favored. One might think that upon being elected, Bush would have compromised his tax cut proposal to align better with public preferences for a smaller tax cut. Democrats in Congress touted such an option. But Bush stuck to his guns.

Events may have interceded to help Bush out. The economy appeared to be stalling after many years of strong growth. Bush then changed tactics in trying to promote his tax cut proposal. Facing a weakening economy, Bush argued that a tax cut could serve to stimulate the economy by putting more money into peo-ple's pockets, which they would then spend on goods and services, giving the economy a boost. Bush even agreed to a retroactive tax rebate for this stimulative effect, even though most of the cuts in his proposal would not take effect for years. Finally, in April 2001, Congress passed a tax cut measure that was almost as large as the one that Bush favored—$1.35 trillion over ten years, compared to Bush's $1.7 trillion. The Reagan and Bush examples show the tenacity of some presidents for some policies or issues that they believe in strongly.

Second, the process of electing presidents may affect the set of problems and issues that presidents bring to office once elected. The election process, while it is about mobilizing voter support, is also a learning process for the presidential candidate. The actions of campaigning bring the candidate into contact with peo-ple who communicate their concerns to the candidate. Moreover, candidates float problems and solutions to prospective voters. Some of those problems and solu-tions will resonate with the public; others will not. Those that do, that seem to help the campaign by rallying voter support behind the candidate, are more likely to be adopted by the candidate as mainstays of the campaign, while those prob-lems and solutions that seem to fall flat and do not evoke a public response tend to be jettisoned. Thus, the search for voter support helps the presidential candi-date sort among the many problems, issues, and solutions that are encountered and raised. Insofar as presidents view themselves as representatives of the peo-ple and their electoral success as being tied to certain issues over others, presi-dents will be predisposed to work on these more "popular" problems than other problems of lesser concern to the voting public.

For example, in his election campaign in 1992, Bill Clinton focused on the economy, which had sunk into a recession in 1991 and seemed slow to pull out of the economic downturn. Clinton found that the economic issue was popular with voters. His campaign headquarters posted a sign to remind the staff of the importance of the issue. The sign read, "It's the economy, stupid." He made economic policy his top priority once he took office, crediting the issue and his stumping on it for his victory.[7]

But Clinton also learned from campaigning that people were concerned about another issue, the cost of health care. Health care costs had been skyrocketing and were taking an increasingly larger bite out of household budgets. Once Clinton set his economic policy in place, he pushed for major health care reform. But Congress failed to approve it, giving Clinton a major policy defeat and harming the reputation of the administration. Some even felt that the Republicans took Congress in the 1994 midterm elections because Clinton pushed on health care, supporting what was styled by critics of the Clinton program as a typical big government Democratic proposal. During much of the debate over the health care reform, Clinton barely budged from his support for universal health care coverage under a government regulatory regime. Perhaps his tenacity for his program came from his campaign, where he learned of public concern with the health issue. But saying that the public is distressed about the state of health care coverage is not the same as saying that the public supported a large-scale government program. Clinton was probably right about public concern but wrong about what the public would support in terms of policy. The larger point is that the process of electing presidents may elevate some issues, as it did with the economy and health care in the Clinton case.[8]

Interest groups, too, may affect the selection of problems for presidential candidates. Interests groups offer several important election resources, including endorsements, campaign workers, and campaign donations. All may be important to the eventual electoral success of a presidential campaign, and in the same ways voters may affect the presidential agenda, interest groups may influence which problems, issues, and solutions presidents spend their time on.

Different types of interests tend to associate with one or the other party. Thus, we find that labor unions, minorities, women, and pro-choice and environmental groups often align with Democrats. Not surprisingly, Democratic presidents have tended to promote policies that those groups favor. In the Republican column, we find big and small business, anti-abortion groups, and the religious right. Republican presidents quite commonly push for policies that groups from this set favors. For example, Ronald Reagan issued a policy through an executive order that prohibited clinics that received federal money from suggesting abortion as an option, which was dubbed as the "gag" rule. Upon taking office in 1993, Bill Clinton reversed the gag rule, a policy that pro-choice groups supported. The party-president-interest group connection probably goes a long way toward explaining why these presidents took the policy stances they did on this issue. Sometimes too an unfriendly interest group or the opposition party may raise an issue to which the president must respond.

[7]See Bob Woodward, *The Agenda: Inside the Clinton White House* (New York: Simon and Schuster, 1994) for the story of Clinton's economy policy.

[8]Clinton's health care proposal has received a lot of attention. For the story of how it captured Clinton's attention, see Jacob S. Hacker, *The Road to Nowhere: The Genesis of President Clinton's Plan for Health Security* (Princeton, N.J.: Princeton University Press, 1996).

Lastly, members of the president's own election campaign, as well as others who offer advice, may be an important source of ideas about problems to deal with. Some advisers look to problems and solutions merely as a way of winning the election. The substance of the problem or solution is less relevant to these election strategists than the electoral benefit that might accrue from pursuing certain issue directions.

Other advisers, in contrast, may have more of a substantive orientation, believing that some problems and issues are more important than others and that the candidate (and president) should select those issues to work on, even if little short-term electoral benefit may be derived from them. Often advisers of this type have special policy expertise, say, in foreign affairs, economics, or another policy area. Consequently, they tend to look at problem selection as more of a substantive policy process than a political or electoral process. Not surprisingly, the division between "election or popularity at any cost" versus "good policy" often arises within presidential administrations and is a major source of intra-administration strife.[9]

A classic example of such a division occurred in the Clinton administration in 1995 and 1996. In 1995, Bill Clinton's presidency was in trouble. He lost the health care reform debate, as we have discussed. Then the Republicans took both houses of Congress, and they began to push for their "Contract with America," a set of ten policies that had been selected because Republican-sponsored polls found them to be popular with the public. One of those policies concerned welfare reform, a policy that Bill Clinton also ran on in 1992, promising to "end welfare as we know it," although Clinton was not precise about what he meant or how he intended to do that.

With the reelection campaign little more than a year away and his prospects for reelection appearing dim, Clinton hired political consultant Dick Morris to devise a campaign strategy aimed at his reelection. Morris was a respected political consultant who had worked for both Democrats and Republicans. Policy expertise was not Morris's strong suit, but election strategy was. Morris designed a strategy called triangulation, in which Clinton would adopt the problems and some of the positions of the opposition, as long as they were popular with the public. Doing this would eliminate the issue as something that the Republicans could use against Clinton in the 1996 election campaign.

Welfare reform was ideally suited to these needs. Welfare reform was popular with the public, Clinton had offered welfare reform in his 1992 campaign, and the Republicans began to hammer at Clinton's inability to produce welfare reform. The Republicans began to push for a policy that would give states more control over some welfare programs and reduce federal influence. Also, the Republican program would limit a person to five years on the welfare rolls (over a lifetime), instead of the unlimited time that had been allowed, and limit continuous welfare eligibility to two years.

[9]Karen Hult, "Strengthening Presidential Decision-Making Capacity," *Presidential Studies Quarterly* 30 (March 2000): 27–46.

Welfare policy experts in the administration criticized the Republican proposal, saying it was not only unfair but also would unduly harm those who would be pushed off of the welfare rolls, because those people lacked the job and other skills to survive. Clinton was sympathetic to the criticism that his welfare experts aimed at the Republican proposal, but he decided to go along with the more sweeping reform. In fact, he strongly presented himself as the proponent of welfare reform. Here, political needs bested policy considerations. Several top welfare experts in the administration resigned in protest, and liberal welfare advocates, often very supportive of the administration, chimed in with their criticisms.[10]

Whether the welfare reform issue aided Clinton's reelection is open to dispute. The economy was strong, and he won handily over Republican Bob Dole, the veteran Kansas senator and 1976 Republican vice presidential candidate. This is a good example of the debate between politics and policy, and the role of advisers of both types in helping to identify problems or issues for the president to address, as well as what types of policy solutions presidents may adopt.

As we see, there are many sources of problems for presidents to work on, from those that are the ongoing activities of government, to unanticipated events, to the president's own policy agenda. The sheer number and scope of problems that seek presidential attention can be overwhelming. No president has the resources, either individual or organizational, to tackle all problems that seek attention. Thus, presidents must choose among the many problems that vie for their attention. They must identify some problems as top priorities, problems on which they will expend time and resources. Other problems will be downgraded, perhaps being deferred until a later time or even forgotten altogether. How problems are prioritized and solutions selected are other important aspects of the presidential policy making process.

BUILDING THE PRESIDENT'S AGENDA: PRIORITIZING PROBLEMS AND ISSUES AND ADOPTING SOLUTIONS

As the discussion of ongoing governmental activities and unanticipated events shows, presidents do not always have a free hand to do whatever they please when it comes to making policy decisions. Very often the problems with which they must deal come to them from unexpected places. One of the difficult and important leadership tasks of the president is to keep control of his policy agenda.[11] How do presidents decide which problems will be high priorities and which will not? And how do presidents find solutions to these priorities?

---

[10]For the welfare policy story, see R. Kent Weaver, *Ending Welfare as We Know It* (Washington, D.C.: Brookings Institution, 2000).

[11]The literature on how presidents build their agendas is growing. Major works include Paul C. Light, *The President's Agenda: Domestic Policy Choice from Kennedy to Clinton* (Baltimore: Johns Hopkins University Press, 1999); Charles O. Jones, *The Presidency in a Separated System* (Washington, D.C.: Brookings Institution, 1994); and Jeffrey E. Cohen, *Presidential Responsiveness and Public Policy Making: The Public and the Policies That Presidents Choose* (Ann Arbor: University of Michigan Press, 1997). The classic study of the origins and institutionalization of the president's program is Richard E. Neustadt, "Presidency and Legislation: Planning the President's Program," *American Political Science Review* 49 (December 1955): 980–1021.

Prioritizing the Policy Agenda

Several factors will determine the **priority** that a problem or issue will receive. These boil down to basically three categories: the importance of the problem, the president's goals, and the availability of policy solutions. Simply put, important problems that meet the president's goals and have solutions are more likely to be high administration priorities than problems that do not possess these characteristics.

Problem Importance   What makes a problem important? Importance may be viewed through both an objective as well as a perceptual lens.[12] Objectively, importance often refers to how many people a problem affects. The more people affected, the more important and thus the higher the priority for that problem. Therefore, issues of whether or not to enter a war or the state of the national economy, problems and issues that affect the entire population, commonly attain the highest priority.

A problem may also be thought to be important, based on objective criteria, when its effects are thought to be consequential, as opposed to modest or trivial. Nothing is likely to be more consequential than loss of life. Hence, we return to the importance of foreign policy, military action, and the prospect of war as important problems. Similarly, problems that affect the economic standard of living and quality of life are also highly likely to be thought of as important. Again, the state of the national economy, as well as problems such as environmental pollution and health care, usually are considered to be important. Problems that have consequential effects, and affect large numbers of people are particularly attractive to presidents; such problems are hard to keep off of the president's priority list.

Thus, we can understand why Ronald Reagan emphasized economic policy and defense as opposed to other issues when he became president. The same can be said of economic policy and health care reform for Bill Clinton. But saying that presidents are attracted to significant problems that affect large numbers of people does not imply that they will not attend to problems of lesser consequence or importance. But rather, these big and consequential problems will often easily become presidential priorities.

At times, presidents may try to resist being dragged into a problem that is big or potentially big. A good case in point is George W. Bush and the issue of high electricity prices in California. In the late 1990s, California deregulated much of its electrical utility industry. The hope was that market forces would be more efficient in supplying energy at a better price. But several forces converged in 2000 that rapidly boosted the price of energy in California, and many feared increasing prices into the future. Some attributed the rise in energy prices to the deregulation policy itself, which energy companies took advantage of by selling their energy outside of California, where prices were higher. This created shortages in the California markets, which put pressure on prices. But other forces were also at work,

---

[12]On the importance of problems, see Deborah Stone, *Policy Paradox and Political Reason* (Glenview, Ill.: Scott Foresman, 1988); Jack L. Walker, "Setting the Agenda in the U.S. Senate," *British Journal of Political Science* 7 (October 1977): 423–45; and Kingdon, *Agendas, Alternatives.*

including the strong and rapidly growing economy, which increased demands for energy. Also a hot summer in 2000 led to increased air conditioner use, which added to the demand for electrical energy. Bush resisted calls to cap energy prices, something that only the federal government and its regulators had the authority to do. First of all, California went for Al Gore and not George Bush in 2000, which may have reduced his sympathy for the state. But Bush also saw the issue as a state one, not a national one, and he preferred to let markets correct the problem, rather than use federal regulatory authority, which he and some of his supporters in the energy industry tended to dislike. Bush talked about energy in his presidential election campaign, but his perspective was to increase the supply of energy and make the United States less dependent on foreign energy sources. His idea was to allow U.S. energy companies greater access to potential energy sources within the United States, sources that were being denied to them because of environmental and other regulations. This included a large tract of land in northern Alaska, the Arctic National Wildlife Refuge, which was protected by statute.

Bush felt that getting involved in the California issue would embroil him in a no-win situation. California's governor, Gray Davis, a Democrat, was hurting in the polls because of the issue, a situation that would favor a Republican opponent. Equally important, entering the California energy issue would divert Bush and the public from his energy policy, which emphasized increasing domestic supply. Thus, for a host of reasons, Bush resisted engaging in an issue that possessed many of the marks of an issue that presidents naturally get involved in. Luckily for Bush, pressure on him to intercede in California waned as prices dropped due to the slowing economy, a cooler summer in 2001 reduced demand for air conditioning, and energy companies increased power supplies to California, perhaps fearing stronger governmental action against them.

Policy importance may also be defined through a perceptual lens. Thus, some people will think that a problem is important, while others will not. Defining a problem's importance by objective criteria usually means that most people agree on the relevance of the "objective criteria." However, a problem may be important not by an objective standard but because some people perceive it to be important.

What might make a president perceive a problem to be important that does not possess the earmarks of objective standards? First, presidents, by their location in government, may possess more information about a problem than the general public or even members of Congress. The veil of secrecy that surrounds so much foreign policy often keeps a problem out of public view but on the president's radar screen. Consequently, it may take presidential leadership to convince the public that a problem is consequential. Sometimes presidents are successful in leading the public, as George H. W. Bush was when Iraq invaded Kuwait, but there are many occasions when presidents are not able to convince the public that a problem is as important as they say. Jimmy Carter was often faced with public skepticism and cynicism as he tried to raise the issues of energy shortages and conservation.[13]

---

[13]On the ability of presidents to increase public concern with problems and issues, see Cohen, *Presidential Responsiveness.*

Also, if the public thinks that a problem is important, presidents are likely to as well. Presidents are apt to be responsive to the public this way for several reasons. First, the idea that the president is the nation's representative creates a motivation for presidents to respond when large segments of the public see a problem as important. Second, presidents may feel that if they are not responsive, it will come to haunt them by reducing their popularity or harming their chances for reelection.

Historically, the economy and foreign policy have been the two most important problems to the mass public. Polls show that this is the case most of the time. From time to time, the Gallup Poll has asked people what they think is the most important problem facing the nation. On figure 13-1, the line marked "Public" adds together the percentage of poll respondents mentioning an economic or a foreign policy problem from 1953 through 1989. For almost every year in the series, more than 50 percent identify either an economic or foreign policy problem as being the most important. On only two occasions, 1964 and 1969, did less than 50 percent of the poll respondents cite economic or foreign policy. In 1969, the total was nearly that high at 48 percent. The figure for 1964 was only 37 percent, but that was an unusual year, with civil rights cited by nearly one-half of the respondents as the nation's most important problem.

Figure 13-1 also traces presidential attention to these two policy areas in State of the Union speeches. We can assume that presidents will talk more about issues that are important to them, while less important issues will receive less presidential attention. To arrive at the "presidential" line on figure 13-1, the number of sentences that mention economic or foreign policy issues are added together, and that total is divided by the total number of sentences that refer to policies. This gives us a presidential attention percentage, which we can compare with the public attention percentage. Looking at figure 13-1, which displays both of these trend lines, shows how clearly they track each other. (The Gallup polls come from the most recent poll before the president's speech. Thus, we can suggest that presidents are following public opinion and not leading it.)[14] While the correspondence between how important a problem is to the public and the amount of attention that a president pays to that issue is not perfect, it is remarkably close, given that so many elements factor into the president's decision to rank an issue as a high priority.

Presidential Goals   Beyond the importance of an issue, whether defined objectively or perceptually, presidents may select problems because of their goals. Three major **presidential goals** are often identified: electoral-popularity goals, policy goals, and historical-reputational goals.[15]

---

[14]The correlation between the two series is .42, which is statistically significant. For more on these data and the relationship between public opinion and presidential policy choice, see Cohen, *Presidential Responsiveness*, pp. 31–53.

[15]This borrows heavily from Light, *President's Agenda*.

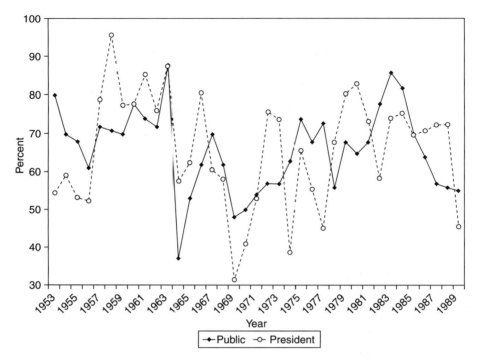

FIGURE 13-1
Presidential and Public Attention to the Economy and Foreign Policy, 1953–1989

Presidents in their first term commonly strive for reelection to a second term, and throughout their tenures, presidents prefer to be popular than unpopular. Just as the popular appeal of a problem or issue in an election campaign may lead presidents to adopt the problem, so too may similar popularity factors lead presidents to elevate a problem to high-priority status once in office.

A second goal that may motivate presidential selection of policy priorities is presidents' sense of desirable public policy. Presidents often bring to office a sense of what they would like to accomplish. As noted, Ronald Reagan wanted to reduce the size of government, which he viewed as a burden, and to restore the military, which he felt had been weakened. Consequently, these two problems were his highest priorities. And as the economy slipped into a deep recession in 1982 and 1983, in part because of Reagan's economic policies, Reagan refused to abandon them and instead urged the country to "stay the course," intoning that the economy would improve if given the time. Few presidents are as loyal and persistent to a set of ideas as Reagan.

Lastly, some presidents are motivated by a sense of history, by a sense of the legacy that they might leave the country. For example, Lyndon Johnson judged that his support for civil rights policy would cost him fifteen points in the polls but that his "grandchildren would be proud of what he had done for blacks."[16] Bill Clinton's push for major health care reform may have stemmed from a similar motivation: wanting to leave a major mark on American society and perhaps even wanting to be compared with Franklin Roosevelt and Lyndon Johnson, other presidents credited with establishing important social reforms.

Available Solutions   Presidents may decide not to pursue a problem because no good policy solution exists.[17] A policy solution might not exist for several reasons. The first is the lack of technology. Many problems are not even thought to be legitimate public concerns because the technology necessary to resolve or alleviate them does not exist.

Second, when the public is not in the right policy mood, an acceptable solution may not exist either.[18] The public tends to cycle over time from being somewhat conservative to somewhat liberal in its policy inclinations. It is most unlikely that the public will accept a solution that is at odds with (the) prevailing (public) sentiment. Presidents, and other politicians, want to avoid defeat and thus are not likely to propose solutions that run against the public mood.

Of course, presidents and candidates for the presidency have offered policy solutions at variance with public sentiment. In 1984, Democratic presidential candidate Walter Mondale tried to convince the public that tax increases were needed to reduce the ballooning federal budget deficit. According to many observers, Ronald Reagan soundly trounced him in the election because of that stance, although tax increases did follow, as Mondale predicted. And Bill Clinton suffered a major defeat of his health care reform initiative, which emphasized a greater federal government role in providing and regulating health care, when it ran into public sentiments that opposed bigger government.

In general, though, successful politicians are able to sense what the public will accept and thus tend not to propose solutions too far afield from that. Recall, Mondale was defeated, and Clinton regrouped, paying very close attention to prevailing winds of public opinion. With welfare reform, as we discussed in the section "The President's Personal Policy Agenda," Clinton finally accepted and supported relatively conservative reforms. Thus, presidents often avoid placing problems as high priorities when no available or acceptable policy solution exists, either because of a lack of technology or because the public mood is not supportive of a solution alternative.

Selecting Solutions

Once the president has prioritized the problems that he will deal with, how does he go about selecting the policy solutions to address those problems? We have already remarked that the absence of solutions often keeps a problem from being

[16]Cited in Stephen Skowronek, *The Politics That Presidents Make: Leadership from John Adams to George Bush* (Cambridge: Belknap Press, 1993), p. 340.

[17]On the importance of available solutions, see Kingdon, *Agendas, Alternatives.*

[18]On the public mood, see Kingdon, *Agendas, Alternatives,* and James A. Stimson, *Public Opinion in America: Moods, Cycles, and Swings* (Boulder, Colo.: Westview, 1991).

TABLE 13-1 PRESIDENTIAL LIBERALISM, 1953–1989

President (Party)	Percentage liberal
Eisenhower (R)	65.7
Kennedy (D)	83.1
Johnson (D)	66.9
Nixon (R)	35.1
Ford (R)	25.9
Carter (D)	56.6
Reagan (R)	10.4
Bush (R)	37.3

Source: Jeffrey E. Cohen, *Presidential Responsiveness and Public Policy Making: The Public and the Policies That Presidents Choose* (Ann Arbor: University of Michigan Press, 1997), p. 252.

viewed as a high priority. And we have stressed the constraints on presidential policy making, at least in selecting problems to work on. Although constraints exist in selecting policy solutions, presidents seem here to have some greater degree of personal choice than in problem selection.

The president's own political beliefs and ideas, the political context, and the advice that he receives all affect the solutions that he selects when addressing a problem.[19] The president's own beliefs and ideas are of greater importance in selecting solutions than in selecting problems to work on, and presidents may often discount the political context, that is, the public mood, because they believe that they can lead the public to accept their solutions to a problem.

Presidential Beliefs Many presidents come to office with definite beliefs about public policy. The stronger those beliefs, the greater the likelihood that those beliefs will affect the policy solutions that presidents adopt. Thus, we have mentioned the tenacity of Ronald Reagan with regard to his economic policy. Because of his strongly held beliefs, he refused to change course despite a faltering economy in 1982.

According to two researchers, almost all policy solutions can be identified as more or less liberal or conservative.[20] Liberals tend to support greater government involvement in a policy solution, while conservatives tend to prefer less government and more reliance on markets and individuals to solve problems. Some presidents veer in the liberal direction, while others hold a more conservative stance, and still others stand between these two opposites; these we will call moderates.

In general, Democrats have been liberal and Republicans conservative. Table 13-1 lists the liberalism scores of presidents Eisenhower through George H. W. Bush. These figures come from the State of the Union address sentences that we

[19]Light, *President's Agenda.*

[20]Keith T. Poole and Howard Rosenthal, *Congress: A Political-Economic History of Roll Call Voting* (New York: Oxford University Press, 1996).

discussed as part of figure 13-1. Each sentence that mentions a policy or issue was classified as liberal, conservative, or neither. The number of liberal sentences compared to the total of liberal and conservative sentences gives us a percentage liberal score.

We see from this table that the Democrats all lean in the liberal direction (we can view 50 as the midpoint between liberal and conservative). Kennedy is most liberal here, with a score of over 80, while Johnson trails at 67 and Carter at 57. Johnson's score is lower than Kennedy's only because of Vietnam. Without Vietnam included, Johnson equals Kennedy in his liberal tendencies. Carter is another story. Where Carter took traditionally liberal positions on foreign and civil rights policy, he was less liberal in economic policy. Carter's moderate stance on economic policy was one major source of strife with the Democrats who controlled Congress at the time.

In contrast to the liberal leanings of Democratic presidents, Republicans lean in a conservative direction. This is most clear with Reagan, who scores a 10, while Nixon, Ford, and Bush are all conservative, although less extreme than Reagan. Eisenhower may be an anomaly here, with a score that is more liberal than conservative. In fact, his score of 66 is almost the same as Johnson's and ten points more liberal than Carter's! How can this be? Just like Carter, Eisenhower was liberal on some issues and conservative on others. His economic policy preferences squared within Republican conservatism, but he held more liberal views on foreign affairs.

Bill Clinton is another interesting case. Some have accused him of being a Republican but calling himself a Democrat, pointing, for instance, to his support for conservative welfare reforms as an indication of his conservativeness. Others, in contrast, point to his health care program and support for gays in the military as evidence that he is a liberal. It is perhaps best to characterize Clinton as moderate, in the sense that he willingly would adopt either a liberal or conservative policy solution, depending in part on political circumstances more than political belief.

At times, presidents change their views on public policy issues. For example, Clinton accepted conservative approaches on welfare, probably more because of political needs than because of his orientations toward policy solutions. Richard Nixon is an even more unusual case, especially with regard to economic policy. Nixon came to office with relatively set ideas about economic policy, following traditional Republican approaches that stress less government and freer markets. However, in 1971, he changed course radically, instituting wage-price controls, the most extreme form of regulation and a policy never before used in the United States, except during war.

Nixon here seemed to display a higher regard for political needs than policy conviction. Inflation was heating up, the United States had important balance of payments issues with foreign nations, Nixon's polls were dropping, and the presidential election campaign was only a year away. These factors, in combination, may have led Nixon to the wage-price control policy. But we may also see here a president who is not so wedded to an idea that he is unwilling to try something new to solve a problem. It may be the case that Nixon truly believed that wage-price control policy would solve the nation's emerging economic problems, although most historians and scholars of the Nixon presidency do not believe that theory, instead viewing him more as a political opportunist.[21] The Nixon case is instructive, however, because it demonstrates that when a president does not possess firmly held beliefs about a policy, he is apt to change his views on the policy when circumstances or other considerations change.

The Political Context   Even presidents with strong beliefs about policy will sometimes be swayed by the political context, and presidents known for political compromise might stick to a policy line. For example, Ronald Reagan refused to support means testing for Social Security benefits—the idea that the rich should get lower benefits than the poor because they do not need it. Means testing was compatible with some conservative ideas, especially those that would reduce or contain the size of government. But Reagan decided against any scaling back of Social Security benefits because of the popularity of the program. Perhaps no governmental program is as popular as Social Security, and Reagan feared that any attempt to limit it would be politically disastrous. Thus, Reagan decided against one policy solution that was compatible with his belief that government was too big.[22]

In contrast, Bill Clinton, who conventional accounts assert often seemed to have his finger on the public pulse and would do little without strong public backing, did not back down on the policy of allowing gays to serve in the military, despite strong public opposition.[23] Why did Clinton refuse to back down and take the political heat, even encountering political opposition from some of the most respected leaders of his party in Congress as well as most of the higher ranks of the military? Without being definitive, it might be that Clinton believed in the right of gays to serve in the military. Another possible answer is that Clinton received campaign support from gays and thus during the campaign committed himself to this policy course. Finally, under intense political pressure, the administration concocted the "Don't Ask, Don't Tell" policy, which preserved the right of gays to serve although not as openly as many gay activists preferred. Here, we see two elements of the political context that might affect presidential solution choice—the public mood, as we have discussed, and campaign commitments.

[21]Allen J. Matusow, *Nixon's Economy: Booms, Busts, Dollars, and Votes* (Lawrence: University Press of Kansas, 1998).

[22]Paul C. Light, *Still Artful Work: The Continuing Politics of Social Security Reform* (New York: McGraw-Hill, 1994).

[23]Actually, considerable debate exists on just how responsive Bill Clinton was to public opinion. One argument contends that Clinton was obsessed with public opinion, not to follow it but to find out about public beliefs so that he would be better able to lead the public to follow his policy choices. See Larry R. Jacobs and Robert Y. Shapiro, *Politicians Don't Pander* (Chicago: University of Chicago Press, 2000). For a related argument that presidents do not follow the public's substantive policy preferences, see Cohen, *Presidential Responsiveness*.

Advice   As we discussed in Chapter 9, presidents now have at their disposal a large staff apparatus that can supply them with information and advice on policy alternatives and their political implications. However, we should note that presidents always have sought advice, and the fact of the large staff operation in the White House Office, Executive Office of the President, and the bureaucracy should not imply that modern presidents rely more on advice than presidents of earlier times.

Very early in the Republic's history, George Washington sought policy advice from both members of Congress and the Supreme Court. Both institutions refused to serve as formal advisers to the president, cautioning Washington about the separation of powers and the independence of each branch from the others. Thus, Washington built an executive branch advising apparatus by convening a cabinet, composed of the people whom he had appointed to head the several government departments then in existence. Alexander Hamilton became, perhaps, the most important of these advisers.

Andrew Jackson, who operated in a political context in which elections had become more important, collected advice more informally than Washington in what has been termed his **kitchen cabinet.** While this set of individuals, who tended to be long-time associates and friends of Jackson, surely offered policy advice, their forte was to advise on the political consequences of actions.

In the 1930s, before the development of the EOP, FDR collected a **brain trust,** a set of advisers across the whole spectrum of policy and politics. FDR's "brain trusters" often were long-time associates and political allies, but others were just very bright people whom FDR brought into government to help him with the dilemmas posed by the Great Depression.

Our major point is that presidents have always sought advice but the advising system, even today, is very fluid, as presidents can shape it to some extent to meet their needs. In general, it appears that presidential reliance on advice, whether from staff or other sources, increases as presidential interest and knowledge about a policy area declines. By way of example, Richard Nixon prided himself on his knowledge and understanding of international politics. Thus, even though Henry Kissinger, his secretary of State, was an influential voice in foreign policy making, in the areas of domestic and especially economic policy, where Nixon was less interested and schooled, we see the influence of advisers increasing. Presidents differ in terms of which policy areas they hold an interest in and possess knowledge of. Hence, across presidents, we will see differences by policy area in regard to the role and influence of advisers; when presidents display the interest and possess the knowledge about a policy area, they often will rely on advisers less, reserving decision making to themselves.

Presidents also will differ in how much attention they will pay to political as opposed to policy advice. Often advisers from the two realms differ. Political advisers tend to lack the knowledge and familiarity with specific policy problems and issues, and thus tend to be unable to suggest policy alternatives. Rather, they will focus on the political implications of policy actions and decisions. In mirror-like fashion, policy experts will often be less attuned to political implications, focusing instead on policy outcomes. Unfortunately, good policy is not always the same as good politics, and presidents will differ in how much play they will give to political versus policy considerations.

Ronald Reagan, because he came to office with a definite set of ideas about public policy, usually focused on policy over politics. In part, this derived from his belief that his policies would work well and would in time become popular. For Reagan, good policy made for good politics. Jimmy Carter initially began his term of office with a similar belief. However, Carter was less fortunate than Reagan. His policies did not appear to the public to be effective, nor were they particularly popular. As the administration aged, Carter turned from policy emphasis to a greater appreciation of political implications, but he was still unable to generate politically appealing policies. This is one reason he was defeated for reelection and Reagan was reelected.

Organizing Advising Systems for the President   Is there a best way to organize presidential advisers and staff? Although the entrenchment of the institutionalized presidency, with its large staff, compels the president to attend to some job duties that he might otherwise forego, when it comes to advising systems, which we should view as a subset of presidential staff, presidents pretty much organize their policy and political advisers in the way that they feel best suits their needs and working style.

Beginning with FDR, three basic advising styles have been used. The lack of staff prior to Roosevelt's presidency makes discussion about advising styles of earlier presidents less pertinent. The three styles have been called the 1) **competitive,** 2) **collegial,** and 3) **hierarchical** (see figure 13-2).[24]

FDR exemplifies the competitive approach to organizing his advisers, and no president since has used such a pattern in such a pure form. The basic structure of competitive advising puts advisers into direct competition with each other. They may, for instance, hold overlapping authority and sometimes differing policy views. At times, FDR would also give the competitors contradictory assignments. Competitive advising creates conflict and disagreement across advisers. To resolve their differences, the competitors would often seek a resolution from the president.

Thus, information would find its way to the president, who would act as final arbiter. Such information would likely be highly reliable, as competitors have no reason to hide from the president their gripes or criticisms about their rivals. The competitive approach assumes that each person will transmit only positive information about themselves to their superiors but will send critical information about competitors. FDR felt that such a system was necessary to ensure that he would

---

[24]The original formulation comes from Richard Tanner Johnson, *Managing the White House: An Intimate Study of the Presidency* (New York: Harper and Row, 1974). These managerial styles are discussed and critiqued in John P. Burke, *The Institutional Presidency* (Baltimore: Johns Hopkins University Press, 1992), pp. 3–115. For an application to several presidencies, see Robert J. Thompson, "Contrasting Models of White House Staff Organization: The Eisenhower, Ford, and Carter Experiences," *Congress and the Presidency* 19 (Autumn 1992): 113–36.

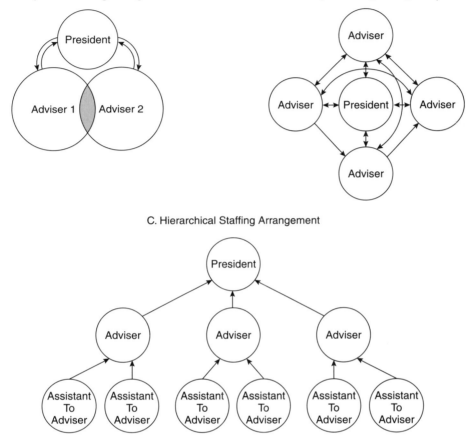

A. Competitive Staffing Arrangement

B. Collegial Staffing Arrangement

C. Hierarchical Staffing Arrangement

FIGURE 13-2
Presidential Staffing Systems

receive the best and most reliable information possible but also that he would re-main the final decision point in any dispute. The competitive system, thus, would maximize FDR's knowledge and control over the people who worked for him.

The competitive advising system places great burdens on the president, con-suming his time and energy. As government has grown, it may not be possible for such a system to operate effectively without overloading the president. In fact, many complained about FDR's approach to advising during the Second World War, and over time FDR's competitive approach gave way to a more structured method of advising presidents.

The hierarchical staff model differs fundamentally from the competitive ap-proach. Eisenhower has often been thought of as using the hierarchical style, modeling on the military chain of command system with which he was so familiar. Here, the lines of communication are channeled and structured. Subordinates communicate to their superiors, and these superiors communicate up the chain of command to their superiors until one reaches the president himself. As information is communicated from the bottom to the top, details are filtered out and information from one level is integrated and summarized at the next higher level. Only information that is deemed of significance to the president is transmitted to the next level. In this system, presidents control subordinates through command, that is, giving orders to be carried out by personnel at the next lower level.

The hierarchical model places fewer demands on presidential time and energy, preserving these resources for decision making rather than for resolving intrastaff conflict and gathering information—the hallmarks of the competitive approach. The major problem with the hierarchical model is that information that might be important to the president might not reach him, as it is filtered out. Especially, information on failure and problems is likely to be filtered out, as people have few incentives to transmit information that may reflect poorly on them. Also, information might not reach the president because subordinates want to protect the chief executive. Because staff may withhold information out of either self-interest or loyalty, presidents using a hierarchical advising system might be information-deficient and become isolated. Unlike the competitive approach, which maximizes presidential contacts, the hierarchical system tends to minimize or reduce presidential contact with others.

The third approach has been termed collegial and was first associated with John Kennedy. Kennedy reacted to the demands, conflict, and inefficiency of FDR's competitive approach and to the limited information basis of Eisenhower's hierarchical model. He sought a system that would retain the president's access to information while reducing the tensions of the competitive model.

The collegial approach has often been characterized as a spokes-in-the-wheel system, with the president as the center and advisers ringing around him. Rather than spur competition, the collegial system creates incentives for cooperation and teamwork. Brainstorming is emphasized, and advisers are treated as equals. However, like the competitive approach, collegial advising may be highly inefficient, absorbing lots of presidential time and energy.

And unlike competitive advising systems, collegial systems may become prone to groupthink. **Groupthink** is a tendency for advisers to adopt the same policy, to think alike, and usually not to question the policy that has emerged as the consensus position. Thus, groupthink is characterized by high levels of adviser identification with each other and with the advising group, along with low levels of criticism or disagreement.[25] The collegial system, which encourages advisers to

[25]The original discussion of groupthink can be found in Irving Janus, *Victims of Groupthink: A Psychological Study of Foreign-Policy Decisions and Fiascoes* (Boston: Houghton, Mifflin, 1972). On groupthink in the Johnson administration, see Kevin V. Mulcahy, "Rethinking Groupthink: Walt Rostow and the National Security Advisory Process in the Johnson Administration," *Presidential Studies Quarterly* 25 (Spring 1995): 237–50. For an argument that groupthink was not pervasive in the Johnson White House, see David M. Barrett, "The Mythology Surrounding Lyndon Johnson, His Advisers, and the 1965 Decision to Escalate the Vietnam War," *Political Science Quarterly* 103 (Winter 1988–89): 637–63.

work as a team and downplays individual competition for power and influence, is a major source of groupthink. The problem with groupthink is that the best policy option may not be followed because advisers give agreement and working together a higher priority than developing the best policy option, which might entail intragroup discord, criticism, and disagreement.

Presidents, advisers, and scholars have looked for a solution that would keep a lid on disruptive conflict among presidential advisers yet provide the president with several possible policy options, each backed up with sound reasoning and information.[26] **Multiple advocacy** has been offered as one such approach. In multiple advocacy arrangements, different advisers take on the task of advocating different policy options. It is important to note that in multiple advocacy arrangements, the power and influence of an adviser are not to be tied to whether his or her policy option is adopted but rather to the quality of the advice presented to the president. In some instances, a person may be assigned the role of "devil's advocate," in which the person's task is to try to attack, undermine, and reveal the problems and pitfalls of the policy option that seems most popular and most likely to be adopted by the president.

One difficulty in implementing a multiple advocacy staffing system is that it requires a president who is able to select a policy course from several that are presented to him. In other words, a decisive president is needed. Second, the president must also be competent to handle the information provided to him in making his policy choice. Presidents with little understanding or interest in a policy or the policy options presented might not be well suited to using multiple advocacy for that particular policy area. Third, for multiple advocacy systems to work, presidents must be open to a variety of information. The firmer the president's preconceived beliefs about a policy and how to handle it, the less impact multiple advocacy arrangements will have on presidential decision making, in part because advisers may be afraid to challenge the president's beliefs.

Also, to be effective, a multiple advocacy system must have the right kind of advisers. Its effectiveness does not totally rely on the president. In particular, advisers must be secure enough to present options that might not be adopted. In other words, they must be secure enough in themselves, their political careers, and their relationship with the president to propose and support an option that might not be adopted and may thus make them appear to be on the losing side. Getting advisers to play such a role in a political environment such as that in Washington, D.C., which places so much emphasis on winning, is not easy.

Clearly, each advising system has its pluses and minuses. No ideal way seems to exist to organize advice for the president. Hence, presidents tend to adopt the system that seems to best suit their styles, personalities, and preferences.[27] In gen-

---

[26]Alexander George, "The Case for Multiple Advocacy in Foreign Policy," *American Political Science Review*, 66 (September 1972): 751–85. On presidential attempts to use multiple advocacy, see Alexander Moens, "The Carter Administration and Multiple Advocacy," *International Journal* 45 (Autumn 1990): 913–48.

[27]On the inability to be able to apply one staffing style for all presidents and all occasions, see Bruce Buchanan, "Constrained Diversity: The Organizational Demands of the Presidency," *Presidential Studies Quarterly* 20 (Fall 1990): 791–822.

eral, Democrats tend to be predisposed to using the collegial approach while Republicans show a penchant for the hierarchical model.

Flexibility in advising systems seems to be what is called for, that is, organizing the advising system that is optimal for each case that crops up. Although preferring to operate normally with a hierarchical system, Eisenhower would break out of that structure and seek information independent of the chain of command when the occasion called for it.

Still, it is not clear that how a president organizes his advising system has much impact on the quality of decisions, although such organizational styles do affect the processes of decision making.[28] Politics and the president's personal preferences will have the biggest impact on the substance of policy decision making. Advising is important in providing information that may help presidents weigh the alternatives that come to them. When solid scientific and technical information exists about the consequences of an alternative, such information is likely to be incorporated into presidential decision making. When uncertainty about consequences exists, no organizing process can act as a substitute, and under such uncertainty presidents are likely to fall back on what they believe to be the best alternative. Here again, presidential preferences will loom large in selecting solutions to policy problems.

CYCLES IN PRESIDENTIAL POLICY MAKING

One theme that permeates this chapter is that presidents do not have complete discretion in deciding what to do. The expectations of others, such as the public and Congress, as well as statutory requirements, force a certain proportion of presidential activity. Political and policy forces may compel presidents to select some problems over others when building their policy agendas. Presidents seem to have the greatest discretion and freedom of choice in selecting policy solutions, but even here, they are constrained by political forces, uncertainty about the consequences of many policy solutions, and the problems associated with different advising arrangements.

One of the greatest hindrances to effective policy making is that fact that despite the large staffing structure, each new administration begins anew. Little learning is transmitted from one administration to the next, in part because there is no permanent staff for the presidency at the highest levels (although at lower levels, there are career people, especially in the OMB). The positions of the institutional presidency tend to remain intact, but the people in those positions change with each new president, if not faster. For instance, Reagan had seven national security advisers in his eight years as president. Although that is an extreme case, turnover is rapid of even highly placed people in the administration.

One factor that improves decision making is experience. As presidents often cannot or do not seem to be able to use the experience of previous administrations as a guide, most presidential learning occurs within administrations. One

[28]Bert A. Rockman, "Organizing the White House: On a West Wing and a Prayer," *Journal of Managerial Issues* 5 (Winter 1978): 453–64.

barrier to learning from previous administrations is that the new president often defeated an incumbent president (or the nominee of the party that had held the White
House) to assume office. A new administration is likely to scoff at a predecessor
that it defeated in the election. Also, the personalization of the office usually requires that a president who succeeds one from his own party must still distinguish
himself and carve out a new identity. For both of these reasons, then, learning
mostly occurs within administrations, not across.

If learning—that is, experience—improves presidential policy making, then the
longer the president is in office, the better the decisions that will be made. Ineffective policies and decisions will more likely be avoided, and politically unpopular or risky approaches will be taken less often. Thus, we can talk of a **cycle of
increasing effectiveness** of presidential policy making.

But many presidents also seem to face a **cycle of decreasing resources.**
That is, as their administrations age, the resources that are so necessary to gain
acceptance of presidential policies dwindle. For instance, the president's party
almost always loses seats in Congress during the midterm election. Second, most
presidents also have lower popularity later in their administrations than earlier.
And as the presidential clock ticks and the time in office runs down, Congress
and the bureaucracy may delay acting on presidential policies with the hopes
that the president will leave office before it has to act. Time is a precious resource, and the two-term limitation greatly restricts this resource to presidents.
Thus, just as presidents are getting better at their job, they are less able to get
people to follow their lead.

If this is true, then we can offer some policy advice to presidents and learn
something about the quality of policy making in American government. First, if
presidents are to get anything accomplished in terms of policy, they must act fast,
while they still possess the resources to influence the political system and persuade people to follow their lead. This "move it or lose it" advice also means that
presidents do not have the time to reflect and build better policy.[29] One consequence is that the policies likely to be implemented may not be as good as they
could be and may create as many problems as they seek to solve. If popular discontent with American government is due to the ineffectiveness of policy, then
one cause of such ineffective policy might be this convergence of these two cycles that affect the presidency: increasing effectiveness but decreasing resources.

PRESIDENTS AS THE ENGINE OF POLICY CHANGE: MANDATES FOR CHANGE AND INNOVATIVE CHANGE

At least since Franklin Roosevelt, presidents have been thought to be a major source
of policy change. The election of a new president to office is an opportunity for changing the nation's policy course. A new president builds a new administration, replacing his predecessor's appointees, even when that predecessor was of the same party.

---

[29]Light, *President's Agenda;* and James Pfiffner, *The Strategic Presidency: Hitting the Ground Running,* 2d ed. (Lawrence: University Press of Kansas, 1996).

This influx of new people may bring new ideas. Also, the election of a new president marks a symbolic starting over. Even a president who succeeds one from his own party may decide that his election allows him to redirect the policies and tone of his predecessor. Upon taking the oath of office in 1989, George H. W. Bush intoned that his administration would be "kinder and gentler," a vague reference to Ronald Reagan, whose administration was often characterized as extreme and doctrinaire. Lastly, the election of a new president may mark change in public opinion. New issues may have cropped up, and the public mood may have shifted. A new president may be thought to bring to office these new public sensibilities.

This is the standard view of presidents and policy change. But not each new president tries to promote much policy change. Some opt to maintain the status quo, and others may not have the opportunities and resources to change policy direction, no matter how much they might want to. In this concluding section of this chapter, we will discuss two factors that influence whether presidents can stimulate policy change or not: whether they think that they have a mandate, and trends over the past several decades that have dampened the president's ability to promote significant policy change.

Mandates and Change

A **mandate** is a claim by an elected politician that the public wants him or her to change existing policy.[30] Politicians love to be able to claim a mandate because it suggests that they are acting as the representative of their constituents, which is the entire nation in the case of the president. With such public backing, it is hard for other politicians to resist the president's call for change.

Not every president, however, can or does claim a mandate for change. For instance, neither John F. Kennedy in 1961 nor Jimmy Carter in 1977 nor George H. W. Bush in 1989 claimed a mandate for significant policy change. In contrast, Lyndon Johnson in 1965, Ronald Reagan in 1981, Bill Clinton in 1993, and George W. Bush in 2001 all claimed a mandate to change policy.

One would guess that because the party of the presidency changed hands from Republican to Democrat with Kennedy's election, Kennedy would claim a mandate for change. Two circumstances dictated otherwise. First, he won with less than 50 percent of the vote, when third-party votes are included, and his lead over Richard Nixon, the Republican candidate, was slim, less than 1 percent. In no way could he say that he had strong public backing. Second, the Democrats in the House lost twenty seats with the election of Kennedy, and Democrats in the Senate picked up only one seat. House Democrats, thus, looked upon Kennedy as he entered office as perhaps more of a liability than an asset. Under these circumstances, Kennedy could not claim a mandate for change.

Jimmy Carter, like Kennedy, ushered in a change in the party controlling the White House, but his election victory also was narrow. He won barely 50 percent

[30]Patricia Heidotting Conley, *Presidential Mandates: How Elections Shape the National Agenda* (Chicago: University of Chicago Press, 2001).

of the popular vote, and his lead over Gerald Ford was a modest 2 percent. More-over, House and Senate Democrats picked up only one seat in each chamber. Carter's election did not strengthen the Democratic Party. In most districts, Carter actually ran behind members running for election to Congress. In these senses, Carter too was seen as a liability.

For different reasons, George H. W. Bush did not claim a mandate. First, he won a strong electoral victory over Michael Dukakis, 53.4 percent to 45.6 percent, nearly an eight-point lead. But Congress remained in Democratic hands at nearly the same seat ratios as before. Equally important, Bush won election in part because of the success of the Reagan administration, where he served as vice president. Bush could not repudiate Reagan's policies, although he still had to distinguish himself from Reagan. He did this by offering himself as a moderate version of Reagan.

Mandate-claiming presidents tend to enter office with a large electoral victory. This was the case for Johnson in 1965 and Reagan in 1981. Also, under Reagan, Republicans gained control of the Senate, which many pointed to as another in-dication of Reagan's popular and political appeal.

Clinton, like Kennedy, won with less than 50 percent of the vote in a three-way race, and his lead over Bush, the incumbent, was only about 5.5 percent. Then why did Clinton, who received only 43 percent of the vote, claim a mandate? The primary reason was that the position of the Democrats in government improved—after years of divided government, the presidency, the House, and the Senate were under Democratic control. Still, while the Democratic majority in the Senate in-creased by two seats, House Democrats lost six seats. It is not surprising that un-der these circumstances, Clinton was unable to get some of his major policies, such as health care reform, enacted.

George W. Bush's circumstances are quite similar to Clinton's. His election vic-tory was modest, to say the least—the narrowest victory in U.S. history—and Al Gore, the Democratic candidate, actually received more popular votes nationally. But with Bush's election, the Republicans took control of the presidency and both houses of Congress (until Senator Jeffords left the Republican Party), although they lost seats in the election. United government drove Bush to claim a mandate for change, just as it did Clinton.

As Clinton found, this is a fragile basis on which to build a mandate. Presidents are best able to see the calls for change being enacted when they possess strong public backing, as demonstrated with a solid election victory, and when their party is strong in Congress. In this sense, presidents are agents of major policy change only under certain circumstances.

Trends Depressing the Potential for Significant Policy Change

Trends over the past two decades have also limited the president as a source of major policy change. Table 13-2 presents some numbers that outline the nature of the policies that presidents have made their highest priorities, since Kennedy.[31] In

---

[31]Paul C. Light, "Domestic Policy Making," *Presidential Studies Quarterly* 30 (March 2000): 109–32.

TABLE 13-2   PRESIDENTIAL AGENDAS, KENNEDY THROUGH CLINTON

President	% Large proposals	% New proposals	% Large-new proposals	Average number per year	Total number for president
JFK/LBJ	53	62	36	13	53
LBJ	55	60	39	23	91
Nixon	35	71	28	11	65
Ford	50	44	25	8	16
Carter	54	61	39	10	41
Reagan	43	60	36	4	30
Bush	19	28	12	6	25
Clinton (I)	48	36	27	8	33

Source: Paul C. Light, "Domestic Policy Making," *Presidential Studies Quarterly* 30 (March 2000): 109–32.

looking at presidential policy proposals, it is useful to distinguish them by how large they are and how innovative or new they are. Large programs either affect a lot of people or are very expensive. "New" or "innovative" means that the proposal is a new way of attacking a problem or raises a whole new problem to address.

Bill Clinton's health care program was large but not innovative, as it applied a regulatory model to solve the health care problem, an approach that had been used many times before. Similarly, George W. Bush's tax cut is large but not innovative, essentially building on tax cuts of the past. In contrast, Bush's faith-based initiative is innovative, although small (or perhaps medium in size). It will not cost much federal money, but it is innovative in the use of charitable groups to dispense federal welfare programs (a tactic also used in Lyndon Johnson's War on Poverty).

Looking at table 13-2, we see that the percentage of presidential policy proposals that are both large and innovative has declined over the years. Reagan is clearly a transitional president in this regard. His percentage of large-innovative programs is as high as that of Kennedy and of Johnson, the leaders here, but the total number of proposals that he offered is the smallest, only four per year, one-half or less than the volume of each president from Kennedy through Carter. Under Bush and Clinton, the number of proposals per year increased modestly but was still less than that of presidents Kennedy to Carter. Perhaps more significant, the number of large-innovative proposals dramatically shrank with Bush and Clinton.

Why have presidents become so much less bold over the past twenty years in offering policy proposals? Several factors seem to be at work here. First, divided government was the rule for most of this period. With divided government, the prospects for securing passage of large and innovative programs are slight. Thus, presidents may not be asking for much, because they do not think that they can get much. Second, for most of this period, the government labored under high deficits. With deficits large, it is unlikely that government can afford to add new, expensive programs without either cutting existing programs or increasing taxes to finance the new programs. Such was not likely to happen, and thus presidents did not ask for much. Third, government seemed to have expanded into almost all realms of modern life by the 1980s. There was little new territory for social programs to till. As a result, the focus of the political system changed from offering new areas for government to address to reforming those areas in which government already was involved. Finally, the expansion of interest group activity since World War II has increased the risk that major proposals will be attacked by various interest groups and, therefore, defeated.

Some people claim that the modern presidency has diminished as a policy leadership post from its heyday perhaps around 1970.[32] We see some of that in the figures on table 13-2, and have pointed out some of the reasons for this. The future will tell if this diminished presidency is but an interlude or a harbinger of the future.

KEY TERMS

collegial staffing   389
competitive staffing   389
cycle of decreasing resources   394
cycle of increasing effectiveness   394
FDR's brain trust   388
groupthink   391
hierarchical staffing   389

Jackson's kitchen cabinet   388
mandate   395
multiple advocacy   392
presidential goals   382
president's agenda   372
priority   380
unanticipated events   373

DISCUSSION QUESTIONS

1. What is the president's agenda? What are the sources of items for the president's agenda? How much of the president's agenda is under his direct control and how much is forced on him? What are some examples of presidents who were able to control their agenda? What are some examples of presidents who were less able to control what was on their agendas?
2. How does the president establish the priorities that make up his agenda? How much control does the president have over what will be his top policy priorities? How much influence do outside factors have in making some issues high priorities?
3. What are the president's goals in deciding which policies to pursue and make high priorities? Does each president have the same goals? Compare what you think the goals of several presidents were. If their goals were changed to other goals, would they have had different policy priorities?

[32]"The Incredible Shrinking Presidency," *Time,* 7 June 1993; David M. Shribman, "The Shrinking Presidency; Why? The Times, the Congress, the Media, the Economy," *Boston Globe,* 25 January 1998, p. E3; and Francine Kiefer, "For US Presidents, It's an Era of Modest Agendas," *Christian Science Monitor,* 28 January 1999, p. 2.

4. How do advisers affect the president's agenda? What are the major sources of division or conflict among advisers over what to include in the president's agenda and what policy solutions to follow once the agenda items are selected?
5. Describe the major ways of organizing the president's staff. What are the benefits and the costs of using one system over another? Is there a best way to organize the president's staff?
6. How do the cycles of increasing effectiveness and decreasing resources affect presidential policy making? How do these cycles affect the quality and effectiveness of the policies of government? Is there any way to break these cycles?
7. Discuss the conditions under which the president serves as a major engine of policy change. How do presidential mandates affect how ambitious the president's agenda will be? What other factors affect the ambition and innovativeness of the president's policy agenda?

SUGGESTED READINGS

John P. Burke, *The Institutional Presidency*. Baltimore: Johns Hopkins University Press, 1992.

Jeffrey E. Cohen, *Presidential Responsiveness and Public Policy Making: The Public and the Policies That Presidents Choose*. Ann Arbor: University of Michigan Press, 1997.

Patricia Heidotting Conley, *Presidential Mandates: How Elections Shape the National Agenda*. Chicago: University of Chicago Press, 2001.

Alexander George, "The Case for Multiple Advocacy in Foreign Policy," *American Political Science Review* 66 (September 1972): 751–85.

Larry R. Jacobs and Robert Y. Shapiro, *Politicians Don't Pander*. Chicago: University of Chicago Press, 2000.

Irving Janus, *Victims of Groupthink: A Psychological Study of Foreign-Policy Decisions and Fiascoes*. Boston: Houghton, Mifflin, 1972.

Richard Tanner Johnson, *Managing the White House: An Intimate Study of the Presidency*. New York: Harper and Row, 1974.

Charles O. Jones, *The Presidency in a Separated System*. Washington, D.C.: Brookings Institution, 1994.

John W. Kingdon, *Agendas, Alternatives, and Public Policies*. Boston: Little, Brown, 1984.

Paul C. Light, *The President's Agenda: Domestic Policy Choice from Kennedy to Clinton*. Baltimore: Johns Hopkins University Press, 1999.

Stephen Skowronek, *The Politics That Presidents Make: Leadership from John Adams to George Bush*. Cambridge: Belknap Press, 1993.

14

THE PRESIDENT
AND ECONOMIC
AND BUDGETARY
POLICY MAKING

THE FOUNDATIONS OF PRESIDENTIAL
ECONOMIC POLICY RESPONSIBILITY

The Constitution does not make the president responsible for economic policy, nor does it bestow on him any policy-making authority over economic policy. Yet, ever since the presidency of Franklin Roosevelt, economic policy has been among the president's highest priorities. When Bill Clinton took the oath of office in 1993, among his first actions was to reorganize the economic policy advising staff in the White House by creating the National Economic Council (NEC). We discuss the NEC in more detail in the section on "Coordinating Macroeconomic Policy Advice." Clinton also made passing his budget, which included important provisions to deal with the economic doldrums that the nation was in, his first legislative priority. George W. Bush, like Clinton, made economic policy the centerpiece of his early administration with his tax cut reforms, which he argued were necessary to help stimulate a sluggish economy. The terrorist attacks of September 11, 2001, produced additional economic problems, particularly for the airline industry, which faced virtual collapse without governmental assistance. Numerous other examples exist of presidents moving economic issues to the top of their agenda.

Economic policy comes in many varieties, but most presidential attention is focused on the **macroeconomy,** that is, the nation's economy as a whole. Thus, issues such as trends in unemployment, inflation, income growth, economic productivity, and the effect of federal spending and taxing on those economic indicators command a large amount of presidential attention. Two factors are important in explaining the high degree of presidential concern with the macroeconomy. First, the public expects the president to be involved and holds him responsible for the state of the nation's economy. Also, over the years, presidential responsibility has become institutionalized, with statutory requirements and the accumulation of staff resources to aid him in directing macroeconomic policy.

Despite these public expectations and statutory burdens placed on the president, the president possesses only a limited ability to steer economic policy. The U.S. government employs primarily two economic policy instruments: **fis-**

cal and **monetary** tools.[1] Fiscal tools refer to the taxing and spending decisions of government, the latter also known as the budget. Presidents share fiscal tools with Congress because changes in tax policy must be legislated and the budget is created through a legislative process. In fact, the House of Representatives is constitutionally empowered to initiate all tax legislation. We discuss the intricacies of budget building in more detail in "The Budget Process and the Presidents" section.

Monetary policy is a tool that regulates the amount of money in the economy and how much it costs to borrow money. But monetary policy is even further removed from direct presidential input than fiscal policy tools because it is the responsibility of the Federal Reserve Board (Fed), an independent agency. Presidents have no direct say over the decisions that the Fed makes. At most, the president may influence Fed decisions through the people whom he nominates to serve on it, but Congress has a role to play here as well through its confirmation power.

Economic policy repeats a common story about the modern presidency—the public holds him responsible for the state of the economy, but he does not possess the governmental authority to do as he pleases about economic policy. Moreover, the stakes for presidents are high in economic policy. Presidents have not been reelected to office because of a poorly performing economy, with George H. W. Bush and Jimmy Carter being two recent examples. A robust economy may benefit presidents in otherwise unforeseen ways. Bill Clinton was probably able to weather the storms of the Monica Lewinsky scandal and impeachment proceedings against him because of the health of the economy, public optimism about the economy, and public satisfaction with what they saw as his management of the economy.

THE EVOLUTION OF THE PRESIDENT'S ROLE IN ECONOMIC POLICY

Public Expectations

Public expectations about the president and the economy began in earnest with the Great Depression.[2] That economic cataclysm undermined the public's faith in the market's ability to correct problems. The severity of the Depression was unprecedented in American life. Although the nation had experienced economic panics and distress before, none could match the depth and duration of the Depression of the 1930s. When Franklin Roosevelt was elected president in 1932, the Depression was already three years old and showed few signs of abating, despite President Herbert Hoover's protestations that "prosperity was just around the corner." In 1933, unemployment stood at 24.9 percent, and between 1929 and 1932,

---

[1]For an overview of economic policy making in the United States, see Jeffrey E. Cohen, *Politics and Economic Policy in the United States,* 2d ed. (Boston: Houghton-Mifflin, 1999).

[2]See, for instance, Samuel H. Beer "In Search of a New Public Philosophy" *The New American Political System,* ed. Antony King (Washington, D.C.: American Enterprise Institute, 1978), pp. 5–43; and Fred I. Greenstein, "Change and Continuity in the Modern Presidency,' in *The New American Political System,* ed. Antony King (Washington, D.C.: American Enterprise Institute, 1978), pp. 45–86, esp. pp. 47–53.

the gross national product declined (in constant 1987 dollars) from $827 billion to $603 billion, a decrease of 27 percent.[3] Typically, economic downturns are short-lived, usually lasting less than a year. The Great Depression lasted until the end of the decade, however, and many economists believe that it was not until America entered World War II in 1941 that the economy finally pulled out of it.

Within this context, the public began to look elsewhere than the capitalist economy for relief. Most eyes focused on the new president. Franklin Roosevelt offered little in the way of concrete policies to deal with the Depression. Rather, he focused public attention on himself and tried to instill public confidence in him, despite the uneven performance of his administration with regard to the economy. He seemed quite successful in this regard, with generally high polls, although he generated more support from those at the bottom of the economy than at the top, which makes sense, since he targeted his policies to help those suffering most from the Depression's ills.[4]

The economy improved somewhat during his administration, even though a recession occurred in 1938 on top of the already existing Depression. Roosevelt's key achievement, however, was not so much improving economic performance but changing the way the public viewed the government's role with regard to the economy.[5] No longer would laissez faire, the doctrine of minimal government involvement in economic affairs, rule. Since FDR's presidency, the government has been heavily involved in managing the economy and is held responsible for its performance, with most of this new-found public attention focusing on the president.

Presidents respond to this public expectation because they fear the electoral and popular consequences of not doing so. For example, George H. W. Bush was roundly criticized for his seeming insensitivity to public concerns about the recession while he was in office.[6] His popularity levels declined precipitously during the recession of 1991, which probably contributed to his defeat for reelection in 1992.

The consequences of a poorly performing economy are readily apparent on presidential popularity and electoral prospects. Studies indicate that presidential popularity moves with the macroeconomic cycle. As the economy declines, popularity dips.[7] Similarly, economic distress is often cited as one reason for presidential reelection defeats, as was the case for Van Buren in 1836, Carter in 1980, and Bush in 1992.

[3]These figures are from Harold W. Stanley and Richard G. Niemi, *Vital Statistics on American Politics,* 4th ed. (Washington, D.C.: Congressional Quarterly Press, 1994), pp. 416, 431.

[4]Matthew A. Baum and Samuel Kernell, "Economic Class and Popular Support for Franklin Roosevelt in War and Peace," *Public Opinion Quarterly* 65 (Summer 2001): 198–229.

[5]Scholarship on FDR and the New Deal is extensive. See, for instance, James MacGregor Burns, *Roosevelt: The Lion and the Fox* (New York: Harcourt, Brace, 1956); Mario Einaudi, *The Roosevelts: A Rendezvous with Destiny* (Boston: Little, Brown, 1990); and Albert U. Romasco, *The Politics of Recovery: Roosevelt's New Deal of Upheaval* (Boston: Houghton Mifflin, 1960). On the New Deal, see Anthony J. Badger, *The New Deal: The Depression Years* (New York: Noonday Press, 1989); and Carl N. Degler, ed., *The New Deal* (Chicago: Quadrangle Books, 1970).

[6]Michael Duffy and Dan Goodgame, *Marching in Place* (New York: Simon and Schuster, 1992).

[7]For a good review and analysis of the impact of the economy on presidential popularity, see Michael B. MacKuen, Robert S. Erikson, and James A. Stimson, "Peasants or Bankers? The American Electorate and the U.S. Economy," *American Political Science Review* 86 (1992): 597–611.

The Institutionalization of the President's Macroeconomic Responsibilities

As a consequence of these public expectations, presidents gradually took on important institutional responsibilities for the macroeconomy. The development of institutional resources for the president to use when dealing with the economy actually began long before the Depression, although the original intention was not directly tied to macroeconomic concerns. The first step was the passage of the **Budget and Accounting Act of 1921.**[8]

The Budget and Accounting Act established an executive budget. This meant the president was responsible for submitting a budget to Congress each year. Congress would then take the president's budget proposal and amend it, with much of the detail work done by the appropriations committees of both houses. (The congressional budget process was amended in 1974, as we describe in the "Reforming the Budget Process: The 1974 Budget Act" section of this chapter.) A staff agency to help the president prepare the budget, the **Bureau of the Budget (BOB),** was also created. In 1970, BOB became the **Office of Management and Budget (OMB).** As the budget became an instrument of macroeconomic policy, both the BOB/OMB and the budget-building process became important in formulating macroeconomic policy. Still, even before this macroeconomic role, the early Bureau of the Budget was, according to Allen Schick, successful in helping the federal government control finance and expenditures.[9]

The creation of the Executive Office of the President in 1939, which we discussed in Chapter 9, is also important, but unlike the Bureau of the Budget, the EOP was not designed to help the president with economic policy making. Its creation was a result of the recognition that the president needed formal staff assistance to manage the bureaucracy and the office of the presidency. The EOP became a place, however, where economic policy advisers to the president would be located, especially the Council of Economic Advisers and the National Economic Council, which we discuss in the section on "Coordinating Macroeconomic Policy Advice."

Formal recognition of governmental and presidential responsibility for the economy came in 1946, when the **Full Employment Act** was enacted.[10] This act specified that it was the policy and responsibility of the federal government "to use all practical means to . . . promote maximum employment, production, and purchasing power" and economic growth with stable prices, that is, without inflation. For the first time, the government went on record as being responsible for

---

[8]On that act, see Larry Berman *The Office of Management and Budget and the Presidency, 1921–1979* (Princeton, N.J.: Princeton University Press, 1979), pp. 3–6; Allen Schick, *The Federal Budget: Politics, Policy, Process* (Washington, D.C.: Brookings Institution, 1995), pp. 35–37; and Aaron Wildavsky, *The New Politics of the Budgetary Process,* 2d ed. (New York: HarperCollins, 1992), pp. 64–66.

[9]Schick, *Federal Budget,* p. 35. In particular, taxes, spending, and the public debt all declined in the 1920s.

[10]The politics and debates of the passage are detailed in Stephen Kemp Bailey, *Congress Makes a Law: The Story Behind the Employment Act of 1946* (New York: Columbia University Press, 1950). A more concise and contemporary account is found in John P. Frendreis and Raymond Tatalovich, *The Modern Presidency and Economic Policy* (Itasca, Ill.: Peacock, 1994), pp. 32–37.

the state of the economy and pledged the use of its agencies and powers to ensure economic health. Thus, the government could now *intervene* in the economy. Ensuing policy debate centered not on the legitimacy of government intervention in the economy but on the degree of such intervention and whether it
was the wisest policy course. The act also helped to fuel public expectations
about government's role in the economy.[11]

The Full Employment Act placed specific economic responsibilities on the
president. Sixty days after the beginning of each new Congress, he was required
to submit a report on the state of the economy, now known as the annual *Economic Report of the President.* The act also gave the president advisers to help him
in this task by creating the Council of Economic Advisers, which became part of
the EOP. The act also created the Joint Economic Committee of Congress.

Finally, in 1978, Congress passed the **Humphrey-Hawkins Act,** which further
increased the government's responsibility for the economy.[12] Sponsors of that act
intended to use the federal government as employer of last resort to attain an unemployment rate of 3 percent by 1983. Since the passage of the act, presidents
have ignored the full employment timetable, as other economic problems became
more pressing and as economists began to argue that a rate closer to 6 or 7 percent is a more reasonable target, since employment at a higher rate would risk fu-
eling inflation.[13]

POLICY ADVICE FOR THE PRESIDENT: THE ECONOMIC SUBPRESIDENCY

With the institutionalization of presidential macroeconomic responsibilities
came economic policy advisers for the president. These agencies that advise
the president on economic matters have come to be called the **economic subpresidency.**[14] Four agencies comprise the economic subpresidency: the Office of Management and Budget, the Council of Economic Advisers, the Department of the Treasury, and the Federal Reserve Board. Three of these
agencies are under the direct control of the president, because they are located
in the executive branch. The fourth, the Fed, is an independent regulatory
commission over which the president has only limited control. Scholars have
included the Fed as part of the economic subpresidency because of its role in
economic policy making, but it is one step removed from the president when
compared to the other three agencies.

[11]Howare E. Shuman, *Politics and the Budget: The Struggle Between the President and the Congress,*
3d ed. (Englewood Cliffs, N.J.: Prentice-Hall, 1992), pp. 161–63.

[12]On Humphrey-Hawkins, see Frendreis and Tatalovich, *Modern Presidency,* pp. 37–38.

[13]See Charles L. Schultze, *Memos to the President: A Guide Through Macroeconomics for the Busy
Policymaker* (Washington, D.C.: Brookings Institution, 1992), pp. 126–27, 155–62.

[14]The concept of the economic subpresidency was first offered in James E. Anderson and Jared E.
Hazelton, *Managing Macroeconomic Policy: The Johnson Presidency* (Austin: University of Texas
Press, 1986). A good discussion is found in George C. Edwards, III, and Stephen J. Wayne, *Presidential Leadership: Politics and Policymaking,* 3d ed. (New York: St. Martin's, 1994), pp. 411–14; and Fre-
dreis and Tatalovich, *Modern Presidency,* pp. 49–64.

Office of Management and Budget

The Office of Management and Budget (OMB) was created in 1921, when, as already mentioned, it was called the Bureau of the Budget. It was originally housed in the Department of the Treasury, but with the creation of the Executive Office of the President in 1939, it was moved to EOP. In 1970, Richard Nixon reorganized the Bureau of the Budget into the Office of Management and Budget, and the director assumed cabinet-level status.[15]

The principal task of the OMB is to help the president in preparing the annual budget. The OMB surveys each agency of the federal government each year about its budgetary needs. After compiling agency budget requests, the OMB makes recommendations to the president about whether agency budgets should be increased or cut.

Early in its history, the Bureau of the Budget played a passive role, focusing on accounting issues, such as whether money was being properly spent. In the 1940s and early 1950s under Harry Truman, it began to acquire policy-advising responsibilities. For instance, it expanded the power of **legislative clearance,** in which it would require each agency to submit its legislative proposals for review. The bureau would then determine if each proposal was consistent with the president's program and recommend action on the proposal to the president.[16] Similarly, the bureau began to review bills that Congress passed to recommend to the president whether he should veto or sign the legislation. Again, it used the standard of whether the legislation was consistent with the president's program in making its recommendation.

In the 1980s, the OMB began the task of **regulatory clearance.** (Ronald Reagan added this task to its other chores.) Regulatory clearance is similar to legislative clearance in that it requires each proposed regulation to be sent by its sponsoring agency to the Office of Information and Regulatory Affairs of the OMB. Using cost-benefit analysis, this office determines if the proposed regulation's benefits outweigh its costs. If so, the agency can proceed with issuing the regulation. If not, the agency is instructed to revise or drop the proposed regulation.[17]

---

[15]On the OMB in general, see Berman, *Office of Management*. For a review of the reorganization of the BOB into the OMB, see Allen Schick, "The Budget Bureau That Was: Thoughts on the Rise, Decline, and Future of a Presidential Agency," *Law and Contemporary Problems* 35 (1970): 519–39; and Hugh Heclo, "OMB and the Presidency: The Problem of Neutral Competence," *Public Interest* 38 (1975): 80–98.

[16]On the development of legislative clearance, also called central clearance, in the BOB, see Richard E. Neustadt, "Presidency and Legislation: The Growth of Central Clearance," *American Political Science Review* 48 (1959): 641–71. Also see Robert S. Gilmour, "Central Legislative Clearance: A Revised Perspective," *Public Administration Review* 31 (1971): 150–58. A broad overview is found in Stephen J. Wayne, *The Legislative Presidency* (New York: Harper and Row, 1978), esp. chap. 3.

[17]A very large literature on regulatory clearance in the OMB now exists. See Barry D. Friedman, *Regulation in the Reagan-Bush Era: The Eruption of Presidential Influence* (Pittsburgh: University of Pittsburgh Press, 1995), for a general overview. Also useful is Howard Ball, *Controlling Regulatory Sprawl: Presidential Strategies from Nixon to Reagan* (Westport, Conn.: Greenwood, 1984); Edward P. Fuchs, *Presidents, Management, and Regulation* (Englewood Cliffs, N.J.: Prentice-Hall, 1988); and William F. West and Joseph Cooper, "The Rise of Administrative Clearance," in *The Presidency and Public Policy Making,* ed. George C. Edwards, III, Steven A. Shull, and Norman C. Thomas (Pittsburgh: University of Pittsburgh Press, 1985), pp. 192–214.

Over time, the Office of Management and Budget has acquired duties beyond budgeting and has become in a sense a central staff agency for the presidency. But the agency's primary and most time-consuming task is still budgeting. As a consequence, the OMB is most concerned with the budgetary implications of macroeconomic and budgetary policy and the role of the federal deficit. Due to its budgetary task, it is often antagonistic toward increasing the deficit, and over the years, the agency has developed a reputation for taking the knife to federal spending and trying to find ways of reducing federal expenditures. At the same time, however, it has looked kindly on programs important to the president, thus mixing political concerns with its budgetary caution.[18] We discuss the role of the OMB in budget making in more detail in the section on "The Modern Budgeting Process in the Executive."

With the acquisition of a policy-advising role, plus legislative and regulatory clearance roles, the OMB has become politicized. Politicization means that the OMB is thought to speak for the president and thus is not considered as politically neutral as it was during the first half of its existence.[19] As a consequence, the OMB's estimates of revenue and spending projections are not considered to be reliable. Rather, they are thought to be either too rosy or too pessimistic, depending on the president's needs.[20] As we discuss in the "Congressional Budget and Impoundment Control Act of 1974" section, Congress created the Congressional Budget Office to provide it with more politically neutral budget estimates and projections.

The directors of the OMB have become important advisers to the president, especially over the past decade and a half, as the federal deficit has loomed so large. The deficit problem of the 1980s and 1990s, plus the accumulation of policy advising responsibility, has moved the OMB director into the forefront of presidential policy advisers. In recent years, many OMB directors have been among the most visible spokespersons for the administration, public personalities in their own right and highly influential within administration policy-making circles.

David Stockman, Ronald Reagan's first budget director and a former member of Congress, played such a role, spearheading the Reagan package of budget and tax cuts in 1981. Richard Darman, George H. W. Bush's budget director, was likewise influential. Bill Clinton's OMB directors have also been politically visible. Leon Panetta, a former member of Congress who served on the congressional budget committee, became such an important player in the Clinton administration that he moved over to become Clinton's chief of staff. Alice Rivlin, a well-respected economist who had been the director of the Congressional Budget Office, replaced him.

Mitchell E. Daniels, Jr., is George W. Bush's director of the OMB. Before being named to that post, Daniels worked for the drug firm Eli Lilly as senior vice president of corporate strategy and policy, but he possesses considerable gov-

[18]See Frendreis and Tatalovich, *Modern Presidency,* pp. 57–60.

[19]See Heclo, "OMB and the Presidency," on this point.

[20]For a revealing portrait of this problem from an insider, see David Stockman, *The Triumph of Politics* (New York: Harper and Row, 1986).

ernmental experience. In the early 1980s, he served on Sen. Richard Lugar's (R-Ind.) staff, and from 1984 to 1987 worked in the Reagan administration as an assistant to the president and as the administration's liaison to the nation's state and local officials.

Council of Economic Advisers

The **Council of Economic Advisers,** as already mentioned, was created in 1946 with the enactment of the Full Employment Act. The CEA's duties include studying the condition of the economy, using that analysis to advise the president on economic policy matters, and helping the president prepare his annual economic report. It was hoped that the CEA would provide the president with a broad picture and understanding of the economy from advisers not captured by bureaucratic or special interests.[21]

The major focus of the CEA is the macroeconomic performance of the economy, in contrast to the OMB's emphasis on government budgets and deficits. Thus, the CEA is most concerned with unemployment, inflation, economic growth, and productivity. Moreover, its macroeconomic emphasis leads it away from concern with particular economic sectors and the government programs aimed at those sectors, and it may take stands against some programs and policies it feels will adversely affect the macroeconomy. In this regard, the CEA also advises presidents on the implications of policies on economic sectors, especially with regard to regulation. For instance, the CEA under Carter argued against some environmental regulations because of the expected effect on the economy.[22] The CEA has been an advocate of applying cost-benefit analysis to regulatory policy as a way of incorporating macroeconomic concerns into regulatory policy making.[23]

The CEA is a unique organization within the federal government. Almost all members of the CEA have been academic economists, and the staff is relatively small, ranging from about thirty-five to sixty-five. Currently, the staff of the CEA numbers in the mid-thirties.[24] It represents no constituency and holds no statutory powers, nor does it administer any programs or laws. Thus, the CEA is in a precarious position. Its role is purely advisory, and there is nothing to make presidents listen to its advice.

What is remarkable is that a body composed of academics, often lacking in political experience, has at times become highly important and influential within presidential administrations. In part, this is a function of the type of people whom

[21]Discussions of the CEA are found in Edward S. Flash, *Economic Advice and Presidential Leadership: The Council of Economic Advisers* (New York: Columbia University Press, 1965); Erwin C. Hargrove and Samuel C. Morley, eds., *The President and the Council of Economic Advisers: Interviews with CEA Chairmen* (Boulder, Colo.: Westview Press, 1984); and Herbert Stein, *Presidential Economics: The Making of Economic Policy from Roosevelt to Reagan and Beyond,* 2d ed. (Washington, D.C.: American Enterprise Institute, 1988).

[22]Fuch, *Presidents, Management,* pp. 64–67.

[23]Ibid., pp. 23–24.

[24]Frendreis and Tatalovich, *Modern Presidency,* pp. 49–55, 318–19.

presidents have appointed to the CEA. Not surprisingly, they often reflect the political and policy leanings of the president. Thus, the CEA members under Republican presidents are often economically conservative, while Democrats usually appoint more liberal people to that body. Presidents have often found their advice useful.

The height of the CEA's influence came with the Kennedy administration. Kennedy's CEA advisor was Walter Heller, an economist from the University of Minnesota. Heller was trained in graduate school when **Keynesian economics** was becoming the intellectual standard. Among the many innovations of Keynesian thinking was the need for government intervention to regulate the macroeconomy. Keynesian policy, which is named after British economist **John Maynard Keynes,** is an orientation that argues that adjustments in government spending policy—whether the government should run a deficit or surplus or be in balance—can affect the state of the economy.

Heller wanted to educate the new president on Keynesian modes of thinking about economic policy and was successful in that task. Kennedy came to the presidency with little training in economics but with a keen sensitivity to the importance of the economy to his reelection hopes in 1964. Heller convinced him to push for a tax cut in 1963 because the economy seemed to be underperforming and there was fear that it would slip into recession. Even though a tax cut would mean increasing the budget deficit, Kennedy accepted Heller's recommendation. Congress passed the tax cut, and the economy did well.[25] Later, Ronald Reagan used the Kennedy tax cut as a model for his own tax package in 1981. In 2001, George W. Bush argued that a tax cut would help stimulate the economy, employing this Keynesian insight to justify his tax policy.

The prestige of the CEA climbed because of the success of the tax cut, and its influence continued during the Johnson and Nixon administrations. However, with the stagflation of the 1970s, the budget deficits of the 1980s and 1990s, and the massive trade imbalance of the past two decades, the CEA has receded in influence as other agencies—notably the OMB, the Treasury, and the Federal Reserve Board—have begun to eclipse it.

Still, in recent decades, presidents have found that they can use the advice of the CEA to counter the demands of interest groups for more programs, more government regulation, and the like. This has become important as the deficit has limited the ability of government to respond to these demands. The CEA has given the president reasons to resist them, and the reasons appear "above politics," rooted in economic analysis and what is best for the economy and the nation.

Department of the Treasury

The third member of the economic subpresidency is the **Treasury Department,** one of the original cabinet posts created during the Washington administration. The tasks of the Treasury Department are to collect government revenues, pay

---

[25]Edward S. Flash, "Conversion of Kennedy from Economic Conservative to Economic Liberal," in *J.F. Kennedy and Presidential Power,* ed. Earl Latham (Lexington, Mass.: D.C. Heath, 1972), pp. 76–81.

government bills, secure government credit, borrow money, and administer the nation's balance of payment with other nations.[26]

Treasury secretaries usually present a conservative and fiscally responsible position to the president. Thus, they often oppose expansion of the government deficit and prefer a stable and sound dollar. In recent years, as the trade gap has widened, Treasury secretaries have become very concerned about the balance of payments problem—the fact that more money is leaving the country in trade and other spending than is coming in.

The business community in the United States, especially big business, often views the Treasury as its emissary to the administration. Thus, the secretary of the Treasury often has a business, banking, or finance background, as presidents accede to this expectation. This is the case for thirteen of the seventeen men who have served in that post since 1946. Presidents most often appoint people to the Treasury Department to send signals to the business sector that business interests will be represented in the administration at the highest levels.[27]

This is most critical for Democratic presidents, whom the business sector often regards with trepidation. Democrats are not thought to be the natural allies of business, and business feels that Democratic administrations are more likely than Republican ones to increase government spending, allow inflation, and impose high taxes on business and the wealthy. To allay these fears, Democratic presidents have sought Treasury secretaries who are conservative, who hold business values, and who are acceptable to business.

Thus, John Kennedy appointed Douglas Dillon to be his Treasury secretary. Dillon, a Republican, had served in the Eisenhower administration in the State Department and worked on Wall Street. Carter had two business executives serving in that capacity for him: W. Michael Blumenthal, chief executive officer of the Bendix Corporation, and G. William Miller who had also served as chair of the Federal Reserve Board. Bill Clinton took the same tack, first appointing Lloyd Bentsen and then Robert Rubin. Bentsen, a former Democratic senator from Texas, was chair of the Senate Finance Committee and, before his Senate career, was a business executive. Rubin, also a Democrat, was a Wall Street financier.

Republican presidents are usually less constrained in selecting a cabinet secretary and quite often choose a person with strong ties to big business. For example, Paul H. O'Neill was named by George W. Bush to be his Treasury secretary. O'Neill's immediate previous job was heading ALCOA, the largest aluminum manufacturing corporation in the United States, but before his stint in private industry, O'Neill extensively worked in government, primarily at the OMB (1967–1977) and the Veterans Administration (1961–1966).

---

[26]Treasury's role in economic policy making is reviewed in Colin Campbell, *Managing the Presidency: Carter, Reagan, and the Search for Executive Harmony* (Pittsburgh: University of Pittsburgh Press, 1986).

[27]Frendreis and Tatalovich, *Modern Presidency,* pp. 55–57, 320–21.

Federal Reserve Board

The **Federal Reserve Board** is an independent regulatory commission that was created in 1913. The Fed, as it is commonly called, is concerned with monetary policy, that is, the nation's money supply. The independent status of the Fed makes it unique among the bodies in the economic subpresidency. The president nominates the members of the seven-person board, subject to senatorial confirmation, as is the case with cabinet-level departments, but Fed members cannot be removed from office by the president. Moreover, they serve long terms—fourteen years—to further their independence from the president and from politics more generally.[28]

Typically, members of the Fed are bankers or have business experience. There have also been many academic economists in the Fed, and they are often selected to chair the board. Due to the combination of its members' experience in the finance sector and its responsibility to regulate the money supply, the Fed usually takes a conservative position on economic policy.[29] Thus, the Fed tends to oppose budget deficits, and its top priority is combating inflation and promoting price stability.

To fight inflation, the Fed often resorts to tight money and countercyclical policies. **Tight money** means restricting the supply of money in the economy, as well as setting higher interest rates. **Countercyclical policies** aim to slow the economy when inflation is running high—for example, by increasing interest rates. Such policies often run afoul of the interests of politicians, both in the White House and Congress, who feel pressure from the electorate for easier money, lower interest rates, and a growing economy. Sometimes the Fed has used tight money to squeeze inflation out of the economy, with recession occurring as a consequence.[30]

When this happens, elected politicians try to avoid blame for the recession by citing Fed action, and on occasion, members of Congress have called for stronger political controls on the Fed to make it more responsive to "political realities."[31] Reform efforts have not been successful, however, because many in Washington value the independence of the Fed. It is able to make hard economic policy choices because of this independence, choices that elected politicians would not be able to make.[32]

[28]A history and discussion of the Fed can be found in Carl H. Moore, *The Federal Reserve System: The First 75 Years* (Jefferson, N.C.: MacFarland, 1990); Richard H. Timberlake, *Monetary Policy in the United States: An Intellectual and Institutional History* (Chicago: University of Chicago Press, 1993); Donald Kettl, *Leadership at the Fed* (New Haven: Yale University Press, 1986); and William C. Melton, *Inside the Fed: Making Monetary Policy* (Homewood, Ill.: Dow-Jones-Irwin, 1985). A good journalistic account is found in William Greider, *Secrets of the Temple: How the Federal Reserve Runs the Country* (New York: Simon and Schuster, 1987).

[29]Frendreis and Tatalovich, *Modern Presidency,* pp. 61–64, 324.

[30]This seemed to be the case when Paul Volker was chair of the Fed during the late 1970s and early 1980s. Michael G. Hadjimichalakis, *The Federal Reserve, Money, and Interest Rates: The Volker Years and Beyond* (New York: Praeger, 1984).

[31]On political control of the Fed, see Kettl, *Leadership at the Fed;* John T. Woolley, *Monetary Politics: The Federal Reserve and the Politics of Monetary Policy* (Cambridge, England: Cambridge University Press, 1984); and Michael D. Reagan, "The Political Structure of the Federal Reserve System," *American Political Science Review* 55 (1961): 64–76.

[32]A recent study on the ability of politicians to influence Fed policy is Irwin L. L. Morris, *Congress, the President, and the Federal Reserve* (Ann Arbor: University of Michigan Press, 1999).

The current chair of the Fed, Alan Greenspan, has served in that capacity since 1987, being named to the post by three presidents, Reagan, Bush, and Clinton. Greenspan is an economist by training and education but has had considerable government experience as well. From 1974 to 1977, he served as chairman of the Council of Economic Advisers under Gerald Ford, and from 1981 to 1983, he was chairman of the National Commission on Social Security Reform for Ronald Reagan; he held other economic policy posts in the Reagan administration before Reagan named him to chair the Fed.

COORDINATING MACROECONOMIC POLICY ADVICE

The four major economic policy advisers in the president's economic subpresidency have different institutional locations, with differing perspectives and backgrounds, each of which may lead to different advice for the president. For example, the CEA is most concerned with economic growth and the business cycle, often supporting fiscal and budgetary means to those ends. The OMB is most concerned with containing the federal budget and promoting the president's program. CEA and OMB officials will be liberal or conservative, depending on the president in office. Generally, they will be more liberal under Democratic presidents. The Treasury Department is most concerned about government revenues, the soundness of the dollar, and government credit. The budget, in particular whether the United States runs a deficit or surplus, has important implications for government credit and the dollar. Similarly, the Fed is concerned about the dollar but also about inflation and stable economic growth. Most often, Treasury and Fed officials are conservative. This usually holds even when Democrats occupy the White House.

With such a variety of disparate advice and with economic performance being so important for the success of presidential administrations, presidents have sought to make sense of and coordinate these many voices. These coordination efforts have not been firmly institutionalized into government, and presidents possess considerable latitude in how they use these coordinating mechanisms, yet institutionalization patterns and processes have developed and begun to take hold in government economic policy making.[33]

Kennedy made the first efforts at coordinating economic policy making. He organized an informal committee composed of the Treasury Department, the CEA, and the OMB, which was called the **Troika.** It was later expanded to include the Fed, making it a **Quadriad.** This committee had regular meetings at the secretarial and subsecreterial levels. Johnson continued Kennedy's system.[34]

---

[33]General treatments of presidential coordination of economic policy making are found in Thomas, Pika, and Watson, *The Politics of the Presidency*, 381–386; Edwards and Wayne, *Presidential Leadership*, pp. 414–16; and Frendreis and Tatalovich, *Modern Presidency*, pp. 65–72. A comparison across presidents is Michael A. Genovese, "The Presidency and Styles of Economic Management," *Congress and the Presidency* 14 (1987): 151–67; Joseph Pilca, John Maltese, & Norman Thomas, *The Politics of the Presidency*, 5th ed (Washington, DC: Congressional Quarterly, 2002), pp. 345–348.

[34]Economic policy making under Johnson is discussed in Anderson and Hazelton, *Managing Macroeconomic Policy*.

Nixon used a different approach.[35] He preferred to centralize policy advice under one person, an economic policy-making "czar." John Connolly, former governor of Texas and a former Democrat, served as Nixon's Treasury secretary from early 1971 to mid-1972. He was succeeded by George Schultz, who formerly served as Treasury secretary and head of the OMB. Nixon designated Schultz as the assistant to the president for economic affairs.

The Watergate scandal forced Gerald Ford to distance himself from Nixon, which included ridding the presidency of many of Nixon's organizational innovations. Still, economic policy stayed at the top of Ford's agenda, as it had been on Nixon's, because inflation was beginning to spin out of control. Ford instituted a new approach to coordinating economic policy with the creation of the **Economic Policy Board (EPB).**[36] The EPB included an array of cabinet departments beyond the economic subpresidency. Most important, it was given institutional resources to operate, including an executive director and an executive committee, which met regularly. During the slightly more than two years that it existed, the EPB met 520 times and discussed over fifteen hundred agenda items.

The EPB operated openly, presenting to the president all the viewpoints that its members expressed. Because of this, EPB members and others involved in economic policy making had little reason to go around the EPB to get to the president or to undermine the EPB and its position. By operating in such a pluralistic manner, however, it is not quite clear that the EPB helped the president in making economic policy. The EPB presented the president with many policy options from which to choose, and some claimed that it wasted presidential time by not prioritizing issues and by allowing less than important ones to reach the president.

Jimmy Carter used a similar coordinating body, called the **Economic Policy Group,** but he did not rely on it as heavily as Ford had relied on the EPB.[37] Nor did the Economic Policy Group meet regularly. Carter fell back on less formal ways of making economic policy, relying on whichever adviser was trusted at the time.

Reagan coordinated his economic policy advisers with the **Cabinet Council on Economic Affairs** (CCEA). The CCEA included an array of cabinet secretaries, including those from Treasury, State, Commerce, Labor, and Transportation, as well as the OMB director, the CEA chair, and the U.S. trade representative. It met several times a week, often with President Reagan chairing the meeting. The meetings helped to build an administration outlook on problems and issues, creating a sense of teamwork and shared fate. However, the CCEA fell into disuse as Reagan began to miss meetings. His absence led others to also miss CCEA meetings.

[35]Nixon's approach is discussed in A. James Reichley, *Conservatives in an Age of Change: The Nixon and Ford Administrations* (Washington, D.C.: Brookings Institution, 1981).

[36]The EPB is discussed in detail in Roger B. Porter, *Presidential Decision Making: The Economic Policy Board* (New York: Cambridge University Press, 1980). A comparison of Johnson's and Ford's styles is found in John W. Sloan, "Economic Policymaking in the Johnson and Ford Administrations," *Presidential Studies Quarterly* 20 (1990): 11–125.

[37]Carter's style is discussed in James E. Anderson, "Managing Macroeconomic Policy: The Carter Experience," *The Presidency Reconsidered,* ed. in Richard Waterman (Itasca, Ill. Peacock, 1993), pp. 247–73. Also see Campbell, *Managing the Presidency.*

In its place, Reagan began to meet informally with trusted advisers, as problems dictated. Bush continued this informal approach.

Clinton, like several of his predecessors, saw economic policy as the key to having won the election; thus, it was his highest priority when he took office. In one of Clinton's first actions as president, he formed a new economic policy-making agency, the **National Economic Council** (NEC). It was created by executive order on January 25, 1993.[38] The NEC was modeled after the National Security Council, which oversees security, defense, and foreign policy. The NEC is a high-level, interagency body with staff assistance.

The president chairs the NEC, and the vice president and eight cabinet secretaries (State, Treasury, Agriculture, Commerce, Labor, Housing and Urban Development, Transportation, and Energy) hold seats. The administrator of the Environmental Protection Agency, chair of the CEA, director of the OMB, and U.S. trade representative are also formal members of the NEC. Plus, others not normally thought of as economic policy advisers, such as the national security adviser and the assistant to the president for science and technology, hold formal member status. Finally, two presidential assistants, one each for economic and domestic policy, are members, as are "any other officials of the executive departments and agencies as the president may from time to time designate." It is important to note that due to its independent status, the Fed is not a member of the NEC. Other than the president, there are seventeen formal representatives on the NEC.

The NEC has four principal functions: "1) to coordinate the economic policy-making process with regard to domestic and international economic issues, 2) to coordinate economic advice to the president, 3) to ensure that economic policy-making decisions and programs are consistent with the president's stated goals, and to ensure that those goals are being effectively pursued, and 4) to monitor implementation of the president's economic policy agenda."[39] Also, the presidential assistant for the economic policy, who coordinates the NEC, is given status comparable to that of the national security adviser and the presidential assistant for domestic policy, though the executive order states that the Treasury secretary retains the rank as senior economic official in the administration. Finally, the NEC is given staff support.

Early accounts suggest that the presidential assistant for economic policy has turned into an important presidential adviser. This is partially a function of the first incumbent, Robert Rubin, a strong and forceful personality with a generally conservative orientation toward economic policy.[40] Rubin proved so important to the Clinton

---

[38]The executive order is numbered 12835.

[39]This is a direct quote from the executive order.

[40]A portrait of Rubin is found in Gwen Ifill, "The Economic Czar Behind the Economic Czars," *New York Times,* 7 March 1993, p. 14. See also Ann Reilly Dowd, "Clinton's Point Man on the Economy," *Fortune,* 3 May 1993, pp. 75–79; Steven Greenhouse, "When Robert Rubin Talks," *New York Times,* 25 July 1993, p. F1; John B. Judis, "Old Master: Robert Rubin's Artful Role," *New Republic,* 13 December 1993, pp. 21–25; and Paul Starobin, "The Broker," *National Journal,* 6 April 1994, pp. 878–83.

administration that he was named to replace the outgoing secretary of the Treasury,[41] Lloyd Bentsen. Under Rubin's leadership, the NEC was actively involved in technology policy,[42] it sought to cut subsidies to commercial shipping,[43] and it moderated the administration's position on the massive health care reform proposal of 1994.[44] The NEC seemed to be so successful and useful to Clinton that it began to eclipse other economic policy advisers, especially those who headed cabinet departments.[45]

George W. Bush has retained the NEC, naming Lawrence Lindsey to head it, with the title of assistant to the president for economic affairs. It is important to note that Lindsey was also named the head of the CEA, an indication of the decline of the CEA and the rise of the NEC. Lindsey is an academic economist by training, having taught at Harvard University from 1984 to 1989. But he also has much experience in government and is closely tied to the Republican Party. From 1981 to 1984, he was a senior staff economist for tax policy in the Council of Economic Advisers. From 1989 to 1991, he was a special assistant to the president for policy development, and he was a member of the Federal Reserve Board from 1991 to 1997. During the 2000 presidential campaign, he was an adviser to Bush on economic issues.

The NEC is an important institutional development in economic policy advice for the president. Under Clinton, it was given staff, strong leadership, and presidential backing, and Bush's naming of Lindsey to both the NEC and the CEA suggests its continued importance. However, it may not persist as an important policy-advising body for future presidents.

This is because different presidents have different approaches to policy making. Moreover, institutionalizing economic policy through such a coordinating mechanism as the NEC may result in tying the president to a specific policy course. The president then may have less room to alter course because of the negotiation process among the various advisers that is a part of any attempt at coordination. Presidents have felt a need to be able to respond to changing economic conditions. Thus, coordinating bodies are more symbolic in importance. Lastly, presidents are held responsible for economic policy, a responsibility that they cannot share with anyone. This degree of responsibility limits how much advice presidents will take from such bodies and how important someone such as the head of the NEC will become to the president.

Although the NEC head may provide the president with good economic advice, presidential economic policy making is a function of politics as well as economics. Presidents prefer to take advice from those to whom they choose to listen, not from an institutionalized and often rigid body. In the end, presidents will make their own economic policies.

[41]The former head of the CEA, Laura D'Andrea Tyson, was named as Rubin's successor in February 1994.

[42]See Will Lepkowski, "Technology Policy," *Chemical and Engineering News* 71 (1993): 6–7.

[43]"U.S. Seeks to End Ship Subsidies," *Facts on File,* 15 July 1993, pp. 525–26.

[44]"Who Makes Policy?" *The Economist,* 8 January 1994, pp. A25–26.

[45]Fred Barnes, "Cabinet Losers: Bentsen, Riley, Pena: Victims of Clinton's Style," *New Republic,* 28 February 1994, pp. 22–27; and Paul Magnusson and Owen Ullmann, "Robert Rubin's Capital Gain," *Business Week,* 28 March 1994, pp. 148–50.

THE BUDGET PROCESS AND THE PRESIDENT

The budget is the major instrument of fiscal policy. Using the budget as a fiscal policy instrument may help the government modulate cycles in the economy. That is, the budget may help pull the economy out of a **recession,** when unemployment is high and demand for goods and services is low. Similarly, the budget may help quell **inflation.** Inflationary periods are noted for a rapid rise in prices, which is caused by demand for goods and services outstripping the supply of goods and services.

Several aspects of the budget make it a useful instrument for adjusting the economy. For instance, running a deficit or surplus may help deal with recession and inflation. Government may help stimulate an economy in recession by running a deficit (spending more than it takes in). Deficits can be created by either increasing government spending or cutting taxes. In either case, money can be poured into the economy to adjust supply and demand. As the supply of money increases, the demand for economic goods and services will also rise, and the economy will grow. When the economy is inflationary, government can help cool it off by running a surplus. Running a surplus helps pull money out of the economy, dampening demand. To run a surplus, government can reduce its spending or increase taxes or both.[46]

Beyond the impacts of deficits or surpluses on the economy, the large size of the federal budget also has important implications for the economy. In fiscal year 2000, the federal government budget amounted to about 18 percent of the economy, or roughly $2 trillion.[47] The government comprises a large component of the economy, and thus, what government does in terms of its budget will affect the economy.

A third aspect of the budget is also important. The budget tells us not only how much money the federal government spends but where it will spend it. We learn much about the priorities of government from the budget. Owing to its importance, the president and Congress spend considerable time on developing the nation's budget, perhaps more than on any other single policy decision or activity.

The Budget Process in the Nineteenth and Early Twentieth Centuries

Presidents have not always been highly interested and active in the budget process. Before 1900, presidents often played little or no part in developing revenue and spending proposals.[48] Presidents sometimes requested additional funds for some programs, called for spending restraint, or proposed new revenue

---

[46]For more on the budget as a fiscal policy instrument, see Cohen, *Politics and Economic Policy,* chap. 8.

[47]State and local government spending amounted to another 10 percent of the economy, or roughly $1 trillion.

[48]Louis Fisher, *Presidential Spending Power* (Princeton, N.J.: Princeton University Press, 1975), chap. 1–2; Lance LeLoup, *Budgetary Politics,* 4th ed. (Brunswick, Ohio: King's Court, 1988), chap. 5; David Nice, *Public Budgeting* (Belmont, Calif.: Wadsworth, 2002), pp. 59–63; Allen Schick, *The Federal Budget* (Washington, D.C.: Brookings Institution, 1995), chap. 4.

policies. But presidential involvement was sporadic and often selective, focusing on a limited number of issues.

Instead, agencies submitted funding requests directly to the Treasury Department, which compiled and relayed them to Congress. Agency personnel generally had the right to ask Congress for whatever level of funding they believed was appropriate. The need to retain the president's goodwill and the fear of a presidential veto often made agency officials consider presidential sentiments, however, in preparing their requests.

In the 1890s, that system came under increasing strain. From 1894 through 1914, the national government ran budget deficits roughly half of the time. This was an important change, because throughout most of the nineteenth century, the United States ran surpluses, and the major policy dispute between Democrats and Republicans in the thirty years after the Civil War centered on the size of the surplus. The national government created several new programs that gave financial aid to the states. The amount of aid was initially small, but the new programs created financial commitments that could not easily be eliminated and might grow over time. The heavy costs of World War I added to the government's financial woes, leading to truly massive deficits that needed to be dealt with. On the revenue side of the equation, the Supreme Court struck down the federal income tax in 1895, a decision that produced a controversial effort to amend the Constitution. Thus, the large and growing federal budget and the rise of large deficits, which were due mainly to wars, produced growing concern that the traditional system of federal budgeting was inadequate.

Reformers at all levels of government advocated stronger executive leadership in many aspects of government, including budgeting. The reformers contended that strong executives would counteract the parochialism created by agencies, interest groups, and legislative committees, as well as the local interests that are often influential in America's legislatures. According to the reformers, a strong executive would have a broader viewpoint and could coordinate budgetary decisions across different agencies, stand up to selfish interest groups and party bosses, and, therefore, curb wasteful spending. A visible chief executive, such as the president, must answer to the general public and would foster greater accountability for budgetary decisions.

Many members of Congress opposed greater presidential involvement in the budget process. They knew that legislative control over finances was a traditional foundation of legislative influence, and some members noted that most of the constitutional provisions involving financial matters were in the article dealing with Congress, not the article dealing with the presidency. Greater presidential involvement in budgeting might weaken the power of Congress considerably.

Establishing the Executive Budget

Demand for budgetary reforms continued, however, and in 1921, Congress enacted the Budget and Accounting Act. The new law required the president to develop and submit a budget proposal to Congress each year. The proposed budget would include both revenue and spending recommendations. Because this would

be an immense and difficult task and because presidents might have little experience or interest in budgeting, the act also created the Bureau of the Budget to
help the president develop the budget proposal and help implement the budget
after adoption. The BOB was originally part of the Treasury Department.[49]

Under this process, the BOB gave agencies guidelines for developing their
budget proposals. These guidelines would reflect the president's budget priorities
and, to varying degrees, assessments of what would have a realistic chance of being adopted by Congress. Agencies would then submit budget requests to the
BOB, along with supporting information to justify their requests.

Because of fears that agencies might ignore the president's budget guidelines
and seek whatever level of funding agency officials wanted, the BOB instituted a
process called central legislative clearance in the 1920s. This process required that
agency proposals for legislation and agency expressions of viewpoints regarding
legislation (such as testimony during congressional committee hearings) must, if
the proposals or expressions might affect the budget, be submitted to the BOB
for review. Only proposals judged to be in line with presidential priorities could
be presented to Congress. Expressions of agency viewpoints could be submitted
to Congress without being consistent with the president's programs, but such
views would be accompanied by comments from the BOB indicating that these
views were not in accord with the president's. Central clearance was not always
enforced consistently in its early years, the 1920s, but it reflected an effort to give
the president more influence over budgetary decisions.

Some members of Congress and some agency personnel disliked the fact that
central clearance allowed the president to conceal information from Congress, although central clearance may also help protect Congress from some financial
pressures. Note, however, that central clearance does not necessarily stop informal communications between federal agencies and Congress. A quiet telephone
call, an e-mail message, a "chance" meeting at a social gathering, information relayed through an interest group—these and many other techniques are used to
undercut the central clearance process. Especially when the president and most
members of Congress have different budgetary priorities, some agencies may use
unofficial communications with Congress to weaken presidential influence.[50]

In 1939, the BOB was moved from the Treasury Department to the new Executive Office of the President. This change emphasized that the BOB was the president's representative in the budget process. At this same time, the BOB's duties
were broadened to include developing proposals to improve federal management
and gathering information on agency performance. That broadening reflected a
changing emphasis in government budgeting, with more attention being paid to
agency activities and management than to just what was spent.

[49]Leloup, *Budgetary Politics,* chap. 4; Richard Neustadt, "Presidency and Legislation: The Growth
of Central Clearance," *American Political Science Review* 48 (1954): 641–51; Nice, *Public Budgeting,*
pp. 60–62; Margaret Wyszomirski, "The De-Institutionalization of Presidential Staff Agencies," *Public
Administration Review* 42 (1982): 448–58.

[50]On these and other budgeting games and strategies, see Roy T. Meyers, *Strategic Budgeting* (Ann
Arbor: University of Michigan Press, 1994).

The Modern Budgeting Process in the Executive

The BOB was reorganized and renamed in 1970. The new Office of Management and Budget retained its former responsibilities but added more emphasis on better management of federal agencies. In subsequent years, the OMB gained more responsibility for persuading Congress to adopt the president's budget proposals, largely because of White House fears that many federal agencies could not be trusted to support the president's policies. In addition, political appointees gradually gained greater influence within the OMB, a development that produced complaints of eroding expertise and credibility.[51]

Critics also complained that the OMB continued to focus primarily on relatively short-term budgetary issues at the expense of longer-term management concerns. A series of reforms and reorganizations, culminating in the OMB 2000 reorganization (announced in 1994), have tried to strengthen the OMB's management efforts, with somewhat mixed results.[52]

The Executive Budget Cycle: Developing Budget Estimates   Since the mid-1970s, developing the president's budget proposal has taken roughly nine to ten months, usually beginning in early spring, to be ready by early in the next year. The OMB, the Council of Economic Advisers, and top officials in the Treasury Department, sometimes joined by other advisers, make projections of future economic conditions, the costs of current commitments, future revenues, and the likely costs or savings resulting from new White House proposals. The OMB sends departments and agencies guidelines for preparing their budget requests.

Agencies then develop their proposals, which may be modified during departmental hearings. New economic forecasts and additional policy changes that might affect agency budgets sometimes arrive during this process. Agency and departmental personnel sometimes try to balance obtaining what their programs need and presenting an image of reasonable adherence to presidential priorities. That is especially difficult for agencies that have few friends in the White House.

Further hearings are held in the OMB, often with an emphasis on making agency requests conform more closely to presidential policies. Although the president has the last word on the budget proposal, OMB officials normally reflect presidential preferences. As a result, agencies that appeal OMB decisions to the president will rarely succeed.

Trying to enforce the president's budgetary policies is often a difficult job. If people in an agency think that the OMB's (and the president's) policies endanger vital programs, they may conceal information, leak stories to the news media, seek protection from interest group allies, or run to Congress for protection. If the OMB appears too friendly toward an agency and its programs, other White House

---

[51]On the development of the OMB, see Larry Berman, *The Office of Management and Budget and the Presidency, 1921–1979* (Princeton, N.J.: Princeton University Press, 1979); and Shelley Lynn Tompkin, *Inside OMB: Politics and Process in the President's Budget Office* (Armonk, N.Y.: M. E. Sharpe, 1999).

[52]Office of Management and Budget, *Changes Resulting from the OMB 2000 Reorganization* (Washington, D.C.: General Accounting Office, 1996).

officials, including the president, may begin to doubt the loyalty of OMB personnel. If the OMB is not sufficiently responsive to presidential priorities, the president may begin to rely on other staff units, at least for important decisions. But if the OMB appears too subservient to the chief executive, others, such as members of Congress, may start to question the reliability of the office's budgetary analyses. This last possibility in fact became a reality and has harmed the OMB's reputation, as well as its role in the budget process.

From its creation in 1921 as the Bureau of the Budget through the 1960s, the budget office developed a reputation for not only serving the president but for the quality of its expertise and its nonpartisan stance. The BOB/OMB developed an ethic of serving not only the individual president in office but also the office of the presidency.

However, presidents, especially Richard Nixon and those who followed, desired an agency that would be highly attuned to their needs. To accomplish this, Nixon began to insist on the loyalty of his administrative appointees. Loyalty to the president would be ensured by politicizing the appointment process. In other words, only those who were loyal to the president and his administration's goals would be appointed to office. Some critics charge that such politicization undermines the expertise of government agencies, a point that we discussed in detail in Chapter 11 on the president and the bureaucracy.

Not only did Nixon politicize the appointments to the budget office, but he reorganized it to gain further control over the agency. Thus, in 1970, the BOB was reorganized into the OMB. With that reorganization, not only did the number of political appointees, as opposed to career bureaucrats, increase at the budget office, but the task of the budget office shifted from helping the president build the budget to management and budgetary control of the departments and agencies of the federal government. While these actions may have helped make the OMB more responsive to the president, they also undermined the OMB's reputation as an expert agency.

Critics of the OMB have sometimes complained that it manipulates its economic and budgetary analyses to help promote the president's policy goals. Those suspicions found some corroboration in 1981, when Reagan's first budget director, David Stockman, admitted that the economic forecasts that helped justify the administration's 1981 budgetary proposals had been manipulated to show that no deficits would result. More recently, the OMB's analysis of Clinton's health care reform proposals in 1994 concluded that they would save roughly $60 billion over seven years. By contrast, the Congressional Budget Office (CBO) concluded that the proposals would cost an additional $70 billion. And in building his first budget, Clinton, understanding the suspicion surrounding OMB budget and economic estimates, offered to use CBO's estimates instead. In fact, one can argue that the CBO was created in part because the OMB's economic and budgetary estimates had become unreliable, because they were designed more to further the president's goals than to predict what might happen in the near future.[53]

[53]Nice, *Public Budgeting,* chap. 4, 6; Rubin, 2000, pp. 191–92; Allen Schick and Felix LoStracco, *The Federal Budget* (Washington, D.C.: Brookings Institution, 2000), pp. 55–56; Wildavsky and Caiden, 2001, p. 78; Aaron Wildavsky and Naomi Caiden, *The New Politics of the Budgetary Process,* 4th ed. (New York: Addison-Wesley-Longman 2001), p. 78.

The Executive Budget Cycle: Sending the President's Budget to Congress   By January or February, the president's budget proposal is usually ready (although changes may follow) and sent to Congress. Some presidents devote considerable time and attention to developing the budget, but other presidents may leave almost all of the work to the OMB and, consequently, be unfamiliar with many of their own budget proposals. For instance, Jimmy Carter and Bill Clinton were heavily involved in the details of budgets. In contrast, Ronald Reagan would set basic administration policy and delegated responsibility to his subordinates and advisers to ensure that the budget in its specific details reflected his priorities and goals.

Since the 1970s, a **current services budget** has accompanied the budget proposal to Congress. The current services budget includes the expected costs of current programs in the next fiscal year. The current services budget is an attempt to project what the future cost of a program would be if nothing about the program changed. Projecting the future costs of current programs is sometimes difficult. Should we allow for inflation? How much should we consider likely changes in program workload—more retirees on Medicare or more visitors to national parks, for example? Slightly different assumptions used to project future costs may greatly alter the current services budget for a program. That current services estimate may affect whether the president's proposal for an agency appears to be a funding cut or an increase. If the current services estimate does not account for inflation or underestimates changes in the expected future workload, the estimate may be viewed as a cut. If it overestimates inflation or the future workload, it may be viewed as an increase.

In most years, the president's budget request is a pretty good predictor of the revenue and expenditure policies that ultimately become law. In some cases, that pattern reflects presidential influence over final budgetary decisions, but in other cases, the similarity between proposal and final result reflects congressional influence on the president or pressures acting on both the White House and Congress.

However, while the overall budget totals that the president sends to Congress are close to those that Congress finally enacts, Congress may change spending levels for particular agencies and programs to ones that differ radically from the president's request. For instance, Congress may cut one agency, while increasing spending levels for another by the same amount. During the 1980s, Democrats in Congress often wanted to reduce President Reagan's spending on defense while at the same time boost spending on domestic programs.

Presidential and Congressional Interaction in the Budget Process

The budget process is fundamentally a legislative one. Before a budget can become operative, it must be enacted into law. Thus, it is important to consider the congressional role in budgeting and the interactions between the president and Congress in making the budget.

Congress influences the president's budget proposals in several ways, both formally and informally. The legislation authorizing a program may, for all practical purposes, make funding for that program immune to control within the budget process by making the spending legally required. Unless revised authorization legislation can be passed, the money must continue to flow. This is most important in the case of **entitlement programs.** Entitlement programs are those that give people certain rights to government benefits if they are qualified. Social Security and Medicare, as well as many veterans programs, are entitlements. It is important to note that entitlements do not have spending caps. For example, if more people than were projected decide to retire early and take their Social Security benefits, the government still has to provide the benefits to them.

Congress may also affect the president's budget proposals whenever White House or agency personnel anticipate Congress's probable reaction to the proposals. Sometimes the White House may trim (or increase) a request to increase its chances of passage. In other cases, the White House may try to offset expected congressional changes. For example, the president might increase the amount requested for a program in anticipation of likely congressional cuts, or the president might recommend less than he actually wants if Congress is expected to add funds to the request.[54]

Of course, members of Congress may detect that behavior and try to offset it with deeper cuts for agencies whose requests are padded and more generosity for programs with unrealistically low budget requests. Presidents usually avoid recommendations that appear unrealistic to members of Congress and, therefore, will not be taken seriously, although Reagan sometimes had that problem during his second term, with budgets that were sometimes pronounced "dead on arrival."[55]

Members of Congress may also lobby White House officials in hopes of influencing presidential budget requests. This may occur with the member taking the initiative or in response to White House efforts to gain congressional support for a forthcoming budget proposal or some other issue. In either situation, the member of Congress indicates an interest in some budgetary concern, such as financial assistance for farmers or higher defense spending. Ignoring those sentiments can be risky for the president, especially if they are shared by many members.

Reforming the Budget Process: The 1974 Budget Act

Until the mid-1970s, the president held the upper hand in budgeting. Although conflict between the president and Congress over the budget broke out on occasion, the budget process was no more conflictual than other types of legislation. By the mid-1970s, however, conflict between the president and Congress over the

[54]Schick, *Federal Budget,* p. 60–61; Aaron Wildavsky, *The Politics of the Budgetary Process,* 2d ed. (Boston: Little, Brown, 1974), pp. 21–24.

[55]Schick, *Federal Budget,* pp. 60–61.

budget erupted and culminated in a major reform of the budget process, the **Congressional Budget and Impoundment Control Act of 1974.**

There were several sources of the increased budgetary tension between the president and Congress. First, the rise in spending associated with the passage of Lyndon Johnson's Great Society programs in the 1960s put additional stress on the budget. Added to this source of increased costs were the costs of the war in Vietnam. The United States attempted a policy of "guns and butter" in the late 1960s and early 1970s that led to large increases in the costs of government. At the same time, the economy began to stall, which limited the resources that government could tap into to pay for the growing cost of government.

Richard Nixon's presidency exacerbated these tensions already inherent in the budget process. To control the costs of government, Nixon impounded funds for several programs that Congress had already authorized spending. These included Housing and Urban Development Department grants, federal housing programs, water pollution funds, and some farm programs. **Impoundments** occur when presidents refuse to spend money that Congress has authorized and appropriated. While impoundments can be and have been justified, for instance, because a program is costing less than anticipated or is no longer needed, Nixon impounded funds for programs that he disliked but happened to be popular with some members of Congress, in particular Democrats.[56]

The Congressional Budget and Impoundment Control Act of 1974 was Congress's attempt to hem in Nixon and to reassert itself in the budget process. To that end, Congress reformed the way it approached budgeting. It created two new committees, the Budget Committees, to oversee the budget process in Congress. The **Budget Committees** would be responsible for budgetary totals. The appropriations committees would still exist, but now they were constrained by the budgetary totals or targets that the Budget Committee and Congress imposed.

Under the 1974 budget act, each congressional chamber would have a budget committee. These committees would focus on broad budget issues, such as desired levels of revenue and spending, the appropriate surplus or deficit, and the allocation of funds across the major areas of federal governmental responsibility. The budget committees were created because of disagreements over the White House's budgetary priorities and because critics felt that Congress needed to place more emphasis on coordinating its various budgetary decisions. The budget committees and the budget resolutions they propose offer a rival to a president's budget recommendations and sometimes provoke considerable conflict that slows completion of the budget.

The **Congressional Budget Office (CBO),** a staff agency, was created to analyze the condition of the economy, forecast future revenues and program costs, and evaluate the effectiveness of federal programs. One major reason for the CBO's creation was that many members of Congress felt that they could not trust the budgetary and economic analyses provided by the White House. Some reformers

---

[56]See Howard E. Shuman, *Politics and the Budget: The Struggle Between the President and Congress,* 3d ed. (Englewood Cliffs, N.J.: Prentice-Hall, 1992), chap. 7.

also believed that expert budgetary advice would help Congress to make better decisions, particularly in light of the growing complexity of the budget and the economy. The CBO's budgetary analyses make members of Congress less dependent on the OMB's information, although much of the time, the two offices' studies generally agree.

The act also created a new budgetary process timetable. The timetable is quite complex, and in practice, Congress has violated and/or changed the timing targets quite often. According to the timetable as presented in the act, fifteen days after Congress convenes each year in January, the president is to submit a budget to Congress. By May 15, Congress is to take action on its first concurrent resolution. The concurrent resolution is a nonbinding budget target. It sets guidelines for total spending and revenues, the desired deficit or surplus, and the allotment of spending across several broad categories. The resolution contains less detail than the president's budget proposal but reflects congressional sentiments regarding broader budgetary issues. On September 15, the second concurrent resolution was to be passed although Congress has usually abandoned the second resolution in recent years. From May until this date, the congressional appropriations committees also work on their spending totals. These must be reconciled with the second (or first, if there is no second one) concurrent budget resolution by September 25. The new fiscal year is then to begin on October 1.

If spending and revenue bills do not match the congressional budget resolution, the 1974 budget reform provides for a remedy: the reconciliation bill. It may revise the budget resolution or modify revenue or spending guidelines. The reconciliation bill may also direct authorization committees to develop proposals to modify authorization legislation. The Reagan administration, working in concert with a coalition of congressional Republicans and conservative Democrats, used the reconciliation bill to adopt a number of budgetary provisions in 1981—a development that surprised many observers, including some members of Congress. Reconciliation has not often served as a vehicle for presidential leadership, however.

If the White House and Congress are unable to complete work on an appropriations bill by the start of the new fiscal year (a common occurrence since the mid-1960s), a **continuing resolution** is used to provide funding for the affected agencies and programs until a regular appropriation bill can be adopted. The continuing resolution may expire within a few days if enactment of the spending bill is expected soon. If more time is needed, the continuing resolution may last much longer—sometimes for an entire year. Some agencies have been funded continuously by continuing resolutions for several years in a row.[57]

Members of Congress have often fought over the budget resolution, particularly in the House. Before 1974, members of Congress could avoid explicit decisions on total revenues and spending and the level of the deficit or surplus. This was because spending decisions were made through an appropriations process. The appropriations committee was divided into numerous subcommittees, each

---

[57]Lastly, the act restricted presidential impoundment ability, although it granted the president the power to withhold spending under specified circumstances.

of which submitted separate appropriations bills to Congress for passage. At no point in the appropriations process was total federal spending considered. The new budget process did this through the budget resolutions and reconciliation process.

Assessing the Reformed Budget Process

Making budgetary decisions with the new process has often been difficult in a context of slow economic growth such as occurred during the 1970s and the recession of the early 1980s and early 1990s, growing party polarization in Congress, frequently divided party control between the presidency and Congress, and increased interest group conflict. The wrangling that resulted from these factors often delayed action on everything in the budget. In 1998, Congress failed to enact a budget resolution due to many disagreements over budgetary issues.[58]

Thus, over time, with numerous exceptions, the process of developing budget proposals has shifted from a relatively bottom-up process that was centered in the appropriations committees to a more top-down process in which the president, top congressional leaders, Congressional and the Budget Committee play the most prominent roles.

Presidents have often found that exerting influence over the budget has been difficult since the early 1970s. Several factors contribute to the difficulty. As noted above, the growing activity of interest groups with conflicting priorities, the frequent division of party control between the White House and Congress, and the growing polarization of the parties have led to increased political conflict over many budgetary issues. The erratic performance of the economy and sluggish revenue growth in the 1970s and 1980s made satisfying multiple demands difficult, and the rising share of the budget consisting of uncontrollable spending hampered efforts to fund other programs. Large budget deficits from the 1980s through the late 1990s provoked further conflict. Congress and the White House were often unable to complete action on all of the spending bills before the beginning of the new fiscal year. Moreover, numerous accusations of failing to honor commitments, deception, and unreasonableness have been hurled back and forth between Capitol Hill and the White House.

Tackling the Deficit Issue

In the late 1970s, government began to run up large deficits. The size of the deficit ballooned in the 1980s, becoming a major source of friction between the president and Congress, as well as between Democrats and Republicans. The budget deficits that plagued the government across the 1980s and into the mid-1990s have several sources.

[58]Norman Ornstein, Thomas Mann, and Michael Malbin, *Vital Statistics on Congress* (Washington, D.C.: American Enterprise Institute, 2000), p. 168; James Thurber, "New Rules for an Old Game: Zero-Sum Budgeting in the Postreform Congress," in *The Postreform Congress,* ed. Roger Davidson (New York: St. Martin's, 1992), pp. 257–78.

First, Ronald Reagan asked for major and permanent tax cuts in 1981, which Congress enacted. The tax cuts limited the ability of government to raise revenue without resorting to new taxes, which are usually unpopular with voters. Reagan argued that the tax cuts would not undermine government revenues, as his detractors asserted, but rather would stimulate economic growth. With a larger economy, government revenues would increase as the economy grew. This idea is termed **supply-side economics** and was the foundation of economic policy under the Reagan administration.

At the same time that Reagan sought tax cuts, he also sought spending increases, primarily in defense. To offset the combination of major tax cuts and defense spending increases, domestic programs would have to be cut drastically. Although many domestic programs suffered large cuts, support from interest groups, public outcry, and Democrats in Congress limited how deeply these cuts could be made.

Another factor of prime importance was the increase in entitlement spending, especially Social Security and Medicare programs. The driving force behind spending for these and similar programs was demographic change. Simply put, the number of retired and elderly people was increasing at a fast rate, and they were living longer than the elderly had in the past. Thus, the number of people eligible for Social Security and related programs swelled. Given the popularity of the program, which is often called the "third rail" of American politics (in reference to electrified rails used to power some mass transit systems; "touch it and you die"), President Reagan decided not to try to contain it, although he briefly toyed with the idea of reforming Social Security to control its rapidly rising costs.[59]

Compounding these factors was the increase in the government's interest payments on its debt. The government finances its deficit by borrowing money. Like everyone who borrows money, the government must pay interest on the loan. As the deficits grew year after year, so did the government's interest payments.

Because of these factors, the deficit grew across the 1980s and into the 1990s, becoming perhaps the most important national policy issue. To help contain the deficit and put the national government on a firmer and more responsible fiscal course, a series of budget reforms and innovations, beginning in the middle of the 1980s, was begun.[60] In 1985, Congress adopted the **Gramm-Rudman-Hollings Act,** which created a series of gradually decreasing budget deficit targets for 1986 through 1990 and a goal of a balanced budget in 1991. If the budget deficit exceeded the target for the year by more than a set amount, automatic spending cuts (following fixed rules) would trim spending until the target was met. The Supreme Court struck down some features of the law, and many members of Congress found that the deficit targets were unrealistic. Consequently,

[59]See Paul C. Light, *Still Artful Work: The Continuing Politics of Social Security Reform,* 2d ed. (New York: McGraw-Hill, 1994).

[60]See John Gilmour, "Summits and Stalemates: Bipartisan Negotiations in the Postreform Era," in *The Postreform Congress,* ed. Roger Davidson (New York: St. Martin's, 1992), pp. 233–56; Robert Lee and Ronald Johnson, *Public Budgeting Systems,* 6th ed. (Gaithersburg, Md.: Aspen, 1998), pp. 230–58; and Aaron Wildavsky and Naomi Caiden, *The New Politics of the Budgetary Process,* 3d ed. (New York: Longman, 1997), chap. 5–6.

1987 reforms established a slightly revised process and a new set of deficit targets, ending with a balanced budget in 1993. The early targets were officially met by using unrealistic budgetary forecasts and a variety of devices—critics called them "gimmicks" or "smoke and mirrors," such as "magic asterisks" that set an amount of savings to be achieved by cuts that would be identified later.

By 1990, many officials believed that the deficit targets chosen in 1987 could not be reached; however, concerns over the deficits continued. The White House and Congress responded by enacting the **Budget Enforcement Act of 1990 (BEA).** The new law raised additional revenue and projected spending cuts but provided for greater flexibility than did Gramm-Rudman-Hollings. The BEA did not apply to emergency spending, an omission that led to several disputes regarding what constitutes a genuine emergency. The BEA also exempted changing costs of entitlement programs if the changes were caused by an increased workload, such as more retirees applying for Social Security.

The BEA set expenditure limitations for discretionary programs (that is, the relatively controllable spending items), but the limits could be modified for inflation and changing program workloads. This provision produced several conflicts over whether particular agency budgets were actually growing or being cut (as traditionally viewed), depending in part on how the adjustment factors were defined. The law created separate funding pools for defense programs, international assistance, and domestic programs for the first three years to prevent supporters of those three sets of programs from trying to take one another's money. In addition, the BEA required that any policy changes affecting revenues or "direct spending" (mainly those expenditures that are largely uncontrollable by the appropriations process, such as entitlements) could not produce larger deficits. Any expenditure increases covered by this requirement would have to include revenue or expenditure adjustments for other programs to offset the increased spending. Policies resulting in revenue cuts must be offset by spending cuts or increases in other revenue sources.

Budgetary conflict continued after enactment of the BEA because the fundamental political and economic pressures continued to plague the White House and Congress. One symptom of that conflict is the various budget "summits" held by the White House and congressional leaders to negotiate budget agreements since 1990. The most dramatic episode occurred in 1995 to 1996, when President Clinton vetoed two bills and government was shut down for a short while.

The 1995–1996 Budget Showdown   The 1995–1996 budget showdown was a singular event in the Clinton presidency and federal budgeting. The seeds of the showdown trace to Clinton's failed attempt to gain enactment of his health care reform package. Several negative consequences to Clinton's presidency resulted. First, the Republicans successfully branded Clinton as a typical "tax and spend" liberal Democrat who was out of touch with the nation. Clinton's polls suffered as well, registering among the lowest levels of his presidency up to then. To add to Clinton's woes, the Republicans took over the House of Representatives for the first time since the early 1950s. Under the leadership of Newt Gingrich, who became the first Republican speaker in fifty years, the congressional Republicans charged forward with their program, which they called the "Contract with America." One element of the Contract was to balance the federal budget within seven years.

To that end, Congress passed a continuing resolution with spending totals much lower than Clinton wanted. Because of mounting deficits, the federal government was reaching its debt limit. The debt limit is a legislative cap on how much money the federal government can owe and borrow. With that limit nearing, new legislation had to be passed, but Congress attached raising the debt limit ceiling to language that would first require the federal government to balance the budget. In effect, Republicans in Congress hoped to corner Clinton into balancing the budget.

Clinton publicly charged that the Republican tactics were akin to "terrorism." The president's offensive seemed to pay off. First, public support for him rose, in part because of his resolve with the Republicans. Twice, he had allowed the government to shut down, once for six days and again for nineteen days, vetoing a continuing resolution and the debt limit bill. He also painted Republicans as willing to sacrifice the environment and cut Medicare spending, while upholding the interests of the rich.

With the president and Congress at an impasse, a compromise was reached in which both sides claimed victory. Congress passed a continuing resolution to allow government to operate, but instead of requiring the balanced budget to immediately take effect, new language only forced the president to agree that the budget would be balanced in seven years. The Republican's Contract used the seven-year time frame, but seven years is a long time in politics.

Clinton came out of the episode in a strengthened position. His polls were high, and the Republicans appeared too extreme for most Americans. This set the foundation for his landslide reelection victory in November 1996. The Republicans grew somewhat timid in challenging the president, fearing that he would again lead the public to think of them as extremists.[61]

From Deficit to Surplus   By fiscal year 1998, the federal government achieved a modest budget surplus for the first time since late 1960s. Budget forecasts also indicated continuing budget surpluses for a number of years into the future. A number of factors contributed to the budget surplus. First, reforms in spending, as we have noted (especially the 1990 budget agreement), seemed to have put a lid on spending growth. Second, across the 1980s and 1990s, government increased taxes. Clinton's first budget in 1993, for instance, called for major tax increases, and many tax increases were passed in the 1980s after the enactment of the Reagan tax cuts. Third, the economy grew, especially in the mid- to late 1990s. More important, it grew much faster than government. The increase in the size of the economy presented the government with more revenues.

[61]Gilmour, "Summits and Stalemates"; David Maraniss and Michael Weiskopf, *Tell Newt to Shut Up!* (New York: Touchstone, 1996), pp. 146–205; Schick and LoStracco, *Federal Budget,* pp. 199–201; Wildavsky and Caiden, 2001; 174–185.

By the late 1990s, the issue was no longer how to solve the deficit issue. It became, instead, what should be done with the surplus. Several approaches were offered. These included spending increases for such items as a drug prescription plan for seniors on Medicare and paying off some of the federal debt, thereby reducing the size of federal interest payments. Doing so would free up more money that could be spent on programs, instead of servicing the debt. Lastly, many supported cutting taxes. President George W. Bush opted for major tax cuts, which Congress approved in 2001. We discussed the Bush tax cuts in some detail in Chapter 10 on the president and Congress.

However, the rosy budget scenario seemed to alter course as quickly as it came. By late summer 2001, it was apparent that the economy was slowing down and that an economic recovery might be slow to come. The smaller economy meant that government revenues would also shrink, but Congress passed large tax cuts the previous spring. There seemed to be little money left in the budget for new or expanded programs that Bush had promised, such as the drug prescription plan, education spending, and enhanced defense programs. Democrats even began to charge that Bush was fiscally reckless because of his tax cut and that the criticisms that they had earlier levied against his tax cut were coming true.

Since the economy is always cycling from growth to slowdown, one cannot be certain, even in the near term, about the budget. Debate between the president and Congress over the budget will continue, in good times and bad, as our discussion illustrates.

CHANGING THE BUDGET AFTER IT IS ADOPTED

For a variety of reasons, presidents may want or need to revise the budget after it has been enacted. Revenues may exceed or fall short of expectations, and the financial needs of various programs may also deviate from expectations. A newly elected president may want to change the budget already in place—a budget that may reflect the priorities of the previous administration and Congress. Different parts of the budget are often adopted at different times, and the later decisions may make revisions in the earlier decisions appear desirable. Political agreements reached earlier may unravel as groups unhappy with specific decisions press for revisions.

The most controversial changes in an adopted budget usually involve funding cuts. For many years, presidents have sometimes declined to spend money appropriated by Congress. That practice, called impoundment, traditionally involved limited amounts of money and usually some degree of consultation with Congress. During the Nixon administration, however, the amounts impounded were large, and Congress was rarely consulted.

Congress responded by attempting to clarify and regulate the president's impoundment power. The Budget and Impoundment Control Act of 1974 created two types of impoundments: **rescissions** and **deferrals.** Rescissions, which are permanent, can be proposed by either the president or Congress. Rescissions must be approved by both houses of Congress; most presidential rescission requests have been rejected since the law took effect, and the savings resulting from approved rescissions have been small relative to the size of the federal budget. Deferrals, which are temporary impoundments, can be used only for routine administrative problems, such as a project falling behind schedule.[62] Even if funds are impounded, they may be restored at some future date.

The president's impoundment powers temporarily expanded in 1996, when Congress passed new legislation. The law provided that within five business days after passage of a spending bill, the president could propose deletion of individual projects funded by the bill, regardless of whether the projects were listed in the spending bill or the committee report accompanying it. The cuts became effective unless Congress passed disapproval legislation within thirty days. If the president vetoed the disapproval legislation, Congress could override the veto by a two-thirds vote in both houses. Clinton used the authority to trim a modest amount of federal spending, but the Supreme Court concluded that the new power violated constitutional provisions for passing legislation and struck down the law in 1998.[63]

Presidents may also modify portions of the budget after they have been adopted, by shifting funds from one part of the budget to another. The needs of one program may increase unexpectedly while another's needs decrease, or an agency may have unexpected expenses for one thing, such as supplies, while managing to save money in some other area of operations. Relatively modest reallocation of funds can be done in two ways. Reprogramming reallocates funds within an appropriations account (which is defined in the appropriations bill); transfers between accounts are used to move funds from one account to another. Transfers are more likely to be politically sensitive, and heavy use of transfers and reprogramming may anger members of Congress, particularly if they are not consulted in advance or if their wishes are ignored.[64]

If an agency or program needs additional funding during the fiscal year or if people are not satisfied with the funding level originally approved, a supplemental appropriation can be used to provide additional funds. Supplemental appropriations are enacted through the same processes used to adopt other legislation. From the mid-1980s through the mid-1990s, concerns over the budget deficits and conflicts between the White House and Congress kept supplemental appropriations at a relatively low level, with the exception of the costs generated by the war in the Middle East in 1991.[65]

[62]Comptroller General, *Memo to the President of the Senate and the Speaker of the House of Representatives* (Washington, D.C.: General Accounting Office, 1998); and Schick and LoStracco, *Federal Budget,* pp. 250–55.

[63]Bruce Oppenheimer, "Abdicating Congressional Power: The Paradox of Republican Control," in *Congress Reconsidered,* 6th ed., ed. Lawrence Dodd and Bruce Oppenheimer (Washington, D.C.: Congressional Quarterly Press, 1997), pp. 381–84; and Michael Nelson, *The Evolving Presidency* (Washington, D.C.: Congressional Quarterly Press, 1999), pp. 247–52.

[64]Donald Axelrod, *Budgeting for Modern Government* (New York: St. Martin's, 1995), p. 235; Fisher, *Presidential Spending Power,* chap. 5; LeLoup, *Budgetary Politics,* pp. 231–32.

[65]Irene Rubin, *The Politics of Public Budgeting,* 3d ed. (Chatham, N.J.: Chatham House, 1997), pp. 231–38; and Schick, *Federal Budget,* pp. 130–31, 166.

PRESIDENTS AND ECONOMIC AND BUDGETARY POLICY

Economic policy has remained a top presidential priority since Franklin Roosevelt's presidency, if not before. Elections are won or lost based on the state of the economy. Presidents go down in history as great leaders or failures in part because of the state of the economy while they were in office. But as this chapter shows, although the public makes presidents politically responsible for the economy, presidents do not possess many tools to steer it. Monetary policy, which regulates the supply and cost of money in the economy, is regulated by an independent commission, the Federal Reserve Board. Fiscal policy, which concerns government taxing and spending, is shared with Congress. As this chapter demonstrates, Congress and the president do not always agree on fiscal policy. Thus, this chapter has highlighted important themes of this text: the mismatch between public expectations for presidential leadership and the control of policy tools given to the president. Still, as we also have pointed out, presidents, while constrained, are not without resources in dealing with these issues. The example of the 1995–1996 budget showdown illustrates how even a president seemingly down on his luck and supposedly destined to be a one-term president can emerge from conflict with Congress in an enhanced position and win a landslide reelection.

Aside from the politics of economic and budget policy, one must also recognize the importance of these policies to a nation's citizens. How well government steers the economy determines to a large extent the economic quality of life of its citizens. In this sense, the results of economic policy have not only important but also profound political implications for people's lives.

KEY TERMS

Budget and Accounting
   Act of 1921   403
budget deferrals   428
Budget Enforcement Act of
   1990 (BEA)   426
budget rescissions   428
Bureau of the Budget (BOB)/
   Office of Management and
   Budget (OMB)   403
Cabinet Council on
   Economic Affairs   412
Congressional Budget and
   Impoundment Control Act
   of 1974   422
Congressional Budget
   Committee   422

Congressional Budget
   Office (CBO)   422
continuing resolution   423
Council of Economic Advisers   407
countercyclical policies   410
current services budget   420
Economic Policy Board (EPB)/
   Economic Policy Group   412
economic subpresidency   404
entitlement programs   421
Federal Reserve Board   410
fiscal policy tools   401
Full Employment Act of 1946   403
Gramm-Rudman-Hollings Act   425
Humphrey-Hawkins Act of 1978   404
impoundments   422

DISCUSSION QUESTIONS

1. Discuss the evolution of economic policy-making responsibility in the presidency. When and why did the presidency assume so much responsibility for making economic policy?
2. Discuss the institutionalization of economic policy making within the executive. What does this tell us about the modern presidency in comparison to the pre-modern presidency? How effectively is economic policy making institutionalized in the executive? How much leeway does the president possess to make economic policy outside of these institutional bodies that also hold economic policy-making responsibility?
3. What are the major units of the economic subpresidency? Compare their missions and the advice that they offer the president. Which have been most important to the president over time? How able is the president to influence these advising bodies?
4. Describe the development of the budget process. What factors have led to changes in the way the budget is made at the federal level? How has the president's influence over budget making been affected by changes in the budget process?
5. Discuss the evolution of the budget office. Where has it been located in the federal executive? Why has it been moved? Why was it renamed from the Bureau of the Budget to the Office of Management and Budget? What else was changed with its renaming? What role does the OMB now play in budgeting and other policy areas for the president?
6. What are the major tensions between the president and Congress over budget policy? How do economic conditions, deficits and surpluses, and politics affect those tensions?

SUGGESTED READINGS

Larry Berman, *The Office of Management and Budget and the Presidency, 1921–1979*. Princeton, N.J.: Princeton University Press, 1979.

Jeffrey E. Cohen, *Politics and Economic Policy in the United States*, 2d ed. Boston: Houghton-Mifflin, 1999.

John P. Frendreis and Raymond Tatalovich, *The Modern Presidency and Economic Policy*. Itasca, Ill.: Peacock 1994.

Irene Rubin, *The Politics of Public Budgeting*, 3d ed. Chatham, N.J.: Chatham House, 1997.

Charles L. Schultze, *Memos to the President: A Guide Through Macroeconomics for the Busy Policymaker.* Washington, D.C.: Brookings Institution, 1992.

Howard E. Shuman, *Politics and the Budget: The Struggle Between the President and the Congress,* 3d ed. Englewood Cliffs, N.J.: Prentice-Hall, 1992.

Herbert Stein, *Presidential Economics: The Making of Economic Policy from Roosevelt to Reagan and Beyond,* 2d ed. Washington, D.C.: American Enterprise Institute, 1988.

Aaron Wildavsky and Naomi Caiden, *The New Politics of the Budgetary Process,* 3d ed. New York: Longman, 1997.

15

THE PRESIDENT AND
FOREIGN POLICY MAKING

Since the nation's inception, the president and the administration have been held responsible for international affairs. Although the president takes the lead in foreign policy formulation and implementation, Congress still possesses important foreign policy powers and responsibilities. Again, as we observed for other policy areas, the Constitution structures the role of the president and the other branches of government in the foreign policy realm. But the fact that the president sits atop the executive branch provides him with several advantages in foreign policy making that he does not so clearly enjoy in other policy areas. Moreover, the public expects presidential leadership and responsibility in foreign policy, an expectation that is perhaps stronger than for any other policy area.

In this chapter, we will discuss the president's role in foreign policy making. As we have done for most topics discussed throughout this text, we begin with the Constitution. Then we will discuss two major aspects of foreign policy making, diplomacy and war making. The middle section of the chapter focuses on advisers to the president in foreign policy, followed by discussions of the presidential advantage over Congress in foreign policy making and the basis of presidential decision making in foreign policy.

THE CONSTITUTION, THE PRESIDENT, AND FOREIGN POLICY MAKING

Traditionally, executives, be they kings, dictators, or presidents, direct a nation's foreign policy. The idea that it is best if one person is in charge of foreign policy is a long-standing assumption. As Alexander Hamilton argues in Federalist No. 70, energy and dispatch in the executive come from its unitary nature. Such "energy in the Executive is the bulwark of the national security" and is "essential to the protection of the community against foreign attack."

Also, placing foreign policy in the hands of one top-level leader allows a nation to speak with one voice in its dealings with other nations. This helps avoid confusion about the nature of a nation's foreign policy, which will supposedly cut down on misunderstandings between nations. Furthermore, centralizing foreign policy responsibility in the executive helps a nation hide its secrets from current and potential adversaries. The more people involved in making foreign policy, the more likely that secrets about such sensitive matters as troop deployment, new weapons development, strategy, and spies may be revealed to adversaries. Keeping its adversaries in the dark about its war making capability, strategies, and foreign policy goals provides the nation with an advantage in dealing with potentially hostile nations.

This unitary responsibility for foreign policy is recognized in the Constitution, but Congress is given an important role to play as well.[1] The underlying principle is that the president is solely responsible for conducting the nation's foreign affairs, although both branches share in the formulation of foreign policy. Thus, once a policy course has been decided, the president should be given a relatively unencumbered hand. As we will see, this is not always the case.

Presidents tend to subscribe to the **sole organ theory** of foreign relations. The sole organ theory argues that the president alone speaks for the nation in the conduct of foreign affairs. The Supreme Court sanctioned this perspective with its famous *U.S.* v. *Curtiss-Wright* decision in 1936. In that decision, the Curtiss-Wright Corporation was accused of violating an arms embargo that Franklin Roosevelt had set against two warring Latin American nations. In its defense, the corporation argued that Congress could not delegate such power to the president. But the Court sided with the president, arguing that the powers of the United States in foreign affairs were rooted in the nation's sovereignty, as well as in the Constitution. Furthermore, the Court argued that the president could exercise his foreign policy-making powers expansively, except when constitutional provisions denied the president a free or unfettered hand. Ever since this decision, the Court has generally granted the president leeway in the conduct of foreign affairs.[2]

Table 15-1 presents a breakdown of Supreme Court support for the president in foreign policy cases from 1934 through Bill Clinton's first term of office in 1996. The figures show how strongly the Court has upheld the president's position on such cases. Of the 170 cases that the Court heard during this period, it sided with the president on 103 (61 percent) of them. Furthermore, the Court supported every president except for FDR and LBJ over half of the time. FDR often ran into difficulty with the Court across many issues, especially from 1933 until 1938. Thus, it may make sense to look only at the presidents after FDR. From Truman through Clinton, the Supreme Court supported the president 67 percent of the time.

---

[1]The literature on the constitutional foundations of presidential foreign policy making is huge. See David G. Adler and Larry N. George, *The Constitution and the Conduct of American Foreign Policy* (Lawrence: University of Kansas Press, 1996; Thomas M. Franck, *Political Questions/Judicial Answers* (Princeton, NJ: Princeton University Press, 1992); Michael J. Glennon, *Constitutional Diplomacy* (Princeton, N.J.: Princeton University Press, 1990); Louis Henkin, *Constitutionalism, Democracy and Foreign Affairs* (New York: Columbia University Press, 1990); Harold Hongju Koh, *The National Security Constitution* (New Haven: Yale University Press, 1999). For overviews of Congress's role, including presidential-congressional relations, see James Lindsay, *Congress and the Politics of U.S. Foreign Policy.* (Baltimore: Johns Hopkins University Press, 1994); and Cecil V. Crabb, Jr., and Pat M. Holt, *Invitation to Struggle: Congress, the President and Foreign Policy,* 2d ed. (Washington, D.C.: Congressional Quarterly Press, 1984).

[2]Kimi Lynn King and James Meernik, "The 'Sole Organ' Before the Court: Presidential Power in Foreign Policy Cases, 1790–1996," *Presidential Studies Quarterly* 28 (Summer 1998): 666–87. Other studies also find that the courts are highly supportive of the president in foreign policy matters; see Craig R. Ducat and Robert L. Dudley. 1989. "Federal District Courts and Presidential Power During the Postwar Era," *Journal of Politics* 51 (February 1989): 98–118; and Jeff Yates and Andrew Whitford, "Presidential Power and the United States Supreme Court," *Political Research Quarterly,* 51 (June 1998): 539–50.

TABLE 15-1   PRESIDENTIAL SUCCESS IN FOREIGN POLICY CASES BEFORE
THE SUPREME COURT, 1934–1996

President	% Won	% Lost	Number of cases
Roosevelt	27.6	72.4	29
Truman	69.4	30.6	36
Eisenhower	50.0	50.0	12
Kennedy	58.3	41.7	12
Johnson	36.8	63.2	19
Nixon	68.2	31.8	22
Ford	87.5	12.5	8
Carter	100.0	0.0	12
Bush	84.6	15.4	13
Clinton	71.4	28.6	7

Source: Kimi Lynn King and James Meernik, "The 'Sole Organ' Before the Court: Presidential Power in Foreign Policy Cases, 1790–1996," *Presidential Studies Quarterly* 28 (Summer 1988): 666–87.

The Constitution recognizes two major types of foreign policy-making powers: diplomatic and war making. Diplomatic powers involve making treaties, designating ambassadors, recognizing other nations, and receiving their diplomats and representatives. War making powers involve declaring war, commiting troops, and commanding the armed forces.

TREATY MAKING, DIPLOMACY, AND THE PRESIDENCY

The **treaty making power** is located in Article II, Section 2, Paragraph 2 of the Constitution. Its key provision reads that the president "shall have the Power, by and with the Advice and Consent of the Senate, to make Treaties, provided that two-thirds of the Senators present concur." Also, the same paragraph grants the president the power to appoint ambassadors, again subject to senatorial consent.

What does it mean that the Senate can advise the president over treaty making? Does advising extend to treaty negotiations with other nations, or does it begin only when the president has submitted the treaty to the Senate? Constitutional language implies that the Senate may advise in the negotiation phase of treaty making, although the Constitution is silent about the form that such advising may take.

In 1789, George Washington tried to get Senate advice on a treaty being negotiated with an Indian tribe. Washington met with the Senate and presented a draft of the treaty, but the Senate refused to commit itself. This soured Washington on involving the Senate in treaty negotiations. Subsequent presidents would not try to involve the chamber as a whole in the negotiations process, although at times presidents would informally meet with Senate leaders for their advice. Presidents might also seek Senate advice on the membership of the treaty negotiation team; sometimes members of the Senate would be appointed as treaty negotiators, and sometimes presidents offered the Senate the power to veto any proposed treaty team member. The form and extent of Senate participation in the negotiation phase have been left up to presidents, who tend to decide on Senate involvement case by case. On controversial and important treaties, however, presidents who disregard a role for the Senate in the negotiation phase sometimes find it difficult to gain Senate acceptance of the treaty.[3]

Once a treaty is submitted to it, the Senate may amend the treaty. Doing so requires returning to the other nation to renegotiate the new language. The treaty need not be resubmitted to the Senate if the other nation agrees to the changes. The Senate may also express **reservations** about language contained in a treaty. Reservations usually define what the Senate considers to be the limits of the obligations of the United States under the treaty. While a reservation does not require renegotiation of a treaty, if the other nation objects to the reservation, it might reject the treaty. The Senate may also state its **understandings** of a treaty, which expresses the Senate's interpretation, usually of a term used in the treaty. For instance, an understanding might define in technical and precise language the type or size of weapon to which an arms control treaty refers. Once the Senate has consented to a treaty, the president can sign it, which ratifies the treaty, putting it into effect. However, the president may also withhold his signature, which keeps the treaty from being implemented.

Presidents may also terminate a treaty. In 1978, President Carter terminated the Mutual Defense Treaty of 1954 with the Republic of China (Taiwan) when the administration established full diplomatic relations with the People's Republic of China (mainland China). Several members of Congress, including Barry Goldwater of Arizona, sued the administration, but the Supreme Court dismissed the case. Thus, while the Court did not overturn Carter, neither did it formally legitimize through a decision that the president has a constitutional power to terminate treaties.[4]

But presidents do not have the power to change an interpretation of a treaty. In 1985, the Reagan administration wanted to go ahead with its "Star Wars" missile defense program. That program, however, violated parts of the 1972 Antiballistic Missile Treaty of 1972 with the Soviet Union. After wrangling with Congress for a year, the administration modified its program to stay within existing treaty guidelines and interpretations.[5]

Lastly, we must not forget the role of the House of Representatives. Although the lower chamber does not possess any formal role in accepting treaties, its responsibilities in appropriating money and legislating may affect the terms of treaty negotiation as well as treaty enforcement. Sometimes treaties require disbursement of money for them to take effect. For instance, the Arms Control treaty that the United States and Russia entered into in the late 1980s required the dismantling of some nuclear weapons and the disposal of nuclear warhead material. To do this required a congressional appropriation to the relevant agencies of government, the Defense and the Energy departments.

[3]See Richard M. Pious, *The Presidency* (Boston: Allyn and Bacon, 1996), pp. 407–8.

[4]James P. Pfiffner, *The Modern Presidency*, 3d ed. (Boston: Bedford/St. Martin's, 2000, p. 185.)

[5]Ibid, p. 185.

TABLE 15-2   SENATE ACTION ON TREATIES, 1949–1996*

President (years)	Ratified	Pending	Withdrawn	Rejected
Truman (1949–1952)	63	76	11	0
Eisenhower I (1953–1956)	63	69	2	0
Eisenhower II (1957–1960)	36	50	8	1
Kennedy (1961–1963)	25	62	1	0
Johnson (1963–1968)	69	91	5	0
Nixon (1969–1974)	79	126	1	0
Ford (1975–1976)	29	47	0	0
Carter (1977–1980)	50	165	0	0
Reagan I (1981–1984)	74	95	6	1
Reagan II (1985–1988)	47	198	0	0
Bush (1989–1992)	72	188	0	2
Clinton (1993–1996)	66	81	0	0
Total	673	1,248	34	4

*Also includes protocols and convertions, which require Senate consent.

Source: Calculated from Lyn Ragsdale, *Vital Statistics on the Presidency: Washington to Clinton,* rev. ed. (Washington, D.C.: Congress Quarterly Press, 1998), pp. 321–22.

Presidents and Treaties

The United States has entered into over sixteen hundred treaties with other nations across its history, but the Senate has rejected only twenty treaties that the president has submitted to it for consideration. These numbers would seem to suggest that presidents are nearly always successful in gaining acceptance of treaties. However, underlying these numbers are frustrations for the president. For example, about 150 treaties have been withdrawn since the end of the Second World War. Moreover, the Senate has rewritten language in nearly one-third of treaties.[6] Table 15-2 lists congressional action on treaties from Truman in 1949 through Clinton in 1996.

Of the 673 treaties submitted from 1949 though 1996, only thirty-four (5 percent) have been withdrawn, and merely four have been rejected. Presidents tend to withdraw treaties when it appears that the Senate will reject them. In some instances, presidents renegotiate the treaty with the other country to make it acceptable to the Senate.

Rejected treaties tell us much about the role of the Senate in the treaty process. In October 1999, the Senate rejected the Comprehensive Nuclear Test Ban Treaty. This was a major treaty and a stunning defeat for President Clinton, who was looking for a major international accomplishment as his term of office neared its end. News reports compared this defeat to the one that Woodrow Wilson suffered in 1920, when the Senate rejected the Treaty of Versailles, which concluded the First

[6]These figures come from George C. Edwards, III, and Stephen Wayne, *Presidential Leadership,* p. 475.

World War and established the League of Nations, the precursor of the United Nations. Thus, the Senate is not averse to rejecting important treaties. At least in modern times, the Senate rejects and presidents are more likely to withdraw treaties when the opposition party controls the Senate, such as was the case with Clinton and the Comprehensive Nuclear Test Ban Treaty. Although partisanship and party competition may partially explain why opposition-controlled Senates may reject a treaty, it is also possible that true policy disagreements exist when the Senate and the president are of different parties, a point that we made in Chapter 10 on presidential-congressional relations.

The length of time it takes the Senate to decide on treaties may also frustrate presidents. As the numbers in table 15–2 show, many treaties stay pending from one year to the next, indicating that the Senate had not taken action on the treaty at year's end. Some treaties can languish in the Senate for years. Unlike regular proposed legislation, which dies at the end of the two-year legislative session and must be reintroduced in the next Congress, treaties are privileged because they remain active from one Congress to the next.

Pending treaties may pile up for several reasons. The Senate may simply have a large number of treaties or other issues to deal with. Sometimes the lengthy process is a function of the Senate modifying the language of a treaty. Other times, the Senate may be unwilling to challenge a president directly by rejecting the treaty, because doing so may have implications for presidential conduct of foreign policy, but support for the treaty is still short of the two-thirds majority needed for passage. Under such circumstances, presidents may ask the Senate to delay action to have time to lobby members to support the treaty. Lastly, the Senate may just be waiting out the president, forcing him to withdraw the treaty. Because of these and other frustrations with the treaty process, presidents have turned to two devices to conduct foreign policy, the fast track and executive agreements.

Fast Track

Fast track authority applies to economic policy, especially trade agreements with other nations. The aim of the fast track is to force Congress to take action on the economic agreement speedily and to reduce Congress's ability to micromanage international economic policy. Presidents fear that because members of Congress might feel pressure from local interests groups to secure advantages and protections in any international economic agreement, they might derail international economic agreements. "Fast tracking" an agreement helps protect the agreement because it forces a vote by a specified date and prohibits Congress from amending the agreement. Using fast tracking however, must be negotiated with Congress on each agreement; it does not cover all economic pacts.[7]

[7]Glen Sussman and Byron W. Daynes, "The Impact of Political Ideology on Congressional Support for Presidential Policy Making Authority: The Case of the Fast Track," *Congress and the Presidency* 22 (Fall 1995): 141–53; Richard S. Conley, "Derailing Presidential Fast-Track Authority: The Impact of Constituency Pressures and Political Ideology on Trade Policy in Congress," *Political Research Quarterly* 52 (December 1999): 785–99; and Karen Schnietz and Timothy Nieman, "Politics Matter: The 1997 Derailment of Fast-Track Trade Authority," *Business and Politics* 1 (August 1999): 233–51.

Fast track authority has existed since Gerald Ford was president, but when it was originally passed, Congress required that it be periodically reauthorized. In 1994, fast track authority expired, but Bill Clinton did not seek its reauthorization until 1996. Circumstances in Congress had changed, and opponents of fast track authority had strengthened. Thus, Clinton was not assured that he would get back fast track authority.

For one, powerful liberal groups within the Democratic Party, such as environmentalists and labor, stiffly opposed fast track, in part because of the North Atlantic Free Trade Agreement which was passed in 1993. That agreement created a free trade zone composed of the United States, Canada, and Mexico. Environmentalists were critical of Mexican environmental policies, and labor unions feared competition to U.S. workers from less costly Mexican workers. In passing NAFTA, the president agreed to side agreements with Mexico on environmental and labor issues, but in the ensuing years these two groups remained critical of Clinton's efforts.

On the opposite side of the political spectrum, Clinton faced a Republican Congress. Republicans traditionally have supported free trade, and thus, Clinton expected that they would support him on the fast track issue. But relations between Clinton and congressional Republicans were quite sour, and Clinton could not convince them to support reauthorization of fast track authority. On the fast track vote in 1997, Congress refused Clinton's request for extension of that power; he received only twenty-nine of 207 Democratic votes in the House. For the remainder of his term, Clinton lacked fast track authority, and as yet George W. Bush has not asked Congress to renew it.

Executive Agreements

Executive agreements allow presidents to enter into agreements with other nations but do not require Senate or congressional approval.[8] Thus, an executive agreement is a device to circumvent the Senate and its power to reject treaties. For example, the Senate refused to approve an agreement that Theodore Roosevelt had negotiated with Santo Domingo. Frustrated by the Senate delay, Roosevelt signed an executive agreement with that nation, thereby countering the Senate rejection.[9]

Executive agreements date to the earliest days of the Republic. The first was signed in 1792, a postal agreement between the United States and Canada.[10] Compared to treaties, executive agreements are quite numerous. Table 15-3 lists the number of executive agreements since 1789. Since 1949, there have been 11,219 executive agreements with foreign nations, compared to 673 treaties. Many executive agreements are quite routine and often involve department-to-department

[8]Charles Lipson, "Why Are Some International Agreements Informal?" *International Organization* 45 (Autumn 1991): 495–538.

[9]See Pious, *The Presidency,* p. 409.

[10]Ibid., p. 410.

TABLE 15-3 TREATIES AND EXECUTIVE AGREEMENTS, 1789-1996

Year	President	Number of treaties	Number of executive agreements
1789–1889		275	265
1889–1932		431	804
1932–1944	Roosevelt	131	369
1945–1952	Truman	132	1,324
1953–1960	Eisenhower	89	1,834
1961–1963	Kennedy	36	813
1964–1968	Johnson	67	1,083
1969–1974	Nixon	93	1,317
1975–1976	Ford	26	666
1977–1980	Carter	79	1,476
1981–1988	Reagan	125	2,840
1989–1992	Bush	67	1,371
1993–1996	Clinton	97	1,137

Source: Adapted from Harold W. Stanley and Richard G. Niemi, *Vital Statistics on American Politics,* 5th ed. (Washington, D.C.: Congressional Quarterly Press, 1999).

relationships across countries. They cover the full spectrum of foreign policy, however. From 1949 to 1996, 20 percent of executive agreements, or 2,248, have been concerned with natural resources and environment issues. Following in order of frequency are agricultural executive agreements (2,098, or 18.7 percent), foreign trade (1,556, or 13.9 percent), social welfare and civil rights (1,321, or 11.8 percent), government economic management issues such as banking, postal services, and labor (1,243, or 11.1 percent), and defense (1,090, or 9.7 percent). The remainder divide between foreign aid and cultural agreements.[11]

Executive agreement use expanded in the twentieth century because of the increasing U.S. presence and involvement in international affairs. Many executive agreements are no more than elaborations of treaty provisions and are meant to help the process of fulfilling treaty obligations. In 1969, Congress tried to limit presidential use of unilateral devices for conducting foreign policy with its National Commitment Resolution. That resolution stated that the United States could not enter into commitments with another nation without congressional action. Presidents have not felt bound by that resolution, arguing instead that executive agreements carry the force of law and are obligations of the United States.

But presidents have also kept executive agreements secret from Congress, including some defense agreements. To counter such actions, Congress passed the **Case Amendment** in 1972, which requires the secretary of State to forward texts of all executive agreements to the Senate within sixty days of their signing. In

[11] These figures are calculated from Lyn Ragsdale, *Vital Statistics on the Presidency: Washington to Clinton,* rev. ed. (Washington, D.C.: Congressional Quarterly Press, 1998), pp. 326–29.

1977, Congress reduced the time limit to twenty days. While the Case Amendment is meant to curb presidential foreign policy-making without congressional knowledge, it did not go so far as to prohibit or stop presidents from making foreign policy unilaterally through such devices as executive agreements. However, if Congress lacks the knowledge that the president has entered into an executive agreement with another nation, Congress is powerless to do anything about that agreement. The Supreme Court has also limited presidential use of executive agreements. For instance, executive agreements cannot be inconsistent with prior congressional legislation, and they cannot undermine the constitutional rights of U.S. citizens. However, the Court has generally been supportive of presidential use of executive agreements.

THE CONSTITUTION, THE COMMANDER IN CHIEF, AND WAR-MAKING POWERS

The Senate has a vital role to play in treaty making, although the president takes the lead in that process. When it comes to war-making powers, the Constitution grants presidents even stronger powers, although Congress still has a major role.

Article II, Section 2, Paragraph 1 of the Constitution outlines the president's defense and **war-making powers:** "The president shall be Commander in Chief of the Army and Navy of the United States, and of the Militia of the several States, when called into active service of the United States." Congress, however, is granted major powers related to the making and conduct of war. In Article I, Section 8, Congress is given the power to "declare war" and "raise and support Armies," "provide and maintain a Navy," and "provide for calling for a Militia." Moreover, Congress is given the power to create the military services, to determine their organization and funding levels, to procure weapons, to establish military grades, and to write a code of military justice. The president and Congress share responsibility for filling the military's commissioned officer ranks. The president nominates such officers, subject to senatorial confirmation.

Clearly, the Constitution invests the power to declare war with Congress rather than the executive. Outside of this strict war declaration power and the others already noted, the Constitution is ambiguous about war making. For instance, what would happen if the nation were attacked? How should the nation respond? Who should be in charge? To take care of such circumstances, the founders at the Constitutional Convention replaced the phrase "make war" with "declare war" because they wanted the president to have the power to repel attacks and defend the nation. They recognized that rapid action was necessary under such circumstances, and the nation could be severely harmed if it had to wait for congressional action before it could respond to an attack.

But recognizing this potential threat and the implied presidential responsibility does not completely resolve the ambiguities over who is to do what outside of a declared war. For example, can the president use military forces to repel attacks on American personnel and property that are located outside of the nation's boundaries? Can the president initiate an attack to thwart an attack by another nation? Can the president commit U.S. troops because of treaty commitments? Can the president employ the U.S. military to force other nations to do what he wishes? The Constitution is silent on these contingencies and questions, nor did the debates at the Constitutional Convention provide clear guidance concerning these and related matters.[12] As a practical matter, presidents have been given a relatively free hand to interpret their powers and use the military as they see fit with one major exception, the War Powers Act, which we discuss in the section on "The War Powers Resolution of 1973."

Moreover, while Congress possesses considerable authority over the military, the president's commander-in-chief designation allows him direct supervision of the armed forces. Congress may decide the size of the military, its organizational structure, and its weapons systems, but the president will command the actual use of the armed forces. In the military chain of command, the president sits at the top and possesses the power to command the military.

It is important to note that the president's commander-in-chief power also ensures civilian control of the military. In 1986, the Goldwater-Nichols Act reformed the military chain of command, which would run from the president to the secretary of Defense, then to the military commanders. This system bypasses the Joint Chiefs of Staff, which has no direct authority to issue commands either. The president, however, has no authority to issue orders to any military personnel other than those designated as commanders of military units. This safeguards against presidential use of the military for nondefense purposes.

In 1974, during the Watergate crisis Secretary of Defense James Schlesinger seemed to understand the importance of keeping the military one step removed from direct presidential command. He issued an order that no military office was to obey a direct command from President Nixon. All commands from the president had to travel through the proper chain of command. That meant that Nixon's orders had to be transmitted through the office of the secretary of Defense and then to the military commander.

The Presidential Use of Armed Forces

Congress has declared war only eight times since the nation's inception: the War of 1812, the Mexican-American War, the Spanish-American War, World War I, and World War II, the last involving four separate declarations of war. However, presidents have committed to the use of military forces over 230 times across the nation's history. Obviously, presidents use the military outside of the formally declared war.

Most of the occasions when the president used the armed forces without prior congressional approval involved minor incidents and were aimed at pirates, criminals, and terrorists; evacuation, rescue, and assistance for U.S. citizens abroad; protection of U.S. property; and enforcement of blockades and quarantines. But some times, the incidents were more consequential, for instance, war and police

---

[12]Pious, *The Presidency,* pp. 441–43.

actions such as Vietnam and Korea, and support for UN and other peacekeeping missions, such as in the Balkans in the late 1990s.[13]

A declaration of war, however, was not issued for the Persian Gulf War in 1991, although President Bush asked for congressional support. Iraq had invaded Kuwait in 1990. In support of Kuwait, Bush convinced Saudi Arabia to allow two hundred thousand U.S. forces to be stationed there, while the United States decided to use economic sanctions against Iraq to try to force Iraq's withdraw from Kuwait. After several months, it became obvious that economic sanctions alone would not prove effective. Bush decided on a more forceful policy, one that would involve military action against Iraq. He rallied support from a large number of other nations and wanted to double the size of the U.S. contingent in Saudi Arabia.

Although he felt that he could take action without formal congressional support, the size of the impending military operation and the memory of U.S. involvement in Vietnam led Bush to seek Congress's backing. The risk for Bush's policy, however, was that Congress would not go along or would only weakly support his policy. Many people still remembered Vietnam, fearing the use of U.S. troops on such a scale in a ground war so far from the United States. The congressional debates were televised, and Congress decided to support Bush's policy with a resolution, rather than a declaration of war. Support was stronger in the House (250 to 183) than the Senate (52 to 47).

In 1999, President Clinton decided to take military action against Serbia, which had been engaged in a campaign of "ethnic cleansing" against Kosovars in the Kosovar region. As in the Persian Gulf War, an alliance of many nations was involved; in this case, members of NATO. But unlike in the Persian Gulf War, Clinton decided against sending in ground troops. Instead, U.S. military actions would involve mostly aerial bombing. Nor did Clinton seek formal congressional support as Bush did. Despite criticisms of Clinton's policy from congressional Republicans, Congress did not attempt to stop the bombing mission, which lasted for months. Finally, the Serbian government backed down, allowing the Kosovars to return to their homes, and the bombing stopped, although NATO troops were deployed in the region to protect the Kosovars.

In the years since the end of the Second World War, Americans have gotten used to American troops being sent to other countries to fight, however much they may dislike using troops this way. But it is not true, however, that the United States used its troops in these ways only with the end of the Second World War and the onset of the Cold War, as the isolationist theory asserts. That theory suggests that the United States was not highly involved in international affairs before the Second World War and that it was reluctant to use its troops in those prewar years. Rather, presidents deployed U.S. troops very frequently, even in the nineteenth century. Presidents committed U.S. troops without prior congressional consent or declaration of war ninety-eight times from 1789 until the Spanish-American War in 1898 and another sixty-five times before the outbreak

---

[13]See ibid., pp. 446–47, for more detail on types of U.S. military intervention.

of World War Two.[14] This is nearly one deployment per year in the nineteenth century and almost 1.5 deployments per year in the 1900-to-1940 period. The rate per year for the 1900-to-1940 period is almost the same as the rate of troop commitment overseas since the end of the Second World War.

Two propositions have been advanced to explain why presidents commit troops so often.[15] The first of these is the **external threat argument.** This idea suggests that presidents respond to the actions of foreign nations that have threatened the United States, its citizens, or its property with the deployment of troops. In other words, international crises stimulate a military response from the United States. The United States, however, does not use troops to respond to each international crisis. Rarely will the United States engage in such a provocative action directly against the Soviet Union or other major powers that might lead to war. The United States is more prone to use troops when the president and his advisers feel that target nation will back down when faced with U.S. troops. In the case of major nations, the United States is more likely to resort to diplomacy.

Also, presidents are more likely to use troops when recent past uses were ineffective. Here, presidents may be concerned about the U.S. reputation—whether other nations feel that the United States possesses the means and the resolve to take military action. The fear is that if the United States appears to be a paper tiger,

[14]Jerel A. Rosati, *The Politics of United States Foreign Policy,* 2d ed. (New York: Harcourt Brace, 1999), pp. 16–17.

[15]The literature on the presidential use of troops is massive. The following paragraphs are based on findings from these studies: Richard J. Stoll, "The Guns of November: Presidential Reelections and the Use of Force, 1947–1982," *Journal of Conflict Resolution* 28 (June 1984): 231–46; Charles W. Ostrom and Brian Job, "The President and the Political Use of Force," *American Political Science Review* 80 (June 1986): 541–66; Patrick James and John R. Oneal, "The Influence of Domestic and International Politics on the President's Use of Force," *Journal of Conflict Resolution* 35 (June 1991): 307–32; T. Clifton Morgan and Kenneth N. Bickers, "Domestic Discontent and the External Use of Force," *Journal of Conflict Resolution* 36 (March 1992): 25–52; Patrick James and Athanasios Hristoulas, "Domestic Politics and Foreign Policy: Evaluating a Model of Crisis Activity for the United States." *Journal of Politics* 56 (May 1994): 327–48; Bradley Lian and John R. Oneal, "Presidents, the Use of Military Force, and Public Opinion," *Journal of Conflict Resolution* 37 (June 1993): 277–300; James Meernik, "Presidential Decision Making and the Political Use of Military Force," *International Studies Quarterly* 38 (March 1994): 121–38; Patrick James and Athanasios Hristoulas, "Domestic Politics and Foreign Policy: Evaluating a Model of Crisis Activity for the United States," *Journal of Politics* 56 (May 1994): 327–48; John R. Oneal and Anna Lillian Bryan, "The Rally 'round the Flag Effect in U.S. Foreign Policy Crises, 1950–1985," *Political Behavior* 17 (December 1995): 379–401; Karl R. DeRouen, Jr., "The Indirect Link: Politics, the Economy and the Use of Force," *Journal of Conflict Resolution* 39 (December 1995): 671–95; James Meernik and Peter Waterman, "The Myth of the Diversionary Use of Force by American Presidents," *Political Research Quarterly* 49 (September 1996): 573–90; Kevin H. Wang, "Presidential Responses to Foreign Policy Crises: Rational Choice and Domestic Politics," *Journal of Conflict Resolution* 40 (March 1996): 68–97; Jean Sebastian Rioux, "U.S. Crises and Domestic Politics: Crisis Outcomes, Reputation, and Domestic Consequences," *Southeastern Political Review* 25 (June 1997): 199–229; Benjamin Fordham, "Partisanship, Macroeconomic Policy, and U.S. Uses of Force, 1949–1994," *Journal of Conflict Resolution* 42 (August 1998): 418–39; Patrick James and Jean Sebastian Rioux, "International Crises and Linkage Politics: The Experience of the United States, 1953–1994," *Political Research Quarterly* 51 (September 1998): 781–812; David Mervin "Presidents, Precedents and the Use of Military Force," *Journal of American Studies* 32 (December 1998): 483–502; James Meernik, "Modeling International Crises and the Political Use of Military Force by the USA," *Journal of Peace Research* 37 (September 2000): 547–62; and Karl Derouen, Jr., "Presidents and the Diversionary Use of Force: A Research Note," *International Studies Quarterly* 44 (June 2000): 317–29.

lacking the will to exert itself, other nations would engage in more risky international ventures, challenging the United States and its allies more frequently and more provocatively. Thus, presidents may deploy troops to act as a deterrent to other nations that are not the direct target of the U.S. troop use.

The second major reason for the presidential commitment of troops is the **domestic or internal politics model.** This idea is that domestic political pressures lead presidents to or dissuade them from using troops. One important variant of the domestic pressures idea is that presidents deploy troops to divert public attention from other issues that are causing trouble for them—what is often referred to as the **diversionary use of force.** Thus, some contend that when the president is doing poorly in the public opinion polls, he will deploy troops with the intention of rallying public support behind him. As we discussed in Chapter 8 on public opinion, there is little support for this idea. Presidents do not seem more inclined to use troops when their polls are low, nor does the use of troops seem to boost public support for the president.

A related idea focuses on the impact of the **electoral cycle.** The electoral cycle or **October surprise** idea suggests that presidents might use troops as the election nears with a motivation similar to that in the diversionary idea, that is, that troop deployment will result in greater public support, in this case votes. In general, recent research has found little support for either the diversionary or electoral cycle ideas.[16]

Other studies have looked at the impact of the economy on presidential use of troops. When the U.S. economy is in worse shape, presidential troop use seems to increase. It is not clear why this is the case, however. One suggestion argues that when the economy is weak, presidents commit troops to divert public attention from the economy. This idea is closely related to the diversionary idea. But it might also be the case that when the United States is economically weakened, foreign nations may take extra risks in their international behavior, seeing the United States as somewhat more vulnerable and less capable of responding decisively. Thus, an economically weakened United States affects the behavior of other nations, leading to more international crises to which the United States then responds by deploying troops. Similarly, an economically weakened United States may indicate economic stress throughout the globe. As other nations suffer economically, they may engage in more risky and provocative behaviors, which in turn, stimulate a U S. response by the use of troops. Thus, several factors seem to affect the presidential use of troops. A combination of external threat and internal domestic politics seems to lead presidents to use troops.

The War Powers Resolution of 1973

Rarely is there much public or congressional outcry against presidential use of armed forces, except, however, when the commitment lasts for a long time and U.S. casualties begin to mount. With the massive losses incurred during the

[16]See the studies cited in endnote 15.

Vietnam War, critics began to feel that Congress should restrain unbridled presidential use of the armed forces, especially in incidents that might be prolonged, involve high casualty levels, and potentially lead to war. Especially in the latter case, Congress was fearful that by committing U.S. armed forces to hostilities without congressional consent, the president might force the United States into a war. The public held similar attitudes about the use of military forces in the post-Vietnam era.[17]

To preserve Congress's role to declare war and to reassert some authority over presidential use of troops, Congress passed the **War Powers Resolution** in 1973. In passing this resolution, Congress overrode President Nixon's veto. The War Powers Resolution, sometimes also referred to as the War Powers Act, does not deny presidents the power to commit troops. Instead, the resolution constructs a process in which presidents must consult with Congress and gives Congress the ability to alter presidential policy. The resolution also tries to define clearly the extent and limits of presidential war-making power.

Under the War Powers Resolution, American troops can be used in hostilities when 1) Congress declares war, 2) when Congress grants the president statutory authority to use troops, and 3) when emergencies exist, for instance, when the United States, its territories, or its armed forces are under attack. Further, the act requires that the "President, in every possible instance, shall consult with Congress before introducing United States Armed Forces into hostilities," but this provision does not define what constitutes "consultation." Must it be formal? Must the president consult with all members of Congress? Presidents have tended to ignore the consultation requirement of the resolution and sometimes do no more than inform several members of Congress that they are going to take military action the next day. The resolution further requires regular consultation between the president and Congress as long as U.S. forces are engaged in hostilities. Again, this provision fails to define the manner of consultation, who in Congress is to be consulted, and what makes up regular consultation.

Perhaps the most important provisions of the resolution give Congress the power to end the president's use of troops after he has deployed them. The resolution requires that the president withdraw U.S. troops sixty days after they have been committed, unless Congress grants an extension. A grace period of thirty days may be added to ensure the safe pullout of U.S. troops. Rarely has the sixty-day deadline been triggered because most presidential uses of armed forces without congressional consent have not lasted that long. One study found that of the twenty-five times that presidents submitted reports to Congress as required under the resolution, the sixty-day deadline was reached only once.[18]

But the resolution also enables Congress to force the president to withdraw armed forces before the sixty-day deadline. As the resolution reads, "[A]t any time

[17] Bruce W. Jentleson, "The Pretty Prudent Public: Post-Vietnam American Opinion on the Use of Military Force," *International Studies Quarterly* 36 (March 1992): 49–74.

[18] Ellen C. Collier, "War Powers Resolution; Presidential Compliance," *Congressional Research Service Issues Brief IB81050* (Washington, D.C.: Congressional Research Service, 1991).

that United States Armed Forces are engaged in hostilities outside of the territory of the United States, its possession and territories, without a declaration of war or specific statutory authority, such forces shall be removed if the Congress so directs by concurrent resolution." A concurrent resolution is a type of legislative veto.

Unlike regular legislation, which requires a presidential signature or congressional override of a presidential veto for enactment, a legislative veto does not require any presidential action for it to take effect. Rather, the intent of a legislative veto is to stop the executive from taking action unless Congress permits the executive to act. In contrast, legislation usually provides the authority for the executive to take action.

In 1983, the Supreme Court declared legislative vetoes unconstitutional in its famous ***Chadha v. INS* decision.** Congress amended the War Powers Act in 1983 in response to require a joint resolution of Congress that, unlike a legislative veto, must be submitted to the president. The president can then veto the resolution, while a two-thirds majority in both houses is necessary to override. Thus, with support of merely one-third of one chamber, the president can continue using the military outside of the United States as he sees fit. Clearly, the joint resolution provision weakens Congress's hand vis-à-vis the president.

The War Powers Act does not seemed to have redressed the imbalance between the president and Congress with respect to the use of U.S. armed forces, as its advocates had hoped. Only once since 1973 has Congress tried to assert itself under the War Powers Act. In September 1982, President Reagan committed U.S. troops as peacekeepers to Lebanon. They remained there until March 1984. But in reporting to Congress upon committing the troops, Reagan informed Congress that he did not intend U.S. troops to become engaged in hostilities. That troops would not fight circumvented the sixty-day deadline of the War Powers Act.

However, in October 1983, a terrorist attack killed 241 Marines at a U.S. base in Lebanon. Questions began to be raised about the policy of keeping troops in that troubled nation. Some members of Congress began to challenge the administration under the provisions of the War Powers Act, but a compromise was reached between the president and Congress. Congress would allow the president to maintain troops in Lebanon for up to eighteen months if the president would sign a joint resolution that agreed that hostilities between U.S. troops and foreign combatants had begun, which activated the War Powers Act. Under the compromise, the sixty-day clock was suspended and an eighteen-month period put in its place.[19]

Generally, presidents have skirted the act by refusing to acknowledge hostilities, which would trigger the act. Forces may be deployed to protect shipping, maintain order, protect innocent lives, or a number of other justifications without an explicit statement that hostilities exist. Moreover, presidents have also refused to legitimize the act, because doing so would limit their freedom of action. Still, presidents have not completely ignored the requirements of the act and have tended to consult with Congress, at least informally. Completely ignoring the act might incite Congress to strengthen its role in foreign policy even more. For the

[19]Rosati, *Politics of United States Foreign Policy,* p. 350.

most part, the act has not tied the president's hands very much, not because it lacks teeth but because Congress lacks the willpower to rein in the president.[20] The fact that most hostilities since the Vietnam War have also been of short duration has also quieted congressional critics of presidential use of the military. Perhaps more important, by the late 1980s Congress had given up on the War Powers Resolution for a system of congressional authorization. Congress moved to this system because of suggestions that the courts might hold key provisions of the act unconstitutional.[21]

THE PRESIDENT AND THE FOREIGN POLICY ESTABLISHMENT

A large and well-developed establishment exists to help the president in making foreign policy. Some of that establishment dates to the founding era, such as the Department of State and the departments of War and Navy, which preceded the Defense Department. In modern times, the National Security Council serves as the formal body with major advising responsibilities to the president in foreign policy. Presidents are not bound to rely on these organs, however, and can direct foreign policy by themselves or with the help of other advisers of their choosing. The expertise of the many formal foreign policy advisers, however, makes them particularly valuable to the president in making foreign policy.

The National Security Council

Before the Second World War, the president could turn to only a small number of foreign policy advisers in government. This group consisted of the secretary of State and that department's diplomats, embassy staff, and top-level personnel. Also counted among government advisers to whom the president could turn were the naval and military officers who had relevant backgrounds, such as having served as attachés to embassies or in foreign nations; this group was small in number. Lastly, presidents could and did turn to private businesspeople and others with experience outside of the United States.

The demands of the Second World War and the ensuing Cold War were too great for such a limited establishment. Presidents needed expertise across a wider array of foreign policy issues, stretching around the entire globe and ranging from diplomatic, to defense, to economic issues. Moreover, the State Department and

---

[20]See Christopher A. Ford, "War Powers as We Live Them: Congressional-Executive Bargaining Under the Shadow of the War Powers Resolution," *Journal of Law and Politics* 11 (Fall 1995): 609–708; James Meernik, "Congress, the President, and the Commitment of the U.S. Military," *Legislative Studies Quarterly* 20 (August 1995): 377–392; Erik Gartzke, "Congress and Back Seat Driving: An Information Theory of the War Powers Resolution," *Policy Studies Journal* 24 (Summer 1996): 259–86; Louis Fisher and David Gray Adler, "The War Powers Resolution (1973): Time to Say Goodbye," *Political Science Quarterly* 113 (Spring 1998): 1–20; Richard J. Harknet and Norman C. Thomas, "The Precedence of Power: Determining Who Should Authorize Military Force," *Congress and the Presidency* 25 (Spring 1998): 1–21; and Michael E. Smith, "Congress, the President, and the Use of Military Force: Cooperation or Conflict in the Post-Cold War Era?" *Presidential Studies Quarterly* 28 (Winter 1998): 36–51.

[21] See Pious, *The Presidency,* pp. 464–65 for details on the major court cases and actions.

military staffers often advised the president from the perspective of their own bureaucracy's interests and needs, rather than from the president's. To help rectify this situation, Congress passed the **National Security Act** in 1947.

The National Security Act is among the most important pieces of legislation ever enacted; it reformed the foreign policy advising establishment along several fronts. The military branches were reorganized into the Department of Defense, which we discuss more fully in "The Department of Defense" section in this chapter. Intelligence gathering was formalized in the creation of the Central Intelligence Agency (CIA). And a **National Security Council** was established, which would centralize advisers from the various relevant agencies, as well as provide the president with his own national security adviser, who was to be placed within the White House structure.

Under the National Security Act, the NSC was to serve as a way to bring together the various presidential foreign policy advisers in one setting. Formally, the NSC was to provide three functions: foreign policy advice to the president, long-range foreign policy planning, and coordination among the various units engaged in foreign policy making. Moreover, the NSC was seen as a way to rationalize foreign policy decision making.

The felt need to rationalize stemmed in part from Franklin Roosevelt's management style. Roosevelt did not organize his foreign policy advisers into a tightly knit unit with well-defined duties Rather, his style was more chaotic, with many channels of communication coming to him and little coordination across his advisers. Quite often different advisers did not know what others were advising or what duties they were carrying out. This system supposedly generated not only confusion and conflict among staffers and advisers, but some thought overburdened the president. Other critics suggested that in a two-front war, Roosevelt's system led to inefficiency and undermined the effectiveness of U.S. military efforts.

The ramifications of FDR's system became all too apparent when Harry Truman became president. Truman had been left out of most foreign policy making during his short stint as Roosevelt's vice president. Further, he had little foreign policy experience during his tenure in Congress. He was seemingly ill-prepared to take over the reins of making foreign policy. Building a support structure that a president could rely on was thought to be one way of helping a president like Truman, who lacked much experience in foreign policy. But such a system was also expected to help presidents in the post-World War II era, who faced a larger range and variety of foreign policy issues than earlier presidents. And the realities of Cold War international relations, the rivalry between the United States and the Soviet Union, and the possession of nuclear weapons made foreign policy a more important issue, with graver consequences, than perhaps at any other time in U.S. history.

Originally, the members of the NSC included the president; the secretaries of State, Defense, Army, Navy, and Air Force; and the chair of the National Security Resources Board, which was responsible for emergency planning and civil defense. Later, the vice president, the national security adviser, and the Joint Chiefs of Staff were added. Also, the NSC is home to a national security staff. Currently, the NSC is composed of the following people: the president, vice president, secretary of defense, secretary of the treasury, secretary of state, and director of the Arms Control and Disarmament Agency, the U.S. Ambassador to the United Nations, and three senior White House staffers. The chairman of the Joint Chiefs of Staff and the director of the Central Intelligence Agency serve as advisors.

During the Cold War, the national security adviser emerged as perhaps the president's leading foreign policy adviser. President Eisenhower created the post of **national security adviser** to supervise the national security staff, the staffing arm of the NSC that is located in the Executive Office of the President. Several reasons account for the importance of the national security adviser during the Cold War era. First, unlike other foreign policy advisers, the national security adviser is situated in the White House and not in a bureaucratic agency. The national security adviser's constituent, therefore, is the president and not an agency with a long history, traditions, and perspectives. Moreover, the national security adviser oversees a small staff, which is responsible for helping the president respond to immediate events and manage the day-to-day affairs of foreign policy. Thus, a great deal of interaction occurs daily between the president and the national security adviser over matters of utmost concern to the president. Traditionally, the national security adviser briefs the president every day.[22]

The national security adviser and staff have proved most useful to presidents in dealing with traditional national security issues, such as use of force or major diplomatic efforts related to such efforts—in other words, the key foreign policy decisions of the Cold War. With the end of the Cold War and the emergence of new issues, such as foreign economic policy, the traditional bureaucratic agencies, such as the State Department, seem to be reemerging in importance to the president, while the national security adviser and staff may be becoming less critical. However, as U.S. foreign policy in the post–Cold War era is still developing, it is still too early to tell what role the national security adviser and staff will play. They provide the president with flexibility, but they lack the depth of expertise on emerging issues that major foreign policy bureaucracies possess.

The Department of State

Historically, the State Department was the lead agency that provided the president with foreign policy advice, but during the Cold War the national security adviser and National Security Council staff often eclipsed State in importance to the president. Several reasons account for the decline of the State Department during the Cold War. First, as foreign relations became more important to the United States, presidential interest in that policy area grew. Foreign policy making in the second half of the twentieth century was pulled out of the State Department bureaucracy and into the White House as a consequence. Second, the development of global communications systems has lessened the president's reliance on the State Department and its network of embassies and overseas offices. Presidents

---

[22]Paul Schott Stevens, "The National Security Council: Past and Prologue," *Strategic Review* 17 (Winter 1989): 55–62; and Anthony Wanis St. John, "The National Security Council: Tool of Presidential Crisis Management," *Journal of Public and International Affairs* 9 (1998): 102–27.

can now communicate with leaders of other nations directly, for instance by secure telephone, without having to use State Department personnel as messengers. Third, the United States in the post–Second World War era has developed its military capability to an extent unparalleled in its history, and presidents have been willing to use military forces to affect foreign policy. Other than the actual deployment of troops into hostilities that we discussed in the section on the War Powers Resolution, one study counted over two hundred instances from 1946 through 1975 in which the United States used a military threat against other nations.[23] Military threats were also common during the George H. W. Bush and Bill Clinton presidencies.[24] The United States thus is not as reliant on diplomacy to secure its foreign policy objectives as it once was.

And with the decline of diplomacy as the major foreign policy instrument, the State Department, the agency with the most diplomatic expertise, declined in prominence as well. Where the United States once viewed diplomacy as the first, and often, only approach to any foreign policy issue, other alternatives, such as military action, began to compete as a favored way of conducting foreign policy.[25]

Neither was the State Department well suited for presidents during the Cold War. Before the Second World War, when the nation was not heavily involved in foreign entanglements and issues, the president could afford to allow the State Department take the lead. But during the Cold War, presidents demanded quick action and responsiveness to their foreign policy concerns. The State Department, a long-standing bureaucracy with a well-entrenched tradition, was often unable to respond quickly or innovatively to new problems. In a sense, the State Department did not adapt very well to changing times or conditions.

Moreover, where the Cold War led presidents to think of foreign policy foremost as a conflict between the United States and the Soviet Union on a global scale, the State Department, because of its structure, tended to view the world in regional or local terms. The State Department is divided into regional bureaus (Africa, East Asia and the Pacific, Europe and Canada, Western Hemisphere, Near East, and South Asia), as well as by some issue areas. Thus, when trouble erupts in a nation or region, State Department personnel, because of their expertise and the geographically oriented structure of the department, tend to analyze the problem from a local angle, focusing on such factors as local history, culture, tradition, economic condition, and so on. At least during much of the Cold War period, presidents and the national security adviser tended to view problems from the perspective of the U.S.-Soviet competition. As a consequence, State Department advice became increasingly irrelevant to the president. Ironically, the very attribute that once gave the State Department its great influence at the highest levels of government, in-depth knowledge of other countries, became a liability in the Cold War era.

[23]Barry Blechman and Stephen Kaplan, *Force Without War: U.S. Armed Forces as a Political Instrument* (Washington, D.C.: Brookings Institution, 1978).

[24]Barry M. Blechman and Tamara Cofman Wittes, "Defining Moment: The Threat and Use of Force in American Foreign Policy," *Political Science Quarterly* 114 (Spring 1999): 1–30.

[25]Rosati, *Politics of United States Foreign Policy,* pp. 150–51.

With the end of the Cold War, secretaries of State have regained some of the influence and prominence that they lost. Although the military is still relied on heavily, for example, as peacekeepers in places such as Africa and the Balkans, world problems are now viewed more in regional than global terms, and diplomacy has risen again as an instrument of foreign policy. Madeline Albright for Bill Clinton and Colin Powell for George W. Bush are both high-profile secretaries of State and very influential in their respective administrations. At the same time, the most recent national security advisers, Sandy Berger for Bill Clinton and Condoleezza Rice for George W. Bush, seem not only less influential than Albright and Powell but also less influential than former national security advisers, such as Henry Kissinger.[26]

The Department of Defense

Historically, the U.S. military establishment was kept small during peacetime. In the late 1930s, the U.S. Army was about the size of Spain's, although the United States had a much larger population and was arguably a potential world-class power, where Spain was not. Consequently, the military was not very influential in providing foreign policy advice to the president.

After the conclusion of the Second World War, however, the U.S. military did not recede to the small size that was common during peacetime. Unlike at the end of the First World War, the United States was thrust into an active leadership role among nations with the close of the Second World War. New weapons of war—missiles and nuclear weapons—posed a new threat. The Soviet Union, which had come to possess such weapons shortly after the war ended, challenged the United States, and a Cold War heated up between the two nations. Some even blamed the isolationism and military weakness of the United States after the First War World for contributing to the Second World War, a viewpoint that furthered strengthened support for maintaining a large military establishment after World War II ended.

The structure of the U.S. military, however, was not capable of organizing and coordinating the vast military resources demanded by the Cold War. That structure was fragmented into two services, the Army and the Navy, each possessing cabinet-level departments. Competition between the two branches was ever present. Coordination across the military branches was thought necessary if the United States was to be effective in countering the Soviet Union.

As noted in the section on the National Security Council in this chapter, the National Security Act created the Department of Defense. The Army and Navy were merged into one cabinet department, and an independent Air Force, also located in the Defense Department, was established. Each military branch would report to its own civilian authority (e. g., secretary of the Army), who would report to the secretary of Defense. The tradition of civilian control of the military remained, but it was hoped that centralization of the different services into one department would help to better coordinate the several military branches. To aid in that coordination, the **Joint Chiefs of Staff (JCS)** was created.

---

[26]Kissinger became secretary of State after having served as Nixon's national security adviser and for a time held both posts simultaneously.

The JCS consists of the six highest-ranking military officers: the chairman, the vice chairman, the chief of staff of the Army, the chief of naval operations, the chief of staff of the Air Force, and the commandant of the Marines. The president appoints the chair of the JCS, who serves a four-year term, and the JCS has a staff of up to four hundred officers, who are loaned by their respective services.[27]

Despite the centralizing structure of the Defense Department and the JCS, coordination of the branches is still difficult. Each branch tends to compete for its budget share, new weapons systems, and priority status. Traditional service rivalries still exist, and rarely do the services speak with one voice when advising the president. To help this situation, the 1987 Goldwater-Nichols Act enhanced the JCS chairmanship. It provided the chairman with a vice chairman and his own staff. As a result, the JCS chair has emerged in recent years as the preeminent military adviser to the president.

One might think that military advisers would be highly likely to recommend use of military forces, but studies conclude that it is the civilian heads of the Defense Department who are more ardent in advocating using military forces.[28] The Vietnam War undermined the confidence of the military leaders when strong political and public backing was lacking. Moreover, military leaders prefer to use the military only when well-defined military targets and objectives exist. Often foreign policy issues are not so well or clearly defined, and many actions are taken with political reasons or objectives in mind.

Defense Department personnel have also gotten more skilled at the art of diplomacy and often look at diplomacy as an important tool for national security. One reason that diplomacy has received a warmer reception in Defense is that at least since the Second World War, U.S. military personnel have had more contact with leaders from around the world, both military and nonmilitary. Another reason is that many military officers spend some time stationed outside of the United States, which increases their contact with and understanding of other nations. In several instances, high-ranking officers have become secretaries of State, such as George C. Marshall for Harry Truman, Alexander Haig for Ronald Reagan, and Colin Powell for George W. Bush.[29] This is perhaps an indication of the usefulness of a military experience in building diplomatic skills and a diplomatic career.

The Central Intelligence Agency

The United States was relatively late to develop its intelligence capabilities in foreign policy. Great Britain had developed its intelligence service around the beginning of the twentieth century, and most European nations developed theirs in the 1920s and 1930s. The United States did not give much attention to intelligence for foreign policy until the Second World War. In the years after that war,

---

[27]Rosati, *Politics of United States Foreign Policy*, p. 180.

[28] Richard Betts, *Soldiers, Statesmen, and Cold War Crises* (Cambridge: Harvard University Press, 1977).

[29]Haig served only a short time, from January 1981 to July 1982. He caused some controversy when President Reagan was shot and hospitalized in 1981, asserting before the media that he was in charge. He was forced to step down shortly after.

however, the U.S. intelligence-gathering effort grew tremendously. The **Central Intelligence Agency** is the most important agency devoted to intelligence for foreign policy. But although the CIA is the lead agency in intelligence work, a number of other intelligence agencies also exist.

These include the **National Security Agency,** which operates in the Department of Defense, having its roots in the Army's Signal Corps. The NSA has two major tasks. The first is to protect the nation's security systems. In 1984, computer security for the government was added to this first task. The second task is to monitor foreign signals of all types, often through satellites and other high-technology devices.

Each military branch also operates an intelligence unit (e. g., Army, Navy, and Air Force Intelligence). The National Reconnaissance Office, also located in the Department of Defense, operates the nation's aerial surveillance operations, while the Defense Intelligence Agency, another Defense Department unit, was created in 1961 to coordinate the many and varied military intelligence operations. The State Department runs its own intelligence operation, and the Federal Bureau of Investigation is also involved, although the FBI is limited to operating within the United States and its territories. In all, the intelligence community of the United States is diffuse and decentralized.

The CIA is the lead agency in intelligence, despite the competition from so many other agencies, because of its size and its relationship to the president. The CIA is perhaps the largest of the intelligence agencies. Maybe more important, the director of Central Intelligence, unlike the heads of the other intelligence agencies, reports directly to the president.

The CIA was created in 1947 with the passage of the National Security Act. It grew out of an existing agency, the Office of Strategic Services, which had been created during the Second World War. The CIA performs all three basic intelligence functions: data collection and analysis, counterintelligence, and political and paramilitary intervention, sometimes termed covert operations. It consists of four divisions: intelligence, science and technology, administration, and operations. Although the bulk of agency personnel work in the intelligence division, which collects and analyzes data, the CIA is most famous for covert operations, which is one duty of the operations division.

Covert operations is an important, if little known or understood aspect of foreign policy, because it has been hidden from the public as much as possible. From its beginning in 1947 until the Vietnam War, the CIA ran many covert operations. Some were aimed at toppling regimes unfriendly to the United States, propping up friendly regimes, and even covertly interceding in elections in other nations so the winner would be a U.S. ally. Although no one has been able to provide a definitive count, one study lists thirty-two major covert operations from 1947 to 1973.[30]

With the conclusion of the Vietnam War, public sentiment turned against involving the United States in a policy aimed merely at stopping communism. That was the major rationale for many covert operations during the preceding decades. Moreover, illegal operations came to public light, further embarrassing the CIA

[30]Rosati, *Politics of United States Foreign Policy,* p. 232.

and the intelligence community. During the 1970s, covert operations were scaled back. With the election of Ronald Reagan, who viewed the world in relatively stark United States–versus–Soviet Union terms, recalling the perspective of Cold Warriors in the 1950 and 1960s, covert operations began to increase in number and ambition. Covert operations supported the Contras in Nicaragua. This became a significant and controversial policy. In 1982, Congress passed the Boland Amendment, which severely curtailed operations in Nicaragua, especially those aimed at overthrowing the Sandinista government. The Reagan administration claimed that the Sandinistas were communists and were supported by the Soviet Union. Rarely had a covert operation been debated so openly.

Despite the Boland Amendment, covert operations against the Sandinista regime continued illegally. These were run out of the White House, rather than the CIA, and involved arms sales to the Contras, who opposed the Sandinistas. However, rather than coming directly from the United States, arms were sold to the Contras via third parties, including Iranians. A major scandal erupted when this secret operation was made public, the infamous Iran-Contra scandal. President Reagan denied knowledge of the diversion of arms sales from the Iranians to the Contras, although the operation was directed by high-ranking officials in his administration. However, he claimed responsibility for the secret operation and instituted reforms that he thought would prevent similar operations from being run from the White House without presidential knowledge. During this period, 1986 and 1987, Reagan's polls suffered heavily, mostly because of the scandal.

The need for covert operations and secrecy in the conduct of foreign policy runs counter to the need of a democracy for information about the policies that the nation's leaders are pursuing. Without such information, the public cannot make an informed judgment about whether to support continuation of the policies. But informing the public about policies that require secrecy may harm national security. A delicate balance exists between the nation's right to know and its security.

Other Presidential Foreign Policy Advisers

Although the national security adviser, the State and Defense departments, and the CIA are usually the most important foreign policies advisers to the president, they do not exhaust the advisers in this area to whom a president can turn. Economic issues have become increasingly important in foreign policy. This is due to the increased amount of trade between the United States and other nations and the globalization of the economy. Some have claimed that a new type of policy area is emerging, one that links domestic economic concerns to foreign policy and is termed **intermestic policy.**[31] An example of an intermestic issue is the North Atlantic Free Trade pact between the United States, Canada, and Mexico. Labor unions tended to oppose NAFTA because of fears that Americans workers would not be able to compete with cheaper Mexican labor and would

[31]On intermestic policy, see Franz Gress, "Interstate Cooperation and Territorial Representation in Intermestic Politics," *Publius* 26 (Winter 1996): 53–72; Jeff Newnham, "New Constraints for U.S. Foreign Policy," *World Today* 51 (April 1995): 72–74; and John D. Stempel, "Losing It: The Decentralization of American Foreign Policy," *Journal of State Government* 64, no. 4 (1991): 122–25.

lose jobs to Mexico. Intermestic issues may involve more than domestic economic concerns, as the NAFTA case again illustrates. U.S. environmentalists also tended to oppose the free trade pact because they viewed Mexican environmental standards as being lax compared to U.S. and other standards that they wanted to see adopted. Environmentalists feared that U.S. manufacturers would relocate to Mexico to avoid the more stringent U.S. standards.

As a result of the rise of economic concerns in foreign policy, the president now turns to those with expertise in economic matters for advice on these foreign policy matters. Three of these stand out: the secretary of the Treasury, the U.S. trade representative, and the Federal Reserve Board. We discuss the Treasury Department and the Fed in more detail in Chapter 14 on economic policy. Their main concerns are the value of the dollar in international markets, interest rates, and the balance of trade. For the past several decades, the United States has been running large trade deficits with other nations.

The Office of the U.S. Trade Representative was created in 1962. Over time, it has grown in prominence. In 1974, it was elevated to cabinet-level status, and the U.S. trade representative was given the rank of ambassador. In 1980, the office was given responsibility for setting and administering overall trade policy, in effect centralizing almost all trade negotiations through this office. The rise of this office gives a sense of the changes in foreign policy to include economic concerns.

The Utility of the President's Foreign Policy Advising Team

The formal structure of the National Security Council was meant to provide the president with information necessary for making foreign policy decisions and to coordinate the various agencies involved in making foreign policy. The NSC has not, however, turned out to be all that useful for presidents.

First, presidents sometimes find the formal structure of the NSC too rigid. It brings together a large number of advisers in one place, but some presidents prefer to work in smaller groups and among advisers whom they trust and with whom they have developed a personal bond. For example, George H. W. Bush met daily with his National Security Adviser Brent Scowcroft, sometimes several times a day. They developed a strong friendship and could be frank and open with each other; their close relationship continued after the president left office in 1993.

Second, the various agencies do not always work together well or with the interests of the president in mind. Sometimes, competition arises between foreign policy advisers from different agencies as they jockey to take the lead. This **bureaucratic interests** perspective that advisers may bring to the table may undermine the usefulness of their advice for the president.[32] In part because advis-

---

[32] On the bureaucratic politics model, see Graham Allison, *Essence of Decision* (Boston: Little, Brown, 1971). For recent applications of the bureaucratic politics model, see Edward Rhodes, "Do Bureaucratic Politics Matter? Some Disconfirming Findings from the Case of the U.S. Navy," *World Politics* 47 (October 1994): 1–41; Lauren Holland, "The U.S. Decision to Launch Operation Desert Storm: A Bureaucratic Politics Analysis," *Armed Forces & Society* 25 (Winter 1999): 219–42; and Paul T. Mitchell, "Ideas, Interests, and Strategy: Bureaucratic Politics and the United States Navy," *Armed Forces & Society* 25 (Winter 1999): 243–85.

ers who work in the bureaucratic agencies (e. g., State, Defense, the CIA) tend to view issues from the perspective of their agency, they do not always see matters from the president's perspective. Perhaps only the national security adviser, who works in the White House and outside of the traditional bureaucracy, is positioned to view problems from the president's perspective.

Still, the NSC represents a quantum leap in presidential foreign policy-making capability compared to the situation that existed before its creation. While the NSC may not be useful as a formal structure, the many units that comprise it now possess foreign policy-making capability much greater than was the case in the 1940s and earlier. This provides the president with sources of advice that he can draw on when and how he sees fit.

THE PRESIDENTIAL ADVANTAGE IN FOREIGN POLICY MAKING

Presidents seem to enjoy several advantages in foreign policy making that they lack in other policy areas. For instance, as we discussed in "The Constitution, the President, and Foreign Policy Making" section of this chapter, the president possesses greater constitutional authority in foreign than in domestic policy matters, which the courts have generally upheld. Second, the president has access to a large advisory network, including experts throughout the executive branch bureaucracies. Third, the presumed need for secrecy in many foreign policy issues gives the president an information advantage over Congress. Although presidents may provide such information to select members of Congress, that information will not always be widely dispensed throughout Congress. Fourth, the hierarchical structure of the executive branch, with the president sitting at the top, allows the president to take action quickly when necessary. Furthermore, the unitary nature of the presidency means that the president can usually take action more quickly than the collective Congress. Fifth, unlike domestic politics, foreign policy tends to have fewer interest groups actively engaged in the policy-making process. Thus, presidents are less likely to encounter interest group opposition in foreign policy making compared to domestic policy-making.

Sixth, the president is allowed to speak for the nation in foreign policy matters as the nation's representative. Allowing the president this leadership in foreign policy ensures that the nation speaks with one voice to other nations, which is important in the conduct of foreign policy. If several leaders in the United States all claimed to be speaking for the nation in foreign policy matters, foreign nations would like become confused as to who really was in charge. Moreover, not presenting a unified voice in foreign relations would allow other nations to play the U.S. leaders off against each other, much like a child might try to play off one parent against the other.

This is a long list of presidential advantages in the foreign policy arena. Because of these advantages students of the presidency have contended that there are two presidencies, a foreign policy presidency and a domestic policy presidency.[33] This **two presidencies thesis** makes two claims. The first, is that presidents will be more successful with Congress in the passage of foreign than domestic policy legislation. Second, presidents will be highly successful in foreign policy; that is, they will rarely lose in Congress on foreign policy matters.

Most studies have found that presidents indeed win in Congress more frequently on foreign policy than domestic policy, but the two presidencies thesis applies more to minority- than majority-party presidents. Majority-party presidents win frequently in both foreign and domestic policy votes, because they possess similar levels of support from members of their party in Congress across all types of issues. In contrast, minority-party presidents face stiff opposition on domestic issues from the congressional majority. But on foreign policy matters, the opposition majority tends to support the president, leading to higher presidential success rates on foreign than domestic policy for minority-party presidents.

The second major claim of the two presidencies thesis is that presidents will always realize high levels of success on foreign policy. However, studies that have looked at presidential success in Congress from the early 1950s to the present have found that presidential success levels on foreign policy have been falling at least since the mid-1970s.[34] Several factors have been suggested to account for this decline in presidential success in foreign policy.

One idea suggests that in the aftermath of the Vietnam War, the bipartisan coalition on foreign policy broke apart. The Vietnam War raised debate over the conduct of U.S. foreign policy and whether the United States should use military force to combat communism. One side of the debate suggested that the traditional Cold War policy of containment should remain as the foundation of U.S. foreign policy. **Containment policy** basically meant that the United States would oppose

---

[33]The literature on the two presidencies thesis is extensive. The idea originally appeared in Aaron Wildavsky, "The Two Presidencies," *Trans-Action* 4 (December 1966): 7–14. A comprehensive collection is found in Steven A. Shull, ed., *The Two Presidencies: A Quarter-Century Assessment* (Chicago: Nelson-Hall, 1991). Recent studies include Leon Halpert, "Presidential Leadership of Congress: Evaluating President Reagan's Success in the House of Representatives," *Presidential Studies Quarterly* 21 (Fall 1991): 717–35; Russell D. Renka and Bradford S. Jones, "The 'Two Presidencies' Thesis and the Reagan Administration," *Congress and the Presidency* 18 (Spring 1991): 17–35; James M. Lindsay and Wayne P. Steger, "The 'Two Presidencies' in Future Research: Moving Beyond Roll-Call Analysis," *Congress and the Presidency* 20 (Autumn 1993): 103–17; Karen Toombs Parsons, "Exploring the 'Two Presidencies' Phenomenon: New Evidence from the Truman Administration," *Presidential Studies Quarterly* 24 (Summer 1994): 465–514; David Rohde, "Presidential Support in the House of Representatives," in *The President, the Congress, and the Making of Foreign Policy,* ed. Paul E. Peterson (Norman: University of Oklahoma Press, 1994), pp. 76–101; Richard S. Conley, "Unified Government, the Two Presidencies Thesis, and Presidential Support in the Senate," *Presidential Studies Quarterly* 27 (Spring 1997): 229–40; and Richard Fleisher, Jon R. Bond, Glen S. Krutz, and Stephen Hanna, "The Demise of the Two Presidencies," *American Politics Quarterly* 28 (January 2000): 3–25. For an interesting study that compares presidential speeches to the public on foreign versus domestic policy, see David Lewis, "The Two Rhetorical Presidencies: An Analysis of Televised Presidential Speeches, 1947–1991," *American Politics Quarterly* 25 (July 1997): 380–95. On the general advantage of presidents in foreign policy making with Congress, see Paul E. Peterson, "The President's Dominance in Foreign Policy Making," *Political Science Quarterly* 94 (Summer 1994): 215–34; and James Meernik, "Presidential Support in Congress: Conflict and Consensus on Foreign and Defense Policy," *Journal of Politics* 55 (August 1993): 569–87.

[34]See, for instance, Fleisher, Bond, Krutz, and Hanna, "Demise of the Two Presidencies."

the spread of communism. The other side of the debate, **coexistence,** suggested that the United States should accept that some nations would be communist and try to reduce tensions with the Soviet Union and seek arms reductions treaties.

Others see the decline of presidential success coming later, in the 1980s, after the Soviet Union fell and the Cold War ended. Without the specter of a communist Soviet Union, the threat of nuclear war seemed to subside. The **end of the Cold War thesis** maintains that the reason that presidents were so successful in foreign policy during the Cold War era was the possibility of nuclear war. Such a prospect was so threatening that politicians of both parties put aside their differences to build a bipartisan consensus on foreign policy. Important events, such as the Cuban missile crisis of 1962, underscored the dangers of the world during the Cold War. With the end of the Cold War, there was no longer such a strong justification to set aside differences over foreign policy. As a result, presidents encountered greater opposition on foreign policy in Congress during the post–Cold War era.

A third idea, related to both of those already presented, is that foreign policy became increasingly tied into partisan divisions. That is, Democrats and Republicans began to divide on foreign policy issues just as they had done on domestic policy issues. For instance, Democrats and Republicans often differed on how much money should be budgeted for defense purposes. Republicans, on average, preferred higher levels of defense spending than Democrats.

Democrats and Republicans also differed on whether or not U.S. troops should be used as peacekeepers around the globe. Republicans preferred to limit U.S. troop use to those areas that were thought to be strategically vital to the United States. Democrats, in contrast, often supported using troops to help stabilize democracies around the world, even in regions that were not so strategically vital. For example, Clinton sent troops to Somalia to help stabilize the political situation and later sent ground troops to Bosnia and Kosovo in the Balkans. In contrast, Republicans support the **Powell doctrine,** which was developed by Colin Powell during the Persian Gulf War. The Powell doctrine argued that U.S. troops should be used mainly when important U.S. interests and security are at stake and when the public will support U.S. military action. Further, enough troops should be on hand to ensure success. Powell's view is that the humanitarian use of troops, such as in Somalia, limits their availability on these other, supposedly more important missions.

Moreover, in the 1980s and 1990s, the distance between the parties on all types of issues grew, leading some to contend that the parties were now polarized in opposition to each other. With the parties so polarized, presidents had a harder time seeking the support from opposition party members on foreign policy matters.

PRESIDENTIAL DECISION MAKING IN FOREIGN POLICY

Thus far in this chapter, we have focused our attention on the substance of presidential foreign policy making. In this concluding section, we turn our attention to the processes of presidential foreign policy decision making, especially with regard to foreign policy crises. Foreign policy crisis decisions are among the most consequential that a president can make. Such decisions may lead to better rela-tions with other nations or may undermine those relations. The reputation that a president develops as a result of major foreign policy crises may affect how other nations see him, which may affect his ability to deal with other nations and their leaders. Perhaps most important, how a president handles foreign policy crises may determine whether or not the United States enters into hostilities with other nations, including war, which put lives at stake. Thus, presidential decision mak-ing in foreign policy crises is of great consequence.

All presidents will face foreign policy crises whether or not they are prepared to deal with such events. Some presidents are better prepared to deal with for-eign policy crises than others. For example, George H. W. Bush had extensive for-eign policy experience before becoming president, having served as ambassador to China, director of the CIA, and vice president. Thus, not only was he well sea-soned in foreign policy before becoming president, but his interests also led him more toward foreign policy than domestic issues.

In contrast, most modern presidents have come to office with less experience in foreign policy. Of the last five presidents, four (Carter, Reagan, Clinton, and George W. Bush) were governors and lacked even national government experi-ence. With the end of the Cold War, foreign policy concerns among the public have receded. Candidates who stress their foreign policy qualifications no longer have the advantage with voters that Cold War-era presidential candidates had. It is likely that into the future, candidates more versed in domestic issues will have an advantage in gaining the nomination and being elected. Thus, we are likely to continue the trend of electing presidents with little foreign policy experience.

One implication of the lack of foreign policy experience is that new presi-dents early in their term may be more likely to make costly foreign policy mis-takes. For example, John F. Kennedy plunged into the ill-fated Bay of Pigs in-vasion of Cuba in 1961, not long after taking office. The fiasco lead him to revise how he made foreign policy decisions, including to whom he listened and from whom he took advice.

Although Bill Clinton did not face a major foreign policy crisis early in his administration, he came to office without much foreign policy experience and seemingly with less interest in foreign than in domestic policy matters. But the longer he stayed in office, the greater his confidence seemed to grow in han-dling foreign policy concerns. His greatest crisis probably came with the Balkans, especially Kosovo in 1997 and 1998. Finally, after delaying acting in hopes that the major European nations would take the lead against the Miloso-vich regime in Serbia, Clinton ordered massive bombing against the Serbians to force them to back away from their policy of "ethnic cleansing." Many in the United States criticized the Clinton bombing policy, either thinking it would be ineffective or viewing it as too bold.

Those who thought that bombing alone would be ineffective pointed to the limited effect of bombing in the Vietnam War: how, despite its intensity, it did not seem to undermine the willingness of the North Vietnamese to continue their struggle against the United States. Others have even suggested that the massive bombing of Japan and Germany in the Second World War was of limited utility. Despite years of bombing, German war production hardly seemed to suffer. The large losses of troops on the Russian front were thought to be more important in weakening Germany.

Others attacked the Clinton policy from a different direction, feeling that the bombing mission would be but the first step in an escalation of U.S. involvement in the Balkans. Ground troops would have to be sent to fight in a land war, and these critics thought that the United States was not prepared to fight a land war there. Despite these criticisms, Clinton persisted with his policy, and finally, the Serbians backed down. We might expect, then, that presidents will learn on the job and that they will become better foreign policy crisis managers as time goes on.

Foreign leaders may take advantage of the inexperience of new presidents, too, fomenting crises early in the term. For instance, a small event early in George W. Bush's term is instructive. Shortly after he took office in 2001, an American spy plane and a Chinese military jet collided. The Chinese pilot was killed and his plane destroyed, while the U.S. plane was so damaged that it had to make an emergency landing on Chinese soil. China detained the American military personnel and the airplane, actions which the U.S. government protested, wanting release of the crew and the damaged plane. The Chinese government, however, insisted on receiving an apology from the United States, claiming that the United States had caused the incident, but the U.S. response was weaker than what the Chinese government had demanded.

An international incident brewed, one with potential implications for two large nations that were often at odds over such issues as the Middle East, arms sales, and China's treatment of dissidents and pro-democracy advocates. But China and the United States were also major trading partners, each benefiting from the volume of trade between them.

It seemed that the Chinese might have been testing the resolve of the new president, who lacked foreign policy experience. Bush allowed his secretary of State, Colin Powell, who was well experienced and possessed a strong reputation, to take the lead in resolving the dispute. After several weeks of negotiating, a compromise was reached over wording acceptable to both sides, because neither was willing to assume responsibility. Then the Chinese released the U.S. crew and the plane.

Thus, the early period of a new presidency may be a dangerous time. As a consequence, it may be all the more important that presidents deal with their first major foreign policy crisis effectively. The consequence of not doing so is that it may invite leaders of other nations to challenge the administration.

Presidents may get better at handling foreign policy crises as the administration ages because they not only gain personal experience but learn which staffers are helpful or not in crises. Some staffers may have special talents that are useful, and the president may be likely to use them during a crisis. Others may have particular agendas that presidents may find they can deal with during normal circumstances but cause problems during a major emergency or confrontation.

Moreover, as an administration ages, presidents interact with foreign leaders more. They learn more about them, and this knowledge may help them in making decisions during a crisis. In many cases, it is relatively predictable that a region of the world or a nation beset with problems will likely be involved in foreign policy emergencies. Currently, the Middle East and the Balkans are two world hot spots that are likely to generate crisis events of one sort or other. A president may have encountered a particular foreign leader from a previous visit or interacted with that leader in other ways, such as at summits, in diplomatic negotiations, and the like. All of these interactions may inform the president about the preferences and attributes of that leader. Such knowledge may help a president in deciding what to do in a crisis involving that leader—whether the president should push hard, seek a compromise, allow the other leader to save face, or so on. For these and the other reasons already mentioned, presidents should become better foreign policy crisis managers the longer they are in office.

One way for new presidents to compensate for their lack of experience is to rely on advisers who are knowledgeable, expert, and veterans in foreign policy making. George W. Bush seems to have followed this path, especially with his appointment of Colin Powell as his secretary of State and Donald Rumsfeld as his secretary of Defense. Both served in high-level foreign and defense policy assignments for other presidents. Ronald Reagan initially appointed Alexander Haig as his secretary of State; Haig was a former general who also served for a while as the U.S. liaison to NATO headquarters. Reagon also chose George H. W. Bush as his vice president. And Lyndon Johnson, another president without much foreign policy experience, relied heavily on John F. Kennedy's foreign policy team when he became president after Kennedy was assassinated.

Yet, such reliance on experienced advisers is no guarantee of effective crisis decision making, as the Bay of Pigs case illustrates. Despite Kennedy's highly experienced foreign policy advising staff, the Bay of Pigs invasion was ill-considered and mishandled. One danger of an inexperienced president and an experienced staff is that the president may listen too much to important staffers. Instead of weighing their advice, the president may follow the staff. This may have happened to Lyndon Johnson, who followed the advice of top advisers such as MacGeorge Bundy and Dean Rusk, who argued for greater involvement in Vietnam. Some accounts suggest that Johnson was swayed by their arguments because he saw them as being more knowledgeable about foreign policy matters.[35] Thus, there seems no magic formula to help presidents when dealing with a foreign policy crisis early in their term.

Also, despite the large and varied advising apparatus that presidents can call on during a foreign policy crisis, most presidents seem to restrict the number of advisers who have access to them. A smaller, closer working group is collected to deal with foreign policy crises. Presidents tend to select for this working group those advisers whom they feel comfortable with and trust, as well as some who clearly possess expertise that is relevant to the situation at hand. Such a process of winnowing advice to a small group has benefits and costs in decision-making crises.

---

[35]Larry Berman, *Lyndon Johnson's War: The Road to Stalemate in Vietnam* (New York: W. W. Norton, 1991).

A major benefit of a small crisis working group is that the president can act more quickly with a smaller group than a larger one. Working with a smaller group reduces the risk of leaks, which might help unfriendly powers gain an advantage. Another benefit is that the president can restrict the group to those whom he trusts. Also, the president may keep from becoming overloaded with too much information and too many perspectives by restricting his advice during a crisis.

There are major costs to restricting advice to the president. Presidents may cut themselves off from some information that may be useful. Further, a tightly knit, small working group may develop groupthink tendencies, which we discussed in Chapter 13 on presidential decision making. Groupthink may lead the president and his advisers down the wrong path in the crisis. For example, pre-existing assumptions about the foreign leader and the policy of the foreign nation might not be challenged, even though these assumptions may be wrong, when groupthink processes are at work. Similarly, new information may be discounted or ignored. And a false sense of confidence may develop between the president and his advisers that they are selecting the correct option.

No formula exists for presidents to apply when dealing with foreign policy crises. Whether the president includes or excludes certain people from the crisis management team has both costs and benefits to decision making, as we have discussed. Crises by definition are complex, threatening situations. What worked in one situation may not work in the next, and what works for one president may not work for another. Thus, it is hard to advise presidents in particular about what to do other than that they be open to adjusting how they deal with foreign policy crises and learn what works best for them.

CONCLUSION

Foreign policy has been important to the transformation of the presidency. Although the founders envisioned that the president would take the lead in making foreign policy, they did not expect that foreign policy would come to be as important as it did during the Cold War. The founders granted the president seemingly extraordinary powers in foreign policy, such as war making, but these were aimed mostly at dealing with crises that require speed and decisive action. During the Cold War, the nation seemed perpetually at crisis, with the threat of nuclear war always in the background. As a consequence, the presidency rose in prominence to a degree unexpected and unanticipated.

Presidential advantages in foreign policy spilled over into other policy areas, as presidents could claim that national security required them. Dwight Eisenhower promoted the interstate highway system in the 1950s for just such reasons, and Bill Clinton argued for strict regulation of computers for similar reasons. We get a sense of the pull of national security arguments when we discussed the tendency of the opposition party in Congress to support the president on foreign policy matters during the Cold War.

The end of the Cold War may affect the presidency. Some journalists contend that the presidency is much diminished, compared to its prominence during the Cold War.[36] Congress is now more likely to challenge the president on foreign policy than during the Cold War. For example, in 2000 the Republican-controlled House supported Bill Clinton on only 40 percent of roll call votes that Clinton took a position on, compared to 51 percent on domestic policy roll calls.[37] The future will tell how much this changed world environment affects the presidency in foreign policy making, as well as more generally.

KEY TERMS

bureaucratic interests and foreign
   policy advice   456
Case Amendment of 1972   440
Central Intelligence Agency   454
Chadha v. *INS* decision   447
coexistence   459
containment policy   458
covert operations   454
diversionary use of force   445
domestic or internal politics model
   of troop commitment   445
electoral cycle theory of
   troop commitment   445
end of the Cold War thesis   459
executive agreements   439
external threat argument
   of troop commitment   444

fast track authority   438
intermestic policy   455
Joint Chiefs of Staff (JCS)   452
National Security Act of 1947   449
national security adviser   450
National Security Agency   454
National Security Council   449
October surprise and
   troop commitment   445
Powell doctrine   459
sole organ theory   434
treaty making power   435
treaty reservations   436
treaty understandings   436
two presidencies thesis   458
war making powers   441
War Powers Resolution of 1973   446

DISCUSSION QUESTIONS

1. Compare the president's role in treaty making with his role in diplomacy. Over which does Congress seem to have the most influence? How supportive is Congress of the president in these two areas of foreign policy making?
2. How do executive agreements differ from treaties? What is the constitutional or statutory basis for allowing presidents to enter into executive agreements? Why have presidents found executive agreements to be a useful foreign policy-making device? How has Congress reacted to presidential use of executive agreements?
3. Why did the founders recognize a difference between declaring and making war? How does this distinction affect the president's ability to wage war? What can and has Congress done to limit presidential war-making powers?

[36]David M. Shribman, "The Shrinking Presidency; Why? The Times, the Congress, the Media, the Economy," *Boston Globe* 25 January 1998, p. E3; and Francine Kiefer, "For U.S. Presidents, It's an Era of Modest Agendas," *Christian Science Monitor* 28 January 1999, p. 2.

[37]David Nather, "Presidential Support: Clinton's Floor Vote Victories Yielded Few Accomplishments," *Congressional Quarterly Weekly Report* 6 January 2001, p. 52.

4. How extraordinary is the presidential commitment of U.S. troops abroad? Has the propensity of presidents to commit troops abroad increased over time? Why do presidents commit troops? Do domestic considerations enter into the president's decision to commit troops?

5. Who are the president's major foreign policy advisers? How do their positions in government affect the type of advice that they provide to the president? How have their advising roles changed over time?

6. Discuss the different foreign intelligence agencies of the federal government. Why are there so many? How do their roles differ? Are some more important than others?

7. Does the president have advantages in making foreign policy over domestic policy? If so, how and why? If not, why not? If he has advantages in making foreign policy, have they remained potent over the years? If not, why not?

8. How is foreign policy crisis decision making different from other types of policy making? What can we do to ensure that presidents make optimal decisions in foreign policy crises? Do presidents get better at making decisions in foreign policy crisis as they serve in office longer or as they encounter more foreign policy crises?

SUGGESTED READINGS

David G. Adler and Larry N. George, *The Constitution and the Conduct of American Foreign Policy*. Lawrence: University of Kansas Press, 1996.

Barry Blechman and Stephen Kaplan, *Force Without War: U.S. Armed Forces as a Political Instrument*. Washington, D.C.: Brookings Institution, 1978.

Cecil V. Crabb, Jr., and Pat M. Holt, *Invitation to Struggle: Congress, the President and Foreign Policy,* 2d ed. Washington, D.C.: Congressional Quarterly Press, 1984.

Harold Hongju Koh, *The National Security Constitution*. New Haven: Yale University Press, 1990.

James Lindsay, *Congress and the Politics of U.S. Foreign Policy*. Baltimore: Johns Hopkins University Press, 1994.

Paul. E. Peterson, ed., *The President, the Congress, and the Making of Foreign Policy*. Norman: University of Oklahoma Press, 1994.

Jerel A. Rosati, *The Politics of United States Foreign Policy,* 2d ed. New York: Harcourt Brace, 1999.

Steven A. Shull, ed., *The Two Presidencies: A Quarter-Century Assessment*. Chicago: Nelson-Hall, 1991.

INDEX